ARGENTINA

URUGUAY

CHILE

BRAZIL

S

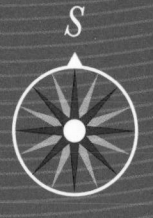

Mary Kate —

Thanks for your wonderful hospitality. Until the next time

Salute!

Jeff White

WINES OF THE SOUTHERN HEMISPHERE

THE COMPLETE GUIDE

THE COMPLETE GUIDE

WINES
OF THE
SOUTHERN
HEMISPHERE

MIKE DESIMONE & JEFF JENSSEN
FOREWORD BY MICHEL ROLLAND

STERLING EPICURE
New York

STERLING EPICURE
New York

An Imprint of Sterling Publishing
387 Park Avenue South
New York, NY 10016

STERLING EPICURE is a trademark of Sterling Publishing Co., Inc.
The distinctive Sterling logo is a registered trademark of Sterling Publishing Co., Inc.

A complete list of picture credits appears on pages 558 and 559.

Designed by Christine Heun

ISBN 978-1-4027-8625-9

Some of the terms in this book may be trademarks or registered trademarks. Use of such terms
does not imply any association with or endorsement by such trademark owners, and no association or
endorsement is intended or should be inferred. This book is not authorized by, and neither the authors
nor the publisher are affiliated with, the owners of the trademarks referred to in this book.

Every effort has been made to have the facts about the wineries, including the contact information,
as up-to-date and accurate as possible. The authors would welcome any input should anything
differ from what's showing in these pages. They can be reached at www.worldwineguys.

Distributed in Canada by Sterling Publishing
c/o Canadian Manda Group, 165 Dufferin Street
Toronto, Ontario, Canada M6K 3H6
Distributed in the United Kingdom by GMC Distribution Services
Castle Place, 166 High Street, Lewes, East Sussex, England BN7 1XU
Distributed in Australia by Capricorn Link (Australia) Pty. Ltd.
P.O. Box 704, Windsor, NSW 2756, Australia

For information about custom editions, special sales, and premium and corporate purchases,
please contact Sterling Special Sales at 800-805-5489 or specialsales@sterlingpublishing.com.

Manufactured in the United States of America

2 4 6 8 10 9 7 5 3 1

www.sterlingpublishing.com

This book is dedicated to our friends, family, and our colleagues in the world of wine—you all know who you are—who encouraged us, held our hands, tasted with us, traveled with us, cooked for us, pushed us when we were just too tired, and understood when we stayed in to write. We thank you all from the bottom of our hearts and the bottom of our wine glasses.

Salud, Prost, Santô, Cheers!

CONTENTS

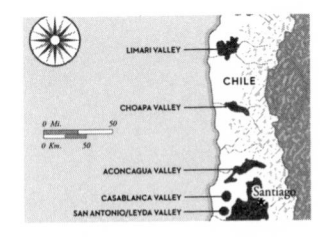

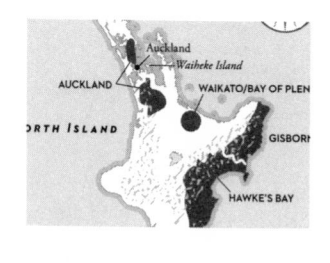

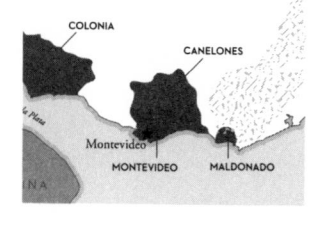

FOREWORD

The time has come for a book about the wines of the Southern Hemisphere.

To write a book only on the wines of the Southern Hemisphere is a great idea: Nobody has ever done this before. I like this idea very much because I personally decided to visit the Southern Hemisphere 25 years ago, when I was asked to become a consultant at Bodegas Etchart. Now I consult for close to twenty wineries in Argentina, Chile, and South Africa.

Argentina, the first Southern Hemisphere country that I visited, has beautiful vineyards in the Andes Mountains. After my original contact with these beautiful vineyards, I then went to Chile, which has amazing vineyards between the Andes and the Pacific Ocean. My life as a consultant also brings me to South Africa, which is amazing as well. It has the most beautiful views from any vineyard in the world. Unfortunately I don't work in Australia and New Zealand because then I would have three harvests at the same time. Even though I am a "flying winemaker," I am not that crazy; I can't spread myself over three continents at the same time.

The Southern Hemisphere has a long history of winemaking, but has become especially important in the past 25 years. We now have so many good vineyards producing fantastic wines from Carmenere, Malbec, Syrah, and many other varieties.

To write this book now is a wonderful idea, because the wine-drinking public may not know what is happening around the globe. At this time only Bordeaux is selling cases of wine for US$700 in high volume—maybe in the future we will see other countries, especially those from the Southern Hemisphere, selling large volumes of well-crafted wines at the prices they deserve.

I hope that you enjoy this book, because it is extremely well done. It is a large volume of work, and very informative. This book will serve as a guide to your exploration of this vast region. After reading, you need to taste the wines from these countries and enjoy them for your own pleasure.

Michel Rolland

INTRODUCTION

At about the same time that Christopher Columbus discovered the "New World" in his quest to find a shorter route to Asia, the Incas, in tandem with the Huarpes, were digging a series of irrigation canals in the foothills of the Andes Mountains. Today, those same canals are used to supply water to the vineyards of Mendoza, Argentina; without the ingenious system of funneling snowmelt, this modern-day wine region would be nothing but arid desert. This brings into focus the fact that the "New World" isn't really that new at all—and also causes us to reflect that the wines thought of as "New World" aren't all that new either. With the exception of wines from North America, almost everything labeled "New World" is from the Southern Hemisphere. The history of winemaking in these countries parallels European colonization and stretches back hundreds of years: Wines that originate south of the equator are not necessarily new; they are simply unfamiliar to many American, European, and Asian wine drinkers and to those living on other continents in the hemisphere.

Winemaking moved from Europe to the Southern Hemisphere in a variety of ways, but much of it was tied to the Catholic Church, either directly or indirectly. In South America and New Zealand, the earliest grapes were planted by missionaries, for both sacramental and table wine, while in South Africa and Australia, persecuted Protestants played an important role in the development of a viable winemaking industry. Although there are analogous forces that shaped the history of wine in each country, varying factors within individual nations, including ethnic backgrounds of settlers, economics, transportation, and of course terrain and climate, all had a hand in causing distinct differences in the style of wine each one produces.

You will find detailed history and much more between the covers of this book, but for the moment, fast-forward with us to the twenty-first century, as we discover that wine lovers—especially young millennials—are drinking more and more wine every year. Research shows they are drinking wine from a variety of countries and regions, not just Old-World Europe. This trend has led to an amazing jump in worldwide consumption of wines from the Southern Hemisphere, whose share increased from a mere 3 percent in 1990 to 27 percent in 2009. The major wine-producing countries below the equator are Argentina, Australia, Chile, New Zealand, and South Africa, each of which boasts a multitude of wine regions, varietals, styles, and outstanding producers. In 2009, Australia surpassed France in the amount of wine imported into the United States, placing Australia just behind Italy. If current trends continue,

Chile and Argentina will also have surpassed France by the time you are reading this, moving wines from countries in the Southern Hemisphere into three of the top five import positions in the US market.

Unfortunately, wine drinkers looking for definitive information on their newfound favorites are not likely to receive much help from other authorities on the subject: writing devoted to these wines is nowhere near keeping up with recent bottlings making their way to wine shops and restaurants. A quick scan of some of the major titles in the world of the vine reveals a paltry number of pages covering the Southern Hemisphere. What this means is that other wine books generally devote 8 percent or less of their total page space to the five main wine-producing countries of the Southern Hemisphere, and many omit Brazil and Uruguay completely or mention them only in passing. Even web searches, whether by hemisphere, country, or region, fail to turn up much objective information; many sites are sponsored by consortiums, importers, and producers.

While we believe that there are few "firsts" left in the world, we are very excited to present *Wines of the Southern Hemisphere: The Complete Guide*, the first comprehensive book ever written on this subject. In order to compile all of this information in a single volume, we traveled extensively throughout the Southern Hemisphere, visiting wine regions, vineyards, and wineries. On some days we toured and tasted at up to seven wineries, and even in our "downtime," we took copious notes on wines purchased at restaurants and wine bars. Many a glass was tasted over dinner with a proud winemaker, and many were tried at trade and private tastings around the globe.

More than just a simple listing of key countries, regions, and producers, this tome delves into the entire winemaking industry of the Southern Hemisphere, giving readers a historical, geographical, and enological overview, all in what we hope comes across as easy-to-read language. There is something in this book for everyone who enjoys wine, from novice to sommelier alike. We have provided insight from winemakers and experts in each area, in a series of interviews titled "In Their Own Words," and have highlighted local cuisine and recipes, in order to place the wines into a food-friendly context. We also endeavored to cover not only the well-known standouts but also the up-and-comers of each country.

As people who came to love wine long before we ever began writing about it, we hope that our passion comes across through our words and ignites a flame in our readers. Just as Columbus accidentally discovered a New World, it is our hope that everyone who reads our book, whether in total or in part, comes away not only with knowledge but also with the joy of discovery and the desire to learn—and taste—even more.

Mike DeSimone and Jeff Jenssen, The World Wine Guys

"And wine can of their wits the wise beguile,
Make the sage frolic, and the serious smile."

Homer, *The Odyssey*, 8th century BC

ARGENTINA

THE NAME ARGENTINA BRINGS SHARP images to mind: gauchos on horseback across la pampa, sensual tango dancers in Buenos Aires pressing their bodies against one another, slabs of grass-fed beef charred to perfection at an *asado* in Patagonia, and a glass of inky purple Malbec, with flavors of cherry, plum, and chocolate, at a high-end wine bar in Mendoza. The last image is the goal of a lot of tourism these days, though it would not have been possible were it not for the Spanish first, and then the French. Argentina first

became home to grapevines in 1557, when cuttings were brought to Santiago del Estero by Spanish conquistadores and priests. The first grape varieties planted were Moscatel and Uva Negra, the grape (or a mutation thereof) that is known here as Criolla and is called Pais in Chile and Mission in California.

It is believed that the Incas arrived in current-day Mendoza only about one hundred years before the Spanish; at that time, they assisted the indigenous Huarpe people to establish a network of irrigation canals using snowmelt from the nearby Andes. The Spaniards might have bypassed this area altogether in their conquests were it not for this system of water-bearing channels: the high-altitude desert would be completely unsuitable for agriculture or much of anything else had these two peoples not collaborated on this ingenious method of bringing water to their crops. Mendoza was actually part of Chile until 1873, when it became part of the Viceroy of Rio de la Plata, the forebear of modern-day Argentina.

In 1853—almost three hundred years after the first grapes were planted—the Quinta Nacional de Agricultura, or National Vine Nursery, was created in Mendoza, under the direction of Michel Aimé Pouget, a Frenchman who had lived in Chile. The Quinta Nacional was succeeded by the National School of Agriculture in 1872, which was then replaced by the National School of Viniculture in 1896. Its role was to bring vine cuttings into the country for experimental purposes. Most of these vines came from France. Most famous among them is Malbec, but into the early twentieth century, hundreds of varieties were imported and nurtured, including Alicante Bouchet, Cabernet Franc, Cabernet Sauvignon, Gamay, Grenache, Malvasia, Moscato, and Pinot Noir.

Although grapes are grown and wine is made from the far north of the country (in the Calchaquí Valley) and through the south (in Patagonia), Mendoza (in the middle of the country) is the most important wine region, producing over 70 percent of Argentina's wine. However, it was only in 1885 that Mendoza really assimilated into the rest of the country, with the advent of the railroad from Buenos Aires. Prior to this, goods were transported by mule-drawn carts. Even with the tortuous mountain passes that lie between the two cities, Mendoza is much closer to Santiago, at 208 kilometers, (129 miles) as the crow flies, than it is to Buenos Aires—958 kilometers (595 miles) away—if you could travel in a straight line. However, once the train arrived, trade between Mendoza and Chile came to a standstill, and produce from Mendoza, including wine, olive oil, fruit, and grain was sold throughout Argentina and also exported to Europe. The train also brought immigrants, mainly from Spain and Italy, to Mendoza, and these newcomers brought their culinary heritage, love of wine, and winemaking knowledge with them.

At the same time that some of today's major wineries were founded, Spanish and Italian transplants were making homemade jug wine from grapes grown on their family farms. In addition to names deriving from Spain, you will note a high proportion of Italian surnames among Argentina's wine families.

Today, Argentina is the fifth largest wine producer in the world, behind France, Italy, Spain, and the United States. Its seven wine regions produced a total of 1.375 million liters in 2010, and exported 230,600 liters that same year; major export markets include the United States, Canada, Brazil, the United Kingdom, Scandinavia, Russia, Holland, Mexico, and China. Argentines are the eighth largest per capita wine consumers in the world, each drinking an average of 31 liters per year. Compare that to neighboring Chile, at just below 14 liters per person, and Brazil, at only 2 liters. Argentina ranks ninth in surface area cultivated with grapevines, with 228,575 hectares (564,821 acres) planted.

The eighth largest country in the world, with a population of 38 million, Argentina enjoys a diversity of landscapes—from towering mountains to wide expanses of plain, from arid desert to lush wetlands. This offers a wide array of environments suitable for grape growing.

The wine lands of Argentina cover a vast swath of land in the far west of the country, closest to the Andes, between 22 and 42 degrees southern latitude, covering a distance of about 2,400 kilometers (1,500 miles). But what undoubtedly has the strongest effect on the quality of Argentine wine is altitude; Argentina boasts the highest vineyard in the world, the Hess Collection's Colomé Vineyard, at about 3,000 meters (9,850 feet) above sea level, as well as the world's highest collective vineyard altitude, with an average height of 823 meters (2,700 feet). One of the primary benefits of increased altitude is greater fluctuations in diurnal temperature variation, meaning the difference between day and night temperatures. Heat from sunlight increases sugar and other complex flavors during the ripening process, while night-time cold preserves the grapes' natural acids. In Mendoza, vineyards climb from 457 to 1,700 meters (1,500 to 5,600 feet).

Altitude also brings cooler temperatures; for every 100-meter (328-foot) increase in height above sea level, there is an average decline of approximately 0.5 degree Celsius (1 degree Fahrenheit). What this translates to is that from the lowest altitude in Mendoza (457 meters [1,500 feet]) to the highest (1,700 meters [5,600]) we have a disparity of more than 1,200 meters and can thus expect, on average, a temperature variation of a little over 6 degrees Celsius (12 degrees Fahrenheit).

The general climate in western Argentina also contributes to the area's wine quality. Rainfall is generally low (except in the south), averaging 102 to 203 millimeters (4 to 8 inches) per year. External irrigation is provided when necessary, but the dry condition of the air and soil is not conducive to the diseases and pests that would otherwise harm ripening grapes.

Soils close to the Andes are mainly alluvial gravel and sand with a mixture of clay, layered over volcanic bedrock. One of the major risks in springtime is hail; it is not unusual to see an elaborate framework of tight-strung nets attached to trellis posts, in order to protect grapes from this frozen threat.

From north to south, the main regions of Argentina are Salta, La Rioja, Catamarca, San Juan, Mendoza (which is further subdivided into five subregions,) Neuquén, and Río Negro. Ninety-five percent of the grapes grown for wine production come from Mendoza and San Juan. That said, the vineyards of San Juan tend to be planted with grapes such as Pedro Giménez and Criolla, which generally produce a low-quality table wine sold into the domestic market. In contrast, although Neuquén, Río Negro, and Salta are comparatively sparsely planted, they produce and export a disproportionate quantity of high-end wine. La Pampa, the flat plain known for cowboys and cattle ranching, is now also home to a smattering of wineries.

Two waves of innovation had considerable effects on Argentine viniculture. The first began at about the same time the railroad reached Mendoza: over the next 15 or so years, a handful of operations were founded, including Trapiche in 1883, Bodegas Escorihuela in 1884, La Rural in 1889, and Catena in 1902. Indeed, throughout the twentieth century total vine plantings in Argentina increased dramatically, but much of the resultant output was poor-quality wine destined for domestic consumption.

At the same time, a small number of producers not only thrived but blossomed, making excellent wines that served a growing demand for high-quality wine among Argentina's elite. None of these wines were exported—between a harsh dictatorship and a steady stream of internal financial crises, Argentina was in no position to extend its potential outlet beyond its own borders. Although Argentine wine was unknown in the world at large during this time, per capita wine consumption within the country had grown to over 90 liters per person a year by 1970. A few bottlings made their way out of Argentina in the 1990s, but with an influx of international consultants—such as Paul Hobbs, Alberto Antonini, and Michel Rolland— assisting in both vineyards and wineries, and an increase in wine knowledge among sommeliers and consumers, by the time the Argentine peso was devalued in 2002 the stage was set for the wines of Argentina to take the world by storm.

Mention Argentine wine and almost everyone immediately thinks of Malbec, the grape that put Argentina on the map. It was first introduced here with Michel Pouget's cuttings in 1853, and it was found to thrive in the dry soils of the Andean foothills. A large portion of Malbec plantings were ripped out in the 1980s and replaced with Criolla, to be made into inexpensive, low-quality wine. In the 1990s, as the Argentine economy strengthened, there was a shift toward the production of high-caliber wine, and Malbec—with its intense flavor structure and opulent tannins—became the preeminent Argentine variety. Now accounting for 12 percent of all the grapes grown in Argentina, it has winemakers (and their marketing managers) around the world scrambling to find the next übervariety that will unseat Argentine Malbec from its international throne.

The white variety that almost seems indigenous to Argentina is Torrontés, which is grown in 3.7 percent of Argentine vineyards. Just over 8 percent of all the grapes grown in Argentina are the Bonarda variety, followed closely by Cabernet Sauvignon at just under 8 percent. A good range of international varieties thrive here, including Chardonnay, Syrah, Merlot, Tempranillo, Chenin Blanc, Pinot Noir, Sauvignon Blanc, Sémillon, and Viognier. Small amounts of Bequignol, Barbera, and Riesling are also farmed here. Pedro Giménez and Criolla are grown on a large scale but are strictly made into domestic jug wine.

Argentina's Instituto Nacional de Viniviticultura, or INV, regulates the wine industry. If a single variety is listed on a label, at least 80 percent of the wine in the bottle must be of that variety. For example, a bottle labeled "Malbec" may contain 80 percent Malbec and 20 percent of other grape varieties, without listing them on the label. Producers of premium Bordeaux-style blends generally list the component grapes by percentage.

Wine made from Malbec also has "Controlled Denomination of Origin" (*Denominacíon de Origen Calificada*, DOC) status in a few regions, which means that if a bottle is labeled with the DOC name, the grapes must come from that area. The first declared Malbec DOC was Luján de Cuyo in 1993, followed quickly by San Rafael.

The terms "Reserva" and "Gran Reserva" were defined in March 2011. To be labeled "Reserva," wine must be made using 135 kilograms (298 pounds) of grapes per 100 liters. Red Reserva wine must age for a minimum of 12 months, and white and rosé must age for a minimum of 6 months. Gran Reserva wine requires at least 140 kilograms (309 pounds) of grapes per 100 liters of wine. Red wines called "Gran Reserva" require a minimum of 24 months aging prior to release, while white or rosé Gran Reserva wine must age for 12 months. These regulations take effect as of the 2011 vintage.

MAJOR GRAPE VARIETIES

BONARDA

The second most widely planted grape in Argentina, Bonarda blankets 18,758 hectares (46,352 acres) of vineyards, or just over 8 percent of the total planted area. It appears to be the same grape known in France as Corbeau and in California as Charbono; Bonarda also seems to be related to the Italian Bonarda Piemontese and Bonarda Novarese, although due to regional mutations, it is unclear exactly what the relationship is. As a late-ripening red variety, Bonarda is one of the last to be harvested. Until recently, it was the most widely planted grape in the nation and was often made into inexpensive table wines. Now, buoyed by the success of Malbec, winemakers are turning to Bonarda to produce red wines of high quality. It is a deep purple on the vine and in the glass, and flavors include cherry, plum, dried fig, cassis, and fennel. Bonarda grows throughout all Argentine wine regions, but the highest concentration of Bonarda vineyards are found in Mendoza, La Rioja, and San Juan.

CABERNET SAUVIGNON

Trailing right behind Bonarda and Torrontés Riojano, Cabernet Sauvignon is farmed on 17,737 hectares (43,829 acres), making up just under 8 percent of the total grapevines in the country. It is grown in the Salta, La Rioja, Catamarca, San Juan, and Mendoza regions, with variations in flavor profile due to geography and climate. It typically tastes of black cherry, cassis, pencil lead, spice, and tobacco. Its aging potential is due to the tannins extracted from its thick skin and seeds. Cabernet Sauvignon from Salta will tend to have blackberry and green pepper characteristics, while Mendozan Cabernet will feature more cherry notes.

CHARDONNAY

From its home in France, Chardonnay has done quite well in Argentina, where its 6,578 hectares (16,254 acres) comprise almost 3 percent of all the grapes grown within the country. Chardonnay's Granny Smith apple and lemon flavors are at home whether in a crisp, steel-fermented version, a full-bodied, well-oaked style, or a sparkling wine. Its tropical fruit notes are emphasized when grown in warm regions, while colder temperatures bring out Chardonnay's minerality. The majority of it—5,406 hectares (13,359 acres)—is cultivated in Mendoza, followed by San Juan with 848 hectares (2,095 acres). In addition, small amounts of Chardonnay flourish from stem to stern of Argentina's wine lands.

CHENIN BLANC

Chenin Blanc is planted in small amounts throughout Argentina. Grown on 2,856 hectares (7,057 acres), it constitutes about 1.5 percent of Argentine grapes. A native of the Loire Valley in France, Chenin Blanc is a late-ripening white varietal. On its own, it carries flavors of peach, pear, and apple and is noted for both its high acidity and strong minerality. It has long been used in Argentina as a blending grape, to add acidity to other white varieties, but recently Chenin Blanc has found its way into a sizable number of single varietal bottlings.

CRIOLLA

A general category of grape that also includes Torrontés, Criolla usually refers to Criolla Grande, a red wine grape used to make intensely colored white or rosé wines. In Argentina it thrives on about 23,000 hectares (56,834 acres) of land. A relative of California's

Mission and Chile's País, Criolla's most notable characteristic is that it does well under poor conditions, leading to high yields perfect for mass production of low-quality wine. It is a descendant of the original cuttings brought to South America by the Spanish conquistador Hernán Cortés.

MALBEC

Malbec is Argentina's chart-topping variety. It carpets 28,000 hectares (69,190 acres), or slightly more than 12 percent of all the vineyards in the land. The majority of Argentine Malbec grows in the Mendoza region. It has a strikingly dark purple color—both as a finished wine and on the vine—and has primary flavors of black cherry, plum, and chocolate, with extra highlights of violet and licorice. Originally from France, where it is usually blended in small amounts with other grapes (most notably in Bordeaux), Argentine Malbec thrives on its own in a variety of styles. A fresh, fruity type benefits from a short time in oak and is available from multiple producers at reasonable prices. In general, as we move up the price scale, we see an increase in the time spent in barrel and the age of vines. We begin to note oak flavors of vanilla and spice in addition to primary fruit flavors, while the natural tannins of the grape are enhanced by tannins derived from oak. Many of these premium Malbecs spend one to one and a half years in barrel and are sourced from single vineyards.

At the upper end of the spectrum we find Malbec vinified into what is known as an "Icon" wine, representing the finest expression of fruit, terroir, and craftsmanship. Hand-selected grapes from old vines are fermented in small quantities, aged at least 24 months in barrel and one year in bottle before release, and are among the most expensive—and delicious—wines the country has to offer. Malbec is also blended with other grapes, mostly other Bordeaux varieties such as Cabernet Sauvignon, Merlot, Cabernet Franc, and Petit Verdot. Argentine Malbec grape clusters are smaller and tighter than those found in France.

MERLOT

The lion's share of Merlot grows in the Mendoza region, though it thrives in the Neuquén and Río Negro regions as well. With just shy of 2,833 hectares (7,000 acres) under vine, it makes up a little over 3 percent of the vines in Argentina. Deep, inky violet in color, Merlot tastes of rich cherry, blueberry, elderberries, mint, and eucalyptus. Its lower tannins bring softness when blended with Malbec or Cabernet Sauvignon.

PEDRO GIMÉNEZ

The most extensively cultivated white grape in Argentina, Pedro Giménez is farmed on 13,476 hectares (33,300 acres), or approximately 6 percent of the land under vine. It is a type of Criolla that may or may not be related to Spain's Pedro Ximénez, but is nonetheless also used to make fortified wine.

PINOT NOIR

The new star of the South, Pinot Noir has flourished for many years in the Mendoza region, where it was often used to make white and rosé sparkling wine. Old bush vine Pinot Noir from Neuquén and Río Negro now produce premium reds. Its color ranges from medium to deep red, and Pinot Noir's typical flavor profile of cherry and chocolate is balanced by strong acidity. Its 1,680 hectares (4,151 acres) of vineyard amount to 0.75 percent of all those in Argentina.

SANGIOVESE

The 2,258 hectares (5,580 acres) of Sangiovese, one of the varieties introduced by nineteenth-century Italian immigrants, embody 1 percent of all the grapes grown in Argentina. It tastes primarily of cherry, strawberry, and violet; Sangiovese can also display tomato leaf or mint characteristics, which are usually associated with *terroir*. Although it is generally thought that Argentine Sangiovese is inferior to the Tuscan variety, the combination of increased quality in Argentine wine in general and a renewed interest in the variety has led to the availability of limited quantities of choice Sangiovese coming out of Argentina.

SAUVIGNON BLANC

Modest in quantity but not in flavor, Sauvignon Blanc—with its essences of citrus, tropical fruit, green pepper, and fresh herbs—grows on 2,278 hectares (5,629 acres), most of it (around 80 percent) in the Mendoza region. Sauvignon Blanc makes up 1 percent of all grapevines planted in Argentina. It makes crisp, clean, usually unoaked white wines. Some Sauvignon Blanc is also grown in the Neuquén and Río Negro regions.

SÉMILLON

Only 956 hectares (2,362 acres) of Sémillon—not even one-half of one percent of the national grape cultivation—grace the vineyards of Argentina. Most of it grows in the Uco Valley of Mendoza, with smaller but still significant amounts in Río Negro, in Patagonia. White wines made with Mendozan Sémillon tend to run toward the aromatic end of the spectrum, with flavors of peach, honey, and light spice, while Sémillon from the south exhibits apple with a hint of forest floor.

SYRAH

This "northern Rhône" red variety (thought to have originated in the Middle East) is propagated on 13,100 hectares (32,371 acres), or around 6 percent of vine land in Argentina. It is often blended with Malbec to add freshness of fruit and richness of mouth feel. As a single varietal, it can be vinified into a powerful "fruit bomb," or alternatively into a wine of delicate complexity. Regardless of style, in a glass of Syrah we would expect to taste plum, black cherry, anise, pepper, and some touches of smoke or earth. The wine will be a deep violet with red highlights. Grown throughout the country, Syrah is most abundant in the Mendoza, San Juan, Catamarca, and La Rioja regions.

TANNAT

The red wine grape most associated with Uruguay—brought to South America by nineteenth-century Basque settlers from its native France—Tannat is noted for its flavors of blackberry, cherry, and raspberry and strong tannic structure. Traditionally used in blending, it has been bottled as a single varietal for a little more than 10 years. It is only grown to any degree in Salta, near Cafayate, where some plantings date back to the 1970s.

TEMPRANILLO

A transplant from its native Spain, Tempranillo is cultivated in the Mendoza region. Its 6,568 hectares (16,230 acres) are almost 3 percent of all the grapes grown in Argentina. With deep ruby color and flavors of cherry, plum, cassis, chocolate, and tobacco leaf, it is bottled on its own or with Bordeaux varieties. Its name comes from the Spanish *temprano,* meaning "early," a reference to the fact that Tempranillo ripens early in the harvest season.

TORRONTÉS

Argentina's signature white grape, and the only truly native Argentine variety. Torrontés is noted for its delicate aromatics and rich flavor profile of rose petal, white flowers, peach, and light spice. There are four types of Torrontés in Argentina; only one, Torrontés Riojano, is used for fine wine. It grows on 8,442 hectares (20,861 acres), or about 3.7 percent of total planted area. (The other types of Torrontés are Torrontés Sanjuanino, Torrontés Mendocino, and Torontel.) All are distinct crossings of Mission or Criolla Chica with Muscat of Alexandria—varieties brought by the original Spanish settlers. If you buy a bottle of wine simply labeled "Torrontés," it will be the Riojano version, because this is the one that makes wine with the finest flavor and aromatics. Widely cultivated across the land, Torrontés is found in the Mendoza, San Juan, La Rioja, and Salta regions. Of these, the best expression of Torrontés is said to come from high-altitude Salta, especially the area closest to Cafayate.

VIOGNIER

An almost miniscule amount—only 748 hectares (1,848 acres), which is one-third of one percent of overall vine plantings—of Viognier is under cultivation in Argentina, mainly in Mendoza. Its distinctive aromatic nose and flavors of fruit and flowers carry through, regardless of whether it is vinified only in stainless or aged in oak as well. Plantings are small, but Viognier is a variety that Argentine winemakers enjoy working with.

ARGENTINA

CHILE

PARAGUAY

BRAZIL

SALTA

CALCHAQUÍ VALLEYS

CATAMARCA

LA RIOJA

SAN JUAN

UPPER MENDOZA RIVER — NORTHERN MENDOZA

UCO VALLEY — MENDOZA

EASTERN MENDOZA/
CENTRAL VALLEY

URUGUAY

Buenos Aires

SOUTHERN MENDOZA

LA PAMPA

NEUQUÉN

RÍO NEGRO

ATLANTIC
OCEAN

PACIFIC
OCEAN

N

0 Miles   400

0 Kilometers   800

© 2012 Jeffrey L. Ward

WINE REGIONS

CALCHAQUÍ VALLEYS

This enchanting 520-kilometer-long (323-mile) network of valleys runs through the provinces of Salta, Tacuman, and Catamarca, in Argentina's northwest. The Calchaquí Valleys are not an official wine region; they are grouped together more for tourism purposes than as a wine designation. Their landscape takes in the imposing beauty of the Andes, valleys filled with archeological riches and natural wonders, and a series of crystalline rivers offering exhilarating rapids and placid lakes formed by dams. Vineyards and jungle waterfalls soar at altitudes unknown anywhere else in the world. Devotion to Jesus and the Virgin Mary exists alongside celebrations honoring Pachamama, the Earth Mother worshiped by the original inhabitants of the Andes.

The Calchaquí Valleys are crossed by many waterways, including the Calchaquí, Las Conchas, Chusca, Sali, Los Sosa, and Santa Maria Rivers. Pre-Columbian and Spanish colonial towns and cities punctuate the dramatic scenery, including Salta, Cafayate, Santa Maria, San Carlos, Cachi, and Molinos. Some of the loftiest—in terms of both quality and altitude—wineries in Argentina are located along the Calchaquí Valley Wine Route, which runs through the Salta and Catamarca regions; wineries are listed by specific region. Tourism options abound; whether your taste runs toward white-water rafting, horseback riding, sightseeing, tasting wine, or spending the night in a neo-rustic inn, the Calchaquí Valleys offer activities to suit your desire.

SALTA

The origins of the name *Salta* are unclear, but the favored explanation—that it derives from the Aymara tribe's word for "very beautiful"—makes sense to anyone who has ever been here. This region in the far northwest of Argentina is home to the highest vineyards in the world, which vary in altitude from 1,280 to 3,005 meters (4,200 to 9,860 feet) above sea level. Salta boasts a variety of climates, including tropical forests, Andean deserts, and warm weather valleys. It boasts two beautiful colonial Spanish cities, Salta in the northeast and Cafayate in the south. The city of Salta, founded in 1582 as a trading post between Lima, Peru, and Buenos Aires, is 1,268 kilometers (788 miles) from Cafayate. Some of the first successful grape plantings in Argentina took place here in the sixteenth century.

Fifty-three percent of the grapes grown here are red varieties. Malbec and Cabernet Sauvignon each comprise 20 percent of the total regional production; the balance consists of Tannat, Bonarda, Merlot, and Syrah. Almost all of the white grapes grown here are Torrontés, with small amounts of Chardonnay and Sauvignon Blanc rounding out the total. It is said that the finest Torrontés in the country is crafted here. Most production in Salta centers around Cafayate, which is the geographic center of the Calchaquí Valley. Named for an indigenous tribe, the city was founded in 1840 on the site of a Spanish mission.

The high altitude, hot, sunny days, and cool nights are the basis for grape-growing and wine production of the highest quality. A relatively dry region, Salta receives only 203 millimeters, or 8 inches, of rainfall in a given year. The *el parral* trellis system is used abundantly here, seen in over 60 percent of vineyards. Vines are trained into pergolas 2 meters (6.5 feet) in height, shielding the delicate Torrontés from the harsh effects of the hot sun and allowing the grapes to develop the best expression of flavor. Salta's 2,300 cultivated hectares (5,683 acres) scarcely make up 1 percent of total Argentine wine production, but there is no doubt that this distinct *terroir* is valued by wine lovers and winemakers alike.

COLOMÉ

Ruta Provincial 53 Kilometer 20, Molinos, Salta, +54 38 6849 4200, www.bodegacolome.com

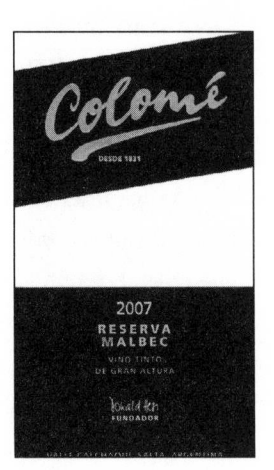

In 2002, Donald M. Hess retired as CEO of Hess Family Estates, but not before falling in love with Argentina in 1999 and buying the property that would become his beloved Finca Colomé. His love of art is well known, and in April 2009, the bodega inaugurated a museum honoring California artist James Turrell, which displays five decades of his work. Colomé Estate Malbec 2008 is composed of

85 percent Malbec, 8 percent Tannat, 3 percent Cabernet Sauvignon, 2 percent Petit Verdot, and 2 percent Syrah. It is dark garnet red, with notes of black fruits, baking spices, clove, and fresh ground black pepper. On the palate it is silky smooth and full-bodied. The finish is lingering with persistent vanilla notes. Colomé Amalaya 2008 is a blend of 75 percent Malbec, 15 percent Cabernet Sauvignon, 5 percent Syrah, and 5 percent Tannat. It is garnet ruby red in color, with notes of red cherries, red raspberries, and vanilla bean in the bouquet. In the mouth it is spicy and vibrant. Colomé Reserva 2007 is a blend of 90 percent Malbec and 10 percent Cabernet Sauvignon. It is dark red in the glass, and the bouquet consists of ripe red and black fruits with a touch of spice. In the mouth it is powerful and elegant with a lingering finish. Only 4,800 bottles were made in 2007.

VASIJA SECRETA

Ruta 40 s/n, Cafayate, Salta,
+54 38 6842 1850,
www.vasijasecreta.com

Casa Cordova y Murga Vasija Secreta is the oldest winery in the Cafayate Valley. It was established in 1857. It is well known for its mineral-driven Torrontés, as well as red wines including Malbec and Tannat. Located at an altitude of 1,650 meters (5,413 feet) above sea level, Casa Cordova y Murga also grows Sauvignon Blanc, Merlot, Chardonnay, and Cabernet Sauvignon. When you are there make sure to pre-arrange a lunch and tasting. The chefs will prepare a delicious wine-paired meal focusing on typical Andean cuisine with Creole touches. Vasija Secreta VAS Torrontés 2010 is medium straw-colored, with aromas of rose petal and geranium. It tastes crisp with flavors of pineapple and rose petal and a geranium leaf finish. Vasija Secreta Lacrado Malbec 2009 is medium garnet, with aromas of cherry, white chocolate, and orange peel. On the palate it has a bright fruitiness with flavors of cherry, orange peel, and licorice. The finish is pleasant.

YACOCHUYA

Finca Yacochuya, Cafayate, Salta,
+54 3868 421 233,
www.sanpedrodeyacochuya.com.ar

Arnaldo Benito Etchart bought the winery that was later to become Yacochuya in the early twentieth century and began selling wine under his family name. Etchart Wines were successful in the domestic market and maintained a strong presence in the international market. In 1988, the family brought in renowned consultant Michel Rolland, and the first product of their collaboration was released the following year. In 1996, the company was sold to the Pernot Ricard Group and began exporting its premium wine, Yacochuya M. Rolland five years later. The property is home to one of the highest wineries in the world at 2,035 meters (6,677 feet) above sea level, and is 16 hectares (39 acres) in size. Nine hectares (22 acres) are devoted to Malbec, 4 hectares (10 acres) to Cabernet Sauvignon, 2 hectares (5 acres) to Torrontés and 1 hectare (2 acre) to Tannat. San Pedro de Yacochuya Torrontés 2008 has aromas of white flowers and tropical fruits. In the mouth it is crisp and dry. San Pedro de Yacochuya Tinto 2006 is made with 85 percent Malbec and 15 percent Cabernet Sauvignon and has beautiful fruit aromas framed in light oak. It's a big and delicious wine with a lovely finish.

CATAMARCA

Catamarca—in the northwest of the country—is south of Salta and west of La Rioja. It borders the Andes and Chile to the west. Eleven hundred and thirty kilometers (702 miles) from Buenos Aires, the region's capital city, San Fernando del Valle de Catamarca, was created as a Spanish outpost called Londres (London) in 1558 and was then settled permanently under this new moniker in 1683. The name Catamarca means "stronghold on the hillside" in the native Quechua language.

Eighty percent of the terrain consists of mountains; 70 percent of regional inhabitants live in or near the capital. Because of the rugged landscape, Catamarca was isolated until the railroad arrived in 1888, and among the first immigrant groups to arrive at that time were those from Lebanon and Iran. Both groups quickly turned to farming in the fertile valleys fed by Andean snowmelt.

Catamarca houses a treasure-trove of pre-Columbian and colonial Spanish archeological sites. The Church of the Virgin of the Valley is visited by tourists and religious pilgrims alike, and local handicrafts such as pottery and woven ponchos make great souvenirs to take home—alongside prized bottles of Torrontés, Malbec, Syrah, and Cabernet Sauvignon. Until recently, most of the local fruit of the vine was destined to be made into cheap jug wine or raisins, but an uptick in the number of boutique wineries has seen a sharp increase in Catamarca wine quality. Ecotourism, adventure tourism, and wine tourism provide a host of activities for visitors.

Vineyards sit at altitudes of 1,106 to 2,194 meters (3,300 to 7,200 feet) in this semiarid region. Annual rainfall averages 431 millimeters, or 17 inches. Average summer temperatures are between 22 and 38 degrees Celsius (72 and 100 degrees Fahrenheit). The main wine-producing areas are the Fiambala Valley, in the west, and the eastern Santa Maria, which is in the Calchaquí Valley. The area has a total of 2,583 hectares (6,383 acres) of grapevines, almost half of which are vinified into rustic local wine. Over 13 percent of the grapes grown here are Torrontés, and just over 12 percent are Cabernet Sauvignon. Syrah is the next most cultivated, at 9 percent, followed by Malbec, at 6 percent. Bonarda and Merlot are also grown here. Most of the boutique wineries of Catamarca have not yet made their presence known in the international market.

CABERNET DE LOS ANDES

Ruta 41 s/n, Pampa Blanca, Catamarca,
+54 3833 425 308,
www.tizac-vicien.com

Founded by Carlos Arizu and Pedro Vicien Arizcuren in 2000, Cabernet de Los Andes is making quality biodynamic and organic wines at altitudes of 1,500 to 2,000 meters (4,921 to 6,562 feet) on the slopes of the Fiambala Valley. Its varieties include Bonarda, Malbec, Syrah, Torrontés, and Cabernet Sauvignon. Vicien Cabernet de los Andes Bonarda Reserve 2007 has initial notes of red berries, red plums, and a touch of fruit conserves. It is full-bodied with a lingering finish. Vicien Cabernet de los Andes Malbec 2007 has aromas of ripe red berries and herbs. It is dry in the mouth with a long finish.

LA RIOJA

One of the first areas in which the Spanish missionaries planted grapes, the full name of the province's capital city is Todos los Santos de la Nueva Rioja, or "All the Saints of the New Rioja." The city now known as La Rioja is 1,167 kilometers (725 miles) north of Buenos Aires. The surrounding landscape offers arid deserts and lush green valleys, some of the highest mountains in the Americas, and broad, wind-swept plains. In addition to grapes, olives, peaches, and cherries are also grown here. The province offers an assortment of leisure activities, including hiking, skiing, ecotourism, and a unique gastronomic circuit, Rioja Flavors, which exposes visitors to local farmers and producers of wine, olive oil, preserves, lamb, and small game. Talampaya National Park, a Unesco World Heritage site since 2000, is awash with natural beauty, the remains of dinosaurs, and evidence of the first humans to inhabit the continent.

In May 2011 Argentina won the right in international court to use the words "La Rioja Argentina" on bottled wine from this region. That right had been legally disputed for 12 years by the Spanish, who claimed exclusive right to the word "Rioja" in regard to wine.

The most important area for wine here is the Famatina Valley; wine is also produced in

Nonogasta, Chilecito, and Antinaco. Average rainfall is a mere 129 millimeters, or 5 inches annually, and the highest altitude vineyard is at 1,719 meters (5,640 feet). Summer temperatures vary between 20 and 35 degrees Celsius (68 and 95 degrees Fahrenheit). The *el parral* trellis system is also used in La Rioja, as its protective self-canopy provides necessary shade for the ripening of grapes.

Red and white wine grapes each make up 40 percent of total cultivation; another 10 percent is comprised of grapes of either color destined for rosé, and another 10 percent are set aside to be eaten as table grapes or raisins. The number one grape variety in La Rioja is Torrontés—35 percent of Riojan grapes are the Argentine native. By contrast, Cabernet Sauvignon—the next most popular variety—accounts for only 13 percent, followed by Syrah (9 percent), Bonarda (8 percent), and Malbec. Moscatel of Alexandria has a presence in Rioja, and small amounts of Merlot are also found here.

BODEGAS SAN HUBERTO

Calle Virgilio Ferreira, Castro Barros, La Rioja,
+54 3827 494 040,
www.bodegassanhuberto.com.ar

One of the first Argentine bodegas to open a winery in China, San Huberto has always

been a bit in front of the curve. The company maintains wineries in Luján de Cuyo and La Rioja and owns 350 hectares (865 acres) in both. It also has contracts with growers in La Rioja and Mendoza for an additional 200 hectares (494 acres) of Cabernet Sauvignon and Malbec. In China, it has planted in the Huailai region and will sell into the domestic Chinese market and to other Asian countries. San Huberto Cabernet Sauvignon Reserva 2007 is deep garnet colored, with aromas of cherry jam, black pepper, and sweet red cherries. In the mouth there are sweet, rounded tannins and a finishing note of mocha. San Huberto Syrah Reserva 2007 is deep violet red in the glass with nice viscosity. It has aromas of red plum, cherry, and chocolate. On the palate it has flavors of sweet blackberry jam and a touch of chocolate. It has sweet tannins and a lingering finish. San Huberto Nina Petit Verdot 2006 is purple and inky, with notes of cherry and red plum in the nose. The palate is big and has a long finish.

LA RIOJANA

La Plata 646, Chilecito, La Rioja,
+54 3825 423 150,
www.lariojana.com.ar

Begun as a cooperative in 1940, La Riojana consists of 451 members, most of whom are small to medium grape growers and wine producers. In 1998, the company received its ISO 9000/2000 certification and has been working within international guidelines of organic production. It is located in the Famatina Valley and has an annual capacity of 64,152,700 liters of wine. Its wines have won awards in national and international wine competitions including the International Wine Challenge. La Riojana Raza Malbec 2003 is deep red in color, with aromas of red plums, dried cherries, chocolate, and a touch of cigar box. It is full-bodied and round on the palate with a fair amount of complexity. It has a long, persistent finish. La Riojana Santa Florentina Cabernet Sauvignon 2008 is purplish red in color, with notes of red fruits, plums, and red raspberries. It is balanced and smooth in the mouth and has a persistent finish.

SAN JUAN

The San Juan valleys have the benefit of one of the sunniest climates on Earth, with only 30 days per year of cloud-cover. Minimal rainfall of 102 millimeters, or 4 inches, per year is supplemented by the San Juan River and irrigation derived from melting Andean snow. San Juan is divided into five valleys: Calingasta, Pedernal, Tulum, Ullum, and Zonda. The last is also the name of a strong wind that is important to the region; the Zonda Wind, derived from high-altitude polar currents, initiates much of the winter precipitation that provides water during the long, dry summer. A devastating earthquake in 1944 damaged much of the capital city of San Juan, which is now much more of a modern city than many of its colonial neighbors. It was a San Juan native, Domingo Faustino Sarmiento, who hired the agronomist Miguel Pouget to found the National Vine Nursery in 1853.

San Juan is Argentina's second largest producer of wine, behind Mendoza. It has 41,492 hectares (102,529 acres) under cultivation. Its vineyards grow at altitudes ranging between 700 meters (2,297 feet) in the Tulum Valley and 1,340 meters (4,396 feet) in the Pedernal Valley, the two most important areas of quality wines in San Juan. Tulum's soils are comprised of clay, sand, and silty loam, while Pedernal's are alluvial layered over stone. Seventy-eight percent of the grapes from San Juan make it into wine bottles; the remainder are eaten as fresh table grapes or raisins. Almost half of the grapes destined for wine are vinified into inexpensive table wine.

Syrah is San Juan's star variety and covers 9 percent of vineyard land. Bonarda, Cabernet Sauvignon, and Torrontés Sanjuanino—a relative of the more common Torrontés Riojano—each comprise about 6 percent of total grape cultivation. Unlike in other regions, a bottle labeled "Torrontés" from San Juan will contain Torrontés Sanjuanino, not Riojano. Malbec is also at home here, accounting for slightly more than 5 percent. Smaller but still significant amounts of Tannat, Chardonnay, and Sauvignon Blanc flourish in the vineyards of San Juan. Besides grapes, olives also play an important role in San Juan's agriculture; the Olive Production Museum offers the gourmet traveler a wide array of local food products. The nearby Ullum Dam Reservoir is a popular spot for locals and tourists to enjoy a day of swimming, sailing, or windsurfing.

AUGUSTO PULENTA

Finca Las Rosas, San Martín County, San Juan,
+54 264 420 2553,
www.augustopulenta.com

Augusto Pulenta, one of founder Don Angelo Pulenta's sons, was born in 1906 and raised working in the estate's vineyards. The company later evolved to become the wine giant Peñaflor Trapiche. In 1997, Augusto's son Mario sold his stock in the original family business and founded Augusto Pulenta, which he proudly named after his father. Today Mario and his sons oversee 200 hectares (494 acres) of vines and continue the family legacy of fine-wine production through hard work, tradition, and a touch of modern technology. Augusto Pulenta Valbona Malbec Roble 2008 is deep garnet colored, with aromatic notes of espresso, red berries, and cocoa. On the palate it has a large presence and a persistent finish. Augusto Pulenta Valbona Cabernet Sauvignon Roble 2008 is more of a ruby red color. The nose offers smoked meats, ripe fruits, and a vanilla frame. In the mouth it is Rubenesque and intense. Augusto Pulenta Augusto P. 2007 is deep red in color. Sweet vanilla and oak notes give way to aromas of dried fruits and ripe black plums. In the mouth it is viscous and rich with a persistent finish. Only 5,000 bottles of this tribute wine were made and, given the quality, that's a shame.

CALLIA

Avenida José Maria de los Rios, s/n,
Pie de Palo, Caucete, San Juan,
+54 264 496 0000,
www.bodegascallia.com

When you drive down the entrance to the winery, you can't help but notice the intricate stone walls with their iridescent colors. Built in the ancient Incan style, Callia owners hired Peruvian stonemason and artist Percy Cuellar to create this masterpiece with carefully selected stone from a neighboring quarry. The head winemaker is José Morales, and the chief agronomist is Rodolfo Perinetti. Together, they craft wines from the estate's 321 hectares (793 acres), 241 (596) of them in Tulum Valley and the remaining 80 (197) in the Pedernal Valley. Bodegas Callia Grand Callia 2006 is a blend of 40 percent Shiraz, 20 percent Malbec, 20 percent Merlot, and 20 percent Tannat. It is dark red with inky purple hues. On the nose you detect anise,

coconut, and ripe black fruits. The palate offers a creamy mouthfeel with round, soft tannins. On the finish, there is a touch of spice. Bodegas Callia Magna Malbec 2008 is deep red with a touch of blue. It has aromas of fruit conserves and a hint of spice. In the mouth it is big and offers flavors of ripe fruits and sweet tannins. Bodegas Callia Alta Shiraz-Malbec 2009 is made up of 70 percent Shiraz and 30 percent Malbec. It is ruby red and has aromas of cassis and red cherry. In the mouth it is like velvet, and the smooth tannins linger for a long time.

GRAFFIGNA

Colón Norte 1342, Desemparados, San Juan,
+54 264 421 0669,
www.graffignawines.com

Started in 1870 by Italian immigrant Santiago Graffigna, Bodegas y Viñedos Graffigna is an

important winemaking name in Argentina's history. Santiago is well known for many firsts in his adopted land, and his entrepreneurial vision included extending the railroad to San Juan, so that he could get his wine distributed to the city of Buenos Aires. Graffigna Centenario Reserve Malbec 2008 is dark red with purple tones. It has a nose of dark fruits, blackberry, and black plums, with just a touch of freshly ground black pepper. In the mouth it has ripe tannins and finishes with a smidgeon of espresso and cinnamon toast. Graffigna Centenario Cabernet Sauvignon 2007 is garnet red colored, with a touch of anise overlying aromas of black plums. In the mouth it's fruity with a hint of black pepper. The tannins are soft with a long finish.

FINCA LAS MORAS

Avenida Rawson s/n, San Martín, San Juan,
+54 261 520 7200,
www.fincalasmoras.com.ar

Finca Las Moras vineyards were restructured by renowned vineyard expert Richard Smart in 1993. Its name is taken from the mulberry trees that surround the vineyards. The Finca's holdings, which total 960 hectares (2,372 acres), are located in Tulum, Pedernal, and Zonda. Finca Las Moras Black Label Cabernet-Cabernet 2008 is a blend of 50

percent Cabernet Sauvignon and 50 percent Cabernet Franc. It is deep red in color and has aromas of dark fruits, black pepper, and a whiff of chocolate. In the mouth it has silky texture and fine-grained tannins. Finca Las Moras Mora Negra 2007 is 70 percent Malbec and 30 percent Bonarda. It is purplish red and has deep fruity notes in the bouquet. In the mouth you can feel the ripe fruits on your tongue. The tannins are mild, and the finish pleasant, with a touch of chocolate to make you smile. Las Moras Reserve Tannat 2008 is deep, dark red, with notes of herbs, touches of mint and eucalyptus underlying dark blackberries and cassis. On the palate you notice the firm tannins, but they give way to a pleasant, long finish.

MENDOZA

From the first grape cuttings carried from Spain by Jesuit priests in the mid-sixteenth century through the creation of the National Vine Library and the arrival of trains three hundred years later, to the present day, Mendoza not only has retained its position as the wine capital of Argentina but also has been recognized in 2005 as one of the Great Wine Capitals of the World. By road, Mendoza is 1,049 kilometers (652 miles) from Buenos Aires, which is a long way—but it is a longer way still from the days of wine held in leather wineskins transported by oxcart to the cosmopolitan capital city of Mendoza and the state-of-the-art equipment installed in the otherwise traditional wineries of this esteemed region. With total vineyard area of 160,704 hectares (397,108 acres), Mendoza is the number one wine-producing region in the country, and home to a staggering quantity of wineries vying for a share of the domestic and international market.

Ciudad de Mendoza del Nuevo Valle de la Rioja, now simply shortened to Mendoza, was established in 1561. Prior to that, it had been inhabited by the Huarpe, Puelche, and Inca peoples. Together, the Huarpes and Incas developed a series of irrigation canals (later expanded by Spanish settlers) that are still in use today as the primary source of vineyard water throughout most of Mendoza. A calamitous earthquake in 1861 destroyed much of the city and killed 5,000 people; the city was rebuilt with the broad avenues and tree-lined plazas it is known for today. Mendoza is the center of wine tourism for the region and is also a stopping off point for climbers on their way to nearby Aconcagua, which at 6,959 meters (22,831 feet) is the tallest mountain in the Americas. Besides winery visits and stays at vineyard hotels and *estancias*, Mendoza also draws travelers for its proximity to horseback riding, rafting, hiking, mountain biking, and skiing. Today, metropolitan Mendoza has a population of almost 900,000; 88 percent of the populace live in the nearby suburbs of Godoy Cruz, Guaymallén, Las Heras, Luján de Cuyo, and Maipú.

The region's vineyards start at an altitude of 457 meters (1,499 feet) and peak at 1,700 meters (5,577 feet) above sea level. Average annual rainfall is 203 millimeters, or 8 inches, which is less than a quarter of the annual rainfall in Bordeaux and about a third of what is received in Burgundy or the Napa Valley. About half of the vines here are trained to the *el parral* system; the 2-meter-high (6.5-foot) pergolas shield grapes from the heat of the sun. Mendoza is divided into five subregions: Northern Mendoza, Eastern Mendoza, Upper Mendoza River (also called the Mendoza River Area), Uco Valley, and Southern Mendoza. Each is further divided into departments, several of which hold prized *terroir* (the Argentine version of Saint-Émilion or Pauillac), such as Upper Mendoza's Luján de Cuyo or Uco Valley's Tupungato.

NORTHERN MENDOZA

Containing the departments of Guaymallén, Las Heras, Lavalle, San Martín, and a portion of Maipú, Northern Mendoza is the lowest area in the region, with average vineyard altitudes of 600 to 700 meters (1,968 to 2,297 feet). The Mendoza River provides water, and average summer temperature is 25.6 degrees Celsius (78 degrees Fahrenheit). Local rosé wines are produced here from the Criolla Grande, Cereza, and Moscatel Rosado grape varieties. The area around Lavalle is now undergoing vineyard rehabilitation, replacing table and jug grape varieties with international varieties suitable for fine wine. Bonarda is planted in 14 percent of Northern Mendoza vineyards. Syrah accounts for over 9 percent of grape cultivation, and Cabernet Sauvignon, Torrontés, and Malbec each make up between 4 and 5 percent of area production.

CAVAS DEL 23

Godoy Cruz, Rodeo de la Cruz,
Guaymallén, Mendoza,
+54 9261 527 2292,
www.cavasdel23.com.ar

Named for the antique winery built in 1923, Cavas del 23 is the dream come true of Alfredo Meyer and Alejandro Jausoro. They purchased the clay and reed structure along with 36 hectares (89 acres) of vines in 2002 and have since focused on making high-quality wines. The winemakers are Roberto Anglat and Oliver Ruhard. They make two ranges of wine, Beviam and Imperio de Sentidos. Cavas

del 23 Beviam Cabernet Sauvignon 2007 is deep ruby red and has aromas of blackberry, black plums, and a touch of spice. In the mouth it's full and fruit-forward with a lingering finish. Cavas del 23 Beviam Reserve Malbec 2007 is purple colored, with aromas of red cherries, red raspberries, and red plums. On the palate the structure is balanced and the tannins ripe. Cavas del 23 Imperio de Sentidos Malbec Rosé 2009 is a brilliant pink color, with light fruity notes of strawberries and red fruits. In the mouth it's playful and delightful—perfect as an aperitif.

CICCHITTI

Buenos Vecinos 57, Rodeo de la Cruz,
Guaymallén, Mendoza,
+54 261 491 0845,
www.bodegacicchitti.com

Founded in 1928, Bodega Cicchitti underwent a major expansion in 2001. The winery now has capacity for 1,120,000 liters, and in 2010 it earned organic status. Cicchitti Torrontés 2009 is straw yellow in color, with aromas of citrus blossoms and spice. In the mouth it is round and has balanced acidity. Cicchitti Malbec 2007 is ruby red with a violet tint and has aromas of ripe red plums, red raspberries, and blackberries. It is round on the palate with sweet tannins. Cicchitti

Blend 2008 is composed of 60 percent Malbec, 30 percent Cabernet Sauvignon, and 10 percent Merlot. It is ruby red with dark black tints. It has aromas of black fruits, black plums, and cassis and is powerful yet friendly on the palate. The finish is smooth and lasting, with a touch of vanilla.

LOS TONELES

Bandera de Los Andes 1393,
Guaymallén, Mendoza,
+54 261 449 0850,
www.bodegalostoneles.com

One of the few historic urban wineries within the city of Mendoza, Bodega Los Toneles was built in 1922 and remains a cultural landmark. It is popular as an event space and can hold up to 1,200 people. The restaurant and wine bar are also a local favorite. Its wines have won awards in many international competitions. Juan Pablo Micheleni leads the winemaking team. Los Toneles makes quality wines using Malbec, Cabernet Sauvignon, Chardonnay, and Torrontés varieties. We just happen to be partial to this winery's Malbecs. Toneles Tonel 22 Malbec 2010 is light purple, with aromas of black plums, dark cherries, and purple flowers. It is ample-bodied in the mouth with a balanced structure. Toneles Gran Tonel 137 Malbec 2009 is purple reddish in color, with notes of red plums, red raspberry, and violet in the bouquet. There are top notes of mocha and cigar box as the wine hits your back palate. The finish is long and luxurious.

REYTER

Carril Urquiza 2019, San Francisco del Monte,
Guaymallén, Mendoza,
+54 261 426 5698
www.bodegareyter.com.ar

Bodega Casa Vinícola Reyter began in 1888. It is one of the few remaining wineries near the city of Mendoza. In 2005, Casa Reyter expanded its visitor center to house art and sculptures made by local Mendozan artists as well as artists from other regions of Argentina. A hotel is currently under construction. Casa Vinícola Reyter Finca La Martina Malbec 2007 is reddish purple in the glass, with notes of red plum, red raspberry, and vanilla. In the mouth there's a burst of fruit with round, sweet tannins. Casa Vinícola Reyter Finca La Martina Chardonnay 2007 is straw yellow, with aromas of fresh tropical fruits. In the mouth it's round and pleasant with a fresh finish.

SANTA ANA

General Roca y General Urquiza s/n,
Villa Nueva, Guaymallén, Mendoza,
+ 54 261 520 7219,
www.bodegas-santa-ana.com.ar

We bet Luis Tirasso would be surprised to see how large his dream has grown. He emigrated from Italy in 1891, and today his Santa Ana wines are available in more than 45 countries. The company owns a significant portion of the vineyards used to produce its quality wines, and the owners are especially proud of the La Mascota vineyards in the Cruz de Piedra region of Maipú. There they grow Cabernet Sauvignon, Malbec, Shiraz, Chardonnay, Viognier, and Sauvignon Blanc. Winemaker Rodolfo "Opi" Sadler has capacity for 12,000,000 liters of wine in Santa Ana's cellars. Santa Ana Homage Opi Malbec 2008 is made in his honor. It is red-purplish in color, with aromas of red fruit, cherry, vanilla ice cream, and a touch of cocoa powder. In the mouth it's big and bold with a lingering finish that pleases with a touch of dark chocolate. Santa Ana Cabernet Sauvignon 2007 is dark red with violet highlights. It has aromas of red fruits and a touch of green pepper and coffee. In the mouth it's balanced and persistent. Santa Ana La Mascota Chardonnay 2006 is light yellow, with notes of pineapple, pear, and tropical fruits. It's round in the mouth with a pleasant finish.

EASTERN MENDOZA/ CENTRAL VALLEY

On a broad plain crossed by the Mendoza and Tunuyán Rivers, Eastern Mendoza encompasses the Junín, La Paz, Rivadavia, San Martín, and Santa Rosa departments. One of the most densely planted areas of the country, Eastern Mendoza has vines that sit at altitudes of 600 to 750 meters (1,968 to 2,461 feet). About half of the grapes grown here are

Criolla varieties aimed at the bargain domestic market, but replanting efforts are underway, and the balance (toward higher quality wines) is expected to shift in coming years. There has also been marked progress in vineyard management, irrigation, and winemaking technology. As in Northern Mendoza, Bonarda is the number one variety, blanketing about 12 percent of the area's 72,000 hectares (177,916 acres). Malbec accounts for about half the amount of Bonarda, followed by Syrah and Cabernet Sauvignon, which each comprise 5 percent of Eastern Mendoza's vines. Tempranillo brings up the rear, at 4 percent of total volume. This is the hottest area of Mendoza, with deep, sandy soils.

NOFAL

Rufino Ortega 453, Alto Verde,
San Martín, Mendoza,
+54 261 420 0976
www.bodeganofal.com.ar

Established in 1950 by Gabriel Nofal, Bodega y Viñedos Nofal continues today under the direction of his daughters Ercilia, Beatriz, Nora, and Teresa Nofal Alonso. Winemaker Carlos González is one of the few high-ranking men in the company. He makes excellent wines from the family's Malbec, Tempranillo, Syrah, Sangiovese, Bonarda, Cabernet Sauvignon, and Barbera d'Asti varieties. The family owns vineyards in Los Sauces-Tunuyán and Alto Verde, San Martín. Bodega Nofal Tempranillo 2006 is garnet, with notes of strawberry jam, black plums, and cassis. It is pleasant on the palate and has a lasting finish. Bodega Nofal Santa Ercilia Cabernet Sauvignon 2006 is ruby red in the glass, with aromas of green and red pepper and dark berries. In the mouth it's a big wine with balanced freshness and smooth tannins.

UPPER MENDOZA RIVER

The Upper Mendoza River region (also called simply Mendoza River) is home to not only the capital city but also some of the finest wineries in all of Argentina, distributed among the departments of Maipú, Godoy Cruz, and Luján de Cuyo. The Uco Valley and Upper Mendoza River regions battle it out for title of "best," an honor that can only be bestowed based on a winery by winery or even bottle by bottle survey. Maipú contains even more narrowly defined districts famous for their excellent wine, including Barrancas, Coquimbito, and Lunlunta. Within the Luján de Cuyo DOC we find the Agrelo, Las Compuertas, Perdriel, and Vistalba districts. There is a wide range of vineyard altitudes here—from 650 to 1,050 meters (2,132 to 3,445 feet). The Mendoza River region holds some of the most highly prized farmland in the world for the cultivation of grapes. Malbec leads the pack, ensconced on 33 percent of the regions' 26,000 hectares (64,247 acres). Cabernet Sauvignon barely accounts for half that amount, with 15 percent of vineyard soil. Bonarda accounts for 6 percent, and Merlot and Chardonnay are tied at 4.5 percent each. Syrah and Tempranillo each make up just over 3 percent of Upper Mendoza's total.

ACHAVAL-FERRER

Calle Cobos 2601, Pedriel,
+54 261 489 2247,
www.achaval-ferrer.com

In 1998 six friends—four Argentines and two Italians—decided to make wine together.

In 1999 they had their first harvest. Their wines have been well received in domestic and international press, and Achaval-Ferrer now exports to more than forty countries. The group owns about 30 hectares (about 74 acres) of vineyards and has contracts with grape growers for approximately 40 hectares (99 acres) more. The chief winemaker is co-owner Roberto Cipresso. His Achaval-Ferrer Finca Altamira Malbec 2008 is reddish purple, with aromas of red and black fruits. It has good heft on the palate with pleasant grippy tannins in the finish. Achaval-Ferrer Finca Mirador Malbec 2008 is purplish-red, with aromas of black plums, blackberries, and a touch of minerality. It is full-bodied in the mouth with a persistent finish.

ALTA VISTA

Alzaga 3972, Luján de Cuyo, Mendoza,
+54 261 496 4684,
www.altavistawines.com

Alta Vista is part of the Edonia Group, a French company owned by the d'Aulan family of Piper-Heidsieck fame. The company makes wine in France and Hungary as well as in Argentina. We met with Philippe Rollet who explained to us that grapes are sourced from the company's Alizarine, Azamor, Serenade, Albaneve, and Temis vineyards in

ALTOS LAS HORMIGAS

9 de Julio, Mendoza,
+54 261 424 3727,
www.altoslashormigas.com

Luján de Cuyo and Uco Valley. It is widely believed to be the first winery in Argentina to produce a single-vineyard wine (Alta Vista Single Vineyard, produced in 2002). Alta Vista wines are consistently highly scored by *Wine Spectator*, *Wine Enthusiast*, and *The Wine Advocate*, and we agree that these are fantastic wines. Alta Vista Terroir Selection Malbec 2007 is garnet with a violet rim and has aromas of grandma's strawberry jam and red raspberries. In the mouth it is a fruit bomb with flavors of red cherry, dried black cherry, and red raspberry exciting your palate before a long luxurious finish. Alta Vista Alto 2007 is dark garnet with deep violet reflections, aromas of rich ripe red fruits, black plums, chocolate, coffee, black raspberries, and a hint of anise. It's big, bold, and yet elegant in the mouth with an amazingly long finish.

Altos las Hormigas (ALH) translates literally as "ants heights." It lovingly draws attention to the fact that this *terroir* is actually owned by ants and other naturally occurring insects. When vines were first planted in 1996, the ants found the young tender shoots too delicious to pass up, and the team had to find organic ways to cohabitate with the ants. The good news is now that the vines are 15 years old, the ants have moved on in search of younger, more tender foods. Altos las Hormigas has assembled an impressive team, including Alan Scerbanenko, Antonio Terni, Antonio Moreschalchi, Carlos Vazquez, and winemakers Attilio Pagli and Alberto Antonini.

Together they make award-winning wines that are consistent high scorers in *Decanter* and *Wine Spectator*. ALH Malbec Clásico 2010 is ruby colored with a violet rim. It smells of black plums, red cherries, cocoa, and toasted coconut. It has smooth mouthfeel, fine tannins, and a persistent finish. ALH Vista Flores Single Vineyard 2006 is almost black colored with a violet rim. It has aromas of blackberry, white flowers, honeysuckle, and dark cherries. It has smooth tannins and a lingering finish.

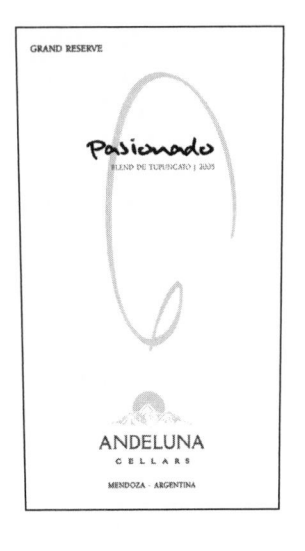

ANDELUNA CELLARS

Ruta Provincial 89, Gualtallary,
Tupungato, Mendoza,
+54 2622 423 226,
www.andeluna.com.ar

Founded in 2003 by Ward Lay, whose father started Frito-Lay and was the director of PepsiCo in the United States, Andeluna Cellars has won many international trophies and awards. Bodegas Andeluna Cellars was named for the Argentine moonlight that shines at the foot of the Andes. The winery receives over 5,000 visitors each year to its tasting room, cellar, wine bar, and open kitchen restaurant, and many guests return for the cooking classes on offer. Winemaking is directed by Silvio Alberto, who works with international consultant Michel Rolland. Andeluna Grand Reserve Malbec 2006 is deep red with a purple rim. The bouquet offers ripe red fruit, floral notes, cocoa, and a touch of cigar box. In the mouth it's a big wine with rounded sweet tannins. Andeluna Grand Reserve Pasionado 2005 is comprised of 36 percent Merlot, 34 percent Malbec, 20 percent Cabernet Sauvignon, and 10 percent Cabernet Franc. It's dark red, with aromas of licorice, black pepper, and red fruits such as red raspberry and red plums. In the mouth it's full-bodied and well structured. Andeluna Grand Reserve Cabernet Franc 2006 is ruby red, with aromas of red berries and a touch of red and black pepper. It has good weight and well-structured tannins. The finish is luxurious and persistent.

AVE

Emilio Civit 40, Perdriel, Mendoza,
+54 261 15454 7112,
www.proyecto-mas.com

Former Milan journalist Iacopo Di Bugno and Tuscan-born London banker Mario Pardini have taken on the daunting task of revitalizing a 40-hectare (99-acre) wine estate in Perdriel. They have lovingly restored the circa 1905 farmhouse that they call home. Some of AVE's vines are more than 95 years old, some are about 30, while others are only a few years old. When not playing music with their band Snob, Di Bugno and Pardini make excellent wines—with the help of consultant Alberto Antonini and winemaker Mariano Vignoni—from Malbec, Cabernet Sauvignon, Cabernet Franc, and Chardonnay vines. AVE Premium Malbec 2007 is bright ruby colored, with aromas of saddle leather, blackberries, cassis, and cigar box. It is big and bold in the mouth with chewy tannins. AVE Premium Malbec 2009 is garnet, with notes of black fruits, black raspberry, and a touch of smoke. It's voluminous in the mouth with a bit of grip. This is a wine that calls out for a nice thick steak!

BENEGAS

Cruz de Piedra, Maipú, Mendoza,
+54 261 496 0794,
www.bodegabenegas.com

Tiburcio Benegas bought his first vineyard, El Trapiche, in 1883 and is widely credited as the founder of the Mendoza wine industry. A tumultuous history of partnerships, acquisitions, and buyouts brings us to the current president, Frederico J. Benegas Lynch, who was born in 1951 and is a descendant of Tiburcio. Lynch and consulting winemaker Michel Rolland craft wonderful wines worthy of international acclaim. Benegas Lynch Cabernet Franc 2005 is made from 100-year-old vines. In the glass it is ruby garnet, with aromas of black fruits, peppermint, and cocoa. In the mouth it has silky smooth tannins and a cooling sensation on the finish. Benegas Malbec 2006 is garnet with a violet rim and has notes of black cherry and cassis with a sweet tannic finish.

CATENA ZAPATA

Calle Cobos s/n, Agrelo,
Luján de Cuyo, Mendoza,
+54 261 413 1100,
www.catenazapata.com

As you enter the gates of Bodega Catena Zapata and continue down the driveway through rows of meticulously kept vines, you can't help being amazed by the imposing Mayan temple before you. Built in 2001, the structure houses the winery, barrel cellar, offices, tasting room, and restaurant. Nicolas Catena is the third-generation family winemaker. In the early 1980s he was one of the pioneers who believed that world-class wine could be produced in Mendoza. His daughter, Laura, continues the family tradition as part-time winemaker, part-time emergency room physician. We enjoyed a wonderful lunch with Señor and Señora Catena who not only entertained us with delightful conversation and delicious food, but also invited one of Argentina's top concertina players

to entertain us with emotionally charged tango music. Catena Zapata has received high scores from many international publications and was named New World Winery of the Year, 2010, by *Wine Enthusiast*. Catena Chardonnay 2008 is straw colored, with aromas of luscious tropical fruits and citrus blossoms. In the mouth it has flavors of grapefruit and lemon rind with refreshing acidity. Catena Alta Malbec 2007 is reddish-purple, with black notes. Blackberry, black plum, and cassis are all found on the nose. On the palate this Malbec possesses a balanced weight and supple texture. The finish is characterized by fine tannins and refreshing mineral notes.

CHEVAL DES ANDES

Thames y Cochambamba,
Luján de Cuyo, Mendoza, +54 261 488 0058,
www.chevaldesandes.com

A thoroughbred with a wonderful pedigree, Cheval des Andes is a joint venture between Bordeaux's Château Cheval Blanc and Argentina's Terrazas de los Andes. Director Pierre Lurton is also the director of Cheval Blanc and president of Château d'Yquem in France. We had the pleasure of dining with winemaker Nicolas Audebert and enjoyed a vertical tasting of Cheval des Andes. We were honored to be the first journalists to taste

his recently bottled Cheval des Andes 2007. According to Nicolas, "It is comprised of a majority of Malbec and Cabernet Sauvignon with touches of Cabernet Franc and Petit Verdot." It is deep red violet in the glass with a bright rim. The nose revealed black cherry, raspberry, rhubarb, bacon, and spice. In the mouth it has flavors of black cherry, cassis, plums, and herbes de Provence. The tannins are firm and well structured. Nicolas said this wine "should age well for at least five and up to twenty years." We can't wait to try it again. Cheval des Andes 2006 is composed of 60 percent Malbec, 35 percent Cabernet Sauvignon, and 5 percent Merlot. It is deep blue violet in the glass, with aromas of dark fruits, cassis, and eucalyptus. The palate reveals black cherry, blueberry, clove, and white pepper. Cheval des Andes 2004 is a blend of 55 percent Malbec, 43 percent Cabernet Sauvignon, and 2 percent Petit Verdot. It is inky violet in color,

with a nose of cassis, stewed cherries, chocolate, espresso, and wet river stones. In the mouth it has flavors of stewed fruit, truffle, and a touch of acidity.

DOMINIO DEL PLATA

Cochabamba 7801, Agrelo,
Luján de Cuyo, Mendoza,
+54 261 498 9200,
www.dominiodelplata.com.ar

Internationally acclaimed winemaker consultant Susana Balbo realized her lifelong dream in 1999 by building her own winery in the heart of Luján de Cuyo. Her partners include Jorge Galante, Pablo Teubal, and Pedro Qüerio. Together they make quality wines with an international taste profile, while respecting the local *terroir*. Dominio del Plata produces 3,000,000 bottles per year; a fair share of which is exported to the United States. Dominio del Plata Susana B. Malbec 2008 is purple in color, with aromas of black raspberry, dark cherries, and a touch of mint. The palate is full of ripe black plums, mocha, and again mint. The mid palate is velvety, while the rear palate displays lingering tannins. Dominio del Plata BenMarco Malbec 2007 is composed of 90 percent Malbec and 10 percent Bonarda. It is purple in color, with aromas of espresso and red plums. It tastes full-bodied, rich, and persistent. Dominio del Plata

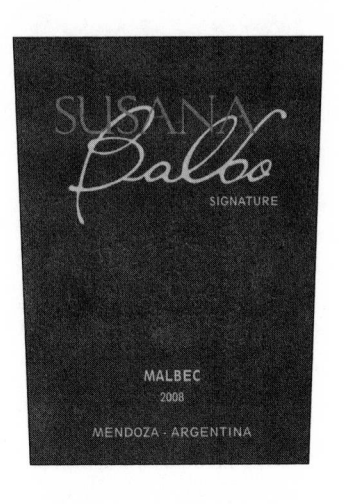

BenMarco Expresivo 2007 is a blend of 50 percent Malbec, 15 percent Syrah, 15 percent Bondarda, 10 percent Cabernet Sauvignon, and 10 percent Tannat. It is inky purple, with aromas of black cherries and dried red cherries. It tastes of cinnamon, cassis, and black cherry. The tannins are ripe, and the way it persists in the mouth is lovely.

Estate Cabernet Sauvignon 2009 is garnet red, with aromas of black raspberry, black plums, baking spice, pencil lead, and green pepper. It is medium-bodied with balanced acidity. Doña Paula Estate Malbec 2009 is deep purple, with notes of black cherry, black plum, anise, and Mediterranean herbs. It has sweet tannins and a persistent finish.

DOÑA PAULA

Avenida Colón 531, Mendoza,
+54 261 429 0741,
www.donapaula.com

In 1997, the Chilean Claro group expanded its business across the Andes and into Argentina. Its first harvest was in 1999, and since then the company has purchased high-altitude vineyards. Winemaking is directed by David Bonami and Edgardo del Popolo. Doña Paula

ESCORIHUELA GASCÓN

Belgrano 1188, at the corner of
Pte. Alvear, Godoy Cruz, Mendoza,
+54 261 424 2698,
www.escorihuelagascon.com.ar

Don Miguel Escorihuela Gascón emigrated from Aragón, Spain, in 1880 when he was only 19 years old. Four years later he purchased 17 hectares (42 acres) of land, planted vines, and built his first winery. He was considered visionary by many and crazy by a few when he built a nine-story building in Mendoza—the tallest at that time—on an earthquake fault line. Public opinion leaned more toward visionary when his building was one of the few that withstood the earthquake of 1927. Today, the quality wines of Escorihuela Gascón are made by winemakers Gustavo Marín and Lucia Valeretti. Visitors to the bodega should not miss lunch or dinner at Restaurant 1884, with Chef Francis Mallmann at the helm. Señor Mallmann has been called "The Alain Ducasse of Argentina." Having dined at both chefs' establishments, we can tell you that Francis gives Alain a run for his money! The wines of Escorihuela Gascón paired perfectly with the meat-heavy Argentine cuisine. We loved the Escorihuela Gascón Reserva Malbec 2009. It was red violet in color, with notes of red fruits, black plums, red raspberries, and a touch of spice. It's big in the mouth with soft tannins—and was the perfect wine to enjoy with a thick, juicy steak. Familia Gascón Rosé 2010 works perfectly as an aperitif. It's a brilliant salmon pink color, with aromas of red fruits and strawberries. It has balanced acidity and is quite refreshing—the kind of wine that keeps you coming back for more.

FABRE MONTMAYOU

Roque Saenz Peña, Vistalba, Mendoza,
+54 261 498 2330,
www.domainevistalba.com

Bordeaux-born Hervé Joyaux-Fabre moved to Argentina in the early 1990s to search for a vineyard. He purchased old Malbec vines that were planted in 1908 and built his Bordeaux Château style winery in Luján de Cuyo. Fabre Montmayo Cabernet Sauvignon 2009 is ruby red, with aromas of black plums, black raspberries, and a top note of menthol. It is full in the mouth with smooth tannins. Fabre Montmayou Reserve Chardonnay 2010 is straw colored, with notes of tropical fruits and toasted brioche. It is medium-bodied and has a fresh finish.

FINCA DECERO

Bajo las Cumbres, Agrelo, Mendoza,
+54 261 524 4748,
www.decero.com

Thomas Schmidheiny, a descendent of the prominent Swiss family, fell in love with the Agrelo subregion in the early 1970s. He named Finca Decero for the Spanish meaning of the words, "from zero—or from scratch." His wines have been rated highly by *Wine Advocate*, *Wine Enthusiast*, and *Wine Spectator*. Winemaking is under the direction of Marcos Fernandez, while Matias Cano manages the vineyards.

Chef Matias Podesta runs the restaurant, serving regional and international cuisine from locally sourced produce. Finca Decero Malbec 2009 is garnet colored, with aromas of red fruits and crystallized violet candy. It is big in the mouth with velvety tannins. Finca Decero Syrah 2009 is purplish colored, with aromas of blackberry, blueberry, cocoa, espresso, and clove. It's a mouth-filling wine with a smooth tannic finish.

on Cabernet Sauvignon and Malbec. Kaiken Ultra Malbec 2008 is dark garnet in the glass, with aromas of black fruits, black plum, cocoa, and espresso. It is luscious on the palate and has a silky tannic finish with lingering notes of black licorice, anise seed, and mocha. Kaiken Cabernet Sauvignon 2009 has aromas of dark plums and black olive tapenade. It lingers on the palate with aftertastes of cocoa and vanilla toast.

KAIKEN

Callejón de la Virgen, Vistalba, Luján de Cuyo,
+54 261 524 3160,
www.kaikenwines.com

LAS PERDICES

Ruta 7 s/n, Agrelo, Luján de Cuyo, Mendoza,
+54 261 498 8208,
www.lasperdices.com

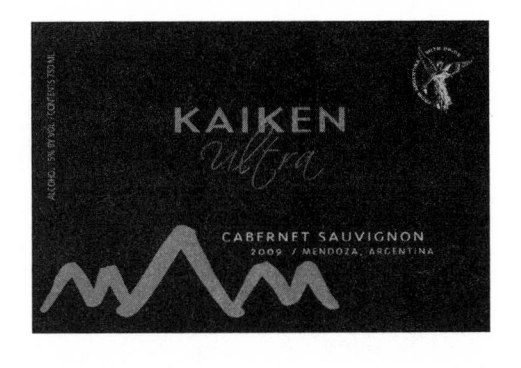

Named for the wild geese indigenous to Patagonia, Kaiken is owned by the Montes family of Chile. Aurelio Montes is the winemaker for some highly rated, good-value wines. Kaiken concentrates predominantly

In 1952 Andalucian-born Don Juan Muñoz López named his vineyard Las Perdices because of the large number of partridges in the area. Today the company has vineyards in Agrelo and Barrancas and produces wines from Pinot Noir, Malbec, Cabernet Sauvignon, Viognier, Sauvignon Blanc, and Pinot Grigio. Las Perdices Malbec 2009 is reddish purple and has aromas of red and blackberries. It is soft in the mouth with smooth tannins and a taste of black cherry on the finish. Las Perdices Cabernet Sauvignon 2008 is garnet colored, with notes of cherry, green pepper, and freshly ground black pepper in the bouquet. There is a touch of black currant to the smooth finish.

LA RURAL

Montecaseros 2625, Coquimbito, Mendoza,
+54 261 481 1032,
www.rutiniwines.com

Don Felipe Rutini, an immigrant from Le Marche, Italy, began planting vines in Coquimbito in 1885. He named his winery La Rural, and today the La Rural Rutini Museum of Wine is probably the most important wine museum in the Americas. It has more than 66,000 visitors each year and more than 4,500 winemaking relics. We were amazed at the collection of winemaking implements, vats, storage casks, and corkscrews. In 1994, Don Felipe's grandson entered into a partnership with Catena Zapata's owner, Nicolas Catena, and the winery underwent a total renovation.

Rutini owns vineyards in five different areas in Mendoza, and we also had the opportunity to visit their new state of the art winery in Tupungato. Rutini Chardonnay 2009 is bright yellow, with aromas of tropical fruits, pineapple, and mango. It is soft and fresh in the mouth, with a touch of vanilla on the finish. Rutini Malbec 2008 is reddish purple, with aromas of dark fruits, black plums, and touches of smoke and toasted brioche. It is concentrated in the mouth with a soft tannic finish. Trumpeter Malbec 2009 is named for the myth about the woman who turns into a swan. It's deep, red violet colored, with aromas of blueberry, blackberry, and chopped green herbs. On the palate it has flavors of blueberry, black cherry, menthol, and a hint of eucalyptus.

LUIGI BOSCA

San Martín 2044, Mayor Drummond,
Luján de Cuyo, Mendoza,
+54 261 498 1974,
www.luigibosca.com.ar

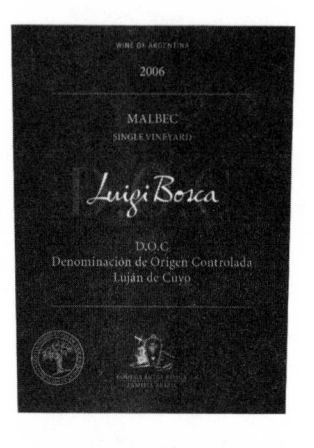

Leoncio Arizu founded Bodega Luigi Bosca Familia Arizu in 1901. He arrived from Navarra, Spain, in 1890 and joined his uncle Balbino, who was already involved in the Argentine wine trade. His children and children's children became involved in the family business and today his descendants still run the company. In 1991 the winery underwent a major renovation and was modernized. The family was instrumental in establishing Luján de Cuyo as Argentina's first DOC in 2005. Luigi Bosca Reserva Pinot Noir 2007 is bright ruby red, with fruit notes high in the glass. Especially noted are red raspberries and red cherries with a touch of candied violet. In the mouth there are flavors of strawberries, milk

chocolate, and again that delicious violet note. It is velvety and has an elegant finish. Luigi Bosca Finca Los Nobles Cabernet-Bouchet 2005 is a field blend of the two varieties. It smells of green bell pepper and boysenberry and boasts tannins that are concentrated yet silky. Bodega Luigi Bosca DOC Malbec Single Vineyard 2006 is inky purple in color, with aromas of black cherry and black plums. It tastes of cocoa, coffee, and blackberry jam and exhibits a restrained yet lovely tannic structure.

MAURICIO LORCA

Perdriel, Luján de Cuyo, Mendoza,
+54 261 496 1240,
www.mauriciolorca.com

Mauricio Lorca worked as a winemaker for many notable bodegas before opening his own winery. Former employers include the large houses of Catena, Luigi Bosca, and Finca La Celia. Despite great demand for his fine-winemaking skills, he recently decided to venture out on his own. Mauricio Lorca Gran Lorca Poetico 2006 is a blend of Malbec, Syrah, and Petit Verdot. It is garnet-red colored, with aromas of red and black raspberries and black cherries. It is big and bold on the palate but finishes with elegant tannins and a touch of cocoa. Mauricio Lorca Fantasia Torrontés 2009 is greenish-yellow. It has strong stone-fruit characteristics, a touch of white flowers, jasmine, and a hint of honeysuckle. It has a crisp, clean finish.

MENDEL WINES

Terrada 1863, Mayor Drummond, Luján de Cuyo,
+54 261 524 1621,
www.mendel.com.ar

Winemaker Roberto de la Moto joined the team at Mendel Wines and, together with vineyard manager Santiago Mayorga Boaknin, took over the stewardship of 80-year-old Malbec vines. The company also grows other varieties on its three vineyards in Perdriel, Finca de los Andes, and Mayor Drummond. Mendel Malbec 2007 is purplish-red, with aromas of purple flowers, dark cherries, and black plums. It is smooth in the mouth, with balanced acidity and lingering flavors of anise and vanilla. Mendel Unus 2007 is a blend of 70 percent Malbec and 30 percent Cabernet Sauvignon. It is dark red with a violet rim and has notes of fresh red cherries, red plums, black raspberries, and black currants. It has a nice top note of dark spices like cinnamon and nutmeg. It is a balanced wine with chewy tannins and a persistent finish.

NAVARRO CORREAS

San Francisco del Monte 1550,
Godoy Cruz, Mendoza,
+54 11 5776 2800,
www.ncorreas.com

The Correas family has owned vineyards and grown grapes since the mid-1800s, but it was not until the 1970s that Edmundo Navarro Correas decided to stop selling his family's grapes to other wine producers and to instead make quality wines under his family name.

The original winery was located on Pedro Molina Street in Maipú, but in 2004, Bodega Navarro Correas opened Cava Godoy Cruz, and in 2009, it opened a second winery at Finca Agrelo. Navarro Correas Colección Privada Malbec 2008 is inky purple in color, with aromas of red fruit, anise, and smoked meats. It is medium-bodied in the mouth, with soft tannins and a fair level of acidity. Navarro Correas Alegoría Gran Reserva Malbec 2007 is deep ruby garnet, with aromas of black plums, earth, mushrooms, black raspberries, and dark cherries. On the palate it is smooth with a lingering finish. Navarro Correas Alegoría Gran Reserva Cabernet Sauvignon 2006 is ruby red, with notes of cigar box, black pepper, and cassis in the nose. The palate presents full ripe fruits with balanced acidity and structured tannins.

NORTON

Ruta Provincial 15 Kilometer 23.5,
Perdriel, Luján de Cuyo,
+54 261 490 9700,
www.norton.com.ar

Englishman Edmund J.P. Norton purchased the land that was to become the first winery south of the Mendoza River in 1895. He fell in love with Argentina and planted vines that he imported from France. The bodega now owns 680 hectares (1,680 acres) of vines and is owned by Austrian businessman Gernot Langes-Swarovski. The wines have achieved a high level of acclaim; in 2006, *Wine Spectator* named it one of the "Top Wineries" in the world. Bodega Norton Finca Perdriel Centenario 2005 is ruby garnet in color. On the nose it has layers of spice, porcini mushroom, freshly ground nuts, and black fruits. In the mouth it is complex, yet restrained and elegant. Bodega Norton Finca Perdriel Single Vineyard 2005 is a blend of 60 percent Malbec, 28 percent Cabernet Sauvignon, and 12 percent Merlot. It is ruby colored and has a touch of spice in the bouquet. In the mouth it has generous amounts of red and black fruits with a persistent finish. Bodega Norton Malbec DOC 2006 is purplish-red, with notes of black plum, freshly ground black pepper, and black raspberries. On the palate it is smooth and silky and has great tannic structure.

PASCUAL TOSO

Carril Barrancas s/n, Barrancas, Maipú, Mendoza,
+54 11 4866 2250,
www.bodegastoso.com.ar

After leaving his hometown, Canale d'Alba, in Piedmont, Italy, Pascual Toso established his first winery in Guaymallén, San José, in 1890. He built his second winery, Las Barrancas, in the early 1900s and set out to grow the best grapes to make the finest wines. In 2001, the winery hired Californian, Paul Hobbs, who together with chief winemaker Rolando Luppino, is making wines that receive international acclaim. Pascual Toso wines are exported to more than thirty countries including the United Kingdom, United States, and Canada. The winery owns 346 hectares (855 acres) of vines and has the capacity for 7,000,000 liters. It utilizes two distinct bottling lines for still wines; one can support 7,000 bottles per hour, and the other bottles 3,000 per hour. The company also has a separate bottling line for sparkling wines with a capacity of 7,000 bottles per hour. Pascual Toso Alta Reserve Syrah 2007 is ruby red with a purple rim. On the nose there is spice, black fruits, and a touch of toasted coconut. In the mouth it is velvety with sweet tannins. Pascual Toso Reserve Malbec 2008 is red garnet, with aromas of black and red fruits. The tannins are a bit firm, but sweet and balanced. Pascual Toso Malbec 2008 is garnet colored, with aromas of black plums, anise, and blackberry. In the mouth it has a licorice characteristic with grippy, masculine tannins.

PULENTA ESTATE

Ruta Provincial 86 Kilometer 6.5,
Alto Agrelo, Luján de Cuyo,
+54 261 420 0800,
www.pulentaestate.com

After their father, Antonio, sold his share in Trapiche in 1997, Hugo and Eduardo Pulenta built Pulenta Estate in 2002. It has 135 hectares (334 acres) of high-quality vines in the center of Luján de Cuyo. The owners' love of fast cars, especially Porsche, is well known, yet they chose to build an austere, restrained winery utilizing modern technology and traditional methods—to be respectful of the environment. Pulenta Estate La Flor Sauvignon Blanc 2009 is bright yellow with green tints. It displays aromas of grapefruit and citrus peel. It

DELICADOCOLORRO
JOCONAGRADABLE
SAROMASSILVESTR
ESCOMOFRES**MA**AC
EREZAYGUIND**LB**AE
QUILIBRADAAC**EC**ID
EZTANINOS**ROSE**SU
AVESREDO**2010**ND
OREFRESCANTEMO
DERNOBALANCEAD
OELEGANTEUNTUO
SOEXCELENTEAPER
ITIVOPUNTOFINAL

• punto final
malbec
rose

has a bright acidity and fruity presence in the mid palate and is crisp and clean on the finish. Pulenta Estate Gran Cabernet Franc 2008 is deep red with purple tinges and has a nose of mint, black and red pepper, sweet fruit, and spice. In the mouth it is fruity with round, ripe tannins. Pulenta Estate La Flor Malbec 2009 is deep red with violet tints. It has notes of ripe fruits and purple flowers with a top note of tobacco leaf. In the mouth it is a full-bodied wine with mild tannic structure.

RENACER

Brandsen 1863, Luján de Cuyo, Mendoza,
+54 261 524 4416,
www.bodegarenacer.com.ar

We arrived at Bodega Renacer just in time to watch the sun set behind the majestic Andes Mountains that back right up to the Bodega Renacer vineyards, owned by Patricio Reich. We were comfortably seated on the lawn with him, his lovely wife, his son, Patricio, and winemaker Pablo Profili, enjoying a refreshing glass of Renacer Sauvignon Blanc 2009 as the last glint of sun turned the sky pink, then red, and finally purple before the light of the moon dominated the night. Renacer wines are highly rated by the top wine magazines including *Decanter, Wine Enthusiast, Wine Spectator,* and *The Wine Advocate*. Its wines, especially Renacer Punto Final Clásico and Punto Final Reserva, have won multiple awards and many gold medals. International winemaker Alberto Antonini is a consultant to the winery. Renacer Malbec Rosé 2010 is light pink in color, with classic strawberry notes in the bouquet. It fills your mouth with cherry flavors and has a refreshing finish. Renacer Enamore 2008 is a blend of Malbec, Cabernet

Sauvignon, Cabernet Franc, Bonarda, and Syrah. It is inky purple, with aromas of spice and a cherry pie fresh from the oven. On the palate delightful flavors of clove, anise, black cherry, and blackberry explode in your mouth before a silky smooth finish. Renacer Punto Final Clasico Malbec 2008 is deep red with a heavy viscosity in the glass. The nose offers raspberry and chocolate, while your palate is excited by well-balanced dark fruits, coffee, licorice, clove, and a delightful, grippy finish. Buy this wine to drink now and to lay down for a treat in the years to come.

ROSELL BOHER

Peuyrredón 1210, Chacras de Coria,
Luján de Cuyo, Mendoza,
+54 261 496 1775,
www.rosellboher.com

The idea of Cavas Rosell Boher started in 1996, when a group of winemakers came together to produce quality sparkling wines using only the traditional Champenoise method. In 1999, they renovated Don Bernardo Martinez's turn-of-the-century winery and began making limited production, artisanal, high-quality sparkling wines. The company also makes well-respected still wines from Chardonnay, Sauvignon Blanc, Syrah, Cabernet Franc, Cabernet Sauvignon, Merlot, Malbec, Pinot Noir, and Tempranillo. Cavas Rosell Boher own 98 hectares (242 acres) of vines in Maipú, Vista Flores, and Tunuyán. Rosell Boher El Niño Malbec 2004 is inky reddish-purple, with aromas of dark fruits and mocha. On the palate it presents copious flavors of dark fruit and has a bit of heft. The finish is persistent and pleasant. Rosell Boher Brut NV is made from 60 percent Pinot Noir and 40 percent Chardonnay. It is pale yellow with persistent small bubbles. The nose reveals tropical fruits and a touch of toasted brioche. In the mouth it has nice body and is rounded, with a refreshing finish of pink grapefruit. Rosell Boher Rosé is made from 100 percent Pinot Noir and has a light aroma of strawberries and cream with a hint of yeasty bread. It is refreshing on the palate and has flavors of cherries and red raspberries. The pleasant finish begs you to come back for another sip.

RUCA MALEN

Ruta 7 Kilometer 1059, Agrelo,
Luján de Cuyo, Mendoza,
+54 261 562 8357,
www.bodegarucamalen.com

Begun in 1998 by Jacques Louis de Montalembert and Jean-Pierre Thibaud, Ruca Malen is named after the Mapuchan word for "young girl's house." Two of the winery's

product lines also have origins in the Mapuche language; *Yauquen* is a reference to the ritual "art of sharing," and *Kinien* is a word used to describe "unique." We have had wonderful dinners with Ruca Malen's team, who certainly understand "the art of sharing" when bottles are opened and enormous platters of meat are brought to the table. They also shared the legend of the Young Girl's House. As the story goes, a defiant woman looked straight into the eyes of a god and immediately fell in love. Unfortunately, the god could not stay on earth, so he built her a house where she could live for eternity. He also left her a magic potion—a nectar—that she could drink to summon the memory of him and not be alone. Ruca Malen Cabernet Sauvignon 2007 might just be that nectar. Magically red in color, the nose offers complex and intense aromas of blackberries, black plums, and baking spices. In the mouth

it has a silky smooth mouthfeel and wonderful concentration of tannins. The finish goes on to eternity—it's a magical wine indeed. Yauquén Malbec 2009 is inky purple red, with aromas of black cherries and red plums. In the mouth you can taste touches of violet, caramelized plums, and vanilla. The finish is lively and persistent. Kinien de Don Raul 2004 is a combination of 78 percent Malbec, 11 percent Merlot, and 11 percent Tempranillo. It is garnet red, with notes of blackberries, red raspberries, and toasted almonds. On the palate the fruit comes alive with a frame of vanilla and light oak. The finish is long-lasting.

SEPTIMA

Ruta Internacional 7 Kilometer 6.5,
Agrelo, Mendoza,
+54 261 498 5164,
www.bodegaseptima.com

Bodega Septima is owned by the Spanish group Codorniu, who own multiple wineries around the world. It has 135 hectares (334 acres) in full production at the Agrelo vineyards, which sit at an altitude of over 1,000 meters (3,280 feet). It grows many European varieties including Malbec, Cabernet Sauvignon, Chardonnay, Sémillon, Gewürztraminer, Sauvignon Blanc, Tempranillo, Syrah, and Tannat. Bodega Septima Septimo Dia Malbec

2008 is red garnet in the glass, with aromas of red cherries, red raspberries, and a touch of rosemary. The tannins are soft and sweet and have good balance. Bodega Septima Septimo Dia Cabernet Sauvignon 2008 has a deep red appearance with a violet rim. On the nose there is red pepper and cassis. In the mouth, red fruits come out with a touch of espresso. The tannins are round and the finish persistent. Bodega Septima Chardonnay 2009 is pale yellow, with notes of tropical fruit, mango, and citrus flowers. In the mouth it is fresh and fruity. If you visit Bodega Septima, make sure to arrive hungry. Restaurant Maria, under the direction of Graciela Hisa, offers fantastic cuisine on an outdoor terrace—try to be there for the sunset. The view of the Andes is as unforgettable as the desserts.

SINFIN

Ruta Provincial 50, no. 2668, Maipú, Mendoza,
+54 261 491 4409,
www.bodegasinfin.com

Owner Carlos Caselles employs international viticultural consultant and Master of Wine María Isabel Mijares to assist him at Bodega SinFin. Family-owned since 1975, Bodega SinFin has a beautiful and interesting philosophy about wine. The owners believe that "wine transcends, moves, and conquers," and

they try to create emotions within each bottle that are released at the moment the cork is extracted. Bodega SinFin Guarda Cabernet Sauvignon 2009 is garnet red in the glass with aromas of red and black fruits framed by vanilla. Generous in the mouth, this Cabernet has sweet tannins and a long finish. Bodega SinFin Guarda Sauvignon Blanc 2010 is yellow with green hues. It has aromas of tropical fruit, mango, grapefruit, and just a touch of green spring asparagus. It is refreshing and light in the palate. Bodega SinFin Guarda Malbec 2009 is ruby colored, with notes of black fruits and mint. In the mouth it's pleasing with a lasting finish.

TAPIZ

Ruta Provincial 15 Kilometer 32, Agrelo,
Luján de Cuyo, Mendoza,
+54 261 490 0202,
www.tapiz.com.ar

Bodega Tapiz was built for Kendall Jackson in the mid-1990s. Tapiz was purchased by Patricia and Jorge Ortiz, owners of Finca Patagonicas, in 2003, when Kendall Jackson sold its Argentine holdings. The family also owns Club Tapiz, Casa Zolo, and Aceite Tapiz, producers of fine olive oil. Tapiz Viognier 2010 is straw colored, with aromas of white stone fruits, yellow peaches, and ripe apricots. It is medium- to full-bodied in the mouth with a clean finish. Tapiz Bonarda 2010 is deep red, with aromas of black raspberries, red raspberries, and wild strawberries. It is soft in the mouth with sweet tannins and a smooth finish.

TERRAZAS DE LOS ANDES

Thames y Cochambamba s/n, Perdriel,
Luján de Cuyo, Mendoza,
+54 261 488 0058,
www.terrazasdelosandes.com

Moët Hennessy sent Renaud Poirier to Argentina in the mid-1950s to scout for new wine *terroirs*. He was impressed with the soils of Luján de Cuyo, so Moët Hennessy purchased a winery from Sotero Arizu, one of the forefathers of Argentina's wine industry. Terrazas de los Andes grows many European varieties, such as Malbec, Cabernet Sauvignon, Syrah, Chardonnay, and Merlot. The winemaking is under the watchful eyes of Herve Birnie-Scott, as well as Nicolas Audebert, who also makes wine at the group's prestigious Cheval des Andes. We were lucky enough to taste not only Terrazas de los Andes wines at dinner with Herve and Nicolas, but Cheval des Andes as well. Terrazas de los Andes Reserva Torrontés 2010 is pale straw colored, with a light touch of smoke and Earl Grey tea in the top notes of the bouquet. Aromas of citrus flowers, ginger, pineapple, and a bit of pink grapefruit are here too. In the mouth it is crisp and refreshing with a persistent finish. Terrazas de los Andes Reserva Malbec 2008 is deep red with garnet highlights. The bouquet reveals black plums, blackberries, and a hint of candied violet. In the mouth it tastes of fresh berries, pencil lead, and dried raspberries. The finish is pleasant with soft tannins and a lingering persistence.

TRAPICHE

Nueva Mayorga s/n, Coquimbito,
Maipú, Mendoza, +54 261 520 7605,
www.trapiche.com.ar

Trapiche is one of Argentina's oldest and largest wineries. It has the greatest share of the international market; Trapiche exports wine to more than eighty countries. It has a total

TRIVENTO

Pescara 9347, Maipú, Mendoza,
+54 261 413 7100,
www.trivento.com

capacity for 30,000,000 liters and grows grapes on 1,000 hectares (2,471 acres) of its own vineyards. It also works with more than two hundred contract growers in a variety of winegrowing areas around the country. November 2008 marked the company's 125th anniversary, and to celebrate, it reopened the doors of the newly renovated winery. Trapiche Broquel Bonarda 2007 is deep red with a violet rim. It has aromas of red fruit, cherries, and raspberries. On the palate it is big and fruity, with ripe, soft tannins. Trapiche Malbec Single Vineyard Viña Federico Villafañe 2006 is deep ruby colored, with notes of pepper, anise, and black raspberries in the bouquet. In the mouth it is ample and has a sweet tannic structure. Trapiche Finca Las Palmas Chardonnay 2007 is pale straw colored, with aromas of citrus flowers and tropical fruits. In the mouth it is lively with a sweet finish.

Trivento is named for the three winds—the Polar, the Zonda, and the Sudestada, which bless the vines of the Mendoza region. Trivento was established in 1996 by Concha y Toro, and the wines quickly found their way onto wine shop shelves around the world. Trivento Amado Sur Torrontés 2010 is golden yellow colored, with notes of crystallized violet and rose petals, along with touches of white peach in the bouquet. It is fresh in the mouth with balanced acidity. Trivento Amado Sur 2009 is a blend of 73 percent Malbec, 15 percent

Bonarda, and 12 percent Syrah. It is deep red with a violet rim and has aromas of cherry, black currant jam, and red fruits. It is big in the mouth with soft tannins and a persistent finish.

VIÑA ALICIA

Terrada y Anchorena, Mayor Drummond, Mendoza,
+54 261 498 7385,
www.vinaalicia.com

Alicia Mateu Arizu, wife of Alberto Arizu, and her youngest son Rodrigo Arizu founded Viña Alicia in 1998 with the intention of creating château-style wines.

Its grapes are sourced from its San Alberto and Viña Alicia vineyards in Luján de Cuyo. Viña Alicia Syrah 2007 is dark purple, with aromas of dark fruit jam, blackberry compote,

and smoked sausage. In the mouth the fruit flavors come on strong and lead up to a finish of well-rounded tannins. Viña Alicia Malbec 2007 has aromas of pencil lead, black plum, and cigar box. It is full-bodied with slightly grippy tannins. Although it is nice to drink now, this wine will certainly improve with age.

VIÑA AMALIA

Finca La Amalia, San Martín, Carodilla, Luján de Cuyo, +54 261 436 0677, www.amalia.com

In 1997, Hugo Basso, a descendant of Adolfo and Tullo Basso—who founded La Purisima and later Bodega Santa Ana—bought and remodeled a small winery in Carodilla. Today Hugo and his sons run the winery he named Viña Amalia. The owners bring years of wine-making experience to crafting delicious wines. Viña Amalia Malbec 2006 is ruby garnet colored with a violet rim. Aromas of black-berries, black plums, and baking spices lead to a mouthful of fresh fruit and a soft tannic finish. Viña Amalia Cabernet Sauvignon 2004 is just hitting its stride with aromas and flavors of dark fruit cocktail and fruits of the wood. There are ripe tannins and a long finish.

VIÑA COBOS

Costa Flores y Ruta 7, Perdriel, Luján de Cuyo,
+54 261 479 0130,
www.vinacobos.com

Luis Barraud, fourth-generation Franco-Argentine winemaker, and his winemaker wife, Andrea Marchiori, traveled to the United States in 1997, met Californian winemaker Paul Hobbs, and became friends. The three are now partners in Viña Cobos in Luján de Cuyo. Viña Cobos Felino Chardonnay 2009 is a brilliant yellow color. It has aromas of white flowers, tropical fruits, and white stone-fruits. It has nice mouthfeel with a balanced finish. Viña Cobos Marchiori Vineyard Malbec 2007 is deep red, with notes of crystallized violet, cigar box, dark fruits, and ripe black raspberries in the bouquet. It is mouth-filling with fine tannins and a pleasing, persistent finish.

VISTALBA

Roque Sáenz Peña, Vistalba, Mendoza,
+54 261 498 9400,
www.carlospulentawines.com

Carlos Pulenta built Bodega Vistalba, his modern *Criollo*-style winery, in 2002. The estate's beautiful La Posada Lodge is a great place to lay your head after a long day of visiting wineries, and with Restaurant La Bourgogne on site—under the direction of French-born chef Jean-Paul Bondoux—you don't have to get in your car to enjoy a delicious meal. Vistalba Corte B is a blend of 63 percent Malbec, 22 percent Cabernet Sauvignon, and 15 percent Bonarda. It is dark ruby garnet, with notes of black raspberries, smoked meat, forest floor, and black plums in the bouquet. It is soft in the mouth with a long chewy finish. Vistalba Corte A is comprised of 87 percent Malbec, 8 percent Bonarda, and 5 percent Cabernet Sauvignon. It is garnet colored, with aromas of black cherries, toasted brioche, and cassis. In the mouth it is full-bodied with ripe fruit flavors and silky tannins in the finish.

ZUCCARDI

Ruta Provincial 33 Kilometer 7.5,
Maipú, Mendoza,
+54 261 441 0000,
www.familiazuccardi.com

We visited Zuccardi and enjoyed the family's wine, hospitality, and delicious empanadas. José Alberto Zuccardi and his family were the consummate hosts. José Alberto's father Alberto Zuccardi planted the first vines in 1963 and built the family winery in 1968. Today José Alberto is handing over the reins of the company to his sons Sebastian and Miguel and his daughter Julia, for whom the Zuccardi Santa Julia wines are named. Zuccardi's Casa del Visitante

from the Uco Valley departments of Tupungato, Tunuyán, and San Carlos. Tupungato contains the districts of La Arboleda and Gualtallary; Tunuyán's prominent district is Vista Flores; and La Consulta is in San Carlos. Adventure tourism, the Historic Apple Tree Region, and a collection of both traditional and state-of-the-art wineries vie for the attention of visitors to this beautiful place. Hot days and cold nights provide optimal ripening conditions for more than 20,000 hectares (49,421 acres) of vineyards. These are planted with an assortment of international varieties. The most significant is Malbec, which makes up 35 percent of the Uco Valley's total. Second in command is Cabernet Sauvignon, comprising 15 percent of grape plantings. Chardonnay and Merlot each account for about 9 percent of vineyards here, while Tempranillo accounts for 7.5 percent. Bonarda has 5 percent, ahead of Syrah and Pinot Noir, each at just under 4 percent. Last, but certainly not least, is Sauvignon Blanc, which grows on 2.5 percent of the Uco Valley's alluvial soils.

has a wonderful restaurant featuring locally sourced produce, including the family's olive oil. The Cava de Arte features regularly updated exhibitions by local artists. The Zuccardi's also host classical music performances at the winery. We found the range of wines to be of excellent quality and quite delicious. Zuccardi Q Malbec 2009 is dark ruby garnet, with notes of black plum and sweet dark cherries. It is fruity and spicy in the mouth with a firm tannic finish. Zuccardi Emma Zuccardi Bonarda 2009 is purplish-red with fruity aromas of red cherries and black raspberries. It is fruit-forward in the mouth with soft, smooth tannins.

UCO VALLEY

Its majestic landscape, position at the foot of the Andes, and average vineyard altitudes of 1,000 meters (3,280 feet) almost seem a mere backdrop to the premium quality wines emanating

ALMA NEGRA

Ernesto Catena Vineyards,
+54 114 331 1251,
www.almanegrawines.com.ar

Alma Negra translates literally as the "dark soul." It is meant to represent the dark side

of every human personality. Artist and wine-maker Ernesto Catena sources grapes from the best vineyards in La Consulta, Altamira, and Tupungato. He is the son of Nicolas Catena, and after living abroad in New York City, London, Cambridge, and California, he returned home to Argentina to perfect his craft. We sat at the enormous antique dining table in his historic family home and tasted his Alma Negra wines. Alma Negra Bonarda 2007 is deep red violet colored, with aromas of black cherry, vanilla, violet, lavender, and jasmine. In the mouth it is a fruit bomb, exploding with flavors of blueberry, black cherry, and violet. It has a long, smooth finish. The composition of Alma Negra *Gran Misterio*—meaning "great mystery"—is Ernesto's secret. Each year the composition and blend changes, depending on his artistic inclinations and instincts. His Alma Negra Gran Misterio 2007 stains the glass

with an inky purple color. Aromas of black raspberry, blueberry, juniper berries, and crystallized violets engulf your senses. The palate is teased by fluctuating flavors of blueberries, talcum powder, black raspberries, and herbes de Provence. This is a truly great wine!

CLOS DE LOS SIETE

Clodomiro Silva s/n, Vistaflores, Tunuyán,
www.monteviejo.com

Michel Rolland is the preeminent international wine consultant. He is extremely familiar with growing grapes and making wines of exceptional quality in South America. Because of this, in 1998, he assembled a group of seven well-known French wine families, purchased Campo Vista Flores, and named the project Clos de los Siete, or "Vineyard of Seven." The other investors at that time included Laurent Dassault, Benjamin de Rothschild, Edmond de Rothschild, Phillipe Schell, Jean-Michel Arcaute, Catherine Pere-Verge, the d'Aulan family of Champagne Piper-Heidsieck, and the Cuvelier family. The concept is fascinating. Each family grows grapes and vinifies their own wines. Michel then personally blends the wines from the seven plots and creates a wine of great character and exceptional expression of *terroir*. Clos de los Siete 2008 is dark ruby garnet in color. It is a blend of 56 percent Malbec, 21 percent Merlot, 10 percent Cabernet Sauvignon, 11 percent Syrah, and 2 percent Petit Verdot. It has inviting aromas of black currants, black plums, and fine saddle leather. It is big on the palate with nice grip and finishes with balanced tannins. As an added bonus, there is a very pleasant lingering persistence of dried cherries at the back of your throat.

CUVELIER LOS ANDES

Clodomiro Silva s/n, Vistaflores, Tunuyán,
+54 261 405 5610,
www.cuvelierlosandes.com

Part of the prestigious Clos de los Siete group, the Cuvelier family from Bordeaux is no stranger to the world of wine. The family business began with H. Cuvelier et Fils, the famous French wine merchant, in 1804. The family also owns the prestigious Bordeaux estates Château Leóville Poyferré in the Medoc and Château Le Crock in Saint-Estèphe. Cuvelier los Andes Grand Malbec 2006 is deep ruby red purple, with notes of black fruits, black plums, and fresh strawberries in the bouquet. On the palate the black fruits come alive with a note of raspberry confiture and a touch of anise. The finish is long and pleasant. Cuvelier los Andes 2007 is a blend of 73 percent Malbec, 19 percent Cabernet Sauvignon, and 8 percent Merlot. It is purple in the glass, with aromas of smoked meats, Chinese five-spice powder, black cherry, and a touch of campfire. It has an abundance of fruit on the palate and a persistent finish.

DIAMANDES

Clodomiro Silva s/n, Vista Flores, Tunuyán,
+54 261 476 5400,
www.diamandes.com

Belgian-born Alfred-Alexandre and Michele Bonnie purchased 130 hectares (321 acres) of land in 2005 and joined Michel Rolland's Clos de los Siete project. They had visited Argentina before and were impressed with the natural beauty, so purchasing vineyards was not a new thought to them. Prior to this, the couple acquired Château Malartic-Lagravière and Château Gazin Roquencourt in France. In December 2010, the family was pleased to

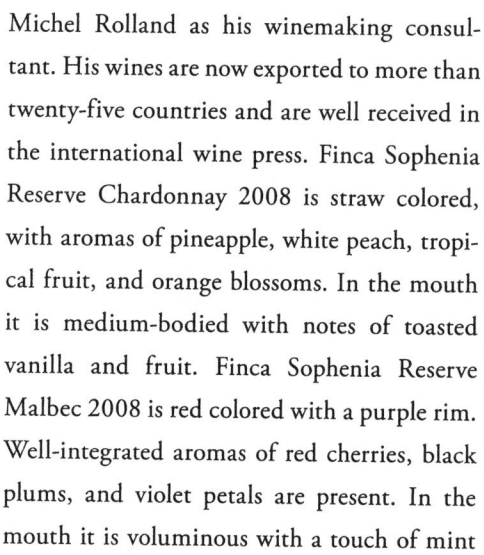

inaugurate their state-of-the-art, gravity fed, environmentally friendly Bodega DiamAndes winery. DiamAndes Gran Reserva 2007 is a blend of 70 percent Malbec and 30 percent Cabernet Sauvignon. It is reddish-purple, with aromas of dark fruits and anise. In the mouth it is full-bodied with focused tannins and a lovely persistence of black licorice.

FINCA SOPHENIA

Ruta Provincial 89 Kilometer 12.5,
Gualtallary, Tupungato,
+54 2622 489 680,
www.sophenia.com.ar

Roberto Luka had the vision to purchase 130 hectares (321 acres) of land in Tupungato in 1997 and make wine that would achieve international recognition. To that end he hired Matias Michelini as his winemaker and

Michel Rolland as his winemaking consultant. His wines are now exported to more than twenty-five countries and are well received in the international wine press. Finca Sophenia Reserve Chardonnay 2008 is straw colored, with aromas of pineapple, white peach, tropical fruit, and orange blossoms. In the mouth it is medium-bodied with notes of toasted vanilla and fruit. Finca Sophenia Reserve Malbec 2008 is red colored with a purple rim. Well-integrated aromas of red cherries, black plums, and violet petals are present. In the mouth it is voluminous with a touch of mint in a persistent finish.

FLECHAS DE LOS ANDES

Vista Flores, Tunuyán, Mendoza,
+54 261 420 4515

A partnership between Baron Benjamin de Rothschild of the famous French winemaking

FRANÇOIS LURTON / J&F LURTON

Ruta Provincial 94 Kilometer 21,
Vista Flores, Mendoza,
+54 261 441 1100,
www.jflurton.com

family and Laurent Dassault of Bordeaux's Château Dassault, Flechas—or "arrows"—de los Andes winery is an architectural dream set against the majestic Andes Mountains. The interior of the winery was designed by Phillippe Druillet, who used local craftsmen to execute his ideas. Flechas de los Andes Gran Malbec 2009 is reddish purple, with aromas of cigar box, ripe black plums, crystallized violet, and ripe blackberries. It is full-bodied in the mouth with abundant fruit and a touch of spice on a persistent finish.

François Lurton and his brother Jacques entered into a winemaking partnership in Argentina with the Catena family in 1992 and by 1996 had opened their own winery, Bodega J&F Lurton. The family has extensive wine knowledge and history and makes wine not only in Argentina but also in Chile, Spain, Portugal, and France. Bodega J&F Lurton Pinot Gris 2010 is straw colored, with aromas of citrus blossoms and white flowers. It is crisp and clean on the palate. Bodega J&F Lurton Gran Lurton Cabernet Sauvignon 2007 is purple red in the glass, with notes of red fruits, red raspberries, and black plums in the bouquet. The flavors are concentrated on the mid palate with a pleasant grip to the tannic structure.

GOUGUENHEIM

Calle La Gloria s/n Tupungato,
+54 911 708 0044,
www.gouguenheimwinery.com.ar

With 42 hectares (104 acres) of prime Tupungato and Escondido vineyards to his name, winemaker and owner Patricio Gouguenheim produces 110,000 bottles of Malbec, Merlot, Cabernet Sauvignon, Syrah, and Torrontés in the shadow of the snow-capped Andes. Under the tutelage of internationally acclaimed winemaker Susana Balbo, Gouguenheim produces value-driven wines from his high-altitude vineyards, which sit at 1,100 meters (3,609 feet) above sea level. Blessed with exquisite *terroir* and benefiting from warm days and cool nights, Gouguenheim does what he can to keep costs down in the winery, such as using oak staves in steel tanks rather than oak barrels to soften his value-driven reds. Gouguenheim Momentos Torrontés 2010, made with grapes from La Rioja, is a pale silver confection, with a nose of mango, white flowers, and a touch of spice. On the palate it is elegantly floral, with flavors of Turkish delight and geranium, and

bright citrus batting cleanup. Gouguenheim Estaciones Cabernet Sauvignon 2009 is classic dark cherry colored, with bright fruit fragrances and a touch of white pepper. In the mouth it reveals well-balanced fruit and spice, with black cherry, black raspberry, licorice, clove, and cinnamon leading up to a long, grippy finish. Gouguenheim Bonarda-Syrah 2008 is a 50-50 blend with a classic Crayola red violet color. Fragrances of fruit, spice, and a hint of earth open on the tongue to flavors of slightly tart cherry, blueberry, orange peel, and baking spices.

MONTEVIEJO

Clodomiro Silva s/n, Vista Flores, Tunuyán,
+54 2622 422 054,
www.monteviejo.com

Owned by Catherine Pere-Verge, Monteviejo is part of the esteemed Clos de los Siete group. Pere-Verge also owns Château La Gravière, Château le Gay, and Château Montviel in Bordeaux. She sources her grapes from her 125 hectares (309 acres) of vineyards on her Argentine estate. Marcelo Pelleriti makes the wines with Michel Rolland. Monteviejo Festivo Torrontés 2009 is straw colored, with aromas of ginger, white peach, and grapefruit rind. It has balanced acidity in the mouth with a clean finish. Monteviejo Festivo Malbec

2009 has notes of red cherries, red raspberry, and black raspberry. It is concentrated on the palate with a sturdy tannic backbone and pleasant finish.

NOMADE WINES

Avenida San Martín s/n, La Consultua,
Valle de Uco,
+54 911 4437 9728,
www.nomadewines.com

The concept of Nomade Wines came to Tomás Achával in a dream. As the previous CEO of Bodegas Chandon and Terrazas de los Andes, both Louis Vuitton Moët Hennessy properties, his dream was bound to come true. The company relies on Gabriela Celeste and winemakers from the Michel Rolland Eno-Rolland Team, with Roberto Simonetto carrying out the daily activities at the Mendoza winery. Nomade makes wines under the Nomade label and 7 Lunas label, which signifies that seven moons pass from the time vines flower until the time of the harvest. Nomade Mendoza Malbec 2006 is deep red, with aromas of red fruit, black plums, dried prune, and crystallized violet petals. It exhibits great balance in the mouth with smooth, round tannins.

O FOURNIER

Calle Los Indios, La Consulta,
+54 2622 451 579,
www.ofournier.com

Founded in 2000, the O Fournier group produces wine in Argentina, Chile, and Spain. The company owns three estates in Argentina with 94 hectares (232 acres) of vineyards. The new winery is positioned to use the Andes Mountains as a spectacular backdrop; tours are given in English, Spanish, and Italian each day. The bodega's Urban Restaurant is under the capable command of Chef Nadia Haron de Ortega, who pairs local and international cuisine with O Fournier wines crafted by José Mario Spisso, the chief winemaker. O Fournier B Crux Sauvignon Blanc 2010 is pale straw, with aromas of tropical fruits, citrus blossoms, and a slight vegetal note. In the mouth it is fruity, clean, and astringent. O Fournier Alfa Crux Malbec 2007 is reddish–purple, with aromas of black plums, strawberries, and cassis. It is generous in the mouth with a fruity persistent finish.

SALENTEIN

Ruta 89 Kilometer 14.5, Los Árboles,
Tunuyán, Mendoza,
+54 2622 429 000,
www.bodegasalentein.com

Bodegas Salentein's winery was designed in the shape of a cross, with four distinct bi-level wings meeting in the middle and the circular central chamber forming an amphitheater. The tasting room has beautiful frescos painted on the ceiling using natural paints made from stones ground by local villagers. Bodegas Salentein is a privately owned estate of 2,000 hectares (4,942 acres), the Killka Center for Culture and Arts, the Chapel of Gratitude, and beautiful Posada Salentein, which offers visitors a relaxing escape from daily life. Bodegas Salentein Los Leones Cabernet Sauvignon 2008 is ruby colored, with aromas of bell pepper, red fruits, and black pepper. On the palate it is well structured with ripe, sweet tannins. Bodegas Salentein Finca El Portillo Sauvignon Blanc 2009 is yellow with hints of green. The nose is pleasant with tropical fruits, white peaches, and a touch of guava. It is fresh in the mouth with lingering acidity. Bodegas Salentein Numina Malbec-Merlot 2005 is a blend of 60 percent Malbec and 40 percent Merlot. It is dark colored, almost black, with rich, ripe dark fruit notes. On the palate it is well structured with firm tannins and a pleasant long finish.

VAL DE FLORES

Vista Flores, Tunuyán,
www.rollandcollection.com

Only one wine is made from Val de Flores' 50-year-old Malbec vines. The project is a joint venture between Dany and Michel Rolland and Philippe Schell. The handpicked fruit comes from a small vineyard near the Clos de los Siete property, and during fermentation, the grapes are hand plunged: this is truly an artisanal wine. Val de Flores 2004 is dark ruby garnet red, with integrated aromas of black plum, black raspberry, porcini mushroom, and espresso. In the mouth there is a rich, creamy sensation with ripe fruit overtones, fine tannic structure, and a wonderfully long finish.

SOUTHERN MENDOZA

Blessed with water from the Atuel and Diamante Rivers, Southern Mendoza is a haven for nature lovers. It sits at the base of the Andes chain with gently sloping hillsides ranging between 400 to 800 meters (1,312 and 2,625 feet) above sea level. Twenty-two thousand hectares (54,363 acres) of grapes flourish here, almost half of which are Criolla varieties. Its two departments are San Rafael and General Alvear. Among varieties cultivated for fine wine, Bonarda leads the way, blanketing 11 percent of all the vineyards in Southern Mendoza. Cabernet Sauvignon is grown in 8 percent of this subregion's vineyards, with Malbec hot on its heels at 7.5 percent. Syrah covers 7 percent of cultivated plots. Chenin Blanc has a strong presence here, making up 4 percent of total grape plantings.

GOYENECHEA

Sotero Arizu s/n, Villa Atuel, San Rafael,
+54 2625 470 181,
www.goyenechea.com

Founded in 1868 by Spanish brothers Santiago and Narciso Goyenechea, the company claims to be the oldest independent, family-owned winery in Argentina. In 1993, they were one of the founders of the Council of Controlled Denomination of Origin San Rafael, reputed to be the original Argentine DOC. Today, the fifth generation of the family runs the business. Goyenechea Chardonnay 2010 is medium straw colored, with aromas of pineapple and white flowers. In the mouth it tastes of green apple, pear, and a touch of rose petal. Goyenechea Quinta Generación Malbec 2007 is dark garnet, with aromas of cherry, chocolate, and lemon peel. On the palate it has nice fruit, dark berries, light citrus notes, good balance of spice and fruit, and a finish of spice, licorice, and sage. Goyenechea Quinta Generación Cabernet Sauvignon 2007 is dark garnet, with notes of black cherry, smoked meat, and Mediterranean herbs in the bouquet. In the mouth the smoked meat taste comes out. It has great mouthfeel and is big and chewy.

NEUQUÉN

Nine hundred and eighty-seven kilometers (613 miles) south of Buenos Aires as the crow flies—but more like 1,200 kilometers (745 miles) away by road—the lush green valleys of Neuquén, which is within Patagonia, offer a stunning antidote to the irrigated deserts of the northern wine regions. In an area better known for its national parks, thermal waters, volcanic structures, paleontological remains, and tourism, 1,631 hectares (4,030 acres) of land have been turned over to viticulture, mostly since 1997. At that time, developer Julio Vola acquired 3,200 hectares (7,907 acres) of land near San Patricio del Chañar, provided improvements to the infrastructure—including a 20-kilometer–long (12-mile-long) irrigation canal—planted vineyards with a variety of grape cuttings and sold 200-hectare (494-acre) plots to investors, with the stipulation that each build a new winery.

Although total plantings are still small—combined, Neuquén and Río Negro account for less than 1 percent of total Argentine wine production—the emphasis here is on high-profile, high-quality wine. Vineyards lie at an altitude of about 200 meters (656 feet), and total rainfall within the year averages 178 millimeters, or 7 inches. Malbec is the most broadly planted variety, covering 34 percent of all the vineyards in the region, followed by Merlot and Cabernet Sauvignon, each accounting for about 18 percent of plantings. Pinot Noir does extremely well in the cooler climate of Patagonia and graces approximately 12 percent of the planted area. Cooler-climate whites thrive here as well: Chardonnay makes up 7 percent of the total, while Sauvignon Blanc makes up almost 5 percent.

FAMILIA SCHROEDER

San Patricio del Chañar, Neuquén,
+54 11 5252 4465,
www.familiaschroeder.com

Building of the winery screeched to a halt when the Schroeder family discovered the remains of a Titanosaur believed to be millions of years old in the soil beneath their proposed building. By the size of the bones, experts believe that this dinosaur would have weighed more than 16 tons. The family has named one of its wines "Saurus," in honor of the find, and have built a special cellar for visitors to view the bones. The Schroeders are growing Torrontés, Pinot Noir, Malbec, Cabernet Sauvignon, Sauvignon Blanc, and Chardonnay on their 120 hectares (297 acres) of vineyards. The family's restaurant, also called Saurus, serves international and Argentine cuisine among the vines. Saurus Rosa de los Vientos NV Sparkling wine is made from Pinot Noir and has a delicate pink color with *petit perlage*. It has notes of strawberry and lemon peel on both the bouquet and palate. Sauras Select Pinot Noir 2007 is deep cherry red, with aromas of sweet fruit and white chocolate. In the mouth it is delicate and elegant and finishes with a taste of buttered brioche. Familia Schroeder Pinot Noir-Malbec 2005 is deep inky red-violet. It is elegant in the mouth, with flavors of blueberry, sweet fruit, and a touch of spice. The tannins are silky, and the finish is bright.

NQN

Ruta Provincial 7, Picada 15,
San Patricio del Chañar, Neuquén,
+54 29 9489 7500,
www.bodeganqn.com.ar

Owner Luis María Focaccia has one of the newest wineries in the province of Neuquén. His vision was to have a structure that would facilitate modern winemaking technology but still fit into the Patagonian landscape. He planted Malbec, Cabernet Sauvignon, Merlot, Pinot Noir, Sauvignon Blanc, and Chardonnay, which have already proven to do well in southern Argentina. Winemaking is under the watchful eye of Sergio Pomar and together with Luis, the team strives to make well-priced, high-quality wines. NQN Malma Malbec Reserve 2007 is inky purple—think blueberry syrup-colored. It has notes of blueberry, black cherry, and orange zest in the bouquet. In the mouth it has flavors of blackberries, blueberries, and espresso with grippy tannins but a bright finish. NQN Pinot Noir 2010 is medium cherry red, with notes of cherry, thyme, and confectioners' sugar in the nose. The palate reveals cherry, white chocolate, lemon peel, and smooth tannins. Colección NQN Blend 2007 is composed of 60 percent Malbec and 40 percent Cabernet Sauvignon. Only 1,000 cases of this wonderful wine are produced, and that is a shame.

It is inky purple in color, with a fruity, almost violet floral nose. The palate explodes with a fruit bomb of blueberry, blackberry, and other dark, sweet fruits. The finish is smooth and silky with notes of chocolate and Mediterranean herbs.

VALLE PERDIDO

Ruta Provincial 7, San Patricio del Chañar, Neuquén,
+54 11 6091 7777,
www.valleperdido.com.ar

Named for the sixteenth century legend of "the lost valley" where seekers can find the "hidden enchanted city," Valle Perdido Patagonia is committed to making quality wines at the bottom of the earth. Always striving for more, Valle Perdido named architect Rodrigo de Marchi and interior designer Monica Nario responsible for the renovation. The winemaking team consists of Martin Caruso Coll, Martin Diletti, and consultant Alberto Antonini. The five-star Valle Perdido Hotel has just been named one of the Small Luxury Hotels of the World. It has 18 rooms, a gourmet restaurant, wine and tapas bar, and a wine spa. Valle Perdido Reserva Patagonia Malbec 2006 is deep red violet in color, with aromas of red fruit, fruit jam, espresso, and mocha. In the mouth it is juicy with sweet tannins and a long finish. Valle Perdido Cubas Patagonia Malbec 2006 is ruby red in color, with notes of spice, cooked red fruits, and roasted espresso beans in the bouquet. In the mouth there are strong but round tannins.

LA PAMPA

La Pampa is a large, lightly populated province in Patagonia mainly known for types of farming other than viticulture. Its major industry is cattle ranching, but sheep, goats, and pigs are also raised here, along with wheat, sunflowers, and other grain. This is the home of Argentina's *gauchos*, the free-spirited cowboys who gallop on horseback wearing broad-brimmed hats and brightly colored ponchos. La Pampa is not officially recognized as a wine region yet, but it is considered up and coming. It has more than one hundred hotels and guest houses, and ten *estancias,* or "ranches," where ecotourism and horseback riding are the primary leisure activities. Despite its immense size, a very small amount of land is turned over to grape farming. At present 14 mostly small wineries have a total of 271 hectares (670 acres) under cultivation. They are situated near the town of "25 of May," named for the day that Argentina's fight for independence from Spain began. The region itself tends to sit at low elevations of 40 to 100 meters (131 to 328 feet) above sea level, while vineyards and wineries are centered around the *Alto Valle Rio Colorado,* or "High Valley of the Red River." This river is the main source of irrigation in a region that receives 178 millimeters, or 7 inches, of rainfall on average per year. There are also some small vineyard plantings in the neighboring province of Chubut.

BODEGA DEL DESIERTO

Alem 855, Buenos Aires,
+54 11 4314 0744,
www.bodegadeldesierto.com.ar

Named for the literal translation of "from the desert," Bodega del Desierto is surrounded by 160 kilometers (100 miles) of desert. It is the first winery located in the La Pampa province of Patagonia and has 140 hectares (346 acres) of vineyards. Varieties planted include Viognier, Sauvignon Blanc, Chardonnay, Merlot, Syrah, Pinot Noir, and Malbec. The winemaking team consists of Sebastian Cavagnaro and consultant Paul Hobbs. Bodega del Desierto Syrah 2006 is medium garnet to dark ruby in color and has bright fruit and freshly chopped herbal notes. In the mouth flavors of cherry, blueberry, chocolate-covered espresso beans, and star anise are noted. The finish is pleasant and long. Desierto 25/5 Cabernet Franc 2006 is a deep garnet color, with fruit aromas such as strawberry and cherry. It is well balanced with dark fruit, rich spice, licorice, clove, and jalapeño notes on the palate. Desierto Pampa Blend Cabernet Sauvignon-Merlot-Cabernet Franc 2006 is deep garnet colored. It has notes of black cherry, light spice, violet, and lemon peel. In the mouth there is dark fruit, baking spices, and medium acidity before a long, tannic finish.

RÍO NEGRO

The southernmost wine-producing area in Argentina, Río Negro has vines that date back to the early twentieth century—though the old estates have only been rehabilitated in recent years, drawing the wine world's attention to this fertile land of fruit orchards fed by the river of the same name. This 119-kilometer-long by 8-kilometer–wide (73-mile-long by 5-mile-wide) valley features vineyards planted with bush vines, which still rely on the ancient practice of flood irrigation to bring much-needed water to its clay soils. Vineyard altitudes range from 396 to 457 meters (1,299 to 1,499 feet) above sea level, and average annual rainfall is 203 millimeters, or 8 inches. This is an enormous region of great natural beauty, where fewer than two people per square kilometer (0.4 square mile) share space with more

than 150 species of birds, beautiful beaches leading to cold, clean water, and a series of valleys populated by cattle, sheep, and apple and pear trees.

Average summer temperatures vary between 12 and 26 degrees Celsius (54 and 80 degrees Fahrenheit). Merlot accounts for the highest concentration of grapevines, at about 15 percent, barely trailed by Malbec, which makes up 14 percent of plantings. Syrah is planted on almost 6 percent of vineyard area, and Cabernet Sauvignon and Pinot Noir are each cultivated on slightly more than 4 percent of arable soil. Río Negro Pinot Noir is regarded as the finest in the country due to its acclimation to this cold weather region, which also supports small plantings of Sauvignon Blanc, Sémillon, and Viognier.

BODEGA CHACRA

Mainqué, Río Negro,
+54 2941 605 125,
www.bodegachacra.com

Piero Incisa della Rocchetta, a descendant of the Tuscan family that brings the famous Italian cult red wine Sassicaia to the world, purchased an abandoned vineyard of Pinot Noir vines in 2004. The vines were originally planted in 1932 and were lovingly nurtured back to life to produce his "Treinta y Dos"

BOTTLE N°. _____ OF 4878

CHACRA

2009 PINOT NOIR
- TREINTA Y DOS -
PATAGONIA - RIO NEGRO

ELEVE ET PRODUIT EN PATAGONIE PAR PIERO INCISA DELLA ROCCHETTA · ALC 13.5% VOL.

Barda Pinot Noir 2010 is medium cherry red, with aromas of dried red cherries, black cherries, and cherry cola. There is a whiff of Mediterranean herbs with a prominent rosemary top note. Soft and supple, this wine invites you in for another sip.

wine. Piero has since purchased two other old vine Pinot Noir vineyards. One was planted in 1955—hence his "Cincuenta y Cinco"—and the second was planted in 1967—soon to be released as "Sesenta y Siete." He also produces a limited quantity of Merlot under the Mainqué label. We were invited to Piero's New York City apartment where he prepared tapas paired with his wines. Bodega Chacra Treinta y Dos Pinot Noir 2009 is a limited production of only 5,868 numbered bottles—we drank bottle number 2,611—which is cherry red in color and has aromas of ripe red fruits, red raspberries, and a touch of vanilla. In the mouth it is fruit-forward yet restrained. It is generous and ample with a lovely persistent finish. Bodega Chacra Cincuenta y Cinco Pinot Noir 2009 is medium red and has notes of red cherries, red plums, and hint of cherry vanilla ice cream in the bouquet. It has a fair amount of heft to the palate with a pleasing fruit-focused finish. Bodega Chacra

HUMBERTO CANALE

Chacra 186, General Roca, Río Negro, Patagonia, +54 2941 433 879, www.bodegahcanale.com

Bodega Humberto Canale was founded by Señor Canale in 1909. After the *La Conquista del Desierto* or "Desert Conquest," it was possible for European immigrants to move south and subsequently grow grapes in Argentina's Patagonian region. Humberto Canale was considered one of the pioneers of Patagonian viticulture. Four generations later, Guillo Barzi Canale and his son Guillermo continue the family tradition. They grow Cabernet Sauvignon, Pinot Noir, Merlot, Malbec, Cabernet Franc, Sauvignon Blanc, Sémillon, Torrontés, and Viognier. The family runs a two-day training course for restaurant professionals, or for those just wanting to learn more about wine and wine service. They are happy to accept visitors and will help you arrange a rafting trip down the Río Negro—if such things take your fancy. Bodega Humberto Canale

Grand Reserve Pinot Noir 2006 is ruby red with a purple rim. The nose presents notes of fruit with touches of spice and vanilla. In the mouth it has a medium weight with soft, velvety tannins. Bodega Humberto Canale Centenium 2005 is a blend of Merlot, Cabernet Franc, and Malbec. It was released in 2009 to pay homage to great-grandfather Humberto. It is deep red in the glass, with aromas of cooked red fruits and fresh blackberries with touches of spice and mocha. In the mouth it is big and bold with mature sweet tannins. The finish is delightful and persistent.

NOEMIA

Ruta Provincial 7 Kilometer 12,
Valle Azul, Río Negro,
+54 9 2984 530412,
www.bodeganoemia.com

Noemia is named for the Condesa Noemi Marone Cinzano of the Italian Cinzano wine producing family. The project is a partnership between Noemi and Danish winemaker Hans Vinding-Diers. Vinding-Diers had the good fortune to grow up in Bordeaux and remembers tasting a fine wine with school lunch at the age of six years old. That event led to a love of wine and a love of the wines of Bordeaux. He is excited to present his Noemia "2" 2007, a Bordeaux-style blend of 85 percent Cabernet

Sauvignon and 15 percent Merlot to the world. Too bad only 1,500 bottles and 30 magnums were produced. It is dark red with hints of violet and has aromas of red fruits and licorice. On the palate it has good heft and a lingering finish. This is a totally delightful wine. Bodega Noemia Patagonia Malbec 2009 is garnet purple in color, with notes of dried figs, pencil lead, black fruits, and cassis and slightly grippy tannins. Bodega Noemia J. Alberto 2010 is a combination of 95 percent Malbec and 5 percent Merlot. It is deep reddish-purple and has notes of licorice, red fruit confiture, and fresh black plum. In the mouth it is voluminous with a pleasant finish.

PATAGONIA VALLEY

Ruta Nacional 22 Kilometer 1013, Río Negro,
+54 9 11 4426 4740,
www.rivus.com.ar

Owner and winemaker Augusto Ripoli is making some very *terroir*-expressive wines down at the foot of South America. The winery's brand name, Rivus, comes from the Latin word for "river" and pays homage to the Río Negro, which collects snow melt from the Andes Mountains and provides fresh water to the vineyards. Patagonia Valley Rivus Sauvignon Blanc 2008 is pale straw, with touches of lemon peel and minerals on the nose. In the mouth it is clean, with flavors of grapefruit and pineapple. The finish is lightly floral. Patagonia Valley Rivus Pinot Noir is medium to dark cherry colored. It has aromas of vanilla, cherry, and orange peel: think cherry vanilla ice cream. In the mouth it has flavors of cherry, tart cherry, and a touch of cocoa powder. It has a nice tannic structure and finishes with a Mediterranean herbal note. Patagonia Valley Rivus Malbec Grand Reserva is garnet red with a touch of violet in the rim. The nose gives an initial aroma of bright fruit, black pepper, and baking spices. It has a good balance between fruit and spice with flavors of raspberry, black cherry, clove, licorice, toasted oak, and vanilla.

RECIPES

ZUCCARDI'S ARGENTINE EMPANADAS

❋

Recipe courtesy of the Zuccardi Family Bodega

❋

SERVES 6-8

Empanadas are a source of national, local, and family pride in Argentina. Ask any Argentine and he will tell you that Argentine empanadas are better than empanadas from any other country, and that empanadas from his town are better than the empanadas from any other town, and of course that his mother's empanadas are better than anyone else's mother's empanadas.

We had the pleasure of dining with the Zuccardi family, and we can certainly vouch for their claim to make the best empanadas. We are happy that they agreed to let us share their recipe in our book. These are *great* empanadas—and the perfect start to a meal at home, or at the Zuccardi's Casa del Visitante Restaurant, which combines the best of Argentine and Italian tradition. Enjoy them with a glass of Zuccardi Serie A Malbec 2009.

FOR THE DOUGH

2¼ pounds all-purpose flour

2 tablespoons salt

1½ sticks butter (12 tablespoons) butter

3 ounces lard or vegetable shortening

2–4 tablespoons cold water

Cornstarch, as needed

2 egg yolks, whisked, for brushing

FOR THE MEAT FILLING

¼ cup olive oil

4 large onions, diced

2 pounds ground beef

½ teaspoon salt

½ teaspoon pepper

½ teaspoon paprika

¼ teaspoon oregano

6 eggs, hardboiled and chopped

MAKE THE DOUGH

Put the flour and salt into a bowl. Using your fingers or two knives, blend the butter and fat into the dry ingredients until small crumbs appear. Add the water, a little at a time, and gently mix together with a fork until a ball forms. Sprinkle a flat surface with cornstarch and stretch the dough into a large flat disc. Using a rolling pin, roll out the dough until it is ¼-inch thick. Sprinkle the top of the dough with cornstarch and fold the dough into four layers. Transfer to a plate and let rest in the refrigerator, loosely covered with a towel for one hour.

When ready to use, with a rolling pin again, roll out the dough until it is ¼-inch thick. Using a cookie cutter (or a glass, or a coffee mug), cut the dough into rounds. Transfer rounds to a platter and cover with plastic wrap. Refrigerate until ready to fill.

MAKE THE MEAT FILLING

Heat the oil in a large cast-iron skillet over medium-high heat until hot but not smoking, then add the onions and cook, stirring occasionally, until softened. Add the ground beef and cook, stirring occasionally, until browned. Add the salt, pepper, paprika, and oregano and stir to combine. Add the chopped eggs, and stir gently to combine well. Remove from heat.

TO ASSEMBLE

Preheat the oven to 375°F.

Transfer the pastry rounds to a flat surface sprinkled with cornstarch. Place a tablespoon of the ground meat mixture in the center of the rounds. Using your fingertips, wet the edges of the pastry with cold water. Fold the dough over the filling to form half-moon shapes and crimp the edges with the tines of a fork to seal. Using a pastry brush, brush the tops with egg yolks.

Bake the empanadas in the oven until golden brown, about 15–20 minutes. Transfer to a rack to cool for 5 minutes before serving.

UCO VALLEY TROUT
WITH FRESH CORN SOUFFLÉ

❋

Recipe courtesy of Facundo Belardinelli,
chef at Posada Salentein, Mendoza

❋

SERVES 6

Chef Facundo Balardinelli uses only the freshest local beef, pork, fish, and lamb, and sources seasonal fruits and vegetables to create quality cuisine. The chef recommends pairing this regional specialty with Salentein Reserve Chardonnay 2009 because he feels that it has a smooth texture, good acidity, citrus characteristics, and mineral notes. Having enjoyed this dish, we couldn't agree more!

This recipe uses two great ingredients that are native to the Uco Valley: fresh trout and sweet corn. This native American favorite, maize, provides great balance to the trout fillet. The delicate flavor of Uco Valley trout enhances any meal, rather than competing with the other components on the plate.

FOR THE SOUFFLÉ

Butter and flour for coating
  the soufflé dish
1 cup fresh corn kernels (cut
  from 2 ears)
2 tablespoons olive oil
1 medium grilled red onion,
  cut into small cubes
1 small clove garlic, cut into
  small cubes
1 medium red pepper, cut
  into small cubes
1 medium tomato, seeded
  and diced
3 ounces mozzarella cheese,
  cut into bits
Salt and freshly ground pepper,
  to taste
Chopped basil leaves, to taste
1 tablespoon butter
1 tablespoon flour
½ cup milk
2 egg whites

FOR THE TROUT

Olive oil for coating baking pan
  (or skillet)
Fresh trout fillets—about
  3 pounds total
Salt to taste
Lemon juice to taste
1 stick (8 tablespoons) butter,
  cut into pieces
Parsley for garnish
Lemon wedges for garnish

MAKE THE SOUFFLÉ

Preheat the oven to 450°F.

Generously butter and flour the soufflé dish. Cook the corn in boiling water for 7 minutes and drain. Heat the olive oil in a heavy skillet over moderate heat until hot but not smoking, then add the onion, garlic, and red pepper and cook, stirring, until softened. Add the cooked corn, the tomatoes, and the cheese and stir to combine, then season with salt, pepper, and chopped basil, and set aside.

In a heavy saucepan, create a roux: Heat the butter until melted, then add the flour and cook it through (but be careful not to burn it). Slowly add the milk in a stream to create a paste and set aside.

In a bowl, quickly whisk egg whites with a pinch of salt until stiff. Add the corn mixture to the roux, then fold in the egg whites. Pour the mixture into the prepared soufflé dish and bake the soufflé in the oven until browned, about 20 minutes. Serve immediately with the trout.

COOK THE TROUT

Preheat another oven to 400°F.

Put a little olive oil in a metal baking pan, and place the trout fillets, skin side down, in the pan. Top the fillets with salt, lemon juice, and butter and bake in the oven for about 5 minutes. (Alternatively, if you do not have 2 ovens, you can cook the trout in a hot skillet).

TO SERVE

Transfer the fish to a serving platter and garnish with parsley and lemon wedges. Serve the soufflé as an accompaniment.

GRILLED BEEF TENDERLOIN WITH CHIMICHURRI SAUCE

✳

Recipe courtesy of Lucas Bustos,
chef, Bodega Ruca Malen

✳

SERVES 4-6

Lucas Bustos turns out some wonderful cuisine at his restaurant at Bodega Ruca Malen. The restaurant was recommended by Michael Schachner in the February 2011 issue of *Wine Enthusiast* as a winery restaurant "that's a hit." Many Argentines covet their recipe for Chimichurri, but after a few glasses of wine, we were able to coax Chef Bustos into giving us his secret formula. The restaurant has soaring ceilings and plate glass windows that look out over a sea of grapevines. Chef Lucas recommends serving this recipe with Ruca Malen Kinien Cabernet Sauvignon 2002. He likes the way that the spice, complexity, and smoky aromas of the wine pair with the beef.

FOR THE CHIMICHURRI SAUCE

¾ cup extra virgin olive oil

2 teaspoons sweet paprika

1 teaspoon chili flakes

8 dried figs, diced

½ cup black olives, pitted
    and sliced

1 ear of corn, kernels removed

2 tablespoons red wine vinegar

FOR THE GRILLED BEEF

Salt

Pepper

4 (8-ounce) tenderloin steaks

MAKE THE CHIMICHURRI SAUCE

Heat ½ cup olive oil in a cast iron skillet over moderate heat
until hot but not smoking, then add the paprika, chili flakes,
dried figs, olives, and corn, stirring to combine well, and cook
until warmed through, about 5 minutes. Remove from heat and
add remaining ¼ cup olive oil and vinegar, Let the sauce rest
while the steaks are cooking.

GRILL THE BEEF

Prepare a hot grill for grilling.

Salt and pepper the steaks and grill them over hot coals to the
desired temperature. Transfer the steaks to a cutting board and
let rest for 5 minutes.

TO SERVE

Slice steaks, arrange on a serving platter, and drizzle
Chimichurri sauce over the entire platter. Serve immediately.

IN THEIR OWN WORDS

LAURA CATENA

Laura Catena is one of the winemakers and family owners of Catena Zapata and an emergency room physician. Harvard educated, Catena has long been involved in the world of wine. She enjoys working with her father and the other winemakers at Catena Zapata. When she is not at home with her husband and three children in San Francisco, she can be found walking through the vineyards, working in the wine cellar, analyzing wine in the laboratory, or in the boardroom blending wine with her father.

How did you get involved in the world of wine?
My father used to take me as his translator on his trips to Bordeaux when I was in college at Harvard. I fell in love with wine and the stories behind it. I was always very independent so at that age I didn't see myself going into the family business. I was always the kind of kid who rescued animals and stood up for the unpopular kids at school—I decided to study medicine because I was convinced that I wanted to do a profession where my contribution to other people's lives was clearly palpable. Little by little, I started to get involved in the family winery, and soon enough I was practicing medicine part time and leading our viticultural research department. One thing led to another, and now I am president. I am really proud of

our family's role in bringing recognition to Argentine wine, and I realize that providing interesting jobs for all the wonderful staff at our winery is also an important contribution.

What are some of the biggest changes you have seen in winemaking since you began your career?
Viticulture in Mendoza is different than anywhere else because of the high altitude (we have a rare combination of extremely cold nights, dry air, very poor soils, and intense sunlight). So we can never apply what is known in other parts of the world because our *terroir* is so different. Coming to this realization and doing all the research, trial and error, and mistakes that it takes to figure out how to

get highly expressive wines from this unique climate has been my biggest challenge. Also, taking a gamble on Malbec in 1994, when nobody thought that Malbec had the stature of Cabernet Sauvignon, Merlot, or other important world varieties.

What are some of the exciting changes that you see happening specifically in your country?
Argentines and Argentine wine drinkers abroad are starting to appreciate the regional differences among the different regions of Mendoza and other wine-producing provinces of Argentina. There is nothing more exciting than tasting Malbec from Altamira for example and comparing it to Malbec from Agrelo, Tunuyán, Vista Flores, or even Malbec from Salta, Patagonia, or the Argentine province of La Rioja.

Where else in the world have you studied, trained, or worked a harvest? How did that influence your winemaking?
I have tasted wines all over the world but never made wine at another winery. But working as a physician in the emergency department has taught me how to work in a team and pay attention to details, and this has been very helpful in running the winery.

Which varieties are you working with? Are you experimenting with anything new?
Yes, I never grow tired of Malbec because it is so different depending on where you grow it. But I am also very excited about extreme high-altitude chardonnay—we are planting a new vineyard of chardonnay at 1,829-meter [6,000-feet] elevation—and also working on our red blends with Malbec, Bonarda, Cabernet Franc, and Petit Verdot. Also, we are working in other winemaking provinces—red blends in the province of La Rioja and Torrontés in Salta. This is all very exciting.

Are there any new areas that you have identified for potential vineyard sites?
Higher in Gualtallary, Tupungato at 1,829-meter [6,000-feet] elevation in Mendoza for Chardonnay and Pinot noir, and perhaps also some very ageable, concentrated and high-acid Malbec, and the province of La Rioja for red blends. Also, we are very excited by the whole area of Eugenio Bustos and El Cepillo in the southern Uco Valley where we have planted three new vineyards in the last five years—we are planting Cabernet Franc in addition to Malbec in these areas because it adds another dimension to the Malbec and Cabernet Sauvignon wines.

What challenges have you faced as a wine-maker or winery owner?

Balancing my job as winemaker with not wanting to give up being a doctor and being a mother of three children! And a wife to my saintly husband.

What is your winemaking philosophy?

Preserve the salient characteristic of each site—whether you decide to bottle in a single vineyard or in a blend, "edgy" wines are better than "perfect" wines.

What would you hope people say about your wine?

That it is different than any other wine they've tasted before and, of course, also delicious!

Do you think that the market should influence winemaking, or do you think that winemaking should influence the market?

Both things happen inevitably, but I don't believe in making wines for a specific style—people eventually get bored with this.

Besides your own wine, what are some of your favorite wines? What do you like about them?

I love white Bordeaux wines with a little age such as Pavillon Blanc and very old wines from Bordeaux because I prefer old wine aromas and the smoothness that comes from ageing.

What is your opinion on screwcap versus cork closures?

I love screwcaps for whites because they are so practical for wines that you put in the fridge. For fine reds, I still enjoy that nervous moment, especially when opening an old bottle, when you wonder if the cork will crumble or if you'll be able to get it out in one piece. What a silly thing to like, but I do.

If you could invite anyone from history, living or dead, to your home for dinner, who would it be? What food would you serve? What wine would you serve?

I would invite Nelson Mandela—he seems like someone with such an amazing vision and life of service who still likes to have a good time. I would serve him Catena Zapata Malbec Argentino with a big piece of steak with chimichurri sauce.

If you were to stay home tonight for a relaxing evening, drinking wine while watching a movie, which movie would you watch?

I would watch an Almodóvar movie, probably *Tacones Lejanos*, I think it's *High Heels* in English—I love all the songs in this movie and the passion and flawed lives (like those of all of us) of the characters in the movie.

How do you like to spend your time away from the winery?
At home with my husband and children baking or playing soccer, swimming, or just going to the park.

Do you collect wine? If so, what is in your cellar?
Yes, my collection is very eclectic. I have quite a few old Argentine wine bottles from the '90s, then lots of red Bordeaux, white Burgundy, and a fair amount of Super Tuscans.

If you weren't involved in wine, what would you be doing?
Full-time emergency doctor—my other profession—and writing books.

PIERO INCISA DELLA ROCCHETTA

Piero Incisa della Rocchetta is the owner of Bodega Chacra. He's a member of an Italian winemaking family with holdings in Umbria, Sicily, and Tuscany—his family owns Tenuta San Guido, the producer of the world famous Sassicaia red wine. Piero purchased his own piece of Argentine vineyards in 2004, named it Bodegas Chacra, and winemaking history was born on the other side of the world.

How did you get involved in the world of wine?

I think at around five years old, my grandpa had us taste some wine at the dinner table, some of it was French, some other was his own wine.

What are some of the biggest changes you have seen in winemaking since you began your career?

We went from finesse and *terroir* to extraction and "opulence" in the span of a quarter of a century.

What are some of the exciting changes that you see happening specifically in your country?

A closer attention and a more intimate relationship with the vineyard and its *terroir*.

Where else in the world have you studied, trained, or worked a harvest? How did that influence your winemaking?

I was born into a Tuscan wine family—growing up with harvests and playing in vineyards as a child. My winemaking team has worked vintages in Europe, South Africa, and, of course, Patagonia. Personally, my experiences in Oregon expanded my approach to cool-climate Pinot Noir.

Which varieties are you working with? Are you experimenting with anything new?

In Patagonia we are working primarily with old ungrafted selections of Pinot Noir and also some Merlot.

Are there any new areas that you have identified for potential vineyard sites?

No, at the moment I am quite obsessed with what we have!

What challenges have you faced as a winemaker or winery owner?

Two of the most fascinating and rewarding challenges are adapting to the unpredictability of Mother Nature—hail, hungry pigeons, ants, hares' appetites, frost, et cetera—and understanding human nature—balancing my team's emotions, finding solutions for their struggles, and finding that fine line between friendship and working relations.

What is your winemaking philosophy?
Listen to Mother Nature and to my winemaker, Hans Vinding-Diers.

What would you hope people say about your wine?
Can I buy some more please?

Do you think that the market should influence winemaking, or do you think that winemaking should influence the market?
Neither, I think winemaking should be influenced by the *terroir* and its characteristics.

Besides your own wine, what are some of your favorite wines? What do you like about them?
Sassicaia, the quintessential expression of elegance and finesse, and Domaine de la Romanée-Conti—legend has it that Luis XV, king of France, was prescribed a bottle a day by his doctor to cure gout.

What is your opinion on screwcap versus cork closures?
I think the jury is still out.

If you could invite anyone from history, living or dead, to your home for dinner, who would it be? What food would you serve? What wine would you serve?
Queen of England, Gandhi, God, and Richard Pryor. White rice, our own, Bodega Chacra "Cincuenta y Cinco" 2010 vintage, it has only 11.5 percent alcohol; it might please God.

If you were to stay home tonight for a relaxing evening, drinking wine while watching a movie, which movie would you watch? Which wine would you drink? Explain.
I don't really watch movies, but if I did I would probably not drink wine, I prefer to have wine with dinner and share it with a friend.

How do you like to spend your time away from the winery?
Traveling and swimming in warm waters without sharks.

Do you collect wine? If so, what is in your cellar?
I don't, I have the good luck to have friends that are very generous with me.

If you weren't involved in wine, what would you be doing?
Gardening.

NICOLAS AUDEBERT

Nicolas Audebert is the winemaker at Cheval des Andes. He is the winemaker and primary liaison between the French-owned Château Cheval Blanc and Argentine-owned Terrazas de los Andes. Before heading south to Argentina, he spent five years as a winemaker at Krug, Veuve Clicquot, and Moët & Chandon.

How did you get involved in the world of wine?

I studied agronomy and enology in Montpellier following a personal passion for wine. I wasn't born into wine, but I always knew I needed to work with nature, with big spaces, to have contact with noble things. I quickly came to realize that wine is the most extraordinary agricultural product of all. Nothing else is so inclusive. I work with the soil and the seasons, yet I am also making an emotional product, something which inspires its customers and which has three thousand years of history and culture.

What are some of the biggest changes you have seen in winemaking since you began your career?

I have seen the use of technology increase in the world of winemaking. What I love with Argentina is that more and more wineries use the latest technology but keep a respect for tradition and *terroir*. One foot in Australia, one foot in France, so to speak.

What are some of the exciting changes that you see happening specifically in your country?

Argentina is booming in the right direction with higher quality and rediscovering of old Malbec vineyards that can produce profound and complex wines. I truly believe Argentina is producing and will increasingly produce world-class wines.

Where else in the world have you studied, trained, or worked a harvest? How did that influence your winemaking?

My early work experiences were in Champagne, with Krug. In Champagne, you know exactly what works. That's the way that great things have been created in the past. From this Champagne experience with prestigious and historic brands, I have learned the respect for tradition and balance, elegance and complexity, as key characteristics a great wine must have. It's a perfect job if you like certainty and security. But I wanted more adventure, the chance to create something new.

In 2006 Pierre Lurton, the director of Château Cheval Blanc, called me into his office and asked me if I would like to take charge of Cheval des Andes. I didn't hesitate.

Which varieties are you working with? Are you experimenting with anything new?

I am working mainly with 80-year-old Malbec vines and 50-year-old Cabernet Sauvignon. We have Petit Verdot, Merlot, and Cabernet Franc as well. We use the traditional Bordeaux varieties to create a "grand cru" from the Andes.

At the core of Cheval des Andes is the art of blending. Every year with Pierre Lurton, we get together and try to make the perfect blend. I have fantastic Malbec, and it would be very easy to bottle that on its own. But that's not the Cheval Blanc philosophy. Malbec is a virtuoso soloist, but it's just one instrument, like a violin. If you add, say, a double bass, and a saxophone, suddenly you have harmony, you have vibration. That's what we want when we blend in Cabernet Sauvignon and use a little bit of Petit Verdot, Merlot, and Cabernet Franc. The skill of blending different grape varieties and different parcels—that search for perfect balance—comes from Cheval Blanc. At the end, every flavor is there, but nothing overwhelms. If you taste anything obtrusive, I've failed.

Are there any new areas that you have identified for potential vineyard sites?

There are some very exciting vineyards in Altamira, the south part of Mendoza, but right now we are very happy with our vineyards and are not looking to expand.

What challenges have you faced as a winemaker or winery owner? What is your winemaking philosophy?

Creating a modern fine wine is easier in Argentina than in Europe. There isn't the weight of tradition and legislation that is always there in France. It's an adventure here, especially since I am working with a new *terroir*. I can change, experiment, and move forward. What I have here is a precious stone, but it's a precious stone that has never been cut or polished. That's what I want to do. I don't have the arrogance or pretension—even though I'm French—to say I've gotten there yet. There's further to go. But I wouldn't want to be anywhere else in the wine world. Up here in the Andes, I can lead from the front.

What would you hope people say about your wine?

That it has delivered them emotion and pleasure. If we talk about what you look for in a wine, there are a thousand answers. It depends of the time, the vibe, the people you are with, of the weather, if you are in Hong Kong and it's 100 degrees and humid or on top of the Andes in the snow, whether it's two in the afternoon or two in the morning . . .

Do you think that the market should influence winemaking, or do you think that winemaking should influence the market?

I don't know, but I would say that one should make wine with passion. The elaboration of the wine, its assemblage, is an art. A great wine is made with a vision of a style, a vision of taste, and nobody has a perfect formula. I have the chance to play with a unique *terroir* and create a unique style; I sincerely hope the market will enjoy it.

Besides your own wine, what are some of your favorite wines? What do you like about them?

Well of course I like Cheval Blanc because of its elegance, finesse, and silkiness. As mentioned earlier, wines need to be very different depending on the time of day

et cetera. I like a lot of different wines depending on the occasion, with a sweet spot of course for Champagne, white Burgundies, great Bordeaux, and of course great Argentine wines!

What is your opinion on screwcap versus cork closures?

I wouldn't use screwcap for Cheval des Andes, but I don't think there is any problem for screwcaps for white wines that are made to be drunk young.

If you could invite anyone from history, living or dead, to your home for dinner, who would it be? What food would you serve? What wine would you serve?

I would invite Johann-Joseph Krug, the founder of Krug Champagne, to enjoy an Argentine Asado with the recent Krugs and Cheval des Andes.

How do you like to spend your time away from the winery?

I love to travel with my wife and four kids to places of beauty where I can learn and discover the beauty of the planet. I went recently to the "Isla de Pascua" (Easter Island) and came back a new man.

Do you collect wine? If so, what is in your cellar?

I don't collect wine per se. I drink way too fast to collect wine!

If you weren't involved in wine, what would you be doing?

I would play polo full time as a professional. As mentioned earlier I need to be outdoors, and I learned to love this sport in Argentina!

AUSTRALIA

AUSTRALIA IS LARGE—VERY LARGE. TO PUT this country—which is both an island and a self-contained continent—into perspective, consider that it is about the same size as the 48 contiguous United States of America. When most people think of Australia, they picture wide-open spaces. And not just any wide-open spaces but barren outback with outcroppings of red rock, broad beaches with killer waves, or kangaroos hopping across a broad plain. None of these is incorrect, but none gives you the whole picture. To place Australia's wide-open spaces in context, think about the fact that only 22,617,000 people live there, or 7.3 percent of the population of the United States. If we look at a map of Australia, we see that almost all of its cities are on or near the coast, and for good reason; these are the areas surrounded by fertile farmland that supported the early settlers here. Much of interior Australia is either barren desert or tropical rainforest, which, while intensely scenic, is not entirely hospitable to human habitation and/ or cultivation. If we can describe Australia's neighbor, New Zealand, as mysteriously beautiful, then we would definitely call Australia ruggedly handsome.

When most people—or most people outside of Australia, at any rate—think of Australian wine, they think of Shiraz. Not just any Shiraz, but a big, bold, juicy, overripe Shiraz, with flavors of fruit, pepper, and spice that explode in the mouth. Again, this is correct, but it is nowhere near the whole picture. Australia is a nation of more than 60 wine regions in six states, spread across the country, but all comparatively close to the coast. It is also a country that grows more than a hundred different grape varieties—from that big, juicy Shiraz to delicate aromatic whites, such as Riesling and Pinot Gris, and everything in between, including elegant Syrah, Shiraz's alter-ego. Australia has some of the world's oldest soils and oldest vines. As phylloxera ravaged the grapevines of Europe in the nineteenth century, some of the young vines of Australia—insulated at the time due to Australia's distance from the rest of the wine-growing world—thrived. When it comes to wine, this is indeed a complex land "Down Under."

Wine grapes first came to Australia in January 1788, on board the eleven ships of the First Fleet, which left Portsmouth, England, on May 13, 1787. England could no longer send convicted criminals to the newly independent United States of America, so the recently discovered New South Wales seemed an opportune prison outpost. Under the leadership of Captain Arthur Phillip, the First Fleet stopped at Tenerife, in the Canary Islands, Brazil's Rio de Janeiro, and Cape Town, South Africa, before sailing across the Indian Ocean toward Australia. Provisions—including grapevine cuttings—were picked up in Cape Town, where grapes had by then been successfully cultivated for more than a hundred years.

The first settlement was established a few kilometers from modern day Sydney, in Botany Bay, where Captain James Cook had been the first European to set foot on the "new" continent. Prior to British colonization, Australia, which features some of the oldest soils on the planet, had been inhabited for more than forty-thousand years by aboriginal peoples, or Native Australians. Australia is the flattest and driest of any inhabited continent, and while the native population was adept at surviving the land's harsh environmental conditions, the early European settlers took decades to properly adapt. Lack of available water posed a major problem for the earliest European pioneers; for this and other reasons, the original grape plantings did not flourish for long.

As British and European emigration continued, other homesteaders were more successful at both grape growing and winemaking. Gregory Blaxland, one of a trio who led the first inland expedition over the Blue Mountains, made wine in Australia in the early 1820s. He too had brought cuttings from South Africa, and his efforts paid off with the win of a silver medal at a London wine competition in 1822, and a gold medal in 1828. He sold wine both within Australia and in the UK market.

The person who had the largest influence on the history and/or establishment of Australian wine was James Busby, a Scotsman who studied viticulture in Spain and France before bringing vine cuttings from those two countries to Australia and New Zealand in 1832. Many of the varieties thriving in Australian vineyards today owe their popularity—and, in some instances, their specific heritage—to the man who is considered the "Father of Australian Viticulture." Two of his published works are "A Treatise on the Culture of the Vine," written in 1825, and "A Manual of Plain Directions for Planting and Cultivating Vineyards and for Making Wine in New South Wales," first printed in 1830. Busby's collection of vines numbered 543 when he set out on his voyage and of those 362 survived. They were planted and propagated in the Sydney Botanical Garden.

Winemaking got its start in South Australia, near Adelaide, when German Lutherans fled religious persecution in their homeland and settled in the Adelaide Hills and Barossa Valley from the 1830s into the 1850s. Although as a whole they had not grown grapes in their homeland (an area that is now part of Poland), they found the farmland conducive to vineyards, and a new industry was born. Descendants of many of these settlers are still making wine in the Barossa today, including the Henschke family in Barossa's Eden Valley, founded by Johann Christian Henschke in 1861; Seppeltsfield, founded in 1851; and Jacob's Creek, which began as Johann Gramp's Orlando Wines in 1847, with vineyards planted on the banks of Jacob's Creek. Penfolds' origins date to 1844, and Yalumba, the oldest family-owned winery in Australia, was established in 1849 by Samuel Smith, a British brewer.

A few decades after James Busby introduced vines into New South Wales, there were almost 700 hectares (1,730 acres) of grapevines planted in the Hunter Valley. A combination of economic downturns, law changes, and phylloxera (mainly in Victoria) devastated the industry toward the turn of the twentieth century, though some vines in both Victoria and New South Wales' Hunter Valley survived. (Importantly, phylloxera has never made it into South Australia, the reason why many of Australia's—and the world's—oldest vines still grow there.)

After phylloxera, it took many years for the Australian wine industry to regain its footing. Two world wars bracketed the Great Depression, and for many decades almost all the wine made within the country was sweet, fortified wine for domestic consumption. Production of dry Australian table wine began to (slowly) take flight again in Australia in the 1920s, but it wasn't until the 1970s that Australia reentered the global wine market in force. Despite economic setbacks in the 1980s and at the end of the first decade of the twenty-first century, Australian wine has increased exponentially in both quality and quantity and is now a major player in the world wine market.

Today, grapes are cultivated and wine is made in 60 wine regions across six Australian states. From west to east they are Western Australia, South Australia, Victoria, Tasmania, New South Wales, and Queensland. In addition to regions you probably know, such as Barossa Valley, McLaren Vale, and the Hunter and Yarra Valleys, are dozens more, plus multiple subregions, adding up to well over one hundred Geographic Indications—all of which may be listed on a wine bottle. Some have been producing for 150 years; others are new kids on the block. But one thing is for sure: if you are

on the lookout for an exquisite, high-caliber wine, regardless of variety or price, you don't have to look any further than the Australia aisle at your local wine shop.

Australia is home to a staggering number of wineries—2,477 at last count, which produced 1.5 billion (!) liters of wine in 2010. Vineyards are planted on 156,632 hectares, or 387,046 acres. That's 605 square miles, or about the size of the entire metropolitan area of Bangkok, Thailand. (And if that doesn't seem that large, bear in mind that more than 9 million people live in Bangkok.) Official data is kept on more than 40 grape varieties, from Shiraz—whose 43,676 hectares (107,926 acres) amount to 28 percent of all the vineyards in Australia—to Touriga Nacional, whose 55 hectares (136 acres) contribute a miniscule amount of wine to the annual total, but whose presence in vineyards is both a reminder of the old "Port-style" wine that was produced here for more than a hundred years and a nod to the new generation of winemakers and viticulturists who place site selection and varietal compatibility at the forefront of their plans to carry the industry through the new century.

Of the 1.5 billion liters of wine produced in Australia from the 2010 vintage, 781 million liters, or a little more than half, was shipped overseas. The top five international markets are the United Kingdom (272 million liters),

United States of America (207 million liters), Canada (56 million liters), People's Republic of China (55 million liters), and New Zealand (28 million liters). Australia's 156,632 hectares (387,046 acres) place the nation in twelfth place for total vineyard acreage the world over, yet they are in sixth place for total wine production and are in second place in the Southern Hemisphere, behind Argentina. Annual per capita wine consumption is 23 liters per person, placing Australia at eleventh place in the world for total consumed alcohol per person.

As already mentioned, Shiraz is the number one grape grown in Australia. Next in line is Chardonnay, which grows on 28,037 hectares (69,281 acres), followed by Cabernet Sauvignon on 26,400 hectares (65,236 acres), Merlot (10,073 hectares; 24,891 acres), and Sauvignon Blanc (7,114 hectares; 17,579 acres). If Australia has a signature white grape, it is Sémillon, whose 6,305 hectares (15,580 acres), or 4 percent of total vineyards, seem small in comparison to its outsized reputation among lovers of fine Australian wine.

On the label of a wine from Australia, varietal claims are optional, meaning the producer is not required to list the variety. However, if a single variety is stated, 85 percent of the wine in that bottle must be of that variety. For example, some producers add a small amount, usually less than 5 percent, of uncredited Viognier to Shiraz, in order to add softer, more floral notes to the aroma and taste. Multiple varieties may be stated, but they must be listed in descending order; if a wine is 70 percent Merlot and 30 percent Cabernet Sauvignon, the label must read "Merlot-Cabernet Sauvignon."

A Geographical Indication (GI) is the official description of an Australian wine zone. The GI system was established in 1993 so that Australia could be in compliance with European Union laws regarding wine imported into the EU. When a Geographical Indication is stated, 85 percent of the wine must come from the stated area. GIs may refer to zones, or a large area of land without any specific attributes, a region, or a subregion. Both regions and subregions must be single tracts of land, made up of at least five independently owned wine grape vineyards, each at least five hectares, producing five hundred metric tons of wine grapes within a year. Both the region and subregion must be entered in the Register of Protected names. Up to three GIs are permitted on a bottle, for example, a zone or state, a region, and a subregion.

The vintage listed on a wine bottle is a statement of the harvest year. At least 85 percent of the wine must come from that harvest year, meaning a wine labeled 2011 must have at least 85 percent wine from grapes harvested in 2011, but the addition of up to 15 percent wine from another year, such as 2010 or 2012, is allowable. Brand names may not be misleading as to the origin, age, or identity of the wine. Australian wine law does not specifically regulate the labeling or production of organic wine; there are several private certifying bodies that substantiate the use of the term "Organic."

The vast size of Australia and the disparity between its wine regions cannot be overstated. By car, the distance from Perth, in Western Australia, to Brisbane, in Queensland, is 4,384 kilometers, or 2,724 miles. Just taking the three closest and most populated (in a vineyard sense) states—South Australia, Victoria, and New South Wales—into consideration still leaves a vast swath of land to contemplate. The distance by road between Adelaide and Sydney is 1,427 kilometers, or 887 miles, and takes in 54 wine regions including the five top wine-producing (in volume terms) zones: Big Rivers, Lower Murray, North West Victoria, Limestone Coast, and Fleurieu. This same drive takes in a wide range of different climates, altitudes, soils, and suitabilities.

In our travels, we are continually asked by Aussie winemakers what they can do to get the word out to consumers about the quality of Australian wine, and our response is always the same: "Don't!" To talk about Australian wine as if it is just one thing is the equivalent of talking about wine from the United States as if it is one category, without taking into account the regional differences in *terroir*, climate, varieties, and winemaking styles. When you walk into your local shop and have a hankering for a bottle from Down Under, be aware that a lot of gems are hiding under that big white sign that says "Australia." Be on the lookout for Riesling from Tasmania or Clare Valley, Sémillon from the Hunter Valley, Shiraz from the Barossa, or Margaret River Chardonnay. The beauty of wine from the New World is that there are fewer rules and regulations. Within reason—and limitations provided by Mother Nature—winemakers are striving to put the best quality product into bottles for your enjoyment and pleasure. Today, over 70 percent of all the wine produced in Australia, including many premium labels, is bottled under screwcap. There is a pioneering spirit and a willingness to try new ideas in Australia; if winemakers aren't afraid to experiment a little, shouldn't you be willing to give something new a try?

MAJOR GRAPE VARIETIES

BARBERA

With its strong fruit flavors of cherry, black raspberry, and blueberry, often with notes of spice and vanilla picked up in the barrel, this Italian variety usually grown in Tuscany and Piedmont has adapted well in Australia. It was originally brought over in the 1960s with cuttings from University of California, Davis, and now is found in bottlings from a range of regions including Mudgee, King Valley, Beechworth, Hunter Valley, Canberra District, and McLaren Vale. Although at this time, it is grown in very small amounts, covering only 120 hectares (297 acres) as of 2010, Australian Barbera is a wine to keep your eye on.

CABERNET FRANC

On its own, Cabernet Franc tastes of cherries and strawberries with strong notes of paprika and black pepper. It can also include flavors of cigar box and violets. In Australia, it is mostly mixed in small amounts with Cabernet Sauvignon and Merlot in Bordeaux-style blends. Because it is mainly used as a blending grape, plantings of Cabernet Franc in Australia are not high. Its 608 hectares (1,502 acres) are about 0.4 percent of the nation's grapevines.

CABERNET SAUVIGNON

Offspring of Cabernet Franc and Sauvignon Blanc, Cabernet Sauvignon is one of the most widely planted grapes in the world. It is generally noted for its tastes of black cherry, cassis, plum, violet, and pencil lead; vanilla and butterscotch flavors are imparted during barrel aging. Depending on the region, Australian Cabernet Sauvignon can also bear notes of mint and eucalyptus, or green pepper and jalapeño, or even chocolate. Some of the best Cabernets come out of Margaret River, Coonawarra, Yarra Valley, McLaren Vale, Barossa Valley, and Mudgee. It is also frequently blended with Shiraz, Merlot, and Cabernet Franc, with each grape adding its own special character to the mix. Cabernet Sauvignon is the second most abundant red grape in Australia, behind Shiraz, and the third most popular in total, right below Chardonnay. It covers 26,400 hectares (65,236 acres), or about 17 percent of total planted area.

CHARDONNAY

One of the most abundant varieties in both Australia and the world, Chardonnay was brought to Australia by James Busby with his 1832 cutting collection, but it took about 140 years for this green-skinned varietal to make a major impact here. Australian Chardonnay runs the gamut of styles, from lean and mineral-driven to oak-aged and buttery. Classic Chardonnay will exhibit flavors of green apple, melon, peach, and citrus fruit, though it can also taste of buttered toast, vanilla, or soft spice. Chardonnay from inland areas such as Murray Darling, Riverina, and Riverland tends to have warmer-weather tropical "sunshine in a bottle" flavors, while lime and lemon will dominate cool-climate examples from Adelaide Hills, Mornington Peninsula, and Tasmania. Turn to Coonawarra, Margaret River, Yarra Valley, Geelong, Tumbarumba, and Hunter Valley for sophisticated, barrel-aged Chardonnay. In Australia, this versatile grape is often blended with Chenin Blanc and Colombard—though almost never at the premium end of the market. The second most populous varietal in the nation, Chardonnay accounts for 18 percent of all the wine grapes grown in Australia. It is cultivated on 28,037 hectares (69,281 acres).

CHENIN BLANC

This native of France's Loire Valley has a long history in Australia, possibly dating back to James Busby's assemblage of vines imported here in 1832; the earliest documented vineyards were planted in the early 1860s. Most styles feature notes of apple, melon, and honeysuckle, and its high acidity nicely balances out any residual sugars in off-dry or sweet versions. It is a favorite of winemakers in Western Australia, especially Peel and Swan Valley. In 2010 Chenin Blanc vines were less than 1 percent of Australian vineyard land, taking root on 549 hectares (1,357 acres).

COLOMBARD

Cultivated in France for Cognac and Armagnac, Colombard is often grown in Australia to add acidity and fragrance to affordable Chardonnay blends. In a single varietal version—usually from Adelaide Plains or Murray Darling—expect flavors of apricot, peach, and lemon zest with floral touches. This white grape makes up 1.5 percent of Australian cultivation; it is planted on 2,278 hectares (5,629 acres).

DURIF

Called Petite Syrah in California, Durif has been a mainstay of the Port-style wines of Rutherglen for almost a hundred years, where it is now also used to make deeply colored, powerful dry wines tasting of plum and blueberry with hints of spice and mint. Due to its high level of tannins, this varietal is noted for its long aging potential. Durif is planted on 442 hectares (1,092 acres); the majority of that in Rutherglen. One of its parents is Syrah, and the word *petite* in its American moniker is French for "small," referring to the size of the grapes on the vine.

GEWÜRZTRAMINER

An immigrant from the cold-weather Alpine regions of Italy, Germany, and France, this aromatic white wine is vinified from grapes that are pink to red on the vine. Its flavors of lychee and rose petal, and its lush mouthfeel, make Gewürztraminer the ideal choice with the spicy and slightly sweet pan-Asian cuisine of Australia. It thrives in cooler climates, which bring out the best of Gewürztraminer's floral notes and luscious acidity. Sometimes called by the out-of-date name Traminer Musqué, it is grown in small amounts in the Adelaide Hills, Clare Valley, Eden Valley, Hunter Valley, Tasmania, Alpine Valleys, and Yarra Valley. Its 884 hectares (2,184 acres) make up 0.6 percent of Australia's vineyards.

GRENACHE

One of the most extensively planted red grapes in the world, Grenache was used to make fortified Port-style wine in Australia for many years. A late-ripening grape, it does best in hot, dry climates in order to concentrate its sugars to the fullest. Its flavor profile combines cherry, blackberry, and cassis with spice, tobacco, and earth; it can also have a candied-fruit character about it. In Australia it is often used in GSM blends along with its Rhône Valley cohorts Syrah and Mourvèdre. Grenache was among the Busby vine collection, but the cuttings that proved more important were those ferried in by Dr. Christopher Rawson Penfold in 1844, the year he founded his eponymous winery. Bush vines up to 150 years in age still grow and produce in South Australia. The finest examples are produced from the Barossa Valley, Clare Valley, and McLaren Vale. Cultivated on 1,795 hectares (4,436 acres), 1.2 percent of all the vines in Australia bear Grenache.

MARSANNE

Beloved by wine geeks the world over, Marsanne is a white Rhône varietal that seems to have hit its stride in the vineyards of Australia. It was first cultivated about 150 years ago in Victoria, and what may be the oldest Marsanne vines in the world have flourished here since 1927. Its essences of peach, honeysuckle, and a touch of baking spice are joined in the mouth by a burst of fresh acidity. It is most often found in blends, although excellent Marsanne comes out of Goulburn (grown on 80-year-old vines) and the Yarra Valley in Victoria. It is grown on 244 hectares (603 acres).

MERLOT

Down Under, Merlot's soft tannins and fresh flavors of cherry, blueberry, and mint are often found blended with Cabernet Sauvignon; the addition of the blue-black grape softens Cabernet's strong tannins and adds brightness in the glass. Cabernet Sauvignon-Merlot blends often emanate from warm, inland areas such as Riverland, Riverina, and Murray Darling; however, like the Barossa Valley and McLaren Vale, these regions are starting to bottle it straight up as well. A more earthy style is also being bottled in Margaret River and the Yarra Valley, where the cool climate contributes to a stronger tannic structure and herbal characteristics. Top-quality examples of varietal Merlot are still a rarity, but on the rise. Covering 10,073 hectares (24,891 acres), about 6.5 percent of all the grapes grown in Australia are Merlot.

MOURVÈDRE

An essential component in popular GSM, or Grenache-Syrah-Mourvèdre Rhône-style blends, for most of its Australian history Mourvèdre was used in sweet fortified wines. Mourvèdre's berry-rich flavor backed by elements of spice and licorice has recently been discovered for enjoyment on its own, especially when vinified from old bush vines. New South Wales and South Australia boast the highest concentration of plantings; some of the choicest representations are from the Barossa Valley. You will almost always see it listed on a label under the name Mourvèdre, although it is also known here by one of its Spanish aliases, *Mataro*. It's grown on 729 hectares (1,801 acres) in Australia, accounting for almost 0.5 percent of grape plantings. The world's oldest Mourvèdre vines grow in the Barossa Valley (planted in 1853).

MUSCAT

Many different species of Muscat are grown in Australia, including Muscat of Alexandria, Muscat Rouge à Petit Grains, and Muscat Blanc à Petit Grains, or Brown Muscat. Although for winemaking purposes Muscat is a white grape, berries of this varietal can be pink or reddish brown on the vine. Rutherglen in northeast Victoria is world-renowned for its delicious sweet wines made from Brown Muscat, with rich flavors of apricot, honey, and lemon zest. Muscat was among the first varieties to be planted in Australia, and its fame here stretches back to the late nineteenth century. It is made into both off-dry and sweet wine. Combining the three most common species of Muscat, it is grown on 3,113 hectares (7,692 acres), or 2 percent of Australian vine land.

PINOT GRIS/ PINOT GRIGIO

Doing double duty, this white variety goes by its Alsatian name and by its Italian moniker, depending on style and winemaker preference. Pinot Gris has been cultivated in Australia since 1832, but it is only in the past 10 to 15 years that it has begun to become a star in its own right. This aromatic white—whose color on the vine runs from bluish gray to light brownish pink, hence the *gris* ("gray" in French) in the name—exhibits flavors of pear, lemon, and apple with light floral notes and crisp minerality. It is made in both an unoaked, easy-quaffing style (Pinot Grigio) and a riper, fuller, spicier version (Pinot Gris). Neither is meant for aging. Cool coastal regions such as Tasmania and Mornington Peninsula are best bets for fine Pinot Gris. Its 3,518 hectares (8,693 acres) account for over 2 percent of all the vineyards in Australia.

PINOT NOIR

Taking its name from its pinecone-like clusters and its color—*noir* is French for "black"—Pinot Noir is known as the famed red grape of Burgundy, yet it has made its home all around the world. Its best successes are achieved in cool climates, and the finest bottlings are being produced in Adelaide Hills, Geelong, Great Southern, Mornington Peninsula, Gippsland, Macedon Ranges, Yarra Valley, and Tasmania.

You can anticipate tasting blackberry, cherry, chocolate, coffee, light spice, and orange zest. Although the berries are very dark on the vine, the resultant wine is usually more of cherry to medium garnet in color. Age does wonderful things to Pinot Noir in a couple of ways; more mature vines yield wines with increased depth and complexity, and aging in the barrel and bottle add notes of vanilla and Mediterranean herbs. Pinot Noir makes up a little more than 3 percent of the cultivated vineyard area in the country, with 5,061 hectares (12,506 acres).

RIESLING

Formerly the most broadly planted white variety in Australia, until bested by Chardonnay in the 1990s, Riesling is made in both dry and sweet styles. Its globe-shaped yellow-green berries, sometimes partially tinted purple, flourish in cool climates. It is found in South Australia's Eden Valley, Barossa Valley, and Clare Valley, Western Australia's Great Southern and Frankland River regions, Victoria's King Valley, Great Western, Strathbogie Ranges regions, and Tasmania. Combining strong flavors of pure fruit with high acidity, Australian Riesling tends to have an unctuous mouth feel, with tastes of lime, lemon, and peach supported by floral and spice notes. Bottlings from the Clare and Eden Valleys are noted for their sharp citrus flavors and clean acidity, while

Tasmanian Riesling tends to develop more perfumed characteristics. Riesling also finds its way into some excellent "stickies," or sweet dessert wines, with flavors of peach, honey, and orange blossom. Riesling plantings on 4,184 hectares (10,339 acres) are a little less than 3 percent of Australia's vineyard holdings.

SANGIOVESE

The famous grape of Italy gets its name from the Latin *sanguis Jovis*, or "blood of Jove." Young versions carry flavors of black plum, strawberry, tart cherry, and orange peel, and careful aging can bring on secondary characteristics of earth, tar, and truffles. Cultivation in Australia began in the 1960s, and Sangiovese now makes its home in the King Valley, McLaren Vale, the Adelaide Hills, Canberra, and Mudgee. It is sometimes fashioned into refreshing rosé. With 612 hectares (1,512 acres) planted, Sangiovese makes up 0.4 percent of Australia's grape cultivation.

SAUVIGNON BLANC

This French variety has found a new home across the Southern Hemisphere and is now one of the most popular grapes in Australia, both in the vineyard and the glass. Differing styles emerge from different regions; generally, flavors of tropical fruit and citrus will be joined by green pepper, asparagus, and fresh-cut herbs on the nose and in the mouth. Sauvignon Blanc is grown in almost every region of the country, but has a particular affinity for the soils and climate of the Yarra Valley, Adelaide Hills, Margaret River, Orange, and Tasmania. In Margaret River, it is often blended with Sémillon, creating wines with structure and elegance. *Sauvignon Blanc* is French for "savage white," which was originally a reference to its proliferation throughout France, but which can also be applied to the more herbal styles. Sauvignon Blanc makes up 4.5 percent, or 7,114 hectares (17,579 acres), of Australian grapevines.

SÉMILLON

Sémillon is almost as popular in Australia as it is in its home country, France. Known for its flavors of lemon and pear in dry styles, moving to peach, honey, and vanilla in botrytized sweet wines, Sémillon is planted across the whole of Australia, where it arrived almost two hundred years ago. In the Hunter Valley, it was known for many years as "Hunter River Riesling." Sémillon from this region is known for its ability to mature in the bottle into a wine with complex notes of honey and roasted nuts. Younger versions from the Hunter are crisp and lean, with flavors of citrus and Granny Smith apple. Barossa Valley Sémillon showcases flavors of peach and mango, and Margaret

River's seems to combine the best of both of these styles. Riverina is becoming known for its sweet Sémillon with layers of flavor. Sémillon vines cover 6,305 hectares (15,580 acres) in Australia, or 4 percent of all vineyards.

SHIRAZ

Called "Syrah" almost everywhere else in the world, this is a grape that no visitor to Australia can miss. Whether bottled on its own or in a Rhône-style GSM blend with Grenache and Mourvèdre, Shiraz is far and away Australia's most popular variety. Australian Shiraz is often a full-on powerhouse, from the first scent of blackberry, blueberry, violet, spice, and black pepper, to tastes of black cherry, cassis, jalapeño, chocolate, and espresso, to its long, chewy finish. Aged Shiraz tends to take on flavors of earth, tobacco, and truffle as well; this is a wine that begs to share the table with grilled red meat. The most widely planted grape in the country, Shiraz from the Barossa Valley, Eden Valley, Heathcote, Beechworth, Canberra, Great Western, McLaren Vale, Margaret River, and the Hunter Valley earn high points with critics and consumers alike. Winemakers sometimes add small amounts of Viognier to Shiraz to add more floral notes to the nose and palate. Cuttings of Shiraz, or more technically, Syrah, were among James Busby's 1832 selection. If you come across a bottle labeled Syrah, expect a more elegant, French-style wine. A whopping 28 percent—or 43,676 hectares (107,926 acres)—of Australian vineyards are home to Shiraz!

TEMPRANILLO

A long way from Ribera del Duero and Rioja in northern Spain, Tempranillo is now being cultivated in a few pockets of Australian vineyard land. With strong tannins, wild berry, and spice notes as its calling card, Tempranillo is now grown in many regions including McLaren Vale, Alpine Valleys, Canberra, Margaret River, and the Barossa Valley. The 618 hectares (1,527 acres) planted with Tempranillo in Australia make up only 0.4 percent of total vines in the country—though even this figure is a sharp increase on where Tempranillo was in Australia 10 or even 5 years ago.

VERDELHO

A white grape widely grown in Portugal, Verdelho is made into sweet, fortified wines on the island of Madeira and into a crisp white elsewhere in the country. It was first brought to Australia to be used in fortified wines mimicking Madeira's, but it has since achieved acclaim for dry versions with crisp flavors of citrus and jasmine coming out of the Hunter Valley and Western Australia's Swan Valley. Verdelho vines grow on 1,593 hectares (3,936 acres), or slightly more than 1 percent of the nation's vineyards.

VIOGNIER

An aromatic white known for its floral aroma and flavor balanced with clean acidity, this immigrant from France is making its mark in Canberra, McLaren Vale, Mornington Peninsula, and Eden Valley. Planted on 1,451 hectares (3,585 acres), Viognier makes up a little less than 1 percent of Australia's grapevines.

ZINFANDEL

With the success of Australian Shiraz, it's no wonder Australian viticulturists are planting vineyards with Zinfandel, another variety known to produce fruit-forward, sometimes high-alcohol, wines. Zinfandel carries powerful flavors of raspberry, blackberry, licorice, and black pepper; cooler climate versions tend to be more restrained, with hints of bell pepper as well. Although early editions of Australian Zinfandel had a brash "fruit bomb" quality about them, a newer style with lower alcohol and more elegant, herbal characteristics is emerging. Seek out bottles from Margaret River, Adelaide Hills, and Hilltops. Plantings remain tiny, with 155 hectares (383 acres) of Zinfandel in 2010.

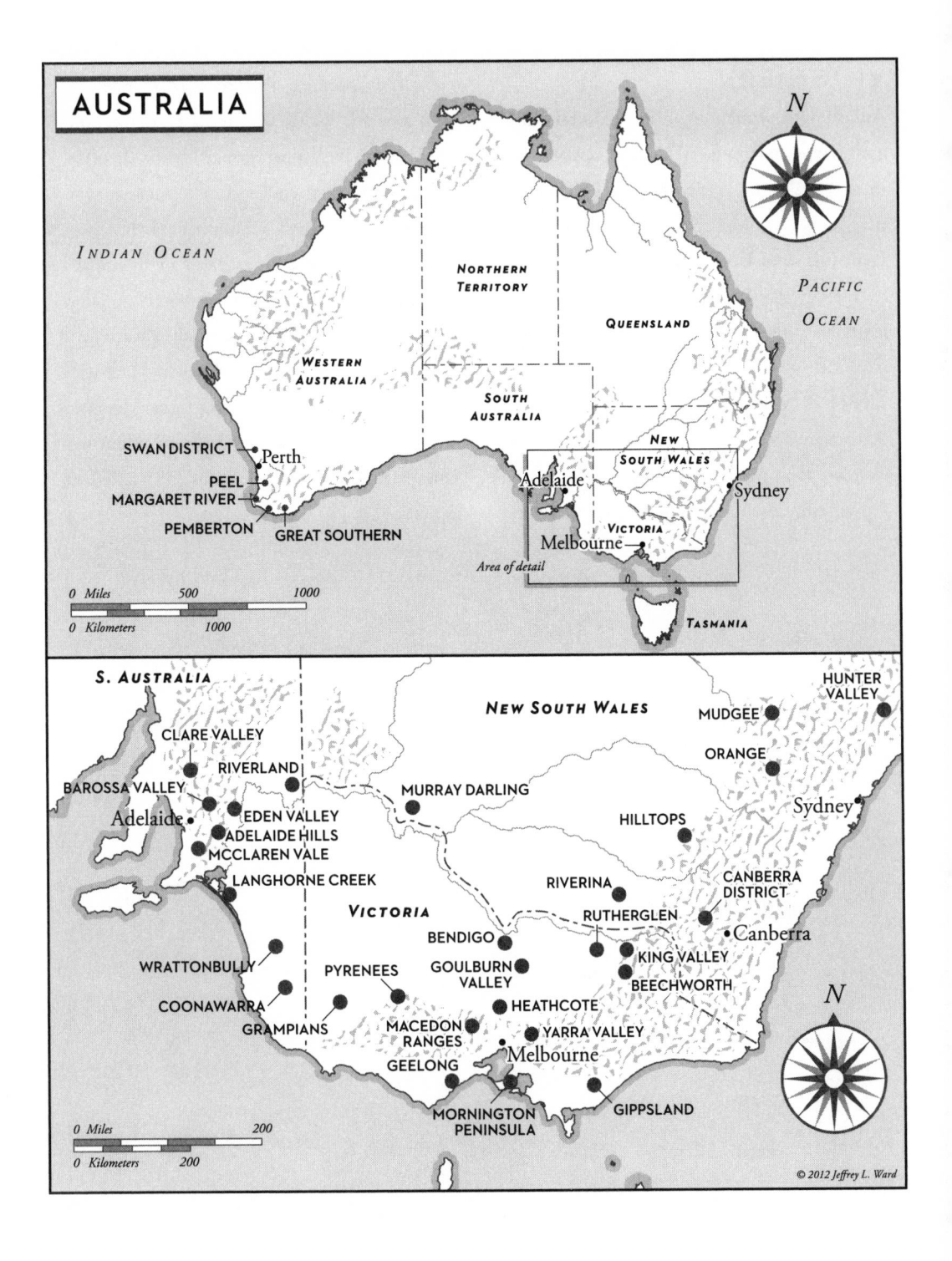

AUSTRALIA

INDIAN OCEAN

PACIFIC OCEAN

NORTHERN TERRITORY

QUEENSLAND

WESTERN AUSTRALIA

SOUTH AUSTRALIA

NEW SOUTH WALES

SWAN DISTRICT • Perth
PEEL
MARGARET RIVER
PEMBERTON
GREAT SOUTHERN

Adelaide

VICTORIA

Melbourne

• Sydney

Area of detail

0 Miles 500 1000
0 Kilometers 1000

TASMANIA

N

S. AUSTRALIA

NEW SOUTH WALES

HUNTER VALLEY

MUDGEE

ORANGE

CLARE VALLEY
RIVERLAND

BAROSSA VALLEY
Adelaide •
EDEN VALLEY
ADELAIDE HILLS
MCCLAREN VALE
LANGHORNE CREEK

MURRAY DARLING

HILLTOPS

Sydney

VICTORIA

RIVERINA

CANBERRA DISTRICT

RUTHERGLEN

• Canberra

WRATTONBULLY

PYRENEES

BENDIGO

GOULBURN VALLEY

KING VALLEY

BEECHWORTH

COONAWARRA

GRAMPIANS

MACEDON RANGES

HEATHCOTE

YARRA VALLEY

GEELONG

Melbourne

MORNINGTON PENINSULA

GIPPSLAND

N

0 Miles 200
0 Kilometers 200

© 2012 Jeffrey L. Ward

96

WINE REGIONS

WESTERN AUSTRALIA

The largest state in Australia, Western Australia spans the western third of the country. Its winemaking regions are almost all clustered in the southwest, coastal area of the state, although some are closer to the state capital, Perth. Between 20 and 30 percent of Australia's premium bottled wine is produced in Western Australia, though the state only grows about 7 percent of Australia's wine grapes. Western Australia regions include Swan District, Perth Hills, Peel, Geographe, Margaret River, Blackwood Valley, Pemberton, Manjimup, and Great Southern. Although wine has been made along this coast for many years, it was Dr. John Gladstone's report, "The Climate and Soils of Southern Western Australia in Relation to Vine Growing," published in 1967, that first highlighted the area in general, and especially Margaret River, as a place to make wine. Since then, the rush has been on, and vineyard totals have risen on an annual basis from the Swan Valley near Perth to Albany in the South and Geraldton in the North. Total planted hectares in Western Australia amount to 11,822 hectares (29,213 acres), almost evenly divided

between red grapes, on 5,791 hectares (14,310 acres) and white, which cover 6,031 hectares (14,903 acres). Western Australia is known for Cabernet Sauvignon, Cabernet-based blends, Chardonnay, and Sauvignon Blanc–Sémillon blends.

GREAT SOUTHERN

This large region—which runs 150 kilometers (93 miles) north to south and 100 kilometers (62 miles) east to west—is dominated in the interior by stands of soaring eucalyptus trees and on the coast by towering cliffs, wide beaches, and the roaring surf of the Southern Ocean. It is divided into five subregions: Albany, Denmark, Frankland River, Mount Barker, and Porongurup. The two most important are Frankland River and Mount Barker. There are more than forty wineries in the region, with a focus on Cabernet Sauvignon, Pinot Noir, Riesling, Sauvignon Blanc, and Shiraz. Both gravelly sandy loam and granitic sandy loam soils are found throughout the region. Rainfall is generally low, varying from 287 millimeters, or 11 inches, in Mount Barker to 354 millimeters, or 14 inches, in Denmark, usually falling throughout the spring and summer growing season. Albany's altitude is 75 meters, or 246 feet, above sea level; Denmark's is 50 to 150 meters, or 164 to 492 feet; Frankland River's altitude ranges from 200 to 300 meters, or 656 to 984 feet; Mount Barker's vineyards are at levels between 180 and 250 meters, or 590 to 820 feet; and Porongurup's are at the highest average altitude, running from 250 to 300 meters, or 820 to 984 feet. In 2010, Great Southern's vineyards totaled 2,861 hectares, or 7,070 acres.

ALKOOMI

1141 Wingebellup Road, Frankland River,
+61 8 9855 2229,
www.alkoomi.com.au

Judy and Merv Lange planted their first vines in Frankland River in 1971. Today, their daughter, Sandy, and her husband, Ron Hallet, are at the helm of this family-owned winery. Named for the Aboriginal word meaning "a place we choose," Alkoomi grows 12 varieties of grapes on its 102 hectares (252 acres) of vineyards. Alkoomi Chardonnay 2009 is straw colored, with notes of yellow peach and citrus blossom in the bouquet. In the mouth it is creamy with bold citrus flavors. The finish is fresh and luxurious. Alkoomi Cabernet Sauvignon 2007 is dark red with a violet rim. It has aromas of cassis, black cherry, and

a touch of vanilla. On the palate flavors of dark plum and cassis are pronounced before a balanced tannic finish.

FERNGROVE

276 Ferngrove Road, Frankland River,
+61 8 9855 2378,
www.ferngrove.com.au

Founded in 1998 by Murray Burton, Ferngrove regularly receives high scores, accolades, awards, and trophies. In 2006 alone, it was the proud recipient of six trophies and 74 medals. Its wines are available in North America, the United Kingdom, Europe, and Asia. Visitors to Ferngrove can rent fully equipped chalets with views over the vines. Ferngrove Sauvignon Blanc 2008 is straw colored with greenish tints. It has aromas of tropical fruits and lemon zest on the bouquet and flavors of guava and grapefruit in the mid palate. It finishes clean with balanced acidity. Ferngrove Merlot 2008 is ruby garnet colored, with aromas of blackberries, cassis, and purple flowers. In the mouth the fruit flavors are concentrated before a smooth tannic finish.

FOREST HILL

Corner of South Coast Highway
and Myers Road, Denmark,
+61 8 9848 0003,
www.foresthillwines.com.au

Established in 1965 by Betty and Tony Pearce, Forest Hill is Western Australia's oldest cool-climate vineyard. Tim Lyons and his family acquired Forest Hill, and today the property has 80 hectares (198 acres) of planted vines. The vineyard is managed by Lee Haselgrove, and the chief winemaker is Bordeaux-born Clemence Haselgrove. Forest Hill Block 5 Cabernet Sauvignon is dark garnet with a purple rim. On the nose aromas of black plums, red raspberries, and licorice are pronounced. There is also a secondary note of cigar box and mushroom. In the mouth the berry flavors come through, with a touch of powdered cocoa on the finish. Forest Hill Block 1 Riesling is bright yellow, with aromas of citrus peel, orange blossoms, and wet river stones. It is bright and expressive in the mouth with a clean finish.

FRANKLAND ESTATE

Frankland Road, Frankland,
+61 8 9855 1544,
www.franklandestate.com.au

Barrie Smith and Judi Cullam are sheep farmers/wool producers turned winery owners. They were bitten by the wine bug after touring France in 1985 and working two harvests at Château Sénéjac in Bordeaux. Today, their son Hunter and daughter Elizabeth are involved in the family business. If you visit the estate, you'll be greeted by Queen Gladys—a Guinea fowl—and her flock, who eat bugs and pests that otherwise might damage the vines. In 2010, the family was proud to have their Isolation Ridge Vineyard designated as Australian Certified Organic. Frankland Estate Isolation Ridge Riesling 2010 is straw colored with green tints. The bouquet reveals lime rind, white flowers, and wet river rock. It is light and fruity on the mid palate with a crisp mineral-driven finish. Frankland Estate Isolation Ridge Shiraz

2008 is dark red with a purple rim. Aromas of black plum, black raspberry, and a touch of finely ground black pepper give way to elegant fruit flavors on the palate with a tight-grained tannic finish.

Shiraz 2008 is deep inky purple, with a nose of stewed plums, black pepper, and truffle. In the mouth a strong tannic structure supports black fruit flavors as they play against Chinese spice and freshly ground pepper.

LARRY CHERUBINO WINES

30 Salisbury Street, Subiaco,
+61 8 9382 2379,
www.larrycherubino.com.au

In the past, Larry Cherubino received accolades and awards for the wines he made at Hardys Tintara, Houghton, and New Zealand's Craggy Range. In 2005, he and partner Edwina set up Larry Cherubino wines, producing three labels: the entry-level Ad Hoc, mid-range The Yard (focusing on vineyard expression), and the upper-tier Cherubino. Since striking out on his own, the praise continues to flow from the international and Australian wine press. Sourcing from family-owned vineyards throughout Western Australia, Cherubino considers himself a "hands-off" winemaker, allowing the fruit in his Riesling, Cabernet Sauvignon, Shiraz, Sauvignon Blanc, Sémillon, and Chardonnay to speak for itself. The Yard Channybearup Vineyard Chardonnay 2010 is crisp, clean, and lean, with flavors of pink grapefruit, key lime, and river rocks. Cherubino Frankland River

PLANTAGENET

Lot 45 Albany Highway, Mount Barker,
+61 8 9851 3111,
www.plantagenetwines.com

In 1968, Englishman Tony Smith—a descendant of the Plantagenets—purchased a farm in Western Australia's Plantagenet Shire and planted his first Shiraz, Cabernet Sauvignon, and Riesling vines. Plantagenet's first vintage was 1974; the Mount Barker winery was built in 1975. Since that time, additional vineyards have been purchased. The original 8.6 hectares (21 acres) has grown to 126 (311 acres) and the three primary varieties have been joined by Chardonnay, Pinot Noir,

Sangiovese, Cabernet Franc, Merlot, Viognier, and Sémillon. Winemakers John Durham and Andries Mostert produce wine in four ranges: the value-driven Hazard Hill; core Omrah Brand, which begin in the late 1980s with a hallmark unwooded Chardonnay; the high-end Plantagenet label, which focuses on premium fruit; and limited release Museum Wines. The company was purchased in 2000 by Lionel Samson and Son, with Tony Smith staying on as chairman and brand ambassador. Plantagenet Riesling 2009 shows purity of fruit on the nose and in the mouth. Aromas and flavors of lemon and lime are joined by white floral notes and a touch of spice; clean minerality lingers on the finish. Plantagenet Cabernet Sauvignon 2008 is bright red violet in the glass, where it gives off fragrances of cassis, spice, and truffle. On the palate intense cassis is supported by anise, black olive, and cooling spices, leading to a rewarding finish.

MARGARET RIVER

Although European settlement started here in the 1830s, it took until the late 1960s into the early 1970s for this area with a reputation for forestry, dairy farming, and the back-to-the-land movement to become known as prime wine country. Margaret River is now a popular destination for casual wine tourists and wine geeks alike—not to mention surfers. A three-hour drive south of Perth, bounded to the west by the Indian Ocean and to the east by the undulating hills of the Leeuwin-Naturaliste, this 90-kilometer–long (56-mile-long) region is known for its abundant natural beauty.

Originally noted for intense Cabernet Sauvignon and Chardonnay, Margaret River has since expanded its repertoire to include Sémillon-Sauvignon Blanc blends and Shiraz. Located in the extreme southwest of the country, it is home to almost 160 wineries. Surrounded by ocean on three sides, Margaret River enjoys a maritime climate; cooling sea breezes provide grapes with badly needed moisture and relief from the heat of long, sunny days. In the spring and summer seasons, total rainfall is 200 millimeters, or 8 inches. Altitudes are fairly constant, at about 40 meters (131 feet) above sea level, although rolling valleys and a network of small creeks provide an abundance of microclimates. A bountiful supply of native flowers, shrubs, and trees provide a moderating buffer from strong ocean winds. Soils are gravelly sandy loam overlaying a substratum of granite. Margaret River was home to 5,189 hectares (12,822 acres), of vineyards in 2010. Although there are no officially designated subregions, wineries often refer to six unofficial subregions, which do show differences in climate and soil. They are Carbunup, Karridale, Treeton, Wallcliffe, Wilyabrup, and Yallingup.

CAPE MENTELLE

331 Wallcliffe Road, Margaret River,
+61 8 9757 0812,
www.capementelle.com.au

Cape Mentelle is one of the first wineries in Margaret River and perhaps *the* one that put the region on the map after its flagship Cabernet Sauvignon won the Jimmy Watson Trophy (an Australian prestigious red wine award) back-to-back in 1983 and 1984. Cape Mentelle now has 200 hectares (494 acres) of vineyards under the management of viticulturist Ashley Wood. Winemaker Robert Mann works with estate-grown fruit to produce varietal Cabernet Sauvignon, Shiraz, Zinfandel, and Chardonnay, as well as Bordeaux-style red and white blends. Cape Mentelle Chardonnay 2009 expresses scents of citrus, honeysuckle, and baking bread. On the tongue, pink grapefruit and lemon zest meld

with notes of marzipan. Cape Mentelle Shiraz 2009 is deep red in color, with a bouquet of blueberries, black cherry, and spiced chocolate truffles. Flavors of blackberry, black currants, fennel, and fresh ground pepper wrap themselves around a strong tannic backbone.

CULLEN

Caves Road, Cowaramup,
+61 8 9755 5277,
www.cullenwines.com.au

Shortly after Margaret River was announced as a suitable climate for viticulture, Diana and Kevin Cullen planted a test plot on their sheep and cattle farm with vines. The results were so positive that they planted an additional 7 hectares (17 acres) with the only vines available at the time, Cabernet Sauvignon and Riesling. This was 1971, and since then their plantings have expanded to include Chardonnay, Sémillon, Sauvignon Blanc, Pinot Noir, Merlot, and Cabernet Franc. Daughter Vanya came aboard as winemaker in 1989, and in 2004 their vineyards were certified biodynamic. Vanya has won winemaker of the year (at the *Australian Gourmet Traveller Wine* magazine awards), and both of her parents have been honored for their service to the industries of winemaking and viticulture. Many of the original vines still produce

CULLEN

MARGARET RIVER

Diana Madeline
2009

PRODUCT OF AUSTRALIA.
750mL

EVANS AND TATE

Corner of Caves and Metricup Roads, Wilyabrup,
+61 8 9755 6244,
www.evansandtate.com.au

low yields of extraordinary quality grapes. Cullen Vineyard Sauvignon Blanc Sémillon 2010, a blend of 66 percent of the former and 34 percent of the latter, has a nose of lemon, lime, papaya, and toasted hazelnut. Lemon, pineapple, and vanilla custard coalesce on the tongue through the zesty finish. Cullen Diana Madeline 2009, the estate's flagship wine, is a blend of 88 percent Cabernet Sauvignon, 6 percent Cabernet Franc, 4 percent Merlot, and 2 percent Malbec. It is deep red violet to the eye. Aromas of black cherry, cassis, and violet candy carry on in the mouth, aided by a gorgeous tannic structure and sustained finish.

Not many tasting rooms have comfy leather sofas, a beckoning fireplace, and stunning views across beautifully planted vineyards. The problem is that once you've tried a few of Evans and Tate's award-winning wines, you may not want to leave—ever. Owned today by the McWilliam's family, John Tate and John Evans acquired the Gnangara estate in 1968 and changed the name to Evans and Tate. One in five wines produced in the Margaret River region is made by Evans and Tate. Evans and Tate Redbrook Margaret River Cabernet Sauvignon 2008 is garnet colored with a violet rim. It has aromas of savory herbs, cassis, and black plums. It is soft and generous in the mouth with a solid tannic spine and a persistent finish. Evans and Tate Gnangara Shiraz 2009 is deep ruby red, with aromas and flavors of dark fruits, black plums, and a touch of mushrooms. The finish is textured and persistent.

HOWARD PARK

Miamup Road, Cowaramup, Margaret River,
+61 8 9756 5200,
www.howardparkwines.com.au

John Wade, one of the pioneering few who went west in 1986, set out to make premium quality Cabernet Sauvignon and Rieslings for the discerning consumer. Today, Howard Park remains a family-owned winery currently run and owned by Amy and Jeff Burch. Its wines have received international acclaim and been highly rated in both domestic and international publications. Howard Park Leston Cabernet Sauvignon 2009 is dark reddish–purple, with aromas of black raspberries, black plums, and cassis. There is a top note of toasted brioche. It is big, fruity, and bold on the mid palate with a balanced tannic finish. Howard Park Riesling 2010 is pale straw with

a greenish hue. Notes of Anjou pear, mandarin orange, and lemon zest tickle your nose and tongue before it delivers a crisp, mineral-driven finish.

LEEUWIN ESTATE

Stevens Road, Margaret River,
+61 8 9759 0000,
www.leeuwinestate.com.au

In 1972, California legend Robert Mondavi chose the site that became home to Denis and Tricia Horgan's Leeuwin Estate. They planted their original vines in 1974 and opened the doors of their winery, which now includes an award-winning restaurant and art gallery, in 1978, with Robert Mondavi staying on as consultant and mentor. They currently produce three ranges of wine, the lauded Art Series, the Prelude Vineyard range, and the Siblings label.

Among the three, there is a dizzying array of varieties and blends. The second generation of Horgans is now working with Denis and Tricia, who were pioneers in winemaking and wine tourism in the region. Charter flights can be arranged from Perth Airport to the estate's private airstrip. Leeuwin Estate Art Series Riesling 2010 is pale straw in color and flecked with green highlights. A nose of lime juice and honeysuckle is a prelude to the ripe citrus fruits, floral, and spice, which are suspended in a richly textured wine with a refreshing bite of acidity. Leeuwin Estate Art Series Cabernet Sauvignon 2006 reveals heady aromas of black cherry and cassis mingling with floral notes, licorice, and cigar box. In the mouth the cherry and cassis are interwoven with chocolate-covered espresso bean, thyme, and fennel. Slightly grippy tannins and animated acidity make for an enthralling finish.

MOSS WOOD

926 Metricup Road, Wilyabrup,
+61 8 9755 6266,
www.mosswood.com.au

Bill and Sandra Pannell, excited by the study citing Margaret River as a prime viticultural area, bought a plot of land and began a Cabernet Sauvignon nursery in 1969. One year later they planted their first two hectares (five acres) of that variety. Their inaugural vintage of Moss Wood Cabernet Sauvignon was 1973. Keith Mugford came aboard as winery manager in 1978, moving up to winemaker within a year. In 1985 he and wife, Clare, bought the vineyards and winery from the founders. Since then their holdings have expanded to six vineyards, including Ribbon Vale, which is the name of one of their labels. Primary varieties grown are Cabernet Sauvignon, Pinot Noir, Chardonnay, Sémillon, and Merlot. Moss Wood Chardonnay 2009 is medium straw in color, with a nose of ripe peach, jasmine, and roasted almonds. Rich mouthfeel lays the groundwork for a palate of peach, lemon curd, and butterscotch—with just the right spray of acidity. Moss Wood Cabernet Sauvignon 2008, deep garnet in the glass, exudes fragrances of cassis, blueberry preserve, bitter chocolate, and Turkish delight. Elegant flavors of blackberry, blueberry, dark chocolate, and toasted vanilla bean are enmeshed in lush tannins—which guide your palate toward a sustained finish.

VASSE FELIX

Corner of Tom Cullity Drive and Caves Road,
Cowaramup,
+61 8 9756 5055,
www.vassefelix.com.au

Said to be the first vineyard and winery in Margaret River, Vasse Felix was founded when Dr. Tom Cullity planted vines in 1967. The current proprietors of this beautiful winery (with an acclaimed restaurant, art gallery, and performance space) are the Holmesà Court family. Winemaking is under the direction of Virginia Willcock. The upper tier wines are bottled under the Heytesbury label, which features special barrel selections in its Chardonnay and Bordeaux blends. At the opposite end is the Classic series, which simply includes a Shiraz/Cabernet Sauvignon blend and a Sémillon/Sauvignon Blanc blend. The Estate Range produces premium bottlings of Cabernet Sauvignon, Merlot, Shiraz, Chardonnay, Sauvignon Blanc, and Sémillon, both in varietal expressions and in blends. From the Estate Range, Vasse Felix Chardonnay 2010 has aromas of lemon and just-baked vanilla cookies. In the mouth it is citrus-forward, with flavors of lemon, lime, and grapefruit. Oak-derived vanilla and spice chime in, and the textured mouthfeel is complemented by a splash of finalizing acidity. Also from the Estate Range, Vasse Felix Cabernet Sauvignon 2008 is blended with 8 percent Malbec. Deep red in the glass, the nose reveals cassis, violet, Mediterranean herbs, and a suggestion of spice. Powerful in the mouth, the palate is awash with raspberry and cassis alongside harmonious notes of cooling herbs, white chocolate, cigar box, and violet.

XANADU

Boodjidup Road, Margaret River
+61 8 9758 9500
www.xanaduwines.com

After purchasing successful wineries in the Yarra Valley, Grampians, and Coonawarra, the Rathbone family set their sights on Margaret River. In 2005, they purchased Xanadu Estate—named after a line from Coleridge's poem "Kubla Khan," not the Olivia Newton-John movie and theme song—which had been planted in 1977. Winemaker Glenn Goodall perfected his craft in New Zealand, South Africa, and California before settling in Margaret River to work with Cabernet Sauvignon, Shiraz, Chardonnay, Sémillon, Viognier, and Sauvignon Blanc. The entry-level Next of Kin range offers a value-oriented introduction to the wines of Xanadu, while the Estate range offers premium expressions of estate-grown fruit. Xanadu Stevens Road

Chardonnay 2009 exhibits stone fruit, citrus, and brioche on the nose, while the palate opens to reveal ripe pear, grapefruit, and soft vanilla enmeshed in a creamy mouthfeel with a spirited citrus finish. Xanadu Limited Release Cabernet Sauvignon 2007 is deep garnet in the glass, with aromas of black currants, cherry, and Christmas spice. Its full-throttle palate is full of cassis, blackberry, and mocha. Strong tannins are the driving force behind the tenacious finish.

PEEL

Named for Thomas Peel, who brought three ships filled with British emigrants here in 1829, the Peel region sits between Perth Hills to the north and Geographe to the south. Peel is less than an hour south of the Western Australian capital, Perth. Although the first vineyards planted here date back to 1857, it was only in 1974 that the first commercial vineyard was planted, on the site of the former Peel Estate. Shiraz is the grape that Peel built its reputation on, although the region is known for Chenin Blanc, Chardonnay, and Cabernet Sauvignon. In addition to grapevines, Peel is also home to a variety of premium fruit and vegetable farms. The coastal climate enjoys cool, wet winters and hot, dry summers; spring and summer rainfall averages 160 to 280 millimeters, or 6 to 11 inches, depending on distance from

the coast and altitudes, which range from sea level to 290 meters (951 feet). Soils in the east tend to be old granite and gravel soils, while those closer to the western coast are sedimentary alluvial soils and sandy limestone. In the coastal area, abundant ground water reserves are found 15 meters (49 feet) below the surface.

PEEL ESTATE

290 Fletcher Road, Karnup,
+61 8 9524 1221,
www.peelwine.com.au

Will Nairn, who remains Peel Estate's senior winemaker, established the first vineyard in the region when he planted grapes in 1973, followed by a winery in 1980; his first vintages were produced at a friend's winery. His 16 hectares (40 acres) are planted with Shiraz,

Chenin Blanc, Zinfandel, Cabernet Sauvignon, Chardonnay, Verdelho, Cabernet Franc, and Merlot. The Traditional range is a grouping of individual varietals, while the Classics features both dry blends and sparkling wine. Peel Estate Shiraz 2004 is deep ruby with a bright rim. The nose is full of jammy fruit and sautéed bell pepper, while in the mouth stewed plums and black cherries are incorporated into a strong tannic structure suggestive of earth and spice.

PEMBERTON

Pemberton is known as karri tree country—these tall eucalyptus trees grow to 90 meters (295 feet). Despite an influx of vineyards since the 1980s, over 85 percent of the region remains planted with native vegetation. Home to only 20 wineries, Pemberton has quickly developed renown for its award-winning wines, including Chardonnay, which is the most widely planted here, followed by Merlot and Pinot Noir. There are two main soil types: granitic gravelly sand and loam, on the higher slopes near the town of Pemberton, and deep red fertile loam. The first sits over clay and the second over coarse-grained metamorphic rock. There is a total of 654 hectares (1,616 acres) of vineyards in Pemberton. Spring and summer rain averages 340 millimeters, or 13.5 inches, and average vineyard altitude is 174 meters (570 feet) above sea level.

PICARDY

Corner of Vasse Highway and
Eastbrook Road, Pemberton,
+61 8 9776 0036,
www.picardy.com.au

Bill, Sandra, Dan, and Jodie Pannell run Picardy, and since 1993 all of their wines have been made from single-vineyard, estate-grown grapes. Picardy is named after a region in the north of France, and the family strives to make quality French-style wines in Pemberton. Picardy Chardonnay 2009 is straw colored, with aromas of white peach, slate, and freshly cut pampas grass. It exhibits nice minerality in the mouth with a clean finish. Picardy Shiraz 2009 is reddish-purple, with aromas of black fruits and black plums. There is balanced acidity in the mouth and a fine tannic finish.

SALITAGE

Vasse Highway, Pemberton,
+61 8 9776 1771,
www.salitage.com.au

John and Jenny Horgan own and run Salitage, a highly regarded boutique winery in Pemberton. John worked with Robert Mondavi in the late 1970s, and in 1985 he was a part owner of Domaine de La Pousse d'Or in Burgundy, so he knows a thing or two about Chardonnay and Pinot Noir. Visitors to Salitage can relax in one of the Salitage Suites, set among a secluded stand of trees on the property. Patrick Coutts is the winemaker. Salitage Chardonnay 2009 is straw colored, with notes of white peaches, honeydew melon, and citrus blossoms. It is generous in the mouth with a touch of citric acidity before a fruity finish. Salitage Pinot Noir 2009 is medium cherry red, with hints of white pepper and licorice over a red cherry and black raspberry fruit core. It is smooth in the mouth with flavors of dark cherry and cherry preserves. The finish is persistent and pleasant.

SWAN DISTRICT

Western Australia's oldest wine region, the Swan District was first planted with vines in 1829. Until the 1970s, it was the only wine region of note in Western Australia, and for most of its history the focus was on fortified wine. This area was settled in waves by English, Italian, and Croatian immigrants, each of which brought their culinary and winemaking traditions to Australia. The Swan District is home to about 30 wineries, and the region's main varieties are Shiraz, Chenin Blanc, Chardonnay, and Verdelho. The Swan District's hot Mediterranean climate receives relief from the heat via a southwest afternoon sea breeze known as the Fremantle Doctor. Rainfall during spring and summer is low, averaging 145 millimeters, or a little less than 6 inches. Deep alluvial soils predominate in the region, with variances in the amount of limestone, gravel, or clay from subregion to subregion. The main subregion is Swan Valley. Most vineyards are at an altitude of 45 meters (just under 150 feet) above sea level. The Swan District has 823 hectares (2,034 acres) of vineyards.

JOHN KOSOVICH WINES

180 Memorial Avenue, Baskerville,
+61 8 9296 4356,
www.johnkosovichwines.com.au

Established in 1922 as Westfield Wines, the winery changed name in 2003 to honor John Kosovich's fiftieth harvest. It is the third oldest winery in the Swan Valley and was awarded Best West Australian Small Wine Producer in 2004. It has one of only two original underground cellars in the Swan Valley—dug in 1922 by John's father without the use of machinery. Kosovich Cabernet Sauvignon 2009 is garnet colored with aromas of black fruit front and center with touches of mint and cocoa on the side. In the mouth, blackberry flavors come forward while soft tannins bring the fruit flavor home. Kosovich Late Picked Verdelho 2009 is straw colored with green hues. It has aromas of white flowers, spice, and a hint of dried apricot. It is full in the mouth with a slightly sweet finish. This wine is lovely with food or as an aperitif.

SANDALFORD

3210 West Swan Road, Caversham,
+61 8 9374 9374,
www.sandalford.com.au

In 1840, John Septimus Roe, Western Australia's first Surveyor General, was rewarded by Queen Victoria with 810 hectares (2,002 acres) of land along the Swan River in Caversham. He named the property Sandalford and set to work planting grapevines. At first, he supplied his neighbors with wine and over time developed a reputation for the quality of his fortified Port- and Sherry-style wines. In 1970, his descendants bought an additional 280 hectares (692 acres) in the up-and-coming Margaret River region and

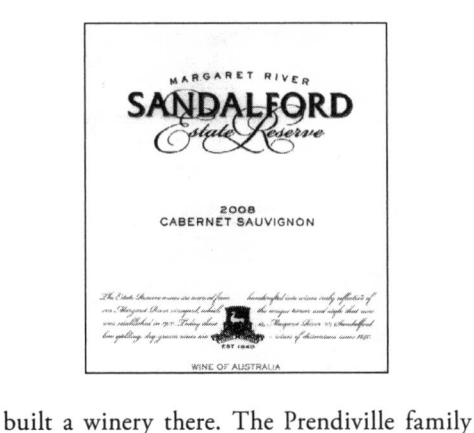

built a winery there. The Prendiville family purchased both estates and wineries in 1991. Each winery features top-notch tourist facilities, including a tasting room and restaurant. A summer concert series is held on the grounds of the original Caversham location. Chief winemaker Paul Boulder trained in Bordeaux, France, and Penedes, Spain, before working at several wineries across Australia, eventually landing at Sandalford. The majority of its wines, in five different ranges, are dry table wines, but fortified and sweet wines are still an important part of the portfolio. Sandalford Estate Reserve Sauvignon Blanc Semillon is a blend of 91 percent Sauvignon Blanc and 9 percent Sémillon. Almost clear to the eye, on the nose it reveals scents of clean citrus mingling with floral notes. In the mouth, citrus continues, buttressed by fresh flavors of chopped herbs and white flowers. Clean, acidic minerality is very pleasing to the palate. Sandalford Estate Reserve

Cabernet Sauvignon 2008 is deep cherry red, with aromas of cassis, herbes de Provence, and violet candy. In the mouth, wild raspberry and blackberry are incorporated into a silky network of tannins with vanilla, spice, and earthy notes close at hand.

SOUTH AUSTRALIA

South Australia is the nation's "grape basket," producing the majority of its wine. It sits in the center of southern Australia and has a whopping 73,409 hectares (181,398 acres) of grapevines—almost half of all the vineyards in Australia. It is home to some of the oldest grapevines in the country (and the world), thanks to quarantine regulations that saved it from phylloxera, which destroyed vineyards to the east. Red grapes outnumber white at a margin greater than two to one; there are 51,506 hectares (127,274 acres) of red grapes and 21,903 hectares (54,123 acres) of white varieties.

South Australia is home to three of the top-producing (volumewise) grape zones in the country: Lower Murray, Limestone Coast, and Fleurieu. The Murray River zone contains one wine region, Riverland, which is Australia's largest single producing wine region. The Limestone Coast encompasses the regions of Coonawarra, Mount Benson, Mount Gambier, Padthaway, Robe, and Wrattonbully.

Fleurieu is a compact zone with five wine regions, all close to Adelaide: Currency Creek, Kangaroo Island, Langhorne Creek, McLaren Vale, and Southern Fleurieu. The Barossa is a 1,970-square-kilometer (761-square-mile) zone that encompasses both the Barossa Valley and the Eden Valley. It includes the towns of Angaston, Lyndoch, Nuriootpa, and Tanunda. Other regions in South Australia are Adelaide Hills, Adelaide Plains, Clare Valley, and the Southern Flinders Ranges.

Founded in 1837 as a British colony, South Australia was settled by immigrant families, not convicts. The capital city is Adelaide, home to 1.3 million people. Adelaide's suburbs spread 20 kilometers (12 miles) from the city center and now encroach on farms and vineyards in McLaren Vale and Adelaide Hills.

ADELAIDE HILLS

A mere 20-minute drive from Adelaide—a large city with a small-town feel—Adelaide Hills is home to 90 wineries and a total of 4,034 hectares (9,968 acres) of grapevines. It's a picture-perfect region filled with rolling hills, charming villages, and roadside fruit stands— Adelaide Hills is perfect for a day of touring in wine country. Vines were first planted in 1839 in the gray brown loamy soil of the region. Adelaide Hills boasts a cool climate, mainly due to altitudes that run between

400 and 500 meters (1,312 to 1,640 feet). As would be expected, the cool climate is ideal for Sauvignon Blanc, Riesling, Chardonnay, and Pinot Noir; the last two are made into sparkling as well as still wine. In addition, Cabernet Sauvignon and Merlot are cultivated here. Rainfall through the spring and summer averages 310 millimeters, or 12 inches.

GEOFF WEAVER

2 Gilpin Lane, Mitcham,
+61 8 8272 2105,
www.geoffweaver.com.au

Anyone who has turned a hobby into a career will tell you it was one of the best decisions ever made. Geoff Weaver is no exception. He and wife Judy planted their first Riesling and Chardonnay vines in 1983, while Geoff was working as a winemaker for local wine giant Hardys. By 1988, when Geoff was promoted to head winemaker at Hardys, his own vineyard had grown into much more than a hobby, although he was still only able to devote bits and pieces of time to the enterprise. In 1992, faced with the choice between ongoing financial security at Hardys or cutting loose and pursuing his dream, Geoff chose the latter, and today his Riesling, Chardonnay, Pinot Noir, Sauvignon Blanc, and Bordeaux-style blends are considered among the finest in the region.

Weaver Sauvignon Blanc 2010 is pale straw in color and gives off scents of pear, pineapple, and mango. In the mouth it exhibits clean flavors of lime, passionfruit, pineapple, and a suggestion of geranium, with rich mouthfeel and a snappy acid finish. Geoff Weaver Pinot Noir 2008 is cherry red in the glass, with a nose of cherry, nutmeg, and clove. A palate of cherry, raspberry, dark chocolate, and oregano frolic among soft tannins through the extended finish.

PETALUMA

389 Mount Barker Road, Bridgewater,
+61 8 8339 9200,
www.petaluma.com.au

In the mid-1970s Brian Croser started looking for areas to plant vines in the Adelaide Hills. He is widely credited for being the first person to do so, save for the German

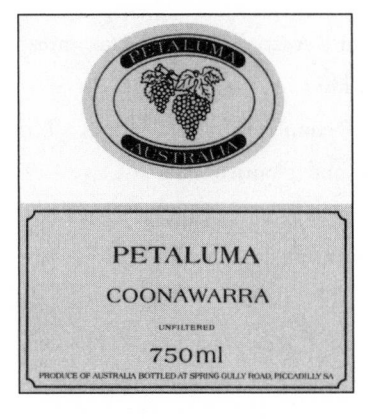

immigrants who planted long-forgotten vines in the early 1800s. Petaluma is now part of the Lion Nathan Group with Andy Hardy as the head winemaker and Mike Mudge, with whom we met, as the winemaker. The historic Bridgewater Mill is the site of the Petaluma tasting room and beautiful restaurant. Opened in 1983, Mike describes the cuisine as "Modern Australian with an Asian twist, because the chef likes to experiment with Vietnamese and Japanese dishes." Petaluma Hanlin Hill Clare Valley Riesling 2010 is pale straw, with lifted notes of white flowers, honeysuckle, and apricot and with mineral notes of flint and shale. It is crisp and clean in the mouth, with balanced acidity. Petaluma Coonawarra 2008 is a blend of 60 percent Cabernet Sauvignon, 31 percent Merlot, and 9 percent Shiraz. It is cherry garnet red, with aromas of black pepper, white pepper, spice, cassis, blackberry, and cola. In the mouth, ripe, red fruits come forward while tobacco and saddle leather ride in behind for a lingering finish. Petaluma Cane Cut Riesling 2010 is golden yellow, with strong notes of ripe apricots, apricot preserves, and yellow peaches. It tastes like grandma's fresh-baked peach pie and has a clean fresh-fruit finish with amazing length.

SHAW + SMITH

Lot 4 Jones Road, Balhanna,
+61 8 8398 0500,
www.shawandsmith.com

Prior to the construction of their winery in 2000, cousins Martin Shaw, winemaker, and Michael Hill Smith, Master of Wine, used the facilities down the road at Petaluma. Originally they were known for their Sauvignon Blanc, but today they are also widely known for high-quality Chardonnay and Shiraz. They also make small amounts of Riesling and Pinot Noir. Michael Hill Smith says, "There is a really good traditional/modern split in Australia. We are modern winemakers making modern wines. Ten years ago we decided to produce varietal wines that work the best in this region—we just didn't want to make another wine, we wanted to make a wine that expresses the best qualities of the variety and the best qualities of our site and climate." Shaw + Smith recently added Tolpuddle Vineyards in

Tasmania to the estate's holdings. We're looking forward to tasting some of these wines on our next visit. Shaw + Smith M3 Chardonnay 2009 is golden yellow, with aromas of stone fruits, butterscotch, and vanilla. It has a luxurious mouthfeel with balanced acidity and a long elegant finish. Shaw + Smith Pinot Noir 2009 is ruby red, with aromas of red cherry, raspberry, fruits of the wood, and a touch of white pepper. It is full and fruity on the palate with that touch of white pepper tickling the back of your mouth—before a smooth, persistent finish. It's just too bad only 400 cases were made of this delicious wine! In a word, Shaw + Smith Shiraz 2009 is stunning! It is deep inky purple with a hint of violet at the rim. It has big fruit in the bouquet with aromas of red plums, black raspberry, and red cherry. The cherry flavor opens up in the mouth with ripe, balanced tannins and an elegant finish.

BAROSSA VALLEY

The Barossa Valley's tradition of grape growing and winemaking stretches back to 1842, when Silesian settlers—German Lutherans fleeing religious persecution—flocked to this broad valley. Six generations later, descendants of the original winemaking families have been joined by talented newcomers and an old-is-new artisanal food culture. Its 10,315 hectares (25,489 acres) of vineyards are shared by more than 150 wineries. The Barossa Valley is known for its robust Shiraz as well as Riesling, Chardonnay, Sémillon, Grenache, Mourvèdre, and Cabernet Sauvignon. It is possibly the most famous Australian wine region in international markets; to many people, Barossa Valley Shiraz is synonymous with Australian wine. The network of valleys and hills creates a potpourri of slopes and vineyard sites. Soils are predominantly clay loam to sandy, all with poor fertility. Colors vary from red to brown to gray. Altitudes vary as well, between heights of 250 meters to 370 meters (820 to 1,213 feet). The Barossa is a broad plateau, so its elevation is not apparent to casual observers. Spring and summer rainfall averages 160 millimeters, or slightly more than 6 inches. If a bottle of wine is simply labeled with the general zone name "Barossa," grapes may come from either the Barossa Valley or neighboring Eden Valley; to use the GI "Barossa Valley" grapes may only come from this region.

CHARLES MELTON

Krondorf Road, Tanunda,
+61 8 8563 3606,
www.charlesmeltonwines.com.au

After an apprenticeship under Peter Lehmann, Graeme "Charlie" Melton struck out on his own, and since his first vintage in 1984, his

Rhône-style reds have been ranked among the best in Australia. His Winery Block vineyard in Tanunda grows bushvine Grenache planted in 1947, and the Lyndoch's Woodlands vineyard is home to Grenache, Shiraz, and Cabernet Sauvignon. A 29-hectare (72-acre) vineyard was purchased in 2008; plantings of Shiraz, Grenache, and the many varieties that make up Châteauneuf de Pape were begun in 2010. Charles Melton Grains of Paradise 2008 is deep violet in the glass and emits fragrances of fresh and candied berries with a soupçon of baking spice. On the tongue rich blueberry, black cherry, and cassis carry on with clove, cinnamon, and lavender, culminating in a satisfying, tannic-rich finish.

CHÂTEAU TANUNDA

9 Basedow Road, Tanunda,
+61 8 8563 3888,
www.chateautanunda.com

Established in 1890, Château Tanunda is one of Australia's largest châteaus. It was originally called the Adelaide Wine Company, changing to its current name prior to being sold to Seppelt in 1916. Unfortunately, it fell into disrepair after being abandoned for more modern digs, until the Geber family bought it in 1998. Both the interior and grounds have been lovingly restored; in addition

to the Basket Press Winery constructed in 2004, there is a large terrace with views of the Barossa Range, a visitor center and tasting room among the barrels, a ballroom for private events, and a cricket oval. The cellar door tasting room houses the Barossa Small Winemaker Center; besides Château Tanunda wine, visitors can taste wine from artisanal producers who might otherwise have been overlooked. Winemaker Tim Smith uses both estate-grown Cabernet Sauvignon, Shiraz, Riesling, and Chardonnay as well as fruit sourced from small local growers. John Geber's fun-loving daughter Michelle is Château Tanunda's ambassador, and we have enjoyed many a dinner in her company, tasting her family's fine wines. Château Tanunda Noble Baron Cabernet Sauvignon 2008 is deep garnet in color, with aromas of cassis and earth. In the mouth, flavors of black cherry, cassis, portabello mushroom, and light spice are enveloped in soft tannins. Château Tanunda The Château 100 Year Old Vines

Shiraz 2008 is deep, dark, and decadent. Blueberry, stewed plum, and anise fill your nose, and the palate is brimming with black fruit, licorice, and Chinese five-spice powder, which carry on until the lush vanilla custard finish kicks in.

ELDERTON

3-5 Tanunda Road, Nuriootpa,
+61 8 8568 7878,
www.eldertonwines.com.au

Brothers Cameron and Allister Ashmead run the 28-hectare (69-acre) Elderton winery acquired by their parents, Neal and Lorraine. The vineyards were originally planted in 1894. Cameron told us how his father became interested in making wine, "Lorraine and Neal bought this property in 1977, but before that Neal was a civil engineer in Saudi Arabia. Due to the Muslim culture, he could not buy wine, so he started making his own." We had a relaxing lunch with Cameron and his lovely wife, Julie, in their beautiful home among the grapevines. Together, they cooked a delicious pasta dish for us that paired perfectly with their wines. Elderton Friends Eden Valley Shiraz 2010 is garnet colored, with aromas of cherry and black plum. The vibrant fruit flavors delight your palate. Elderton Ode to Lorraine 2008, named for Cameron and Allister's mother, is

a blend of 55 percent Cabernet Sauvignon, 37 percent Shiraz, and 8 percent Merlot. It is ruby colored, with aromas of red fruits and vanilla. In the mouth it's velvety smooth with a pleasant, soft finish. On the other hand, Elderton Neal Ashmead Gran Tourer Shiraz 2009 is a masculine wine, named for their (late) father. It is dark red, with aromas of dark cherry and black plums. It has ripe, balanced tannins with an elegant finish.

FIRST DROP

Williamstown, Barossa Valley,
+61 4 1784 4284,
www.firstdropwines.com

Friends and wine lovers John Retsas and Matt Gant came to the world of wine via different routes. Retsas's European parents served wine at every meal, including homemade Grenache fermented in the bathtub. Gant took a class called "The Historical Geography of Viticulture" in his final year of university, setting him on a life- and career-changing path. The fun-loving Retsas—JR to his friends—heads up the business side of things, while Gant, who was named "Young Winemaker of the Year" in 2004 for his work at St Hallett, brings his enological skills to the table. Gant has worked in the United States, New Zealand, Spain, Italy, and Portugal. First

Drop is known for its Shiraz and Cabernet Sauvignon, but Gant's European experience surely has a hand in the choice of varieties, such as Tinta Amerella, Arneis, Albariño, Nebbiolo, Barbera, Tempranillo, Touriga Nacional, and Monastrell. Previous vintages were produced in borrowed space, but from the 2011 vintage, First Drop has its own purpose-built winery. Fruit is sourced from growers in the Barossa, Adelaide Hills, and McLaren Vale. First Drop Mother's Milk Barossa Shiraz 2009 is bright black cherry to the eye. Enticing aromas of cassis, spice, and confectioners' sugar prepare the taste buds for a delectable rush of cassis, stewed plums, anise, vanilla, and orange zest. First Drop Fat of the Land Seppeltsfield Barossa Valley Shiraz 2008 is rich red violet with a bright red rim. A siren call of cherry, blueberry, and violet on the nose beckons you to taste the ambrosial nectar within your glass, which delivers lush berry, spice, and floral flavors wrapped in gentle tannins with a peppery finish.

GLAETZER

34 Barossa Valley Way, Tanunda,
+61 8 8563 0288,
www.glaetzer.com

The Glaetzer family settled in the Barossa Valley in 1888, having emigrated from

Germany. The family has more than its fair share of winemakers. Glaetzer is now run by Colin Glaetzer and his son Ben, both graduates of the leading Australian enology course at Roseworthy, but Colin's wife, Judith, and his twin brother, John, are also winemakers. Prior to founding Glaetzer in 1995, Colin honed his skills at some of the nation's finest wineries, including Tyrrell's, Seppelt, and Barossa Valley Estate. In addition to his work with the family business, Ben is an active partner in both the Heartland and Mitolo wine brands. The bold graphic labels, designed by Ben, telegraph the fact that although this is a family routed in tradition, they are very much a part of the modern winemaking world. Glaetzer Wallace by Ben Glaetzer 2009 is a blend of 70 percent Shiraz and 30 percent Grenache. In the glass, the color is bright cherry with a red violet rim. Aromas of black cherry, vanilla, and Chinese five-spice powder barely prepare your senses for the sensuous rounded flavors of cherry, blueberry, strawberry, licorice, and clove that follow. Glaetzer Anaperenna by Ben Glaetzer 2009 is a blend of 76 percent Shiraz and 34 percent Cabernet Sauvignon. Red violet in the glass, it exudes aromas of blackberry, blueberry, licorice, and Mediterranean herbs. The palate is filled with succulent black cherry, blueberry, vanilla, coffee, and anise entangled in a web of velvety tannins.

GRANT BURGE

Barossa Valley Way, Tanunda,
+61 8 8563 7471,
www.grantburge.com.au

The fifth generation of his family to be engaged in winemaking, Grant Burge enjoyed an illustrious career before embarking on his own venture with wife, Helen, in 1988. An enterprise of this size, with ten ranges of wines, 440 hectares (1,087 acres) of vineyards, and a brand new destination tasting center usually smacks of corporate ownership, but this remains a family affair. Grant and Helen's oldest son, Toby, is their vineyard manager, and his siblings Amelia and Trent are learning the business as well. Grant Burge The Vigneron Barossa Valley and Eden Valley

Shiraz 2008 is deep black cherry. Fragrances of blackberry, black cherry, allspice, and mocha lead to flavors of black cherry, damson plum, fresh cracked pepper, and Chinese five-spice, with a delicate balance between smooth tannins and brightness. Grant Burge Holy Trinity Grenache Shiraz Mourvèdre 2008, a 44-40-16 percent blend, is dark red violet to the eye, with a classic nose of cherry, cassis, licorice, cinnamon, and violet. In the mouth, dark berries, flowers, and spice continue their motion in the presence of finely honed tannins and bustling acidity.

JACOB'S CREEK

Barossa Valley Way, Rowland Flat,
+61 8 8521 3000,
www.jacobscreek.com

Johann Gramp brought his family from Germany to Australia in 1846 and planted his first vineyard in 1847. He built a homestead in the Barossa Valley; this historic home is now a tasting room, where we met with winemaker Bernard Hickin. Hickin is passionate about "regional expression and what the region does to the variety." He has been Jacob's Creek chief winemaker since 2006 and has been with the company for more than 35 years. When asked what he feels his role at Jacob's Creek encompasses, he responded, "Firstly for me, I have always had a passion for producing great quality wines at a price that is comfortable for the consumer. At Jacob's Creek, we have a role to play for Australia where we speak about the regions of Australia. We want to make them household names. I would love to have people think of Coonawarra Cabernets in much the way that people think about Cabernet Sauvignon from Napa. I want the consumer to be confident about buying quality wines from Australia with regional identity—wines that exhibit the personality of the region." Jacob's Creek Reserve Adelaide Hills Chardonnay 2009 is fermented in French oak, 20 percent of which is new each year. It is straw colored, with light stone fruit aromas. On the palate it is fruity and creamy with a balanced minerality to the finish. Jacob's Creek Reserve Barossa Shiraz 2007 is inky purple, with lifted notes of Dr Pepper over blackberries, black plums, and Christmas fruitcake candied fruits. It has a soft tannic finish and is easy drinking— a great food pairing wine. Jacob's Creek St Hugo Coonawarra Cabernet Sauvignon 2007 is purple inky color with a violet rim. It has wonderful aromas of black olive, plum, cassis, clove, and dark spices in the bouquet. It is a fruit bomb in the mouth with length in the mid palate before finishing with cigar box, cedar, and tobacco leaf.

JOHN DUVAL

Tanunda, Barossa Valley,
+61 8 8562 2266,
www.johnduvallwines.com

John Duval made wine at Penfolds for 29 years and was appointed chief winemaker in 1986. For 16 years, he was therefore considered the guardian of Australia's most prized wine, Penfolds Grange. Since leaving Penfolds in 2002, he has worked on a variety of consulting winemaking projects around the globe, including Ventisquero in Chile. He founded John Duval Wines in 2003 and, despite his other commitments, spends four months each year in the Barossa Valley handcrafting his wines. John Duval Shiraz, Grenache, and Mourvèdre are sourced from some of the oldest vineyards in the Barossa. John Duval Wines Eligo 2008 is 100 percent Shiraz. It's inky violet, with a heady nose of blackberry and vanilla spice. In the mouth, flavors of blueberry, black cherry, anise, and ground pepper commingle with luxurious tannins, leading to a sustained finish.

KAESLER

Barossa Valley Way, Nuriootpa,
+61 8 8562 4488,
www.kaesler.com.au

Winemaker Reid Bosward is living the dream. After stints with the Tyrrell family in the

Hunter Valley and time with Jacques Lurton in France, investors—including Swiss banker Edourd Peter—purchased Barossa estate Kaesler and bankrolled this renowned operation. Bosward works alongside viticulturist Nigel van der Zande. Founded by German immigrants, Kaesler's original vineyards of Shiraz, Grenache, and Mourvèdre date back to 1893; their icon Old Bastard Shiraz is made from a single block planted that year. Among their 92 hectares (227 acres) are other vineyard blocks planted in the 1930s and 1960s. Over dinner at Barossa's Vintners Bar and Grill restaurant, Bosward shared some of his finest bottles with us alongside perfectly grilled steaks. Kaesler Old Bastard Shiraz 2008 is deep red in the glass, with aromas of black cherry, cassis, and smoky spice. In the mouth, invigorating berries, cherries, and plum glide across the tongue, and elegant tannins are livened up by bursts of paprika and black pepper. Kaesler Barossa Valley Stonehorse Shiraz 2009 shows black cherry color with a violet rim. Notes of cassis, blueberry, and black licorice, first apparent on the nose, continue in the mouth to a prolonged but graceful finish.

KALLESKE

6 Murray Street, Greenock,
+61 8 8563 4000,
www.kalleske.com

One hundred and fifty years after their forebears planted grapes in the Barossa, seventh-generation farmers Tony and Troy Kalleske produced the first vintage of Kalleske wine. Troy is the winemaker, and their parents John and Lorraine and brother Kym manage the estate's 48 hectares (119 acres) of vines. The average vine age in their certified organic vineyard is an extraordinary 50 years, while the oldest vines date back to 1875. Varieties include Shiraz, Grenache, Mourvèdre, Cabernet Sauvignon, Sémillon, Chenin Blanc, Petit Verdot, Durif, Viognier, Tempranillo, and Zinfandel. Kalleske Johann Georg Shiraz 2008 is deep purple blue to the eye. It exudes aromas of dark berries, licorice, Mediterranean herbs, and Turkish delight. Powerful flavors of black cherry, blueberry, anise, sage, and violet fill the entire palate, lingering on through a brilliant finish. Kalleske Merchant Cabernet Sauvignon 2009 is red violet in color. Fragrances of black cherry, cassis, dark chocolate, and cooling herbs carry over onto the tongue; this full-bodied wine has a strong tannic backbone and fine acid balance.

PENFOLDS

Penfolds Magill Estate, 78 Penfold Road, Magill,
+61 8 8301 5569,
www.penfolds.com.au

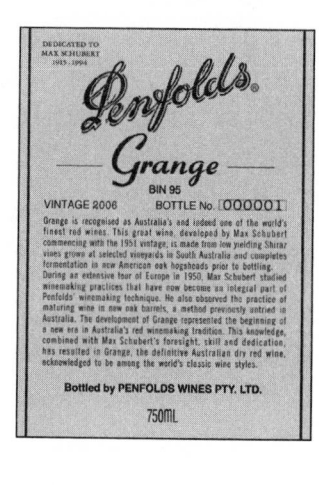

Dr. Christopher Rawson Penfold and his wife, Mary, purchased the historic Magill (then Mackgill) Estate in 1844 and started growing grapes. They made fortified wines that Dr. Penfold prescribed to his anemic patients for medicinal purposes. Mary handled the winemaking while Dr. Penfold tended to his patients. Penfolds wines have always been well respected in Australia, and in 1951 winemaker Max Schubert made the first vintage of Grange, giving the company international recognition. Today Peter Gago is the head winemaker, and Jamie Sach is the Penfolds ambassador. We enjoyed too many Penfolds wines to mention, but here are a few of our favorites: Magill Estate Shiraz 2008 is garnet colored, with aromas of green olives, black plums, and purple flowers. It is feminine on the nose, yet masculine in the mouth, with bright black plum, black raspberry, red raspberry, and crème caramel. It is youthful on the palate with a prolonged finish. Penfolds Bin 389 is lovingly referred to as "baby Grange." The barrels are used the first year for Grange, then the second year for Bin 389. Jamie told us that "This is the wine that many winemakers buy because at one tenth of the cost of Grange, it has excellent quality to value ratio." Penfolds Bin 389 2009 is a blend of 52 percent Cabernet Sauvignon and 48 percent Shiraz. It is inky ruby colored, with aromas of blackberry, blueberry, and light spices. In the mouth, black cherry, licorice, and candied violet delight your palate before the long, silky, tannic finish. Penfolds Grange 2006 is composed of 98 percent Shiraz and 2 percent Cabernet Sauvignon and is black cherry colored. There are intermingled aromas of raspberry, blueberry, smoked meats, nutmeg, black licorice, and freshly ground espresso. In the mouth, flavors of blueberry, licorice, menthol, Mediterranean herbs, cherry cola, and candied cherry excite your palate. The finish is luxurious—we hated having to put our glasses down!

PETER LEHMANN

Para Road, Tanunda,
+61 8 8563 2100,
www.peterlehmannwines.com

Winemaker Ian Hongell told us, "We are very happy with the quality of this year's (2011) harvest, even though it has been a very difficult harvest with a lot of rain. There are lots of positive things, but for many winemakers, there will be a lot of heartache." Hongell predicted that the 2011 wines "are going to be more feminine in style." He has been with Peter Lehmann for 13 years and is the liaison for the US market. The company started when winemaker Peter Lehmann gathered a group of investors in 1979. Peter Lehmann Wines benefits from being able to buy the best grapes from 185 contract growers. Peter Lehmann Mentor Cabernet Sauvignon 2006 is dark garnet colored, with aromas of cherry cola, cooling herbs, eucalyptus, sage, black currant, and black raspberries. In the mouth it's a generous wine with heft to

the mid palate. It finishes with violet floral characteristics. Peter Lehmann Eight Songs Shiraz 2006 is garnet colored in the glass. Aromas of red fruit compote, chocolate, coffee, espresso, and mocha lead to an opulent wine with soft tannins and a persistent finish. Peter Lehmann Stonewell Shiraz 2006 is dark red; mineral notes from the red clay, iron-rich earth in the vineyard are evident in the nose along with aromas of black currant, dark chocolate, vanilla, cassis, black plums, and a hint of smoked meat. This flagship wine is a muscular Shiraz with an elegant, smooth, tannic finish.

SCHILD ESTATE WINES

1 Lyndoch Valley Road, Lyndoch,
+61 8 8524 5560,
www.schildestate.com.au

Schild Estate was established in 1952 when Ben Schild bought the Three Springs Farm in the

Rowland Flat subregion of the Barossa. Under the leadership of his son Ed, Schild Estate has grown to include 162 hectares (400 acres) of premium Barossa vineyards. Winemaker Scott Hazeldine works alongside the second and third generation of Schild family members to produce award-winning Shiraz, Cabernet Sauvignon, Pinot Noir, Riesling, and Sémillon. Schild Estate Barossa Cabernet Sauvignon 2009 is dark black cherry with a red rim. The black cherry continues straight through the nose and onto the palate, where it is joined by licorice and clove. Its smooth tannins and bright fruit-filled finish are a winning combination. Schild Estate Moorooroo Shiraz 2006, from a vineyard planted in 1847, is blue violet with aromas of blueberry pie and clove. A fruit-filled entry of cherry and blueberry widens to delicious notes of buttered cinnamon toast on the side palate.

SEPPELTSFIELD

Seppeltsfield Road, Seppeltsfield,
+61 8 8568 6217,
www.seppeltsfield.com.au

When you visit Seppeltsfield the first thing you notice is the two thousand or more date palm trees that line the entrance. Grateful employees that were not let go during the Great Depression planted these as a gift to the family. Silesian-German Joseph Ernst Seppelt emigrated to Australia in 1849, and by 1867 his full-scale winery was up and running. Seppeltsfield is known for its fortified wines and especially for its Para Tawny Ports that are released only after one hundred years of barrel aging. We enjoyed the 1911 (yes, 1911) vintage after a wonderful dinner with a group of Barossa winemakers. It had aromas of stewed fruits, dried raisins, and blackberry pie. In the mouth it had great heft and concentrated flavors of dried Sultana raisins and dried plums. It was an immensely satisfying way to end a perfect meal.

ST HALLETT

St Hallett Road, Tanunda,
+61 8 8563 7000,
www.sthallett.com.au

In speaking of the 2011 harvest, winemaker Toby Barlow told us, "All the Barossa winemakers are waiting to see how the red wines, especially Shiraz, progress after malolactic fermentation occurs." He expects "bright, fresh aromatics this year, but the challenge will be to see how the tannins develop." St Hallett was established in 1944 by the Lindner family, who initially concentrated on fortified wines. In the 1970s and 1980s, it shifted its focus to quality table wines.

STANDISH WINE COMPANY

100 Barritt Road, Lyndoch,
+61 4 0736 6673,
www.standishwineco.com

Barlow continued, "In making our Blackwell range of wines, which are named after Stuart Blackwell—St Hallett winemaker for over 30 years—our philosophy is to get rich black fruit character and full body with a bit of that raisin-edged taste." St Hallett Barossa Blackwell Shiraz 2008 is a stunning purple color, with aromas of black cherry, paprika, white pepper, and raisins. It is big and jammy in the mouth with flavors of leather, red fruit, dried raisins, tobacco, blackberries, and fruit compote. It has a long smooth tannic finish. St Hallett Barossa Old Block Shiraz 2004 is inky indigo purple colored, with notes of truffles, saddle leather, black olives, and Porcini mushrooms. It's a fruit bomb in your mouth with finishing flavors of anise and Chinese five-spice powder. There are lightly gripping tannins on the finish; it's a great wine.

We had dinner with the affable Dan Standish, a sixth-generation Barossa grape grower and now winemaker. Standish told us that he learned how to prune vines from his grandfather when he was six years old. His wine philosophy is, "I am simply trying to convey what the vineyard has endured in the past year—with a message in a bottle." By our accounts 2007 was an amazing year, and Standish's wines are some of the best Australian Shiraz that we have ever had. Standish Borne Bollene Shiraz 2007 is deep purple—think purple velvet—with heady aromas of blackberry, blueberry, cassis, purple flowers, and hints of smoked sausage. In the mouth it explodes with flavors of mixed berry conserves and purple flowers. It has great heft and elegant ripe tannins. Standish Andelmonde Shiraz 2007 is inky purple in the glass with tinges of red. It has concentrated dark fruits, cassis, and a whiff of cigar box as a top note. This is a big, bold-but-balanced Shiraz that is drinking wonderfully now—though if you can resist the temptation, by our reckoning, it will only get better. This is another super wine from Dan Standish.

TORBRECK

51 Roennfeldt Road, Marananga,
+61 8 8568 8123,
www.torbreck.com

In the early 1990s during a government-sponsored vine-pull operation, winemaker Dave Powell fell for a vineyard filled with nearly useless ancient bushvine red Rhône varieties. He nurtured them back to health and began a share-farming setup with the vineyard's owners. He bought the property in 2002 and named his winery Torbreck after a forest in Scotland. He's since planted new vineyards with Shiraz and white Rhône varieties. Torbreck The Steading Blanc 2009, a blend of 55 percent Roussanne, 25 percent Marsanne, and 20 percent Viognier, gives off extravagant perfumed aromas of jasmine, rose petal, toasted almonds, and lemon curd. A gentle interplay of rich mouthfeel and sharp minerality is the setting for flavors of citrus, marzipan, and Turkish delight. Torbreck The Steading 2007 is comprised of 60 percent Grenache and 20 percent each of Shiraz and Mataro (Mourvèdre) from Dave's original old bush vines. Deep garnet in color, it gives a nose of raspberry, herbes de Provence, and portabello mushroom. On the palate three-berry parfait with notes of truffle, star anise, and violet are suspended in a web of smooth tannins and vivid acidity.

TWO HANDS

Neldner Road, Marananga,
+61 8 8562 4566,
www.twohandswines.com

Businessmen Michael Twelftree and Richard Mintz put their heads together and formed Two Hands in 1999. Twelftree started in wine as an exporter and, after a few years of selling other people's wines, decided to make and sell his own. Since then Two Hands has received numerous accolades from various domestic and international publications. Its winemaker is Matthew Wenk, whose experience includes stints in the Languedoc and Sonoma Valley. Two Hands Ares Barossa Valley Shiraz 2008 stains your glass with dark purple black ink and has complex aromas of dark plums coated in cocoa powder, grandma's beef stew, pencil lead, and top notes of cigar box. In the mouth this big wine gives up dark fruit flavors with a second wave of anise and dark chocolate before the elegant yet restrained finish. This is what Shiraz from the Barossa should taste like! Two Hands Coach House Block Cabernet Sauvignon 2007 is purple, with aromas of cassis, currants, and olive tapenade. It has pleasantly sweet, ripe fruit characteristics that coat your tongue before a lovely balanced tannic finish.

WOLF BLASS

97 Stuart Highway, Nuriootpa,
+61 8 8568 7311,
www.wolfblass.com.au

Wolfgang Blass first made wine in the Barossa in 1966. Forty-five vintages and multiple awards later, the brand Wolf Blass—now owned by Treasury Wine Estates—is one of the largest wine-producing companies in Australia. It produces five different ranges, from the easy-drinking Yellow and Red Labels through the Grey, Black, Gold, and Platinum Labels. Wolf Blass Gold Label Riesling 2008 is pale straw with golden highlights. Aromas of lime sorbet with floral notes give way to flavors of lemon and lime with a pinch of anise. Wolf Blass Gold Label Barossa Shiraz 2007 is dark garnet in the glass. The nose exhibits fragrances of raspberry, black cherry, and licorice. In the mouth, rich velvety tannins and bright acidity wrap around fruits of the wood, spice, and cigar box flavors.

YALUMBA

Eden Valley Road, Angaston, SA 5353,
+61 8 8561 3200,
www.yalumba.com

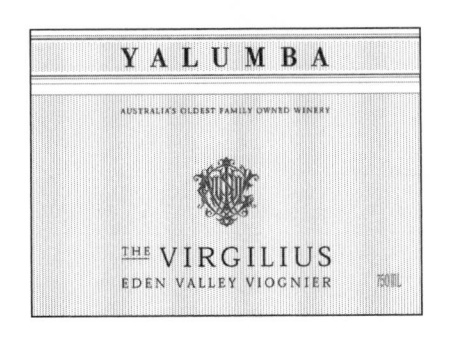

Founded by Samuel Smith in 1849, Yalumba is Australia's oldest family-owned winery. From the Aboriginal word *yalumba* meaning "all the land around," the company is owned today by Robert Hill Smith, his younger brother, Sam, and their mother, Helen Hill Smith. Its iconic "Clock Tower" building in which we tasted the company's wines was built in 1909. Yalumba is known around the world for its award-winning wines and its pioneering use of screwcaps. Yalumba Patchwork Shiraz 2007 is dark red colored, with aromas of dried black and red fruits, mushrooms, wet earth, and cigar box. It is generous on the palate with a lingering finish. Yalumba Eden Valley Virgilius Viognier 2009 is pale straw colored, with aromas of lemongrass, ginger, white peach, and white flowers. It's a luxuriously heady bouquet. In the mouth it's full and voluptuous with a smooth finish.

CLARE VALLEY

Less than two hours north of Adelaide—in the Mount Lofty Ranges—the Clare Valley is famous for its picturesque landscape and exceptional Riesling. Vineyards were first planted here in the 1840s. Today there are 4,924 hectares (12,167 acres) of grapevines and 50 wineries. Clare Valley's hot summers are tempered by cool late-day breezes and cold nights, providing optimum ripening conditions not only for Riesling but also for Sémillon, Shiraz, and Cabernet Sauvignon. Soils differ in the two main subregions: Watervale's limestone base is overlaid with red topsoil, while Polish Hill River is distinguished by its broken slate soils. The northern end of the valley features fertile deep alluvial soils that do not require irrigation. Rainfall from spring through summer is 200 millimeters, or 8 inches, and vineyards are at altitudes ranging between 400 to 500 meters (1,310 to 1,640 feet) above sea level.

GROSSET

Auburn, Clare Valley,
+61 8 8849 2175,
www.grosset.com.au

Owner and winemaker Jeff Grosset opened his winery in 1981. He began his career making wine in Germany and then returned to Australia to work at Lindemans. We had a wonderful opportunity to sit down and chat with Grosset at his winery. He proudly admits, "My winemaking style is influenced by Germany and France. When I was 15, my parents had just discovered wine, and I remember loving the Rieslings the best. When I was asked to go to Germany—I just felt like it was meant to be. I think I found my niche by specializing in white wine, but don't get me wrong, I love our red wines too. For example, our Pinot Noirs are crushed by foot, and I think that makes a better wine. We make a total of 10,000 cases per year, and we want every wine to be a standout." Grosset makes wines that are highly rated by Australian and international publications, and we think that he is making some of the best Rieslings in Australia. His partner, Stephanie Toole, is the owner and winemaker at Mount Horrocks, the neighboring winery. Grosset Springvale Riesling 2010 is very pale yellow, almost clear in the glass. It offers white floral, stone fruit, lime, and lemon notes in the bouquet and great focus in the mouth. It has an elegant finish with pronounced minerality. Grosset Off-dry Riesling was first released in 2010 and only 1,200 cases were made. It is pale straw, with light floral aromas, white stone fruits, and lavender. There is a touch of sweetness in the mouth, but it's combined with a tight grip of acidity. The finish is taught, complex, and crisp with a faint hint of sweetness. Grosset Pinot Noir 2009 is cherry red in color, with aromas of fruits of the wood, raspberries, red cherry, cocoa powder, and a whiff of confectioners' sugar. It is elegant and fruit-forward with a soft, velvety smooth finish. We both agree that this is one kick-ass Pinot Noir!

JIM BARRY WINES

Craig Hill Road, Clare,
+61 8 8842 2261
www.jimbarry.com

Jim Barry, the first qualified winemaker to work in the Clare Valley, started Jim Barry Wines with his wife, Nancy, in 1959. Jim Barry Wines, the home of such esteemed labels as The Armagh Shiraz, The McRae Wood Shiraz, The Florita Riesling, and The Cover Drive Cabernet Sauvignon, is now run by Jim's son,

Peter Barry; his wife, Susan; and their children—although Nancy still keeps a watchful eye on them all. Grapes for Jim Barry wines are sourced from estate-owned vineyards at four different locations in the Clare Valley, plus a Cabernet Sauvignon vineyard in Coonawarra. Jim Barry The Lodge Hill Dry Riesling 2010 is almost clear in the glass. Lime sorbet and lemongrass dominate both the nose and the palate, although in the mouth this bone dry, crisp wine is joined by fragrant touches of orange blossom. Jim Barry The Benbournie Cabernet Sauvignon 2004 is inky black cherry to the eye and exhibits aromas of blueberry and jalapeño pepper. Plush tannins support intense flavors of black cherry, cassis, spice, and jalapeño. Jim Barry The Armagh Shiraz 2006 is deep red violet, with fragrances of blueberry, vanilla, and paprika. Expressive flavors of cassis, blueberry preserves, and stewed prunes are enhanced by hints of truffle and summer farm stand.

KILIKANOON

Penna Lane, Penwortham via Clare,
+61 8 8843 4206,
www.kilikanoon.com.au

Owner and winemaker Kevin Mitchell was born in the Clare Valley and has worked at various other wineries. His relatives were

dairy farmers in the 1950s, and in the 1970s, his grandfather started planting vines on their sloped land. The name Kilikanoon is from a Celtic word meaning "nut grove on a slope." Mitchell acquired the winery in 1997 and now produces 500,000 bottles per year. We visited Kevin and tasted a few of his wines, and he told us, "The fact that my wine comes from the region in which I was born, means that I want to make wines that are expressive of the *terroir*. Our reds in Clare are bigger than many other Australian regions—I prefer a bigger wine, a wine that is more generous." Kilikanoon Killerman's Run Shiraz is named after a local hermit who played the banjo and made his own wine. "His friendly ghost still visits the vineyard, and if you listen real close, you can still hear the banjo," Mitchell reckons. Killerman's Run 2009 is garnet red color, with notes of red fruit and leather on the nose. In the mouth, flavors of dark fruits, black raspberries, chocolate, and black plums dance on

your tongue, before an apparition of mocha appears on your back palate. Kilikanoon Covenant Shiraz 2008 is reddish-purple in color. Its notes of licorice, black plum, and anise invite you into the glass to explore more about this wine. It is big, but there are restrained fruit flavors in the mid palate, cooling herbs and mint notes in the finish—and taut gripping tannins. Kilikanoon Oracle Shiraz 2008 is a brilliant purple color, with aromas of cooling spices, currants, coffee, dark chocolate, and stewed fruits. This is a big wine that coats the inside of your mouth and has strong, yet elegant, tannins in the finish.

MOUNT HORROCKS

Old Railway Station, Curling Street, Auburn,
+61 8 8849 2202,
www.mounthorrocks.com

Winemaker and owner Stephanie Toole makes delicious boutique wines from her estate-grown grapes in the Clare Valley. She purposefully limits her production to 4,500 cases per year to achieve single-vineyard wines of the highest quality. Mount Horrocks Watervale Riesling 2010 is pale yellow and has aromas of lemon blossoms and a fair bit of minerality. It is crisp and clear in the mouth with a beautiful finish. Mount Horrocks Clare Valley Cabernet Sauvignon 2009 is ruby red, with notes of green pepper, almost jalapeño, in the bouquet. There is nice spiciness that tickles the nose overlying a black cherry backbone. On the palate black cherry and jalapeño come to life moments before the peppery finish.

TAYLORS/WAKEFIELD

Taylors Road, Auburn,
+61 4 0445 6249,
www.wakefieldwines.com

Established in 1969, Bill Taylor Senior and his sons, John and Bill, purchased 178 hectares (440 acres) of land near the Wakefield River in the Auburn area of the Clare Valley. In 1973, they nervously entered their first wine competition and walked away with the trophy for the best red wine in the show. In the last four years they have won eleven trophies in competitions around the world. The company is known as Taylors in Australia and as Wakefield in the US and UK markets. Winemaker Adam Eggins, who has been with the company for 10 years, led us through a tasting of Taylors wines. Taylors Wakefield St Andrews Riesling 2010 is straw colored, with lifted aromas of lime and tropical fruits. It has rich mouthfeel and seamlessly blends fruity acidity and creamy texture. Taylors Wakefield Sauvignon Blanc 2009 is pale yellow, with aromas of passionfruit, guava, sweet Cavaillon melon, and jasmine. In the mouth it's crisp, but with rounded edges and a balanced acidic finish. Taylors Wakefield St Andrews Cabernet Sauvignon 2006 is inky purple with a violet rim. It has notes of cherry cola, cigar box, spicy pepper, and freshly ground white and black pepper. It has an elegant finish of fine and persistent tannins with a touch of candied violet flowers post palate.

TIM ADAMS

Warenda Road, Clare,
+61 8 8842 2429,
www.timadamswines.com.au

Tim Adams and his wife, Pam, started Tim Adams Wines in 1987. Tim is still the chief winemaker, and Pam, who was working as a registered midwife when she and Tim met, is the general manager. Grapes come from 12 different sites throughout the Clare Valley, some estate-owned and others owned by valued friends. Varieties include Grenache, Shiraz, Sémillon, Cabernet Sauvignon, Riesling,

Pinot Gris, Tempranillo, and Malbec. Tim Adams Reserve Riesling 2008 exhibits bright fragrances of lemon and grapefruit. On the palate full mouthfeel and invigorating acidity set the stage for flavors of mixed citrus fruits and a subtle hint of floral spice. Tim Adams The Aberfeldy Shiraz 2008, from a single vineyard of vines dating back to 1904, is brilliant violet red in the glass and gives off aromas of cherry, mocha, and Christmas baking spices. Flavors of cherry, black plum, Chinese five-spice powder, and butterscotch are suspended within soft-grained tannins.

COONAWARRA

Part of the Limestone Coast zone, Coonawarra is in the far southeast of the state of South Australia, 96 kilometers (60 miles) from the ocean and close to the border between South Australia and Victoria. The red earth of Coonawarra and regular cloud cover offer the region's Cabernet Sauvignon, Riesling, Shiraz, and Chardonnay vines blessed conditions for ripening. Home to almost forty wineries, Coonawarra's vineyards blanket a total of 6,110 hectares (15,098 acres). Elevations are low, at an average of 60 meters, or just shy of 200 feet, above sea level. Average rainfall between April and October is 220 millimeters, or 8.5 inches. The region is renowned for its distinctive red soils.

BALNAVES OF COONAWARRA

Main Road, Coonawarra,
+61 8 8737 2946,
www.balnaves.com.au

Doug and Annette Balnaves created their first six vintages at a neighbor's facility before building their own winery, with its distinctive bell tower, in time for the 1996 vintage. This is a family affair with adult children Kirsty and Pete also on hand; all four of the Balnaves family work alongside winemaker Peter Bissell. From the original 5 hectares (12 acres), Balnaves now has 56 hectares (138 acres) of prime Coonawarra terra rossa soil. Balnaves of Coonawarra Chardonnay 2009 is pale straw to the eye. The nose reveals aromas of white peach, lime, and toasted almonds. In the mouth, fresh flavors of lemon sorbet and tangerine zest combine with notes of fruitcake; the creamy mouthfeel benefits from a spray of acidity. Balnaves of Coonawarra Shiraz 2008 exudes fragrances of black cherry and blackberry with a pinch of black pepper.

Ripe flavors of cherry, blackberry, white chocolate, and floral spice are nestled within smooth tannins.

BOWEN ESTATE

Riddoch Highway, Coonawarra,
+61 8 8737 2229,
www.bowenestate.com.au

Doug and Joy Bowen have been in the wine business for 35 years, and daughter Emma has now joined her parents in creating small-batch, handcrafted Chardonnay, Shiraz, and Cabernet Sauvignon from their 33 hectares (82 acres) of red Coonawarra earth. Bowen Estate Chardonnay 2010 bears aromas of honeydew melon and white peach, which carry over onto the palate. Good mouthfeel and zesty acidity work toward a rounded finish. Bowen Estate

Shiraz 2009 is red violet to the eye. On the nose blackberry and clove dominate, while in the mouth berries and Damson plum interweave with toasted vanilla and baking spices on a bed of mouth-pleasing tannins.

MAJELLA

Lynn Road, Coonawarra,
+61 8 8736 3055,
www.majellawines.com.au

The Lynn family has a long-standing presence in Coonawarra, having morphed over time from shopkeepers to sheep farmers to grape growers and then to winemakers. In 1960, George Lynn bought the property from his uncle Frank and, along with family member Brian Lynn and friend Eric Brand, planted 2.5 hectares (6 acres) of Shiraz. They have added Cabernet Sauvignon and Riesling, and vineyard holdings now total 60 hectares (148 acres). For many years they were a major supplier of grapes to neighboring Wynns Coonawarra Estate. Brothers Brian and Tony Lynn run the company; their winery was built in 1996, and it is under the talented direction of winemaker Bruce Gregory. Majella Shiraz 2008 is deep red violet to the eye. On the nose soft berry fruit hides behind chocolate, coffee, and cigar box aromas. The palate is just the opposite—rich cherry and blackberry dominate, with background notes of espresso and crème brûlée, making their presence known among soft tannins. The finish shows excellent persistence. Majella Cabernet Sauvignon 2008, deep garnet in the glass, exhibits aromas of black cherry, blackberry, and cooling herbs. Flavors of cherry, blackberry, and vanilla are accented by a pinch of clove through the long, smooth finish.

PARKER COONAWARRA ESTATE

Riddoch Highway, Coonawarra,
+61 8 8737 3525,
www.parkercoonawarraestate.com.au

From their first award-winning vintage in 1988, John and Fay Parker made their mark on Coonawarra. Now Parker Coonawarra Estate is a member of the Rathbone family of wineries, with Peter Bissell and Darren Rathbone as winemakers. It may just be coincidence, but Parker Coonawarra wines receive consistently high marks from the other Parker, Robert. Parker Coonawarra Estate Terra Rossa First Growth 2006, a Cabernet Sauvignon-Merlot blend, is red violet in the glass with a brighter red rim. The seductive fragrance of wild blackberries and raspberries tossed with truffles and spice only hint at the sophisticated palate of berries, anise, and lightly smoked meat, all encased in gorgeous tannins.

WYNNS COONAWARRA ESTATE

Memorial Drive, Coonawarra,
+61 8 8736 2225,
www.wynns.com.au

With a history spanning 150 years, Wynns Coonawarra Estate traces its heritage to John Riddoch, who in the 1860s raised sheep on more than 700 square kilometers (270 square miles) of farmland. Riddoch subsequently divided 800 hectares (1,977 acres) of Coonawarra land into smaller plots in 1890, selling them off to farmers—who planted fruit trees and grapevines. Samuel Wynn purchased Riddoch's winery and vineyards in 1951, 50 years after Riddoch's death. At present, Wynns Coonawarra Estate is the largest single vineyard holder in the region. Vines are under the management of Allen Jenkins, and estate grown Cabernet Sauvignon, Shiraz, Merlot, Chardonnay, and Riesling are crafted into highly regarded wines by famed winemakers Sue Hodder, Sarah Pidgeon, and Luke Skeer. Wynns Coonawarra Estate Michael Shiraz 2005 is inky red violet. Aromas of blueberry, fresh cracked pepper, and Mediterranean herbs prepare the palate for the rich taste of raspberry and blueberry preserves, with notes of vanilla and clove. Wynns Coonawarra Estate John Riddoch Cabernet Sauvignon 2006 is dark ruby to the eye. The nose is filled with intense blackberry and cassis melded with mocha and cooling herbs. In the mouth, dark berry flavors combine with white chocolate, light spice, and forest floor, all enveloped in luxurious tannins.

EDEN VALLEY

The Barossa Valley's next-door neighbor—and part of the Barossa zone—the Eden Valley is famous for some of Australia's most elegant examples of Riesling and Shiraz. Thanks to high altitudes (compared to the Barossa Valley), with vineyards ranging between 380 and 550 meters (1,250 to 1,800 feet) above sea level, the Eden Valley's cool climate assists in the slow ripening of these two varieties, as well as premium Chardonnay and Cabernet Sauvignon. As with the Barossa Valley, the Eden Valley was settled by the Silesians in the 1840s. A good portion of the Eden Valley's 1,978 hectares (4,888 acres) of vineyards and twenty-plus wineries are still tended and operated by the fifth- and-sixth generation family members of the immigrant pioneers. Gently sloping hills and vales are given an average 280 millimeters, or 11 inches, of rain each spring and summer.

HENSCHKE

Henschke Road, Keyneton,
+61 8 8564 8223,
www.henschke.com.au

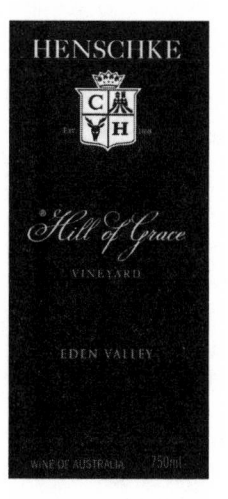

Regarded as one of the finest producers of red wine in Australia, Henschke is best known for its iconic red Hill of Grace Shiraz, named for its vineyard in front of the Gnadenberg Church. The Henschke family continues to provide wine for Communion—an empty jug left on the winery porch signifies the need for a refill. We had the privilege of walking among the vines and visiting the angelic tombstones carved by winemaker Stephen Henschke's great uncle, Julius Henschke. The Henschke family emigrated in 1841 from a German town that is now within the borders of Poland. Henschke winery remains a family-run business with fifth-generation Stephen Henschke in charge of the winemaking and his wife, Prue, in charge of the vineyards. They remarked that there were five or six winemaking families in 1841 and theirs is the only one remaining. Henschke is a traditional yet modern family winery; they were the first in Australia to have the Vino-Lok glass stopper bottling system, and much of their estate vineyards are farmed biodynamically. Henschke Hill of Grace Single Vineyard 2006 is 100 percent Shiraz and dark garnet colored with a violet rim. It has aromas of dried eucalyptus, sage, cooling herbs, and Christmas baking spices, lifted over deep blackberry and black plum fruit notes. In the mouth it is fresh, elegant, velvety, and—dare we say it—heavenly. Hill of Grace Shiraz is made from 145-year-old vines, and there is naturally only a limited quantity of numbered bottles made each year. We apologize that you won't be able to find bottle number 9555 from 2006. Henschke Keyneton Euphonium 2008 is a blend of 75 percent Shiraz, 11 percent Cabernet Sauvignon, 8 percent Merlot, and 6 percent Cabernet Franc. It is ruby red in color with a violet rim. It smells and tastes of black and red fruits, explodes with strong yet gentle tannins, and has an elegant prolonged finish.

PEWSEY VALE

Eden Valley Road, Angaston,
+61 8 8561 3200,
www.pewseyvale.com

In 1839, Joseph Gilbert boarded a ship from his hometown Wiltshire's Vale of Pewsey in England, sailed to South Australia, and acquired 6,070 hectares (15,000 acres) of land. He planted Riesling, Gewürztraminer, and Pinot Gris vines and established Pewsey Vale. We visited with the immensely likable, straight-shooting winemaker and communications director, Jane Ferrari, who works for Yalumba and Pewsey Vale. Ferrari explained, "The soil at the top of the hill comes from the igneous extrusion of erupted lava, and it is a perfect medium to grow Riesling and Chardonnay." Pewsey Vale Eden Valley Riesling 2010 is pale straw colored, with lemon-lime aromas and an explosion of citrus in your mouth. This is one

Riesling that would pair perfectly with oysters. Pewsey Vale Museum Reserve The Contours Riesling 2005 is medium straw colored, with aromas of toasted bread slathered with orange marmalade. It has balanced acidity and a tight finish. Pewsey Vale Museum Reserve The Contours Riesling 1999 is straw colored, with aromas of toasted brioche, apricot marmalade, and dried yellow peach. It is generous in the mouth with a pleasant finish. Ferrari handed us the unfinished bottle and told us to pair it with (local restaurant) Vintners Bar and Grill's sautéed scallops with dried shrimp and pork chili relish. A smart man would never say no to Ferrari, and she was absolutely correct—it was a perfect pairing.

LANGHORNE CREEK

One of Australia's oldest wine regions, viticulture began on the river flat delta of the Langhorne Creek region in 1860. It's now home to 6,053 hectares (14,957 acres) of vineyards and about thirty wineries, noted mainly for Cabernet Sauvignon and Shiraz. Deep sandy loam soils, at altitudes of 30 meters, or about 100 feet, are moistened during the winter using the age-old practice of flood irrigation prior to the growing season. This supplements the small amount of rain that falls mainly in the spring, averaging about 140 millimeters, or 5.5 inches, annually.

BLEASDALE

Wellington Road, Langhorne Creek,
+61 8 8537 3001,
www.bleasdale.com.au

This is one of the oldest family-owned wineries in Australia. Bleasdale owes its existence to sailor Frank Potts' exploration of Langhorne Creek in the 1850s. Five generations of his family have since weathered many changes in the world at large and in the wine drinking preferences of consumers at home and in the international market. A wide range of highly regarded fortified wines is still made here, as are sparkling Shiraz and delicious dry wines crafted from estate-grown Shiraz, Malbec, Cabernet Sauvignon, Verdelho, Riesling, and Chardonnay. Its historic tasting room, an hour from Adelaide, is like a trip back in winemaking history. Bleasdale Potts Catch Verdelho 2010 has a brilliant nose of honeydew melon and spiced peach, opening on the palate to melon and stone fruits with a hint of honeysuckle and vanilla. Bleasdale Generations Shiraz 2008, inky red violet to the eye, gives off aromas of blackberry, anisette, and white pepper. In the mouth, powerful berry, cassis, and baking spices coalesce in a soothing labyrinth of fine-grained tannins.

BREMERTON

Strathalbyn Road, Langhorne Creek,
+61 8 8537 3093,
www.bremerton.com.au

Bremerton Lodge Homestead was built in 1866, and in 1985 Craig and Mignonne Willson turned this historic dairy farm into Bremerton vineyards and winery. They renovated, planted, and began making wine, but in 1992 a flood wiped out their buildings and vineyards. They were not to be beaten so easily. In 1994 they renovated the 1866 barn, which is to this day their cellar door, and a new winery was completed in 2002. Winemaker Rebecca Willson and her sister Lucy took over the running of the business in 2004; they are the driving force behind the family's award-winning Shiraz, Chardonnay, and Cabernet Sauvignon. Bremerton Reserve Chardonnay 2009 gives off scents of lemon and toasted almond. In the mouth, flavors of peach, apricot, lemon, and toast are nicely suspended between complex mouthfeel and racy acidity. Bremerton Reserve Cabernet 2007 is 100 percent Cabernet Sauvignon. Deep ruby red in the glass, it offers a nose of blackberry and portabello mushroom. On the palate blackberry is joined by earth, mocha, and a pinch of cinnamon, all encased in velvety tannins.

MCLAREN VALE

Undulating hills covered with grapevines, a collection of top-notch wineries, and a vibrant wine tourism industry combine to make McLaren Vale a wine lover's dream. Only a short drive from Adelaide and ensconced between the Mount Lofty Ranges and the Gulf of St Vincent, this world-renowned wine region and its 6,636 hectares (16,400 acres) of vineyards offer both rocky coastline and some of the greenest land in South Australia. Over 110 wineries grow Shiraz, Cabernet Sauvignon, Grenache, Sémillon, and Chardonnay in a variety of sites cooled by breezes from the nearby Indian Ocean. As one would anticipate in an area situated between the mountains and the sea, there is a broad array of soil types, including brown sandy loam, gray loamy sand with clay and lime subsoil, and areas of red and black loam. All are appropriate for grape growing. Altitudes vary between 50 meters (165 feet) above sea level closest to the coast and 200 meters (660 feet) toward the Mount Lofty foothills. Between October and April the average rainfall is 180 millimeters, or 7 inches, of rainfall.

CHAPEL HILL

Corner of Chapel Hill and Chaffeys Roads,
McLaren Vale,
+61 8 8323 8429,
www.chapelhillwine.com.au

Chapel Hill has been through many changes over the years. It began life in 1865, as the Christian Bible Church, which fell into disrepair in the 1960s and was restored in the 1970s after being purchased by Professor Tom Nelson. He started Chapel Hill Winery in 1973; it has changed hands three times since. A new winery capable of producing 80,000 cases per year was built in 1994, and in 2000 the Swiss Schmidheiny family, who also own wineries in Argentina and Napa Valley, acquired Chapel Hill and its vineyards. Chief winemaker Michael Fragos came aboard in 2004. Day-to-day winemaking operations are under the command of Bryn Richards, who, besides working elsewhere in Australia, has experience in New Zealand, England, Portugal, and the United States. The engaging Richards met us for dinner at the nearby Victory Hotel and spoke with us about his commitment to the environment and sustainable winemaking—as we tasted through his current releases. Chapel Hill Unwooded Chardonnay 2010 is almost clear to the eye and exhibits aromas of citrus with a pinch of oregano. On the palate its sharp minerality plays against flavors of grapefruit, lemon zest, and Mediterranean herbs. Chapel Hill Bush Vine Grenache 2009 is cherry red in the glass, which when held to the nose exudes black cherry and vanilla notes. Its muscular tannin structure holds beautiful flavors of cassis, blueberry, licorice root, and violets. Chapel Hill The Chosen Gorge Block McLaren Vale Cabernet Sauvignon 2009 is inky black cherry in color with a violet rim. A nose of black cherry, cocoa powder, and confectioners' sugar only hints at an opulent, tannin-drenched palate of ripe cherry, chocolate-covered espresso bean, and Thai basil.

D'ARENBERG

Osborn Road, McLaren Vale,
+61 8 8329 4888,
www.darenberg.com.au

When you arrive at d'Arenberg, its size reminds you of a dairy or factory—but the reality

is anything but. Joseph Osborn founded a 25-hectare (62-acre) grape farm here in 1912; his son Frank increased the family's holdings to 78 hectares (193 acres) and built a winery in 1928. His son, Francis Osborn d'Arenberg, started his own label, d'Arenberg, in 1959 in honor of his mother. Fourth-generation winemaker Chester d'Arenberg preserves old-fashioned winemaking techniques such as foot-treading, open-topped fermenting, and gentle basket pressing to create exquisite wines with fun-loving names from his family's gnarly old vines. Curiously named wines include The Broken Fishplate, The Hermit Crab, The Lucky Lizard, The Last Ditch, The Daddy Longlegs, and The Dead Arm, the latter name derived from vines affected by a fungal disease that shrivels one "arm" of the vine's base until it resembles petrified wood. On-site restaurant d'Arry's Verandah

looks out over a sea of vines and pastoral farmland. d'Arenberg The Dry Dam Riesling 2010 is very nearly clear and gives off aromas of lemongrass, orange blossom, and honeysuckle. In the mouth, flavors of lemon sorbet and jasmine are the first act to zippy acidity and a crisp, clean finish. d'Arenberg The Dead Arm Shiraz 2007 is deep red violet in color. A nose of black cherry and anise only hints at intense flavors of black cherry, fennel, violet, and white pepper showcased within a delicate equilibrium of smooth tannins and vivid acidity.

HARDYS

202 Main Road, McLaren Vale,
+61 8 8329 4124,
www.hardys.com.au

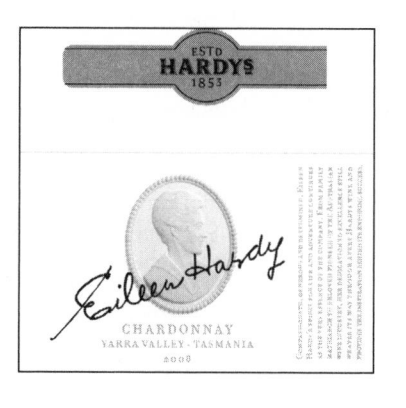

We met with the immensely likable and humble Bill Hardy at his Tintara Winery in

McLaren Vale. He is the great-great-grandson of founder Thomas Hardy, who established Hardys in 1853. He is a consummate story-teller, historian, and a man of great wit. Bill stated, "Hardys is currently the largest wine producer in Australia. We are also the most diverse wine company, because we have vine-yards in more wine regions than any other company. This makes it possible for us to source fruit from so many different areas so that we can make the best product for our customer." We've long been fans of Hardys wines, and our visit with Bill confirmed our fanaticism. Hardys Eileen Hardy Chardonnay 2008 is made from Chardonnay grapes grown in the Yarra Valley and Tasmania and is named for Bill's grandmother, Eileen, who was given the Order of the British Empire award in 1977 for her service to the wine industry. It is medium straw colored, with aromas of mango, white peaches, stone fruits, tropical fruits, and amazing top notes of soft vanilla and oak. It is creamy and fruity in the mouth with a lingering finish. Hardys Stamp Shiraz 2009 is ruby red and is a great fruit-forward Shiraz. Put some steaks on the barbie, and open a few bottles. Hardys Nottage Hill Chardonnay 2010 is named for Bill's uncle. It is a great Chardonnay with aromas of stone fruits and citrus flowers. It has refreshing acidity and a long finish.

KANGARILLA ROAD

Hamilton Road, McLaren Flat,
+61 8 8383 0533,
www.kangarillaroad.com.au

A winemaker with more than 20 years expe-rience, Kevin O'Brien and his wife, Helen, started Kangarilla Road in 1997. Many of its 12 hectares (30 acres) of vines are more than 20 years old, and Kevin's skill as a winemaker shows through in the estate's highly regarded wines. With a background in public relations, promotions, and fashion, Helen's sensibilities are reflected in the beautiful black-and-white labels, which feature a single leaf of the grape variety contained within the bottle. The winery's name comes from the name of the road that leads to the small local village of Kangarilla, which in turn takes its name from an Aboriginal word referring to an "abundance of local resources." With equal amounts of knowledge and congeniality, Kevin presented his wines to us over a long, enjoyable dinner in McLaren Vale. Kangarilla Road Black St Peters McLaren Vale Zinfandel 2009 is rich black cherry in the glass, with aromas of fruits of the wood and capsicum. Opulent flavors of fresh black cherry, blackberry, butterscotch, and five-spice powder lay the groundwork for strapping tannins and a powerful finish. Kangarilla Road McLaren Vale Cabernet Sauvignon 2009 is deep red violet in color, and its bouquet features notes of cassis and black raspberry. A delectable palate of cassis, stewed prunes, pickled jalapeño, oregano, thyme, and sage is accompanied by luscious tannins and an enduring finish. Kangarilla Road Q Shiraz 2007, a single-vineyard offering, is blue black to the eye. Its nose reveals scents of three berry preserves with a suggestion of hot pepper. Its rich mouthfeel and flavors of blueberry, black pepper, capsicum, and vanilla lead into an elegant, rewarding finish.

KAY BROTHERS

Kays Road, McLaren Vale,
+61 8 8323 8201,
www.kaybrothersamerywines.com

Herbert and Fredrick Kay bought the plot that became the Amery Vineyard in 1891 and within 18 months cuttings of Cabernet Sauvignon, Malbec, Hermitage, and Riesling had gone into the ground. By 1895, they had planted 40 hectares (99 acres) and built a winery, which remains the province of winemaker Colin Kay. Colin works alongside winemaker Andy Coppard and vineyard manager Waz Oakley, who cares for vineyards still growing many of the original vines. Kay Brothers Amery Vineyards Block 6 Shiraz 2008 is lustrous dark purple, with fragrances of cassis, blueberry, cracked pepper, and portabello mushroom. Complex flavors of cassis, damson plum, chocolate-covered espresso bean, and anisette arranged among luscious tannins pave the way for a prolonged finish.

MITOLO

Corner of Johns and Angle Vale Roads, Virginia,
+61 1300 571 233,
www.mitolowines.com.au

A love of food and wine comes naturally to Italian-Australian Frank Mitolo, who founded Mitolo Wines in 1999. He and business partner and winemaker Ben Glaetzer produce the Jester range, which offers a good value-to-price ratio, and the Mitolo series from vineyards in McLaren Vale and the Barossa Valley. Mitolo Serpico Cabernet Sauvignon 2007 is a rule-breaker, much like the New York City police officer it is named in honor of. Restrained fruits of the wood take a back seat to complex spice, cracked pepper, and smoked meat; a rigid tannic spine supports lush layers of flavor. Mitolo Savitar Shiraz 2007 is inky, dark purple and exudes fragrances of black currant, cherry, portabello mushroom, and fresh ground pepper. These carry over to the palate as well, where a healthy dose of tannin and complex mouthfeel culminate in a superb finish.

MOLLYDOOKER WINES

Coppermine Road, McLaren Vale,
+61 8 8323 6500,
www.mollydookerwines.com

Sarah and Sparky Marquis, both progeny of winemaking families, met at university and began writing their own history. They started out growing grapes and crafting wines for friends in the business, and by 2006, when they founded Mollydooker—Aussie slang for "left-handed"—they had worked at five highly praised wineries. Using the produce of their own three vineyards, and fruit sourced from trusted friends, they today produce 60,000 cases per year of some of the highest scoring wines in the country under the Mollydooker label. Their irreverent, fun-loving spirit belies the quality of wines they produce. The wines bear names such as Gigglepot, Blue Eyed Boy, Enchanted Path, Carnival of Love, and The Scooter. Sarah and Sparky have developed and trademarked the Marquis Fruit Weight Scale; they use it to determine which wine each particular parcel of grapes should go into. Mollydooker Velvet Glove Shiraz 2009 is aptly named; it possesses both powerful tannins and velvety smoothness, which enfold extravagant flavors of blueberry, black currant, and a complex mix of spices pinched from Grandma's pantry. There is nothing funny about Mollydooker Gigglepot Cabernet Sauvignon 2009; from its deep violet red color to its rich nose of cassis and mint, through its bold tannic structure and tastes of black cherry, dried currants, and mocha, this is a wine which you will take very seriously, even as a satisfied smile spreads over your lips.

PRIMO ESTATE

McMurtrie Road, McLaren Vale,
+61 8 8323 6800,
www.primoestate.com.au

In 1953, Primo Grilli emigrated to Australia from the Le Marche region of Italy. In 1973 he planted his first grapevines in Australia. His eldest son, Joseph—who now runs the winery with his wife, Dina—studied enology at Roseworthy College. He graduated in 1979, the same year the Primo Estate winery was built. Combining New World ingenuity with Italian winemaking techniques, Joe Grilli quickly became known for his outstanding wines. Primo Estate's 37 hectares (91 acres) of vineyards, almost evenly divided between McLaren Vale and Adelaide Plains, are home to Shiraz, Merlot, Cabernet Sauvignon, Pinot Grigio, and Nebbiolo. It was one of the first Australian wineries to produce olive oil, and in addition to the high marks received for its Primo Estate and JOSEPH dry wines, it is well known for sparkling red and botrytized sweet wine. A beautiful modern winery and tasting center were constructed in 2006. JOSEPH Angel Gully Shiraz 2008 is deep purple, with aromas of blueberry, blackberry, and spiced herbs. On the palate it shows flavors of berries with black pepper and jalapeño, which all coalesce in a long, mineral-rich finish. JOSEPH Moda Cabernet Sauvignon Merlot 2008 is inky black cherry in the glass, with a tantalizing nose of berry preserve, cassis, tobacco, and spice. Lavish layers of fruit intertwined with clove, licorice, chocolate, vanilla, and earth are encased in gorgeous tannins.

SPRING SEED WINE COMPANY

Gaffney Road, Willunga,
+61 8 8556 2441,
www.springseedwineco.com.au

Peter and Anthea Bosworth first planted vines in the early 1970s, and now their Spring Seed Wine Company is in the hands of their son Joch, who is the viticulturist and winemaker, and his partner, Louise Hemsley-Smith, who takes charge of both marketing and their two young daughters, Celia and Peggy. Brightly colored labels bearing images from antique seed catalogs grace single-vineyard bottlings of Shiraz, Cabernet Sauvignon, Chardonnay, Viognier, Sauvignon Blanc, and Mourvèdre, from their 28 hectares (69 acres) of organically certified vineyards. Joch and Louise also head up the Battle of Bosworth brand. We had the pleasure of tasting their well-crafted range with Louise at the nearby Victory Hotel—its sweeping views of the Gulf St. Vincent were eclipsed by her wonderful personality and delicious wines. Spring Seed Wine Company Four O'Clock Chardonnay 2010 is a crisp, clean riot of fruit. Light yellow in the glass with a bright rim, its nose of lemon and lime opens to include peach, apricot, and an inkling of spice blessed with racy acidity. Spring Seed Wine Company Scarlet Runner Shiraz 2010 is run through with black cherry—you will note it in the color, fragrance, and taste. On the nose it is accompanied by delicate vanilla and punchy black pepper, and in the mouth blueberry and licorice play their parts, leading up to a long, bright, and spicy finish. Battle of Bosworth Preservative Free Shiraz 2010 is like a fresh slice of blueberry pie. Bright red violet to the eye, it has a vibrant nose of fruit, while on the palate blueberry and vanilla flavors duke it out for the number one spot.

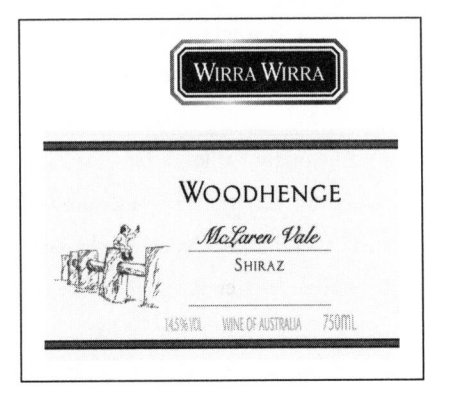

WIRRA WIRRA

McMurtrie Road, McLaren Vale,
+61 8 8323 8414,
www.wirrawirra.com

When you drive through the large wooden structure called "Woodhenge" and see an enormous wooden catapult near the front door, you know that you're in for a different winery experience. We met with two friendly blokes, Andrew Kay, managing director, and Paul Smith, winemaker, for a tour and tasting of Wirra Wirra. They told us the name Wirra Wirra is aboriginal for "between the gum trees." They recounted the winery's history between sips of their delicious wines. The original 1800s winery was rebuilt in 1969 by Richard Gregory Trott, who was considered "part crazy, part maverick, and part visionary." He liked to load up his catapult with wine bottles (sometimes full and sometimes empty,) rocks, or whatever was available and shoot it in the direction of his neighbor's property. Smith added, "Wirra Wirra has a long history of taking wine seriously but having fun at the same time." Wirra Wirra Scrubby Rise 2009 is a blend of 50 percent Shiraz, 35 percent Cabernet Sauvignon, and 15 percent Petit Verdot. It's named for an imaginary hill in front of the winery. Smith said, "This is another one of Trott's jokes, because there is no hill anywhere near the winery." It is dark purple in the glass, with notes of dark fruits, blackberries, and black plums, with touches of coconut and vanilla in an oak frame. It's big and bold in the mouth with soft balanced tannins. Wirra Wirra Catapult 2007, ingeniously named after Trott's weapon of war, is a blend of 95 percent Shiraz and 5 percent Viognier. It is ruby garnet in color with vibrant yet restrained dark fruit notes. There is a touch of violet floral perfume as a top note. On the palate it is elegant with balanced tannins. Wirra Wirra Woodhenge Shiraz 2006 has aromas of black fruits, dark fruit jam, cocoa, dark choco-late, and anise. In the mouth the flavors of fruit come out followed by espresso and licorice in the post palate.

RIVERLAND

Riverland was Australia's largest region planted with grapes until it was overtaken by Riverina, in New South Wales, in 2010. The Riverland has a total of 20,402 hectares (50,414 acres) under vine. The vineyards follow the banks of the Murray River and are set against a dramatic background of limestone cliffs. For such a large region, there are very few winer-ies—about twenty—though there are over thirteen hundred individual grape farmers, who sell their fruit to some of the biggest names in Australian wine, including Pernod

Ricard, Hardys, and Australian Vintage. In recent years, some smaller-scale wineries have sprung up in the valley, creating a complex mix of vineyard sizes and winemaking styles. Chardonnay is the number one grape in the region—and indeed, plantings of this variety outnumber plantings of Chardonnay in all the other regions of South Australia combined. Other grapes grown here are Shiraz, Cabernet Sauvignon, and Merlot, although many other varieties crop up each season. The continental climate is characterized by hot, sunny days and cool nights. Lower river valley soils are sandy loam over clay, while higher slopes feature sand over limestone and clay. Average altitudes are low in this river valley—about 20 meters (66 feet) above sea level. Rainfall in spring and summer averages 135 millimeters, or barely more than 5 inches.

WRATTONBULLY

Settled in 1842 and known for its Grade "A" lamb and beef for most of its history, this Limestone Coast region's first vines were planted in the 1960s, though it didn't really come to fame as a winemaking area until the 1990s. Terra rossa soils overlay limestone; its natural limestone Naracoorte Caves are a World Heritage site. Mineral-rich loam and clay provide nourishment for Cabernet Sauvignon, Shiraz, Merlot, Tempranillo, and more recently, Chardonnay. There are 2,832 hectares (6,998 acres) of these vines growing at elevations ranging between 75 and 150 meters (250 to 490 feet). Average growing-season rainfall is 210 millimeters, or a tad more than 8 inches.

TAPANAPPA

Piccadilly Road, Crafers, Wrattonbully,
+61 4 1984 3751,
www.tapanappawines.com.au

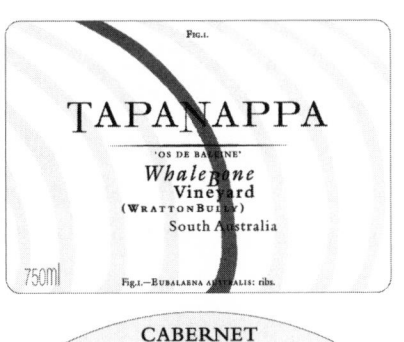

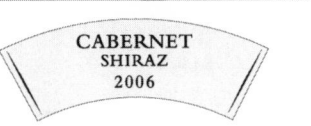

Famed Australian *"terroir-ist"* Brian Croser, the founder of Adelaide Hills' Petaluma Winery and Argyle in Oregon, teamed up with two esteemed names in the world of French wine, Bordeaux's Cazes family and Champagne's Bollinger family. Their goal is to craft exquisite, single-vineyard and regional wines from the finest sites. Their Whalebone

Vineyard in Wrattonbully is home to Cabernet Sauvignon, Merlot, Cabernet Franc, and Shiraz, while the Tiers Vineyard in Piccadilly Valley is planted with Chardonnay. On the Fleurieu Peninsula, Pinot Noir is grown on the Foggy Hill Vineyard. Tapanappa Whalebone Vineyard Cabernet Shiraz 2006 is a blend of 60 percent Cabernet Sauvignon, 30 percent Shiraz, and 10 percent Cabernet Franc. It is deep red violet in color and emits aromas of blackberry, blueberry, eucalyptus, and black truffle. On the tongue the silky tannins are a satisfying base for flavors of blackberry, black cherry, licorice, cedar, black pepper, and a trace of violet. Tapanappa Tiers Vineyard Chardonnay 2008 gives off scents of stone fruits and honeydew with a whiff of buttered toast. In the mouth, peach and melon play host to almond paste and pastry crust in an intricate dance of creamy mouthfeel and exhilarating acidity.

VICTORIA

In the southeast corner of Australia, Victoria is the smallest mainland state (the island state of Tasmania is smaller) and is also the most densely populated. Seventy-five percent of Victoria's inhabitants live in the cosmopolitan state capital, Melbourne. The state was first planted with grapevines in 1854 and was known for years for fortified wine and liqueur. It is divided into five large zones, each of which has multiple regions. The zones are Central Victoria, North East Victoria, North West Victoria, West Victoria, Port Phillip, and Gippsland. Central Victoria is comprised of Heathcote, Bendigo, Goulburn Valley, and Strathbogie Ranges. North East Victoria includes Alpine Valleys, Beechworth, King Valley, Glenrowan, and Rutherglen. North West Victoria is the third highest producing wine zone in all of Australia; it contains two regions, Swan Hill and Murray Darling. Murray Darling spreads north and straddles the border of New South Wales. Western Victoria's regions are Grampians, Henty, and Pyrenees, while Port Phillip, closest to Melbourne, is made up of the Yarra Valley, Macedon Ranges, Sunbury, Geelong, and Mornington Peninsula. Gippsland is a self-contained zone to the east of the state.

Although Victoria has more wineries—over six hundred—than any other wine-producing state, it ranks third in overall production, mainly due to the absence of large bulk-oriented growers. Total plantings in the state amount to 26,498 hectares (65,480 acres). Plantings of red wine grapes on 15,353 hectares (37,938 acres) outrank white plantings on 11,145 hectares (27,540 acres).

BEECHWORTH

The town of Beechworth, in northeast Victoria, was established in 1853 on the discovery of gold, and three years later the first vines were planted. The town of Beechworth is perched on a steep hillside, as are most of its 65 hectares (160 acres) of vines, which sit at altitudes ranging between 300 to 720 meters (985 to 2,360 feet). Viticulturists and winemakers at the ten wineries in the region generally use natural practices in the vineyards and handcraft wines using Chardonnay, Pinot Noir, Sauvignon Blanc, and Shiraz. Soils at the lowest altitudes are sandstone, mudstone, and shale transitioning to volcanic granite on the higher slopes. Pinot Noir thrives at the highest elevations, which provide the overnight coolness necessary for appropriate ripening. Average rainfall is 460 millimeters, or 18 inches, during the growing season. Limited water resources are a barrier to major viticultural expansion in the region.

SAVATERRE

929 Wangaratta Road, Beechworth,
+61 3 5727 0551,
www.savaterre.com

Owner and winemaker Keppell Smith was on a mission to find the perfect Australian *terroir*, and he seems to have found his spot close to the town of Beechworth. Using a combination of biodynamic and traditional French techniques, since 1996 he has applied his knowledge and love of wine to each handcrafted bottle of Pinot Noir and Chardonnay, with Shiraz expected to be released soon. Savaterre Chardonnay 2008 is a delightful contradiction. It is at once bright and crisp and also full of complex flavors. Aromas of lemon custard and summer herbs expand on the palate to flavors of grapefruit, nougat, and sliced pear, with a suggestion of toasted cashew.

BENDIGO

Central Victoria's Bendigo region became home to grapevines in 1855, during the height of the Victorian Gold Rush. Thirty wineries produce mostly Chardonnay, Shiraz, and Cabernet Sauvignon. Loamy sand and clay loam soils overlay stony clay; the mineral-poor soils by necessity produce low grape yields, leading to rich concentrations of flavor in the wines. Hot summers give up 267 millimeters, or 10.5 inches, of rain during the growing season. Vineyards are at altitudes ranging between 240 to 390 meters (790 to 1,280 feet). Total plantings in Bendigo are on 788 hectares (1,947 acres) of land.

BALGOWNIE ESTATE

Calder Highway, Bendigo,
+61 3 5449 6222,
www.balgownieestate.com.au

Stuart Anderson's 1969 vineyards were the first new vineyards planted in Bendigo in the twentieth century. He began with 2 hectares (5 acres) each of Cabernet Sauvignon and Shiraz. The estate was purchased by the Forrester brothers in 1999; they established a sister property of the same name in the Yarra Valley in 2002. Balgownie Estate now has 33 hectares (82 acres) of vineyards managed by John Monteath; winemaking in Bendigo is directed by Mark Lane. The Yarra Valley location offers a hotel, day spa, and restaurant, while the original Bendigo estate has a café and rental cottage onsite. Balgownie Estate Chardonnay 2009 exhibits aromas of white peach and honeydew with a touch of toasted almond. In the mouth, flavors of peach, melon, and citrus are joined by buttered toast and a splash of brightness on the finish. Balgownie Estate Shiraz 2008 is deep garnet in the glass, with a nose of blueberry, black cherry, and vanilla bean. On the palate, flavors of blueberry, blackberry, aniseed, and clove overlay a rich tannic structure, leading to a lingering finish.

PONDALOWIE

21 Wellsford Drive, Bendigo,
+61 3 5437 3332,
www.pondalowie.com.au

Husband and wife owner-winemakers Dominic and Krystina Morris decided to open their own winery on a visit to Pondalowie Bay, so they named their Bendigo vineyard and winery in honor of their place of inspiration. Pondalowie is planted mainly to Tempranillo, Shiraz, and Cabernet Sauvignon, with small amounts of Viognier and Malbec. The Morrises' combined experience in Australia, France, and Portugal is put to excellent use with a combination of modern and traditional vinification techniques. They are among a handful of Australian producers turning out Tempranillo to rival that of Rioja and Ribera del Duero. Pondalowie MT Tempranillo 2008 offers a nose of black cherry and blackberry with spice and Mediterranean herbs. In the mouth, fruit remains dominant, joined by pinches of both cooling and savory herbs; silky tannins and vivid acidity bring joy to the tongue.

GEELONG

Geelong has a divided winemaking history. Victoria's first commercial wines were made here by Swiss immigrants in 1845, but after phylloxera struck in the 1870s, it took almost a hundred years for Geelong to reenter the world of wine growing. Chardonnay is its mainstay, primarily as a still wine, but Pinot Noir is also a significant variety, and the two are being vinified into sparkling wines of exceptional quality. Cabernet Sauvignon and Shiraz are also among the varietals raised on Geelong's 526 hectares (1,300 acres) of vines. The ripening period is enhanced by the cooling effect of the waters of Port Phillip Bay and low rainfall during the spring and summer, averaging 250 millimeters, or slightly less than 10 inches. The main soil type is red clay loam over hard clay. Vineyard altitudes range from 20 to 150 meters (66 to 492 feet).

BY FARR

101 Kelly Lane, Bannockburn,
+61 3 5281 1979,
www.byfarr.com.au

Father and son winemakers Gary and Nick Farr have both worked vintages in California, Oregon, and Burgundy, and that experience shines through in both their limited release, estate-grown By Farr wines and their Farr Rising label. They work with Chardonnay, Viognier, Shiraz, and Pinot Noir; each of the three By Farr Pinot Noirs is produced from a single vineyard. By Farr Shiraz 2008 is deep red violet. Its nose of blackberry and blueberry is enhanced by white pepper and light floral notes. In the mouth, blackberry and blueberry continue; muscular tannins carry notes of cracked pepper and portabello mushroom through the sustained finish. By Farr Sangreal Pinot Noir 2008 is deep cherry in the glass, with a nose of cherry and red raspberry and with suggestions of white chocolate and Mediterranean herbs. Flavors of red berry carry over to the palate, interwoven with mocha, thyme, oregano, and earth encased in velvety tannins.

SCOTCHMANS HILL

190 Scotchmans Road, Drysdale,
+61 3 5251 3176,
www.scotchmanshill.com.au

David and Vivian Brown rescued an abandoned dairy farm on Mount Bellarine, an extinct volcano, in 1982. Since that time, they have grown to become the largest producer in Geelong. In addition to estate-grown fruit, its ten labels use grapes sourced from other regions and even from New Zealand. David and Vivian have been joined in the business by family members Matthew and Andrew Brown. Robin Brockett is both the chief viticulturist and winemaker. Varieties here include Shiraz, Pinot Noir, Riesling, Chardonnay, Cabernet Franc, Gewürztraminer, and Sauvignon Blanc. Scotchmans Hill Riesling 2009 exhibits

sublime aromas of lemon-lime and rose petal. On the palate citrus flavors are joined by nougat, baking spices, and precise minerality. Scotchmans Hill Shiraz 2008 is inky violet in the glass, with a nose of cherry, blackberry, licorice, and fresh ground pepper. In the mouth, robust ripe and dried berry flavors are accentuated by fennel, black pepper, and truffle, all wound in sturdy tannins.

GIPPSLAND

Covering a large area from the New South Wales border in the east to the Great Dividing Range in the west, Gippsland offers dramatic coastline and quaint green hills. It is home to more than fifty wineries, with the region's plantings totaling 253 hectares (625 acres). Although the first vineyards were planted here in the late nineteenth century, viniculture in the area dropped off around World War II and didn't make a comeback until the 1970s. It is divided into three subregions: South Gippsland, East Gippsland, and Gippsland West. Soils range from deep sandy loam to gravel and sandy loam. Rainfall between October and April—the growing season—averages between 420 and 530 millimeters, or 16.5 to 21 inches. Chardonnay and Pinot Noir are the staples of Gippsland grape production. Gippsland Pinot Noir is said to be among the finest Australia has to offer. Cabernet

Sauvignon and Merlot are also grown here, mainly for use in Bordeaux-style blends.

BASS PHILLIP

Tosch's Road, Leongatha,
+61 3 5664 3341,
www.bassphillip.com.au

Founder and winemaker Phillip Jones believes that great wine is made in the vineyard. His excellent Pinot Noirs—dead ringers for some of the best Burgundies—are the result of close-planted vines, low yields, no irrigation, and natural winemaking techniques (and no use of pumps or filters). Bass Phillip Estate Pinot Noir 2009 is vibrant cherry in the glass, with fragrant aromas of raspberry and herbes de Provence. On the palate raspberry is mated with wild cherry, white mushroom, aniseed, and fine-grained tannins—which quickly give way to an orange zest finish.

GOULBURN VALLEY

The first vineyards were planted here in 1860; today the Goulburn Valley is blanketed with 1,685 hectares (4,164 acres) of grapevines. It is home to 15 wineries, all with no lack of water—thanks to the Goulburn River, which along with many creeks and ponds, plus 250 millimeters, or 10 inches, of rain each growing season, irrigates the alluvial sandy soils of the region. The main grape grown here is Shiraz, supplemented by substantial plantings of Marsanne, Riesling, Cabernet Sauvignon, and Chardonnay. Vineyard altitudes range between 130 and 350 meters (425 to 1,150 feet). The Goulburn Valley has the highest number of hectares of Marsanne growing anywhere in the world. The Nagambie Lakes subregion is known for its high-quality wines.

MITCHELTON

Mitchellstown Road, Nagambie,
+61 3 5736 2221,
www.mitchelton.com.au

Mitchelton's vines were first planted in 1969, its first vintage was 1973, and its first award was in 1978, just four years after its winery and tower were built on a well-irrigated site on the Goulburn River. It is now part of the Lion Nathan group. Winemaker Travis Clydesdale "came home" to Mitchelton in 2010 after practically growing up on the property—his father worked here for almost 30 years. Viticulturist John Beresford works with the Rhône varietals Shiraz, Grenache, Mourvèdre, Marsanne, Roussanne, and Viognier, providing Travis with grapes for single varietals and blends. The Cursive brand includes three blends: two reds and a white. Mitchelton Shiraz 2007 is inky red violet to the eye and gives off fragrances of ripe black cherry, mocha, and clove. On the palate lavish tannins provide the background for cherry, cassis, chocolate-covered espresso bean, and penetrating spice. From the Cursive range, Mitchelton Airstrip 2007, a blend of 40 percent Marsanne and 30 percent each Roussanne and Viognier, is medium straw in the glass with flecks of gold. Tempting aromas of tropical fruits, rose petal, and lily bulb are an ample introduction to flavors of Clementine, passionfruit, and lemon curd—with a drop of rosewater—all contained in an elegant balance of texture and acidity.

TAHBILK

254 O'Neils Road, Nagambie,
+61 3 5794 2360,
www.tahbilk.com.au

A member of Australia's First Families of Wine, Tahbilk traces its roots to 1860 and founder John Phinney Bear's plan to plant one million grapevines on his 1,214 hectares (3,000 acres) of riverfront property. That goal has still not been reached—there are only 360,000 vines among the 200 hectares (494 acres) of land planted with vines here. These include red and white Rhône and Bordeaux varieties as well as Riesling, Chardonnay, Verdelho, Tempranillo, and Savignan. The original winery, which has since been joined by additional cellars and a

café, was completed in 1860. The Purbrick family purchased the property in 1925; chief winemaker Alister Purbrick has been at the helm since 1979. The balance of this beautiful property remains a popular wetlands and wild-life reserve. Tahbilk Viognier 2010 has a nose of juicy nectarine and jasmine; its weighty mouthfeel means that bright flavors of peach, lemon blossom, and Turkish delight linger on your taste buds for a few extra seconds until doused by a quick spray of brightness. Tahbilk Eric Stevens Purbrick Cabernet Sauvignon 2005 is deep black cherry. A nose of black cherry, cassis, and spice leads into a palate of ripe cherry, stewed plums, and dried berries with Christmas spice and a pinch of dried herbs. Velvety tannins segue into an enduring finish.

GRAMPIANS

A two-hour drive northwest of Melbourne, Grampians is red wine country. The region was previously known as Great Western; many wineries still use this term in their name. The first vines were planted here in 1867, and several of its grape varieties still elude ampelographers' efforts of identification. In addition to flagships Cabernet Sauvignon and Shiraz, Chardonnay and Riesling also do well in this inland, cool-climate region with strong diurnal variations. Vineyards cover 528 hectares (1,305 acres); soils are divided between gray-brown loamy sand and hard, yellow soil overlaying structured clay. Both types have a low pH and require the application of lime to maintain grape yields. The naturally beautiful landscape of the region covers some of the largest hand-dug gold mines in Victoria. Vineyard heights range between 240 and 440 meters (790 and 1,445 feet), and seasonal rainfall prior to harvest is 240 millimeters, or 9.5 inches.

BEST'S

111 Best's Road, Great Western,
+61 3 5356 2250,
www.bestswines.com

In its 145 years, Best's has only changed hands once. Founded by the Best family in 1866, it was purchased by the Thomson family in 1920. Fifth-generation managing director and vineyard manager Ben Thomson has taken the reins from his semiretired father, winemaker Viv Thomson. Among the varieties in their two vineyards are Shiraz, Cabernet Sauvignon, Pinot Noir, Chardonnay, and Riesling. Wines are produced in three ranges: Regional Selection, Great Western, and Icon. Best's Great Western Chardonnay 2009 has aromas of nectarine and barely buttered toast. In the mouth it exhibits ripe stone fruits, lemon, and baking bread, presented within a framework

of rich mouthfeel and brisk acidity. From the Icon range, Best's Great Western Old Clone Pinot Noir 2009 is bright cherry red with a luminous cast. The bouquet gently opens to reveal cherry, raspberry, espresso, and oregano. On the palate, flavors of cherry, toasted vanilla bean, and thyme mingle among soft tannins and spry acidity.

MOUNT LANGI GHIRAN

80 Vine Road, Bayindeen,
+61 3 5354 3207,
www.langi.com.au

Mount Langi Ghiran derives its name from the aboriginal home of the yellow-tailed black cockatoo. It has been home to Shiraz vines since 1870, although they were ripped out and replaced in 1963. It is owned today by the Rathbone family; prior owner Trevor Mast handed over winemaking duties to Dan Buckle in 2003. Pinot Noir, Shiraz, Cabernet Sauvignon, Riesling, Pinot Gris, and Sangiovese grow here. Both Chardonnay and Shiraz are vinified into dry and sparkling wines. Mount Langi Ghiran Riesling 2009 exhibits aromas of grapefruit, lemongrass, and jasmine. In the mouth, lime and Clementine are joined by Turkish delight and honeysuckle. Mount Langi Ghiran Langi Shiraz 2007 is inky red violet; on the nose dark berries, clove, and candied violet mix in a surprisingly delicate bouquet. In the mouth, intense flavors of blueberry, blackberry, licorice, and jalapeño sit within a smooth layer of tannins.

SEPPELT GREAT WESTERN

36 Cemetery Road, Great Western,
+61 3 5361 2239,
www.seppelt.com.au

Seppelt Great Western was christened with this name after being purchased by Benno Seppelt in 1918. The vineyards and winery were sold to him by Hans Irvine, who produced the first sparkling wine here in 1890, after first having bought the property from the estate of founder Joseph Best. With three large vineyards, one here, one in Heathcote, and one in Henty, Seppelt produces whites and reds at various price points, with a focus on Shiraz, both dry and sparkling. Head winemaker Emma Wood was awarded Australia's Young Winemaker of the Year Award in 2006; she works alongside winemaker Jo Marsh. Seppelt Drumborg Vineyard Riesling 2009, made with fruit from a vineyard in Henty, has a nose of lime sorbet with a suggestion of jasmine. Flavors of lemon, lime, and rose petal run the gauntlet between crisp minerality and vivacious acidity. Seppelt St Peters Grampians Shiraz 2007 is deep red violet and exhibits a bouquet of lightly spiced

blueberry pie. On the palate flavors of blackberry, blueberry, clove, allspice, and oregano cavort amidst muscular tannins leading to a sustained finish.

HEATHCOTE

Heathcote, in Central Victoria, is legendary for its premium Shiraz, which is the number one grape planted in the region. Wine lovers are also taking note of other varietals from Heathcote, including Cabernet Sauvignon, Merlot, Chardonnay, and Viognier. The first vines here took root in the 1860s, but gold mining and sheep grazing supplanted winemaking as the region's primary industries until 1960. The Mount Carmel range, with its red calcareous clay soils, offers a natural conduit for winds that blow throughout the growing season, providing a cooling antidote to hot summer sun. Altitudes run between 160 and 320 meters (525 to 1,050 feet), and seasonal rainfall of 280 millimeters, or 11 inches, arrives between October and April each year. There are 1,281 hectares (3,165 acres) of grapevines in Heathcote.

GREENSTONE VINEYARD

Corner of Heathcote-Rochester and McManus
Roads, Colbinabbin,
+61 3 5727 1434,
www.greenstoneofheathcote.com

A collaboration between Australian viticulturist Mark Walpole, David Gleave MW, a wine merchant living in the United Kingdom, and renowned Italian winemaker Alberto Antonini, Greenstone has attracted its share of attention for its Sangiovese and Shiraz. Only half of its 40-hectare (99-acre) Heathcote site is planted to vine, so we can expect more as this project unfolds. Greenstone Heathcote Sangiovese 2007 is deep cherry red, with aromas of black cherry and dried Mediterranean herbs. On the palate grippy tannins and spry acidity are a lovely conduit for flavors of blackberry, black plum, sage, and aniseed.

JASPER HILL

Drummonds Lane, Heathcote,
+61 3 5433 2528,
www.jasperhill.com

Ron Laughton—who worked in the cheese industry prior to setting up Jasper Hill—and his wife, Elva, had a revelation while standing out front of a real estate office window in Heathcote. A small sign reading "Vineyard for Sale" caught their eye and the rest, as they say, is history. Since 1975, they have produced superlative wines from estate-grown fruit; Jasper Hill's three vineyards total 19 hectares (47 acres), planted to Shiraz, Riesling, Grenache, Nebbiolo, and Sémillon. Jasper Hill Georgia's Paddock Riesling 2009 is an exhilarating splash of lemon and pink grapefruit with a suggestion of spice from first whiff through to the rich mineral finish. Jasper Hill Georgia's Paddock Shiraz 2008 is black cherry with a bright rim. Aromas of black cherry, raspberry, and clove lead into flavors of red berry fruit, anise, and chocolate-covered espresso bean with a pinch of dried savory herbs. The strong tannic structure is a natural foil to zesty acidity.

SHADOWFAX

K Road, Werribee,
+61 3 9731 4420,
www.shadowfax.com.au

Shadowfax's One Eye Vineyard, planted in 1968, is the oldest in Heathcote. Vineyard manager Alister Timms cares for One Eye and four other Heathcote vineyards planted with Shiraz; winemaking is under the direction of Matt Harrop. In addition to estate-grown Shiraz, contract vineyards in Geelong, Macedon Ranges, and Beechworth are the source of Chardonnay, Sauvignon Blanc, Pinot Gris, and Pinot Noir. Shadowfax One Eye Shiraz 2008 is deep red violet to the eye and exhibits scents of blackberry, damson plum, and licorice. A palate of blackberry, cassis, anisette, clove, and cinnamon are woven into a network of silky tannins, which lead up to an invigorating finish.

KING VALLEY

The diverse landscapes of the King River's watershed provide fertile soils for a wide array of grape varieties. Expect the unexpected here: besides Cabernet Sauvignon and Chardonnay, you are likely to come across Sangiovese, Barbera, Prosecco, or Tempranillo. Sparkling and fortified wines take pride of place alongside still wine. First planted toward the end of the nineteenth century, King Valley is home to about twenty-five wineries, who share 1,338 hectares (3,306 acres) of vineyards planted in deep red clay loam soils. Many of the grapes grown in King Valley make their way to wineries throughout Victoria, South Australia, and New South Wales. There is a wide range of altitudes, with grapes planted from 155 meters (510 feet) to 860 meters (2,820 feet). Rainfall varies through the region as well, but is on the high side: between 640 and 1,410 millimeters, or 25 and 56 inches, mostly during the spring and summer.

BROWN BROTHERS

239 Milawa Bobinawarrah Road, Milawa,
+61 3 5720 5500,
www.brownbrothers.com.au

John Francis Brown convinced his father to plant their first vineyard in 1885; four vineyards and an equal number of generations later, Brown Brothers grows and vinifies a mind-boggling

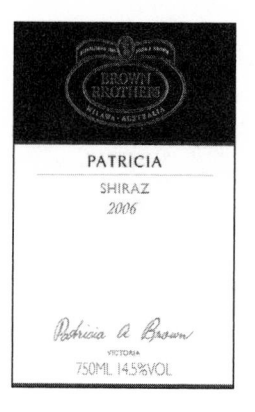

array of varieties. Additional vineyards were acquired and planted in 1968, 1982, 1994, and 1999. Fourth-generation family members still operate the business, including the Epicurean Center, which is open for lunch daily. Brown Brothers Cabernet Sauvignon 2009 is deep garnet in the glass, from which it gives off a bouquet of cassis, herbes de Provence, and portabello mushroom. On the tongue, fine-grained tannins lay the groundwork for flavors of red cherry, black currant, dried herbs, and a pinch of brightening spice. Brown Brothers Patricia Shiraz 2006 is inky red violet to the eye. Aromas of blackberry, blueberry, licorice, and clove give way in the mouth to blackberry, preserved plums, cracked black pepper, and toasted almond.

MACEDON RANGES

Mainland Australia's coolest wine region, Macedon Ranges also features the highest concentration of naturally formed mineral springs in Australia. Home to about forty wineries, Macedon Ranges' cold climate is ideal for both table and sparkling wine produced from Chardonnay and Pinot Noir, and also for Riesling, Shiraz, Merlot, and Cabernet Sauvignon. Cooler temperatures combined with granite-based sandy loam leads to low-yielding vines in this region's 232 hectares (573 acres) of grapevines, which sit at altitudes ranging between 300 and 700 meters (985 and 2,300 feet). Spring/summer rainfall averages about 330 millimeters, or 13 inches.

CURLY FLAT

263 Collivers Road, Lancefield,
+61 3 5429 1956,
www.curlyflat.com

In the 1980s, while studying in Switzerland, Phillip Moraghan developed a love for the Pinot Noir wines of Burgundy. He and his partner, Jeni, bought a small vineyard in the Macedon Ranges region and learned the arts of viticulture and winemaking both here and in the United States. Their vineyard hold-ings have grown to 14 hectares (35 acres) of mainly Pinot Noir, with small plantings of Chardonnay and Pinot Gris. Curly Flat Pinot Noir 2008 is deep garnet in color. A tantalizing nose of cherry, blackberry, white chocolate, and truffle cedes to a berry-dominated palate filled with flavors of cracked pepper, candied violet, peat, and chopped herbs.

HANGING ROCK

88 Jim Road, Newham,
+61 3 5427 0542,
www.hangingrock.com.au

In 1982, John and Ann Ellis chose a plot of Macedon Ranges land known as Jim Jim for their first vineyard. In the intervening 30 years they have grown to become the largest winery in the region. After graduating from Roseworthy in 1971, John went on to work with some of the major players in Australian wine. Ann, the daughter of Murray Tyrrell, is no stranger to the industry she was born into; her career has placed her in the offices and cellars of several of the country's wine-making titans. Well known for its incomparable sparkling brut and exquisite Shiraz, Hanging Rock also produces approachable wines from an assortment of varieties under the Odd One Out label. Hanging Rock Macedon Brut Cuvée XII NV is a blend of 60 percent Pinot Noir and 40 percent Chardonnay from vintages dating back to 1987. A classic "Champagne" nose gives way to tastes of Granny Smith apple and baking bread—which wash across the side palate

in a graceful, mouth-pleasing pas de deux. Hanging Rock Jim Jim Pinot Noir 2008 is black cherry in color. It has a bouquet of cherry and Chinese five-spice powder with a suggestion of smoke. On the palate rich flavors of cherry, dried oregano, thyme, and clove are at play among softly structured tannins.

VIRGIN HILLS

Salisbury Road, Lauriston,
+61 2 4993 3547,
www.virginhills.com.au

After opening Little Reata restaurant in Melbourne, Hungarian-born restaurateur and artist Tom Lazar bought 120 hectares (297 acres) of farmland, which turned out to be the wrong environment for the cherry orchard he had dreamed of planting. Turning adversity into opportunity, he instead planted the land with Bordeaux varieties and Shiraz, thus founding Virgin Hills. It is owned today by Michael Hope; winemaker Steve Hagan hand-crafts 1,000 cases of wine each year, which are available at select restaurants and retailers or via special order. Virgin Hills 2004 is a blend of 60 percent Cabernet Sauvignon, 18 percent Shiraz, 17 percent Merlot, and 5 percent Malbec. It is deep black cherry to the eye, with aromas of ripe cherry, cassis, and white chocolate. In the mouth, silky tannins envelope flavors of black cherry, blackberry, espresso, and cooling herbs.

MORNINGTON PENINSULA

Residents of Melbourne mention "The Peninsula" in the same manner that Bostonians refer to "The Cape." With its rolling dunes, quaint villages, and rugged coast, this strip of land southeast of Melbourne could well play Cape Cod's double in a Hollywood movie—except for mobs of kangaroos bounding through vineyards at dusk. Surrounded by water on three sides, Mornington Peninsula's gentle hills offer a cool climate to more than fifty wineries, whose 772 hectares (1,908 acres) are interspersed with farms and orchards growing fresh produce for the region's many restaurants and roadside stalls. Chardonnay and Pinot Noir reign, although Pinot Gris and Shiraz are making their presence known at local cellar doors and on the wine lists of nearby Melbourne. There are four main soil types, including hard, yellow soil over well-drained clay in the Dromana area, fertile red volcanic soils near Red Hill and Main Ridge, brown sandy loam over clay in the Merricks area, and sandy soils at Moorooduc. Vineyard altitudes range from 25 to 250 meters (80 to 820 feet), and spring and summer rainfall in a given year averages 350 millimeters, or 14 inches.

DROMANA ESTATE

55 Old Moorooduc Road, Tuerong,
+61 3 5974 3899,
www.dromanaestate.com.au

Established 30 years ago by Garry Crittenden, Dromana Estate is now investor-owned. Winemaker Duncan Buchanan is responsible for the flagship Dromana Estate range, the cool-climate varietal Mornington Peninsula range, and the "i" range, which features Italian varieties. The David Traeger line of wines is produced from Goulburn Valley fruit. Dromana Estate Chardonnay 2010 has a nose of stone fruit with light floral notes; on the palate apricot and white peach mingle with vanilla and a hint of toast. Dromana Estate Pinot Noir 2009 is medium cherry in the glass, with aromas of cherry and both cooling and savory herbs. In the mouth it tastes of black cherry, oregano, and espresso, with a suggestion of orange rind on the bright finish.

KOOYONG—PORT PHILLIP ESTATE

263 Red Hill Road, Red Hill South,
+61 3 5989 4444,
www.portphillipestate.com.au

Giorgio Gjergja purchased Port Phillip Estate in 2000 and subsequently purchased Kooyong in 2004. He retained winemaker

Sandro Mosele from Kooyong, who is now the head winemaker of both estates. We had lunch with Mosele in the Port Phillip Estate dining room; its beautiful curved-glass walls have direct views over the vines and distant sea views. Mosele told us, "Kooyong is only ten minutes away from here, but it has a distinctly different *terroir* than Port Phillip Estate. The soil is a base of volcanic red schist that was then covered by a tsunami, which left sedimentary soil on top." Mosele continued, "I am passionate about the vineyards, and I am all about the property and the individual characteristics of each plot of land. I love the styles of Burgundy and Barolo, so these are the things that I am interested in. I want to make wines that are structured, elegant, and have finesse." Port Phillip Estate Salasso Rosé 2010 is made from 100 percent Shiraz and is light pink in color, with a nose of light red fruits. It has soft white peach flavors in the mouth and a clean lemon zest finish. Port Phillip Estate Sauvignon Blanc 2010 is pale straw colored, just a step beyond clear. It has herbal aromas of rosemary and thyme. It is full-bodied and textured in the mouth, with flavors of passionfruit and pineapple before a crisp, clean finish. Kooyong Single Vineyard Faultline Chardonnay 2006 has penetrating minerality with notes of shale and iron. The minerality is joined on the palate with delicious white fruit flavors and a refreshing burst of lemon. Kooyong Pinot Noir 2008 is light cherry red, with aromas of raspberry, red cherry, and vanilla. Very Burgundian in style, the palate is elegant and balanced, with a gentle fruit finish.

MAIN RIDGE

80 William Road, Red Hill,
+61 3 5989 2686,
www.mre.com.au

Rosalie and Nat White planted their 3-hectare (7-acre) vineyard with Chardonnay and Pinot Noir in 1975. In 1980, they produced their premiere vintage at the newly built winery, the first commercial winery on the peninsula. Main Ridge Estate Chardonnay 2009 has a nose of white peach and lemon meringue pie, which on the tongue morphs into mellifluous flavors of nectarine, lemon custard, and hazelnut. Main Ridge Estate Half Acre Pinot Noir 2009 is deep garnet in the glass, with aromas of cherry, clove, and toasted nuts. On the palate a mélange of sweet and slightly tart cherry unites with Mediterranean herbs and a hint of violet encased in subdued tannins.

STONIER

2 Thompsons Lane, Merricks,
+61 3 5989 8300,
www.stoniers.com.au

Stonier was founded in 1978 by Brian Stonier and his wife, Noel. Their first vintage was a few years later, and until their state-of-the-art winery was completed in 1991, they made their wines offsite. Mike Symons has been the winemaker since the 2008 vintage. Prior to that he "went to University in Adelaide, studied winemaking at Montpelier, worked for the Antinori family in Bolgheri, and worked on and off for two years at Petaluma." He manages 60 hectares (148 acres) of Chardonnay and Pinot Noir vines. He took a few hours out of his 2011 harvest to have a chat with us and walk us through a tasting of his wines. Stonier Chardonnay Reserve 2008 is pale straw and has aromas of baked lemon meringue pie and vanilla ice cream with crumbled vanilla cookies. In the mouth there are flavors of white peach and lemon curd. The finish is elegant and persistent with lingering hints of honeysuckle and white flowers. Stonier Windmill Vineyard Pinot Noir 2008 is cherry red to garnet, with aromas of candied apples and red cherries and a touch of vegetal characteristics, presumably from the 40 percent whole-bunch fermentation. It has nice muscular tannins and a pleasing finish.

YABBY LAKE

112 Tuerong Road, Tuerong,
+61 3 5974 3927,
www.yabbylake.com

The Kirby family—key figures in the Australian movie and entertainment industry—became involved with wine in 1992, when they planted their first vineyard on Red Hill on the Mornington Peninsula. In 1998, they acquired their Yabby Lake vineyard in the subregion of Moorooduc. We had coffee one Sunday morning with viticulturist Keith Harris at the vineyards. After a few cups and a nice chat, we tasted through Yabby Lake's range of wines. Keith told us that the winery name comes from the fact that the kids would catch yabbies in the lake. In other English dialects, "yabbies" are known as crawfish or crayfish. Yabby Lake Cooralook Strathbogie Ranges Chardonnay 2009 is pale yellow in color. It has notes of citrus blossoms, lemon curd, and cream, like a lemon crème brûlée, in an inviting bouquet. It is big and creamy in the mouth with a pleasant finish. Yabby Lake Single Vineyard Mornington Peninsula Pinot Noir 2008 is rich garnet colored, with light notes of Moroccan spices, red fruits, and cumin. On the palate there is a restrained fruit character and a long, persistent finish. Yabby Lake Heathcote Estate Shiraz 2008 is garnet to inky purple with a violet rim and has aromas of black fruit and cassis. It is persistent, with a balanced, tannic finish.

MURRAY DARLING

The second largest wine region in Australia, Murray Darling flanks the Murray River in the northwest of Victoria and the west of New South Wales; its wineries and vineyards are in both of these states. A warm-weather, inland region with little rainfall, irrigation—and grapevines—first came to Murray Darling toward the end of the nineteenth century. Wine styles and prices vary, from low-priced, easy-drinking, mass-produced wines to elegant, small-batch wines at the upper end of the price spectrum. There are 8,536 hectares (21,093 acres) of vines in Victoria's portion of Murray Darling and another 7,054 hectares (17,431 acres) across the state border, in New South Wales, bringing the region's total area devoted to grapevines to 15,590 hectares (38,524 acres). The region's primary soil type, calcareous earth, is an alkaline soil high in both calcium and magnesium. The soil itself tends to be cool, contributing to the delayed ripening necessary for acid balance in finished wine. Not only is rainfall low, with 140 millimeters, or 5.5 inches, falling through the spring and summer, but altitudes are as well, with a range of just 55 to 70 meters (180 to 230 feet) above sea level. The main grapes grown in this large river basin are Chardonnay, Cabernet Sauvignon, and Shiraz, although among the region's 15 wineries, some viticulturists with experimental temperaments work with Italian and Spanish varieties.

PYRENEES

Named after the breathtaking mountain range that divides France and Spain, this southern continuation of Australia's Great Dividing Range features an array of microclimates; it is no wonder that more than twenty-five varieties are found in its 903 hectares (2,231 acres) of vineyards. In addition to spicy Shiraz and Cabernet Sauvignon, a host of international reds are grown, with Chardonnay and Sauvignon Blanc rounding out the assortment. About thirty wineries are interspersed with stands of eucalyptus trees; most vineyards are between the towns of Moonambel and Redbank, with a few closer to the town of Avoca. Rainfall in the growing season averages 220 millimeters, or 8.5 inches, and vineyards sit at altitudes ranging between 220 and 375 meters (920 and 1,230 feet).

DALWHINNIE

448 Taltarni Road, Moonambel,
+61 3 5467 2388,
www.dalwhinnie.com.au

Architect David Jones started Dalwhinnie in 1972; his first Cabernet Sauvignon was planted in 1976, and over 20 years those vines were joined by Shiraz and Chardonnay. His son David, who currently owns the winery alongside wife, Jenny, came aboard in 1983.

Dalwhinnie Cabernet Sauvignon 2008 is inky purple. On the nose black cherry and blackberry are joined by notes of clove, eucalyptus, and tobacco. Cherry and blackberry are also evident on the palate, alongside flavors of clove, Mediterranean herbs, and forest floor. Light, grippy tannins and playful acidity set the stage for a refined finish.

RUTHERGLEN

Rutherglen is the king of Australian fortified wine. With a history of winemaking stretching back to the mid-nineteenth century and a family tradition now in its sixth generation in some cases, it is no wonder that the sweet wines of Rutherglen are famous the world over. Its brown loam soils and 300 millimeters, or 12 inches, of rain in spring and summer nourish 872 hectares (2,155 acres) of vine. Twenty wineries mainly work with Muscat Rouge a Petits Grains, (also called Brown Frontignac) and Muscadelle, although a young generation

of winemakers has embraced Shiraz—vinified in both a still and sparkling style—as well as Riesling, Marsanne, Chardonnay, Sangiovese, and Durif, which was formerly used only in fortified wines. Vineyards are mostly at a height of about 170 meters (560 feet).

Rutherglen's most legendary wine is its fortified Muscat, which is classified according to both quality and years of aging. If a bottle is labeled "Rutherglen," the wine has aged for 2 to 5 years; if it is called "Classic," aging has occurred for 5 to 12 years; if the label reads "Grand," it has been aged between 12 and 20 years, while bottles of "Rare" are aged for 20 years or more. Rutherglen Topaque, formerly called Tokay, is mostly vinified from the Muscadelle grape. The name change came about due to European Union regulations concerning the use of the name "Tokay," and the similarity to the "Tokaj" wines of Hungary. Topaque is labeled using the same aging criteria as Muscat. Both Muscat and Topaque are blended nonvintage wines. The first bottle of newly named Topaque was sold on Saturday, April 11, 2009.

ALL SAINTS ESTATE

All Saints Road, Wahgunyah,
+61 2 6035 2222,
www.prbwines.com.au

Its distinctive turreted castle was built in the 1880s, about 20 years after All Saints Estate was founded by George Sutherland and John Banks. Barrels up to one hundred years old contain Muscat and Tokay dating back 80 years, to be used in the estate's finest bottlings, which will be of the "Rare" classification. Siblings Eliza, Angela, and Nicholas Brown, the fourth generation of a winemaking dynasty, currently own All Saints Estate and nearby St Leonards. Winemaking is the province of Dan Crane. All Saints Grand Rutherglen Muscat is medium brown, with a nose of rum raisin ice cream. On the palate flavors of raisins, golden currants, and honey move toward a bright but sustained finish.

CAMPBELLS

Murray Valley Highway, Rutherglen,
+61 2 6033 6000,
www.campbellswines.com.au

While the fifth generation of founder John Campbell's family are currently at work in the vineyards and cellars of circa-1870 Campbells, the sixth generation, the young children of Julie Campbell and husband, Cameron Ashmead,

are growing up in the Barossa, at the Ashmead's Elderton Estate. Fourth-generation brothers Malcolm Campbell, the viticulturist, and Colin Campbell, the winemaker, are in charge of the operation today, which produces both dry and sweet wines from the estate's 65 hectares (161 acres) of vineyards. These are planted with Riesling, Trebbiano, Viognier, Chardonnay, Sémillon, Shiraz, Durif, Tempranillo, Cabernet Sauvignon, Malbec, and local heroes Muscat and Muscadelle. The last two are vinified into exquisite sweet wines according to the regional classification system. Campbells Rutherglen Muscat NV is viscous gold tinged with blood orange. A nose of honeyed raisins leads into flavors of apricot and honey with light floral notes; it is kept from becomingly cloyingly sweet by a nice dash of acidity. Campbells Rutherglen Topaque NV is deep amber in the glass, from which it gives off fragrances of honey and toffee. In the mouth, honey and toffee mingle with candied orange peel and dried fig, which linger until the refreshing finish.

MORRIS WINES

Mia Mia Road, Rutherglen,
+61 2 6026 7303,
www.morriswines.com

George Francis Morris started with 4 hectares (10 acres) of vines in 1859; by 1885, he was up to 81 hectares (200 acres), making him the largest wine producer in the Southern Hemisphere (at the time). Unfortunately, phylloxera arrived a few years later, devastating the vines, and in 1897 George's son Charles had to sell a prize show horse in order to replant the grapes. Winemaker David Morris is the fifth generation of his family to be involved with the business, and he has been responsible for Morris's dry, sparkling and fortified wines since 1993. Fortified wines include Port-style, Sherry-style, and Muscat and Tokay, which are produced in only two versions, varietal and Old Premium, rather than the accepted four-tier system. Morris of Rutherglen Old Premium Amontillado NV, made from 100 percent Palomino, is an elegant Sherry-style wine that is light amber in the glass, with mellow notes of toasted almond brioche. In the mouth, flavors of toasted almond, baking bread, and a spray of seawater endure to the brisk, nutty finish. Morris of Rutherglen Durif 2009 is dark black cherry, exuding scents of black raspberry, clove, and vanilla bean. On the palate blackberry and black cherry are interwoven with butterscotch and a pinch each of baking spice and sage, combined with a smooth base of tannins.

STANTON AND KILLEEN

Jack's Road, Rutherglen,
+61 2 6032 9457,
www.stantonandkilleenwines.com.au

Park View Estate was established by Timothy Stanton in 1855. Almost a hundred years later, Norman Killeen married Timothy's granddaughter Joan Stanton. In the intervening years, Joan's father, Jack, had established Stanton Wines, absorbing his father's Park View Estate. With the marriage of Joan and Norman came the name change to Stanton and Killeen. Today, the seventh generation is on hand in the form of Simon Killeen, who is studying winemaking under the tutelage of Brendan Heath, who stepped in shortly before Simon's father's untimely death in 2007. Dry wines are produced from Chardonnay, Frontignac, Riesling, Cabernet Sauvignon, Shiraz, Merlot, and Durif. Sparkling white and red wines are made, as are Port-style wines and sweet Topaque and Muscat. Stanton and Killeen Vintage Fortified 2005 is a blend of Shiraz, Durif, and three Portuguese varieties. It is deep red in the glass, and a hot—but not unpleasant—nose of raspberry and cassis is in evidence. Strong fruit flavors of blackberry and cassis hold sway over lighter elements of licorice and aniseed.

YARRA VALLEY

Yarra Valley seems to have it all: scenic hills covered with grapevines, an assortment of traditional and modern wineries to please discerning day-trippers from nearby Melbourne, and an international reputation for its Chardonnay and Pinot Noir—made into both still and sparkling wine—as well as Shiraz and Cabernet Sauvignon. But this wasn't always the case. With a history of winemaking reaching back to 1838, Yarra Valley was the cradle of wine in Victoria, but as sweet, fortified wine became the fashion in the 1920s, production dwindled to a dead halt. The valley was reborn to vines in the 1960s, but it's only since the 1990s that the Yarra has regained its reputation as a significant region for fine wine. Eighty wineries call the Yarra Valley and its soils, which vary between sandy clay loam and red volcanic earth, home.

The Yarra Valley is a cool region, due both to the nearby sea and to altitudes, which range from 50 meters to 400 meters (165 to 1,310 feet) above sea level. Summers are dry, with only about 400 millimeters, or 16 inches, of rain falling between October and April; irrigation is the norm. Grapes are cultivated on 2,492 hectares (7,270 acres) of land.

COLDSTREAM HILLS

31 Maddens Lane, Coldstream,
+61 3 5960 7026,
www.coldstreamhills.com.au

Coldstream Hills was founded in 1985 by James and Suzanne Halliday. They planted vines the same year in their Amphitheater and House Block vineyards; the estate's first commercial vintage was in 1988. James is well known in the world of wine, as a journalist and author of more than sixty books on wine. He was honored in 1995 with the Maurice O'Shea Award, Australia's most prestigious individual award, for his Outstanding Contribution to the Australian Wine Industry. Coldstream Hills was sold to Southcorp in 1996 and continues to make wines that are highly regarded by international publications and wine lovers alike. It also happens to make some of our favorite Australian wines. Winemaker and site manager Andrew Fleming guided us through the winery and vineyards and led us through a tasting of

Coldstream Hills Wines. Coldstream Hills Chardonnay 2010 is straw colored, with lovely aromas of citrus blossoms, white stone fruits, and freshly baked lemon tart. In the mouth, the fruit comes forward with just a touch of vanilla. The finish is elegant with a light burst of citrus in the post palate. Coldstream Hills Pinot Noir 2009 is medium red, with aromas of raspberries, red cherries, and cherry vanilla ice cream. The palate is a delightful mix of Turkish delight and clove, with a suggestion of spice at the back of the tongue. Coldstream Hills Reserve Shiraz 2007 is beautiful indigo purple in color with aromas of fresh red plums and black plum preserves. It is well balanced, soft, and supple in the mouth. The finish is elegant and persistent.

DE BORTOLI

58 Pinnacle Lane, Dixon's Creek,
+61 3 5965 2271,
www.debortoli.com.au

We had lunch with winemaker Steve Webber at De Bortoli's Yarra Valley restaurant and were invited to have a glass of wine afterward at his home. We sat on the back terrace overlooking the family's Emu and Lucia Vineyards. For us, one of life's ultimate pleasures is drinking the wine while sitting on the land where the grapes were grown. Webber, who is married to Leanne De Bortoli, was awarded Winemaker of the Year 2007 by *Gourmet Traveller Wine* magazine. He is the consummate host, a talented winemaker, and a fun bloke to have a few glasses of wine with. The family makes wine and owns vineyards in many regions around Australia, including the Yarra Valley, Hunter Valley, King Valley, and Riverina. This makes De Bortoli one of Australia's largest family-owned wine companies. The family business started in 1928, when Vittorio and Giuseppina De Bortoli, immigrants from Italy, made their own table wine out of surplus grapes—at a time when most Australian wine was fortified. Word spread, and Italian immigrants would beg Vittorio to sell them his nonfortified table wines. Soon he was sending wines to other regions of Australia, and De Bortoli family wine gained recognition. Today De Bortoli wines are internationally acclaimed. De Bortoli Yarra Valley Lucia 2007 is a blend of 91 percent Cabernet Sauvignon and 9 percent Sangiovese. It is medium garnet colored, with aromas of bright red fruits, wild black fruits, and savory herbs. It is full-bodied in the mouth with a pleasant tannic grip. Riorret Viggers Single Vineyard Pinot Noir 2008 is named for "*terroir*" spelled backward. The label has artistic renderings of all of the helpful insects found in a vineyard, the ladybug being Webber's favorite. It is a serious Pinot Noir with a cherry red color and aromas of raspberries, red cherries, and cherry cola. On the palate it is silky smooth with an elegant, luxurious finish. It's just a shame that only 500 cases were made. According to Webber, "Twenty-ten is arguably the best year for Pinot Noir in the Yarra Valley." De Bortoli Yarra Valley Pinot Noir 2010 is cherry red, with heady aromas of cooling spices over notes of rich, red fruits and black cherry. In the mouth it has flavors of red cherries, raspberries, and a touch of cherry pie. There's a surprise "pop" of fruit at the back palate and a touch of smoke on the finish.

DOMAINE CHANDON

727 Maroondah Highway, Coldstream,
+61 3 9738 9200,
www.domainechandon.com.au

French Champagne house Moët & Chandon put down Australian roots in 1986 to make *méthode traditionelle* sparkling wine using cold-climate local grapes. It added still wine to the portfolio in 2005. In addition to vineyards here and in Strathbogie Ranges, fruit is sourced from contract growers across Victoria and in Tasmania. Winemaker Glenn Thompson is in charge of sparkling wines; Lillian Carter handles the still collection; winemaker Adam Keath works on both. None of them could get the job done without grapes provided by viticulturist Daniel

Dujic. The estate's Greenpoint Tasting Room and Brasserie is open daily. Chandon Brut NV is a blend of approximately 60 percent Chardonnay and 40 percent Pinot Noir; the exact blend varies from year to year in order to eliminate vintage variation. Expect a medium straw color and enduring *perlage*. On the nose aromas of sliced pear, white peach, and honeysuckle prepare the palate for flavors of ripe stone fruit, green pear, lemon rind, toasted almond, and rising bread.

FIVE OAKS

60 Aitken Road, Seville,
+61 3 5964 3704,
www.fiveoaks.com.au

Former nuclear physicist Wally Zuk and his wife, Judy, bought this 3-hectare (7-acre) vineyard in 1995, when the vines were already

17 years old. They renamed it Five Oaks after the commanding trees that embellish the property. Far from the world of science he left behind, Wally makes small-batch Cabernet Sauvignon, Merlot, Chardonnay, and Riesling. They are members of Smaller Wineries of Yarra Valley, and the ever-smiling Wally met us for dinner and a tasting of several vintages of his handcrafted Cabernet Sauvignon. Five Oaks Cabernet Sauvignon 2009 is deep red violet in the glass, with a nose of black cherry and licorice. On the palate flavors of bright black cherry, cassis, white pepper, and bitter chocolate worked their way toward a rich, tannic finish. Five Oaks Cabernet Sauvignon 2006 is bright black cherry to the eye and exhibits aromas of cherry and chocolate. Flavors of cassis, plums, black cherry, cooling herbs, and milk chocolate are enveloped in a smooth tannic structure.

GIANT STEPS/ INNOCENT BYSTANDER

336 Maroondah Highway, Healesville,
+61 3 5962 6111,
www.innocentbystander.com.au

Giant Steps/Innocent Bystander owner Phil Sexton took a giant leap of faith when he moved from Margaret River to the Yarra Valley, in much the same way that jazz

musician John Coltrane did when he released his first solo album entitled Giant Steps. Phil is obviously a Coltrane fan, and guests of the winery restaurant can hear a variety of cool music in Healesville's hippest hang out. This is one great winery and a trendy visitor experience. You can tour through the winery amid the tanks and barrels or, as you eat, watch the winemaking process through large plate glass windows from your comfy chair. We did both. Giant Steps Tarraford Vineyard Chardonnay 2008 is pale yellow, with aromas of citrus blossoms and stone fruits. In the mouth it's round and refreshing. The finish is crisp and clean with a nice citrus burst in the post palate. We're told that Greg Liney, the vineyard manager, lets the grass grow between the vines all summer, then cuts it just before harvest. He does this because the grape

WINES OF THE SOUTHERN HEMISPHERE

pickers won't go into the vineyard's tall grass for fear of snakes. This is a delicious wine; too bad only 400 cases were made. Innocent Bystander Yarra Valley Pinot Noir 2010 is light cherry red in color, with a nose of red cherry, spice, and raspberry. When it hits your palate, it explodes with Chinese five-spice powder and fruit before filling your mouth with drying tannins.

MAC FORBES

770 Healesville Koo Wee Rup Road, Healesville,
+61 3 9818 8099,
www.macforbes.com

Mac Forbes started working harvests in France at the age of 19 before returning home to Australia in 2004. His wines have a decidedly international style, while staying true to their Australian *terroir*. Mac Forbes wines have received international acclaim, and Forbes himself was nominated for 2011 Winemaker of the Year by *Gourmet Traveller Wine* Magazine. He told us one of his winemaking secrets: "Pick the fruit at the optimum time to express a nice level of minerality in the wines." His team consists of Tony Fikkers, winemaker, and Dylan Grigg, viticulturist. Mac Forbes Woori Yallock Yarra Valley Chardonnay 2008 is medium straw colored, with aromas of white flowers, jasmine, and slate-like minerals. It opens with tropical

fruits that gently caress the palate, leading to a creamy mouth feel and a pleasant, lingering finish. Mac Forbes RS 37 Riesling 2008 has a pale straw, almost clear lemon, color. The nose has gentle aromas of white flowers, honeysuckle, and jasmine. In the mouth there is a nice level of sweetness balanced by the perfect amount of acidity to retain its fresh character. Flavors of green fig, orange blossom, and white peach are present on the finish. We enjoyed this wine with Spicy Sichuan Chicken in Melbourne's Chinatown.

MEDHURST

24 Medhurst Road, Gruyere,
+61 3 5964 9022,
www.medhurstwines.com.au

Ross Wilson, former CEO of Southcorp, and his wife, Robyn, searched for the perfect *terroir* to put down roots. They found the ideal plot of land, planted vines, and asked their son Tom and his partner Christine Petsinis, both architects, to design a state-of-the-art winery. Matt Steel makes the wines. Medhurst Chardonnay 2010 is medium straw colored with aromas of guava and pineapple. This wine does not undergo malolactic fermentation, yet it is creamy and rich in the mouth with a fresh finish. Medhurst Pinot Noir 2010 is brilliant cherry colored, with aromas of cherry preserves and fresh raspberries. On the palate it tastes like a mouthful of Mom's cherry pie. This is a super Pinot Noir.

TARRAWARRA

31 Healesville-Yarra Glen Road, Tarrawarra,
+61 3 5962 3311,
www.tarrawarra.com.au

Marc and Eve Bessen established TarraWarra almost 30 years ago, with winemaker Clare Halloran joining the team in 1996. Known for its Pinot Noir and Chardonnay, TarraWarra also produces Shiraz, Merlot, and white Rhône varietals. TarraWarra Estate Chardonnay 2009 exudes fragrances of peach and nectarine with Chinese five-spice powder. On the palate ripe peach, buttered toast, and light spice cavort with lean minerality and a splash of acidity. TarraWarra Estate Reserve Pinot Noir 2008 is bright cherry red, with a nose of cherry, aniseed, and nettles. In the mouth, complex layers of sweet and slightly tart cherry, chocolate, Mediterranean herbs, and fennel are woven into a base of mild tannins and a finish of orange zest.

YARRA YERING

4 Briarty Road, Gruyere,
+61 3 5964 9267,
www.yarrayering.com

We visited with Tim Hampton, general manager, and Paul Bridgeman, head winemaker, in Yarra Yering's beautifully restored farmhouse set amidst the vines. Besides being an excellent winemaker, Bridgeman can sometimes be found on stage with his band, guitar in hand, rocking out at Yarra Valley's pre and post harvest festivals. Yarra Yering was founded by botanist Dr. Bailey Carrodus in 1969. He produced his first vintage in 1973 and continued crafting quality wines for more than 35 years. He used a variety of avant-garde and unusual winemaking methods that he passed on to Paul Bridgeman in the short time they worked together—before Carrodus's death in 2008. Bridgeman guided us through the winery and gave us a glimpse into his winemaking world. We are sworn to absolute secrecy, but we can tell you that in visiting thousands of wineries, we have rarely seen these techniques utilized. Yarra Yering Chardonnay 2008 is medium yellow in color, with aromas of citrus blossom on the nose and just a hint of pineapple and lemon zest. In the mouth there are bright lemon flavors tempered by a touch of creaminess—think lemon custard with a dollop of fresh whipped

cream. The finish is elegant with a touch of lavender in the post palate. Yarra Yering Underhill Shiraz 2001 is garnet colored, with notes of red cherry, cassis, confectioners' sugar, and red plums that have been softened around the edges. In the mouth, flavors of stewed plums, blackberries, and Chinese five-spice powder delight your palate before the clean bright finish on the tongue. Yarra Yering Agincourt 2005 is a blend of 70 percent Cabernet Sauvignon and 30 percent Merlot. It is garnet colored, with aromas of chopped green peppers, black plums, and dried red cherries. It has a delicious vibrant fruit flavor and a supple texture in the mouth before the long finish.

YERING STATION

38 Melba Highway, Yarra Glen,
+61 3 9730 0100,
www.yering.com

You could call Yering Station Victoria's oldest vineyard. It was planted in 1838 by the Scottish-born Ryrie Brothers. It has changed hands a few times since—and none of the original vines remain—but it is important to note that Yering Station wines won early international awards, including the Grand Prix at the Universal Exhibition in Paris in 1889. We visited this beautiful winery, designed by

Melbourne architect Robert Conti, and tasted wines with chief winemaker Willy Lunn. The Wine Bar Restaurant has stunning views over the Yarra Valley. Lunn is an affable bloke who seems to have a lifetime of experience despite his youthful appearance. He worked at Argyle Winery in Oregon for six years and then a few years at Shaw + Smith and Petaluma. His wines exhibit a marvelous sense of variety and *terroir*. Yering Station Coombe Farm Single Vineyard Chardonnay 2007 is medium straw colored, with aromas of guava, mango, and tropical fruits. In the mouth it is round and generous with an elegant yet cheeky finish— it's a wonderfully pleasant wine. Yering Station Pinot Noir 2008 is medium cherry colored, with aromas of red fruits, pure red cherry, raspberry, and a touch of cocoa powder. It is fruity and fleshy in the mouth with an elegantly restrained finish.

TASMANIA

Tasmania is almost a microcosm of Australia as a whole. It is at once an island, a state, and a wine region. Surrounded by water on all sides, its maritime climate provides ideal conditions for a number of cool-weather varieties such as Chardonnay, Pinot Noir, Riesling, Sauvignon Blanc, Pinot Gris, and Gewürztraminer. Tasmania is noted as the home of Australia's premium sparkling wine industry; accordingly much of the emphasis is on Pinot Noir and Chardonnay. This is a natural paradise with a variety of visitor attractions, from hiking and rafting to fine dining—the latter often featuring a wide range of island-raised meat and produce. There are 1,388 hectares (3,430 acres) of grapevines cultivated here. The island boasts 200 vineyards and 160 producers of wine.

Tasmania is one region, divided into seven wine-growing areas: Tamar Valley, North East, East Coast, North West, Derwent Valley, Huon/Channel, and the Coal River Valley. The island's many mountains protect vineyards from wind and forceful rain. Soils are mostly ancient sandstone and newer combinations of alluvial sediments and porous volcanic rock. Northern Tasmania's vineyards are at altitudes ranging between 80 and 210 meters (265 to 690 feet), while southern Tasmanian vineyards sit slightly lower on average, between 50 and 175 meters (165 to 575 feet). Rainfall from October to April is marginally greater in the south than in the north, but the average across the island is 335 millimeters, or 13 inches.

BAY OF FIRES

40 Baxters Road, Pipers River,
+61 3 6382 7622,
www.bayoffireswines.com.au

Fran Austin is the head winemaker at Bay of Fires. In 2005 Austin was awarded Australian Young Winemaker of the Year in the Qantas/Gourmet Traveller Awards. Bay of Fires makes wine under its own name, but it is also known for its Arras sparkling wines, which have been highly rated in Australian and international competitions and publications. Bay of Fires Pinot Noir 2009 is medium red colored, with aromas of raspberries, black cherries, red cherry conserves, and a whiff of forest floor. It is medium weighted on the palate with smooth tannins and a lingering finish of dried cherries. Bay of Fires Riesling 2010 is straw yellow with greenish tints. On the nose it has notes of lime zest, oregano, rosemary, freesia, and jasmine. In the mouth it is crisp with balanced acidity.

JOSEF CHROMY

370 Relbia Road, Relbia,
+61 3 6335 8700,
www.josefchromy.com.au

Czech-born Josef Chromy left his war-torn village and escaped through Soviet-occupied territories, minefields, and heavily guarded border crossings, to finally arrive in Australia in 1950. He brought with him a strong Eastern European work ethic, winemaking knowledge, and a desire for a better life. In recognition of his rags-to-riches life story, he was awarded the Order of Australia Medal for his contribution to Tasmanian food and wine. Josef Chromy Riesling 2010 is pale straw, with aromas of lime zest, white flowers, and citrus blossoms. It is crisp in the mouth with a balanced fruit finish. Josef Chromy Pinot Gris 2010 has aromatics of white stone fruits, nectarines, and dried Turkish apricots. It is creamy on the palate with a fruit-driven finish.

PIRIE TASMANIA

Waldhorn Drive, Rosevears,
+61 3 6330 1815,
www.pirietasmania.com.au

Dr. Andrew Pirie is known as Australia's first doctor of Viticulture. He identified land in Tasmania as perfect for cool-climate varietals. Dr. Pirie established Pirie Tasmania in 2004, but before this he had established Pipers Brook Vineyards in 1973 and continued through 2002. Pirie Estate Pinot Noir 2009 is medium garnet in color, with aromas of cherry, raspberry, dried black cherries, and a whiff of cooling herbs in a luxurious bouquet. In the mouth it exhibits classic Burgundian heft and a mineral-driven finish.

NEW SOUTH WALES

New South Wales (NSW) was the first state in Australia to be settled by Europeans and the first to be planted with grapevines. Its most well-known wine region is the Hunter Valley, about a two-hour drive north of Sydney, but most of NSW's production takes place in the Big Rivers zone, where grapes are grown for both box wines and low-cost, entry-level wines. New South Wales is divided into eight zones. The most productive in the state—and the entire country—is Big Rivers, which is made up of the Riverina and Perricoota regions, plus portions of Murray Darling and Swan Hill, both of which cross into the neighboring state of Victoria. The Central Ranges zone includes the Cowra, Mudgee, and Orange regions, and the Hunter Valley zone is divided into Upper Hunter and Lower Hunter. The Northern Rivers zone contains the Hastings River region, while the New England Australia region is contained within the Northern Slopes zone. The South Coast zone encompasses the regions of Shoalhaven Coast and Southern Highlands. The Canberra District, Gundagai, Hilltops, and Tumbarumba districts are within the Southern New South Wales zone, while the Western Plains is an undivided wine zone.

New South Wales has the second highest total of hectares devoted to grapevines in the country, behind South Australia, but ahead of Victoria. It is almost evenly divided between red and white varieties. Out of a total of 42,621 hectares (105,320 acres) of vines, 20,959 hectares (51,791 acres) are planted with red varieties and 21,662 hectares (53,528 acres) are covered with white varieties. The state capital, Sydney, is a sophisticated international city with a population of more than four million, and New South Wales is Australia's most populous state—something you couldn't even begin to believe driving through the state's western slopes and plains.

CANBERRA DISTRICT

Crossing between New South Wales and the adjoining—and much smaller—Australian Capital Territory, the Canberra District was first planted with vines in 1971. The region is home to about forty (mainly small) wineries, which have traditionally relied on cellar door sales to visitors from Australia's capital city, Canberra, but which lately have increased dramatically in both reputation and distribution. Canberra, a cool-climate region, is becoming known for Chardonnay, Riesling, Pinot Noir, Cabernet Sauvignon, Shiraz, and Sauvignon Blanc-Sémillon blends. Altitudes fall between 500 and 850 meters (1,640 to 2,788 feet). Many vineyards have views of the distant Snowy Mountains. Most soils are shallow, brown clay loam. The underlying shale and clay tends to have poor water-retention qualities, and irrigation is often necessary, even in a region that receives an average of 360 millimeters, or 14 inches, of rainfall during the growing season. Canberra has about 500 hectares (1,235 acres) of vineyards.

CLONAKILLA

Crisps Lane, Murrumbateman,
+61 8 6227 5877,
www.clonakilla.com.au

In 1971, research scientist John Kirk bought an 18-hectare (44-acre) farm and planted small amounts of Cabernet Sauvignon and Riesling. He persevered despite a severe drought that caused significant vineyard loss in 1973 and produced his first vintage in 1976. Clonakilla, Gaelic for "meadow of the church," was the name of his grandfather's farm in County Clare, Ireland. In addition to the original two varieties, John Kirk's vineyards are also now planted with Shiraz, Chardonnay, Pinot Noir, Cabernet Sauvignon, and Viognier. His son Tim left a teaching career in 1996 to take over winemaking duties; since 2009, Tim has also been Clonakilla's CEO. Clonakilla Viognier 2009 exhibits lovely fragrances of green pear, nectarine, and just-baked gingerbread, which lead to flavors of pear, apricot, lemon blossom, and marzipan. The rich mouthfeel is kept in check by a finalizing smack of acidity. Clonakilla Hilltops Shiraz 2009 is vibrant violet red, with a muscular nose of black cherry, cassis, and anisette. In the mouth, flavors of blackberry, black currant, and Chinese five-spice powder dance on a stage of rich tannins and dazzling acidity and then on through an encore-laden finish.

HILLTOPS

Lush vineyards and bountiful cherry orchards today characterize a region where the first vignerons were Croatian settlers in the late nineteenth-century. After grapevines were abandoned in favor of more profitable crops, the region was revitalized in the 1970s, most notably by the founding of Barwang Vineyards. Today, there are 10 wineries in Hilltops, sharing 492 hectares (1,216 acres) of grapes, almost all of which are planted at altitudes above 450 meters (1,476 feet). The dark red granite clay soils nourish vines laden with Chardonnay, Cabernet Sauvignon, Shiraz, Verdelho, and Sémillon, the last of which is vinified into both dry and sweet styles. Irrigation is a necessity due to the dry, hot summers; altitude-enhanced night-time coolness slows down the ripening process, enabling the development of a proper balance of sweetness/ripeness and acidity in the wines of the region.

GROVE ESTATE

4100 Murringo Road, Young,
+61 2 6382 6999,
www.groveestate.com.au.

In 1989, the Flanders, Kirkwood, and Mullany families pooled resources and talent, and purchased 50 hectares (123 acres) with the goal of becoming contract grape growers. In 1997 the partners decided to hold back some Cabernet Sauvignon to bottle under the Grove Estate label. The 50 hectares (124 acres) of vineyards are planted with Cabernet Sauvignon, Shiraz, Merlot, Zinfandel, Pinot Noir, Chardonnay, Sémillon, and Italian varietals. Brian Mullany is the head viticulturist; winemaker Richard Parker works with the guidance of Clonakilla's Tim Kirk. Grove Estate The Partners Cabernet Sauvignon 2006 is deep garnet to the eye, with scents of blackberry, black cherry, and anisette. On the palate, rich, berry fruit and cool spices are accented by a dash of dried Mediterranean herb flavors; fine-grained tannins make for a smooth finish.

HUNTER VALLEY

The Hunter Valley is Australia's oldest wine region—and its most visited. Just two hours north of Sydney by car, the Hunter Valley is filled with hotels, restaurants, and tourist-friendly wineries; it has the feel of California's Napa Valley. It boasts 3,513 hectares (8,680 acres) of grapevines and includes some of Australia's oldest winemaking families. In addition to its iconic Sémillon, the Hunter Valley also produces world-class Shiraz and Chardonnay, as well as excellent examples of Sangiovese, Tempranillo, Verdelho, and Pinot Gris. About 130 wineries abound here, as do the legends of the Hunter's historic wine-makers—such as Maurice O'Shea, Murray Tyrrell, and Len Evans. Three main types of soil are found in the Hunter Valley: red clay loam, mostly on hills and slopes; deep brown podsol soils, with abundant organic material; and sandy loam over clay, usually found in low-lying areas along narrow waterways. In the Lower Hunter, vineyards are found at altitudes between 200 and 400 meters (656 and 1,312 feet), with average rainfall received from spring into summer, of about 530 millimeters, or 21 inches. The Upper Hunter Valley, so named for latitude, not altitude, has vineyards at heights of 150 to 250 meters (490 to 820 feet) above sea level. Seasonal rainfall is lower as well, with an average of 400 millimeters, or 16 inches.

AUDREY WILKINSON

DeBeyers Road, Pokolbin,
+61 2 4998 7441,
www.audreywilkinson.com.au

Audrey Wilkinson was just a boy when his father died, and he was left to run the family business. Established in 1866, Audrey Wilkinson began exporting wine to London in the early 1900s, where his wines won awards in various competitions. Visitors to the winery can tour the family museum housed in the original winery and stay in its comfortable guesthouses. Audrey Series Hunter Valley Shiraz 2009 is garnet colored, with aromas of dark cherry, black raspberry, purple flowers, and a touch of cocoa. In the mouth it is fruit-driven with a persistent mineral finish. Audrey Series Semillon 2009 is yellow with green tints. It has a nose dominated by lime and lemon zest, and the palate is as refreshing as a lemon-lime Italian ice.

BROKENWOOD

401 McDonalds Road, Pokolbin,
+61 2 4998 7559,
www.brokenwood.com.au

In 1970 three lawyers from Sydney—Tony Albert, John Beeston, and James Halliday—purchased land in the Hunter Valley to grow grapes and make wine as a weekend hobby. The first vintage was 1973, and by 1975 they'd built a winery to keep up with demand. Over the years some partners left, some passed on, and others have joined, but the quest for quality remains the same as in the early years. Brokenwood Graveyard Vineyard Shiraz is the estate's flagship wine; the 2007 vintage has the color of blueberry pie with cherry highlights. Aromas of blueberry, black cherry, jalapeño, and clove are present in a complex bouquet. In the mouth, flavors of blueberry, anise, and clove delight your mouth. This wine is wonderfully full on the palate but not overpowering. Brokenwood Army Block Vineyard Semillon 2010 is almost clear, just a tad darker than tap water. It has a nose of green fig, white peach, and ripe stone fruits. Natural summer fruit sweetness and bright acidity crisscross the palate in refreshing waves. This is a wine that keeps inviting you in for another sip.

GLENGUIN ESTATE

Milbrodale Road, Broke,
+61 2 6579 1009,
www.glenguinestate.com.au

Established by the Tedder Family in 1988, Glenguin Estate now makes quality, organically grown wines. The average age of its vines is 19 years old, but the estate also has vines that are more than 50 years old. Robin Tedder MW is the winemaker, assisted by viticulturist Klauss Hahn and consulting winemaker Rhys Eather. Glenguin Estate Aristea Shiraz 2007 is an amazing example of what Australian Shiraz can be. It is deep red, with lovely aromas of red plum conserves, sweet black plum, and cassis, with top notes of powdered dark cocoa and Madagascar vanilla bean. It is generous on the palate, with luxurious mouthfeel and a pleasantly firm, tannic finish.

HOPE ESTATE

2213 Broke Road, Pokolbin,
+61 2 4993 3555,
www.hopeestate.com.au

Michael Hope introduced us to an Australian experience that we will never forget. After touring the Hope winery and tasting Michael's excellent wines, we jumped into his SUV for a tour of the vineyards. Five minutes later we encountered a mob of kangaroos that was quietly munching on grass just as the sun was beginning to set. We have never seen so many kangaroos—there must have been three hundred of them—mothers with baby joeys in their pouches, young males, old males, and old females. It was the most amazing sight we have ever seen! Michael encouraged us to get out of the SUV and crouch quietly in the grass to observe them. Within minutes, the kangaroos forgot that we were there and continued eating grass—some of them came within three meters (ten feet) to munch the tender grass near our feet! We must have stayed there for an hour—it really ranks up there with one of life's most amazing experiences! Besides being a great guy and avid naturalist, Michael is very active in raising money for breast cancer awareness, having lost his mother to the disease. On the winemaking side, Michael and his team make some really fantastic wines. Hope Estate is 129 hectares (319 acres), acquired in bits and pieces since 1997. It grows Verdelho, Chardonnay, Shiraz, and Merlot. Hope Estate is also known for its Harvest Restaurant and its 19,000-person capacity amphitheater. Recent acts have included Sting, Fleetwood Mac, Eric Clapton, and the Doobie Brothers, who we missed by only one day. (But then again, we most likely would not have seen kangaroos if 19,000 people were singing along to "Without Love— Where Would You Be Now?") Hope Estate Verdelho 2010 is pale straw, with aromas of tropical fruits, pineapple, and citrus rind in the bouquet. In the mouth the mid palate has beautiful richness before the zesty finish. Hope Estate Chardonnay 2009 is medium straw colored, with a nose of citrus blossom, Granny Smith apple, white peaches, and toasted hazelnut. It has a luxurious mouthfeel and a persistent finish. It is the perfect wine to sip while observing kangaroos!

MARGAN

1238 Milbrodale Road, Broke,
+61 2 6579 1317,
www.margan.com.au

Winemaker/owner Andrew Margan worked more than 20 vintages with the late Murray Tyrrell before deciding to open his own winery with his wife, Lisa. The estate's first harvest was in 1997, and the family now owns 129 hectares (319 acres) of vines. Margan Restaurant opened in 2007 and has quickly become a destination for city dwellers from Sydney. Margan Semillon 2010 is pale straw colored with green hues. It has aromas of white flowers, jasmine, honeysuckle, and lemon blossoms, with a background note of wet river rocks. It is crisp on the palate with balanced acidity. Margan Shiraz Saignee Rosé 2010 is candy apple red, with aromas of wild strawberries and just picked raspberries. It has soft acidity and a refreshing finish—it's a great wine for summer quaffing.

MCWILLIAM'S MOUNT PLEASANT

68 Anzac Street, Chullora, NSW +61 2 9722 1200,
www.mcwilliamswine.com

Founded in 1877 by Samuel McWilliam, McWilliam's Wines is one of Australia's oldest family-owned wineries. McWilliam's consistently wins awards and accolades, and in 2009 alone, it walked away with 40 trophies and 889 medals from wine shows around the world. The company owns four wineries in Australia. We visited with Scott McWilliam, the sixth-generation family winemaker, at the family's Mount Pleasant Estate. He is especially proud of his Maurice O'Shea Shiraz 2007, which recently won Australian Shiraz of the Year in a popular Australian wine guidebook. Maurice O'Shea Shiraz is named after Maurice O'Shea, acclaimed as perhaps the greatest Australian winemaker of all. He was the first Australian to study winemaking at Montpelier and made wine at Mount Pleasant between 1921 and 1957. He sold his winery to the McWilliam family in 1945 but stayed on as its winemaker—in the process crafting some of the most legendary of all Australian wines. The 2007 release is ruby red garnet in the glass, with aromas of black cherry, black raspberry, and black plum. It has nice heft on the palate and a savory and elegant finish due to the well-structured tannic backbone. It is sophisticated and restrained.

McWilliam's Hanwood Estate Chardonnay 2008 is medium straw colored, with notes of white peach, Bartlett pear, and toasted brioche. It is soft and gentle in the mouth with moderate acidity. This is a very pleasant chardonnay.

ROSEMOUNT ESTATE

McDonalds Road, Pokolbin,
+61 2 4998 6670,
www.rosemountestate.com.au

Carl Brecht planted the Hunter Valley's first vineyards, which were subsequently purchased by Bob Oatley in 1968. In 1974 Rosemount released its first wines, and while its home is the Hunter Valley, it now makes wine from vineyards all around Australia. In 1999 Rosemount was the first non-American company to win "Winery of the Year" at San Francisco's International Wine Competition. It is now owned by Treasury Wine Estates. Matt Koch is the chief winemaker. Rosemount Estate Diamond Cellars Traminer Riesling 2010 is pale straw colored, with aromas of white flowers, lemon zest, and lime juice. It is crisp in the mouth with a touch of white pepper on the finish. Rosemount Estate Diamond Cellars Semillon Chardonnay 2010 is straw yellow, with a nose of white stone fruits and citrus blossom. It has balanced acidity and a clean finish.

TEMPUS TWO

Corner of Broke and McDonalds Roads, Pokolbin,
+61 2 4993 3999,
www.tempustwo.com.au

The name Tempus Two is from the Latin word *tempus*, meaning "time" and the number "two." Translated as "second time," Founder Lisa McGuigan takes an open jab at the French Appellation Authority who sent her a cease and desist letter because her winery was originally called "Hermitage Road." It seems that the French felt that they owned the rights to the word "Hermitage." Tempus Two winery is a very cool-looking, modern building with a grass amphitheater that is capable of seating

10,000 people—Sir Elton John has performed here to sold-out crowds. Winemaker Scott Comyns has been with Tempus Two since 2003, when he started as a cellar hand. He was promoted to head winemaker in 2008 and has never looked back. He was very friendly and hospitable and a great guy to sit down with, have a chat, and taste a few glasses of his delicious wines. Tempus Two Varietal Sémillion-Sauvignon Blanc 2010 is composed of 85 percent Sémillion and 15 percent Sauvignon Blanc. It is pale yellow in the glass and has aromas of flint, lemon, lime, lemon zest, dried herbs, and cut grass. It is refreshing in the mouth with a clean acidic finish. Comyns told us, "This is our biggest seller in the domestic Australian market." Tempus Two Copper 2009 Wilde Chardonnay is named after Oscar Wilde, because McGuigan loves his quote: "The only thing worse than being talked about is not being talked about." It is a blend of 50 percent Hunter Valley Chardonnay, which Comyns uses "for the fruit flavor," and 50 percent Adelaide Hills Chardonnay, which he uses "for structure and length." It is straw yellow colored, with aromas of white peach, stone fruits, and a bit of apricot. It is generous in the mouth with beautiful length. There is a burst of minerality in the post palate.

TULLOCH

Corner of McDonalds and DeBeyers Roads, Pokolbin,
+61 2 4998 7580,
www.tulloch.com.au

John Younie Tulloch, a merchant, accepted 17 hectares (42 acres) of land as payment for a debt owed to his general store—and thus began the history of Tulloch Wines in 1895. Over the years there was a series of mergers and acquisitions, but today Jay Tulloch, along with his daughter Christina and son Jock, run the company. Tulloch Chardonnay 2010 is straw colored, with aromas of white and yellow stone fruits, buttered brioche, and ripe melons. It is creamy in the mouth with a pleasant lingering finish. Tulloch Cabernet Sauvignon 2009 is deep garnet purple, with notes of anise, cassis, black raspberry, and geranium leaf. In the mouth, juicy fruits prevail before a finish characterized by ginger and cinnamon flavors.

TOWER ESTATE

Corner of Halls and Broke Roads, Pokolbin,
+61 2 4998 7989,
www.towerestatewines.com.au

A boutique winery in every sense of the word, Tower Estate prides itself on its artisanal, handcrafted wines that are limited to 1,000 cases per variety. The estate is also the site of the Relais & Châteaux property, the exclusive 12-room Tower Lodge, whose Roberts Restaurant is considered one of the best gastronomic experiences in the Hunter Valley. Tower Estate Chardonnay 2010 is straw colored, with aromas of orange rind, white stone fruits, and a touch of Madagascar vanilla bean in the enticing bouquet. In the mouth this wine has a creamy texture before a mineral-driven finish.

TYRRELL'S

2313 Broke Road, Pokolbin,
+61 2 4993 3555,
www.tyrrells.com.au

Founded by English immigrant Edward Tyrrell in 1858, Tyrrell's is one of Australia's oldest family-run wineries. Fourth-generation Bruce Tyrrell is the current managing director, with the fifth generation already working in the family business. Tyrrell's currently has 193 hectares (477 acres) of vines in the Upper and Lower Hunter Valley, but the family also maintains vineyards in other regions of Australia and around the world. Winemaking is carried out by a dedicated (and illustrious) team, including Andrew Spinaze, Mark Richardson, Iain Hayes, Chris Tyrrell, and Peter Lane. The family has been making quality wine for more than 150 years, and in 2010 James Halliday named it "Winery of the Year." We had an amazing experience while visiting Tyrrell's that convinced us that screwcaps are a valid closure for wines destined for ageing. We first tried Tyrrell's Vat 1 Hunter Sémillon 1999 bottled under cork. It exhibited honey, lemon, and straw in the nose. In the mouth it showed soft citrus fruits and baked country biscuit. It was a generous wine on the palate. The same wine bottled under screwcap was fresh and bright with flavors of lemon-lime, white peach, green fig, geranium, and violet. It was also generous in the mouth with refreshing fruit flavors and crisp acidity. Our conclusion was that the wine under screwcap had the freshness and excitement of a young wine. We were blown away by the difference between the two wines! Besides Sémillon, Tyrrell's is also known for excellent Chardonnay, Pinot Noir, Shiraz, and Sparkling. They are wines worth seeking out.

WYNDHAM ESTATE

Dalwood Road, Dalwood,
+61 2 4938 3444,
www.wyndhamestate.com

George Wyndham, the father of Australian Shiraz, planted the country's first commercial Shiraz vineyards in 1830. Today the company and the winemaking team—consisting of Nigel Dolan, Tony Hooper, Ben Bryant, and Steve Myer—are committed to continued quality production of Wyndham's wines. The estate has wonderful dinner and concert events with notable opera stars like Dame Kiri Te Kanawa performing under the stars. George Wyndham Langhorne Creek Shiraz 2007 is ruby garnet colored with a violet rim. It has aromas of black raspberry, black plum, cassis, cigar box, and a touch of peppermint. In the mouth it has chewy fruit flavors, smooth tannins, and a persistent finish. Wyndham Estate Bin 222 Chardonnay 2010 is straw colored with green tints. It has a nose of white peach, toasted brioche, and citrus blossoms. It is creamy on the palate with a zesty finish.

MUDGEE

Its name is Aboriginal for "nest in the hills," which makes perfect sense when you see this bowl-shaped region surrounded by a rim of hills. Mudgee is four hours by car from Sydney, but patient drivers and their passengers are rewarded by ever-changing panoramas, high-end restaurants, and guest houses—and some of the finest wine produced in the country. Known primarily for its red wines, Mudgee is also the habitat of a rare Chardonnay clone that may be descended from the cuttings brought to Australia by James Busby in 1832. Mudgee's 3,444 hectares (8,510 acres) of vineyards are among the highest in the country. The western slopes of the Great Dividing Range harbor vines growing between 450 and 1,100 meters (1,475 to 3,610 feet) above sea level. Although summers are hot, cooler temperatures and greater diurnal variation are the natural result of the increased elevation. Due to delayed ripening, Mudgee's harvest can be a full month later than the nearby Hunter Valley's.

The brown soils of the region are mostly sandy loam over clay or mineral-rich sandstone substratum. Rainfall is approximately 360 millimeters, or 14 inches, during the growing season; some sites with inferior water retention require vineyard irrigation. Premier varieties are Shiraz, Cabernet Sauvignon, Chardonnay, Sémillon, and Riesling. Mudgee also does a brisk cellar door trade in a variety of fortified wines.

HUNTINGTON ESTATE

Cassilis Road, Mudgee,
+61 2 6373 3825,
www.huntingtonestate.com.au

Attorney Bob Roberts, a contemporary of noted Australian wine folk James Halliday and the late Len Evans, also left the world of law and let his winemaking dreams lead him to Mudgee, where he started Huntington Estate in 1969. A lover of the great wines of Bordeaux, the Rhône, and Burgundy, he planted his vineyards with Cabernet Sauvignon, Merlot, Sémillon, Shiraz, Grenache, Pinot Noir, and Chardonnay. Bob's daughter Susie joined him in the business in 1993. In 1996, journalist Tim Stevens, a lover of the wines of Huntington Estate, bought the vineyard next door and began making wine; Tim and Bob became friends. Nine years later, when Bob Roberts was ready to retire, Tim Stevens bought the property and took over as winemaker. His 40 hectares (99 acres) of vineyards, divided into 24 blocks, are home to Bob's original vines, which are now more than 40 years old. Tim Stevens Signature Shiraz 2006 is deep red violet. The nose shows aromas of black raspberry, blueberry, mocha, and gingerbread spice. On the palate, juicy fruit is softened by silky tannins; flavors of blackberry, black cherry, dark chocolate, and licorice are held in check by a sprinkling of Mediterranean herbs.

ROBERT OATLEY VINEYARDS

Craigmoor Road, Mudgee,
+61 2 6372 2208,
www.robertoatley.com

Bob Oatley is one of the most important men, if not *the* most important man, in the Australian wine industry. He is widely credited as the Australian who brought Australian wine to the world. He made his first wines at Rosemount Estate in the Hunter Valley in the 1970s; and today his winemaking home is in Mudgee. His wines have been internationally acclaimed by numerous publications, and he has been recognized by Queen Elizabeth II and awarded the British Empire Medal for his contributions to Papua New Guinea's coffee and cocoa industry. Besides making wine, Oatley is passionate about sailing; he owns a fleet of sailboats, called the Wild Oats series, which have won the prestigious Admiral's Cup. He also owns Hamilton Island Resort in Australia's Whitsunday Islands. Robert Oatley Pemberton Sauvignon Blanc 2010 is crisp and clean with a hint of pink grapefruit and freshly mown grass. It is delightful on the palate and has nice length. Robert Oatley Tic Tok James Oatley Cabernet Sauvignon 2009 is completely fruit-forward with aromas of blackberries and black plum. Deep red-violet in color, with flavors of blueberry, black pepper, clove, and coriander seed, it has a firm tannic structure that holds through the persistent finish. Robert Oatley Mornington Peninsula Pinot Noir 2009 is resonant black cherry in color, deeper than your typical Pinot Noir. Aromas of cherry vanilla, wild raspberry, oregano, a touch of spice, and smoked bacon are present in the bouquet. On the palate it is a generous, mouth-filling wine with upfront flavors of smoked meats and Mediterranean herbs—backed by a full complement of juicy red fruits. The finish is long and lasting.

ORANGE

Grape farmers joined fruit orchardists in this beautiful region only as recently as 1980, but the high altitude and varied fertile soils provide optimum ripening conditions to the 1,605 hectares (3,966 acres) of vineyards in Orange. More than thirty wineries cultivate Chardonnay, Riesling, Sauvignon Blanc, Cabernet Sauvignon, Merlot, and Shiraz at altitudes between 600 and 900 meters (1,970 to 2,950 feet) above sea level. While Shiraz is the most widely planted variety in Orange, there is general agreement that Chardonnay is the most important grape in the region. Cabernet Sauvignon and Merlot are usually blended, often with grapes from warmer regions, in order to soften the region's cool-weather herbal characteristics. Moderate seasonal rainfall of around 440 millimeters, or just over 17 inches, often leads to irrigation during the long growing season. In addition to fruit and wine, Orange is also noted for its artisanal cheeses.

PHILIP SHAW

Caldwell Lane, Orange,
+61 2 6365 2334,
www.philipshaw.com.au

Philip Shaw purchased his 47-hectare (116-acre) Koomooloo vineyard in 1988. It is at an elevation of 900 meters (2,953 feet), and is situated on the slopes of an extinct volcano, thus giving it old volcanic and red earth soils. Less than 1 percent of Australia's vineyards are located at altitudes higher than 600 meters (1,969 feet), making Koomooloo one of the highest grape producing vineyards in the country. Philip Shaw The Dreamer Viognier 2010 is straw colored with green hues. It has aromas of dried peaches, fresh apricot, white stone fruits, and a touch of white pepper. It has balanced acidity in the mouth with a pleasant lingering finish. Philip Shaw No. 19 Sauvignon Blanc 2011 is straw with green tints. Notes of tropical fruits, wet river rocks, and guava play in your nose and on your palate. The wine has nice weight with smooth balanced acidity.

RIVERINA

The most widely planted wine region in Australia—as of 2010 when it surpassed Riverland for the first time—Riverina has 21,034 hectares (51,976 acres) of grapevines planted in its alluvial soils. Primarily a large, flat plain in the southwest of New South Wales, Riverina was given this name in the 1850s, but it was discovered as a wine region in 1912 by John James McWilliam. More than half the grapes grown in the state come from Riverina, which also produces 15 percent of all the grapes grown in Australia. Home to fewer than twenty wineries, Riverina is most famous for its botrytized Sémillon. Unlike many other Australian wine regions, groundwater is abundant here and is supplemented by 200 millimeters, or 8 inches, of rain throughout the growing season. Although summers tend to be hot, cooler autumn temperatures enhance the proliferation of the "noble rot," which concentrates the sugars in affected grapes. Sémillon is also produced in a dry style, as is Chardonnay, which is otherwise the most important grape in the region. Shiraz and Cabernet Sauvignon thrive here as well. Although for many years the focus in this region was on quantity, in the last 20 years a shift has occurred, with a large amount of high-quality wine coming out of Riverina.

CASELLA

Wakley Road, Yenda,
+61 2 6961 3000,
www.casellawines.com.au

When Filippo and Maria Casella left Sicily in 1957 and purchased a farm in Riverina in 1965, they could not have imagined that Casella Wines would become the largest family-owned winery in Australia. Second- and third-generation family members work in every area of the company, which is managed by Filippo and Maria's sons, John, Joe, and Marcello. Casella's bottling line is said to be the fastest in the world, with a capacity of up to 36,000 bottles per hour. Grapes are sourced from 33 regions throughout the country, and 15 percent of all the wine exported from Australia is Casella wine. They bottle under the Yellow Tail, Yellow Tail Reserve, Yellow Tail Bubbles, Yendah, and Casella Mallee labels. Alan Kennett is the chief winemaker for the group. Yellow Tail Reserve Cabernet Sauvignon 2008 is deep garnet in the glass. Aromas of black cherry, eucalyptus, and toasted vanilla prime the palate for flavors of ripe cherry, wild raspberry, mint, and lightly buttered toast. Yellow Tail The Reserve Shiraz 2007 is red violet to the eye, with a nose of blueberry, blackberry, and anisette. Flavors of bright berries with a touch of spice and vanilla play on the palate, leading to a pleasant finish.

QUEENSLAND

Also known as "The Sunshine State," this subtropical region is better known for its beaches than for its wines. Queensland was first planted with vineyards at the beginning of the twentieth century, but it took another hundred years before serious viticulture took place in the cooler, high-altitude regions of South Burnett and the Granite Belt. Today, there are 592 hectares (1,463 acres) of grape-vines in Queensland, with almost 60 percent of those in the Granite Belt. The Granite Belt features higher altitudes as well: most of its vineyards are 600 to 1,500 meters (1,970 to 4,920 feet) above sea level, while South Burnett's are only between 300 to 600 meters (985 to 1,970 feet). There are only ten wineries in South Burnett, while about fifty wineries call the Granite Belt home. Both regions use their height to overcome hot summer days, bestowing peak ripening conditions on their crops of Chardonnay, Cabernet Sauvignon, Shiraz, Verdelho, Sémillon, and Viognier. Both areas receive about 500 millimeters, or just under 20 inches, of rain throughout the growing season. As might be expected, the Granite Belt, on the eastern edge of the Great Dividing Range, features granite-based soils overlaid with grayish-brown earth, while South Burnett's soils are mostly clay.

BALLANDEAN ESTATE

354 Sundown Road, Ballandean,
+61 7 4684 1226,
www.ballandeanestate.com

Four generations of the Puglisi family have made wine since 1926. The family grows many varieties, including Viognier, Sylvaner, Shiraz, Sémillon, Sauvignon Blanc, Chardonnay, and Italian native Nebbiolo. Dylan Rhymer is the winemaker responsible for the production of Ballandean Estate's quality wines. Ballandean Estate Reserve Chardonnay 2008 is medium straw colored, with aromas of honeycomb, white stone fruits, and toasted brioche. It is generous in the mouth with a creamy finish. Ballandean Estate Nebbiolo 2009 is red garnet, with notes of black cherry, red cherry, and vanilla. It is fruit-driven in the mouth with a pleasant finish.

ROBERT CHANNON

Amiens Road, Stanthorpe,
+61 7 4683 3260,
www.robertchannonwines.com

Robert Channon wines are well known in Queensland, where they have won Queensland's Best White Wine three times since their first vintage in 2001. Their Verdelho has something of a local cult following. Robert Channon and his wife, Peggy, also grow Chardonnay, Pinot Gris, Cabernet Sauvignon, Merlot, and Pinot

Noir. They farm 8 hectares (20 acres) of vines and make wine with the assistance of winemaker Mark Ravenscroft. Robert Channon Pinot Gris 2008 is pale straw colored, with aromas of lemon zest, jasmine, citrus blossoms, and Granny Smith apple. It is crisp in the mouth with a clean finish.

SIRROMET

850 Mount Cotton Road, Mount Cotton,
+61 7 3206 2999,
www.sirromet.com.au

Sirromet has won some five hundred domestic and international awards since opening in 2000. Adam Chapman handles winemaking, and the award-winning Restaurant Lurleen's is under the capable command of Chef Andrew Mirosch. Sirromet Classic Unwooded Chardonnay 2011 is pale straw colored with green tints. It has aromas of citrus blossoms, wet river rocks, and tropical fruits. In the mouth, flavors of light melon and citrus juice combine with a crisp minerality on the finish. Sirromet Rosé 2010 is 100 percent Cabernet Sauvignon with notes of rose petal, strawberries and cream, and sage. It is soft and smooth in the mouth with a pleasant finish.

RECIVES

SLOW ROASTED PORK BELLY WITH PINK LADY APPLE AND CELERY LEAF SALAD

✳

Recipe courtesy of chefs Nigel Rich and Peter Reschke
of d'Arry's Verandah Restaurant, at the
d'Arenberg Winery in McLaren Vale

✳

SERVES 6

D'Arry's Verandah restaurant has received many accolades. It was named Best Winery Restaurant in the South Australia Restaurant Awards in 2008 and was called the "Best Aussie Dining Experience" by *Wine & Spirits Magazine*. We enjoyed a crazy-fun lunch with winemaker and owner Chester Osborn and can't wait to go back and hang out again. We love most anything pork, especially pork belly, and chefs Rich and Reschke's recipe is one of the best we have had. We enjoyed ours with d'Arenberg d'Arry's Original Shiraz Grenache 2007. Cooking time—allow 2 hours.

FOR THE PORK BELLY

3 pounds pork belly with
   bone removed
Salt
Ground black pepper
1 quart chicken stock
1 bottle d'Arry's Original
   Shiraz Grenache

FOR THE SALAD

1 whole Spanish onion or
   ½ bunch spring onions
1 whole celery root
2 whole Pink Lady apples
1 handful of each: celery leaves,
   arugula, parsley, fresh herbs,
   washed and torn into bite-
   size pieces
Extra virgin olive oil
Wine vinegar
Salt
Ground black pepper

ROAST THE PORK BELLY

Preheat the oven to 350°F. Rub the pork belly all over with salt
and pepper, and place, skin side down, in a heavy roasting pan.
Roast the pork in the oven for 60 minutes. Remove pork from
the oven and reduce the oven temperature to 300°F. With tongs,
flip over the pork belly, skin side up, and pour the chicken stock
over the pork. Return the pork to the oven, and roast until the
meat pulls apart easily, 50 to 60 minutes more. Transfer the
pork to a large bowl. Deglaze the roasting pan with a generous
splash of d'Arry's Original for au jus.

PREPARE THE SALAD

Gather whatever greens, onions, herbs, and apples you might
have in your garden. (We use arugula, flat leaf parsley, celery
leaves, Spanish onion, spring onions, celery root, and Pink
Lady apples.) Finely slice the onion, celery root, and apples, and
transfer to a large bowl. Mix in a handful of fresh celery leaves,
arugula, parsley, and add fresh herbs at your discretion. Add
extra virgin olive oil and good quality wine vinegar, and toss.
Season with salt and pepper to taste.

TO SERVE

Place a nice slab of pork belly on each plate and top with the
salad. Drizzle each plate with au jus and serve immediately.
Enjoy the rest of the d'Arry's Original bottle with the meal.

RABBIT RILLETTES

✳

Recipe courtesy of Chef Simon West of the Kooyong and
Port Phillip Estate winery on the Mornington Peninsula

✳

SERVES 8

Chef West presented his homemade rabbit rillettes at our lunch with winemaker Sandro Mosele. They were an instant hit with all three of us, and we only had to beg for 15 minutes in person and a further two months via e-mail to get the recipe. West's menu changes every day, based on seasonal availability and market freshness. His style is "a modern take on the classics, but more elegant than rustic." Port Phillip Estate's restaurant has white tablecloths, large columns, floor-to-ceiling glass windows and beautiful views over the vines. On a clear day, you can see the ocean and the coast of the Mornington Peninsula. Next door, there's an informal bistro with a bustling tasting room. We can't wait to return to experience West's cuisine paired with Sandro's wines again. This dish goes perfectly with Port Phillip Estate Pinot Noir 2008.

This recipe has two stages, and it can be done ahead of time and stored in jars in the fridge.

TO CURE THE RABBIT

1 cup kosher salt

6 bay leaves

1 tablespoon black peppercorns

1 star anise, lightly crushed

¼ bunch of thyme

2 rabbits, jointed into 8 pieces
(you can ask your butcher
to do this for you)

FOR THE CONFIT

¼ bunch thyme

4 bay leaves

6 cloves of garlic, crushed

1 teaspoon black peppercorns

1 quart duck fat, melted

1⅓ bottle white wine

Vegetable oil, if needed

2 teaspoons green peppercorns

ACCOMPANIMENTS

Brioche

Verjuice jelly

Fresh figs

CURE THE RABBIT

In a large bowl, combine the salt, bay leaves, peppercorns, star anise, and thyme. Cover the rabbit pieces with salt mixture, and leave overnight (12 hours) in the refrigerator to cure.

COOK THE RABBIT

Remove the rabbit pieces from the salt mixture, rinse them thoroughly, and pat them dry. Place the rabbit pieces in a wide pot, add thyme, bay leaves, garlic, and black peppercorns, and cover with duck fat and wine. (If you don't have enough to cover, add any flavorless vegetable oil to make up the difference.) Cook the rabbit over the lowest heat, until meat is tender and falls off the bone, 2 to 4 hours. (Do not let the mixture boil, as it will make the meat tough.) Remove the pot from heat, and let the rabbit cool in the pot to room temperature.

Strain the meat from the duck fat, reserving the fat. Flake the meat with your fingertips into a bowl, and make sure that all bones are removed. Gently work the meat together, add green peppercorns, and pack firmly into sterilized jars or a container. Cover with a thin layer of duck fat and refrigerate overnight.

At Port Phillip Estate, this dish is served on toasted homemade brioche, with verjuice jelly and fresh figs.

CHAR-GRILLED SPATCHCOCK

*

Recipe courtesy of Chef Heath Farrow of
Giant Steps/Innocent Bystander Winery,
in the Yarra Valley

*

SERVES 6-8

Named after John Coltrane's *Giant Steps*—one of owner Phil Sexton's favorite albums—Giant Steps/Innocent Bystander Winery has one of the hippest restaurants in the valley. Plate-glass windows give diners an amazing view of the entire winemaking process—as well as the chef's antics in the kitchen. All of the restaurant's breads and pizzas are made on premise utilizing a sourdough recipe and "starter" that is more than one hundred years old. Winery ambassador Cameron Mackenzie told us over lunch that he has to come in on Christmas Day, when the rest of the winery is closed, "just to feed the starter beast." "Spatchcock" is the Australian name for a type of young chicken that is extremely popular among grill masters in the Yarra Valley.

FOR THE MARINADE AND CHICKEN

1 lemon, zest removed and juiced
5 cloves sliced garlic
¼ bunch chopped thyme
5 bay leaves
1 cup olive oil
3 or 4 small chickens (about
    3 pounds each)

FOR THE GREEN SALSA

1 bunch parsley, chopped
1 bunch cilantro, chopped
½ bunch basil, chopped
5 white anchovies
2 ounces capers
¾ cup caper juice
2 tablespoons minced green
    jalapeño pepper
Salt
Freshly ground pepper

FOR THE SALAD

2 red bell peppers
¼ Spanish onion, finely sliced
1 ripe plum tomato, cut into
    large dice
4 sweet basil leaves, torn
Salt
Pepper

MARINATE THE CHICKEN

Put all the marinade ingredients into a big bowl.

Cut the chicken open as if to butterfly. Remove the wishbone and rib cage and add chicken pieces to the marinade. Marinate chicken for 6 hours.

COOK THE CHICKEN

Prepare a charcoal or gas grill for grilling over high heat.

Remove the chicken from the marinade and grill for 10 minutes on one side. With tongs, flip over the chicken and grill for another 10 minutes. Let the chicken rest another 10 minutes before serving.

MAKE THE GREEN SALSA

Combine all ingredients in a blender, and blend until smooth. Season with salt and pepper to taste.

MAKE THE SALAD

Char the red peppers over an open flame, and remove the skin. Let the peppers cool.

Dice the cooled red peppers and add to a large bowl with onion and tomato. Dress the salad with the salsa, finish with the freshly torn basil leaves, and salt and pepper to taste.

TO SERVE

Divide the salad among the plates, and top with the chicken.

IN THEIR OWN WORDS

MICHAEL HILL SMITH MW

In 1988 Michael Hill Smith was the first Australian to pass the Master of Wine examination. He has been awarded an Order of Australia for his contribution to the wine industry in his country. In 2009 he was named one of the "Top Fifty Movers and Shakers in the Wine World" by *Decanter* magazine. We had the pleasure of sharing a few glasses of Shaw + Smith wine with Michael and his winemaker cousin, Martin Shaw.

How did you get involved in the world of wine?
My forebears established Barossa winery Yalumba in 1849. I'm a sixth-generation Australian winemaker, so you could say it is in the genes. As a child we were served lemonade flavored with Shiraz! I sold out of Yalumba in 1989 and set up Shaw + Smith with my winemaker cousin Martin Shaw the same year. My greatest influence and mentor however was the extraordinary wine man Len Evans, who showed me just how exciting fine wine could be. He inspired me in many ways, and this resulted in me passing the Master of Wine Examination in 1988.

What are some of the biggest changes you have seen in winemaking since you began your career?

The wines of today are better made than those of the past—there are less obvious winemaking faults and far more consistency. World demand is less Eurocentric—great wine can and does comes from any number of countries. Consumers now have a wonderful choice of wines from both the New and Old Worlds. It is a good time for wine drinkers.

What are some of the exciting changes that you see happening specifically in your country?
The rise and rise of Australian wine internationally has been an exhilarating ride for us. We now have a wonderful array of small to medium-sized wineries making regional wines of great diversity and quality. This will only increase in the future. More than ever, winemakers are focusing on regional wines that

show and have respect for their region and site. And finally there has been a significant move to cooler regions—and these regions are now making wonderful Chardonnay, Pinot Noir, and balanced spicy Shiraz—in direct contrast to the traditional, somewhat heavier, styles from warmer regions.

Where else in the world have you studied, trained, or worked a harvest? How did that influence your winemaking?

I am not an enologist but studied:

- Wine Production and Marketing at Roseworthy College, now part of the University of Adelaide
- Advanced Diploma Cordon Bleu School London WSET Diploma in 1986
- Master of Wine Studies 1986–88; Graduated Master of Wine 1988
- 30 years as a wine judge at Australian and International wine shows

All these experiences have helped mold my views on wine and the wines Martin and I aspire to make.

Which varieties are you working with? Are you experimenting with anything new?

Martin and I focus on classical varieties that are best suited to the cool climate of the Adelaide Hills. We make four grape varieties only:

a fresh zingy Sauvignon Blanc, a complex but restrained barrel-fermented Chardonnay, juicy Pinot Noir, and spicy "fruit-pure" Shiraz.

Are there any new areas that you have identified for potential vineyard sites?

We are very excited about Tasmania—we think it has a wonderful climate, and we are just about to purchase an outstanding vineyard in southern Tasmania with a view to making single-vineyard Pinot Noir and Chardonnay.

What challenges have you faced as a winemaker or winery owner?

Keeping focused on making the best wines we possibly can and not being distracted by too many other projects and diversions along the way. Being ruthless on the blending and only including those wines that are good enough for the Shaw + Smith name. Declassifying lesser wines is essential to making the best wines possible.

What is your winemaking philosophy?

Our goal is to make exciting modern Australian wines that rank amongst the best of their type. We do this by careful vineyard selection, low vineyard yields, and attention to detail at every stage of the process.

What would you hope people say about your wine?

Delicious, authentic wines that overdeliver. And most importantly, "let's have another bottle!"

Do you think that the market should influence winemaking, or do you think that winemaking should influence the market?

Winemakers cannot ignore the market, but having said this, most of the winemakers I admire make wines that above all they like themselves—and then somewhat arrogantly expect consumers to share this enthusiasm.

Besides your own wine, what are some of your favorite wines? What do you like about them?

Wines of balance, harmony, great perfume supported by depth of flavor and palate length.

What is your opinion on screwcap versus cork closures?

I am not a screwcap zealot, but I hate cork taint and random oxidation caused by cork. I am a fan of screwcaps for both young and aged wines and wish all of my cellar was safely aging under screwcap.

If you could invite anyone from history, living or dead, to your home for dinner, who would

it be? What food would you serve? What wine would you serve?

My friend and mentor Len Evans—I miss him and would love to see him again! Food would be simple—freshly picked crab, aged sirloin with gratinée potatoes and green beans, cloth-wrapped English Cheddar. We would probably drink old Hunter Valley Sémillon and a bottle of 1962 Penfolds Bin 60A—widely believed to be the greatest Australian red wine ever made.

If you were to stay home tonight for a relaxing evening, drinking wine while watching a movie, which movie would you watch? Which wine would you drink? Explain.

To Catch a Thief and 1978 DRC La Tache. Both classics.

How do you like to spend your time away from the winery?

I love skiing—the perfect family holiday; I love to cook; I am an irregular and poor student of yoga.

Do you collect wine? If so, what is in your cellar?

Aged Australian Riesling and Sémillon. Aged Australian reds such as Grange, Wendouree, Cullen. A fair amount of first- and second-growth Bordeaux—more than I really want.

Not nearly enough Burgundy, but I am currently building stocks of DRC, Rousseau, Raveneau, Leroy, Dujac, Bonneau du Martray, Domaine Leflaive. An increasing amount of good Barolo and Super Tuscan.

If you weren't involved in wine, what would you be doing?

Running a restaurant in a very good ski resort.

PETER BARRY

Peter's father Jim Barry was the seventeenth winemaker to graduate from the prestigious Roseworthy College in 1946. Peter graduated from his dad's alma mater in 1982. He is strongly involved in anything related to his beloved Clare Valley. He is a member of many winemaking organizations, including the Clare Valley Winemakers Incorporated for which he sits on the board. Peter also serves as the chairman of the South Australian Wine Industry Association. We were lucky enough to enjoy his 2010 Watervale Riesling with him, his lovely wife, and family while watching the sun set over the Clare Valley.

How did you get involved in the world of wine?
I was fortunate enough to have been born into a winemaking family. I enjoyed working with my late father from the age of four and continued the relationship until his death. I inherited his passion for wine.

What are some of the biggest changes you have seen in winemaking since you began your career?
Some of the biggest changes I have seen are the advances in the "science" of winemaking through continued research. Modern winemaking machinery, which assists with filtering and filling, as well as viticultural equipment, has changed the way we do things. The use of computers has also had a tremendous impact.

What are some of the exciting changes that you see happening specifically in your country?
There is a growing interest in new varieties and experimental techniques. I find this terribly exciting as it will allow the Australian wine industry to move with our foreign counterparts and become innovators in the field. We are also seeing a return to boutique winemaking practices, which I truly believe is the way forward for our industry.

Where else in the world have you studied, trained, or worked a harvest? How did that influence your winemaking?
I have worked in the Hunter Valley, Barossa Valley, Bordeaux, and China for a brief time. All experiences in life are good, as they shape

the person you are and the actions you take. I now encourage my children to go abroad and work in as many different places as possible.

Which varieties are you working with? Are you experimenting with anything new?

We work with Riesling, Shiraz, Cabernet Sauvignon, and small amounts of Malbec, Sauvignon Blanc, and Sémillon. After visiting Santorini and tasting Assyrtiko I imported cuttings from the island to Australia where they were in quarantine for two years. We will be the first to plant Assyrtiko in Australia this August.

Are there any new areas that you have identified for potential vineyard sites?

Clare has warm days and cool nights so we look for the cooler sites for Riesling, free draining soils. The future is for the next generation, maybe Tasmania, Yarra Valley, or half a hectare in Champagne—would be fascinating but perhaps a bit far away.

What challenges have you faced as a winemaker or winery owner?

As a winemaker and winery owner one must empty tanks ready for next vintage—this is the challenge. The better the quality, the easier it is to sell—thus keep the quality at a consistently high standard and the consumers will always return.

What is your winemaking philosophy?

Our wines are of a consistently high standard, yet I will always strive to make better wines.

What would you hope people say about your wine?

That it brings them enjoyment and stimulates their senses; makes them say "that's very good wine."

Do you think that the market should influence winemaking, or do you think that winemaking should influence the market?

The market does not influence our winemaking—we make our wine and then seek consumers who appreciate our Jim Barry fruit, backbone, and structure.

Besides your own wine, what are some of your favorite wines? What do you like about them?

Wines that represent a place intrigue me— Riesling from the Wachau and Mosel. Chardonnay from Burgundy, and Chablis and Assyrtiko from Santorini. These wines are pure expressions of their region, and I enjoy tasting from many different producers.

What is your opinion on screwcap versus cork closures?

The screwcap is the most consistent closure and the best for Riesling. It is great for the consumer. Screwcaps are the best closure available today for white wine; there is 40 years of research (AWRI) to support this. With red wine our trials are only nine years old, and we are confident that the screwcap will be the answer.

If you could invite anyone from history, living or dead, to your home for dinner, who would it be? What food would you serve? What wine would you serve?

I would gain the greatest pleasure from sitting down with my late father, Jim Barry, and our very large family—they would be disappointed if we didn't invite them. It would be simple fare, probably soup and slow-roasted lamb with vegetables from the garden, gravy, and mint sauce—just cheese for dessert. The wine would be our 1977 Watervale Riesling. This wine is from the first vintage that I worked with my father.

If you were to stay home tonight for a relaxing evening, drinking wine while watching a movie, which movie would you watch? Which wine would you drink? Explain.

The movie I would watch would be *The Dinner Game* by Francis Veber. It's a French comedy about wealthy businessmen who have a game of choosing a person who they consider to be an idiot and inviting them to dinner. It backfires. The wine would be our 1989 The Armagh Shiraz.

How do you like to spend your time away from the winery?

I live with my wife and family on a vineyard and farm, with horses, turkeys, chickens, and pigeons. One of my hobbies is breeding pigs. I also love to cook and entertain for large numbers. I always look forward to our annual family holidays to Robe, where I go cray fishing. I also enjoy traveling overseas to visit our international markets in Europe, North America, and Asia.

Do you collect wine? If so, what is in your cellar?

Yes, I have a large collection of Australian wine and imported wine. I'll never drink my cellar, so I give the keys to my children from time to time to help themselves, they really enjoy drinking wines older than them and that have been sitting in the same place for such a long time.

If you weren't involved in wine, what would you be doing?

I would be involved in agriculture in some form as I really enjoy the land and life in the country.

JAMES HALLIDAY

James Halliday has been writing since 1979 and has contributed to more than fifty-eight books on wine. He is considered by many to be the leading Australian wine authority. He is the Editor-at-Large of *James Halliday Wine Companion* magazine, the author of *James Halliday Australian Wine Companion*, *James Halliday's Wine Atlas of Australia*, and *The Australian Wine Encyclopedia*. He was one of the founders of Brokenwood Winery in the Lower Hunter Valley and thereafter founded Coldstream Hills Winery in the Yarra Valley.

How did you get involved in the world of wine?
In 1956, while at the University of Sydney nominally studying for my Arts Law Degrees, I was in fact actively pursuing other knowledge and pleasure. Part of this was the College Wine Cellar; we were permitted to drink wine in the Great Hall on Wednesday night and Sunday lunch, and the College had a Wine Cellar Club, which I promptly joined. It was with that club that I made my first trips to the Hunter Valley to visit Tulloch courtesy of Harry Brown, then working with Johnny Walker at Rhine Castle. Somehow or other I failed sufficiently in my pursuit of pleasure, thus graduating with my Arts Law Degrees and promptly took off for a year overseas with one of my best friends from St. Paul's College. Armed with a van and camping equipment, we drove all over France, Spain, Italy, and Germany, without paying any particular attention to where we were. At that time, I did not have the faintest idea about fine French wine, and we could not have afforded it even if I had known.

I returned to Sydney in 1962 to seriously commence my law career, and it was only then that it became apparent I had unknowingly been infected with the wine bug. Australian wine (including most obviously Lindemans) started to accumulate under my bed in the house I shared with friends and in my parents' cellar in Bellevue Hill, although I discovered that my mother assumed that anything in the cellar that was not Lindemans was by definition cooking wine, and after the mysterious disappearance of a number of precious bottles, I realized the problem and tore up a sheet to make big, white bows that I put around the necks of the bottles to prevent further unfortunate mistakes.

What are some of the biggest changes you have seen in the world of wine since you began your career?

Throughout the 1940s and '50s there was almost nothing written about wine outside of technical trade publications. Wine criticism as we know it today was likewise nonexistent. Thus my father bought Lindemans Hock, Riesling, Chablis, and White Burgundy without having the faintest idea that each of those four wines was made from Sémillon; he likewise purchased Clarets and Burgundies without knowing that they were both made from Shiraz. You didn't worry about such things at that time; the only consideration was whether the wine was excellent, good, or disappointing.

The other change was the increasing importation (from a very low base) of top-class Burgundy, Bordeaux, etc. picking up pace in the 1960s and '70s, albeit waxing and waning over subsequent decades. A high point of imports was in 1985, when Australia imported more wine by volume and value than it exported. Since then exports have increased exponentially, from a little over A$8 million to well over A$2 billion.

What are some of the exciting changes that you see happening in Australia?

First up, the formal registration of 63 Geo-graphic Indications (the equivalent of French AC or US AVA). While the process of registration applies to areas regardless of their age, the greatest number are of cool- to intermediate- climate regions. The range and quality of Pinot Noir has increased exponentially from a near-zero base in 1980, with Tasmania, Mornington Peninsula, Yarra Valley, Geelong, and Gippsland providing most (although not all) of the excitement. Chardonnay came on-stream from the early 1970s, but it has really only been in the last 25 years that Margaret River and the Yarra Valley have been locked in mortal combat for supremacy with this variety. Within this there is a subtext of a move to earlier picking, less new oak, and exclusion of malolactic fermentation.

Are there any new or untapped areas in Australia that you have your eye on?

There are many parts of Tasmania that as yet do not have vines but (subject to water availability) will grow fabulous grapes in the years ahead. What is more, if global warming proceeds the way the IPCC would have us believe, Tasmania will be air-conditioned by the very cold oceans that surround it and will be unaffected. Other interesting regions have been opening up on the western side of the Great Dividing Range, Tumbarumba in the Australian Alps is one such example, Orange further north (with plantings up to 1,000 meters [3,281 feet] but more to go up if the climate warms) another.

Are you still actively involved at Coldstream Hills?

In May 2000 I resigned as Southcorp Group Winemaker, and these days am responsible only (in a consultancy role) for Coldstream Hills. So far as Coldstream is concerned, it is more a change of title than substance: I continue to be involved as part of the winemaking team, and owning the house which stands at the highest part of the vineyard, overlooking the House Block Chardonnay and the Yarra Valley floor spread out below, there is no chance of my ever leaving this beautiful part of the world.

Do you think that the market should influence winemaking, or do you think that winemaking should influence the market?

Assuming we are discussing fine wine (as opposed to beverage wine) in an ideal world, it should be winemaking that influences the market. There is a further gloss on the question in Australia, where it is constantly being posed thus: Do winemakers make wines to please the show judges, or do the show judges point the way for winemakers to improve their wines? It is a bit of both. Winemaking

and marketing have always been in a fluid and dynamic relationship, and I don't see this changing in the future.

What is your opinion on screwcap versus cork closures?

If one wishes to adhere to a 350-year-old technology that matches cork bark (where, by necessity, every cork is different from every other cork, either to a tiny degree or a much larger degree) and insert it in the neck of a bottle that, by virtue of the way bottles are made, can be precisely calibrated to extremely fine tolerances on the exterior, but is uncertain in the interior, so be it. As the cork producers are so fond of saying, cork is a natural substance, and it is for this reason that it does vary. It is an extraordinary substance with millions of hexagonal gas-filled chambers and is impossible to replicate with synthetics of whatever type. Having denied the existence of problems from TCA emanating from the way corks were made, pointing the finger instead at shipping containers (some truth in that until they stopped using chlorine-type disinfectant), wineries (if they were insane enough to use similar chlorine-based antiseptics) and vineyards (on the ludicrous proposition that trichloranisole is endemic in vineyards, particularly in Australia), the Portuguese reluctantly agreed they had a problem.

By this stage the horse had bolted from the stable, and Australian winemakers were swapping en masse to screwcaps. It is ironic that a significant part of the reason for change was TCA, not random/sporadic oxidation. The Portuguese have root and branch changes to the harvesting, storage, fabricating, and shipping of corks and have succeeded in significantly reducing the level of TCA. If this were the only problem with corks, there would still be substantial use of them by Australian makers to meet the demands of export markets but, having moved from cork to screwcap, Australian winemakers have realised just how unreliable corks are (oxidation problem 1, TCA problem 2, mechanical failure problem 3) and how totally reliable screwcaps are. (Accusations of reduction are shooting the messenger: the cause lies in the wine, not the closure. Reduction is not an issue with well-made wine.)

Thus of the 8,000 or so wines I tasted for the 2011 Australian Wine Companion, 84 percent were under screwcap (up from 79 percent the year before), one-piece natural cork 9 percent (down from 14 percent the year before), Diam 6 percent (up 1 percent), the remaining 1 percent (in approximate order of importance) ProCork, Twin top, Crown seal, Zork, Vino-Lok, and Synthetic. Vino-Lok is an elegant-looking closure with some of the advantages of screwcaps once the bottle has been opened, but is expensive, and the small polyethylene band may or may not retain its elasticity.

And, incidentally, I have, in all seriousness, offered to pay an extra A$100 per bottle above the standard asking price to Domaine de la Romanée-Conti for the wines I buy from it each year to be sealed with a screwcap. Aubert de Villaine knows I am sincere, but of course, is not the least bit tempted to make such a radical move.

What are some of the most prized bottles in your cellar?

Other than the empty ones of greater age and/or provenance, Burgundies from the Domaine de la Romanée-Conti, the oldest from 1942, and a few remaining bottles of vintage (not solera) Madeira from the mid-nineteenth century.

If you weren't involved in wine, what would you be doing?

Obviously, I would still be practicing law.

BOB OATLEY

Bob Oatley is considered to be the man who introduced Australian wine to the world. He began his wine career in the late 1960s at Rosemount Estate in the Hunter Valley. He was the first Australian invited to present his wines at Wine Spectator's Critic Awards (now called Wine Spectator Wine Experience), and he and his wines have won numerous awards, medals, and trophies. He is passionate about racing his *Wild Oats* yacht and has collected many racing trophies including the prestigious Admiral's Cup. He has always been involved in agriculture and was awarded the British Empire Medal by Queen Elizabeth II for his contribution to the Papua New Guinea coffee industry.

How did you get involved in the world of wine?
I have been involved in agriculture all of my life, beginning in Papua New Guinea growing and marketing coffee and cocoa and then in the 1960s embarked on grape growing and winemaking, planting my first vineyard, with my children, in the Hunter Valley.

What are some of the biggest changes you have seen in winemaking since you began your career?
The biggest change has been the rise in quality of everyday wines—through greater emphasis on quality in the vineyards and improved winemaking practices.

What are some of the exciting changes you see happening specifically in your country?
The enormous shift in Australian winemaking culture to focus on high quality is the change that excites me most.

Where else in the world have you studied, trained, or worked a harvest? How did that influence your winemaking?
I have no formal technical education in wine but have, for all my life, been a great student of agriculture and also flavors, firstly in coffee and latterly in wine. For both of these beverages, the most critical aspect is the taste in the mouth—and the thing I most focus upon.

Which varieties are you working with? Are you experimenting with anything new?
I continue to be excited by the evolution of Chardonnay and view our viticultural and winemaking practices as a continuing experiment—areas in which we never stop

developing and hopefully improving. Every day we understand more about our craft.

Are there any new areas that you have identified for potential vineyard sites?

Our primary focus is upon improving our existing vineyards—both preserving the history behind the very old sites (one of our properties dates back to 1858) and evolving the newer plots. Meanwhile, we have discovered a passion for the vineyards of south Western Australia—an exciting new area for us to work with.

What challenges have you faced as a winemaker or winery owner?

Seasonal variation is the challenge we have every year. We must adapt and adjust our plans according to the changing seasons so we can continue to improve our quality.

What is your winemaking philosophy?

We aim to make wines that express their site and variety and most importantly have a taste that appeals to the consumer.

What would you hope people say about your wine?

That they enjoyed drinking it as much as we enjoyed making it.

Do you think that the market should influence winemaking, or that winemaking should influence the market?

Winemakers should always be aware of changing tastes in the marketplace and respond accordingly.

Besides your own wine, what are some of your favorite wines? What do you like about them?

I have a few favorite White Burgundies and also enjoy the red wines of Rioja. In both instances it's the texture and mouthfeel that I enjoy most.

What is your opinion on screwcap versus cork closures?

We are one hundred percent committed to screwcaps.

How do you like to spend your time away from the winery?

I am a very keen sailor and spend as much time as I can spare on the water. In the Australian winter, I head to Porto Cervo on the Mediterranean, a beautiful sailing spot that was the inspiration for our beautiful tropical resort, Quaila, which we recently built on the Great Barrier Reef and where I also have a home. They are my two favorite places to unwind.

If you weren't involved in wine, what would you be doing?

On the water, racing my yacht.

BRAZIL

WHEN MOST PEOPLE THINK OF BRAZIL they think of Rio de Janeiro, the sounds of Astrud Gilberto and Gilberto Gil, and sandy beaches with scantily clad beauties. The fifth largest country in the world, and the fifth largest producer of wine in the Southern Hemisphere (behind Argentina, Australia, South Africa, and Chile), Brazil has a whole lot more to offer than sun, samba, and sand. With a winemaking tradition dating back to the late nineteenth century, the nation's wineries produced over 3.3 million hectoliters (330,000,000 liters) in 2010. Originally growing *Vitis labrusca* grapes—the North American varieties such as Concord and Niagara, generally made into grape juice and jelly rather than into fine wine—the vineyards of Brazil now grow "international" *Vitis vinifera* grapes such as Merlot, Pinot Noir, Malvasia, Cabernet Sauvignon, Chardonnay, Cabernet Franc, Tannat, Malbec, Riesling, Viognier, and Muscat.

A total of more than 88,000 hectares (217,000 acres) of grapes are planted in its five main wine regions, which are, from north to south, Vale do São Francisco, Planalto Catarinense, Serra Gaucha, Serra do Sudeste, and Campanha. Of the five, Serra Gaucha is responsible for more than 90 percent of Brazil's wine production. From the mid-1870s until about 1900, more than two million European immigrants arrived in Brazil, the majority of them from northern Italy. In exchange for passage, they worked on coffee plantations for two years, at the end of which time they were able to purchase farmland at low prices. Most of the Italians settled in the Serra Gaucha region, whose fertile mountainsides closely mimic the hills of Piedmont and Tuscany. Today, Italian-style cooking is the dominant cuisine of the region, and many of the older residents speak a northern Italian dialect interspersed with Portuguese.

More than fifteen thousand families are involved in grape growing and winemaking in Brazil. Grapes are grown in four different states, and there are almost twelve hundred wineries across the land. However, 90 percent of fine-wine production takes place in Serra Gaucha, in the state of Rio Grande do Sul in southern Brazil, and fewer than forty wineries account for 90 percent of all wine produced in the country. While many larger facilities still produce grape juice and cheap jug wines for the domestic market, a growing number of businesses, most of them family owned, now focus on fine-wine production. Dry red wines and sparkling wines, both dry and sweet, predominate, with dry white wines, rosé, and still sweet wines rounding out the national portfolio. Sparkling wines are produced using both the Charmat and traditional Champenoise method. The widespread use of Charmat—also known as *Metodo Italiano*—is easily understandable, given the large numbers of Italian immigrants involved in winemaking here.

Many wineries were founded or moved into the fine-wine business in the last 20 years. The latest generation of Brazilian-Italians is studying business, marketing, winemaking, and languages and making their impact known in the global market. Brazilian wines are now exported to approximately thirty countries. In a 15-year period through the end of 2010, wines from Brazil won more than 2,300 medals at wine competitions around the world. There is no widespread government regulation over allowable grape varieties or geographic vineyard designations, but groups of winemakers are petitioning to be allowed to follow the lead of the recently formed D.O. Vale dos Vinhedos in Serra Gaucha.

MAJOR GRAPE VARIETIES

CABERNET FRANC

One of the genetic parents of Cabernet Sauvignon (along with Sauvignon Blanc), this red variety lends both softness and a peppery characteristic to Merlot- and Cabernet Sauvignon–based blends and is also increasingly seen bottled as a single varietal.

CABERNET SAUVIGNON

This small, dark grape with a thick, pest-resistant skin is known for its flavors of black cherry, black currant, spice, and graphite. Its strong tannins give it the ability to age well, and in Brazil it is bottled both as a single varietal and with a majority of Merlot in Bordeaux-style blends.

CHARDONNAY

Native to France, this white grape with flavors of tropical fruits and green apples finds its way into still and sparkling wines alike. Vinified in stainless steel, its crisp fruit and mineral character shines through, while versions aged in oak tend to lean toward toast, butter, and vanilla.

MALVASIA

Both Malvasia Bianca and Malvasia de Candia flourish in Brazil and are used in both dry white and sweet sparkling blends. Expect flavors of white peach and apricot, with nut-like flavors as the wine ages.

MERLOT

The only red grape that may be labeled as a single varietal in Serra Gaucha's D.O. Vale dos Vinhedos, Merlot is a dark purple-blue grape that bears flavors of black cherry, blueberry, cassis, and mint. Merlot can run the gamut from fruity and vibrant to complex and rich, depending on winemaking technique and amount of age.

MOSCATO

Brazil's shining star in the international market may well be sparkling Moscato, made from a combination of Moscato Bianco, Moscato Giallo, Moscato de Alexandria, and Moscatel Nazareno. Smooth and sweet, with aromas and flavors of white floral blossoms, citrus, and stone fruit, Moscato may also be vinified into still white wine.

PINOT NOIR

The cone-like appearance of its dark purple bunches of grapes gives Pinot Noir its name, taken from the French words for "pine" and "black." Dry red Pinot Noirs tend to have flavors of cherry, chocolate, and citrus zest. Sparkling wines made from Pinot Noir, in both the traditional and Charmat methods, lean toward crisp, clean minerality.

RIESLING ITALICO

This white variety came to Brazil via northern Italy. It is unrelated to the Riesling that predominates in Germany and Austria. Made into both still and sparkling wines, it has traditionally been used as a blending grape but is now seen as a single varietal as well.

SAUVIGNON BLANC

French for "wild white," Sauvignon Blanc in Brazil is more aligned with a restrained French or Italian style than with the grassy, herbaceous New World–style seen elsewhere in the hemisphere. Its crisp, tropical fruit flavors are found bottled alone or blended with Chardonnay and other whites.

BRAZIL

TRINIDAD AND TOBAGO

VENEZUELA

GUYANA

SURINAME

FRENCH GUIANA

COLOMBIA

N

Amazon R.

Manaus

Amazon R.

Natal

B R A Z I L

VALE DO
SÃO FRANCISCO

PERU

Salvador

Brasília ★

BOLIVIA

*ATLANTIC
OCEAN*

CHILE

PARAGUAY

São Paulo

Rio de Janeiro

PLANALTO CATARINENSE

I.P. PINTO BANDEIRA

SERRA GAUCHA

*PACIFIC
OCEAN*

D.O. VALE DOS VINHEDOS

ARGENTINA

SERRA DO SUDESTE AND CAMPANHA

URUGUAY

0 Miles   500

0 Kilometers   500

© 2012 Jeffrey L. Ward

WINE REGIONS

VALE DO SÃO FRANCISCO

Almost 4,025 kilometers (2,500 miles) north of Serra Gaucha, Vale do São Francisco is the wine-producing area of Brazil closest to the equator. Due to the tropical climate—temperatures throughout the year range from 20 to 31 degrees Celsius (68 to 88 degrees Fahrenheit)—each plant bears grapes twice per year. The soil is poor and rocky; this is the only area in the country in which irrigation is widely used. Vineyard altitudes range from 350 to 450 meters (1,150 to 1,300 feet).

Most of the grapes grown are *Vitis labrusca*, for inexpensive table wine and grape juice. However, red varieties such as Syrah, Tempranillo, and Cabernet Sauvignon are raised here, as are whites such as Chenin Blanc, Malvasia Bianca, and Muscat. Of these, Muscat is the most important variety. It is used to make sweet sparkling wines. Producers making quality wine from grapes grown in Vale do São Francisco include Fazenda Ouro Verde of the Miolo group and Vinibrasil.

PLANALTO CATARINENSE

An area settled by Italians and in which Italian dialect is widely spoken, Planalto Catarinense is both the highest and coldest of Brazil's wine regions. Average temperatures range from 9 to 22 degrees Celsius (49 to 71 degrees Fahrenheit) and altitudes range between 900 and 1,400 meters (2,950 to 4,600 feet). Due to both altitude and temperature, harvest takes place between March and April, about two months later than in neighboring Serra Gaucha. Soil type is mainly basaltic, resulting from volcanic activity. The subregion Vale do Rio do Peixe is further subdivided into Friburgo and Caçador. Main types of red grapes are Cabernet Sauvignon, Merlot, and Pinot Noir, and white varieties are Sauvignon Blanc and Chardonnay. Late-harvest ice wines are also made here.

SANJO VINHOS FINOS

Av. Irineu Bornhausen, 677, Martorano,
São Joaquim, SC,
+55 49 3233 0012,
www.sanjo.com.br

A relative newcomer to the winemaking industry in Brazil, Sanjo was founded in 1993 by a group of 34 Japanese immigrants. Originally fruit growers with a strong emphasis on apple varieties, namely Fuji and Gala, the company began planting vines in 2002. It released its first vintages from the 2005 and 2006 seasons. Today the company produces 70,000 liters of wine annually. The vineyards are located in the Serra Catarinense range—one of the coldest regions in Brazil, due to its high altitude. All of Sanjo's vineyards are planted at a minimum of 1,000 meters (3,281 feet) above sea level. Its Maestrale Integrus 2008 is a blend of 85 percent Chardonnay and 15 percent Sauvignon Blanc. It is grown in Sanjo's highest vineyard at 1,300 meters (4,265 feet). Low yields of 1 kilogram (2.2 pounds) of grapes per vine produce an elegant, full-bodied wine with a nose of apricots, white stone fruits, and butterscotch. The Maestrale Cabernet Sauvignon 2006 is ruby red with a violet rim. It offers aromas of red fruits, raspberries, and black plums and is soft and supple in the mouth with balanced tannic acidity.

SANTO EMÍLIO VINÍCOLA

Rua Major Bibiano Rodrigues de Lima 194,
Lages SC
+55 49 3223 0208,
www.santoemilio.com.br

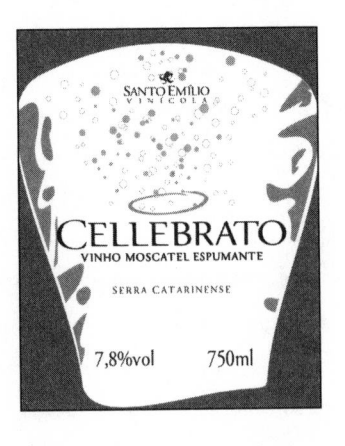

Unlike most Brazilian winemaking families, the Binotto family got its start in freight transport and wood products before diversifying into fine wine. Vineyards were first planted in 2003, and the first harvest and vinification in its state-of-the-art winery took place in 2006. With a young, all-female staff and a fresh approach to winemaking and packaging, Santo Emílio produces wines of a quality as high as their vineyards. At 1,400 meters (4,593 feet), the cold climate is just right for their citrus and herb-scented Sauvignon Blanc. Cellebrato NV, a sweet Moscatel with notes of white peach and honeysuckle, is platinum blonde and bubbly, just like winemaker

Patricia Poggere. Cabernet Sauvignon and Merlot find their way into both Stellato NV, a sparkling rosé brut that tastes of strawberry jam and toasted bread and Leopoldo 2007, an oak-aged blend whose flavors of cassis and stewed fruits are nicely balanced by bright acidity.

SERRA GAUCHA

The largest and most important wine region in Brazil, Serra Gaucha accounts for almost 90 percent of Brazil's fine-wine production. It is a national leader in quality, innovation, and wine tourism—in 2010, 150,000 visitors streamed through its wineries, restaurants, and hotels. The area was mainly settled by Italian immigrants (and some German) in the latter part of the nineteenth century, and most families here say they have been growing grapes and making wine since 1875. Unlike most wine regions around the world, which usually appear parched at harvest time, Serra Gaucha is a rolling landscape of lush green hills, and many vineyards are punctuated by an occasional palm tree. Vineyards sit at 450 to 750 meters (1,475 to 2,450 feet) above sea level. Temperatures run between 11 degrees Celsius (53 degrees Fahrenheit) in winter and 22 degrees Celsius (72 degrees Fahrenheit) in summer.

The majority of white grapes here are Riesling, Chardonnay, Muscat, Malvasia, and Glera (formerly known as Prosecco). Red varieties include Merlot, Cabernet Sauvignon, Cabernet Franc, Tannat, Ancellota, Pinot Noir, Touriga Nacional, and Teroldego. Most are used as single varieties though blends are common as well.

BOSCATO VINHOS

VRS 314, Km 12.5, Nova Padua, RS,
+55 54 3296 1377,
www.boscato.com.br

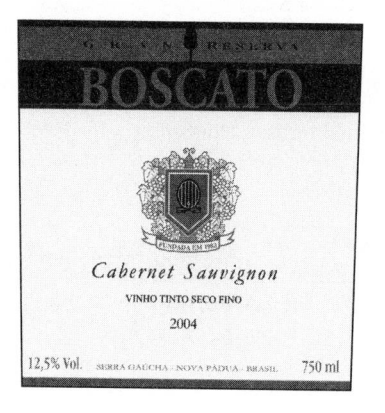

The Boscato family is serious about technology—from their commitment to the most modern equipment to monitoring climatic changes on their vineyard's weather station in Nova Padua. Originally from northern Italy, the family has been making quality wines since 1983. Their Chardonnay 2010 has won gold medals in European competitions and is made in very small quantities. One-third is fermented in oak barrels then transferred to stainless steel. It exhibits a light straw color with green hues and has a nose of tropical fruits such as pineapple and guava. On the palate it is crisp, fresh, and well balanced. Unusual for this region, their Gewürztraminer 2009 is clear to pale yellow in appearance, with a bouquet reminiscent of white flowers and tropical fruits. It is exciting in the mouth, with balanced acidity. Boscato Gran Reserva Cabernet Sauvignon 2004 is dark claret with an iron-tinged rim. The nose reveals blueberry pie and guava jelly. In the mouth, flavors of blueberry, black cherry, guava, and vanilla unfold alongside a restrained tannic structure.

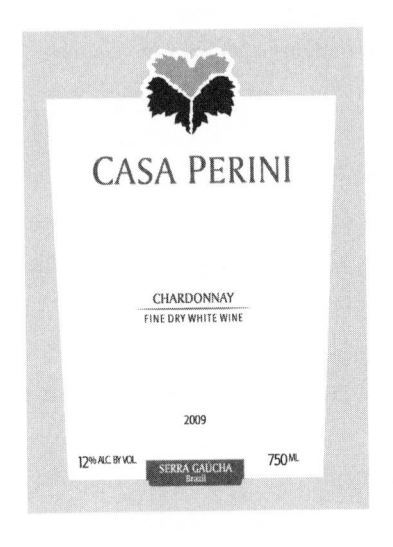

CASA PERINI

Santos Anjos, Farroupilha, RS,
+55 54 2109 7300,
www.vinicolaperini.com.br

The Perinis are one of the few families using the "Y" trellis system in their 92 hectares (227 acres) of vineyards. According to Pablo Perini, this allows increased air circulation and higher sun exposure to his grapes, which results in greater concentration of sugars and color. His Casa Perini Chardonnay 2009 is pale straw—almost clear—with a nose of white melon and peeled Granny Smith apples. Forty percent of the wine ages in oak for two months. On the palate it reveals caramelized pineapple, lemon zest, and jasmine with a well-rounded mouthfeel. Casa Perini Merlot 2008 is a deep claret color with a bright rim. The nose reveals blueberry, black raspberry, and light clove scents. In the mouth, black cherry, cooling spices, and bright fruit are evident.

CHANDON

Rodovia RST 470, Km 224, Garibaldi, RS,
+55 54 3388 4400,
www.chandon.com.br

Brazil's arm of the famed Moët & Chandon Champagne dynasty has been making quality sparkling wines in Garibaldi since 1973. Chandon Reserve Brut NV is made from Chardonnay, Pinot Noir, and Riesling Italico. The nose is rich with green apple and light citrus notes, while on the palate a creamy texture and bright bubbles are evident. Chandon Passion NV is an assemblage of Malvasia Bianco, Malvasia de Candia, Moscato Canelli, and Pinot Noir. The bouquet presents white stone fruits, such as peach and plum, with tropical fruit flavors in the mouth. Chandon Baby Disco Rosé NV is a fun Brazilian twist on Chandon's serious French image. It is sold in a single-serve, 187-milliliter bottle, complete with hot pink print on a disco ball label.

COURMAYEUR

Av. Garibaldina, 32, Garibaldi, RS
+55 54 3463 8517
www.courmayeur.com.br

Named after a village in northern Italy, near the border with France, Courmayeur has been family-operated since its inception in 1976. Eighty percent of its production is sparkling wine, using both the Charmat and traditional methods. Grapes are both estate-grown and purchased from other families. Courmayeur Extra Brut Sparkling NV, a blend of Chardonnay and Pinot Noir, exhibits delicate bubbles, which upon bursting reveal a nose of tropical fruits and brioche. In the mouth, one finds flavors of Granny Smith apple, pineapple, and buttered bread. The Brut Sparkling NV is primarily Chardonnay, with small amounts of Riesling and Pinot Noir. Its bubbles linger a bit longer, as do pleasant flavors of caramelized pineapple and green apple—with touches of jasmine and honeysuckle. Lightly sweet, this makes an excellent aperitif. Courmayeur Muscat Sparkling NV, made from 80 percent Muscat and 20 percent Malvasia di Candia, is almost clear except for a column of rapid, tiny bubbles. Delicious and well balanced, its nose of *dama de noche*, apricot, and light baking spices is further enhanced on the palate by flavors of white peach, geranium leaf, and fig.

PIAGENTINI

Rua Visconde de Pelotas, Caxias do Sul, RS
+55 54 2101 1500,
www.piagentini.com.br,
www.vinhosdecima.com.br

Relative newcomers to Brazil, the Piagentini family emigrated from Italy in the early 1930s. The family sources grapes via what they refer to as the "Multi *Terroir*" method; that is, they purchase fruit from growers in Rio Grande do Sul areas of Caxias do Sul,

Valle dos Vinhedos, Faria Lomos, and Serra Gaucha. In this way, they are not reliant on a single climate, piece of land, or soil type. Although they make Cachaças, liqueurs, grape juice, and bulk table wine, the pride of the Piagentini portfolio is its fine wines under the Piave, Familia Piagentini, Boutique Reserva, and Decima Gran Reserva labels. Its Boutique Reserva Brut NV, a sparkling blend of Chardonnay, Riesling, and Viognier, is medium straw in the glass and capped by a nice moussant. Its fragrance of soft green apple, jasmine, and rose give way to more vibrant apple, baking bread, and light honey flavors in the mouth. Decima Gran Reserva Pinot Noir Rosé Brut NV, made using the traditional Champenoise method, has a golden apricot color and the scent of strawberry preserves on buttered toast. This flavor continues on the palate, complemented by zingy notes of lemon zest. Decima Gran Reserva Tannat 2005 is an inky purple example of the variety. Notes of blackberry and cassis mingle with coffee and tobacco on both the nose and in the mouth.

VINÍCOLA AURORA

Rua Olavo Bilac 500, Bento Gonçalves, RS
+55 54 3455 2001,
www.vinicolaaurora.com.br

Forget everything you ever thought about large co-ops making lots of low-quality wine. Founded in 1931 by 16 Italian immigrant families, Aurora Co-op now boasts 1,100 member families and produces 38 million liters of still and sparkling wine per year. With a team of six winemakers and more than fifteen different labels, the higher-end wines are treated as boutique products within Brazil's largest winery. Its vast plant in downtown Bento Gonçalves is a microcosm of the Brazilian wine industry, turning out everything from old-style jug wine to its Pequenas Partilhas (single-vineyard) Cabernet Franc

2009, whose black cherry and leather notes come to a clean, bright, fruity finish. On the bubbly front, the Brazilian Soul Sparkling Pinot Noir NV tastes of Granny Smith apples and toasted brioche, and those with a sweet tooth will surely enjoy the fig compote and honeysuckle flavors of Aurora Demi-Sec NV, a blend of Riesling, Muscat, and Pinot Noir. The Aurora Varietal line includes nice versions of Merlot, Chardonnay, Riesling Italico, Carmenere, and Cabernet Sauvignon.

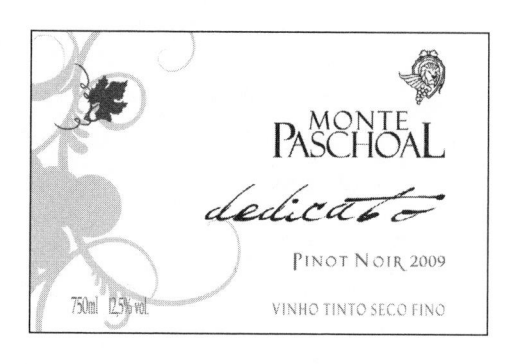

VINÍCOLA IRMÃOS BASSO

Monte Berico, Distrito 2, Farroupilha, RS,
+55 54 2109 7400,
www.vinicolabasso.com.br

Family-owned and run by four brothers, Vinícola Irmãos Basso produces more than 8.5 million liters of wine per year. Grapes are sourced from a variety of regions. The grapes for the sparkling wines come from Monte Belo do Sul and Farroupilha, Merlot and Cabernet Sauvignon come from Serra Gaucha, and Tannat comes from Alto Uruguai. Monte Paschoal Pinot Noir Dedicato 2009 is grown in Farroupilha and is dark cherry in color with an iron rim. The bouquet reveals raspberry, dark chocolate, orange peel, and leather. On the palate it is spicy with bright acidity. Monte Paschoal Sparkling Brut NV is made in the Charmat method from 70 percent Chardonnay and 30 percent Riesling Italico. It is medium straw in color with persistent bubbles. The nose reveals apricot, guava, and baked bread, with flavors of green apple and toasted brioche in the mouth.

VINÍCOLA SALTON

Mario Salton Street, 300, Tuiuty District,
Bento Gonçalves, RS,
+55 54 2105 1000,
www.salton.com.br

Originally called Paolo Salton and Irmãos, brothers Paolo, Angelo, João, Cezar, Luiz, and Antonio Salton began making wine informally, like many Italian immigrants, in a small store-front in downtown Bento Gonçalves. Vinícola Salton was born in 1910 and now produces more than thirty wines in Super Premium, Classic, Espumantes, Frisantes, and Volpi product lines—a far cry from its inception more than a hundred years ago. The winery has storage capacity for 17 million liters of wine in its stainless-steel tanks and more than twelve-hundred French and North American oak barrels. The bottling line can process more than ten thousand bottles per hour. Vinícola Salton Series Cabernet Franc 2006 from Serra Gaucha is fermented and aged in stainless steel and retains intense fruity aromas of mulberry and raspberry, with floral herbaceous notes of violet, eucalyptus, mint, and clover. Full-bodied in the mouth, it has a lasting finish of smoked paprika. The Series Malbec 2007 is made from grapes from the Campanha region near the southern border of Uruguay. It has an intense ruby color and aromas of lily, violet, lavender, and red fruits. It is well balanced in the mouth with soft tannins and a fruit-filled finish.

D.O. VALE DOS VINHEDOS

Vale dos Vinhedos falls within the confines of Serra Gaucha. Its official D.O. status was granted to Brazil's first such region in the spring of 2011. Its 72 square kilometers (28 square miles) are all within Serra Gaucha. While the majority of the vineyards (61 percent) are centered around the city of Bento Gonçalves, a smaller portion (33 percent) are nearer to Garibaldi, and the remainder (5 percent) are clustered near Monte Belo do

Sul. Only grape varieties belonging to species *Vitis vinifera* are permitted to be grown and bottled using the Vale dos Vinhedos designation. Grapes must be grown and wines must be produced and bottled within the geographic limits of the D.O. Allowable red varieties are Merlot, Cabernet Sauvignon, Cabernet Franc, and Tannat. Chardonnay and Riesling Italico grapes are permitted for white wines. For fine rosé or white sparkling wines, Pinot Noir, Chardonnay, and Riesling Italico are allowed. The D.O. is responsible for 20 percent of the fine dry wines and 35 percent of the sparkling wines produced in the state of Rio Grande do Sul.

Dry red wines must be made with at least 60 percent Merlot grapes. The only red wine that may be labeled as a single varietal is Merlot; to be labeled as such it must contain at least 85 percent Merlot. The minimum alcohol content for red wines is 12 percent, and they must be aged a minimum of 12 months before being sold to consumers.

Dry white wines must contain a minimum of 60 percent Chardonnay. Only wines comprised of a minimum of 85 percent Chardonnay may be labeled as such. The minimum alcohol content of white wines is 11 percent, and they may only be sold after six months of aging.

Sparkling wines must be made of at least 60 percent Chardonnay and/or Pinot Noir, and they may be white or rosé. The traditional method must be used, and the wine must remain in contact with yeast for nine months. They are to be classified as Nature, Extra Brut, or Brut.

The only allowable training system for grapevines is vertical trellis. Maximum productivity permitted is 10 metric tons per hectare (4.5 US tons per acre) of grapes for red and white wine, and 12 metric tons per hectare (5.4 US tons per acre) for sparkling wine. Only 2.5 kilograms (5.5 pounds) of grapes per plant are permitted for red wine, while 3 kilograms (6.6 pounds) of grapes per plant are allowed for white wine. The maximum production per plant for grapes intended for sparkling wine is 4 kilograms (8.8 pounds). The harvest of grapes within the D.O. must be performed completely by hand. The only authorized wood for aging of wines is oak. All vineyards and wineries are certified by the Regulatory Board, and all wines are evaluated by the Tasting Commission.

CASA VALDUGA

Linha Leopoldina, Vale dos Vinhedos,
Bento Gonçalves, RS,
+55 54 2105 3122,
www.casavalduga.com.br

Originally from Rovereto, Italy, the Valduga family began planting vineyards in Brazil's

Vale dos Vinhedos in 1875. Three generations later, Juarez, Erielso, and João continue their family's legacy of fine-wine production. Casa Valduga makes both sparkling and still wines as well as grappa and brandy. Its grape varieties include Merlot, Malbec, Cabernet Sauvignon, Chardonnay, Cabernet Franc, Gewürztraminer, Marselan, Riesling, and Sangiovese. Casa Valduga Brut 130 NV is made from Chardonnay and Pinot Noir of which only 5 percent receives a short time in oak. Fermented in the traditional Champenoise method and matured for 36 months, this sparkling wine has a medium gold hue with excellent *perlage*. The bouquet has a pleasant papaya, guava, and tropical fruit nature. Broad and full-flavored on the palate, this is an excellent wine to be served with food or on its own as an aperitif. The Cabernet Franc Premium 2007 receives eight months in oak barrels and is ruby red in color with a violet rim. The nose has intense notes of red fruits including plums, raspberries, and cherries. In the mouth this full-bodied wine has moderate acidity with a persistent tannic finish. It pairs perfectly with game birds and milder pasta sauces.

CAVALLERI VINHOS FINOS

RS 444, Km 24, Vale dos Vinhedos,
Bento Gonçalves, RS,
+55 54 3459 1001,
www.cavalleri.com.br

With 30 hectares (74 acres) of vineyards, Adega Cavalleri Vinhos Finos produces more than 200,000 liters of white, red, and sparkling wines. Utilizing modern pressing technology, it prides itself on extraction of secondary aromas, increased body, and balanced tannic structure in its wines. Its Merlot vines average 9 to 10 years of age and are planted in stone-rich clay soil. Cavalleri Merlot Reserva 2006 shows a deep claret color with a bright rim. It has aromas of cassis, stewed figs, and light spice. On the palate, flavors of tart cherry, cocoa, coffee, and blueberry are evident. Only 6,000 bottles are made per year. Sparkling Moscato Giallo NV is pale yellow, yet almost clear, with aggressive bubbles. The nose reveals ripe honeydew melon and honeysuckle. It is expressive on the palate with flavors of white peach, honeydew, and jasmine.

LIDIO CARRARO

Estrada do Vinho RS 444, km 21,
Vale dos Vinhedos, Bento Gonçalves, RS
+55 54 3459 1222,
www.lidiocarraro.com

A boutique winery in every sense of the word, Lidio Carraro produces top-quality wines without the use of oak in both Vale dos Vinhedos and Serra do Sudeste. Lidio and Isabel Carraro, and their children Patricia, Juliano, and Giovanni, are among a handful of families whose focus is only on high-end wine. Carraro's vineyards in Vale dos Vinhedos produce Elos, with two rich blends, one of Cabernet Sauvignon and Malbec and one of Touriga Nacional and Tannat; and Singular, a series of exquisite single varieties, including Teroldego, Tempranillo, and a notable Nebbiolo. The Lidio Carraro Grande Vindima line, only made in outstanding years, may be made with grapes from either region. It includes a Merlot 2005 from Encruzilhada do Sul—with flavors of blueberry, black cherry, mint, and clove—and Quorum 2006, a blend of Merlot, Cabernet Sauvignon, Tannat, and Cabernet Franc from Vale dos Vinhedos, which tastes of cassis, violet, earth, and coffee. Sul Brasil wines are comprised of the Agnus and Da'Divas labels; all the wines are vinified at the Vale dos Vinhedos location. Lidio Carraro pioneered the use of Thermal

Pest Control, using forced hot air rather than chemical pesticides to eliminate fungi, bacteria, and insects in the vineyard.

MIOLO FAMILY VINEYARDS

Estrada do Vinho, Vale dos Vinhedos,
Bento Gonçalves, RS,
+55 54 2102 1500,
www.miolo.com.br

Since their arrival in Brazil in 1897, the Miolo family has grown grapes and made wine. Today, the family owns six projects in five Brazilian wine regions and has partnered with other companies to expand its production of quality wine. Each year the family receives more than 130,000 visitors to its Val dos Vinhedos location and has tourist facilities at its Lovara and Fazenda Ouro Verde wineries as well. Under the direction of Adriana

Miolo, and with the guidance of internationally acclaimed consultant Michel Rolland, its portfolio consists of sparkling, white, and red wines. Miolo Viognier 2009 is produced from grapes grown at 100 to 300 meters (328 to 984 feet) above sea level and is light yellow with pale green highlights. White flower and apricot are expressed in the nose, with bright acidity on the palate, and a distinct floral finish. Miolo Merlot 2009 is made from manually harvested grapes and fermented in temperature-controlled stainless-steel tanks for 15 days. One-half of the wine is aged in 300-liter American oak barrels. The color is intense purple, with pleasant aromas of ripe red fruit and black plum. It is full-bodied in the mouth with a lingering finish.

PIZZATO VINHAS E VINHOS

Via dos Parreirais, s/n, Vale dos Vinhedos,
Bento Gonçalves, RS,
+55 54 3459 1155,
www.pizzato.net

Plinio Pizzato and his son Flavio continue the family's tradition of making wines in the Vale dos Vinhedos in Bento Gonçalves on 42 hectares (104 acres) of estate-owned vineyards. Before entering the family business, Flavio graduated college with a master's degree in engineering, set up his own software company, then reentered school for a degree in viticultural studies. The fact that he worked in Mendoza, Argentina, before returning home gives his wine an international flavor and may be responsible for the estate's high honors in international competitions. Pizzato's main grape varieties include Cabernet Sauvignon, Merlot, Chardonnay, Pinot Noir, Egiodola, Tannat, and Alicante Bouschet. Its Fausto Cabernet Sauvignon 2008 has a nose of ripe cassis, stewed fruits, leather, and truffles, with supple round tannins in the mouth. Pizzato DNA99 Single Vineyard Merlot 2005 has aromas of blueberry, black cherry, cassis, and vanilla and remains bright, fruity, and lively on the palate.

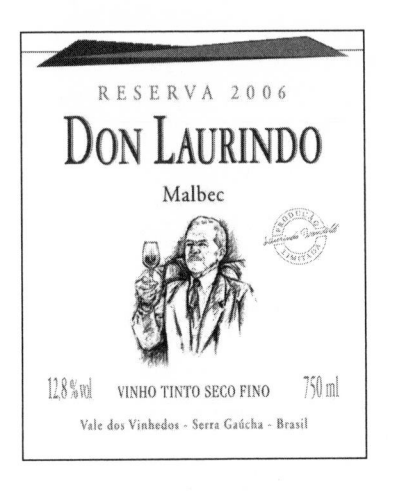

VINHOS DON LAURINDO

Estrada do Vinho, 8 da Graciema,
Bento Gonçalves, RS,
+55 54 3459 1600,
www.donlaurindo.com.br

Don Laurindo Brandelli's grandfather, Marcelino Brandelli, emigrated from Zevio, a small village in the northern Italian province of Verona, in 1887. In 1991, Don Laurindo established Vinhos Don Laurindo to make fine wines—with the help of his sons Ademir, Adelar, Alfonso, and Marcio. The family continues to emphasize small but quality production of Merlot, Ancellotta, Cabernet Sauvignon, Malbec, Tannat, Malvasia de Candia, Chardonnay, and Riesling wines. Their Don Laurindo Malbec 2006 is deep black cherry in color with an intense violet rim. The nose reveals blueberry, chocolate, and eucalyptus, and the palate shows ample yet silky tannins. Don Laurindo Merlot D.O.V.V. 2009 is aged in French oak barrels for 12 months and has a bright ruby color. The bouquet reveals dark cherry, blueberry, tobacco, and black plum. Concentrated, mature tannins give this wine an intense prolonged finish.

I.P. PINTO BANDEIRA

This geographic area is made up of 81 square kilometers (31 square miles) and is also within Serra Gaucha. All wines labeled with this geographic indication must be produced from grapes grown within its limits, and all production, bottling, and aging must be performed there. Rules regarding varieties are less strict than within D.O. Vale dos Vinhedos; more varieties are permitted, and no specific regulations exist at this time for percentages within blends.

Fine sparkling wine is to be made via the traditional method, and grape varieties allowed are Chardonnay, Pinot Noir, Riesling Italico, and Viognier. Moscatel sparkling wine must be comprised of Moscato Bianco, Moscato Giallo, Moscato de Alexandria, Moscatel Nazareno, Malvasia de Candia, and Malvasia Bianca.

Eleven types of grape may be grown for dry white wine: Chardonnay, Malvasia Bianco, Malvasia de Candia, Gewürztraminer, Moscato Bianco, Moscato Giallo, Peverella, Riesling Italico, Sauvignon Blanc, Sémillon, and Viognier. Reds may consist of Ancellotta, Cabernet Franc, Cabernet Sauvignon, Merlot, Pinot Noir, Pinotage, Sangiovese, and Tannat. Vineyards, wineries, and wines must be approved by the Regulatory Council and Tasting Commission.

DON GIOVANNI VINHOS VINHEDOS POUSADA

Linha Amadeu, 28, Pinto Bandeira,
Bento Gonçalves, RS,
+55 54 3455 6294,
www.dongiovanni.com.br

An excellent restaurant and guesthouse make this one winery not to miss. Built in 1932, the main house has seven beautifully appointed bedrooms. The winery is fourth-generation family-owned and produces both sparkling and still wines made from grapes grown in Pinto Bandeira. Don Giovanni Stravaganzza NV Brut is pale straw, with aromas of tropical fruits, pineapple, green apple, and melon. As the winery's entry-level sparkling wine made using the Charmat method, it is refreshing on the palate with balanced acidity. Don Giovanni 12 Month Brut NV is medium straw with gold reflections. Made in the traditional Champenoise method, the nose offers tropical fruits, vanilla, and toasted bread. This sparkler is creamy in the mouth, with honey notes as well as toasted almonds on the finish. Don Giovanni Merlot 2006 has an intense ruby color, with notes of ripe red fruits, tobacco, black pepper, and coffee. It is full-bodied in the mouth with a balanced tannic structure.

VINÍCOLA GEISSE

Linha Jansen, s/n, Pinto Bandeira,
Bento Gonçalves, RS,
+55 54 3455 7461,
www.cavegeisse.com.br

Winemaker and agronomist Mario Geisse has been making fine wines in Rio Grande do Sul since 1979. Originally from Chile, he moved to Brazil to work for Moët & Chandon in 1976 and identified the Pinto Bandeira region of Bento Gonçalves as the ideal area to grow grapes for his quality sparkling wine. All of the wines from Cave Geisse are made in the traditional Champenoise method. His Brut and Nature are made from 70 percent Chardonnay and 30 percent Pinot Noir. Both are fermented for six months with a minimum of two years on lees. The Rosé Brut 2006 is made from 100 percent Pinot Noir grapes, has delicate bubbles, and recalls strawberries and cream on the nose. Terroir Nature 2006 has sublime notes of white flowers and ripe apricot and has a delightful creaminess on the palate. Both the Rosé Brut and Terroir Nature are aged a minimum of three years on lees.

SERRA DO SUDESTE AND CAMPANHA

Located in southern Brazil, near the border with Uruguay, these adjoining regions sit on a plateau with altitudes ranging between 200 meters (650 feet) and 450 meters (1,475 feet). With a moderate climate and dry summers, the climate fosters maturation of grapes with a high level of sugar. Temperatures vary between 12 and 24 degrees Celsius (53 and 75 degrees Fahrenheit). Soil is mainly granite and limestone. The most common red grapes here are Cabernet Sauvignon, Merlot, Touriga Nacional, Tannat, Tinta Rouriz, Alfrocheiro, and Arinarnoua. Prevalent white varieties are Chardonnay, Gewürztraminer, Pinot Grigio, and Sauvignon Blanc. With 2,400 hectares (5931 acres) of vineyards under cultivation, this is Brazil's newest area for winemaking. Lidio Carraro makes some excellent quality wines using grapes that are grown in Serra do Sudeste. While there are not many wineries in this region, it is important to note Cordilheira De Santana, as well as new projects sponsored by the Miolo Family Group.

RECIPE

DON GIOVANNI'S ROASTED CAPON

✳

Courtesy of Beatriz Dreher Giovannini
of Vinhos Don Giovanni Restaurant and Guesthouse

✳

SERVES 8

Each time that we travel to Brazil's Rio Grande do Sul, we almost have to tell ourselves that we haven't boarded the wrong plane and instead flown to one of Italy's wine regions such as Piedmont or Tuscany. The rolling hillsides, architecture, people, language, and cuisine feel more like Italy than South America. On one recent trip, we had the pleasure of having lunch with the owners of Vinhos Don Giovanni and couldn't resist second and third servings of this delicious chicken dish. We also love the interesting history of this preparation.

When the Italian immigrants came to Brazil, they brought with them their love of hunting small game birds. As the indigenous population of rare South American birds dwindled, the government stepped in to preserve various species, so hunters turned to raising delicious chicken known as *Galletto di Primo Canto* on their farms. Translated as "little rooster with the first song," these young male chickens were castrated after their first crow and allowed to fatten in a life of relative luxury—until their demise. This chicken is known for its rich layer of fat and easily crisped thick skin. If it is difficult to find *Galletto di Primo Canto* at your local supermarket, ask your butcher for free-range capon or organically raised young hen.

16 chicken thighs
8 chicken drumsticks
1 teaspoon salt
½ teaspoon pepper
8 medium onions, sliced
1 cup raisins
24 ounces beer

Preheat oven to 350°F.

Place the chicken pieces, skin side down, in a large metal roasting pan and sprinkle with salt and pepper. Add the onions and raisins, spreading evenly. Cover with beer and bake in oven for approximately one hour, or until all of the beer has evaporated.

Transfer the chicken pieces to a baking pan, placing them skin side up. Bake the chicken for 10 more minutes. Turn the broiler on, then finish the chicken under the broiler for a few minutes until crisp. Transfer the onions and raisins to a serving dish, and place the browned chicken on top to serve.

IN THEIR OWN WORDS

MORGANA MIOLO

Morgana Miolo is the export and public relations manager for her family's company, Miolo Wines. She is a fourth-generation Italian-Brazilian living and working in D.O. Vale dos Vinhedos.

How did you get involved in the world of wine?
My passion for the entrancing world of wine is easily explained by my life history. I am a member of the fourth generation of Miolo Family in Brazil, traditional winemakers, with headquarters in the beautiful Vale dos Vinhedos in Bento Gonçalves, where I was born and grew up. Currently, I am involved in efforts to diversify the market served by the company, which already exports to 30 countries.

What are some of the biggest changes you have seen in winemaking since you began your career?
Some of the changes include the use of high technology to produce wine as naturally as possible. The gravity system, for example, and modern fermentation techniques that we use in order to preserve the grapes and make wine as naturally as possible.

What are some of the exciting changes that you see happening specifically in your country?
The discovery of new areas such as Campos de Cima da Serra, Vale do São Francisco, and Campanha region will allow Brazil to produce very good, diverse, and interesting wines.

Where else in the world have you studied, trained, or worked a harvest? How did that influence your winemaking?
I can say that Michel Rolland, who is our consultant since 2003, influenced the winemaking at Miolo with the maceration management. He also helped us to adopt the gravity system of reception of the grapes and worked with our punch downs of the caps during fermentation. We also have a partnership with the French producer Henry Marionnet, who is known as the "Pope of Gamay." He helped us with the carbonic

maceration. In addition, our enologists travel around the world, and I can say that Chile, California, and Australia are some of the places that influence our winemaking process.

Which varieties are you working with? Are you experimenting with anything new?
In Vale dos Vinhedos, we have mainly Cabernet Sauvignon, Merlot, Pinot Noir, and Chardonnay, and we are experimenting in the Campanha region with Nebbiolo, Alvarinho, and Gamay. In Vale do São Francisco, where we have tropical climate, we are experimenting with Tempranillo, Grenache, Mourvèdre, Petit Verdot, and Verdejo.

Are there any new areas that you have identified for potential vineyard sites?
The Vale do São Francisco in the northeast of Brazil in the 8th parallel, as well as the Campanha region in the south of Brazil which lies at the 31st parallel. We are also looking at Campos de Cima da Serra.

What challenges have you faced as a winemaker or winery owner?
I think that it is a big challenge to show Brazilian wines to the world. When we talk about Brazil, the images that come up for most people are Rio de Janeiro and soccer; however, Brazil produces great wines, and people are amazed when they try an exciting Brazilian wine.

What is your winemaking philosophy?
Miolo follows a philosophy of rational wine development, preserving the characteristics of each grape variety and the characteristics of each region where the wine is produced. We also try to extract the maximum potential from the grapes as naturally as possible. Miolo seeks the most advanced technology in the world, maintaining rigorous quality control to preserve the intensity of the fruit.

What would you hope people say about your wine?
That it is surprisingly good!

Do you think that the market should influence winemaking, or do you think that winemaking should influence the market?

Wine is the result of climate, soil, and the influence of man. Having information of how and why the consumer buys wine will help the enologists make wines that fit the market.

Besides your own wine, what are some of your favorite wines? What do you like about them?

I am a great fan of Pinot Noir, it is a special wine, delicate and fruity, very pleasant to drink. I like many Pinot Noirs.

What is your opinion on screwcap versus cork closures?

I am in favor of screwcap for wines that should be drunk now. It is so easy, and it is not complicated. But I do prefer cork closures for those wines that should stay in the cellar or bottle for many years.

If you could invite anyone from history, living or dead, to your home for dinner, who would it be? What food would you serve? What wine would you serve?

I would invite Woody Allen and would serve a special lamb that I have previously prepared for my husband Eduardo, and the wine would be a Sesmarias, our icon wine from Seival State in Campanha region.

If you were to stay home tonight for a relaxing evening, drinking wine while watching a movie, which movie would you watch? Which wine would you drink? Explain.

It would be *A Good Year* with Russell Crowe, I like this movie because it is light, charming, and shows how delightful the wine world is.

How do you like to spend your time away from the winery?

I like to spend time with my little baby, Cecilia, drink wine with friends, and I like to travel to discover new places, people, and cultures.

Do you collect wine? If so, what is in your cellar?

I do not collect wine, but I do have some bottles of wines at home. I don't keep it for a special day because when I open it, it makes the day special.

If you weren't involved in wine, what would you be doing?

Probably running a bar or a restaurant.

CHILE

ON OUR FIRST VISIT TO CHILE, WE WERE struck by the immense beauty of vineyards set against a backdrop of towering peaks. A 4,345-kilometer (2,700-mile) ribbon of land wedged between majestic Andes Mountains and the Pacific Ocean, Chile has a winemaking history dating back to the first Spanish con- quistatores, who arrived in the early sixteenth century. As Chile has an average width of only 177 kilometers (110 miles), it is said that one is never more than a two hours' drive from the ocean, no matter where in the country one may

be. The same claim can be made for vineyards as well. With the exception of the Atacama Desert in the north and Patagonia in the south, grapes are grown and wine is made across a large portion of central Chile.

The grape variety originally grown here is the Pais, or Mission, grape, which was vinified into sacramental wine for use in the Catholic Mass. This grape most likely made its way to Chile via Peru, having first traveled there from Mexico, where Hernán Cortés brought grapes in 1520. Early Chilean vineyards were cared for by Jesuit priests, who were also responsible for winemaking. As wine moved from church into the home, other grapes were grown as well, including Muscat and Torontel, a close relative of Argentina's well-known Torrontés. Although the Spanish colonies in South America were a rich source of gold and precious stones, the home country also relied on them for export income, and it was expected that South America would remain a viable market for Spanish wine. In the mid-seventeenth century, Philip III of Spain limited grape cultivation and prevented Chile, Peru, and Argentina from selling wine back to Spain. Although this severely hurt the fledgling export market for Chilean wine, most winemakers carried on with their craft, selling wine to the domestic market and to neighboring countries.

The phylloxera epidemic of the mid to late nineteenth century first wreaked havoc on vineyards and winemaking in France, but it also caused French winemakers to seek other lands in which to ply their trade. Wealthy Chilean landowners had already begun importing French vines, so at the same time that enologists were moving to Rioja in Spain, bringing along with them their expertise, a similar emigration took place between Bordeaux and Santiago. Grape-growing mainly took place in the Central Valley. Don Silvestre Ochagavia Echazarreta is widely credited as the first Chilean to import and grow French *Vitis vinifera* varieties from Bordeaux, including Cabernet Franc, Cabernet Sauvignon, Malbec, Sauvignon Blanc, and Sémillon. He founded Viña Ochagavia in 1851. About 20 years later, Don Maximiano Errazuriz founded Viña Errazuriz, also using French varieties and employing French techniques. Both continue to make award-winning wine today, as do their contemporaries Undurraga, Concha y Toro, and Cousiño Macul. The area previously known only as Chile's Valle Central (Central Valley) is now subdivided to include the Maipo, Rapel, Curicó, and Maule Valleys.

With a total vineyard area of 118,000 hectares (291,500 acres) divided into 14 regions (plus a new D.O., which is not yet producing wine), Chile offers a wide diversity of altitude and soil types. Chile is the only wine-producing country in the world to be phylloxera-free, in part because of strict quarantine rules for cuttings and plantings brought in from other countries. Although these rules limit the amount of experimentation with different varieties, this is more than compensated for by the *terroir* available in vineyards ranging from 29 degrees latitude in the north to 38 degrees in the south. Distance to the sea or the Andes can account for far greater differences in temperature than proximity to the equator, with altitudes ranging from sea level to more than 2,000 meters (6,562 feet) above.

Wine regions the world over boast of their "sheltered microclimate," but Chile is unique in that it is sheltered to the east by the snow-capped Andes, to the west by the frigid Pacific, to the north by the arid Atacama—the driest desert in the world—and to the south by the ice floes of Antarctica. This isolation, in combination with an almost total lack of humidity and predominantly sandy soil, is given as the primary reason for the absence of phylloxera here. Unlike European vines (or those of Argentina, just across the Andes), which are grafted onto phylloxera-resistant American rootstock, Chile's vines remain ungrafted. This accounts for the high number of "old vine" vineyards throughout the country, as ungrafted vines live longer than those that have been grafted onto rootstock. Chile's warm, dry summers and cold, wet winters—its Mediterranean climate—and large swings between daytime and nighttime temperatures provide a perfect environment for raising strong vines and excellent grapes.

Chile's climate lessens the need for pesticides and fertilizers, so viticulture is naturally "eco-friendly," with many vineyards and wineries using sustainable, biodynamic, or organic growing methods. Chile's wine industry is also in the process of developing a Chilean Code for Sustainable Wine Production. In addition to measuring claims of sustainability, this code will set out guidelines for environmentally friendly systems that are also economically feasible.

The earthquake and subsequent tsunami that hit Chile on February 27, 2010, affected the country's southernmost wine regions, and it is estimated that among the economic losses experienced by the nation as a whole (estimated to be US$30 billion, or about 14.5 trillion Chilean peseos), 125 million liters of wine were lost. There was extensive damage to many winery production and storage facilities, but most vineyards remained untouched. The year 2010 was mourned by many Chileans on a personal level due to this devastating act of nature, but this was also the year that the country celebrated its bicentennial. In the two hundred years since Chile gained independence from Spain, much has changed—most especially in the search for new and exciting wine *terroir*.

Cultivation of grapes for the production of fine wine has spread to the north and the south. The winegrowing area at Chile's center now spans 1,287 kilometers (800 miles), divided into the aforementioned 14 regions. Just over three-quarters of the 118,000 hectares (291,584 acres) under cultivation for winemaking grow red grapes, with the balance made up of white varieties. Cabernet Sauvignon is the most widely planted, accounting for more than 35 percent of total vineyard area. Merlot is the next most popular red, at about 10 percent of total plantings, closely followed by Carmenere. Syrah accounts for approximately 5 percent. Pinot Noir currently makes up less than 3 percent of grapes grown in Chile, but that will most likely change as viticulturists increase plantings in the cool-weather, high-altitude areas in which it thrives.

Chardonnay and Sauvignon Blanc are almost tied for second place of all grapes grown (and first among whites) at just over and under 12 percent. Small amounts of Gewürztraminer, Viognier, and Riesling are also grown, both for single-varietal wines and blending. Muscat and Pedro Ximénez are still grown in the north of Chile, primarily for Pisco distillation.

From north to south, the 14 major regions are Elqui Valley, Limari Valley, Choapa Valley, Aconagua Valley, Casablanca Valley, San Antonio/Leyda Valley, Maipo Valley, Rapel/ Cachapoal Valley, Rapel/Colchagua Valley, Curicó Valley, Maule Valley, Itata Valley, Bio Bio Valley, and the Malleco Valley. Four of the regions in closest proximity to the capital city, Santiago—Maipo, Casablanca, Curicó, and Rapel (divided between Colchagua and Cachapoal Valleys) are responsible for almost two-thirds of all the wine made in Chile. However, some of the most interesting wine comes from the extreme borders of Chile's agricultural territory, especially Sauvignon Blanc and Syrah from Elqui and Chardonnay from

Limari, both in the north, and Pinot Noir from Bio Bio in the south.

French varieties and winemaking techniques altered the face of Chilean wine in the mid-nineteenth century, and the effects of France continue to be felt today. One of the forerunners of the modern Chilean fine-wine revolution, Casa Lapostolle, was founded by Alexandra Marnier Lapostolle, whose family brought Grand Marnier to the world. (Another famous French citizen, Michel Rolland, is Casa Lapostolle's consulting winemaker.) In 2011, Lapostolle was the first producer in Chile to gain full CERES organic certification of its vineyards. In 1988, Baron Eric de Rothschild, owner of Château Lafite Rothschild, took over the Los Vascos estate, which continues as one of Chile's best-known properties. Bruno Prats, former proprietor of famed Château Cos d'Estournel in Bordeaux, is a founding partner of Viñas Aquitania. And Michelle Bachelet, the president of Chile from March 2006 to March 2010, is the great-great-granddaughter of Louis-Joseph Bachelet, a French wine merchant from Chassagne-Montrachet who left France in 1860 to take up winemaking in Santiago.

One of the biggest changes in wine worldwide, felt profoundly in Chile, is the trend of young winemakers visiting opposite hemisphere wine regions in their off-season. We have met Chilean enologists who work harvest and make wine in California, Washington, Oregon, Spain, Italy, and France. These youthful innovators embrace change the same way their forebears embraced Cabernet Sauvignon, Chardonnay, and lots of oak. Winemaking techniques like pre-fermentation cold soaks, whole cluster fermentation, and use of lightly toasted oak are just a few of the tricks they picked up abroad. Drip irrigation has been employed for more than 30 years; this technique allows young winemakers to spread their craft to extreme low-water regions such as Elqui, Limari, Casablanca, and San Antonio. Modern drip irrigation, often controlled automatically by state-of-the-art weather systems, is a far cry from the ancient technique of flood irrigation, in which dammed rivers and lakes were set free over vineyards. This practice was abandoned only recently.

Although Chile and Argentina run neck and neck in terms of export volume to the United States, Chile exports far more of its wine than is consumed back home, sending more than two-thirds of its total production to foreign markets. In 2010, Chile exported a total of 738 million liters of wine. Primary export markets are the United States, United Kingdom, and Canada, and both China and Russia have become important markets as well. Within the current decade, the Chilean wine industry aims to become the leading producer of sustainable and diverse premium wines from the New World. It has set the bar high, expecting to reach exports of bottled wine of US$3 billion by the year 2020.

Chile's system of wine laws came into effect in 1994. This laid out the boundaries of the nation's wine regions and established a series of wine label regulations. There are no restrictions on varieties of grapes that may be grown, techniques that may be employed in winemaking, or viticultural practices. To list a grape variety on a label (as a single or predominant varietal) at least 75 percent of that grape must be present in the wine. To state a vintage year on the label, a minimum of 75 percent of the wine must be from grapes harvested in that year. There is no legal definition of the word *Reserve* in reference to wine, or on a wine label.

Chile has seven Denomination of Origin zones. These are subdivided into the main grape-growing and wine-producing valleys. The newest to achieve Denomination of Origin, or D.O., status, Atacama, is now the northernmost region, although it has yet to produce any wine as of this writing. The majority of grapes grown here were previously either made into Pisco or simply eaten as table grapes or raisins. Atacama is divided into two subregions, Copiapo Valley and Huasco Valley. Only 12 hectares (30 acres) is planted in Copiapo.

Due south of Atacama is the Coquimbo

D.O., which includes Elqui Valley, Limari Valley, and Choapa Valley. The Aconcagua D.O. is made up of the Casablanca Valley and Aconcagua Valleys. The most well-known region, closest to Santiago, is the Valle Central, which includes the four most productive valleys: Maipo, Rapel, Curicó, and Maule. About 650 kilometers (404 miles) south of Santiago, the Southern Chile D.O. includes Itata Valley, Bio Bio Valley, and Malleco Valley. Further south are two new Denominations of Origin: Araucania, which has 11 hectares (27 acres) planted in Victoria, and Los Lagos, whose 6 hectares (15 acres) are planted within the commune of Futrono.

MAJOR GRAPE VARIETIES

CABERNET SAUVIGNON

Chile's preeminent variety—brought here from France in the middle of the nineteenth century—Cabernet Sauvignon has played a leading role in Chile's rise to fame in the world of wine. A descendant of Cabernet Franc and Sauvignon Blanc, Cabernet Sauvignon is a small, dark grape with a thick skin that is resistant to disease and pests. It thrives in all but the coldest climates, though the finest examples of Chile's 38,806 hectares (95,892 acres) of the varietal (which account for over a third of all the wine grapes grown in the country) currently come from Colchagua, Aconcagua, Cachapoal, Maule, and Maipo.

Chile's warm, dry vineyards bring out the best of Cabernet Sauvignon's notes of black cherry, cassis, tobacco, spice, and pencil lead. Those grown in colder, more coastal climates also show greener flavors such as bell pepper and olive. Wine labeled "Cabernet Sauvignon" may be blended with up to 25 percent of other varieties, so what you are tasting could be influenced by Carmenere, Merlot, or Syrah as well. Cabernet Sauvignon aged in oak will also show qualities of toast, vanilla, and cocoa.

Wines made from the grape will range in color from bright cherry red to deep violet.

CARMENERE

Long forgotten in Bordeaux, Carmenere may have become extinct had it not accidentally made its way to Chile in the mid-1800s, mixed in with cuttings labeled "Merlot." This happenstance helped preserve what is on its way to becoming Chile's signature grape, its "answer"—if one is required—to Argentina's Malbec. Cultivated on 8,249 hectares (20,384 acres) (and counting), Carmenere appears perfectly suited to the hot days and cold nights in Chile's alluvial soils.

Its name derives from *carmin*, the French term for "crimson," which describes the leaves on the vine at the end of the season, rather than the dark purple berries that are made into a deep red wine. On its own, Carmenere has the smooth flavors of fruits of the wood, black pepper, and green bell pepper. Light smoke and dried herb characters are also noted. It is widely grown in Maipo, Aconcagua, Cachapoal, and Colchagua. Alone, it's usually best consumed within a few years of bottling; its low acid impedes long aging.

Many excellent versions of Carmenere as a single varietal are now on the market; De Martino is noted for producing the first single-varietal Carmenere in 1996. Cabernet Sauvignon is often added to Carmenere for an injection of structure and acidity.

CHARDONNAY

The second most popular grape in all of Chile—and the most popular white—Chardonnay is extensively grown the entire length of Chilean wine country. However, of late, it has especially thrived in the cool climates of Casablanca, San Antonio, and Limari. Chardonnay generally tastes of tropical fruits or green apples with light hints of butter; the over-toasted flavor that was long associated with chardonnay was due to the amount of time it spent in oak—which also adds the tastes of vanilla and caramel to the wine. The lean, mineral-driven versions coming out of Chile now are either completely stainless-steel fermented or spend just a minimum of time in barrel.

While most of the Chardonnay from Chile's 12,739 hectares (31,479 acres) is made into inexpensive, easy-drinking wine, expansion of vineyard area into the far north and south and a change in winemaking style have contributed greatly to an increase in quality. The light-green grape is especially vulnerable to the effects of *terroir* and the winemaker's

touch. Single-vineyard and Reserva bottlings from Chile are now popping up on wine lists around the world.

MERLOT

For a long time Merlot was made into an unintentional field blend in Chile—it grew alongside Carmenere, and the two were mistaken for one another—until 1994, when it was discovered that the ingredients of "Chilean Merlot" were two distinct varieties. They were then separated. Merlot came to Chile from Bordeaux in the mid-nineteenth century, but didn't become popular here for almost 150 years.

Covering 9,656 hectares (23,860 acres), the dark bluish-purple grape, which takes its name from the French word for "blackbird" (*merle*) tends to carry the flavors of black cherry, blueberries, currants, and mint. Merlot can range from young, fresh, and fruity to rich and deep, depending on where it is grown, how it is made, and how long it is allowed to age. Young Chilean Merlots are considered one of the best bargains in the world of wines, and even more serious, high-end versions, alone or in blends, sell for just a fraction of what their counterparts from France or Italy tend to command. The deep color of the grape carries over into the glass, where Merlot will range in color from intense black cherry to inky purple.

PAIS

The former workhorse of the Chilean wine industry, Pais was number one in the nation until Cabernet Sauvignon—and fine wine in general—supplanted cultivation of the grape brought here by conquistadors and propagated and tended by missionaries in the sixteenth century. About 3,300 hectares (8,155 acres) remain of the thin-skinned fruit, most of which is made into unrefined rust-colored wines sold domestically in large jugs and is not sold internationally at all. If you are visiting Chile, a glass of Pais is worth a try to see what wine tasted like before international varieties, irrigation, and modern technology changed the game for the better.

PINOT NOIR

Twenty-six-hundred hectares (6,425 acres) of Pinot Noir flourish in the colder climates in the north and the south of the country, such as Casablanca, San Antonio, and Bio Bio. In 2010 plantings in Bio Bio were up 50 percent, while in Curicó they were up 40 percent. Pinot Noir takes its name from the French words for "pine" and "black," referring to the cone-like appearance of clusters of Pinot Noir's dark purple grapes. Although Pinot Noir grown in other climates is often turned into wine that is bright cherry red, the severe, sun-filled days of a Chilean summer lead to wines with shades closer to ruby and garnet. This depth of color often belies the delicate elegance of a well-crafted Pinot Noir, whose palate of black cherry and lightly stewed plum is balanced by soft chocolate notes and refreshing acidity. Although many Chilean winemakers hang their hats on Carmenere, Pinot Noir may just turn out to be Chile's "Little Grape That Could."

SAUVIGNON BLANC

The third most widely planted grape in Chile, Sauvignon Blanc is an up-and-comer in the cooler-climate areas of Limari, Casablanca, San Antonio, Aconcagua, and Bio Bio, where cultivation of the bulbous green variety grew by more than 300 percent in the last decade. Wine made from this grape often has one thinking of boiled asparagus or, as the French say, *pipi de chat*; Chilean versions trend toward pear, tropical fruit, and Granny Smith apples. Here its herbal qualities run more in the direction of grass, while clover mineral notes sing through as well.

Blanketing 11,244 hectares (27,785 acres) in Chile, Sauvignon Blanc takes its name from the French words for "wild" (*sauvage*) and "white" (*blanc*). Its savage qualities, often tamed by prudent vineyard management and winemaking technique, are amplified by the cooler regions it now calls home. Much of the low-quality "Sauvignon Blanc" once produced in Chile was a field blend of Sauvignon Blanc and the less flavorful Sauvignon Vert, which lacks Sauvignon Blanc's acidity and aromatic brightness.

SYRAH

Unknown in Chile until the mid-1990s, Syrah is now cultivated on 5,391 hectares (13,321 acres) and has quickly gained cult status as the must-have wine from Chile. Whether planted at high altitudes in the Elqui Valley, the seaside foothills of Colchagua, or the cherished soils of Apalta, the intense sweet blackberry, spice, and black pepper flavors of Chilean Syrah are widely appreciated by connoisseurs of fine red wine. The deeply colored grape is vinified into richly pigmented wines ranging in color from dark red-violet to inky purple. Cooler-climate versions from San Antonio and Elqui develop a fiery complexity whose notes of smoked meat and herbs make it the ideal companion for grilled or roasted foods.

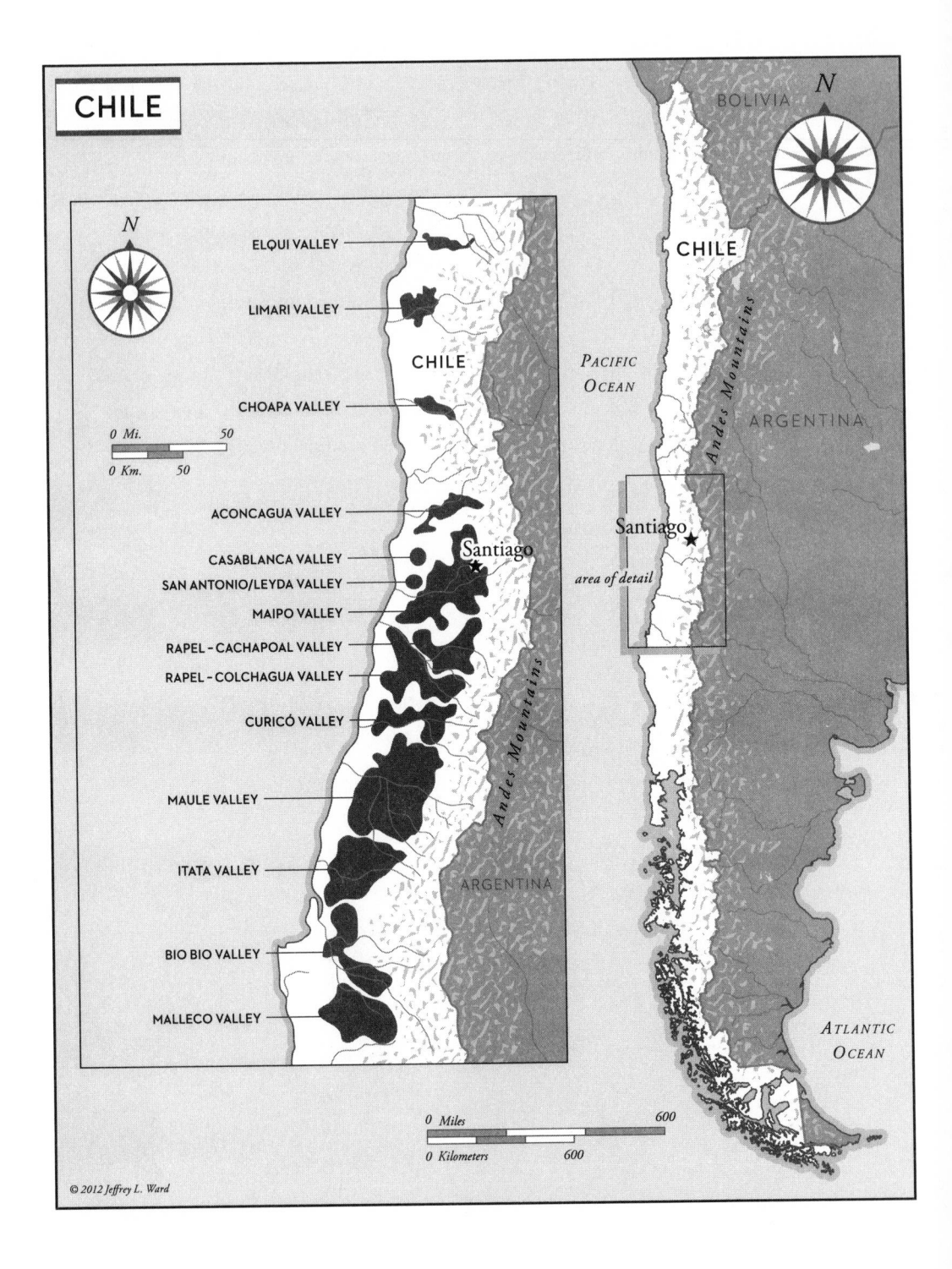

CHILE

ELQUI VALLEY

LIMARI VALLEY

CHOAPA VALLEY

ACONCAGUA VALLEY

CASABLANCA VALLEY

SAN ANTONIO/LEYDA VALLEY

MAIPO VALLEY

RAPEL – CACHAPOAL VALLEY

RAPEL – COLCHAGUA VALLEY

CURICÓ VALLEY

MAULE VALLEY

ITATA VALLEY

BIO BIO VALLEY

MALLECO VALLEY

CHILE

Santiago

PACIFIC OCEAN

Andes Mountains

ARGENTINA

0 Mi.   50
0 Km.   50

BOLIVIA

CHILE

Andes Mountains

PACIFIC OCEAN

ARGENTINA

Santiago

area of detail

ATLANTIC OCEAN

0 Miles   600
0 Kilometers   600

© 2012 Jeffrey L. Ward

WINE REGIONS

ELQUI VALLEY

Five-hundred kilometers (310 miles) north of Santiago, Elqui is at present the northern-most wine-producing region in Chile and is the established valley closest to the Atacama Desert. There are just two main wineries here, although many other wineries have vineyards in the valley. While most Chilean valleys run north-south, the Elqui Valley runs west-east, sitting mainly between the coastal town of La Serena and the inland city of Vicuña. While grapes have been grown here for many years (Vicuña is a center of Pisco production), the first winery to focus on fine-wine production was founded in 1998. Tranque Puclaro, a man-made lake about 60 kilometers (37 miles) east of La Serena, provides water for irrigation. Altitudes vary from 300 meters (984 feet) to just over 2,000 meters (6,562 feet), and average yearly rainfall is 70 millimeters, or 3 inches. The vineyards closest to the coast benefit from daily penetration by the Camanchaca fog, which provides both moisture and a cooling influence on the grapes. More easterly vineyards soar toward the Andes and are blessed with clear skies and lower temperatures. The most popular grape in the valley is Syrah: of a total of 306 hectares (756 acres) under production, 80 (198) of them are planted with this French native. Second most favored is Sauvignon Blanc, planted on 71 hectares (175 acres). Carmenere, which is catching up quickly, is grown on 60 hectares (148 acres). Twenty-five hectares (62 acres) of Cabernet Sauvignon are farmed here. Chardonnay accounts for less than 3 percent of the varieties cultivated in Elqui, followed by about half that amount of Merlot.

FALERNIA

Ruta 41 Kilometer 52, Vicuña,
+56 51 412 260,
www.falernia.com

Aldo Olivier Gramola was only 12 years old in 1951 when his family emigrated to Chile from a small town in the Trentino region of northern Italy. His family planted grapes for Pisco production, becoming the third larg-est producer in the country. Only in 1995, after meeting one of his Italian cousins who remained in Italy to work as a winemaker, did he realize the potential for fine-wine

production. Viña Falernia is Chile's northern-most wine estate and is 520 kilometers (323 miles) north of Santiago, the capital. The soil in this region is composed of glacial deposits, as well as alluvial sand and silt; it is poor for the cultivation of other crops. The climate is semi-arid, making drip irrigation necessary. Viña Falernia has 320 hectares (791 acres) of estate-owned vineyards and oversees approximately 100 hectares (247 acres) of contract growers. Double Guyot trellising is used in most of their vineyards. Falernia Syrah Reserva 2007 is luxu-riously purple with aromas of black pepper and purple flowers. It is fruit-forward on the palate with soft tannins and a balanced equilibrium. Falernia Carmenere Reserva D.O. Elqui Valley 2008 is deep purple in the glass with slight herbaceous notes, green pepper, and cocoa in the nose. Black fruits are evident in the mouth

along with a chocolaty-yet-spicy finish. Falernia Late Harvest Moscatel-Semillión D.O. Elqui Valley 2009 is bright yellow with aromas of stone fruits and white peaches. It's pleasantly sweet on the palate with balanced acidity.

LIMARI VALLEY

Once a power seat of the Inca Empire, Limari is named for the Franciscan monk who first planted grapes here in 1548. Today, the rich soils of the windswept valley have been discov-ered by major players such as De Martino, Undurraga, and Concha y Toro, whose Maycas del Limari brand pays homage to the ancient Inca civilization.

This region was once a haven for red grapes, which used to make up 80 percent of the total production. The Limari Valley is now almost evenly divided between whites and reds. The calcareous, limestone-rich soil and lower average temperatures closest to the Pacific have proven ideal for crisp, mineral-driven versions of Chardonnay, which is now the most prevalent variety planted. Syrah rules the roost toward the Andes, where sunny skies and warm, dry weather bring out the fruit-for-ward, full-bodied nature this grape is known for. About 400 kilometers (249 miles) north-west of Santiago, the valley's largest locality is Ovalle. Running through the center of Limari is the Limari River, whose source is a few kilometers east of this laid-back, almost rural, town. Average rainfall is 94 millimeters, or 3.5 inches, per year. The coastal territory can count on cooling moisture from the Camanchaca fog, but organic viticulture has been embraced in the drier, inland region; drip irrigation is the norm in both areas. Total planted area is 1,755 hectares (4,337 acres). Chardonnay is grown on 541 hectares (1,337 acres), or about a third of the total area under cultivation. The other main white varietal, Sauvignon Blanc, is farmed on 161 hectares (398 acres). Syrah, once the leading grape of the region, covers 328 hectares (811 acres), followed by Cabernet Sauvignon, which is raised on 294 hectares (726 acres). Carmenere is ensconced on 93 hectares (230 acres), while Pinot Noir and Merlot bring up the rear, at 61 hectares (151 acres) and 54 hectares (133 acres), respectively.

fifteenth centuries have been found by workers in the Tamaya vineyards. Another interesting archaeological feature of this region is the *piedras tacitas*, which are believed to be early maps of the stars and constellations. Tamay Chardonnay Reserva 2009 is pale gold in color with a bouquet of white fruits, green apples, and pears. In the mouth it is fresh, has great structure, and finishes with a light minerality and touch of butter. Only 2,000 cases were produced in 2009. Tamaya Malbec-Cabernet Sauvignon-Syrah Reserva 2007 is made from 55 percent Malbec, 24 percent Cabernet Sauvignon, and 21 percent Syrah. It's a purple-ruby color. The bouquet presents ripe fruits, especially blackberry and cassis, with touches of toasted brioche. On the palate expect fine tannins and a wildly fruity finish. Tamaya Cabernet Sauvignon-Syrah-Carmenere Reserva 2008 is a beautiful wine—too bad only 330 cases were produced.

CASA TAMAYA

Avenida Vitacura 5250, Vitacura,
+56 2 658 5040,
www.tamaya.cl

Named for the Diaguita word meaning "high lookout," Tamaya is the highest peak in the region, from which you can take in the view of the entire Limari Valley. Artifacts from the Diaguita culture dating from the eighth to

MAYCAS DEL LIMARI

Avenida Nueva Tajamar 481,
Las Condes, Santiago,
+56 2 476 5567,
www.maycasdellimari.com

The Limari Valley has low rainfall, but grapes here are cooled by strong ocean breezes as well as rolling fog—which consequently allows

TABALÍ

Fundo Santa Rosa de Tabalí, Ruta 45, Ovalle,
+56 2 477 5520,
www.tabali.com

for concentration of the grapes' sugars and flavors. The Limari Valley also benefits from a relatively long growing season. The word *maycas* comes from the Quechua language and translates roughly to "croplands." This region was once the holdings of the powerful Inca Empire, whose famous calendar is glorified on the winery's Reserva Especial labels. The word *Limari* comes from the Franciscan monk credited as the first to plant grapes in this area in 1548. Maycas del Limari is a project sponsored by Concha y Toro. Maycas del Limari Reserva Especial Syrah 2006 has a powerful ruby red color. On the nose you can detect blackberry and blueberry with notes of cocoa and white pepper. It is full-bodied and dense on the palate with expressive flavors of black plums and blackberries. Maycas del Limari Reserva Especial Chardonnay 2007 has an elegant bouquet of citrus, orange blossom, and toasted hazelnuts. It is pale straw in appearance, but on the palate it's luscious and full.

Located south of the Atacama Desert and only 29 kilometers (18 miles) from the Pacific Ocean, close to the entrance of the Enchanted Valley, Viña Tabalí benefits from hot days and cool nights. The valley is virtually an open-air museum with cultural and scientific interest. Inhabited by the Molle people and other notable civilizations from approximately 2000 BC through the seventh century AD, the valley is home to amazing rock paintings such as humans with antennae, snakes, and ceremonial masks. Ancient grinding stones for grain have also been found. Owned by the same parent company as Viña Leyda, Tabalí maintains a different style than its sister to the south. Vines were first planted here in 1993. Viña Tabalí Reserva Especial Syrah 2008 is dark ruby with a light violet rim. Purple flowers, black pepper, and a touch of smokiness are noted on the nose. The palate is round and smooth with flavors of dark cherries and cassis.

The tannins are well structured and the finish is persistent. Viña Tabalí Reserva Especial Pinot Noir 2009 is brilliantly cherry red. The bouquet is full of strawberries and cherries, while on the palate, fresh acidity and fruitiness are expressed. The finish is elegant with a silk-like texture. Viña Tabalí Reserva Especial Chardonnay 2009 has green hues over its rich yellow color. It has strong mineral and tropical fruit aromas and is then full-bodied with a round and ample finish.

CHOAPA VALLEY

No major winery has yet graced the fertile, colluvial soil (combining clay, sand, and volcanic rock) of the Choapa Valley, situated at Chile's narrowest point. Fed by El Rio Choapa, which originates in the Andes, and its tributary the Illapel River, the valley's two main towns are Illapel and Salamanca. The valley has 134 hectares (331 acres) planted with grapes. Known for its Cabernet Sauvignon, this small area is quickly building a reputation for Syrah. Among others, the De Martino family is noted for high-quality Syrah from this region; in fact, its winemaker Marcelo Retamal is the "*terroir hunter*" widely acknowledged as the first to unlock the potential of this high-altitude area wedged between the Andes and Chilean Coastal Range.

DOMAINE DE MANSON

Hijuela 10, Coirón, Casilla 25, Salamanca, IV Región,
+56 2 299 7807, www.domaine-de-manson.cl

One of the smallest commercial vineyards in Chile, Domaine de Manson has 4 hectares (10 acres) on the banks of the Choapa River. Owned by Scotsman George Manson, a retired mining engineer, and his Australian wife, Maureen, the estate prides itself on its use of organic techniques. The estate specializes in the varieties of the northern Rhône: Syrah, Viognier, Marsanne, and Roussanne. In homage to their adopted country, the Mansons also grow Carmenere. Domaine de Manson Coironino Blanco de Oro 2010, made from 100 percent Viognier, is a pale gold nectar and tastes of peach, white flowers, and violet. A blend of 95 percent Syrah and 5 percent Viognier, Domaine de Manson Coironino Coupage 2009 has a fresh, fruity palate of raspberries and strawberries with soft floral undertones. The refreshing, tropical fruit-scented Domaine de Manson Coironino Rosado 2010 is comprised of 52 percent Syrah and 48 percent Viognier. George and Maureen are aided in the vineyard and winery by the Araya brothers, Nelson and Jacob, whose family originally owned the property, and by Jacob's wife, Magaly. Together they manage to bottle almost nine hundred cases of wine each year.

ACONCAGUA VALLEY

Named for the tallest mountain in the Western Hemisphere—the 7,010-meter-high (22,999-foot-high) Mount Aconcagua (which is only 20 kilometers, or 12 miles, away from the region's eastern limit yet sits entirely in Argentina)—the Aconcagua Valley has produced fine wine for more than 150 years. Like the other valleys of northern Chile, Aconcagua Valley's orientation is mainly west to east, running along the twisting length of the river of the same name. The closest city is Valparaíso, nicknamed "The Jewel of the Pacific." The grape-growing area ends just west of this UNESCO World Heritage Site, and the river empties into the ocean a few kilometers north of here. Santiago is a little more than 100 kilometers (62 miles) to the southwest. Within Aconcagua's borders is the city of Quillota, which in the mid-sixteenth century was the property of Pedro de Valdivia, the governor of Chile. This fertile valley has been populated and farmed for more than two thousand years. It was here that Don Maximiano Errazuriz first established Viña Errazuriz in 1870; his motto, "From the best land, the best wine," is still upheld by his descendants and by everyone else who has since planted vines here.

Aconcagua Valley is Chile's warmest region. Its mineral-laden, alluvial soil is made up of silt, clay, sand, and gravel deposited here by a large prehistoric river. Historically, this was the home of the country's finest Cabernet Sauvignon and Merlot, yet the newer vineyards closest to the Pacific are now being associated with Chardonnay and Pinot Noir. Average yearly rainfall is 214 millimeters, or 8.5 inches. Vineyards here are some of the highest in the country, rising to 2,400 meters (7,874 feet). Total area planted is 672 hectares (1,661 acres); approximately three quarters of these produce red varieties, with the balance producing whites. This is a sharp change from just a couple of years ago, when red grapes made up almost 90 percent of the total. Cabernet Sauvignon still holds the top position, blanketing 250 hectares (618 acres), more than double the amount of first runner-up Sauvignon Blanc, which is raised on 102 hectares (252 acres). Merlot is grown on 82 hectares (203 acres), Syrah on 72 hectares (178 acres), Chardonnay on 60 hectares (148 acres), and Carmenere on 54 hectares (133 acres). Although Pinot Noir accounts for an almost imperceptible amount of total plantings, excellent examples are produced by Carmen, Carta Vieja, and Paseo. Errazuriz and San Esteban are standard-bearers for Chardonnay; although their wineries are close to the eastern city of Los Andes, new Chardonnay vineyards have sprung up much closer to oceanfront Valparaíso.

ARBOLEDA

503 Torre Sur, Las Condes, Santiago
+56 2 339 9100,
www.arboledawines.com

A boutique project owned by Eduardo Chadwick, the proprietor of Viña Errazuriz. Arboleda is named for the groves of native Chilean trees that stand in the vineyards. Arboleda's two estates, Las Vertientes and Chilhué, are managed sustainably—to respect the environment, preserve the land for those to come, and consider the health of its workers and end consumers. *Las Vertientes* is Spanish for "the slopes," while *Chilhué*, the indigenous word for "place of the seagulls," is a reference to its position just 14 kilometers (8 miles) from the coast. Winemaker Carolina Herrera joined the team in 2010. Her focus at both university in Chile and France and while working in the Loire Valley has been Sauvignon Blanc. Arboleda Sauvignon Blanc Aconcagua Costa 2009 is sourced from the 1,407-hectare (3,477-acre) Chilhué vineyard. Pale straw in color, its tropical fruit flavors are enhanced by fragrances of green pepper and fresh chopped herbs, with lush mouthfeel and bracing acidity. Arboleda Merlot 2008 is comprised of 90 percent Merlot and 10 percent Carmenere from the Las Vertientes parcel, which is 50 kilometers (31 miles) inland. Aged 12 months in French and American oak, it is the color of black cherries with a bright violet rim. The taste of kirsch and black raspberry mingles with black pepper, smoke, and baking spices. Arboleda Syrah 2009, also from Las Vertientes, is deep purple, and its blueberry and black fruit front notes are nicely balanced by Mediterranean herbs, mace, and a light floral finish.

ERRAZURIZ

503 Torre Sur, Las Condes, Santiago
+56 2 339 9100,
www.errazuriz.com

One of the oldest wineries in Chile, founded by Don Maximiano Errazuriz in 1870, Viña Errazuriz is still family owned. Today it is run by fifth-generation descendant Eduardo Chadwick. The estate's goal is to produce the finest wine possible from estate-grown fruit in the Aconcagua, Casablanca, and Curicó Valleys. In addition to bringing new technology and ideas to the company since joining

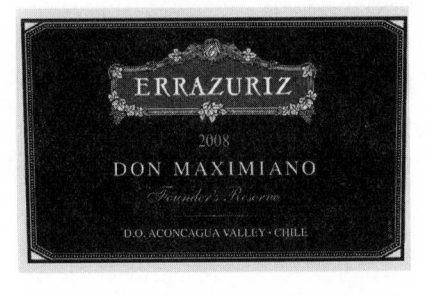

Nutella, and cinnamon toast. Errazuriz Estate Carmenere 2010 has a deep red-violet hue and tastes of black raspberries, paprika, and violets, with just a whiff of eggnog on the finish. Errazuriz Chardonnay Wild Ferment 2010 has flavors of pineapple and guava garnished with vivid jasmine, honeysuckle, and just a hint of shaved white truffle.

the family business in 1983, Eduardo created the winery's first ultra-premium bottling, Errazuriz Don Maximiano Founder's Reserve, in 1988. He also increased the estate's vineyard holdings in Aconcagua and added Syrah and Carmenere to the varieties grown. Errazuriz's seven main vineyards in the heart of Aconcagua cover rolling slopes and the floor of the valley itself and include one organic vineyard. The focus is on Bordeaux varieties: Cabernet Sauvignon, Merlot, Petit Verdot, Malbec, and Syrah, as well as Carmenere and Viognier. The Manzanar vineyard in the coastal area produces cool-climate Sauvignon Blanc, Chardonnay, and Pinot Noir. Winemaker Francisco Baettig has degrees from both the University of Chile and the University of Bordeaux. Errazuriz Don Maximiano Founder's Reserve 2008 is crafted mostly from Cabernet Sauvignon with small amounts of Carmenere, Syrah, and Petit Verdot sourced from the Don Maximiano and Max Vineyards. Glistening ruby red, its swift cherry-raspberry attack is softened by more complex essences of red currant preserves,

SAN ESTEBAN

La Florida 2074, San Esteban, Los Andes
+56 3 448 1050,
www.vse.cl

Viña San Esteban was founded in 1974 by grape-grower José Vicente and his son Horacio, a Bordeaux-trained winemaker who has worked at Château Mouton Rothschild. Located in the eastern Aconcagua Valley, in the foothills of the Andes, the estate's 120 hectares (297 acres) of steep hillside vineyards produce Cabernet

Sauvignon, Merlot, Carmenere, Syrah, Sangiovese, Cabernet Franc, Mourvèdre, Petit Verdot, Chardonnay, Sauvignon Blanc, and Viognier. Grapes grown on their Paidahuen estate benefit from the rocky, fluvial soil along the banks of the Aconagua River and at higher elevations toward the statuesque mountains. Horacio Vicente's second label, In Situ, crafts single-vineyard wines using organic techniques; organic certification was gained in 2009. San Esteban has begun using organic practices in the traditional vineyards too, such as growing cover crops between rows of grapevines and using biodegradable reed rather than plastic to secure pruned vines. Viña San Esteban Classic Chardonnay 2009, fermented and aged in steel to preserve the freshness of the grape, is pale yellow with golden flecks. Its nose of Clementine and green apple yields to honeydew melon and soft pear. Also unoaked is Viña San Esteban Classic Cabernet Sauvignon 2008, whose raspberry preserve and black cherry character are quickly joined by vanilla and a suggestion of spice. In Situ Laguna del Inca Gran Reserva 2008, a blend of 30 percent Cabernet Sauvignon, 40 percent Syrah, and 30 percent Carmenere, memorializes the legend of an Incan princess who died on her wedding day and was buried at the bottom of a lake near the source of the Aconagua River; the waters immediately turned emerald green, the color of the princess's eyes. At the opposite end of the color spectrum, this wine is a dark ruby red. Its luscious cherry scent continues on the palate, accompanied by flavors of anise, gooseberry, and dried mountain herbs.

SEÑA

503 Torre Sur, Las Condes, Santiago
+56 2 339 9100,
www.sena.cl

Spanish for "distinguishing mark" or "personal signature," Seña, began as a joint venture between Eduardo Chadwick and Robert Mondavi and set out to create Chile's first "icon wine." Now solely owned by Chadwick, Seña proved its mettle at the Berlin Tasting of 2004, where a distinguished panel rated Seña 2001 ahead of wine world deities Châteaux Margaux,

Lafite, and Latour. A wooded 350-hectare (865-acre) estate shelters 42 hectares (104 acres) of hillside vineyard in Aconagua's western border, about 40 kilometers (25 miles) from the ocean. Cabernet Sauvignon, Merlot, Malbec, Petit Verdot, Cabernet Franc, and Carmenere grow here on colluvial soils layered with gravel and loam, at altitudes ranging between 290 to 500 meters (951 to 1,640 feet). Biodynamic methods are employed by a team under the direction of viticulturist Jorge Figuereoa and winemaker Francisco Baettig. Seña is a blend of the six varieties grown on the estate—hand-selected from the best blocks in the vineyard, before being submitted to two hand-sortings in the winery. The varieties are vinified separately and then blended before spending 22 months in new French oak. Seña 2008 is deep garnet red with a bright purple rim. A bountiful nose of three-berry parfait endures in the mouth, balanced by gingerbread spice and hints of cedar. This is a wine of elegant complexity.

VON SIEBENTHAL

Calle O'Higgins S/N, Panquehue,
Valle de Aconcagua,
+56 3 459 1827,
www.vinavonsiebenthal.com

Mauro von Siebenthal, formerly a Swiss lawyer, fell in love with Chile and opened Viña von Siebenthal in 1998. He has three main vineyards in Panquehue, all managed using organic farming techniques. A relatively small production of 150,000 bottles per year and his watchful eye are at least partly responsible for numerous international accolades. Von Siebenthal wines are exported to 18 countries from Iceland to Indonesia. Viña von Siebenthal Parcela #7 2006 is a blend of 40 percent Cabernet Sauvignon, 35 percent Merlot, 10 percent Petit Verdot, and 15 percent Cabernet Franc. It is fermented in 100 hectoliter stainless-steel tanks and then aged for 10 months in a combination of French and American oak. It is ruby red with aromas of dark cherries and fruits of the woods. On the palate it is excitingly vibrant with elegant, balanced fruits and smooth, lingering tannins. Viña von Siebenthal Montelig 2005 is a blend of 40 percent Cabernet Sauvignon, 30 percent Petit Verdot, and 30 percent Carmenere. It is aged for 24 months in new French oak. It is a medium ruby red with notes of pencil lead, cassis, and fruits of the wood. On the palate it is beautiful, round, and expressive. Viña von Siebenthal Tatay de Cristobal 2007 is a blend of 90 percent Carmenere and 10 percent Petit Verdot. It is ruby red with a bouquet of coarsely ground black pepper, red and black raspberries, and dried cassis. It is extremely well structured, balanced, and elegant. The finish is long and lovely. Too bad only 1,492 bottles were made.

CASABLANCA VALLEY

Just 75 kilometers (47 miles) due west of Santiago, Casablanca—a coastal, cool-climate valley—is the highest producer among Chile's "new" regions. Often referred to as the Napa Valley of Chile, Casablanca's modern Route 68 connects Santiago and Valparaíso. The valley is easily accessible by car and offers multiple options for wine tourists, including world-class hotels and restaurants. In the not-so-distant past, its sandy soil was mostly home to bramble and scrub—until the 1980s, when innovations in technology met up with an experimental spirit, leading to rapid expansion in viticulture and winemaking. Agustin Huneeus is recognized as the pioneer who put Casablanca on the map: In 1990, there were only 40 hectares (99 acres) of vines planted here. Since Huneeus's founding of Veramonte that same year, total vineyard area has risen to 5,680 hectares (14,036 acres).

Although Cabernet Sauvignon and Carmenere were among the original varieties planted in the Casablanca Valley, production of these varieties has dwindled to almost nothing, having been supplanted by Chardonnay, Sauvignon Blanc, and relative newcomers Pinot Noir and Syrah. Chardonnay, which generally does well in a cool climate such as this, accounts for about 40 percent of plantings, with 2,270 hectares (5,609 acres). Combined with Sauvignon Blanc's 1,932 hectares (4,774 acres), these two white varieties—joined by small amounts of Gewürztraminer and Viognier—make up about 75 percent of the grapes grown in the region. Casablanca's leading red variety is Pinot Noir, cultivated on 710 hectares (1,754 acres), followed by Merlot, grown on 400 hectares (988 acres). There are 180 hectares (445 acres) of Syrah in this region.

Early-morning fog provides moisture in the early part of the day. Late afternoon sunshine provides much-needed warmth. Cold, windy nights and the icy-cold Humboldt Current of the Pacific lengthen the ripening season by almost a month: the harvest in Casablanca takes place in April. Rainfall within the span of a year averages 542 millimeters, or 21.5 inches. The soil on the valley floor tends to be sandy loam or clay loam, while hillsides are covered with gray and black clay. Higher-slope soil is generally red clay. Unlike most of Chile's vineyard valleys, there is no central river; water is found in deep wells, and drip irrigation is employed extensively. The valley is separated into four main zones, from east to west: La Vinilla/Tapihue, Lo Ovalle/El Ensueño, Lo Orozco, and Las Dichas. Additionally, smaller satellite areas are contained within the D.O., such as Lo Orrego and Lagunillas. The main difference from zone to zone is soil type.

CASABLANCA

Rodrigo de Araya 1431, Macul, Santiago,
+56 2 238 0307,
www.casablancawinery.com

Viña Casablanca is a boutique winery established in 1992. With 55 hectares (136 acres) in the Santa Isabel region of the Casablanca Valley, very close to the Pacific Ocean, it produces quality wine under four brands: Cefiro, El Bosque, Nimbus, and Neblus. Winemaker Ximena Pacheco uses Cabernet Sauvignon, Merlot, Pinot Noir, Syrah, Chardonnay, and Sauvignon Blanc to make Viña Casablanca's wines. Grapes for Cefiro Colección Privada Cabernet Sauvignon 2006 come from a level area of Casablanca's Los Nogales estate and is dark garnet with aromas of blackberries, black cherries, and cassis. It tastes full and ample with silky tannins and a long-lasting finish. Viña Casablanca Neblus 2005 is a blend of 60 percent Merlot and 40 percent Cabernet

Sauvignon. It has a bouquet of Christmas baking spices, red currants, and black fruits. On the palate flavors of tobacco, anise, and fruit conserves overwhelm your mouth before velvety tannins calm the fruit bomb that just went off. Viña Casablanca Cefiro Colección Privada Pinot Noir 2007 has a ruby tone with notes of cocoa, red cherries, and fruits of the wood. In the mouth it has a fruity yet restrained presence.

CASAS DEL BOSQUE

Avenida Alonso de Cordova 5151, Santiago,
+56 2 378 5495,
www.casasdelbosque.cl

Founded in 1933 as a family-owned, boutique winery dedicated to the production of high-quality wine, Casas del Bosque still lives up to the family tradition. Located only 70 kilometers (43 miles) from Santiago and 30 kilometers (19 miles) from Chile's principal port—Valparaíso—the family had both

convenience and transportation in mind when it founded here. An amazing 80 percent of production is exported. The family limits their production to 70,000 cases per year, all from grapes grown on 245 hectares (605 acres) in the Casablanca Valley and 13 hectares (32 acres) in the Rapel Valley. The winemaking team consists of New Zealander Grant Phelps and Chileans Milenko Valenzuela and Pilar González. Gran Bosque 2008 is made from 100 percent Cabernet Sauvignon grown in the Rapel Valley. It's a deep garnet red with a bouquet filled with dried fruits, especially cassis and black raspberries. In the mouth this juicy Cabernet delights you with flavors of licorice, baking spices, black cherries, and cocoa. The finish is long and ample. Gran Estate Selection Private Reserva 2007 is made from a blend of 61 percent Syrah, 26 percent Merlot, and 13 percent Pinot Noir. It is a brilliant violet colored wine with lovely aromas of blueberry, fennel, herbes de Provence, and cinnamon buns. On the palate flavors of saddle leather, black truffle, and dark fruit conserves overwhelm your taste buds and prepare them for a multilayered, smooth finish. For a sweeter tooth, try Casa del Bosques Late Harvest 2006 made from 100 percent Sauvignon Blanc. It is a bright gold nectar with heady fruit notes. In the mouth the balance of sweetness and acidity is nicely played.

KINGSTON

Old Corral, Casablanca,
+56 32 274 2916,
www.kingstonvineyards.com

Carl John Kingston—a miner from Central Mine, Michigan—packed up his family, loaded them on a ship in the early 1900s, and headed south to Chile. He was looking for copper and gold but instead settled on a large cattle ranch. Descendants Courtney and Tim Kingston came up with the idea of planting vines in 1994, and much of the company's day-to-day business is managed by the Chilean arm of the family. Consulting winemaker Byron Kosuge spent 14 years working at Saintsbury in Carneros, California, before teaming with Evelyn Vidal, herself a veteran of Napa harvests. Together they make some wonderful wines. Bayo Oscuro Syrah 2008 is deep indigo in color. Its scents of violet and dark fruit invite you deeper into the glass. Round in the mouth, this Syrah's soft tannins are silky smooth. Cariblanco Sauvignon Blanc 2008 is pale yellow with scents of citrus blossoms and fresh-squeezed limes. It is crisp and clean in the mouth with a delightful finish.

LOMA LARGA

Fundo Loma Larga, Casilla 139, Casablanca,
+56 32 274 2098,
www.lomalarga.com

Tour Loma Larga's vineyards on horseback or climb aboard a horse-drawn carriage to see views of the property from the surrounding hillsides. Situated in the beautiful Casablanca Valley, Loma Larga is a winery you shouldn't miss. The family's first vines were carried from Bordeaux and planted in their first estate—Chacra Victoria in what is now the center of Santiago—in the nineteenth century by Don Manuel Joaquín Díaz Escudero Alvarez de Toledo. Modern plantings occurred in 1999 with Cabernet Franc, Malbec, Merlot, Pinot Noir, Sauvignon Blanc, and Syrah. French winemaker Cedric Nicole, a native of the Loire Valley, has worked in New Zealand and Oregon with the same varieties. He strives for concentration of the grape's sugars and nutrients in the berries themselves and uses a variety of internationally recognized techniques, including canopy management, vine positioning, and trellising. His desired acidity is achieved by hot days and cool nights, which allow for slow ripening of the grapes. The average yield here is only 1.8 tons per hectare. French oak is used exclusively, and only 300,000 liters are produced per year. Lomo Larga Unfiltered Cabernet Franc 2008 is indigo-ink colored with a violet rim.

Rose, anise, and graphite aromas lead to flavors of red fruit preserves before a long finish. Lomo Larga Pinot Noir 2009 is deep ruby red with scents of black cherry and candied orange peel, while in the mouth, red fruit persists. Lomo Larga Syrah 2008 is ruby red with aromas of strawberry and caramel. In the mouth, blueberries and blackberries explode before a long tannic finish.

MORANDÉ

Alcantara 971, Las Condes, Santiago,
+56 2 270 8900,
www.morande.cl

Founded in 1996, Morandé is going strong, with exports to more than forty countries on five continents. Winemaking director Pablo Morandé oversees production of grapes sourced from two main estates. The Belén Estate in Casablanca has 130 hectares (321 acres) of Chardonnay, Pinot Noir, Merlot, Sauvignon Blanc, Riesling, Gewürztraminer, Sémillon, and Cabernet Franc. The Romeral Estate in the Maipo Valley has 50 hectares (124 acres) of Cabernet Sauvignon, Carmenere, Cabernet Franc, Merlot, and Petit Verdot. Morandé wines have garnered high scores for more than one of their varieties. Edición Limitada Carmenere 2008 hails from the Maipo Valley and is dark garnet red in color. The bouquet reveals blueberries, purple flowers, cassis, and cocoa. In the mouth there are intense flavors of black fruits, especially plums, along with an element of spice. The finish is long with smooth tannic structure. Edición Limitada Syrah-Cabernet Sauvignon 2007 has aromas of cocoa, earth, and fruits of the wood to complement its red, almost purple, presentation in the glass. The mouth is rewarded with fresh fruit and balanced tannins. Edición Limitada Carignan 2007 comes from unirrigated, 50-year-old vines. It's deep cherry red with notes of kirsch and street vendor chestnuts. In the mouth there is a nice balance of acidity and tannin, with a touch of sweetness.

favorable winds in 2009 when its new winery opened on March 7, just two days before the start of the harvest season. Founded by Felipe Aldunate, Hernán Gómez, Pablo Gómez, Edmundo Eluchans, Jaime Charles, Felipe Larraín, Felipe Morandé, and the Rencoret family, the group hired Álvaro Espinoza and Juan Carlos Faundez to be a part of the winemaking team. Its wines have won international awards and have been rated highly in various markets. Quintay Sauvignon Blanc Casablanca Valley 2008 comes from two distinct areas in the valley and uses three different clones of Sauvignon Blanc. It is pale straw with mineral-accented notes of canned peas and pampas grass. On the palate it is fresh and clean with a bracing finish. Quintay Chardonnay 2008 also comes from two plots in Casablanca Valley, a good portion of which is sourced from northeast-facing Tapihue vineyards. It is straw colored with green hues and has a bouquet of tropical fruits. In the mouth it is well rounded with a mineral finish.

QUINTAY

San Sebastian 2871, Las Condes, Santiago,
+56 2 231 0246,
www.quintay.com

Quintay is the Mapuche word for "sailing with the current." It seems this outfit found

VERAMONTE

Ruta 68, Kilometer 66, Casablanca,
+56 3 232 9998,
www.veramonte.cl

The first time that we visited Veramonte, we were impressed by the beautiful grand scale, Old World, Bordeaux-style architecture of the visitor's center. In contrast, the winery is amazingly state of the art, having been designed by one of Chile's leading architects, Jorge Swinburn. It contains gravity-fed fermenting receptacles and über-modern stainless-steel tanks. Although the winery can handle large volumes of grapes, there is an area where small-lot winemaking occurs. Individual and experimental plots can be vinified separately. On a subsequent visit over lunch, winemaker Christian Aliaga explained his passion for Chilean *terroir*. Before joining Veramonte in 1999, he worked many harvests in the Northern Hemisphere, especially in California and Bordeaux. His wines garner many international awards. Straw-colored Veramonte Sauvignon Blanc Reserva 2009 has aromas of white stone fruits, white flowers, and micro-planed lemon peel. In the mouth it has medium body with Cavaillion melon and citrus blossom flavors and a clean crisp finish. Veramonte Ritual Pinot Noir 2008 is cherry red with aromatic notes of raspberry and red cherry. On the palate it is elegant and refined—a wonderful example of what a Chilean Pinot Noir should be. Veramonte Primus 2007 is composed of 65 percent Cabernet Sauvignon, 20 percent Syrah, 8 percent Merlot, and 7 percent Carmenere. It is dark ruby red with aromas of cigar box,

mint, toasted brioche, and red fruits; then in the mouth it's a juicy, mouth-filling wine that delights with a prolonged tannic finish.

WILLIAM COLE

Camino Tapihue Kilometer 4.5, Casablanca,
+56 32 215 7777,
www.williamcolevineyards.cl

The William Cole winery was built in 1999. It lovingly recalls the style of an old Spanish mission—though looks can be deceiving, as the building houses 92 modern stainless-steel tanks with a capacity of 2.2 million liters. The winery produces four lines of wine—Bill, named after the founder; Columbine Reserva; Alto Vuelo; and Mirador—utilizing Pinot Noir, Cabernet Sauvignon, Carmenere, Syrah, Sauvignon Blanc, and Chardonnay varieties. William Cole Single Vineyard Columbine Reserve Cabernet Sauvignon 2005 is deep garnet with notes of blackberry and mocha. In the mouth it explodes like a chocolate-covered cherry and finishes with long-lasting tannins. William Cole Alta Vuelo Cabernet Sauvignon-Carmenere 2005 is brilliant red with a violet rim. The bouquet has rich, ripe, red fruits with touches of geranium leaf. The palate is pleasing with light vanilla notes and silky tannins.

SAN ANTONIO/ LEYDA VALLEY

The race is on to see who can plant more vineyards—and make the leanest, crispest wine possible—in this cool-climate region 100 kilometers (62 miles) southwest of Santiago. The most coastal of any vine-growing land in Chile, it features breathtaking views of the Pacific from many vineyards—once the morning fog has burned off. It is divided into six subzones, Lo Abarca, Rosario, Malvilla, Llolleo, Cartagena, and Leyda, the last of which seems to be the most significant at the moment. The area achieved D.O. status in 2002. Between minimal water, poor soil, and a primarily cool climate, San Antonio, and Leyda in particular, have turned out to be ideal for the production of bright, high-acid wines with a strong mineral component. Here too, the effects of cool marine air and mists early in the day—both resulting from the frigid Humboldt Current—lengthen

the ripening period of the grapes. Don't be fooled into thinking that weather alone is responsible for the highly drinkable Pinot Noir, Chardonnay, and Sauvignon Blanc coming from San Antonio: certainly the small, rolling hills covered with loam, clay, granite, and quartz gravel have a hand in the outcome as well.

So far it is the boutique producers, of which two have female winemakers (which is in and of itself an innovation in the world of Chilean wine), who are turning heads in this region. Whites outnumber reds by a ratio of three to one. Plantings of Sauvignon Blanc increased almost eight-fold in the last decade and now grace 835 hectares (2,063 acres)—of just over 1,600 hectares (3,954 acres) of vines planted in the region as a whole. That is more than twice the amount of Chardonnay, which covers 340 hectares (840 acres). Following close on Chardonnay's heels (and no doubt set to surpass it) is Pinot Noir, on 327 hectares (808 acres)—quadruple the amount of just a few years ago. Syrah is planted on 45 hectares (111 acres), and a trio of aromatic white varieties—Riesling, Gewürztraminer, and Sauvignon Gris—round out the total plantings with 25, 16, and 10 hectares (62, 40, and 25 acres), respectively. Average annual rainfall is 350 millimeters, or 14 inches. There is a 20 percent chance of frost in the spring.

AMARAL

Avenida Ellodoro Yañez 2962,
Providencia, Santiago,
+56 2 520 4355,
www.amaralwines.cl

MontGras's newest venture in the Leyda Valley produces quality wines on the estate's 650 hectares (1,606 acres). Sauvignon Blanc, Chardonnay, and Pinot Noir grapes are grown in alluvial soils on sloped vineyards. The company hired winemaker Jaime de la Cerda for his expertise with international varieties in France and Argentina. Amaral is already earning high points and scores from many international sources. Amaral Leyda Valley Barrel Fermented Chardonnay 2007 is medium straw in color, comes from vineyards at 200 meters (656 feet) of altitude, and is aged in French oak, 70 percent of which is new. It has aromas of pineapple upside-down cake, toasted almonds, and vanilla. In the mouth it is creamy with well-balanced acidity. Too bad they only made 2,000 bottles; drink now through 2017. Amaral Leyda Valley Chardonnay 2009 is straw colored with a green hue. Fermented in stainless steel with no barrel ageing, the bouquet has aromas of white peach and white flowers. It is crisp and clean on the palate. Amaral Leyda Valley Sauvignon Blanc 2010 is pale yellow with notes of mandarin, tangerine, and lemon blossoms. In the mouth there is a nice balance of acidity and medium-bodied richness.

AMAYNA

Riconada de San Juan, Leyda,
+56 2 428 8080,
www.amayna.cl

The Garces Silva family is serious about wine. Before purchasing Amayna in a privileged location in the Leyda Valley, José Antonio Garces Silva was a businessman with holdings in real estate, livestock, and the financial sector. He hired Francisco José Ponce Sanhueza and Jean Michel Novelle as his winemakers, and the result has been the production of consistent, quality wines, which have earned international accolades. The winery was architecturally designed for both gravity-assisted winemaking and to blend in with the valley's natural environment. It has storage capacity for 120,000 liters in French oak barrels and 285,000 liters in stainless-steel tanks. Annual production is 15,000 cases per year. Amayna Sauvignon Barrel Fermented 2007 is straw colored with notes of ruby red grapefruit, caramelized pineapple, and ripe tropical fruit. The roundness in the mouth comes from 12 months of aging in new French oak barrels. Amayna Chardonnay 2008 has aromas of guava, dried apples, and toasted almonds—with an edge of minerality. On the palate it is delightful, with an elegant finish. Amayna Pinot Noir 2009 is dark ruby with aromas of black fruits and red cherries. The palate is generous with mouth-filling tannic structure and a persistent finish.

CASA MARIN

Las Peñas 3101, Las Condes, Santiago,
+56 2 657 1530,
www.casamarin.cl

As of this writing, Casa Marin is the closest Chilean winery to the Pacific Ocean, with only 4 kilometers (2.5 miles) separating the two. The viña was founded in 2000 by María Luz Marín, and the main winery building was completed in 2004. Casa Marin grows Gewürztraminer in its Casona vineyard, a relatively flat parcel of land with dark, fertile soil, and grows Sauvignon Blanc on the top of a windy hill in its Cipreses vineyard. Sauvignon Gris is grown in its Estero vineyard, while Lo Abarca Hills and Litoral vineyards are home to Pinot Noir vines. The winemaking team includes winemakers from Chile and the United Kingdom. If you visit (and you're so inclined) you can work with the winemaking team in a three-day work program while being housed in basic lodging, or you can forgo the work and simply stay in the private Villa Casa Marin. The winery is located on the Camino Malvilla in the Leyda Valley, but reservations are taken at the main business office in Santiago. The family can

arrange tours to local sites of interest, including the home of Chilean poet, Pablo Neruda. Casa Marin Litoral Vineyard Pinot Noir 2006 is ruby red in the glass with aromas of red and black fruits. Well rounded in the mouth, this is a classic example of what coastal Pinot Noir should taste like. Casa Marin Miramar Vineyard Syrah 2008 is ink colored with notes of sweet blackberry and ground pepper. It is full-bodied on the palate with an easy finish.

LEYDA

Avenida del Parque, 4161,
Ciudad Empresarial Heuchuraba, Santiago,
+56 2 430 5900,
www.leyda.cl

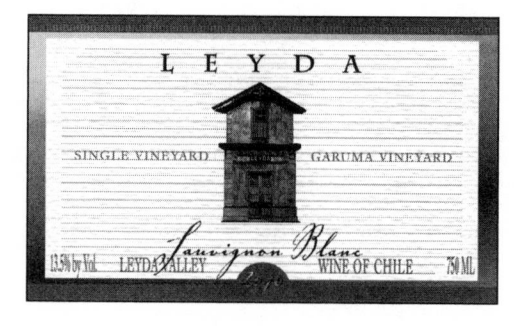

We thoroughly enjoyed our lunch with chief winemaker Viviana Navarrete, who makes quality wines from cool-climate varieties. When we asked if her goal was to craft wines using a French, Argentine, or North American style profile, her answer was a proud, "I am Chilean, and I make Chilean wines in the Chilean Style." The vines here were planted in the mid-1990s. The estate—built on a former pasture—is located on a cool-climate site just 12 kilometers (7 miles) from the Pacific Ocean. Leyda Single Vineyard Garuma Sauvignon Blanc 2010 is pale straw in color with a pronounced minerality on the nose and lovely citrus notes. It is crisp and clean in the mouth, with balanced acidity. Leyda Single Vineyard Las Brisas Pinot Noir 2009 is medium cherry and ruby in the glass with red fruits of the wood on the bouquet. The palate is full-bodied with balanced tannins. Leyda also produces a Reserva/Classic line of wines, made from grapes grown in other regions. Leyda Syrah 2008 is grown in the Colchauga Valley and is a rich ruby color. Notes of black plum and raspberry are evident on the nose, with silky, full-bodied tannins in the mouth.

LITORAL

Avenida Los Leones 382, Providencia, Santiago,
+56 2 233 0318,
www.geowines.cl

Established in 1999, Viña Litoral has 140 hectares (346 acres) of vineyards, 74 hectares (183 acres) of which are planted with Sauvignon Blanc and 24 hectares (59 acres) with Pinot Noir. Chardonnay vines cover 23 hectares (57 acres), while Gewürztraminer and Riesling cover only 2.5 hectares (6 acres) and 1 hectare (2.5 acres), respectively. Four clonal varieties of Sauvignon Blanc are represented, namely 242, 108, 107, and 1, while Pinot Noir is only made from clone 777. Viña Litoral Ventolera Leyda Valley Chardonnay 2008 is straw colored with tropical fruit aromas on the nose. It is round on the palate with light notes of vanilla, due to half of the production receiving six months of oak barrel aging. Viña Litoral Ventolera Leyda Valley Pinot Noir 2008 receives eight months of barrel aging and is ruby red with a bouquet of fruits of the wood. The palate is lush and generous. Viña Litoral Ventolera Leyda Valley Sauvignon Blanc 2008 has lovely vegetal aromas and a crisp, clean finish.

MATETIC

Fundo Rosario, Lagunillas, Casablanca,
+56 2 595 2661,
www.mateticvineyards.com

Matetic Winery is certainly a sight to see when visiting the Rosario Valley. Founded in 1999, the family employed architect Laurence Odfjell to create a stunning building with beautiful surroundings. The family also brought in biodynamic consultant Alan York, consulting winemaker Ken Bernards, and viticultural

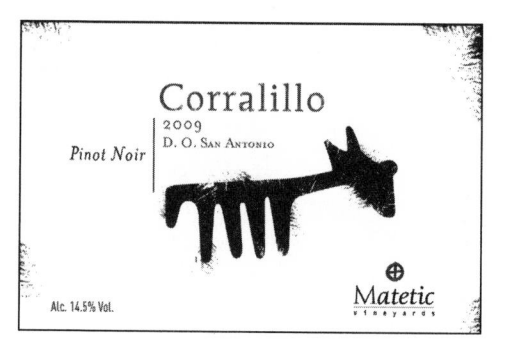

MAIPO VALLEY

The Maipo Valley is claimed to be the only wine region in the world that contains a capital city that also has vineyards within its city limits: Santiago. Although it is not the largest, or even most densely planted of Chile's valleys, Maipo's historical importance to winemaking in Chile, its proximity to Santiago, and its high number of high-profile wineries all combine to make Maipo the center of not just the country but also the world of Chilean wine. Silvestre Ochagavia's first experiments with French varieties here in 1851 were followed by Cousiño Macul in 1861, Santa Rita in 1880, and Viña Undurraga in 1885. Although Cousiño Macul has since relocated its winemaking operations outside of the city (maintaining the original winery for tourism) the descendants of this group of pioneers still make wine in Maipo today.

Like the great river from which the valley takes its name, vineyards stretch from the Andes, just to the east of Santiago, all the way to the mighty Pacific. It is divided into three distinct subzones. Alto Maipo climbs the base of the Andes, with altitudes ranging between 400 and 800 meters (1,312 and 2,624 feet). Vines spend the early part of each day in shade—until the sun peeks over the Andes from the Argentine side, providing

consultant Ann Kraemer. Besides making quality wines, Matetic has a boutique hotel and restaurant and is the site of many weddings, parties, and special events. The restaurant, Equilibrio, is under the direction of Chef Matias Bustos and is worth a stop—whether staying at Matetic's La Casona or simply visiting the winery for the day. Matetic Coralillo Chardonnay 2009 is pale yellow with a greenish hue. The nose has aromas of mango, guava, white peaches, and caramelized pineapple, and in the mouth it's round with a persistent finish. Matetic Coralillo Pinot Noir 2009 is dark ruby red. The bouquet contains black cherry and raspberry notes, and on the palate soft juicy tannins lead to a long finish. Matetic Syrah 2008 is garnet colored with a violet rim. Aromas of black pepper, wet earth, smoked meats, and cooling spices lead to a full-bodied palate with balanced tannins.

high afternoon temperatures. Cool mountain breezes cause a strong drop in overnight temperatures, and it is this disparity in day-to-night climate that provides excellent ripening conditions for the elegant red wines of the region. Central Maipo, the zone immediately bordering the river, sees less rain than the surrounding, more mountainous regions—although the fertile alluvial soils and proximity to running water make up for the drier conditions. Pacific Maipo borders San Antonio but is sheltered from the direct influence of the ocean by its position in the foothills between the Andes and the Coastal Range.

Total hectares planted with grape vines is just shy of 12,000 (29,653 acres). Nearly 85 percent of the varieties here are red. Cabernet Sauvignon is the star of the show, particularly in the Alto Maipo: more than half of the grapes grown in the valley as a whole are Cabernet, which thrives on 6,172 hectares (15,251 acres). Merlot trails behind in a not-even-close second place, covering 1,060 hectares (2,619 acres). Chardonnay is hot on Merlot's heels, blanketing 1,012 hectares (2,501 acres). Fine Syrah (891 hectares; 2,202 acres) and Carmenere (771 hectares; 1,905 acres) are grown here, as are Sauvignon Blanc (671 hectares; 1,658 acres) and a not-so-shabby amount of Cabernet Franc, (255 hectares; 630 acres) used mainly for blending. Most Chardonnay and Sauvignon Blanc are relatively new plantings in the Coastal Region.

ALMAVIVA

Puente Alto, Maipo,
+56 2 270 4225,
www.almavivawinery.com

The name Almaviva comes from the character Count Almaviva in the play *The Marriage of Figaro*, first written by the French playwright Beaumarchais and later set to music by Mozart. As defined by Beaumarchais, *Almaviva* is the act of joining two great traditions to offer pleasure and excellence to the world. In 1997, Baroness Philippine de Rothschild and Eduardo Tagle, CEO of Concha y Toro, signed a partnership agreement to create a wine that would live up to Beaumarchais's definition. The buildings of Bodega Almaviva, in Puente Alto, were designed by Chilean architect Martin Hurtado. Although the winery was not inaugurated until 2000, the first vintage, 1998, became an immediate world success. The winery produces only one wine and has petitioned to use the term *Primer Orden* to describe its product. In Spanish, it roughly translates to a combination of "estate grown" and "Grand Cru," as used in the French winemaking tradition. By definition, Primer

Orden wines are grown, vinified, and bottled on the estate by a team dedicated to producing one wine. Eighty-five hectares (210 acres) of land have been reserved for growing grapes solely for Almaviva, and the estate uses a modern underground drip irrigation system to constantly measure the moisture in the soil. Almaviva 2008 is comprised of 66 percent Cabernet Sauvignon, 26 percent Carmenere, and 8 percent Cabernet Franc. It ages for 18 months in new French oak and is dark ruby red in color. The bouquet opens with notes of cassis, black raspberry, mocha, and anise. On the palate it has a firm tannic structure and a lingering finish. It is a truly beautiful wine.

ANTIYAL

Alto Jahuel, Buin,
+56 2 821 4224,
www.antiyal.com

Considered one of the first "garage wineries" in Chile, Antiyal was started by Álvaro Espinoza and his family in 1996, with the idea that good wines could be made on a small scale while maintaining organic and biodynamic principles. The word *Antiyal* is from the Mapuche language and means "sons of the sun." Álvaro wanted to teach his children and, as he says, "anybody who would listen," that we must take care of our environment

and be stewards of the land—so that we can pass it on to the next generation. Álvaro feels that organic growing methods lead to wine with truer varietal characteristic. He limits his yield to 4 metric tons per hectare (1.8 US tons per acre). He uses compost and manure from his farm as fertilizer for the vines. His first production in 1998 yielded 3,000 bottles of Antiyal, an assemblage of Cabernet Sauvignon, Carmenere, and Syrah. Currently, Alvaro produces 7,000 bottles of Antiyal and 12,000 bottles of Kuyen, which means "moon" in Mapuche. His wines consistently score highly in international publications. Antiyal 2005 has notes of smoked meats, purple flowers, and cassis. Well-structured tannins and a persistent finish are pleasing to the palate. Kuyen 2005 is ink colored with aromas of dark fruits and barbecue meats. It is full-bodied and expansive in the mouth.

CANEPA

Avenida Nueva Tajamar 481, Torre Norte,
Las Condes, Santiago,
+56 2 476 5382,
www.canepawines.cl

José Canepa Vaccarezza emigrated from Genoa, Italy, to Chile in 1914, and almost one hundred years later, the Canepa family claims to be the only traditional Chilean winery today with generations of Italian heritage. The company was extremely forward-thinking and began exporting its wines to Europe in the 1940s. In 1979, it won the title of "Fifth Best Wine in the World" at the Gault and Millau competition in Paris—the top four wines were all French. Its wine labels are handsomely decorated with paintings of ancient Roman mosaics and scenery. Canepa Finisimo Sauvignon Blanc 2009 is pale straw with a floral, citrus, and herbaceous nose. It is vibrant in the mouth with refreshing acidity. Canepa Finisimo Cabernet Sauvignon 2009 has aromas of smoked meat, bacon, black fruit, and saddle leather. It is full-bodied with well-structured tannins.

CARMEN

Avenida Apoquindo 3669, Las Condes, Santiago,
+56 2 362 2122,
www.carmen.com

Founded in 1850 by Christian Lance and named after his wife, Carmen, Viña Carmen is now owned by the Claro Group. The company sources grapes from its own vineyards, which range from Chile's northernmost valleys to its southernmost, near Patagonia. Carmen has vineyards in Elqui Valley, Limari Valley, Casablanca Valley, Leyda Valley, Mapio Alto, Colchagua Valley, Apalta, and Maule Valley. It is the company's philosophy to grow the best grapes with varieties suited for each valley and climate. Carmen Gran Reserva Cabernet Sauvignon 2008 is made from grapes grown in the Maipo Alto Valley. It is made from 95 percent Cabernet Sauvignon and 5 percent Carmenere and has aromas of cassis, graphite, and mocha. In the mouth it is full-bodied with a long finish. Carmen Carmenere Reserva 2009's grapes are sourced from the Colchagua Valley and is a blend of 90 percent Carmenere and 10 percent Carignan. It has aromas of Hungarian paprika, cigar box, and ripe black plums. The tannins are soft and silky on the palate, and the finish is lingering. Carmen Gran Reserva

Sauvignon Blanc 2009 is made from 100 percent Sauvignon Blanc grapes grown in the Leyda Valley. It is almost clear in the glass with aromas of ruby red grapefruit, lemon blossoms, and geranium leaf. In the mouth it is crisp, clean, and refreshing.

CHOCALÁN

Dagoberto Godoy 145, Cerillos, Santiago,
+56 2 208 7401,
www.chocolanwines.com

Viña Chocalán began after wine bottle supplier Guillermo Toro's two-year search for suitable land to grow grapes. It was his life-long dream to make wine that would actually fill the bottles he previously sold. Architect Marianne Balze designed the winery to blend into the natural environment; construction began in 2002. *Chocalán* comes from the indigenous word for "yellow blossom," as many yellow flowers grow wild in the area. Viña Chocalán bottled its first wines in 2003, and today the winery employs all five of Guillermo's children. Fernando Espino and María del Pilar González Tamargo are the winemakers. Together, they have many years of experience; Fernando has worked harvests in France, Spain, and California. Their Viña Chocalán Chardonnay Selección 2010 is a rich golden color with aromas of caramelized

pineapple, citrus flowers, and white peaches. In the mouth it is fruit-driven with a creamy finish. Viña Chocalán Gran Reserva Malbec 2008 is deep purple with notes of pencil lead, vanilla, and dried plums. It has a large volume of flavor in the mouth with a soft tannic finish. Viña Chocalán Carmenere Reserva 2009 is deep ruby with aromas of dried figs, cloves, and cocoa. The palate is pleasant with well-structured tannins. The vineyard and winery are located in Santa Eugenia de Chocalán in the Maipo Valley, but they can be reached through their offices in Santiago.

COUSIÑO MACUL

Avenida Quilin, 7100, Peñalolen, Santiago,
+56 2 351 4181,
www.cousinomacul.cl

We had the pleasure of visiting Cousiño Macul's historic winery and having dinner with Señor Carlos Cousiño, who told us that his is the only remaining nineteenth-century Chilean winery still owned and operated by its original founding family. A sixth-generation descendant of the original founder, he is also very proud that Cousiño Macul is 100 percent family owned and makes its reserve wines using estate-grown grapes. The name Cousiño Macul is derived from founder Matías Cousiño and the ancient word *macul*,

which means "right hand" in Quechua. Señor Cousiño's ancestor, Matías, originally developed one of Chile's richest silver mines and was responsible for building a good portion of the country's railroad. Matías died in 1863, but not before he convinced his son Luis to travel to France in 1860 to bring back rootstock of Cabernet Sauvignon and Merlot from Pauillac and Margaux, Chardonnay and Pinot Noir from Burgundy, and Sauvignon Blanc from Graves. Unfortunately, Luis died young, but his widow, Isidora Goyenechea, hired French winemaker Pierre Godefroy Durand to adapt these French varieties to Chilean soil. Today, Bordeaux-educated Pascal Marty is the head winemaker. He is responsible for the creation of the iconic wine Lota, which he developed to commemorate the 150th anniversary of the winery. Cousiño Macul Lota 2007 is dark garnet with a violet rim. It is a blend of 85 percent Cabernet Sauvignon and 15 percent Merlot. The nose reveals cassis, black plum, and Christmas baking spices. The generous palate offers flavors of black fruits and cocoa. The elongated finish is delightfully smooth. Cousiño Macul Finis Terrae 2008 is an assemblage of 60 percent Cabernet Sauvignon, 30 percent Merlot, and 10 percent Syrah. It is inky purple with notes of blueberries, blackberries, and cassis. Plum and red fruits are found in the mouth along with ripe tannins. Cousiño Macul Antiguas Reservas Chardonnay 2009 is golden in color. The bouquet reveals tropical fruits and light vanilla. It is round in the mouth with nice texture.

CONCHA Y TORO

Avenida Nueva Tajamar, 481, Torre Norte, Piso 15,
+56 2 476 5000,
www.conchaytoro.com

Concha y Toro was founded in 1883 by Don Melchor Concha y Toro on land inherited by his wife. He traveled to France to purchase French varietal rootstock and brought back a French winemaker as well—to craft the young winery's first vintages. Located in Pirque, a short drive from Santiago, the winery is certainly worth a visit to tour the ancient cellars, but if you have limited time and are based in the capital you can visit Concha y Toro's tasting lounge in the Alonso de Cordova

Manuel Rodriguez 229, Isla de Maipo,
+56 2 819 2959,
www.demartino.cl

shopping area. One of the winery's most famous features is the Casillero del Diablo cellar, where Don Melchor effectively stopped his employees from stealing his best wine by telling them that he saw the Devil hiding among the barrels. Concha y Toro was the first Chilean wine to be exported to the United States—in 1963—and ever since it has consistently been a well-rated and good-value choice. Concha y Toro Casillero del Diablo Cabernet Sauvignon 2010 has aromas of stewed fruits, blackberries, and cinnamon. In the mouth it has balanced acidity with a persistent finish. At the higher end of the range, Concha y Toro Don Melchor Cabernet Sauvignon 2007 is extremely concentrated with powerful fruit aromas of dried cherries, black plums, and Mediterranean herbs. It is inky garnet with flavors of kirsch, preserved plums, and black cherries. The finish is smooth with persistent and elegant tannins.

In 2010, De Martino was the only Chilean winery whose wines ranked in the top 100 picks of all three major US/UK wine magazines: *Wine Spectator*, *Wine Enthusiast*, and *Decanter*. *Wine Enthusiast* chose Legado Reserva Chardonnay, *Wine Spectator* chose Legado Reserva Syrah, and *Decanter* chose Legada Reserva Cabernet Sauvignon. One evening over dinner, Marco De Martino explained to us his passion for making fine wines, while using both sustainable and organic methods. Joining us at the table were his winemakers Eduardo Jordan and the famous "*terroir* hunter," Marcelo Retamal. It was truly guys' night out—we were eating grass-fed organic beef at an amazing *churrascaria*, while drinking delicious organic beef-friendly wines. The De Martino winery was founded by Marco's ancestor, Pietro De Martino, who settled on the perfect site, Isla de Maipo, once an island surrounded by different branches of the Maipo River. The current vineyards are located in the bed of one of the river's branches—it dried up after a large earthquake. The family began converting its vineyards from "traditional" to 100 percent organic agriculture in 1998, and two years after obtaining the German Organic Certification in 2001,

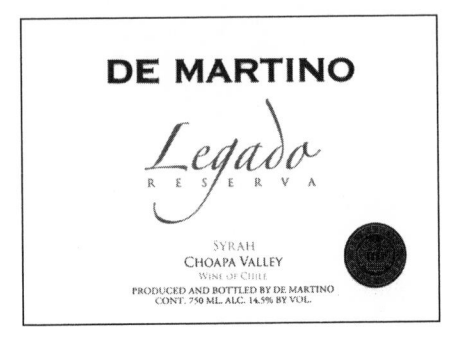

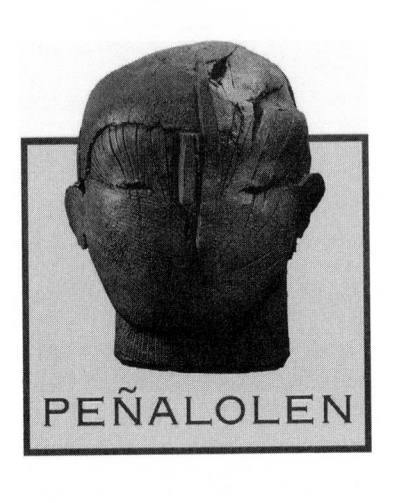

they harvested their first organic grapes. Today, De Martino is the second largest producer of organic wine in Chile. De Martino Legado Reserva Syrah 2008 is brilliant reddish-purple with great legs. On the nose, notes of black-berry and red plums are well pronounced; in the mouth it is full, rich, and can stand up to the thickest steak. It has a long, elegant, tannic finish. De Martino Cabernet Malbec 2008 is a 50/50 blend. It is ruby red with aromas of fruits of the wood, saddle leather, and dark plums. It shines on the palate with amazingly full mouthfeel and a super finish.

DOMUS AUREA

Consistorial 5900, Peñalolen, Santiago,
+56 2 274 8271,
www.domusaurea.cl

Tired of selling their quality grapes to other winemakers, Isabelle and Ricardo Peña enlisted the help of winemaker Ignacio Recabarren and

began making their own wines. Clos Quebrada de Macul is a single, family-owned vineyard. Most of the vines were planted in 1970, with the majority of them Cabernet Sauvignon, though the family also grows Petit Verdot, Cabernet Franc, and Merlot. The family's first wine, Domus Aurea in 1996, quickly became well regarded. In 2003, the family hired consultant Patrick Valette and resident wine-maker Jean Pascal Lacaze with an eye to future markets. Domus Aurea Cabernet Sauvignon 2005 is dark red with notes of black cherry, cocoa, and faint menthol. It is generous in the mouth with round tannins and a long finish. It is a shame the production is so limited. Peñalolen Sauvignon Blanc 2007 is pale straw with aromas of tangerines and fragrant white flowers. It is crisp in the mouth with bracing acidity—a delicious wine on its own or with food.

EL PRINCIPAL

Casilla 420, Pirque, Santiago,
+56 2 854 7023,
www.elprincipal.cl

After the death of his father—Jean-Paul Valette, former owner of Château Pavie in Saint-Émilion—in 1999, his son Patrick Valette and hacienda owner Jorge Fontaine carried on the legacy at Viña El Principal. Fifty-four hectares (133 acres) of the hacienda grow Cabernet Sauvignon, Merlot, Carmenere, and Cabernet Franc. The 1999 harvest (and subsequent harvests) yielded grapes of excellent quality due to Patrick's implementation of proven French viticultural techniques—shoot thinning, precise water control, and a hand-selection grape sorting table. The vineyard is currently owned by a large conglomerate that continues Jean-Paul, Patrick, and Jorge's commitment to quality wine. El Principal

2006 is ruby red with long, beautiful legs. It is 83 percent Cabernet Sauvignon and 17 percent Carmenere, is unfiltered, and spends 18 months in French oak barrels. It has aromas of mocha, cassis, and vanilla toast and is full-bodied with focused tannins. Memorias 2007 spends 14 months in French oak and is a blend of 80 percent Cabernet Sauvignon and 20 percent Carmenere. Aromas of espresso, blackberries, and brioche pave the way for a round-in-the-mouth, full wine with a lasting finish.

HARAS DE PIRQUE

Casilla 247, Pirque, Region Metropolitana,
+56 2 854 7910,
www.harasdepirque.com

When visiting Haras de Pirque you can't help but notice that someone on the estate has an amazing passion for majestic horses. In 1991, Eduardo Matte combined his love of horses with his love of fine wine—and 120 hectares (297 acres) of Cabernet Sauvignon, Merlot, Carmenere, Chardonnay, and Sauvignon Blanc were planted. The other 480 hectares (1,186 acres) of land are an apparent indulgence to his beloved thoroughbreds. Haras de Pirque is a partnership between Eduardo Matte and the Antinori family of Tuscany and is a member of the prestigious group of Chateau Ste. Michelle Estates in Washington State. Haras de Pirque

cocoa, and mint—think grown-up Thin Mint Girl Scout cookies. It is silky smooth in the mouth with an ample tannic structure.

INTRIGA

Avenida Eliodoro Yáñez 2962, Providencia, Santiago, +56 2 520 4355, www.intriga.cl

is committed to environmental responsibility and sustainable practices. All of the estate's grapes are hand-harvested and meticulously sorted to achieve the best-quality wines. Haras de Pirque's horses are internationally famous in the racing circuit—and the trophies are on display to prove it. In addition to exporting wine, the estate is well known for its award-wining studs and breeding horses. Eduardo can often be seen riding around the horse-shoe-shaped winery, in one of the eighteen horse-drawn carriages that he collects. Haras Carmenere 2008 is dark purple with a violet rim and is made from 100 percent estate-grown grapes. Aged for nine months in French oak, it has aromas of garden herbs, cigar box, Mission figs, and black plums. In the mouth it is big and juicy with focused tannins. Hara Albis 2003 is a blend of 73 percent Cabernet Sauvignon and 27 percent Carmenere. It is deep red in the glass and presents with aromas of black raspberry, red cherry, bittersweet

Part of the prestigious MontGras group, Intriga was founded in 1865 by Don Alejandro Reyes. The family brought in Riojan Miguel Ortiz in 1915, who established various practices of preventive viticulture, many of which are still practiced today. Currently the renowned consultant Alberto Antonini assists winemaker Christian Correa in making Intriga's internationally acclaimed wine. Intriga Cabernet Sauvignon 2008 is made from 100 percent estate-grown Cabernet Sauvignon grapes. The average age of the vines is between 10 and 50 years. It spends 23 months in 65 percent new and 35 percent second-use French oak. It is deep garnet with aromas of cassis, dried black cherries, and eucalyptus. In the mouth the rich fruit elements expand and the balanced tannic structure paves the way for a long, refined finish.

ODFJELL VINEYARDS

Camino Viejo a Valparaíso,
Padre Hurtado, Santiago,
+56 2 811 1530,
www.odfjellvineyards.cl

Tired of Bergen's cold and wet climate, Norwegian ship owner Dan Odfjell fell in love with a small corner of the Maipo Valley more than 25 years ago. He planted mostly red varieties, including Cabernet Sauvignon, Merlot, Carmenere, Syrah, Cabernet Franc, and Malbec on his 85 hectares (210 acres) of vineyards. The main winery is in Padre Hurtado, with vineyards located in Ribera Rio Claro (Molina) and Tres Esquinas (Cauguenes.) When you visit Odfjell Vineyards you're likely to be greeted by beautiful Fjord horses. This unique breed was imported by Dan Odfjell over 10 years ago and is known for its gentle nature—Fjord horses are often used therapeutically for children with disabilities. At harvest, all grapes are picked by hand and brought to Odfjell's gravity-assisted winery, designed by Dan's son, Laurence, an architect educated at

Yale. Odfjell Armador Carmenere 2008 has a nose of red and purple flowers with blackberries and dark plums on the palate. The finish is smooth and round. Odfjell Orzada Cabernet Sauvignon 2007 offers notes of cassis and blackberry with chocolate-covered cherries in the mouth—followed by a firm tannic finish. Odfjell Babor Cabernet Sauvignon 2009 is a great value with a bouquet of raspberry and blackberry and a subsequent fruit-bomb explosion in the mouth.

PÉREZ CRUZ

Camino Padre Hurtado, Kilometer 54,
Acceso Fundo Liquai, Liquai,
+56 2 655 1318,
www.perezcruz.com

Pérez Cruz's beautiful winery blends in with the natural environment. Designed by architect José Cruz Ovalle and made of locally sourced radiata pine, it was built for maximum air circulation and minimal energy consumption. The winemaking process is gravity assisted, and the storage tanks and barrels are subterranean, thus requiring less energy for climate control. The estate has more than 250 hectares (618 acres) of vineyards, with 171 hectares (423 acres) of Cabernet Sauvignon, 27 hectares (67 acres) of Carmenere, and 14 hectares (35 acres) of Syrah. The balance of the plantings are Cot, Merlot, Petit Verdot, Mourvèdre, Grenache, and Cabernet Franc. The estate has two distinct soil types; the sloped foothills have colluvial soil with large flat stones, clay, and loam, while the lower lands have alluvial soils formed by an ancient river. Here the stones are smaller, rounder, and mixed with sand and clay; they provide excellent drainage. The winery's management team is committed to corporate social responsibility and has outreach programs that contribute to sustainable economic development in the local population. Viña Pérez Cruz Quelen 2006 is a blend of Petit Verdot, Carmenere, and Cot and has notes of red fruit, tobacco, and dark spices. On the palate the fruit notes are well defined, especially raspberry and cassis. The finish is soft with a slight minerality. Viña Pérez Cruz Cabernet Sauvignon Reserva 2008 has dried fruit, black pepper, and vanilla aromas. In the mouth, ripe, red fruits are noted with concentrated tannins. Viña Pérez Cruz Liquai 2007 is a blend of Syrah, Carmenere, and Cabernet Sauvignon. It has strong aromas of cassis followed by a light cigar box whiff. On the palate, black fruit, chocolate, and persistent, well-structured tannins will delight you.

PORTAL DEL ALTO

Camino el Arpa 119, Alto Jahuel, Buin,
+56 2 821 9178,
www.portadelalto.cl

Alejandro Hernández is well known in the Chilean winemaking community—he taught many of Chile's current winemakers while he was a professor at the country's largest winemaking school, the Universidad Católica de Chile. He founded Portal del Alto in 1971 and has more than 130 hectares (321 acres) of Cabernet Sauvignon, Carmenere, Merlot, Pinot Noir, and Syrah. As a professor, he had access to the school's research laboratory; he grafted the Cabernet Sauvignon rootstock that was brought from France in 1850 by viticulturist Cladio Gay onto his own vines. The estate produces 900,000 liters per year under four brands: Portal del Alto, San Fernando, Maitenes, and Santa Martha. Portal del

Alto Alejandro 2003 is a blend of 90 percent Cabernet Sauvignon, 5 percent Merlot, and 5 percent Syrah. It is ruby red with notes of cassis, dark red fruits, and toasted vanilla bean. In the mouth the fruit opens up and you can feel the firm tannic structure. Portal del Alto Reserva Merlot Cabernet 2007 is a blend of 60 percent Merlot and 40 percent Cabernet. It is deep red with aromas of plums and fresh black figs—and a whiff of white flowers. In the mouth it has a generous body with a medium finish. Portal del Alto Sauvignon Blanc 2008 has a brilliant straw appearance with aromas of jasmine and pink grapefruit. On the palate it is crisp and refreshing.

SANTA CAROLINA

Rodrigo de Araya 1431, Macul, Santiago,
+56 2 450 3000,
www.santacarolina.cl

Señor Luis Pereyra Cotapos founded Viña Santa Carolina more than one hundred years ago. The brand is named after his wife, Carolina. Today, this large company sources grapes from many valleys in Chile, including the Leyda Valley, Rapel Valley, Maule Valley, the Santa Isabel estate in Casablanca, Los Nogales estate in Maipo, Miraflores and Los Lingues estates in Colchauga, and La Rinconada estate in the Cachapoal Valley. The original warehouse designed by French architect Emile Doyeré still stands and was declared a national monument in 1973 for its preserved state and structural beauty. It remains the only building from that era that was built with the antiquated system of using lime and egg whites as mortar. Santa Carolina Barrica Selection Syrah 2008 is a dark ruby garnet with aromas of cocoa, spice, and cassis. On the palate it is complex and full-bodied with a long finish. Santa Carolina Reserva Sauvignon Blanc 2009 is made from grapes sourced in the Leyda Valley. It is bright yellow with a green tint. The nose offers pineapple, tropical fruit salad, and mango. It is bright and refreshing on the palate. Santa Carolina Reserva de Familia Cabernet Sauvignon 2007 is an elegant garnet with notes of blackberry and black cherry. Round, full tannins are present, and it has weighty mouthfeel.

SANTA EMA

Balmaceda 1950, Isla de Maipo,
+56 2 819 9189,
www.santaema.cl

Viña Santa Ema was founded by Italian immigrant Pedro Pavone Voglino in 1917. He bought the land that Santa Ema sits on in 1931. His oldest son, Felix Pavone Arbea began a marketing campaign in 1956 and began exporting wines to Brazil. The company now exports wines to more than thirty countries in the Americas, Europe, and Asia. Santa Ema's primary market is the United States, where they consistently rank among the top 10 Chilean wineries in terms of sales. The company continues to grow exponentially and in 2003 opened its new El Peral winery in Isla de Maipo. Its 3.2 million liter capacity winery is surrounded by 50 hectares (124 acres) of estate vineyards. It is one of the most modern, technologically advanced wineries in Chile today. Winemakers Andres Sanhueza, Irene Pavia, and Rodrigo Blazquez make consistently good, award-winning wines. Santa Ema Amplus Cabernet Sauvignon 2008 is garnet colored with aromas of black plums, blueberries, and cocoa. In the mouth it is big with fine tannins and a long finish. Santa Ema Amplus Sauvignon Blanc 2010 is pale straw with notes of pea shoots, freshly cut asparagus, lemon blossom, and garden fresh herbs. It is crisp in the mouth with a spicy jalapeño edge. Santa Ema Barrel Select 60/40 2007 is made from 60 percent Cabernet Sauvignon and 40 percent Merlot. It is garnet red with aromas of stewed plums and baking spices. It is round in the mouth, with focused tannins and a long finish.

SANTA RITA

Camino Padre Hurtado 695, Alto Jahuel, Santiago,
+56 2 821 9966,
www.santarita.com

Santa Rita 120—one of Santa Rita's most commercially available brands—is named after the 120 Patriots. They were freedom-fighters who were hidden among the barrels of Doña Paula Jaraquemada's wine cellar. She bravely kept their opponents at bay by throwing hot coals at them and shooing them off. This heroic

TARAPACÁ

Isla de Maipo,
+56 2 819 2785,
www.tarapaca.cl

act gave the 120 Patriots time to rest, recuperate, and eventually gain Chile's independence from Spain. Today the estate is owned by the Owens Illinois Company, the world's largest manufacturer of glass bottles. One thousand hectares (2,471 acres) in Maipo, Rapel Lontue, Casablanca, and Apalta are overseen by a team of eight winemakers, headed by Cecilia Torres Salinas and Andres llabaca Andonie. Santa Rita Medalla Real Cabernet Sauvignon 2007 is garnet colored with aromas of toasted vanilla, cassis, and black plums. Bold and round in the mouth, the finish is long lasting. Santa Rita Carmenere 2008 is ruby red with aromas of black plums and blackberries. In the mouth the soft, sensual tannins are delightful. Santa Rita 120 Chardonnay 2009 is yellow straw with aromas of tropical fruits, pineapple, and white peach. In the mouth it is supple with delicate wood flavors on the finish.

Viña Tarapacá Ex Zavala has an interesting history. It is named after the aggressively successful lawyer, the "Lion of Tarapaca," who assisted Señora Zavela in her divorce from her husband and gained her sole ownership of the estate. In 1992, the Fosforos Group took control of Viña Tarapacá and acquired El Rosario de Naltagua, a 2,600-hectare (6,425-acre) estate located in the Maipo Valley. Part of the VSPT group since 2008, it is one of the leading wineries in the Chilean market and exports to more than sixty countries. The winemaking team consists of US-born, UC Davis–educated chief winemaker, Ed Flaherty, and his assistant, Cristian Molina. Tarapacá Zavala Red Blend is only made in what the winemakers consider to be superior vintages. The 2008 is composed of 41 percent Cabernet Franc, 31 percent Cabernet Sauvignon, and 28 percent Syrah and has aromas of black plum, black cherry, and cassis. In the glass it is rich garnet with chewy tannins and a long finish. Tarapacá Gran Reserva Syrah 2009 is deep purple with aromas of stewed blackberries, cherries, and a touch of black licorice. It's rich and supple on the palate with a spicy finish. Tarapacá Etiqueta Negra Cabernet Sauvignon 2009 is 81 percent Cabernet Sauvignon, 9 percent Petit Verdot, 5 percent Cabernet Franc, and 5 percent Syrah. It is deep garnet with a violet rim and has aromas of cinnamon, cigar box, black plum, and black raspberries. In the mouth it is big and jammy, with notes of dark chocolate in the long finish.

TERRAMATER

Luis Thayer Ojeda 236, Providencia,
+56 2 438 0000,
www.terramater.cl

The three Canepa sisters shunned retirement in 1996, built a new winery, and started TerraMater. Their family had been making wine since the early 1930s, so these ladies were not new to the world of wine or the winemaking process. They set out to make low-yield, high-quality wines. Their efforts have certainly paid off—TerraMater consistently wins awards in international competitions. Only 8,000 bottles

of TerraMater Unusual 2007 were made. It is a blend of 45 percent Cabernet Sauvignon, 35 percent Shiraz, and 20 percent Zinfandel and is ruby red to reddish purple. Aromas of red plums, espresso, and chocolate are easily detected. On the palate it has soft tannins and a persistent finish. TerraMater Altum Cabernet Sauvignon 2008 is deep red almost black with whiffs of smoked meat, black pepper, and vanilla found under the stewed black fruit primary scent. In the mouth it has a fruity long finish. TerraMater Altum Shiraz 2008 is deep purple with scents of bittersweet chocolate, prunes, and blackberries. It has elegant, ripe tannins on the finish.

TRES PALACIOS

Magnere 1543, Providencia, Santiago,
+56 2 235 9852,
www.vinatrespalacios.cl

Patricio Palacios traveled the world looking for the mysteries of life—in much the same way as one of his heroes, Don Quixote de la Mancha. Fate brought Palacios to Peru, where he met his wife, Maria Ines Covarrubias. Together they moved to the Maipo Valley and founded Tres Palacios Winery in 1996. They employed winemaker Camilo Rahmer—who makes award-winning wines by extracting the essence of their distinctive *terroir*. Tres Palacios Merlot

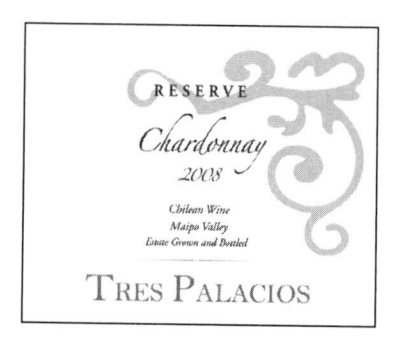

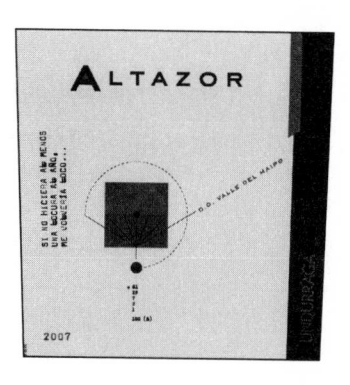

Reserve 2007 is dark reddish purple with notes of anise, ground white pepper, baking spices, and cassis. In the mouth it is round bodied with soft, silky tannins. Tres Palacio Cabernet Sauvignon Family Vintage 2008 is brilliant red with aromas of strawberry and raspberry. On the palate it is fresh and mellow with a lingering finish. Tres Palacios Chardonnay Reserve 2008 is golden yellow. The bouquet has aromas of tropical fruits—such as guava and custard apples. In the mouth it has balanced acidity with a slight mineral finish.

UNDURRAGA

Avenida Vitacura 2939, Vitacura, Santiago,
+56 2 372 2900,
www.undurraga.cl

When Viña Undurraga made its first shipment in 1903, it was one of the first Chilean wineries to export to the United States. Founded in the nineteenth century by Don Francisco Undurraga, the first vines were planted in his

Santa Ana Estate, named after his wife, in the town of Talagante. The company now has 1,200 hectares (2,965 acres) in the Colchagua, Maipo, and Leyda Valleys. The winemaking team is headed by winemaker Hernán Amenábar—with the assistance of internationally renowned wine consultant Álvaro Espinoza. Espinoza's creation, Altazor 2007 is a blend of 61 percent Cabernet Sauvignon, 29 percent Carmenere, 7 percent Syrah, 2 percent Carignan, and 1 percent Petit Verdot. It's purplish-red with aromas of black cherry, cigar box, and mocha. Generous on the palate, Altazor has a balanced, persistent finish. Undurraga T.H. Syrah Limari 2008 is ruby red with notes of red fruits, saddle leather, and smoked meat. It is juicy and full in the mouth with a firm tannic finish. Only 8,555 bottles were produced. Undurraga T.H. Pinot Noir West Casablanca 2008 is transparent garnet with a nose of cherry cola, red cherries, and cooling herbs. In the mouth the cherry becomes more pronounced, with flavors of chocolate-covered espresso beans as an undercurrent. It has a long, refined finish.

VIÑEDO CHADWICK

Avenida Nueva Tajamar 481, Torre Sur, Santiago,
+56 2 339 9100,
www.vinedochadwick.cl

Don Alfonso Chadwick Errazuriz was born in Chile in 1914. He became a lawyer yet worked in the family business of winemaking. He is credited with establishing the first wine brokerage in Chile. He was also considered one of the best polo players in the country and played for the Chilean national team. He constructed a polo field on his Viña San Jose Torconal Estate. He had five children, and his son Eduardo is now the company's president. Eduardo's passion for fine wine is well known in Chile. In fact, he identified the land under the polo field to be perfect soil for growing quality grapes

and—remarkably—had his father's beloved polo field ploughed under and replanted with fine varietal vines. In 1995, he partnered with Robert Mondavi to create his iconic Seña wine. Viñedo Chadwick 2007 is inky garnet with aromas of raspberry, smoke, anise, and Christmas baking spices. In the mouth it is generous and full and teases the palate with red and black fruits. It has an elegant tannic structure and long finish, with a last note of licorice. It is sad that this lovely wine is made in such limited quantities.

VENTISQUERO

Camino La Estrella 401, Rancagua,
+56 7 220 1240,
www.ventisquero.com

We arrived one hour before sunset at Ventisquero's lovely open-air tasting room—which overlooks its Apalta vineyards. Our evening of wine tasting was only made better by the gorgeous view and the stunning sunset over the mountaintops. Although the main winery is in the Maipo Valley, it was a great idea to taste wines in beautiful Apalta. Chief winemaker Felipe Tosso led us through his portfolio of amazing wines, assisted by winemakers Alejandro Galaz and Sergio Hormazabal. Tosso confided that he loves winemaking because it's more than just work—it's his lifestyle. He

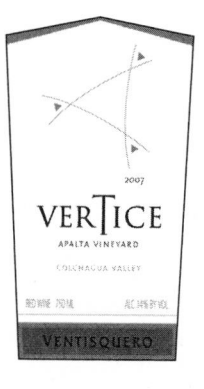

85 percent Cabernet Sauvignon and 15 percent Syrah. It is purplish black with notes of fruit compote and red raspberries. On the palate it is fruity, yet creamy with a persistent finish.

WILLIAM FÈVRE

Avenida Alcalde Hernán Prieto, Pirque,
+56 2 853 1026,
www.william-fevre-chile.com

mentioned that he'd thought about becoming a classical guitarist for a short while, and even considered becoming a tennis pro. We assured him that we—and the wine-drinking public— were happy that he chose winemaking. In addition to the Maipo Valley, Ventisquero has vineyards in Colchagua, Casablanca, Rapel, and Leyda. Ventisquero's Pangea and Vertice wines are a collaboration with Australia's John Duval and have been since 2003. Viña Ventisquero Pangea 2007 is from their Apalta Vineyard in Colchagua Valley and is intense deep garnet red. Aromas of spice, specifically black pepper and baking spices, along with blueberry, raspberry, and pencil lead are present. In the mouth, the tannins are generous, well structured, and have a long finish. Viña Ventisquero Vertice 2007, also from Apalta, is a deep ruby red with notes of vanilla, bittersweet chocolate, red fruits, and blackberries. It is soft on the palate with balanced acidity. Yali Three Lagoons Cabernet Sauvignon 2008 is

Burgundian winemaker William Fèvre sold many of his business interests and holdings to a large conglomerate in 2002, but his contribution to the Chilean wine industry has left a lasting and positive impact. When William Fèvre began business in Chile, his partner Victor Pino's family had deep roots in Chilean winemaking. Together they planted 40 hectares (99 acres) of vineyards, implemented Burgundian techniques in the winemaking process, and made Chilean wines of decidedly Burgundian character. Today the company owns 25 hectares

(62 acres) of Cabernet Sauvignon, Chardonnay, and Pinot Noir vineyards in San Juan de Pirque, 4 hectares (10 acres) of Cabernet Sauvignon in Las Majadas, and 40 hectares (99 acres) of Cabernet Sauvignon, Cabernet Franc, Merlot, and Carmenere in San Luis. William Fèvre Gran Cuvée Pinot Noir 2009 has a French nose of strawberries and red raspberries. It is sublime on the palate, with flavors of red cherry confiture and *fruits de bois* (literally "fruits of the forest," which includes all berries). It has a lingering finish with soft tannins. William Fèvre La Misión Chardonnay 2010 is golden straw yellow with aromas of citrus blossoms and poached pears. In the mouth it has a creamy texture with a clean minerality. It is round in the mouth with a buttery aftertaste.

RAPEL–CACHAPOAL VALLEY

This V-shaped area 80 kilometers (50 miles) south of Santiago has built its reputation on reds. It is the inland, more northerly portion of what was formerly known as the Rapel Valley, and is divided into three subzones: Rancagua, named for the province's capital city, Cachapoal Alto, and Peumo—the latter known for its Carmenere. Cachapoal's position between the Andes to the east and the Coastal Mountain Range to the west keeps the effects of the Pacific at bay. Winters are cool and rainy; the main source of water during the hot, dry summers is the Cachapoal River. This river and its tributaries, the Claro and Graneros Rivers, run into Lake Rapel. Annual rainfall is 340 millimeters, or 13.5 inches, and there is a 32-percent risk of spring frost.

Eighty-four percent of the grapes grown on the region's 9,787 hectares (24,184 acres) are red varieties. Cabernet Sauvignon is most popular, planted on 3,756 hectares (9,281 acres). Carmenere, which has increased by 60 percent in the last few years, follows with 1,538 hectares (3,800 acres). Merlot has declined slightly of late; and now covers 1,431 hectares (3,536 acres). Chardonnay is planted on 813 hectares (2,009 acres), while Syrah, which is on the rise, covers 656 hectares (1,621 acres). Sauvignon Blanc is farmed on 584 hectares (1,143 acres). The area most densely populated with wineries is directly south of Santiago, to the north and the south of the colonial city of Rancagua.

ALTAIR

Fundo Totihue Camino a Pimpinela s/n,
+56 2 477 5598,
www.altairwines.com

A joint project between Chilean giant Viña San Pedro and Laurent Dassault of Bordeaux.

The name *Altair* comes from the Arabic word meaning "flying eagle," but the winery takes its name from the star that shares the same name. Altair, one of the brightest in the Southern Hemisphere, forms a triangle with lesser stars Deneb and Vega, and can easily be recognized in the dark night sky. The wine-making team here creates one of Chile's best Bordeaux-style blends. Visitors to the winery can arrive by car or land their helicopters on Altair's helipad before embarking on a horseback visit to the vines. Altair 2004 is a twinkling red garnet in the glass with aromas of black cherry and cassis. On the palate it delights with flavors of red and black cherry with a touch of cocoa. The finish is long and elegant. Altair 2005 is a deep dark garnet with aromas of cherry, tobacco, and mocha. In the mouth there is balanced acidity, bright fruit, fine tannins, and a lovely persistence.

ANAKENA

Avenida Alonso de Córdova 5151,
Las Condes, Santiago,
+56 2 426 0608,
www.anakenawines.cl

Childhood friends Jorge Gutierrez and Felipe Ibañez planted the first vines in 1999 and today manage more than 400 hectares (988 acres) of vineyard. Anakena has 150 hectares (371 acres) of vineyard in the Cachapoal Valley, 127 hectares (314 acres) in the Leyda-San Antonio Valley, 44 hectares (109 acres) in the Rapel Valley, and 70 hectares (173 acres) in the Colchagua Valley. Its properties in the Rapel and Colchagua Valleys are planted with red varieties including Carmenere, Cabernet Sauvignon, Cabernet Franc, and Syrah, while the vineyards in the Leyda Valley grow cooler-climate varieties, including Chardonnay, Riesling, Gewürztraminer, and Sauvignon Blanc. The impressive winery was designed by architect Luis Uriarte, whose intention was to build a modern structure while maintaining key design elements from the colonial period. Sergio Cuadra is the head winemaker. His Anakena Indo Carmenere 2009 is medium ruby with notes of black fruits, cigar box, and a touch of eucalyptus and mint. In the mouth black fruits shine through with a cocoa finish. Anakena Ona Syrah 2007 is ruby red with a bouquet of black raspberry, freshly ground pepper, and purple flowers. On the palate there is a hint of smoked meat under the bright berry flavors. The finish is pleasant and long lasting. Visitors to the winery can tour the vineyards by horseback and return to have a delicious gastronomic lunch paired with Anakena's wines.

CASAS DEL TOQUI

Fundo Santa Anita, Totihue, Requinoa,
+56 7 232 1870,
www.casasdeltoqui.cl

The corporate marriage between esteemed French wine house Château Larose Trintaudon and the well-respected wine-producing Granella family of Chile began in 1994. Initial plantings included Cabernet Sauvignon and Chardonnay, but today the portfolio includes Pinot Noir, Syrah, Carmenere, Merlot, Sémillon, and Sauvignon Blanc. The wines have gained international attention. Casas del Toqui Chardonnay 2010 is a brilliant straw color with aromas of tropical fruits and oak. On the palate it is full-bodied with a lingering finish. Casas del Toqui Cabernet Sauvignon 2009 is ruby red with aromas of blackberries, raspberries, and dark plums. In the mouth it is full-bodied with round tannins. Casas del Toqui Late Harvest Semillon 2002 is a very pleasing way to end a wonderful dinner. It is golden hued with notes of apricot, honey, and caramelized pineapple. In the mouth there's a nice level of sweetness—kept in check by a refreshing acidity.

CHATEAU LOS BOLDOS

Camino Los Boldos, Requinoa,
+56 7 255 1230,
www.clboldos.cl

Founded in 1991, Chateau Los Boldos now has 201 hectares (497 acres) of vines. The company was purchased by the Portuguese Sogrape Group, whose other brands include Mateus Rosé, Ferreira, Offley, and Finca Flichman. The winery has a storage capacity for 5,000,000 liters of wine and boasts a bottling line that can process 5,000 bottles per hour. Winemaking and viticulture are under the direction of Stephane Geneste and Juan Pablo Aranda. Chateau Los Boldos Grand Reserve Cabernet Sauvignon 2008 is deep purple with a violet rim. The nose reveals red fruits and cassis, while in the mouth there are lovely flavors of ripe fruit, cloves, and soft tannins. Chateau Los Boldos Grand Reserve Merlot 2008 is deep garnet with aromas of red fruits, raspberries, and red plums. Round in the mouth, the finish has notes of vanilla and mocha. Chateau Los Boldos Grand Reserve Carmenere 2008 is garnet colored with a violet reflection. It has aromas of fruit compote and cocoa. Blackberry and black fruits are revealed in the mouth along with sweet tannins.

LA ROSA

Coyancura 2283, Providencia, Santiago,
+56 2 670 0600,
www.larosa.cl

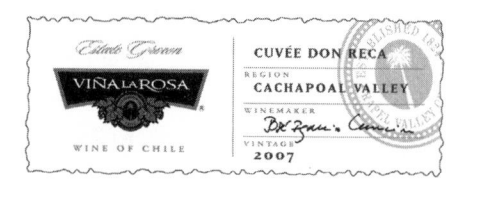

In 1824 proud father Don Francisco Ignacio Ossa y Mercado went shopping for a piece of land that he could pass on to his first-born son. He ended up—unexpectedly—establishing a winery. He purchased what is now known as Viña La Rosa from Chile's first president, Manuel Blanco Encalada. The sale of the estate included a house, winemaking equipment, and a cellar full of barrels. The pre-phylloxera vines had been imported from France years before the destructive aphid attacked Bordeaux. Today, sixth-generation family member Don Ismael runs one of Chile's oldest existing wineries. The winemaking team consists of José Ignacio Cancino and Gonzalo Carcamo. The La Rosa Chardonnay Reserva 2009 is straw colored with a greenish hue. It has aromas of grapefruit, white peach, and green apple. Tropical fruits overwhelm your palate and make you beg for another glass. La Rosa Ossa 2004 is a blend of 30 percent Cabernet Sauvignon, 30 percent Merlot, 20 percent Cabernet Franc, 15 percent Syrah, and 5 percent Carmenere. It is deep garnet red with notes of cedar, mint, raspberry, and a touch of saddle leather. On the palate it is smooth and luxurious with an elegant finish. La Rosa Don Reca 2007 is 52 percent Merlot, 25 percent Cabernet Sauvignon, 18 percent Syrah, and 5 percent Carmenere. Dark reddish-purple in the glass, its aromas of cooling herbs, clove, and red fruits overwhelm your nose. Full-bodied in the mouth, the finish has notes of dark chocolate and black plum.

MORANDÉ

Alcantara 971, Las Condes, Santiago,
+56 2 270 8900,
www.morande.cl

Viña Morandé has been named "Winery of the Year" more than once by leading wine publications. Founded in 1996, its goal has always been to produce distinctive, quality wine. It prides itself on the use of scientific techniques—such as advanced irrigation and vineyard architecture. In 2010, Morandé introduced optical grape selection to replace manual selection and brought in Ricardo Baettig as the winemaking manager. Morandé Edición Limitada Carignan 2007 has aromas of cigar box, anise, saddle leather, and black fruits. In the mouth, flavors of ripe black cherry, blackberry, and pencil lead minerality are noted. The tannins are soft and supple, and the finish is persistent. Morandé Gran Reserva Cabernet Sauvignon 2008 is deep ruby red with aromas of cassis and cocoa. On the palate it is fruit-forward with a nice, smooth finish. Morandé Edición Limitada Cabernet Franc 2008 is garnet red with notes of mocha and dried cherries to both smell and taste. This is a full-bodied wine with nice smooth tannins.

RAPEL—COLCHAGUA VALLEY

Chile's most famous *terroir*, Apalta is the jewel in the crown of the area of the Rapel Valley known as Colchagua Valley. If you face the palm of your left hand away from you and make a "V" with your index finger and thumb, you have Colchagua—with Apalta sitting right in the fleshy part at the midpoint of the two.

The capital city of the region, San Fernando, is at an altitude of 339 meters (1,112 feet), at the base of the Andes. Most vineyards and wineries in this region run from this northeast corner of the valley (near your thumbnail) down through Apalta and up north again toward the coast and Marchegui (the middle joint on your index finger.) Further southwest, closer to the sea (near the second knuckle) are the newer grape-growing areas of Lolol and Paredones, which are now producing innovative cool-climate whites.

Colchagua has historically been known for reds, first from the vineyards in Ninquen and later in Apalta. Eighty-five percent of the land is devoted to red varieties, but whites are on the rise. Both Sauvignon Blanc and Viognier doubled in 2010. Cabernet Sauvignon, although declining, still covers the largest amount of hillsides, with 10,733 hectares (26,522 acres) out of a total 24,603 hectares (60,795 acres) devoted to grapevines in the region. Second most important here is Merlot (also in decline), which is grown on 2,933 hectares (7,248 acres). Carmenere has 2,905 hectares (7,178 acres), Syrah 1,804 (4,458 acres), Chardonnay 1,775 (4,386 acres), and Sauvignon Blanc 1,247 hectares (3,081 acres) and rising. Cabernet Franc and Malbec have just under 500 hectares (1,236 acres) each. Although the amount of Viognier in the region has increased exponentially in the past year, total amount under cultivation is still obscure here.

Snow melt from the Andes—in particular the 4,279-meter-high (14,039-foot) Tinguiririca Volcano—feeds the river of the same name, which starts at the foundation of the volcano and carries water through the valley. Pelagic air currents sweep between the coastal mountains and provide a cooling counterpoint to the hot, sunny days of summer, providing for differences of up to 24 degrees Celsius (40 degrees Fahrenheit) in a 24-hour period. Average annual rainfall is 592 millimeters, or 23.5 inches. Spring brings with it a 33-percent risk of frost. The basaltic soil closest to the Andes gives way to a mixture of loam silt and loam clay as you move west in the valley.

The centrally located amphitheater-shaped group of hills that border the Tinguiririca River—Apalta—garner the lion's share of attention in Colchagua, and rightfully so. The Neyen estate's Carmenere and Cabernet Sauvignon vines date back to 1890. These were followed more than a hundred years later by Aurelio Montes' Carmenere and Syrah plantings in 1993—joined shortly thereafter by Casa Lapostolle's Clos Apalta and Ventisquero. In 2002, the Neyen family built their winery on the site of the late nineteenth century vineyards, which still produce some of the finest wines of the region. The poor, stony soil of Apalta provides lower yields—in some cases 25 percent of what a hectare can support in other areas of the valley—making these celebrated wines even more precious.

APALTAGUA

Avenida Malaga 50, Las Condes, Santiago,
+56 2 365 1539,
www.apaltagua.com

American businessman Edward Tutunjian was vacationing in Chile in 1995 when he fell in love with the country and the people. He returned quickly and purchased his first vineyard, La Pancora. A few years later he purchased a second vineyard in Huaguen and later acquired Viñedos y Bodegas Apaltagua in the Apalta region of the Colchagua Valley. By 2007 he was firmly rooted in Chile and decided to purchase an estate for his family, San Juan de Pirque—a lovely historic home surrounded by 100-year-old trees in the Maipo Valley. Apaltagua Reserva Carmenere 2009 is sourced from the Apalta vineyard and is deep purple in color. It has aromas of red cherry, blackberry, and tobacco leaf, tannins, which are juicy and big, and a finish that is long and lovely. Apaltagua Grial 2003 is made from 100 percent Carmenere and is ruby red with notes of black plum and blackberries on the nose and in the mouth. The finish is persistent. Apaltagua Envero Gran Reserva 2008 is composed of 90 percent Carmenere and 10 percent Cabernet Sauvignon. The bouquet reveals black raspberry, blueberry, cigar box, and a light-oak frame. Big and juicy in the mouth, there are touches of vanilla on the elegant finish.

BISQUERTT

Avenida del Condor, Huechuraba,
+56 2 946 1540,
www.bisquertt.cl

The Bisquertt family looks after the day-to-day happenings at their winery and are very proud of their family tradition. They pride themselves on producing quality wine rather than large quantities of it; all their wines are grown, vinified, and bottled on the family estate. Bisquertt now exports 200,000 cases per year to various world markets. Winemaker Joana Pereira and consultant Felipe de Solminihac are turning out some wonderful wines. Bisquertt Cabernet Sauvignon Reserve 2009 has aromas of cherry, black raspberry, and baking spices. In the mouth it is fruity with a touch of cloves on the finish. Bisquertt Carmenere Reserve 2009 is a blend of 85 percent Carmenere and 15 percent Cabernet Franc. It has notes of Mission fig, freshly ground black pepper, and blackberry on the

nose. The palate is rewarding with rich black and red fruit flavors and a long, pleasant finish. Bisquertt Merlot Reserve is a combination of 86 percent Merlot and 14 percent Malbec. In the glass it is a beautiful garnet color with aromas of strawberries, red cherries, and raspberries. In the mouth there is a touch of baking spices along with silky tannins.

CALITERRA

Avenida Nueva Tajamar, Las Condes, Santiago,
+56 2 203 6346,
www.caliterra.com

Robert Mondavi and Viña Errazuriz founded Caliterra in 1996. It's named for the Spanish words for "quality" (*calidad*) and "land" (*tierra*). They chose the Colchagua Valley because of its Mediterranean climate—characterized by hot, sunny days and cool, gentle breezes at night. Caliterra Estate has more than 1,000 hectares (2,471 acres) in the center of the valley and is one of the valley's largest estates. In 2004, the Mondavi family sold its 50 percent share to Viña Errazuriz, and the company is now solely Chilean-based. Since its inception, the wines have consistently been rated highly by reviewers. Caliterra Tributo Edición Limitada Shiraz-Cabernet Sauvignon-Viognier 2009 is a combination of 55 percent Shiraz, 38 percent Cabernet Sauvignon, and 7 percent Viognier. It is deep purple with a violet rim and has aromas of cassis and black fruits—with top notes of tobacco leaf and fresh ground white pepper. In the mouth there is a lovely presentation of fruits and a lingering finish. Caliterra Tributo Edición Limitada Carmenere-Malbec 2009 is a blend of 68 percent Carmenere and 32 percent Malbec. In the glass it presents as a beautiful deep purple velvet robe with notes of black plums, baking spices, and dried raspberries. Its tannins are silky, and it has a long finish. Caliterra Bio-Sur Carmenere 2010 is grown in organically managed vineyards. It is deep purple and presents aromas of black cherries and black plums. The tannins are a bit gripping now but should evolve to silky smooth in a short time.

CASA LAPOSTOLLE

Avenida Vitacura 5250, Vitacura, Santiago,
+56 2 426 9960,
www.casalapostolle.com

The Marnier Lapostolle family is known for Château de Sancerre in the Loire Valley in France, as well as for producing the world-renowned liqueur Grand Marnier. Casa Lapostolle began in Chile in 1994 when Alexandra Marnier Lapostolle and her husband, Cyril de Bournet fell in love with the Apalta vineyards and joined forces with Don José Rabat Gorchs. Casa Lapostolle boasts an elite group of luminaries for the production of their highly rated wines. Besides Alexandra and Cyril, Jacques Begarie, Patricio Eguiguren, and world-renowned consultant Michel Rolland are part of the team. Casa Lapostolle owns 350 hectares (865 acres) and produce 2,400,000 bottles of wine per year. It has three distinct vineyards growing Cabernet Sauvignon,

Merlot, Carmenere, Syrah, Sauvignon Blanc, and Chardonnay. The Cunaco winery is where the Casa and Cuvée Alexandre lines are produced, while the Clos Apalta winery produces their highly rated Clos Apalta wine. Sophisticated travelers clamor to stay at the Lapostolle Residence, a Relais and Château property consisting of four *casitas* named after grape varieties. Lapostolle Borobo 2006 is a blend of grapes sourced from all three of their vineyards. It is 26 percent Pinot Noir from Atalayas Vineyards in Casablanca, 26 percent Syrah from Las Kuras Vineyards in Cachapoal, 20 percent Carmenere from Apalta Vineyard in Colchagua, and 16 percent Merlot, 10 percent Cabernet Sauvignon, and 2 percent Petit Verdot, all from the Apalta Vineyard. It is garnet colored with aromas of pink flowers, raspberries, and spice. On the palate it is round and has a refreshing acidity. The iconic Clos Apalta 2008 is a blend of 73 percent Carmenere, 17 percent Cabernet Sauvignon, and 10 percent Merlot, all from the Apalta Vineyard. It is purplish-red in color, with a heady aroma of red plums, blackberries, cassis, and herbs. On the palate, the tannins are mouthfilling, smooth, and lead to a long, elegant finish. Cuvée Alexandre Pinot Noir 2008 has a nose of ripe red fruits, cocoa, and dried tobacco leaf. Fruit-forward on the palate, this delicious wine pairs perfectly with duck confit.

CASA SILVA

Hijuela Norte s/n, Angostura, San Fernando,
+56 7 271 6519,
www.casasilva.cl

Emilio Bouchon emigrated from France to Chile in 1892 and soon planted vines and began making wine. Three generations continued the business, but family members began selling their shares in the property—until 1977, when Mario Silva Cifuentes married Maria Teresa Silva Bouchon and began buying back the family estate, including the old cellar. In 1997 their son Mario Pablo urged his father to discontinue the estate's bulk-wine business and concentrate solely on quality wine. Today, the company is run by Mario Pablo and his two brothers, Gonzalo and Francisco, with the assistance of technical director and consultant Mario Geisse and winemakers José Ignacio Mautana and Patricia Gonzales. Casa Silva now makes consistent, highly rated, quality wines. Casa Silva Sauvignon Blanc 2009 is pale straw with notes of Granny Smith apple, tropical fruits, and a touch of minerality. On the palate it is refreshing with a mineral-driven, citric finish. Think lemon zest and ruby red grapefruit. Casa Silva Los Lingues Carmenere 2005 is garnet with a herbaceous top note over black fruit aromas. In the mouth the tannins are sweet and soft, with a touch of mocha in the finish.

CONO SUR

Nueva Tajamar 481, Las Condes, Santiago,
+56 2 476 5090,
www.conosur.com

Named after the winery's position in South America—the southern cone—Cono Sur was established in 1993. It is one of a small number of wineries with a Facebook page and an active Twitter account, but we would expect nothing less from a winery with the motto "No family trees, no dusty bottles, just quality wine." It is the company's vision to produce quality wines conveying the pioneering spirit of the New World. In 2007, it became the first winery in the world to obtain carbon neutral status, and in 2008, it increased its capacity to 3,900,000 liters. Cono Sur Vision Casablanca Valley Chardonnay 2008 is golden yellow with a greenish tint. Aromas of guava, mango, and tropical fruit are present. It is creamy in the mouth, with flavors of mango, white peach, and papaya before a crisp, clean finish. Cono Sur Colchagua Valley Organically Grown Pinot Noir 2009 has a deep ruby, garnet, black cherry color with a ruby rim. The bouquet has scents of black plums, black cherry, and a touch of confectioners' sugar. It is full-bodied in the mouth with flavors of black cherry, stewed plums, black prunes, and chili-infused hot cocoa. The finish is gentle with a rounded tannic structure.

ESTAMPA

Avenida Presidente Kennedy 5757,
Las Condes, Santiago,
+56 2 202 7000,
www.estampa.com

Over a century ago, Spanish-born Don Miguel González Dieguez built a wheat mill next to a church, Our Lady of Carmen of The Flying Estampa. The name of the church is based on the miracle of a pocket-sized religious image, or estampa, which flew out of a salesman's hands, continued to fly for an hour, and landed across the Mapocho River. Like an angel, it landed gently onto the feet of a woman teaching religion to her children. The church was built on this site in 1794 to commemorate the miracle. Today, Don Miguel's descendants—the González-Ortiz family—run the wheat mill cum winery with the assistance of head winemaker José Antonio Bravo. Estampa Estate Bottled Syrah-Cabernet Sauvignon-Merlot Reserve 2007 is 63 percent Syrah, 22 percent Cabernet Sauvignon, and 15 percent Merlot. It is purplish red, with notes of espresso, black plums, and black raspberries. It is concentrated and fruity in the mouth with an impressive finish marked by a touch of mocha. Estampa Gold Syrah-Cabernet Sauvignon-Merlot-Malbec 2008 is a blend of 62 percent Syrah, 22 percent Cabernet Sauvignon, 10 percent Merlot, and 6 percent Malbec. It is a deep garnet, with notes of raspberry, blackberries, and a hint of spice. In the mouth you feel a touch of coffee and anise underlying rich, ripe fruit flavors. The tannins are big and round, and the finish is persistent.

HACIENDA ARAUCANO

Ruta 72 Kilometer 29, Lolol, Santa Cruz,
+56 7 282 4386,
www.haciendaaraucano.cl

French national François Lurton purchased this 200-hectare (494-acre) estate, named after the local people, in 1992. He believes that Colchagua Valley is a "dreamland for fine red wine." He has wholly owned Hacienda Araucano since 2007 and focuses on small-quantity, high-quality boutique wines. Hacienda Araucano Gran Arucano Cabernet Sauvignon 2006 has aromas of blueberry and cassis, with dark berry flavors in the mouth. The tannins are soft and smooth. Hacienda Araucano Clos de Lolol 2006 is a blend of Cabernet Franc, Carmenere, and Syrah with notes of cocoa, spice, and black cherry in the bouquet. In the mouth the cherry flavor comes out along with essence of dark plums. The finish is soft and supple.

KOYLE

Isidora Goyenechea 3600, Las Condes, Santiago,
+56 2 335 1593,
www.koyle.cl

Fifth-generation Cristóbal Undurraga, of the famed Chilean winemaking family, is the head technical director at Koyle. He gained international experience from working at Franciscan Estate in Napa Valley, Rosemont Estate in Australia, and Château Margaux in Bordeaux. His family bought 1,100 hectares (2,718 acres) in the valley for the production of fine wine. The name Koyle is taken from the endangered native Chilean plant (which grows abundantly in its vineyards) and is renowned for its beautiful purple flowers. Koyle Royale Syrah 2007 is 85 percent Syrah, 11 percent Malbec, and 4 percent Carmenere. It is bright purple in the glass, with notes of black cherry, spice, and smoked meats. In the mouth it is

smooth with a textured finish. Koyle Reserva Cabernet Sauvignon 2007 is a blend of 88 percent Cabernet Sauvignon and 12 percent Carmenere. It is dark ruby with aromas of blueberries, mocha, cigar box, and an underlying blackberry note. In the mouth it is balanced with silky tannins.

LA PLAYA

Camino a Calleuque s/n, Peralillo, Santa Cruz,
+56 2 657 9991,
www.laplayawine.com

La Playa was founded in 1989 by the Axelsen family of California and the Chilean Sutil and Errazuriz families. The estate owns 242 hectares (598 acres) of prime vineyard real estate in the Colchagua Valley. The families spent more than $10 million in 2002 on a state-of-the-art winery and the stunning Viña La Playa Winery Hotel. The hotel sits on the banks of the Tinguiririca River, and its eponymous dining room serves international cuisine excellently paired with La Playa's wines. La Playa Chardonnay 2010 is straw yellow with golden-green tones. The nose presents with white peaches, Anjou pears, and peach marmalade. In the mouth it has a bright acidity and a lingering finish of caramelized peaches. La Playa Block Selection Reserve 2008 is a blend of 90 percent Cabernet Sauvignon and 10 percent Petit Verdot. It is garnet ruby with light notes of black tea, baking spices, and black plum jam. On the palate it displays ripe tannins and a persistent finish.

LOS VASCOS

Camino Pumanque Km 5, Peralillo,
+56 7 235 0900,
www.losvascos.cl

Named after the Spanish translation of "the Basques" (*los vascos*), this 2,200—hectare

(5,436-acre) estate was purchased by Domaines Barons de Rothschild-Lafite in 1988. At that time only 220 hectares (544 acres) were planted with vines. Today, Los Vascos has 580 hectares (1,433 acres) of vines in the center of its impressive 3,600-hectare (8,896-acre) property. The estate benefits from a sheltered microclimate, as it is only 40 kilometers (25 miles) from the Pacific Ocean. It sits at an altitude of 130 meters (427 feet) above sea level. Improvements to the hacienda have resulted in the production of two new premium wines, Los Vascos Grande Reserve and Le Dix de Los Vascos. Los Vascos Grande Reserve 2008 is deep ruby red with a complex bouquet of red cherry, black plum, anise, a touch of black truffle, and baking spices. In the mouth it has good volume with a soft finish. Le Dix de Los Vascos 2008 is deep ruby red with a violet rim. The nose has aromas of pure, ripe, red fruits and a touch of toasted brioche and spice. It is soft and full on the palate, with ripe tannins.

MONTES

Avenida del Valle 945, Huechuraba,
+56 2 248 4805,
www.monteswines.com

Montes was founded in 1987 by Douglas Murray and Aurelio Montes. In 1988 they were joined in the venture by Pedro Grand and

Alfredo Vidaurre. Viña Montes has always had an eye on the global market; today 94 percent of its wine is exported to more than seventy-five countries, with the US market importing the lion's share of more than 150,000 cases. Its grapes are grown in three different vineyards: the El Arcangel Estate in Marchigue, La Finca de Apalta Estate in Apalta, and the Los Nogales Micaela y Santa Marta Estates in Curicó. Both the wines and the winery are consistently rated highly. Montes has had the honor of being named the Top Chilean Winery, the Top International Winery, and among the One Hundred Top Wineries Worldwide, by various publications over the past 15 years. Montes Alpha Carmenère 2008 is a blend of 90 percent Carmenere and 10 percent Cabernet Sauvignon. It is dark ruby with aromas of baking spices, blackberry, red fruits, and a touch of vanilla. In the mouth it explodes with fruit and finishes with soft round tannins. Montes Purple Angel 2007 is royal purple with aromas of cedar, tobacco, and cocoa underlying dark fruit in the bouquet. It is a blend of 92 percent Carmenere and 8 percent Petit Verdot. Big and full-bodied in the mouth, with lots of ripe tannins, it finishes with an angelic, smooth persistence. Montes Cherub Rosé 2010 is beautiful iridescent pink. It is made from 100 percent Syrah grapes from the Arcangel Estate. It has aromas of strawberries, pink flowers, and orange zest and is light and fruity in the mouth.

MONTGRAS

Avenida Eliodoro Yanez 2962,
Providencia, Santiago,
+56 2 520 4355,
www.montgras.cl

The Gras brothers—Hernán and Eduardo—and their partner Cristian Hartwig started MontGras in 1993. With their original vineyards in Palmilla, Colchagua, they have quickly made a name for themselves. Wines are made in four categories, Super Premium, Reserva, Varietal, and Organic, and are exported to the United States, Europe, Asia, South America, and the Middle East. The winery has a capacity to produce 6,500,000 liters annually and space for more than 3,500 American and French oak barrels. In 1997, MontGras initiated its Ninquén Project (roughly translated as "plateau on a mountain" in the local dialect), making it the first winery in Chile to plant on a mountain plateau. Approximately 100 hectares (247 acres) of red grape varieties were planted and Hernán proudly maintains: "Ninquén is not just a grape variety, and it's not just a *terroir*. It's a concept that sums up our entire philosophy of quality, handcrafted winemaking." Ninquén 2007 is a blend of 65 percent Syrah and 35 percent Cabernet Sauvignon. It is deep, dark red with aromas of blackberry, licorice, and cigar box in the bouquet. On the palate it is rich and graceful, with ripe fruit flavors. The tannins are big, and the finish is elegant. MontGras Antu Ninquén Syrah 2007 is a blend of Syrah and Cabernet Sauvignon, similar, but different, to Ninquen. It is rich purple, with black fruit, saddle leather, and cooling spice aromas. In the mouth it is well structured with a long finish. MontGras Chardonnay Reserva 2010 is deep yellow, with notes of vanilla, tropical fruits, and caramelized pineapple. It is fruity, creamy, and round in the mouth.

NEYEN DE APALTA

Apalta,
+56 2 240 6300,
www.neyen.cl

Roughly translated from ancient Mapudungun as "Spirit of Apalta," Neyen de Apalta began exporting wines in 2003. The family established its modern-day bodega on the site of an old winery dating back to the late nineteenth century. Both Cabernet Sauvignon and Carmenere vines planted on the estate in 1890 are still bearing fruit and are used to make delicious, high-quality wines. The Rojas family used consultants to assist with its project, and recently Neyen de Apalta merged with Veramonte. This new company now has 676 hectares (1,670 acres) of vines. Today's team includes Christian Aliaga, Paul Hobbs, and Patrick Valette. Neyen 2005 is 70 percent Carmenere and 30 percent Cabernet Sauvignon. The vines used ranged in age from 35 to 115 years in age. It is ruby red in the glass, with aromas of cassis, red fruits, and black plums. In the mouth it has an elegant tannic structure, balanced acidity, and a lasting finish.

VIÑEDOS EMILIANA

Nueva Tajamar 481, Las Condes, Santiago,
+56 2 353 9130,
www.emiliana.cl

Founded as Bodegas y Viñedos Santa Emiliana in 1986, Emiliana has been a leading exporter of quality wines for 25 years. It owns 1,550 hectares (3,830 acres) of land in the Casablanca, Maipo, and Rapel Valleys. In 1998, it was one of the first to use organic and biodynamic agriculture in Chile and founded Emiliana Organico. It received the coveted ISO 14,001 certification in 2001, which has been a great source of pride for the company and its employees. British magazine *The Drinks Business* named them "The Best Green Launch" in March 2011. Viñedos Emiliana Coyam 2009 is a blend of 41 percent Syrah, 29 percent Carmenere, 20 percent Merlot, 7 percent Cabernet Sauvignon, 2 percent Mourvèdre, and 1 percent Petit Verdot. It is

aged for 13 months in French and American oak. It is an inky purplish-red, with aromas of red berries, blackberries, and black plums, along with notes of earth and baking spices. In the mouth it is big and bold, yet finishes with round, smooth tannins. Novas Carmenere-Cabernet Sauvignon 2009 is garnet red, with aromas of black pepper and just-picked strawberries. In the mouth the tannins are firm but well structured—before a long finish.

CURICÓ VALLEY

Grape farming and winemaking are the primary industry of Curicó, where this tiny flavorsome fruit has been grown since the middle of the nineteenth century. The dominant landscape feature here is the ever-present sight of the white-capped Andes, the string of dormant volcanoes to the east, and the undulating coastal hills to the west. The valley takes its name from the indigenous Mapuche word *Kureko*. Meaning "land of black water," it describes the color of the many streams that once crisscrossed the region. Summer days in this sun-filled, dry valley can be as hot as 32 degrees Celsius (90 degrees Fahrenheit), but nights can drop down to the mid-10s (mid-50s), providing superior ripening conditions. Average rainfall is 702 millimeters, or 27.5 inches, with a 43-percent chance of frost in the spring. The western coastal hills limit the influence the Pacific might otherwise have here. Alluvial soils are fed by a web of canals flowing from the Mataquito, Teno, and Lontué rivers.

Overall vineyard plantings decreased 30 percent at the end of the last decade, mainly due to removal of older vineyards to make way for new varieties. The rustic Pais grape, grown for local table wines, has decreased in volume by 90 percent. Total hectares under cultivation is 13,462 (33,273 acres); of that, 60 percent are red varieties and 40 percent are white, but that balance is likely to change as vines continue to be ripped out and replaced. Cabernet Sauvignon, down 45 percent, ranges over 3,822 hectares (9,444 acres), while Sauvignon Blanc is grown on 3,351 (8,281 acres). Merlot covers 1,518 hectares (3,751 acres), succeeded by 1,110 hectares (2,743 acres) of Chardonnay. Carmenere grows on 949 hectares (2,345 acres). Up-and-comers Syrah and Pinot Noir now blanket 321 and 307 hectares (793 and 759 acres) respectively, an increase of 46 percent for the former and 40 percent for the latter.

The city of Curicó, 189 kilometers (11 miles) south of Santiago, is known for its Wine Harvest Festival, held annually from March 15 through March 20. In addition to grapes and wine, Curicó is known for its apples and cherries. This provincial capital city also enjoys a nationwide distinction as the "City of Cakes."

ECHEVERRIA

Avenida Apoquindo 3500, Las Condes, Santiago,
+56 2 232 7889,
www.echewine.com

The Echeverria family emigrated to Chile from Amezqueta, a small town near San Sebastian in the north of Spain, in 1740. In the early 1900s, it established a winery and planted vineyards in Molina in the Curicó Valley. Many of their vines are from pre-phylloxera rootstocks. The family began marketing its wines worldwide in 1992 and has strong export sales in Asia, Europe, and the Americas. Echeverria Cabernet Sauvignon 2009 is made from 100 percent Cabernet Sauvignon grapes and is garnet colored with touches of purple. It has aromas of black plum and ripe strawberry with notes of spice and white pepper. In the mouth it is fruity, well balanced, and has a nice finish. Echeverria Cabernet Sauvignon Limited Edition 2007 is composed of 85 percent Cabernet Sauvignon, 10 percent Syrah, and 5 percent Carmenere. It is purple-red, with aromas of blackberry, black cherry, and red plums countered by touches of black pepper and eucalyptus. It is round and voluptuous on the palate with a persistent finish.

MIGUEL TORRES

Panamerica Sur, Km 195, Curicó,
+56 7 556 4110,
www.migueltorres.cl

With more than three hundred years of wine-making experience in Spain, it was only a matter of time before the Torres family started planting vines in Chile. In 1979, they were the first non-Chilean company to finance vineyard production in the foothills of the Andes Mountains. Its 100 hectares (247 acres) soon grew to 445 hectares (1,100 acres), which today are under the watchful eye of Miguel Torres Maczassek, a fifth-generation Torres winemaker. Torres has vineyards in Manso de Velasco, Cordillera, Maquehua, and San Luis de Alico. A visit to the vineyards and winery will give you a sense of the pride that Miguel has for the beautiful part of Chile that he calls home. The restaurant offers fantastic cuisine with amazing views over the vines. Miguel was kind enough to ask his chef to write down his recipe for Pan-Seared

Grouper. Both men recommend pairing it with Miguel Torres Cordillera Chardonnay 2007. We couldn't agree more. This delicious wine is straw colored, with notes of apple, roasted nuts, and toasted brioche in the bouquet. In the mouth the fresh and delicate acidity gives way to a lasting finish. If you're in the mood for something a bit more filling, like beef or lamb, try them with the Conde de Superunda 2004. It is a blend of Cabernet Sauvignon, Carmenere, Monastrell, and Tempranillo. It is light red in the glass, with notes of red raspberries, purple flowers, such as violets, and light red fruits. It is big in the mouth with a lovely texture. The finish is long with a fine acidity.

VALDIVIESO

Luz Pereira 1849, Lontue,
+56 7 547 1002,
www.valdiviesovineyard.com

Viña Valdivieso dates back to 1879, when Alberto Valdivieso founded Champagne Valdivieso, the first company in Chile and South America to make sparkling wines. Today, the still wines used for Valdivieso's sparklers are made at the company's Lontue winery, which has a storage capacity for 12,201,444 liters of wine (1,800,000 liters of which are matured in French and American oak). The still wines are then transferred to Celia Solar, near Alberto's

original nineteenth century manor house in Santiago, where they undergo second fermentation via both Champenoise method and the Charmat method. The company began making still wines in the 1980s; many of its higher bottlings are extremely well received in the international market. For example, Valdivieso Caballo Loco is a crazy-good wine that is purposefully nonvintage. It has a strong cult following. Half of Edition Number 11 comes from the 2006 vintage, while the other half is a blend of wines from 1990 to 2005. It is dark garnet in appearance, with amazing aromas of cassis, espresso, baking spices, and ripe black cherries. On the palate it is full-bodied with juicy, smooth tannins. Valdivieso Eclat 2007 is a blend of 65 percent Carignan, 20 percent Mourvèdre, and 15 percent Syrah. It has strong red color with a purple rim and has aromas of red fruits, purple flowers, and spice.

In the mouth it opens with a burst of flavor and finishes with lingering tannins.

MAULE VALLEY

The farthest south of D.O. Central Valley, Maule has more land dedicated to grape cultivation than any other Chilean region: its vineyards cover 31,792 hectares (78,560 acres). A sharply contrasted combination of high-end wineries and their more industrial cousins producing bulk wine, Maule is rapidly changing as some older vines are displaced by new plantings and other long-neglected bush vines are being harvested to produce distinct field blends. Old-school Pais and Moscatel are giving way to Cabernet Sauvignon, Syrah, and Chardonnay. At the same time, old-vine Carignan from unirrigated plantings is making waves among wine geeks worldwide.

Most widely planted here is Cabernet Sauvignon, which increased 40 percent in 2010 to a total of 13,418 hectares (33,157 acres). This is roughly triple the amount of the next most populous varietal, Chardonnay, which is grown on 4,451 hectares (10,999 acres), an increase of 175 percent over the previous year. Maule is the only region in which you will note a significant amount of Pais, which even with a decrease of 66 percent still clings to 2,916 hectares (7,206 acres) of hillside and flatlands. Sauvignon

Blanc's 2,060 hectares (5090 acres) rank just ahead of Merlot's 1,968 hectares (4,863 acres), which is closely followed by Carmenere's 1,809 hectares (4,470 acres). The next most popular cultivar, Syrah, accounts for 1,013 hectares (2,503 acres), a jump of 28 percent over the previous year. Trailing far behind are 332 hectares (820 acres) of Carignan, much of which is a *terroir*-specific treasure.

Talca, a bustling industrial city and the region's capital, is 254 kilometers (158 miles) south of Santiago. Talca University's CTVV (Centro Tecnológico de la Vid y el Vino) is a world-class viticultural research center. The soils closest to the city tend to be a mixture of loam and mud, while those in the low-lying longitudinal valleys—which run between the Andes and coastal ranges—are alluvial. Hillside soils tend to be more basaltic and volcanic. Lower-lying soils can be nutrient deficient due to the now-discarded practice of flood irrigation. Frost risk in spring is estimated at 42 percent, and annual rainfall—mainly in winter—averages 735 millimeters, or 29 inches. Daytime summer temperatures hover around 32 degrees Celsius (90 degrees Fahrenheit), and a sharp swing in day-to-night temperatures helps to preserve the acid-to-sugar balance in the grapes. The Maule River—which gave the valley its name—and its tributaries, including the Loncomilla River, are the main source of water. Although the valley is more than 150 kilometers (93 miles) long, most wineries are situated close to Talca.

CALINA

Fundo El Maitén, Camino Las Rastras Km 7, Talca,
+56 7 126 3126,
www.calina.cl

Perched on the top of a slope overlooking the northern aspect of the Maule Valley, Calina makes quality wines, many at value prices. It has consistently been named a "Best Buy" in America's *Wine Enthusiast* and other magazines. Its wines have garnered a variety of awards in international competitions and have been featured on the *Today* show. Gavin Taylor, the winemaker, was born in Paarl and spent his early years in Wellington, South Africa. He earned his Bachelor of Science in Viticulture and Oenology at Stellenbosch University in 1996, traveled to Chile to work a harvest, and fell in love with the natural beauty. The vineyards are managed by Ricardo Marin Irigoyen. Calina Reserva Chardonnay 2009 is straw yellow, with aromas of pear, apple-sauce, and white peaches. In the mouth it is smooth and pleasant and finishes with a touch of honey. Calina Alcance Merlot 2006 has aromas of cherry, cassis, black plums, and a touch of smoked meats in the bouquet. On the palate it has great volume and a pleasant finish.

LA RESERVA DE CALIBORO

La Reserva de Caliboro, Pillay-Caliboro,
www.caliboro.com

Founded by Francesco Marone Cinzano—a descendant of the sixteenth-century Italian family which brought Asti Spumante to the world—La Reserva de Caliboro produces Erasmo wines in Chile. The thick, mud-walled cellars of La Reserva de Caliboro were built at the end of the nineteenth century, and many locals tell stories of how Don Fernando Solar Manzano kept a white owl there, mainly to protect against rodents, but it also played to the mystical claims surrounding the wines. In 2005, Count Francesco Marone Cinzano restored the buildings and cellars after years of neglect. Today, it is a marriage of traditional and modern, with Chilean rural patrimony blended with high-tech Italian winemaking equipment. La Reserva de Caliboro Erasmo 2005 is a blend of 60 percent Cabernet Sauvignon, 30 percent Merlot, and 10 percent Cabernet Franc. It is a deep ruby color in the glass, with aromas of blackberries, baking spices, black plums, and a touch of oak. In the mouth it has elegant, yet firm tannins with a delightful finish.

O. FOURNIER

Camino Constitucion, Km 20, San Javier, Talca,
+56 98 500 6787,
www.ofournier.com

We have had the pleasure of meeting José Manuel Ortega Gil-Fournier in more than one city around the world. He is a pleasant, affable, yet unassuming man whose company goal is to produce 1.5 million bottles of wine in the four different countries of Argentina, Chile, Spain (Rioja and Ribera del Duero regions), and Portugal (Douro Valley). His vision is clear, and his wines have received a multitude of accolades. O. Fournier Centauri Red Blend 2009 is a combination of 45 percent Cabernet

Franc, 25 percent Merlot, 20 percent Cabernet Sauvignon, and 10 percent Carignan. It is garnet red, with notes of red cherry, black pepper, and cassis on the nose. On the palate it is full-bodied and finishes with a touch of cedar. O. Fournier Urban Red Blend 2009 is 50 percent Cabernet Sauvignon, 25 percent Cabernet Franc, 20 percent Merlot, and 5 percent Carignan. It is a pleasing red color, with aromas of tobacco leaf, cassis, black cherry, and a whiff of graphite. Fruit-forward in the mouth, this wine is lovely to drink with a meal or on its own.

TERRANOBLE

Fundo Santa Camila s/n, San Clemente,
+56 7 123 1800,
www.terranoble.cl

We can't wait until 2015, when the Sauvignon Blanc vines that we planted at Terranoble are ready to harvest. We just hope that the wine is a good as the Terranoble Sauvignon Blanc 2009

that we enjoyed while these vines were being planted. It was straw yellow with greenish hues that glinted in the bright sun. The bouquet had notes of white peach and tropical fruits, which was different than the smell of wet dirt that was on our hands. We enjoyed its elegant balance on the palate and the crisp clean finish, but most importantly, it gave us a moment's pause from the back-breaking work of planting vines. We've already scheduled to return to Terranoble for the 2015 harvest. Terranoble was founded in 1993 by Jorge Elgueta, and in 2006, he brought in Wolf von Appen and Patricio de Solminihac. The estate has 360 hectares (890 acres) in Maule, Casablanca, and Colchagua Valleys and stands by the motto: "Wines intended for the consumer from the vineyard to the glass." Terranoble Gran Reserva Cabernet Sauvignon is 90 percent Cabernet Sauvignon and 10 percent Carmenere, with the majority of grapes from the Colchagua Valley and a bit from the Maule Valley. It is red garnet, with aromas of blackberry, black plum, and a whiff of smoked meat—or is that our lunch of barbecued lamb roasting over the open fire now that we're done planting? It is fruit-driven in the mouth with a touch of mocha that lingers before a persistent finish. On a more serious note, Terranoble Lahuen Rojo 2007 is a seriously delicious wine. Comprised of 58 percent Carmenere, 19 percent Syrah, 14 percent Cabernet Sauvignon, and 9 percent Malbec, it is deep garnet with a violet rim. There is a layer of spice top notes over a red berry and black fruit bouquet. In the mouth it is elegant and well structured with a smooth tannic finish.

VIA WINE GROUP

Avenida Presidente Kennedy,
Las Condes, Santiago,
+56 2 229 7939,
www.viawines.com

The idea of the Via Wine Group began when Simon Farr, a UK-based wine merchant, traveled to Chile and met the Coderch family. After years of discussion and searching for the right site, 400 hectares (988 acres) of vineyards were planted at the San Rafael estate in the Maule Valley. Today the group's investors include partners from Chile, Brazil, and the United States. Currently the group owns 1,039 hectares (2,567 acres) of vineyards in Maule,

Curicó, Casablanca, and Colchagua. Wines are produced under a variety of brand names; the two most notable in the US market are Chilcas and Oveja Negra ("black sheep"). The winemakers are Camilo Viani, Edgard Carter, and Claudio Villouta. The company has the capacity to produce 17 million liters of wine per year. Chilcas Red One 2007 is composed of 32 percent Syrah, 30 percent Cabernet Sauvignon, 19 percent Carmenere, 11 percent Cabernet Franc, and 8 percent Petit Verdot. It is red purple, with notes of cassis, dried cherries, and black plums. In the mouth it is full and large, with smooth tannins and a persistent finish. Chilcas Cabernet Sauvignon Reserva 2009 is garnet colored with a purple rim. Notes of blueberry and red fruits are evident, and the mouthfeel is lush and smooth—with a touch of mocha on the finish. Oveja Negra Reserva Chardonnay Viognier 2008 is bright yellow, with notes of tropical fruits, honeydew melon, and orange blossoms. In the mouth it is medium-bodied and has balanced acidity. It's a white wine meant to be paired with food.

ITATA VALLEY

If you're traveling southward, the Itata Valley is the first stop in the Southern Region D.O. As the Coastal Mountain Range lessens in altitude, this valley—less protected than those to the north—feels the effect of ocean-born winds and rain, especially in winter. Grape vines arrived in the valley via the nearby port of Concepción (509 kilometers, or 316 miles, southwest of Santiago) 450 years ago and have been cultivated since. It is only in the last 20 years though that Itata has been considered a source of fine wine.

The number one change here has been the eradication of older vineyards in favor of higher-quality, and more commercial, international varieties. This means that total plantings are down, and the region is temporarily undercultivated. Overall cultivation shows a decrease of 77 percent, with the largest declines in Pais (down 92 percent) and Muscat of Alexandria (down 82 percent.) Despite the downward trend, Muscat of Alexandria—used in Pisco production and for homely, sweet wines—is still the most widely planted in the region; its 928 hectares (2,293 acres) amount to a significant portion of the remaining 2,421 hectares (5,982 acres) of vineyard in the valley. Newly minted Cabernet Sauvignon vines cover a rapidly expanding 326 hectares (806 acres), while the primitive Pais remains on an ever-shrinking 266 hectares (657 acres). Chardonnay is grown on 168 hectares (415 acres), Merlot on 154 hectares (380 acres), Cinsault on 124 hectares (306 acres), and Pinot Noir on 81 hectares (200 acres). Although white varieties account for 53 percent of total grapes grown in Itata, it remains to be seen which varietal will make its presence known as the hallmark of Itata.

The region's capital city, Itata, is 400 kilometers (249 miles) south of Santiago. Its name means "where the sun sits" in the language of its indigenous people. Bernardo O'Higgins, the national hero who led the fight for Chile's independence from Spain, was born here in 1778. The valley is crossed by the Itata and Nuble Rivers. Dry, hot summers are offset by winters that are exactly the opposite; rainfall averages 1,107 millimeters, or 43.5 inches per year. From the Andes to the Pacific, the lush, green landscape vacillates between dense forest and rolling hills—covered with sandy-soiled vineyards.

BIO BIO VALLEY AND MALLECO VALLEY

Two adjoining valleys in the Southern Region D.O., Bio Bio and Malleco, are respectively the southernmost and northernmost areas of the neighboring provinces of Bio Bio and Araucania. They are divided by the Renaico River. Although this was previously thought to have been the farthest south that grapes could be reasonably grown in Chile, they are now joined by D.O.'s Araucania and Lagos, where plantings have not yet yielded a viable harvest.

As in the Itata Valley to the north, vineyard

cultivation at the end of the last decade was reduced here by 76 percent. Both Pais and Muscat varieties showed a momentous downward trend as they were displaced by cool-climate varieties. Meanwhile, Cabernet Sauvignon—which never thrived in the cold, wet south—was replaced by grapes with more affinity to the climate. Red and white varieties are planted here in almost equal proportion, but we will see a change as Chardonnay, Sauvignon Blanc, Riesling, and Gewürztraminer increase, and Pais, already down 95 percent, continues its decline.

A total of 835 hectares (2,063 acres) supports cultivation of grapes in the Bio Bio Valley. The number one varietal is Pinot Noir, which grows on 255 hectares (630 acres), an increase of 50 percent over the prior year. Cultivation of Chardonnay has grown by the same percentage and now accounts for 188 hectares (465 acres). The region's swiftly rising star is Sauvignon Blanc, whose 174 hectares (430 acres) represent an astounding growth of 324 percent. Pais is holding its own on 115 hectares (284 acres), while Riesling's 49 hectares (121 acres) show an upward tick of 50 percent. Gewürztraminer is raised on 21 hectares (52 acres).

The most recent tallies for the Malleco area show that its 17 planted hectares (42 acres) are divided between 9 hectares (22 acres) of Chardonnay and 8 hectares (20 acres) of Pinot Noir.

Despite its proximity to Antarctica, high temperatures in summer soar to over 32 degrees Celsius (90 degrees Fahrenheit). Winters here are cold and wet: average yearly rainfall is 1,276 millimeters, or 50 inches, with a 64 percent chance of spring frost. Both of these figures are the highest recorded for any established Chilean wine region

AGUSTINOS

Avenida Las Condes 11,380, Vitacura, Santiago,
+56 2 240 7600,
www.agustinos.cl

Get into your car, or use our preferred method—helicopter—and head due south just about 500 kilometers (310 miles) from Santiago. You will find yourself in the Bio Bio Valley. It's a bit colder than Santiago, and cool winds always seem to blow all day. The soil at Agustinos is the sand and loam of an ancient riverbed. Agustinos is a part of the VC Family Estates group, one of Chile's successful family-owned food and beverage companies. French-Canadian winemaker Patrick Piuze learned cool-climate winemaking while working with Jean-Marc Brocard in Burgundy's Chablis region, and winemaker Rodrigo Romero worked in both Italy and Napa Valley before Agustinos. All the wines are made from estate-grown grapes. Agustinos has a strong commitment to the environment; it employs solar energy, biodynamic viticulture, and sustainable wastewater treatment. Agustinos Bio Bio Pinot Noir 2008 is ruby red in the glass. On the nose smoked meats and beef jerky are detected along with ripe red fruits. In the mouth it is fruity, juicy, and has a lovely soft tannic finish. Agustinos Bio Bio Chardonnay Reserva 2008 is straw yellow with green hues. It has a bouquet of citrus and tropical fruits, such as papaya and mango. The palate is refreshing and clean with a nice mineral finish. Agustinos Bio Bio Sauvignon Blanc 2009 is almost clear and has notes of tropical fruits, melon, and a touch of cut grass. In the mouth it is refreshing with a bracing minerality.

SOLDESOL

Avenida Consistorial 5090, Peñalolen, Santiago,
+56 2 791 4500,
www.aquitania.cl

Viña Aquitania sources grapes from what it claims is Chile's southernmost wine-producing region. Although no winery exists at this location (650 kilometers, or 405 miles, south of Santiago), the vineyards produce remarkable grapes, and the winemaking team includes wine-world luminaries such as Bruno Prats, Paul Pantallier, Felipe de Solminihac, and Ghislain de Montgolfier. SOLdeSOL Pinot

Noir 2008 is ruby red, with aromas of fresh ripe cherry, dried cherry, and a slight touch of vanilla. It is fruity and flavorsome with an elegant finish. SOLdeSOL Chardonnay 2007 presents with a straw yellow hue and aromas of lush tropical fruits. It is full and round in the mouth with a beautiful finish. Visitors are welcome to taste the wines at Viña Aquitania's main winery in Santiago.

VERANDA

Avenida Las Condes 11,380, Vitacura, Santiago,
+56 2 240 7600,
www.veranda.cl

Montreal-born winemaker Pascal Marchand was drawn to the Bio Bio Valley after studying in Beaune, France, and working in Pommard for Clos des Espeneaux and Clos Jordanne with the famed Boisset family. Veranda makes three product lines in the Bio Bio Valley: Veranda, Oda, and Millerandage. Veranda Oda Miraflores Vineyard Bio Bio Pinot Noir 2007 has dried fruits, namely dried cherry, with a slight earthy note on the nose. A delicate, light cherry color foretells the cherry and juicy red fruit on the mid palate before the long, fruity finish. Veranda Pinot Noir 2008 is ruby red with aromas of dark cherry and black plum. Smooth and fruity on the palate, it delights with a persistent finish.

RECIPES

GRILLED LAMB SKEWERS IN MERQUÉN MARINADE
SERVED WITH A CHILEAN-STYLE MINT SALSA

*

Recipe courtesy Ruth Van Waerebeek,
consulting chef and culinary advisor, Concha y Toro

*

SERVES 4

Ruth is a regular culinary advisor to *Paula*, a Chilean women's and lifestyle magazine, and is the consulting chef for Concha y Toro, creating dishes to pair with its wines. She is the author of two cookbooks, has sailed the Atlantic Ocean on a small, two-person yacht, and worked in kitchens around the world. She became captivated with spice and vibrant flavor while working in the United States with notable chefs, including Norman Van Aken and Douglas Rodriguez. Ruth recently opened a guesthouse and cooking school, Mapu Yampai, in the foothills of the Andes Mountains. She recommends pairing this dish with Concha y Toro Terrunyo Cabernet Sauvignon 2007.

From the northern Andean foothills to the Patagonian grasslands, tender lamb is the meat of choice for the parrilla or Chilean grill, especially when spiced with a pungent and exquisite merquén mixture, then served with a refreshing green mint salsa.

FOR THE MERQUÉN MARINADE

½ cup olive oil

3 tablespoons plain yogurt,
preferably whole milk

2 tablespoons onion, grated

2 garlic cloves, finely minced

1 tablespoon fresh rosemary,
finely chopped

1 tablespoon merquén or other
smoked chili pepper mix
(see note below*)

1½ pounds leg of lamb, deboned
and degreased, cut into
1½-inch cubes

**FOR THE CHILEAN-STYLE
MINT SALSA**

¼ cup scallions, chopped

½ cup fresh mint leaves

¼ cup fresh cilantro leaves

½ jalapeño pepper, seeds
removed

1 clove garlic

3 tablespoons apple cider
vinegar

⅓ cup canola oil

¼ cup cold water

1 tablespoon sugar

Salt to taste

FOR THE LAMB SKEWERS

8 (12-inch) bamboo skewers,
soaked in water for
30 minutes

4 small firm peaches, quartered

24 fresh bay leaves

Vegetable oil for brushing
grill rack

MAKE THE MARINADE AND MARINATE THE MEAT

Combine all the marinade ingredients in an oven-proof glass
baking dish just large enough to hold meat. Add the lamb, mix
to combine, and marinate meat, covered, for up to 2 hours.

MAKE THE CHILEAN MINT SALSA

Put all the salsa ingredients in a blender and blend until
smooth. Taste and adjust the seasonings (this salsa should
be brimming with flavor). Refrigerate until ready to serve or
up to 4 days.

GRILL THE LAMB SKEWERS

Soak skewers and prepare a charcoal, gas, or electric grill
to medium hot.

Thread 3 pieces of lamb, 2 quarters of peach, and 3 bay leaves
loosely on each skewer. Lightly oil the grill rack. Grill skewers,
turning occasionally, until just cooked through, 10 to 15
minutes.

Serve the lamb with mint salsa.

*Note: If merquén, a unique smoked chilli pepper mix from the
indigenous Mapuche Indians, is not available, you can make your own
spice mix using ½ teaspoon dried oregano, 1 teaspoon cayenne pepper,
1 teaspoon smoked paprika powder, ½ teaspoon salt, and ½ teaspoon
ground coriander seeds.

PAN-SEARED GROUPER

Courtesy of Miguel Torres, owner of Miguel Torres Winery

✳

GROUPER WITH BAKED TOMATO CONFIT AND PEANUTS FLAVORED WITH DRIED CHILLI PEPPER, SERVED WITH WHITE BEAN BLINI

✳

SERVES 2

Miguel Torres recommends pairing this dish with Torres Cordillera Chardonnay 2007. Miguel has two restaurants, one in Santiago and the other at the winery in Curicó. We enjoyed their Chilean tapas-style menu in Santiago, while the winery restaurant is more of a three-hour gastronomic affair for lunch or dinner. The décor is elegant yet minimalist, and guests enjoy views of the vineyards while dining.

FOR THE GROUPER

2 (6-ounce) pieces of grouper

½ teaspoon salt

¼ teaspoon ground black
   pepper

Olive oil for cooking

FOR THE BLINI

1 (8-ounce) can white beans,
   drained

2 ounces flour

2 eggs, lightly beaten

1 ounce small shrimp

1 tablespoon chopped cilantro

FOR THE CONFIT TOMATOES

8 ounces ripe tomatoes

½ teaspoon salt

½ teaspoon white pepper

¼ teaspoon dried cilantro

½ teaspoon dried oregano

4 tablespoons olive oil

FOR THE CORN SAUCE

2 ears of corn

1 ounce basil

1 ounce spinach

4 ounces cooking cream

FOR THE GARNISH

2 ounces papaya, julienned

4 ounces spicy roasted peanuts,
   crushed

SEAR THE GROUPER

Season grouper with salt and pepper. Heat a heavy skillet over high heat until hot, then add enough olive oil to lightly coat the bottom of the pan and sear the grouper on both sides. Transfer fish to a hot platter and set aside.

MAKE THE BLINI

Put the white beans in a blender or food processor and process until smooth. Transfer puree to a bowl, add the flour, egg, shrimp, and cilantro and whisk to combine the blini batter.

Heat a pancake griddle until hot. Whisk the batter again and ladle onto nonstick or lightly greased griddle. Cook blini on both sides, then remove and set aside.

MAKE THE CONFIT TOMATOES

Preheat oven to 350°F.

Peel, seed, and roughly chop the tomatoes and transfer to a baking dish. Add the salt, pepper, dried cilantro, oregano, and oil and stir to combine. Bake confit in the oven for 15 minutes.

MAKE THE CORN SAUCE

Blanch the corn in boiling water for 2 minutes, then transfer to a colander and let cool. Cut the kernels off the cobs and process kernels in a food processor or blender. Transfer to a saucepan, add the basil, spinach, and cream, and cook over low heat until heated through, about 5 minutes.

TO SERVE

Cover the bottom of each plate with the corn sauce, place the blini on top, then the grouper. Top with the tomato confit and sprinkle with the papaya julienne and the crushed peanuts.

CHILEAN EGGPLANT STEW

✳

Recipe courtesy of María José Tolosa Habit,
national marketing manager for Montes

✳

SERVES 6-8

This family recipe was created by her grandfather, Mario Habit Constela and has been passed down from generation to generation. If you're lucky, it might be the special of the day at Café Alfredo at the Montes Apalta Winery. Maria recommends serving it with Montes Purple Angel 2007, a blend of 92 percent Carmenere and 8 percent Petit Verdot.

Olive oil
1 red pepper, cut into strips
1 green pepper, cut into strips
1 onion, chopped
8 eggplants
2¼ pounds of fillet steak, cut
    into 4- by 1-inch strips
Salt and black pepper to taste
Oregano to taste
1 (or more) bottle of Montes
    Classic Chardonnay
White rice, cooked

Heat olive oil in a heavy-bottomed copper pot over moderate heat until hot but not smoking, then add the bell peppers and onion and cook, stirring, until golden brown. Transfer vegetables with a slotted spoon to a bowl and set aside. Reserve oil in the pot.

Peel the eggplants, and cut lengthwise into thin slices. Put the slices into the copper pot and brown in olive oil. Transfer the eggplant to a bowl with other cooked vegetables. Reserve any remaining oil in the pot.

Put the strips of meat into the copper pot, add salt, black pepper, and oregano, and cook until meat is browned on all sides.

Return all vegetables to the copper pot. Add enough of the Montes Classic Chardonnay to cover the mixture, and simmer, covered with lid ajar, for about 2 hours, stirring and adjusting spices occasionally.

Serve with white rice.

PISCO SOUR

✳

Recipe courtesy of Waqar 40 Grados Pisco and Puro Chile, New York City

✳

MAKES 1 DRINK

The classic *Pisco Camahueto* is found in every bar and restaurant in Chile, as well as cocktail lounges around the world. The Camahueto is the invention of the Waqar 40 Grados Pisco mixologists and has been formulated to entice the sophisticated yet adventurous connoisseur of Pisco from Chile.

2 slices pineapple, diced

10 basil leaves

½ ounce simple syrup

Crushed ice

2 ounces Waqar 40 Grados Pisco

1 ounce ginger ale

Put the pineapple and basil in a highball glass. Add simple syrup and stir gently. Add ice, then Pisco, and top with ginger ale.

"LET'S TALK ABOUT PISCO"

We think Pisco is an important spirit to discuss here—given that much of Chile's grape production, especially from the northern valleys, is used to make it. Although much of the Pisco mixed into cocktails around the world today comes from Peru, the planting of grapes and the subsequent distillation into alcohol took place simultaneously in what were at the time Spanish territories. Chileans are especially proud of Chilean Pisco and for good reason. According to Professor Hernán Cortés of the Universidad de La Serena, the term "Pisco" was used in common speech and literature in the early eighteenth century to describe grape brandy. In 1870, Juan de Dios Peralta set up a distillery in the town of La Serena and began selling his brand of Pisco. In 1889, his Tres Cruces Pisco, which is still produced today, won an award at the Universal Exposition de Paris—and Chilean Pisco was introduced to the world market. Recently, there has been a resurgence in the artisanal production of the spirit as a softening, mellowing, and rounding of the original harsh-edged classical-style of *aqua ardiente*— or "burning water"—has begun to take hold. Innovative mixologists have discovered the versatility of this sometimes misunderstood spirit and are constantly experimenting with new and exciting cocktails featuring Pisco.

IN THEIR OWN WORDS

EDUARDO CHADWICK

Named one of the most influential people in the wine industry by *Decanter* magazine, Eduardo Chadwick is both the president/owner of Viña Errazuriz and renowned for his tireless support of the Institute of Masters of Wine and the Chilean wine industry in general. In 1995, he had the foresight to partner with Robert Mondavi and created his now famous iconic wine, Seña. In what is now known simply as "The Berlin Tasting," Viñedo Chadwick 2000 and Seña 2001 placed first and second, respectively. Eduardo's passion for fine wine knows no boundaries; having identified the land under his father's beloved polo field to be perfect soil for growing excellent grapes, he had it ploughed under and planted it with high-quality rootstock.

How did you get involved in the world of wine?

Viña Errazuriz is a family run winery, and I got involved back in 1983 when my father invited me to join. At the time it was the very beginning of the wine-quality "revolution" in Chile, and at Viña Errazuriz it was the right time to get started!

At 23 years of age, I had just finished engineering studies at the university and had a couple of years of working experience in other fields, so this represented a new start for me. The very first thing my father did was to send me to the University of Bordeaux for a much-needed crash course in enology!

What are some of the biggest changes you have seen in winemaking since you began your career?

The changes at Viña Errazuriz and in general in Chilean winemaking have been a complete transformation. From a sleepy period before the 1980s (when we were) focused on the domestic market with generic wines, to an actual modern and energetic wine industry that has completely reinvented itself. Developing new *terroirs*, new cool coastal regions, new varieties, building new state-of-the-art wineries, and producing wines for the world markets. Chile has today perhaps one of the most globalized wine industries of the world, exporting 80 percent of our wines to more than a hundred worldwide markets.

What are some of the exciting changes that you see happening specifically in your country?

Chile is defining its character and personality in its wines; offering a great diversity from cool coastal fruity and fresh Sauvignon Blanc with balanced ripeness and acidity to excellent Cabernet Sauvignons and Carmenere blends that are full-bodied with ripe tannins, yet balanced with acidity and offering great elegance and finesse. Chile is offering very unique world-class wines!

Where else in the world have you studied, trained, or worked a harvest? How did that influence your winemaking?

I have traveled the world of wine from Bordeaux, Burgundy, Tuscany, Napa, Australia, New Zealand, to other regions numerous times, many times accompanied by our viticulture and winemaking team. The knowledge and understanding of other world wine regions and winemaking practices has helped us to define our style and the personality in our wines. Understanding our Chilean *terroir* with a global perspective has allowed us to produce truly world-class wines.

Which varieties are you working with? Are you experimenting with anything new?

I am convinced the quality of our Cabernet Sauvignons from Aconcagua and Maipo are unrivaled, as well as our Casablanca and Aconcagua Costa Sauvignon Blanc and Pinot Noir. Carmenere on its own or blended also gives us unique and distinctive world-class wine.

Are there any new areas that you have identified for potential vineyard sites?

We are developing a new area in the Aconcagua Valley located just 12 kilometers (7 miles) from the Pacific Ocean, what is known as *Aconcagua Costa*. Here we are developing our Manzanar vineyard, with a very cool climate and ideal soils for Sauvignon Blanc, Pinot Noir, Chardonnay, and Syrah.

We are also planting a new vineyard site in Aconcagua at 80 kilometers [50 miles] from the coast and 700 meters [2,297 feet] of elevation. The climatic conditions and soils here are ideal for Cabernet Sauvignon, Carmenere, and Syrah varieties.

With these two properties, we are showcasing the great diversity that we can achieve at our Aconcagua Valley, from cool, coastal, fresh, aromatic wines to full-bodied reds of great balance at the interior near the Andes Mountains.

What challenges have you faced as a wine-maker or winery owner?

The greatest challenge we have faced has been to obtain the deserved recognition by the world critics. Our wines have only 20 years of international exposure, and during the early years it was difficult to gain awareness for Viña Errazuriz as a world-class producer. Back in 1995 with Seña, our joint venture with the late Robert Mondavi, Chile started to gain the world-critics' attention, similar to how Opus One helped Napa obtain international respect. Later we developed blind tastings, similar to the "Judgement of Paris," and our Viñedo Chadwick, Seña, and Don Maximiano wines defeated the mythical 100-point vintage 2000 of the first growths Lafite, Margaux, Latour, and Super Tuscans Sassicaia and Tignanello. This is referred to "The Berlin Tasting" (www.theberlintasting.com), of which we have already conducted 12 events in all major wine capitals of the world.

Today most critics around the world recognize Viña Errazuriz's world-class wines for their quality and consistency.

What is your winemaking philosophy?

To make wines that showcase the positive characteristics of the New World: fruit purity, intensity, freshness, together with ripeness and round tannins in reds. We always search for great finesse, elegance, and balanced wines.

What would you hope people say about your wine?

Our wines want to express our Chilean *terroir* with great quality and finesse, but most importantly we hope people will enjoy our wines when drinking them!

Do you think that the market should influence winemaking, or do you think that winemaking should influence the market?

When talking about world-class wines, there is no doubt that style and true *terroir* should be understood and therefore influence the market.

Besides your own wine, what are some of your favorite wines? What do you like about them?

From the world: Brunello di Montalcino Salvioni, Barolos (Scavino, Conterno, Vietti, Mascarello, etc.), Chablis (Domaine Dauvisat among others), Maison Louis Jadot Pinots from Burgundy, Alsace wines (Schlumberger, Trimbach, etc.), Champagne, I can drink bottles and bottles. I'm fond of Roederer, Jordan Estate, Robert Mondavi from California, Henschke from Australia, just to name a few. . . .

What I like about them is they are wines that give pleasure, that I enjoy drinking, and that have a clear sense of place and where they come from.

What is your opinion on screwcap versus cork closures?

I am a screwcap convert; in varietal wines it really helps to preserve the quality and aromatics in perfect condition throughout the life of a wine due to its excellent seal performance. It is of great help for conserving the primary aromas in wines like Sauvignon Blanc, Riesling, Pinot Noir, etc.

If you could invite anyone from history, living or dead, to your home for dinner, who would it be? What food would you serve? What wine would you serve?

I would first like to invite a good friend and enjoy an old bottle of our Viñedo Chadwick, perhaps vintage 2000. And if I were able to invite anyone from history, I would love to have dinner with Nelson Mandela and hear firsthand his amazing struggle to free South Africa from apartheid—a real leader! I would also treat him with a bottle of Viñedo Chadwick 2000!

If you were to stay home tonight for a relaxing evening, drinking wine while watching a movie, which movie would you watch? Which wine would you drink?

I would like to watch *The Way Back* from Peter Weir, drinking a nice bottle of our Seña 2001, which is already showing its greatness.

How do you like to spend your time away from the winery?

Climbing mountains or having fun diving with my four wonderful daughters!

Do you collect wine? If so, what is in your cellar?

I can't say I am a real collector of wine; however, I enjoy drinking wines from other producers and regions to taste their style. I bring wines from my trips around the world and have old vintages of Robert Mondavi Reserve cabernets, old Pinot from Maison Louis Jadot, some Chiantis and Brunellos from my friends of Frescobaldi, among others.

If you weren't involved in wine, what would you be doing?

Thinking how to get into the wine industry!

MARCELO RETAMAL

Marcelo Retamal is considered to be Chile's most important "*terroir* hunter." His work as De Martino winemaker takes him north to south, east to west, down in the valleys and high up into the Andes Mountains of Chile—in search of new sites to plant vineyards and grow grapes. Many experts and several of his contemporaries consider him to be one of the most acclaimed and respected winemakers of his generation. He has twice been awarded "Best Winemaker of the Year" by the Chilean press, and his wines garner high scores in international competitions.

How did you get involved in the world of wine?
My family has vineyards in the south of Chile, so I have always been involved in wine. When I finished school and I had to choose the career to follow, I was clear that I wanted to be a winemaker. In Chile to be a winemaker I had to be an agronomist first. So after finishing this degree, I chose to specialize in enology.

What are some of the exciting changes that you see happening, specifically in your country?
The most incredible change is in the planting of vineyards in new areas of Chile, especially near the sea and in the Andes. These are very different soils and climates. I think that it is a great opportunity for the winemakers to experiment in these areas. There is a lot in Chile to be discovered, and that is very attractive to me.

Where else in the world have you studied, trained, or worked a harvest? How did that influence your winemaking?
When I started to work at De Martino, the owners and I agreed that I could travel every year for one month to understand the different wine-producing areas in the world. I have been to many of the wine-producing areas of France, Italy, Spain, Portugal, New Zealand, Argentina, United States, and Australia. In every trip I have had the opportunity to try an average of over six hundred wines. Each concept, each wine, each landscape, each meal, each culture, and of course the people help me to make better wines. It also humbles me to think that there are so many people in the world making amazing wines and doing amazing things in so many places.

Which varieties are you working with? Are you experimenting with anything new?

I am working with Sauvignon Blanc, Chardonnay, Viognier, Cabernet Sauvignon, Cabernet Franc, Petit Verdot, Petite Syrah, Syrah, Merlot, Carmenere, Malbec, Sangiovese, and Carignan. Today I am working with Cinsault. In southern Chile there are very old vines. They are without irrigation, and we have started with a producer that is 17 kilometers [10 miles] from the sea, so it is a cold climate that produces grapes with good acidity. Here we want to make a Rosé wine fermented in a natural way using a 200–liter handcrafted, clay pottery shaped jar that is called a *tinaja*.

Are there any new areas that you have identified for potential vineyard sites?

To me, a great potential today is in the Andes Mountains. It is a big mountain range that extends through most of Chile. There is a lot of snow in the winter, high altitude, extreme temperatures, and many soils of different geological origins. It is very diverse. In the Elqui Valley, especially the Alcohuaz area, we are making wines that come from grapes grown at 2,000 meters [6,562 feet] of altitude. I am also working in the Maule and Itata Valleys, because there are old vineyards without irrigation. Here we make some exciting field blends, which produce unique wines. Six years ago

we at De Martino began focusing on rescuing these vines, and today we have four wines in the market, two of which are already in the United States, El Leon De Martino (predominantly Carignan) and Las Cruces De Martino (predominantly Malbec and Carmenere.)

What challenges have you faced as a winemaker?

The biggest challenge we have had these years was to carry out the project on the definition and characterization of Chilean *terroir*. Since 1996 we have managed to make wine from more than 350 plots in almost all the places where vineyards are planted in Chile. We are excited about our 300-hectare [741-acre] organic vineyard located in Maipo Valley, in which we mainly grow Carmenere and Cabernet Sauvignon.

The idea is to look at each particular variety and the places that produce wines with more personality and authenticity. Characterizing the geology, soils, climate, and vinifying the grapes in our winery, and measuring the correlation of what we see in the glass with what we see in the vineyard.

What is your winemaking philosophy?

Today, it is very simple: to produce the least standardized wines possible, to reflect a place of origin and honesty. Wines that are food friendly, complex, recognizable, and easy to drink. For our higher-value wines, we have taken out the aromas of oak. These are wines produced in the most natural way possible, without using external yeast.

All our vineyards that we own are organic since 1998, and today we are transferring this experience to our contract grape growers with whom we have long-term relationships. This year we will eradicate the use of herbicides and transform many of the vineyards into organic.

What would you hope people say about your wine?

I hope they say that these are wines that are recognizable and they are food friendly. We hope that they are wines that two people can share and not be bored with the bottle. I want our wines to be recognized as well made and with great personality. I want our simple wines to be recognized as simple and people to recognize the complexity in our complex wines.

Do you think that the market should influence the winemaking, or do you think that the winemaking should influence the market?

Winemaking cannot influence the market; the market gives the winemaker guidelines to make wines that in the end you can sell. The wine business is a business of distribution and not production: the big brands that are suc-cessful today are those with good distribution. Those of us who work in production must work to create products that the consumers like. I am constantly working on developing new product lines, new brands, and new wines that the consumers will like. This is part of our long-term philosophy at De Martino, which we defined in 2011. It is a philosophy that will stand for our company. We understand that once we have defined our philosophy we cannot follow every trend and fashion. We believe that great wines should be faithful to their style.

Besides your own wine, what are some of your favorite wines? What do you like about them?

Tough question! I drink wine every day at home, usually from other producers. Barolo is my favorite; they are wines with personality, and when they are old they are very complex. If I have to choose one, it's Bartolo Mascarello, the great master of classic Barolo—and it is well priced. I think Giuseppe Dolcetto Mascarello can be a great option from the Piemonte area.

What is your opinion on screwcap versus cork closures?

For economic wines I like screwcap; I have no problem. For higher-value wines I like the cork; I think I like the sound of the cork when opening the bottle, and in this sense, there are certain traditions which must still remain, including the costs involved.

If you were to stay home tonight for a relaxing evening, drinking wine while watching a movie, which would you watch? Which wine would you drink?

I think in this case my choice would be beer. Very cold, I like it because it is lighter and less alcoholic. My favorite movies are the *Godfather* series—but I especially like Part Two.

How do you like to spend your time away from the winery?

I like being home. I take care of the garden, I have a barbecue where I like to have a lot of barbecues and invite friends. I like going to the beach, the countryside, cooking. I do not watch TV in general, but if I watch it, it is only to see soccer. I like to watch Spain and Italy play. I also like to watch the PGA tournaments.

Do you collect wine? If so, what is in your cellar?

Instead of collecting wine, I buy a lot of wine and I drink it. I do have many bottles in my house, I bring them back from my travels, but I usually drink them with friends. I don't like to keep bottles as trophies to show my friends. Wine is meant to be enjoyed. I think the only wines I like to save are the great wines from Porto. I have three daughters, and I look forward to the day when they come to my house with their boyfriends and husbands and drink my wines together. Nothing is better than that.

If you were not involved in wine, what would you be doing?

Perhaps in my next life, I would be something different, but I am happy being a winemaker for today.

ALEXANDRA MARNIER LAPOSTOLLE

Alexandra Marnier Lapostolle is the great-granddaughter of Alexandre Marnier Lapostolle, the creator of Grand Marnier. Her family also owns Château de Sancerre in France, and she and her husband, Cyril de Bournet, are the founders of Chile's Casa Lapostolle, producer of the famed Casa Lapostolle Clos Apalta.

How did you get involved in the world of wine?
In short, by love and tradition. The Marnier Lapostolle family has been involved in viticulture and winemaking in Sancerre in the Loire Valley since the seventeenth century. It was a natural step for me to follow that inspiration by creating Lapostolle in Chile in 1994.

What are some of the biggest changes you have seen in winemaking since you began your career?
The diversity of wine that is available in the world today for the consumer. There are so many different areas, styles, varieties. Also, the search for wines that pair the different gastronomic scenes of each country. How that has evolved in such a positive way in most areas where we sell our wines.

What are some of the exciting changes that you see happening specifically in your country?
The wine scene in Chile is very exciting and dynamic at the minute. Chile is finally looking to expand the usual central valley growing area and is looking to promote the diversity of the country that allows us to grow so many different varieties. There is a *terroir*-hunting fever in the country, to discover new *terroirs* and push the boundaries toward the cool Pacific Ocean, in the Andean altitudes, and also the north and south of the country, where there are many different unexplored regions with types of climates and soils that are very promising. Also, there is new respect for the traditional planted areas, where old vines, I mean pre-phylloxera vines, were planted in the early twentieth century. Places such as Alto Maipo with its Cabernet Sauvignon, Apalta in Colchagua with Carmenere, and even Caquenes in Maule, with the old Carignan bush wines. All this is part of trying to make wines that are better in quality and that will bring respect and also a sense of place.

Where else in the world have you studied, trained, or worked a harvest? How did that influence your winemaking?
Of course, my family estate in Sancerre was

the first influence. The *terroir*-driven wines we make there is a philosophy I have also embraced in Chile. We have worked with Michel Rolland as our exclusive consultant here in Chile since the beginning—he has a really wide worldwide experience that he brought with him to Lapostolle.

Which varieties are you working with? Are you experimenting with anything new?
We are well known for our Merlots, Carmenere, and Cabernet Sauvignon from Colchagua, especially those with huge potential in Apalta. We also grow Chardonnay in the cold Casablanca region, next to the Pacific, and Sauvignon Blanc and Syrah from a special estate in the foothills of the Andes. We are experimenting every harvest with varieties and also new techniques both in the vineyards and in the winery. For example, we have a new project called *vin de tunel* with one of our winemakers—it is made in a tunnel in our Apalta winery, hence the name—it is truly handmade from small lots of Syrah and Carmenere. From north to south, our Syrah is showing the great potential of this variety. We are also working with the great range of *terroirs* in Chile from north to south and east to west. We're working with Carmenere from Colchagua, the style is fresh and light. We are looking for restraint and elegance.

Also we are working with co-fermentation in our search for complexity, that is, how fermenting together two varieties from the same *terroir*, can enhance the characteristics of each grape. We find that better balance is achieved with this early relationship that starts with the crushing. This is like the old vineyards that were mixed in the past. We are currently working with Syrah and Viognier, also Merlot and Petit Verdot.

What challenges have you faced as a wine-maker or winery owner?
There is always a new challenge: first establishing the winery in a far away country. Then after realizing the great quality we could get, came another challenge: to sell the wine and convince the consumers that the wines are worth spending their money on. The value of our wines is really great, but Chile is still on the rise, and it is not easy after a certain price point. We then begin our journey onto our sustainable challenges: changing the way we do viticulture was not easy and took years. We started in 2006, and just now after the 2011 harvest, we will be 100 percent certified organic. After that our challenge was to implement the biodynamic approach. Our recent ISO 14001 environmental certification. Well, once you start, there is always something new in our mind and always a new challenge ahead!

What is your winemaking philosophy?

For us at Lapostolle, it is very important to respect the *terroir* and the environment. So we focus on the vineyard and try to keep it simple at the winery: gentle extraction, wild yeast, no corrections, minimal filtration, I can mention among others. We save also energy and reduce our waste, so everybody wins. The idea is to make wines with a sense of place and that are also very gastronomic and food friendly.

What would you hope people say about your wine?

First: that they are delicious! And then, that our wines are elegant, authentic, and focused.

Do you think that the market should influence winemaking, or do you think that winemaking should influence the market?

Well that is a tricky question: the egg or the chicken type. I think they both influence each other, and it depends on the range/volume. If you are making a range of wines with bigger volumes, then the market is important and needs to be taken into account, but keeping your personal touch is important so that the wine will keep its personality. When you're working with small volume, you can be more creative and avant-garde, because in the end, your friends and family will have to drink it!

Besides your own wine, what are some of your favorite wines? What do you like about them?

I prefer wines with an elegant personality. Recently I have enjoyed Angelus 2000, Chave 1991, Harlan Estate 2001. I always loved Leflaive Puligny Montrachet, Meursault Perriere Leroy, Haut Brion, Tertre Roteboeuf, Clos des Papes (both *blanc et rouge*). It is funny because wines reflect the personality of their soil, but most of the time they are produced by people who I like and/or admire.

What is your opinion on screwcap versus cork closures?

I think it is great to have the alternative of choosing which closure you can use. Of course, cork is more natural and has the romantic side. But for wines you will enjoy young and you want to keep the aromatics, the screwcap is a great alternative, and you are sure to avoid cork-taint problems.

If you could invite anyone from history, living or dead, to your home for dinner, who would it be? What food would you serve? What wine would you serve?

Well we just found out that Catherine Middleton at her pre-wedding dinner with her family enjoyed our Casa Sauvignon Blanc 2011. So, I would invite her and William, to stay in our Lapostolle Residence Relais & Châteaux property and enjoy Chile's wonderful seafood along with our Sauvignon Blanc, as a starter! They both have been to Chile to participate in a teen work experience focusing on remote communities in the south, so they know the country well.

If you were to stay home tonight for a relaxing evening, drinking wine while watching a movie, which movie would you watch? Which wine would you drink? Explain.

It all depends on my mood. With a romantic movie, our Cuvée Alexandre Syrah with its luscious aromas and texture is a very sensual wine. With a thriller, our Cuvée Alexandre Merlot, with its tense freshness and restraint . . . great to go along with the rhythm of a thriller movie!

How do you like to spend your time away from the winery?

Exploring the world with our sons.

Do you collect wine? If so, what is in your cellar?

Yes I do. Our wine cellar is too small now. It is in our chalet in the mountains, and it keeps the wines a little too cool, but always at a constant temperature. So the wines evolve very slowly, which is nice. We try to buy every year, from different regions.

If you weren't involved in wine, what would you be doing?

I would be a landscape designer. I love plants and, in particular, vineyards. I love the places where you can grow vineyards, which are always beautiful. The vineyard has a unique effect: it enhances your passion and serenity at the same time. So if I had not been involved in wine, I would have planted gardens, like my grandfather, who designed the most beautiful private botanical garden in France. Life through the seasons is passionate, and when you grow a plant, you hope it will stay for a long time. Like Colbert, who planted oak forests in France to build ships in the seventeenth century, and now we use those oak trees to produce barrels with an exceptional fine grain to age our wines. This oak will now enhance the finesse of our wines. A vivid cycle!

CARLOS COUSIÑO

Carlos's ancestor Matías Cousiño founded the Carlos Cousiño company in 1856. It is among the oldest family-run wineries in Chile. We enjoyed dinner and spirited conversation with Carlos at his family's antique winery in Santiago.

How did you get involved in the world of wine?

I was born into the world. I was raised in the vineyards, and I got fully involved in the management of the winery after the death of my grandfather in 1990 and then even more after my father's death in 1998.

What are some of the biggest changes you have seen in winemaking since you began your career?

The most significant changes were the vinification of individual varieties of grapes that we had in our vineyards, such as Chardonnay and Merlot. We began doing this in the 1980s, but before that time, we did not separate the grapes. On the technical side, the introduction of stainless steel in the late 1970s was significant and then the use of oak barrels in the mid-1980s. In the vineyards, the biggest change has been the increase of planting density and drip irrigation, which we began in 1990.

What are some of the exciting changes that you see happening specifically in your country?

The development of new *terroirs* in areas and regions where we thought that no proper wine could ever be produced.

Are there any new areas that you have identified for potential vineyard sites?

We are constantly looking for new areas where vineyards could be developed in the future. We think Chile presents many very good alternatives.

What challenges have you faced as a winemaker or winery owner?

The challenges have been related to the necessity of considering the whole world as a market for our wines. I would call this the globalization challenge.

What is your winemaking philosophy?

Wine is meant to produce and improve friendship. It therefore has a strong relation to living a common experience, where the table plays a very relevant role. Wine is meant to be enjoyed with food, and both are meant to promote friendship between human beings.

What would you hope people say about your wine?

That they enjoyed the moment in which they were drinking the wine.

Do you think that the market should influence winemaking, or do you think that winemaking should influence the market?

I think it is a great thing that both happen simultaneously. It controls the vanity on both ends.

Besides your own wine, what are some of your favorite wines? What do you like about them?

As we do not produce any, I am always looking for a good Pinot Noir and for Nebbiolo.

What is your opinion on screwcap versus cork closures?

Cork is still part of the enjoyment of wine in a restaurant or a special occasion. For daily drinking, screwcap is fine.

If you could invite anyone from history, living or dead, to your home for dinner, who would it be? What food would you serve? What wine would you serve?

Probably the most fascinating character of modern history is Talleyrand, a bishop in Napoleon's Empire. He then supported the restoration of monarchy under Louis XVIII and negotiated peace in Vienna for the French. Meeting such a character demands more than one course and one wine. To start, a selection of smoked salmon with a slightly oaked Antiguas Reservas Chardonnay. Then some

young veal cutlet with rösti potatoes and vegetables. Lota 2004 seems just the ideal wine for this.

If you were to stay home tonight for a relaxing evening, drinking wine while watching a movie, which movie would you watch? Which wine would you drink? Explain.

La Dolce Vita would be a good choice. A bottle of Sauvignon Gris to start with, according to the crispy and light-hearted beginning. Then some Finis Terrae to help swallow the ending, which would demand a wine with tannins.

How do you like to spend your time away from the winery?

Reading and traveling. As it happens I can do both without having to choose.

Do you collect wine? If so, what is in your cellar?

I do. I have some red Burgundy and just a few bottles of white. I also have a bit more Bordeaux including an '89 Petrus, which I'm longing to drink. I also have some Nebbiolo, but less than what I would like to keep.

If you weren't involved in wine, what would you be doing?

Teaching.

NEW ZEALAND

WINEMAKING DIDN'T START IN NEW Zealand until the middle of the nineteenth century. This isn't surprising, given that the two islands that make up the country are considered to be among the last large land masses to have arisen from the sea, and that it is one of the most recently inhabited countries on the planet. The Maori people, who called New Zealand—or the North Island at least—*Aotearoa*, which means "Land of the Long White Cloud," arrived here about a thousand years ago from Eastern Polynesia. According to Maori legend, the great hero, Maui, fished North Island out of the Pacific Ocean. While there is no consensus on when this happened, geologists agree that the soils of New Zealand are among the youngest on Earth.

It is apparent to anyone who has ever flown over the green islands of New Zealand that its soils are among the most fertile on the planet as well; it has been called the world's largest farm by more than one observer. Its total population is 4.3 million, and one-third of those live in or around Auckland. In fact, 85 percent of New Zealanders (or "Kiwis" as they refer to themselves), live in or near urban areas. The remaining 15 percent share farmland, mountains, beaches, and fjords with a lot of sheep, 40 million at last count, which means that there are 9.3 sheep for each person in the country. It's no wonder then that New Zealand lamb is known worldwide as some of the finest in the world. The reputation of New Zealand's wine is not far behind.

Wine is grown from the top of the North Island to the bottom of the South Island, in eleven distinct winemaking regions. The first European explorer to reach New Zealand, Abel Tasman, arrived in 1642, but it wasn't until 1819 that the first grapevines were planted by Samuel Marsden, an Anglican missionary, in Kerikeri, in Northland, north of Auckland. He believed that prior to converting the Maori to Christianity, he should teach them the enlightening pastime of agriculture. In 1819, Marsden wrote, "New Zealand promises to be very favourable to the vine as far as I can judge at present of the nature of the soil and climate." Although it took years to prove his prediction correct, winemaking in New Zealand is now among the country's major industries.

James Busby, the Scotsman known as the Father of Australian Viticulture, first brought grape cuttings to Waitingi, also in Northland, New Zealand, in 1836. Busby is notable for drafting the Declaration of Independence of New Zealand and the Treaty of Waitangi (which gave Britain dominion over New Zealand while retaining and extending Maori rights), after first studying viticulture and winemaking in Spain and France. As was the case in South America, grapes and winemaking were propagated in New Zealand by the Catholic Church. Bishop Jean Baptiste François Pompallier, the first Catholic Bishop of the South Pacific, brought cuttings from his native France to New Zealand in the mid-nineteenth century. Vineyards were a common sight alongside Catholic mission churches, providing priests with raw material for wine to be used for sacramental purposes and drinking. In 1840 the French government, not recognizing the British claim to New Zealand, established a colony at Akaroa, where early settlers also grew grapes both for the table and to be made into wine. New Zealand's oldest existing vineyard was planted by the Catholic Church in 1851 in Hawke's Bay; today, it is still the site of the highly regarded Mission Estate Winery.

Charles Levet and his son William cleared their property near Rodney of bush and planted grapes—thought today to be the *Vitis labrusca* varietal "Isabella"—in 1863. Theirs was the first commercially successful vineyard and winery in the nation. Most of the early British settlers (as was the case in neighboring Australia, which is over 1,400 miles away) preferred fortified, Port-style wine, which was what the Levet family and their contemporaries provided. Most colonists preferred beer and hard liquor; there was not an enormous demand for wine in nineteenth-century New Zealand. The temperance movement at the time also seems to have made more headway in the young nation than did its incipient wine industry.

Two of the best known vineyards of the late 1800s were William Beetham's in Lansdowne, Wairarapa, and Henry Tiffen's in Hawke's Bay. By the end of the century, Beetham's flourishing winery produced more than eight thousand liters per year, mainly from estate-grown Pinot Noir and Syrah. At the same time, Tiffen was making "Burgundy" from Pinot Noir and Pinot Meunier and "Claret" from Cabernet Sauvignon and Malbec. Both men's wines came to the attention of Romeo Bragato, a viticulturist from Istria who visited Australia and New Zealand in 1895 after receiving a degree in viticulture and enology in Italy—the man later appointed New Zealand's Government Viticulturist from 1902 through 1909. Bragato thought both growing conditions and many of the wines he first encountered in New Zealand to be of very high quality, and many of the subsequent advances in viticultural and winemaking technique in the early twentieth century are attributed to him.

Bragato thought of himself as Italian, but he was from the coastal region of Istria, which is now part of Croatia. It is from here that a large influx of immigrants arrived in New Zealand in the 1890s, to work in the gum fields near Auckland, digging up fossilized tree resin, which the Maori use for jewelry, chewing, and tattoo pigment but which also has a commercial use in varnish. The Croatians first planted vineyards for their own use and then began producing wine for sale. Some of New Zealand's finest wineries are still run by the descendants of Croatian transplants, including the Brajkovich family's Kumeu River, Sir George Fistonich's Villa Maria, and the Babich family's eponymous Babich Winery.

Laws prohibiting or limiting the sale of alcohol, including wine, were in effect in New Zealand to some degree from 1836 until the 1960s. During that time, wine could be purchased only in hotels; when the restrictions were lifted, it could be enjoyed in restaurants, taverns, and cabarets. New waves of European immigration combined with a burgeoning middle class traveling overseas had begun to expose the people of New Zealand to the culture of drinking wine; at the same time, a handful of small producers and one very large producer—McWilliam's, an Australian family-owned business—had been slowly improving the quality of domestic wine. In 1973, Britain entered the European Economic Community and was no longer reliant on meat and dairy products from New Zealand. With a decrease in overseas demand for its traditional agricultural output, farmland was converted to vineyards almost overnight, and many farmers entered the business of "contract grape growing" for large wineries.

Another Croatian immigrant, Ivan Yukich, had planted his first vines near Auckland in 1934. With his sons Maté and Frank, Ivan started Montana Wines in 1961; in 1973, the company expanded into Gisborne and Marlborough. Along with McWilliam's, which had by then merged with McDonald's Wines, Montana dominated the domestic industry. Today, Montana is known as Brancott Estate, and they produce wine at varying price points under a large number of labels. It is claimed that Montana's 1973 Marlborough Sauvignon Blanc ushered in the country's modern wine industry. Around the same time, Montana was also one of the first producers in New Zealand to include the vintage and grape variety on the wine label. As Sauvignon Blanc and other European varieties gained traction, existing vineyards growing Isabella were replanted with Chardonnay and Riesling.

"The Land of the Long White Cloud" is 1,600 kilometers (994 miles) long. With a total area of 268,680 square kilometers (103,768 square miles), it is approximately two-thirds the size of the state of California. North Island, the smaller of its two main bodies of land, holds 75 percent of the country's population, as well as six of its wine-producing regions. From north to south, they are Northland, Auckland, Waikato/Bay of Plenty, Gisborne, Hawke's Bay, and Wairarapa. The sparsely populated South Island is home to the magnificent Southern Alps and Aoraki/Mount Cook, which at 3,754 meters (12,316 feet) is New Zealand's tallest mountain. The South Island is also home to five winegrowing regions: Nelson, Marlborough, Canterbury/Waipara, Waitaki Valley, and Central Otago. Including its many small islands, New Zealand has 15,134 kilometers (9,398 miles) of coastline, providing for the maritime influence so prevalent in its vineyard area.

Besides Sauvignon Blanc, New Zealand is also known for Pinot Noir, Chardonnay, Merlot, Syrah, Pinot Gris, and Riesling. If Marlborough Sauvignon Blanc is what put this lush island nation on the world wine map, exquisite Pinot Noir, Bordeaux blends, and white aromatic varietals will keep it there. Sauvignon Blanc is still the number one varietal, making up 65 percent of all grapes grown, and Marlborough retains its hold on production, accounting for 68 percent of all the wine made in New Zealand. At the same time, some of the most exciting winemaking takes place at the extremes, from the mountainous slopes of Central Otago, where Pinot Noir reigns, to Northland, home to New Zealand's first vineyards, where in addition to Cabernet Sauvignon and Merlot blends, richly scented Viognier and Pinot Gris are making their presence known.

New Zealand's annual rainfall is on the high side: it ranges between 640 millimeters, or 25 inches, and 1,500 millimeters, or 59 inches, depending on region, and on average is evenly spaced throughout the year. One would expect that this would create problems (or would lead to overspraying to deal with pests and mildew), but just the opposite is true. As a whole, the New Zealand wine industry recognizes its obligation to maintain the unspoiled environment that the nation enjoys, as evidenced by the New Zealand Winegrowers' Sustainability Policy, which was announced in 2007. Under this initiative, it is expected that all vineyards and wineries in the nation will operate using sustainable practices (monitored by an independent authorizing body) by 2012. As of this writing, 94 percent of wineries and vineyards are participating. There is also a strong movement toward holistic and organic vineyard management throughout the country. It is predicted that by the end of this decade, 20 percent of vineyards in New Zealand will be certified organic.

The first decade of this millennium saw exponential growth in the New Zealand wine sector. From 2000 through the end of 2010, total number of wineries increased from 358 to 672, while total planted hectares more than tripled, growing from 10,197 hectares (25,197 acres) to 33,408 hectares (82,553 acres) in just nine years. With this increase came a corresponding jump in output; 60.2 million liters of wine were produced in 2000, jumping to 190.0 million liters in 2009. Domestic wine consumption grew as well: At the beginning of the decade, the average Kiwi drank 17.3 liters of wine, and 10.8 of that was from New Zealand. Nine years later, the total average per person was 21.1 liters annually, and 13.0 of those liters were New Zealand wine.

Total wine exports in 2011 were US$915 million from 155 million liters; just over one-third of that went to the United Kingdom, and slightly less than one-third went to Australia (where New Zealand Sauvignon Blanc is loved by consumers and loathed by winemakers in equal measure), with just slightly less than one-third going to the United Kingdom. About 20 percent of exported wine went to the United States. Approximately 5 percent of annual exports was destined for Canada, and smaller but still important amounts were shipped to The Netherlands, Denmark, Germany, Ireland, and Japan.

Soils in most New Zealand regions are alluvial, mainly consisting of sandstone, clay, and gravel left by receding rivers. The maritime climate provides for cooler summers and more moderate winters than might be expected at latitudes from 36 degrees south in Northland to 45 degrees south in Central Otago. To place these latitudes into a Northern Hemisphere perspective, Northland is roughly equivalent to Jerez, Spain, the home of Sherry, while Central Otago is comparable to France's Bordeaux region. It is not latitude alone that creates an environment suitable for the growing of a particular grape, a fact which is clearly borne out by the abundance of Pinot Noir in the mineral-enriched silty, loam soils of Central Otago, rather than Cabernet Sauvignon and Merlot.

The New Zealand Food Safety Authority regulates the wine industry, including what information may appear on a label. Within New Zealand, when a grape variety is listed on the label of a single-varietal wine, the wine must contain at least 75 percent of that variety. For wines that are to be exported to the United States or the European Union, the amount of the stated variety must be 85 percent. When a label lists two varieties in a blend, they must be stated in the order of volume; for example, a bottle labeled "Merlot-Cabernet Sauvignon" will contain more Merlot than Cabernet Sauvignon. When a place is designated on a bottle, such as a region, subregion, or vineyard appellation, a minimum of 75 percent of the grapes must be from the stated area.

New Zealand was among the first countries to bottle its wine using alternative closures. Today, 95 percent of the country's wines are bottled under screwcap.

MAJOR GRAPE VARIETIES

CABERNET FRANC

Cabernet Franc lends dark fruit flavors of cherry, plum, and blackberry with violet notes and a strong dose of green pepper and earth to Bordeaux-style blends. It is grown here in small amounts, totaling only 1 percent of New Zealand's vineyards. The majority of it—more than 80 percent—is found in the Hawke's Bay region, with the balance coming from Auckland, Northland, Nelson, Wairarapa, and Waipara. It was among James Busby's original cuttings brought to Australia and New Zealand. Cabernet Franc covered 161 hectares (398 acres) in 2010 and is expected stay at that amount through 2012.

CABERNET SAUVIGNON

Cabernet Sauvignon accounts for 2 percent of New Zealand's grapes. Ninety-two percent of that is farmed in Hawke's Bay, primarily for blends. It is rarely seen as a single varietal and increasingly plays second fiddle to Merlot in high-end "icon" wines. Expect flavors of plum, cassis, graphite, and mocha from Hawke's Bay, with a lighter, more floral style coming out of Auckland and Northland. It is also grown in Marlborough, Nelson, Wairarapa, and Waipara. James Busby is responsible for bringing this small, dark, thick-skinned variety to Oceania. In 2010, there were 519 hectares (1,282 acres) of Cabernet Sauvignon in New Zealand and an increase of 2 hectares (5 acres) is expected by 2012.

CHARDONNAY

A world traveler, Chardonnay made its way to the South Pacific with James Busby's 1832 saplings, was lost later in that century due to phylloxera, and remerged in the 1970s with the advent of the modern wine industry. About two-thirds of the Chardonnay grown here is made into still wine, while the remainder is vinified into sparkling. Flavors of green apple, citrus, and tropical fruits can swing toward buttered toast with aging in oak barrels. Twelve percent of New Zealand's vines bear this round, green-skinned grape, which grows in conical clusters. Gisborne is home to 39 percent of New Zealand's Chardonnay, followed by Marlborough, which accounts for 29 percent of the varietal, and Hawke's Bay, with 25 percent. The balance is grown in the other seven regions; each produces a modest amount. There were 3,685 hectares (9,106 acres) of New Zealand Chardonnay in 2010; a slight decrease, to 3,792 hectares (9,370 acres), is anticipated by 2012.

GEWÜRZTRAMINER

Gewürztraminer makes up roughly 1 percent of New Zealand's wine production. A native of northern Italy that is also widely planted in Germany and Alsace, Gewürztraminer is noted for its bright acidity and floral notes, especially rose petal. About half of this aromatic varietal can be found in Gisborne, with another quarter coming from Marlborough. About 12 percent of total New Zealand Gewürztraminer is grown in Hawke's Bay and every other region has at least a miniscule portion of cultivation dedicated to this small, pink grape. In 2010, 314 hectares (776 acres) of Gewürztraminer grew here; growers predict a decline to 290 hectares (717 acres) within two years.

MALBEC

Over 80 percent of New Zealand's plantings of this Bordeaux variety is grown in Hawke's Bay. Total plantings are small though, making up a bit less than 1 percent of viticultural production, but its strong tannic structure and flavors of cherry, blackberry, violets, and spice are highly valued by winemakers seeking balance in their blends. It is also found to some degree in Auckland, Gisborne, Marlborough, and Nelson. Malbec is on an upswing; 161 hectares (398 acres) of the grape are expected to be planted by 2012, compared to 157 hectares (388 acres) in 2010.

MERLOT

Merlot is the second most popular red grape in New Zealand; 4 percent of the grapes grown here are this small, dark variety, which takes its name from the French word for "blackbird." Primary flavors are cherry, blueberry, elderberry, eucalyptus, and mint. It is bottled on its own to a small degree, but is mostly mixed with other varieties to create Bordeaux-style blends. A predominantly Right Bank–style is currently in vogue, meaning Merlot gets to stand in the spotlight while the more tannic Cabernet Sauvignon sings backup. The vineyards of Hawke's Bay produce 88 percent of New Zealand's Merlot. While it is found throughout the country, the only otherwise notable amounts of Merlot grow in Gisborne, Marlborough, and Auckland. Merlot covered 1,371 hectares (3,388 acres) of land in 2010; it is anticipated that in 2012 we will find 1,403 hectares (3,467 acres) of Merlot.

PINOT GRIS

Known in Italy as Pinot Grigio, Pinot Gris grapes can range in color from bluish-gray to light brownish-pink; in fact, you may see berries of varying hue within the same pinecone-shaped cluster. French for "gray," gris refers to the grayish color the grapes can have, although it is often appropriate for the silver cast the wine may take on in the glass as well. Its aromatic scent and taste can include lemon, apple, and pear, with sharp minerality and a light floral undertone. Five percent of New Zealand's grapes are Pinot Gris; of which 35 percent grows in Marlborough. Hawke's Bay and Gisborne are each responsible for a little more than 21 percent of total Pinot Gris cultivation. Found in every wine region, it is also making an impact in Auckland, Wairarapa, Nelson, Waipara, and Central Otago. Pinot Gris's 1,763 hectares (4,356 acres) as of 2010 are likely to remain unchanged in 2012.

PINOTAGE

This South African native is a cross between Pinot Noir and Cinsault. Total percentage of Pinotage in New Zealand is 0.5 percent, yet it seems to be a variety that winemakers are excited about. Its flavor profile trends toward blackberry and mulberry, with notes of smoke and leather as well. About half of New Zealand's Pinotage grows in Gisborne and another quarter in Marlborough. Scattered plantings appear throughout the North Island, with tiny appearances in the southern Waipara and Central Otago regions as well. The grape covered 74 hectares (183 acres) in 2010; total coverage is predicted to drop to 68 hectares (168 acres) by 2012.

PINOT NOIR

The most widely planted red grape in New Zealand, Pinot Noir blankets 15 percent of all the vineyards in the nation. Known worldwide as the red grape of Burgundy, this dark purple berry produces wine of a medium cherry to garnet red. Flavors of cherry, blackberry, espresso, and orange blossom are enhanced by New Zealand's maritime climate, dry summers, and cool nights. In the past 15 years, total plantings have increased almost ninefold, to a total of 4,777 hectares (11,804 acres). Although Central Otago Pinot Noir has everybody talking, it is grown in almost equal amounts here and in Hawke's Bay—each accounts for about 17 percent of total Pinot Noir plantings. However, Marlborough is home to the majority of New Zealand's Pinot Noir: 44 percent of it is grown here. More than 7 percent of Pinot Noir is from Wairarapa and Gisborne, with Nelson and Waipara each providing the country with 4 percent of its total. Pinot Noir is showing distinct characteristics in each region. From Central Otago, it tends to exhibit rich herbal notes, bright berry flavors, and a strong tannic structure. Wairarapa Pinot Noir shows off the variety's denser, more full-bodied style, while both Marlborough and Nelson Pinot Noirs are known for their full fruit and tight structure. Pinot Noir from Waipara runs more toward the pepper and spice characteristics associated with the grape. About one-quarter of New Zealand Pinot Noir is made in the sparkling style; the remaining 75 percent is vinified into still wine. From the grape's 4,777 hectares (11,804 acres) in 2010, two-year gains will bring it to 4,828 hectares (11,930 acres) by 2012.

RIESLING

Riesling can run the gamut from bone dry to sticky sweet, but its flavors of lemon, lime, apple, light spice, and honey shine through whatever the style. New Zealand Riesling is best known in its slightly off-dry version, with bright acidity and crisp mineral notes making it a good match for the Pacific Rim cuisine of the country. Bearing bulbous, green-yellow fruit, Riesling thrives in cold-weather regions. It makes up only 3 percent of total New Zealand wine production, but as in other parts of the world it appears to be the variety that

winemakers favor when filling their own glass. Forty-six percent of New Zealand Riesling is grown in Marlborough, followed by Waipara, which grows 36 percent of this aromatic varietal. Nelson and Central Otago both produce around 6 percent. Riesling is found in some small amount in all of New Zealand's other wine regions. Riesling is on the (slight) rise: by 2012, 1,009 hectares (2,496 acres) of New Zealand's vineyards will be planted with it, as opposed to the 986 hectares (2,436 acres) which existed in 2010.

SAUVIGNON BLANC

Sauvignon Blanc is far and away the number one variety in the country: 65 percent of all of the grapes grown on these two large islands are Sauvignon Blanc. Known worldwide for its bold style, Sauvignon Blanc from New Zealand has full-on tropical and citrus fruit flavors, such as passion fruit, mango, lemon, lime, and grapefruit, with pungent flavors of green pepper, fresh cut grass, and chopped green herbs. The variety that alerted the rest of the world to New Zealand's winemaking capabilities was first planted in Auckland in the early 1970s, making its way to Marlborough in 1976. The first vintage produced in any real quantity was 1980; in just over 30 years, New Zealand Sauvignon Blanc, now as ubiquitous as Band-Aids or Kleenex, has taken the world by storm. From 2003 to 2010 it increased from 4,516 hectares (11,159 acres) to 16,910 hectares (41,786 acres). Marlborough is home to 90 percent of New Zealand's Sauvignon Blanc vineyards, which means that to most of the world, Marlborough Sauvignon Blanc is New Zealand Sauvignon Blanc. Just under 5 percent comes from Hawke's Bay, 2.5 percent is grown in Nelson, and although the percentages are tiny elsewhere, plantings by region still outnumber almost every other varietal. Sauvignon Blanc takes its name from the French words for "savage" and "white." Its wild nature shines through in most bottlings from New Zealand. Predictions indicate that by 2012, there will be 17,297 hectares (42,742 acres) of Sauvignon Blanc thriving in the vineyards of New Zealand.

SÉMILLON

With all of the focus on Sauvignon Blanc in New Zealand, it was only a matter of time before this Bordeaux native—which has also made great inroads in Australia—began to be cultivated by savvy winemakers interested in utilizing the weight, structure, and longevity that Sémillon adds to blends. A fairly constant 185 hectares (475 acres) are cultivated in scattered pockets around the country, and although it is rarely seen bottled as a single varietal, that may change as the reputation

of New Zealand's aromatic whites gains traction at home and abroad. Young versions brim with flavors of tropical fruit and lemon-lime, while barrel and bottle aging add notes of toast, honey, and herbs. Late-harvest versions, often with a touch of botrytis, are seen in small numbers as well.

SYRAH

Very little Syrah grows in New Zealand—it makes up 1 percent of cultivated vineyards in the nation—but the small amount of Rhône-style red it produces wows critics and consumers alike. Seventy-eight percent of New Zealand Syrah is planted in Hawke's Bay, where it exhibits intense fruit flavors of plum and cassis, backed by strong tones of black pepper and anise. Just over 8 percent is grown in the Auckland region, particularly on Waiheke Island. Small but still noteworthy amounts of Syrah are cultivated in Northland, Gisborne, Wairarapa, Marlborough, and Waipara. Unlike neighboring Australia, where the same grape is called Shiraz, New Zealand Syrah tends to be a more elegant French style as opposed to the well-known (though not necessarily representative) Aussie fruit bombs. A slight uptick in Syrah's proliferation is envisioned over the two years from 2010 through 2012, growing from 297 hectares (734 acres) to 300 hectares (741 acres).

VIOGNIER

Bearing a perfumed aroma and flavors of apricot, white peach, honeysuckle, and spice, Viognier—far from its home in France's Rhône Valley—has made small but still substantial inroads into New Zealand. Making up less than 1 percent of total plantings, Viognier seems to be overrepresented on restaurant wine lists throughout the country and with good reason: its delicate flavors and bright acidity are well matched with the fresh seafood and Asian spices of this Pacific island nation. Look for bottles from Gisborne, Hawke's Bay, Marlborough, and Auckland. For an insight into Viognier's growing popularity, consider this: from 2010 through 2012, plantings are expected to increase from 163 hectares (403 acres) to 204 hectares (504 acres), a gain of 25 percent.

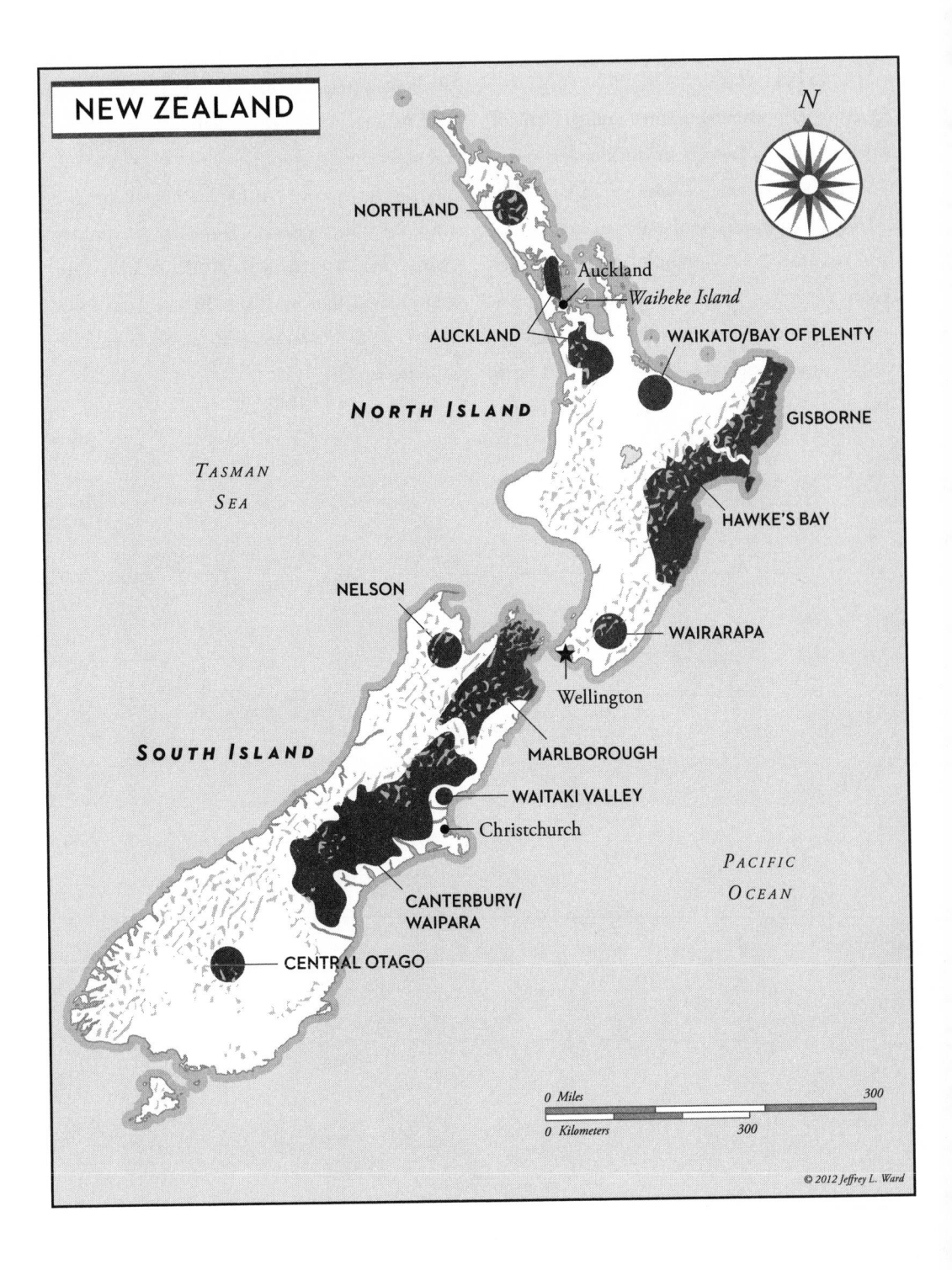

NEW ZEALAND

N

NORTHLAND

Auckland

Waiheke Island

AUCKLAND

WAIKATO/BAY OF PLENTY

North Island

GISBORNE

*Tasman
Sea*

HAWKE'S BAY

NELSON

WAIRARAPA

Wellington

South Island

MARLBOROUGH

WAITAKI VALLEY

Christchurch

*Pacific
Ocean*

CANTERBURY/
WAIPARA

CENTRAL OTAGO

0 Miles   300

0 Kilometers   300

© 2012 Jeffrey L. Ward

346

WINE REGIONS

NORTH ISLAND

NORTHLAND

The northernmost winemaking region on the North Island and New Zealand's only subtropical region, Northland boasted a total of 14 wineries in 2010, double the number it had in 2000. This is the area where Reverend Samuel Marsden planted New Zealand's first grapevines, in 1819, in the Bay of Islands. This is also where the original Croatian immigrants settled and began making wine at the end of the nineteenth century; many wineries and families in the wine business trace their heritage to Northland. In Northland, one is always within 50 kilometers (31 miles) of the sea, and the climate is humid and warm. Northland has the highest average temperatures of any New Zealand wine region. Maximum altitudes are 150 meters (492 feet) above sea level, and a substrata of clay is overlaid with clay and loam soils. Chardonnay is the most widely planted white variety, followed by Pinot Gris and Viognier. Syrah, Cabernet Sauvignon, Merlot, and Pinotage are grown here as well. The western portion of the region, toward

Kaitaia, receives 650 millimeters, or 26 inches, per summer, and to the east, near the Bay of Islands, summer rainfall averages 860 millimeters, or 34 inches.

AUCKLAND

Auckland is known as "The City of Sails," and with good reason: the main part of this city of 1.3 million people sits on an isthmus between the Tasman Sea's Manukau Harbor and the Waitemata Harbor on the Pacific Ocean side, and there truly are sails just about everywhere you look. Auckland's original winemaking subregions—Henderson, Huapai, and Kumeu, which are northwest of the urban center—have a long history of grape growing and winemaking. Croatian gum diggers established many of the wineries in this area. As suburbs, office parks, and industry have encroached on farmland, much vineyard land to the northwest of Auckland has been lost, although the total amount of land planted in the Auckland region has increased, from 461 hectares (1,139 acres) in 2003 to 543 hectares (1,342 acres) in 2010. It is expected to continue climbing too (to 573 hectares, or 1,416 acres, by 2012) due to newer plantings on Waiheke Island and in Matakana and Clevedon.

Waiheke Island is a quick and pleasant ferry ride from the city of Auckland. It was planted in the 1980s with Bordeaux varietals, but since then Syrah and Chardonnay have taken root here as well. Matekana is northeast of Auckland's center and is becoming known for its maritime-influenced Chardonnay and Pinot Gris, as well as Merlot, Cabernet Sauvignon, and Syrah. To the south of the city is Clevedon, the newest area in the region, where viticulturists are mostly working with French varieties, but pockets of Nebbiolo, Sangiovese, and Montepulciano are now found in its gently rolling hills.

Across the region as a whole, Chardonnay is the number one grape grown, covering 121 hectares (299 acres). Merlot, planted on 84 hectares (208 acres), runs a distant second, and Cabernet Sauvignon places third, with 61 hectares (151 acres) planted. Syrah is the fourth most-planted variety in Auckland, thriving on 44 hectares (109 acres), closely followed by Pinot Gris and Cabernet Franc, each of which is grown on 38 hectares (94 acres). The king of New Zealand varieties, Sauvignon Blanc, is a poor country cousin in the Auckland region with only 35 hectares (86 acres) of it farmed here. Auckland's soils are both alluvial and volcanic, with a mix of clay and sandstone. It enjoys warm, humid summers and relatively high rainfall; the northeast of the region receives about 560 millimeters, or 22 inches, per summer, while Waikeke Island averages around 630 millimeters, or 25 inches, each summer. There are 111 wineries in the region. Many of Auckland's wineries vinify local grapes as well as those brought in from other regions.

BABICH WINES

Babich Road, Henderson, Auckland,
+64 9 833 7859,
www.babichwines.co.nz

Established by Croatian immigrant Joseph Babich—who planted his first vineyard in 1912 at the age of 16—Babich is one of the oldest and most respected names in New Zealand wine. Today it owns vineyards—under the direction of second- and third-generation family members—in Auckland's Henderson Valley, Hawke's Bay, Marlborough, and Gisborne. Indeed a staggering array of wines is produced at its winery in Henderson Valley (where all bottling takes place) and at its joint-venture Rapaura Vintners facility in Marlborough. Price and style run the gamut from easy drinking and easy on the wallet to sophisticated, special-occasion wines. Name a variety planted in New Zealand and Babich crafts it into fine wine. Babich Marlborough Sauvignon Blanc 2010 is a nice mouthful of mixed fruit, with flavors of lime, passionfruit, and pear joined by a dash of chopped green herbs. The Patriarch 2009, a blend of 51 percent Cabernet Sauvignon, 24 percent Malbec, and 24 percent Cabernet Franc, is named in honor of founder Joseph Babich. Made from select Hawke's Bay grapes and aged in oak for 13 months, The Patriarch delivers everything you would expect from a super-premium, Bordeaux-style blend. Intense black cherry and blueberry are joined on the nose by anise and a touch of tobacco, all of which carry through on both the palate and to the lengthy finish.

as three more vineyards on this small island, which is a short ferry ride from downtown Auckland. Under the careful eye of vineyard manager Heike Sonnenschein, they have carefully matched varieties to island *terroir* in their Oakura Bay, Whakarite Bay, and Jasa Vineyards. In addition to single varietals and blends, they press their own olive oil and produce honey, which are available at the charming tasting room. Lunch is available on the shaded wooden deck with views of the vineyards and bay. Deep red Kennedy Point Syrah 2009 exhibits strong flavors of cherry and black pepper, supported by notes of shaved truffle and baking spices. It has nice balance of smooth tannins and refreshing acidity. Kennedy Point Cuvée Eve Chardonnay 2009 has a fruity nose of cantaloupe and sliced pear. On the palate these delicate fruit flavors mingle with lightly buttered toast and a dollop of orange marmalade.

KENNEDY POINT

44 Donald Bruce Road, Waiheke Island, Auckland,
+64 9 372 5600,
www.kennedypointvineyard.com

The first certified organic vineyard on Waiheke Island, Kennedy Point Vineyard was planted with Bordeaux varietals and Syrah in 1996. Since then owners Neal Kunimura and Susan McCarthy have added Chardonnay, as well

KUMEU RIVER

550 State Highway 16, Kumeu, Auckland,
+64 9 412 8415,
www.kumeuriver.co.nz

Maté Brajkovich, his sisters, and his parents emigrated from Croatia in 1937. They began growing grapes on a small plot of land and Brajkovich Winery was born. Maté married a lovely woman named Melba, who to this day remains an elegant force of nature. The family later changed the name to San Marino Vineyards in honor of the Dalmatian saint, and in 1986, Maté and Melba's children, Michael, Milan, Paul, and Marijana, changed the winery name once again, this time to Kumeu River, in homage to the river surrounding the property. The winery is only 30 minutes from downtown Auckland and is certainly worth a visit to taste world-class wines that have been named one of *Wine Spectator's* Top 100 Wines, and other journalists have called "the best Chardonnays in New Zealand." The head winemaker is Michael, the oldest son and New Zealand's first Master of Wine. He says, "There are nine grandchildren ranging from 8 to 18 years of age, six boys and three girls, and we're hoping that one, two, or nine of them become involved in the family business." The winery "uses no irrigation at all, and it is also important to note that we only use wild yeast fermentation. We have also been using screwcap since September 2001 and have never looked back." His youngest brother, Paul, a former cricket player, entered the business as the export director in 1990 and is striving "to get the business to about 50 percent export market and 50 percent domestic market."

Kumeu River Pinot Gris 2009 is a light straw color, with aromas of lemon, citrus, and orange flowers. In the mouth there is a fair bit of residual sweetness, but it retains a clean dry finish. Kumeu River Village Chardonnay 2008 is pale straw colored and according to Michael, "It is made in two-thirds stainless steel and one-third old barrels, so there's no real oak influence. It is our desire to make this wine a more Chablis-style Chardonnay." It has clean lemon and lime blossom aromas with a crisp, clean, mineral-driven finish. In contrast, Kumeu River Estate Chardonnay 2008 is medium straw, with aromas of toasted brioche, lemon curd, and a light floral top note. It is elegant and Burgundian in style and has a voluptuous presence on the palate with an elegant, long finish. In speaking about this wine, Michael said, "The Estate Chardonnay is what we have always been about, it is 100 percent barrel fermented, using 20 percent new oak and it is made from vineyards all over the Kumeu region. We were the first winemakers in this region to allow our wines to go through malolactic fermentation, but we always strive to maintain freshness."

MAN O' WAR

Waiheke Island, Auckland,
+64 9 303 9677,
www.manowarvineyards.co.nz

With 60 hectares (150 acres) of small-parcel vineyards spread across Waiheke Island, Man O' War is named for a point on the eastern edge of the island that Captain James Cook, in 1769, designated as a water and wood station, noting that the tall kauri trees would be perfect to make masts for the Royal Navy. Family-owned since 1993, Man O' War has vines that are divided among 90 hillside plots, where the Spencer family and viticultural manager Matt Allen raise Syrah, Sauvignon Blanc, Merlot, Cabernet Franc, Malbec, Chardonnay, Pinot Gris, Petit Verdot, Cabernet Sauvignon, Sémillon, and Viognier. These are bottled both as single varietals and as sophisticated Bordeaux-style blends. Winemaker Duncan McTavish produces two labels, the entry-level Man O' War and the flagship Black Label wines, which are named for battleships. Man O' War Chardonnay 2009 has the scent of Granny Smith apple and baking bread; these continue onto the palate, where they are joined by citrus fruits, lightly buttered toast, and a touch of flint. From the Black Label line, Man O' War Dreadnought Syrah 2009 is deep black cherry, with a nose of bright fruit and layers of turned earth, smoked meat, and white pepper. In the mouth the fruit comes across as black cherry and blueberry, and black pepper morphs into spice for a balanced finish.

MUDBRICK

Church Bay Road, Oneroa, Waiheke Island,
+64 9 372 9050,
www.mudbrick.co.nz

Our rainy boat ride from Auckland's main pier to Waiheke Island was cold, wet, and miserable. Had we been in the Caribbean, we would have called this a tropical storm, or even a hurricane, but the moment we pulled into the island's idyllic harbor, the sun appeared and dried our wet clothing. Waiheke Island is home to a handful of wineries, but Mudbrick's wines and award-wining restaurant—with stunning views over the Hauraki Gulf—should not be missed. Named because the original house, winery, and barn were made from mud-colored bricks, Mudbrick was started in 1992 by Robyn and Nicholas Jones. They were both in their mid-twenties then and had just completed university studies. They decided that they wanted a "better" lifestyle than working as accountants in a nine-to-five Auckland office environment. Their Mudbrick Syrah 2008 is indigo-ink colored, with a nose of baking spices, currants, and cassis. In the mouth it is big and round with a finish of fine-ground white pepper. Mudbrick Reserve Cabernet Sauvignon Merlot 2009 is garnet colored, with aromas of red berries, anise, and a touch of saddle leather. On the palate it is big and fruity and finishes with a touch of spice. Mudbrick Shepherd's Point Syrah 2009 has aromas of black raspberry, black cherry, and purple flowers and delights with a soft, round, tannic finish.

NOBILO

45 Station Road, Huapai, Auckland,
+64 9 412 6662,
www.nobilo.co.nz

Nikola Nobilo emigrated to New Zealand from Korcula Island, Croatia, in 1943 and established his family winery in the Auckland area. His wines gained national and international recognition, and he was awarded an Order of the British Empire Medal in 1994. Nikola passed away in 2007 at the age of 94. The company is now owned and managed by the Constellation NZ group. We had a chance to

NOBILO ICON

MARLBOROUGH
SAUVIGNON BLANC
2010

NEW ZEALAND

meet senior winemaker David Edmonds, cook a meal together, and taste his wines. Edmonds has extensive international experience and has worked in both Germany and California. Nobilo Icon Marlborough Pinot Noir 2009 is deep garnet red, with aromas of black plums, cherries, and cocoa. In the mouth it is big and bold with complex red and black fruit flavors and a silky smooth tannic finish. Nobilo Icon Marlborough Sauvignon Blanc 2010 is pale yellow with greenish tints and has aromas of tropical fruits, pineapple, and ruby red grapefruit. On the palate it displays excellent structure with crisp acidity. It finishes with tropical fruits and bracing minerality.

PASSAGE ROCK

438 Orapiu Road, Waiheke Island, Auckland,
+64 9 372 7257,
www.passagerockwines.co.nz

David and Veronika Evans-Gardner planted their first vines on Waiheke Island in 1994 and within a few years had produced some of this tiny island's most awarded wines. Estate-grown Syrah, Merlot, Cabernet Sauvignon, Cabernet Franc, Pinot Gris, and Viognier are joined by Chardonnay and Gewürztraminer (sourced from Gisborne) to create fruit-driven wines of pure varietal character. Their label's grapevine wreath design is symbolic of the continuing cycle of the seasons and the combination of elements that go into their wonderful wine. The on-site café here is a lovely spot to kick back and enjoy a light lunch paired with house-made wine and beautiful views. Passage Rock Pinot Gris 2010 exhibits a clean nose of pear and apple notes with the faintest hint of spice. On the tongue it tastes of sliced apple and green pear with touches of lemon-scented crème brûlée. Passage Rock Cabernet Sauvignon Merlot Reserve 2008 is deep violet with a bright rim and has a nose of black cherry, cassis, black pepper, clove, and fennel seed. In the mouth it tastes of cassis, stewed plums, cooling herbs, and a smidgeon of asphalt—which dampens the palate momentarily but is brought back to life with a finish of orange rind.

STONYRIDGE VINEYARD

80 Onetangi Road, Waiheke Island, Auckland,
+64 9 372 8766,
www.stonyridge.co.nz

Dr. Stephen White skippered yachts in the Mediterranean and Caribbean, worked in wineries in California and Italy, and fell in love with the wonderful red wines of France, Italy, and California. When he was ready to settle down and make a commitment, he bought land on Waiheke Island, trained in Bordeaux under Peter Sichel, and planted north-facing vineyards growing the "Bordeaux Five," and the "Rhône Three." It is claimed that Stonyridge was the first winery in New Zealand to blend first four and then all five of the Bordeaux varieties: Cabernet Sauvignon, Merlot, Cabernet Franc, Malbec, and Petit Verdot. He was also the first in the country to make a Rhône blend using Grenache, Syrah, and Mourvèdre. A visit to Stonyridge's organic vineyards and restaurant is like a trip to Provence; you can enjoy small plates of food overlooking olive trees and fields of lavender. Stonyridge Pilgrim, a blend with the image of a scallop shell on the label, is named in honor of the pilgrims who pass through the south of France on their way to Santiago de Compostela in Spain. The 2008 is a blend of Syrah, Mourvèdre, and Grenache, with a classic Rhône palate of fruits of the wood, cassis, licorice, and orange zest. Stonyridge Larose 2008, a Cabernet Sauvignon-dominant five varietal Bordeaux blend, has a nose of blackberries, black currant, and Mediterranean herbs that continue onto the palate, where they mingle with anise and hints of dark chocolate before coming to a rich, structured finish.

VILLA MARIA

118 Montgomerie Road, Mangere, Auckland,
+64 9 255 1777,
www.villamaria.co.nz

When George Fistonich founded Villa Maria Winery in 1961, he had no idea what his start-up company would eventually become. He began producing wines from his half-hectare (one-acre) plot in Mangere, and today, Sir George Fistonich—he was knighted in 2009—has vineyards and wineries in four regions around New Zealand and exports to more than fifty countries. It was due to this success that he built a new winery in Auckland, close to the airport, to handle the demands of his domestic and international markets. The winery is in a volcanic basin, which makes it the perfect shape for an outdoor amphitheater. The winery's summer concert series has included big-ticket names such as Simply Red, Diana Krall, Sir Tom Jones (he, incidentally,

was knighted in 2006), and Ronan Keating. The Vineyard Café serves wonderful lunches on the winery's outdoor terrace. We enjoyed the chef's fine cuisine while dining with Sir George and the lovely Lady Gail. It was a perfect late summer afternoon, and the food, wine, and conversation were all delightful. We enjoyed Villa Maria Single Vineyard Ihumatao Verdelho 2008 paired with a locally caught white fish. The wine had lovely floral aromas, with notes of mandarin peel, citrus blossom, jasmine, and ginger. It was complex and textured in the mouth with balanced acidity and a persistent finish. We were honored to have lunch with them again at Aureole, when they visited New York City a few weeks later. We tasted many of Villa Maria's wines and enjoyed them immensely, but we certainly had a few favorites. Villa Maria Cellar Selection Marlborough Chardonnay 2009 is straw yellow, with notes of stone fruits, white peach, and citrus blossoms. In the mouth it is creamy with flavors of cashews and white stone fruits. It finishes with balanced acidity. Villa Maria Single Vineyard Waikahu Chardonnay 2006 is made from fruit grown on the eastern plateau of Maraekakaho and is straw yellow in the glass. It has aromas of flint, stone fruit, and white flowers. On the palate it is creamy and generous before finishing with delightful length.

WAIKATO/BAY OF PLENTY

One of the smallest of New Zealand's wine regions, Waikato/Bay of Plenty is home to 20 wineries and a total of 147 hectares (363 acres) of vines. Both are south of Auckland; Waikato is inland near the small city of Hamilton, while Bay of Plenty is located on the water. The main agricultural pursuit in the area is kiwi fruit. Heavy loam soil layered over clay provides good drainage for this high-rainfall area. Twenty hectares (49 acres) are planted with Chardonnay, 18 hectares (44 acres) with Cabernet Sauvignon, 13 hectares (32 acres) with Sauvignon Blanc, and 10 hectares (25 acres) with Merlot. The remaining 60 percent of the region's vines bear a host of international varieties; within reason, if you can name a grape, there's a good chance a small amount of it is growing here. Average summer rainfall is 700 millimeters, or 28 inches.

MILLS REEF

143 Moffat Road, Bethlehem, Tauranga,
+64 7 576 8824,
www.millsreef.co.nz

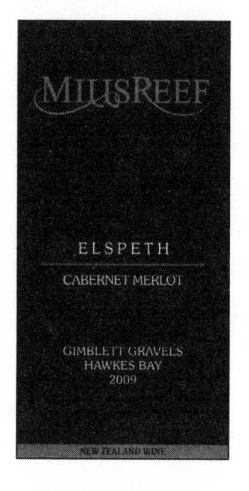

Although most of its fruit comes from Hawke's Bay, the visitor experience at Mills Reef—with the excellent Bordeaux-style and Syrah wine—is worth the trip. Owner/winemaker Tim Preston and winemaker Paul Dawick produce a wide range of wines from the entry-level Mills Reef, mid-tier Reserve, to the premium Elspeth range. The entry level includes varietal Riesling, Sauvignon Blanc, and Chardonnay, plus a blend of Merlot and Cabernet Sauvignon; the Mills Reef Reserve adds varietal bottlings of Viognier, Pinot Gris, Merlot, and a Merlot/Malbec blend to the mix; while the Elspeth line focuses on Chardonnay, Syrah, Cabernet Sauvignon, Merlot, and a blend of the latter two. The entire range is available for tasting at the picture-perfect Art Deco style tasting room near Tauranga. Mills Reef Elspeth Chardonnay 2009, made with estate-grown Gimblett Gravels fruit, has a rich, sensuous mouthfeel and flavors of white peach, nectarine, mango, and lightly toasted almonds. Mills Reef Elspeth Cabernet/Merlot 2009 blends 52 percent Cabernet Sauvignon and 48 percent Merlot, also from Hawke's Bay, into an inky purple wine, with a nose of blackberry, cassis, and mocha. The palate adds a generous dose of Christmas spices and a silky finish.

GISBORNE

On the east coast of the North Island, southeast of Auckland and north of Hawke's Bay, Gisborne is the first city in the world to see the rising sun each day. It is also where the first Maori *Harouta*, or "large canoe," landed—and where Captain James Cook first set foot on New Zealand soil, in 1769. The first commercial vines in Gisborne were planted by the German winemaker Friedrich Wohnsiedler in 1921, but it took another 50 years before viticulture caught on. Today, it is the third largest wine region in the country, after Marlborough and Hawke's Bay, with a total of 24 wineries, plus 87 farmers who grow grapes. Gisborne is divided into several subregions, each with its own distinct microclimate and slightly varied

soil type. The main areas of Gisborne are the Golden Slope, Central Valley, Ormond Valley, Waipaoa, Patutahi, the Patutahi Plateau, and Manutuke. The main soil type is clay loam. Summers bring long hours of sunshine; annual rainfall averages 520 millimeters, or 20 inches.

Total planted vineyard area in Gisborne as of 2010 is 2,083 hectares (5,147 acres). This is expected to decline slightly over coming years, as some varietals that have fallen out of favor are removed and then replanted, but over time totals will remain the same or increase. Chardonnay is far and away the star grape of the region, flourishing on 1,137 hectares (2,810 acres), or 53 percent of planted vineyards. Aromatic varieties are grown here as well; Pinot Gris is the second most abundant grape, on 175 hectares (432 acres), and Gewürztraminer is number four, on 109 hectares (269 acres)—right behind the region's only red grape of note, Merlot, which holds its own on 119 hectares (294 acres). Muscat varieties cover 109 hectares (269 acres) of land. Pinot Noir grows on 81 hectares (200 acres)—but 75 percent of it is made into white sparkling wine, with only 16 hectares (40 acres) dedicated to still red wine. Sauvignon Blanc covers 78 hectares (193 acres), Sémillon 77 hectares (190 acres)—the latter vinified into both an off-dry style and botrytized sweet wine. Pinotage is planted on 33 hectares (82 acres).

MILLTON VINEYARD

119 Papatu Road, Manutuke, Gisborne,
+64 6 862 8680,
www.millton.co.nz

James and Annie Millton started making wine from their estate-grown grapes more than 25 years ago, and to this day, their wines are produced and bottled on their property. All of their grapes are grown using biodynamic techniques. According to James, this involves growing grapes without the use of fertilizers, insecticides, herbicides, or fungicides. The estate also incorporates the use of complex herbal preparations and teas, while carefully watching the phases of the moon and charting cosmic rhythms. The vineyards and grapes are certified organic by BioGro and are certified biodynamic by Demeter New Zealand. Membership in these organizations is considered to be prestigious and requires the most stringent qualifications needed to participate in the specialized wine market. James and

Annie's philosophy is "to produce a selection of specialized table wines, which give an expression of the natural flavors found in the grapes harvested from our vineyards." They are also careful to "enhance the quality of the land and leave it in an improved condition for future generations." As James says, "Wine, after all, is a natural art form to be enjoyed in moderation by all people." Millton Chenin Blanc 2009 is straw gold in color, with aromas of Granny Smith apples and quince. On the palate it is crisp, fruity, and has refreshing acidity. Millton Riesling 2009 is a light straw color, with notes of citrus flowers and lime juice. In the mouth, it has a light residual sugar that is balanced by sufficient acidity, so as not to be cloying. It has a very refreshing finish. Millton Viognier 2010 is pale straw, with notes of honeysuckle and white stone fruits. It is full-bodied on the palate with a pleasing minerality to the finish.

VINOPTIMA

Ngakoroa Road, Ormond, Gisborne,
+64 6 862 5520,
www.vinoptima.co.nz

Nick Nobilo is a pioneer of the modern era of New Zealand wine. In the late 1960s he was one of the leaders in the movement that prompted winemakers to move away from the antiquated style of producing fortified wine.

Vinoptima Ormond Gewürztraminer 2003, received rave reviews. Vinoptima The Grand Vintage Gewürztraminer 2007 is one of Nick's favorite vintages and perhaps one of his best. It is straw colored, with aromas of rich, ripe fruits, kumquat, lychee, and stone fruits. In the mouth it is balanced with a light sense of honey, vanilla, and white melon. The finish is elegant and delightful.

HAWKE'S BAY

His Nobilo Cabernet Sauvignon 1976 was one of the first New Zealand wines to be exported on a large commercial scale to the United Kingdom, and in 2000 he oversaw the transfer of the family company to BRL Hardy. Not one to sit still for too long, he decided to start his own winery in 2000, using the ancient Latin word *Vinoptima* to describe his philosophy for producing highly rated wines. Translated as "best wine," many people in the industry share his opinion that his Gewürztraminers are some of the best produced in New Zealand. The estate consists of almost 10 hectares (24 acres), and all grapes are grown, vinified, and bottled on the property. The original south block vines were planted in 2000, and the north block was planted in 2007. Nick selected five different clones of Gewürztraminer to grow on these parcels, based on his 25 years of experience with the variety. His first release,

Hawke's Bay is New Zealand's oldest existing wine region; it was here that Bishop Pompallier planted his grapevines in 1851. It is also the second largest in the nation, after Marlborough. An earthquake destroyed the town of Napier in 1931; rebuilding took less than three years, and the entire downtown is built in the Art Deco style. Unlike this delightful seaside town, which was re-created almost overnight, it took thousands of years for the four main rivers of Hawke's Bay to form the region's valleys and hillsides—with many types of soil, including clay loam, distinctive well-drained red gravel, sand, and limestone.

Varieties are evenly divided between red and white. Chardonnay is the most abundant grape here, covering 1,164 hectares (2,876 acres), out of a total 4,947 hectares (12,224 acres) in the region. There are 85 wineries in Hawke's Bay, a sharp increase over the 44 that were here in the year 2000. There are also 171 grape growers. New plantings are underway, and if predictions bear out, the total number of hectares will be 5,046 (12,469 acres) by 2012. Merlot is second in command in Hawke's Bay; it is grown on 1,017 hectares (2,513 acres). Merlot is bottled varietally or used as the primary ingredient in Bordeaux-style blends. Sauvignon Blanc is the third most popular grape here—it is planted on 895 hectares (2,212 acres)—and is expected to be grown on 936 hectares (2,313 acres) by 2012. Cabernet Sauvignon, sometimes vinified alone but more often blended with Merlot, is farmed on 387 hectares (956 acres). Pinot Noir plantings cover 376 hectares (929 acres), 58 percent of which is grown specifically for sparkling wine. Pinot Gris is planted on 355 hectares (877 acres), while Syrah—the rising star of Hawke's Bay—currently grows on 204 hectares (504 acres).

The large area known as Hawke's Bay runs along 350 kilometers (217 miles) of Pacific Ocean Coastline, with a total area of 1.4 million hectares (5,405 square miles). Most vineyards are in a 50-kilometer by 30-kilometer (31-mile by 19-mile) zone closest to the towns of Napier and Hastings. There are four rivers running east to west through the territory: the Wairoa, Waiau, Esk, and Ngaruroro Rivers, which have created a series of sheltered valleys. In a given summer, about 400 millimeters, or 16 inches, of rain is expected. The coastal areas benefit most from the effects of the warm maritime climate, especially the Bay View subzone in the northern Esk River Valley and Te Awanga in the south. Hawke's Bay's earliest wineries were in Taradale, Meanee, and Korokipo. The inland areas of Ohiti, Bridge Pa, and Gimblett Gravels were formed by the evolution of the path of the Ngaruroro River as it left behind free draining alluvial soils, silt loam, reddish gravel, and stone. Merlot, Cabernet Sauvignon, and other red varieties do especially well in the broad alluvial plain of Gimblett Gravels, where some of New Zealand's finest wines originate. Te Mata Peak's vineyards are also recognized for their high quality, and the inland vineyards of Central Hawke's Bay—with altitudes climbing to 300 meters (984 feet)—are becoming known for cool-climate Sauvignon Blanc, Pinot Noir, and Pinot Gris.

ALPHA DOMUS

1829 Maraekakaho Road, Hastings, Hawke's Bay,
+64 6 879 6752,
www.alphadomus.co.nz

The name "alpha" is an anagram using the first initials of the Ham family's first names, while *domus* is Latin for "home." This Hawke's Bay winery's home is close to an historic airfield; hence the vintage de Havilland Tigermoth plane on the label. Family member and managing director Paul Ham—the *P* in Alpha—leads a team including vineyard manager Darren Chatterton and winemaker Kate Galloway, who work with estate-grown Chardonnay, Sauvignon Blanc, "old vine" Bordeaux varieties, and more recently planted Rhône varieties from the estate's 20 hectares (49 acres) of land on the Heretaunga Plains. Three tiers of wine are produced: The Pilot, at the entry level, Alpha Domus, at the premium level, and the icon AD range. Alpha Domus The Barnstormer Syrah 2010 has exciting aromas of dark fruits, anise, and freshly ground pepper. In the mouth we taste black cherry, blackberry, mocha, and fennel seed, with hints of vanilla. AD The Aviator 2007 blends 36.4 percent Cabernet Sauvignon, 27.3 percent Cabernet Franc, 22.7 percent Merlot, and 13.6 percent Malbec into a deep red violet confection, with aromas of black cherry, licorice, and tobacco and flavors of raspberry, cassis, chocolate-covered espresso bean, and a dusting of baking spice.

BILANCIA

Stortford Lodge, Hawke's Bay,
+64 6 844 4301,
www.bilancia.co.nz

Bilancia is Italian for "balance"; in this case, it refers to Libra, the Zodiac sign of owners Lorraine Leheny and Warren Gibson. This word can also be used to describe the wine they make from Pinot Gris, Viognier, and Syrah—grown on the estate's 6 hectares (15 acres) of hillside vineyard. Both partners are winemakers who honed their craft around the world before founding Bilancia in 1997. Bilancia Syrah 2008 combines fruit from the La Collina vineyard on Roys Hill with fruit from the esteemed Gimblett Gravels appellation (blended with 6 percent Viognier). Its 20 months in oak was well spent; the finished wine has both the aroma and taste of blackberry, raspberry, and black pepper, lifted by a hint of rose petal and a splash of refreshing acidity. Bilancia La Collina White 2008, a blend of 86 percent Viognier and 14 percent Gewürztraminer, mingles floral and stone fruit scents with bright flavors of green pear, lemon blossom, and Turkish delight.

CJ PASK

1133 Omahu Rd, Hastings, Hawke's Bay,
+64 6 879 7906,
www.cjpaskwinery.co.nz

When pilot Chris Pask flew over the wide Ngaruroro River Valley in the 1970s, he saw the potential in land that has now become some of the most sought-after vineyard territory in the world. He was looking down on Gimblett Gravels. Pask planted his first vineyards here

CRAGGY RANGE

253 Waimarama Road, Havelock North,
Hawke's Bay,
+64 6 873 7126,
www.craggyrange.com

in 1981; he and his daughter Tessa produced the estate's first vintage in 1985. Winemaker Kate Radburnd, the managing director, came aboard in 1991; she now works hand-in-hand with winemaker Russell Wiggins, who joined the team in 2003. Today, CJ Pask owns and manages close to 90 hectares (222 acres) of Gimblett Road vineyards. The gravel-strewn alluvial soils are ideal for Merlot, the estate's primary variety, as well as Chardonnay, Syrah, and Cabernet Sauvignon. Small amounts of Malbec, Pinot Gris, and Viognier round out the estate's plantings. The deep red violet tone of CJ Pask Gimblett Road Merlot 2008 is the first clue as to this wine's intensity. Ripe notes of cherry and blueberry combine on the nose and on the palate, where they are harmoniously joined by flavors of plum, white flowers, and vanilla—with a notable minerality on the smooth finish.

The entrance to the Craggy Range winery is stunning. It is architect John Blair's masterpiece and utilizes shapes commonly found on New Zealand farms. There is a round room resembling a stook of oats and another circular silo-like structure that houses the winery's award-winning restaurant, Terroir. Views of the craggy-peaked mountains from the restaurant windows are as equally amazing as the food. Owned in part by Australian-American TJ Peabody and New Zealand winemaking legend Steve Smith MW, Craggy Range is producing Southern Hemisphere wines of great complexity. Smith, whose official title is viticultural director, explained, "Every wine we make at Craggy is a single-vineyard wine." He gave us an extensive tour of the vineyards, winery, cellar, and restaurant. Craggy Range Te Muna Road Vineyard Martinborough Pinot Noir 2009 is garnet colored, with aromas of red fruits and black cherry—with top notes of savory spices, dried lavender, and purple flowers. In the mouth it is full-bodied with great viscosity. It is balanced, has lovely sweet tannins, and finishes long and elegant. Craggy Range Sophia 2009 is a blend of 65 percent Merlot, 25 percent Cabernet Sauvignon, 7 percent Cabernet Franc, and 3 percent Petit Verdot. The wine is named Sophia because (according to Smith) "all of the partners (in the business) have a special Sophia in our lives. We also all have a crush on (laughing) Sophia Loren, and we honor the Latin word *Sophia*, which means 'wisdom.'" The wine is inky purple, with aromas of dark berries, black cherries, and sage. On the palate it is voluptuous and Rubenesque and reveals flavors of espresso, mocha, and dark chocolate—like a brooding woman who has many secrets and only reveals them when needed. Tightly structured and restrained, Sophia is one of our personal favorites. Craggy Range Gimblett Gravels Les Beaux Cailloux Chardonnay 2009 has aromas of toasted

brioche, white peaches, pears, melted butter, and stone fruits. It is full and viscous in the mouth and reminiscent of a fine Burgundian Chardonnay. It is very well executed, with excellent persistence.

ESK VALLEY

Main Road, Bay View, Hastings, Hawke's Bay,
+64 6 872 7430,
www.eskvalley.co.nz

Esk Valley began its life as Glenvale Winery; its first vineyards were planted and a winery built in 1933, with an emphasis then on fortified wines. Times have changed and so has this boutique winery, which is now owned by Sir George Fistonich of Villa Maria. Glenvale's concrete fermentation vats are still in use, now joined by stainless-steel tanks and French oak barrels. Senior winemaker Gordon Russell works with local Hawke's Bay fruit and Marlborough Sauvignon Blanc to produce the Esk Valley range, Winemakers Reserve wines, and The Terraces, the latter a super-premium wine made only in exceptional years from a 1-hectare (2.5-acre) vineyard on the northwest-facing slopes of the Esk Valley. Esk Valley Hawke's Bay Reserve Merlot Malbec Cabernet Sauvignon 2006 is the dark color of ripe blueberries, which continue on the nose and palate, in combination with cassis, licorice, clove, and violet. It all culminates in a long, silky finish. Esk Valley The Terraces 2006 combines single-plot Malbec, Merlot, and Cabernet Franc, which are harvested and vinified together. This blend of 45 percent Malbec, 40 percent Merlot, and 15 percent Cabernet Franc is inky purple, with a strong nose of black cherry, blackberry, and spicy vanilla. Elegant dark fruits are joined in the mouth by toasted almond, clove, and a touch of paprika; the finish goes on and on, with structured tannins and a final note of brightness.

HAWKES RIDGE

551 Kereru Road, RD 1 Hastings,
+64 6 874 9668,
www.hawkesridge.co.nz

Hawkes Ridge Wine Estate is a small, family-owned vineyard, winery, and olive grove in the Ngaruroro River basin. Unlike many of its neighbors who farm an impossible amount of grape varieties, things are kept simple here, with the spotlight on only a handful: Pinot Noir, Tempranillo, Pinot Gris, Viognier, and Sémillon, the last of which is vinified into both dry and sweet styles. Label art is simple too: a pair of angled curving slashes, symbolizing both the contours of the surrounding hills and the hawks that glide overhead. Tastings

are handled at nearby Triangle Cellars, on Ngatawara Road, which is a cooperative tasting room for Hawkes Ridge, Bridge Pa Vineyard, and Bushhawk Vineyard. Hawkes Ridge Wine Estate Semillon 2009 has bright fruit and is generous and round in the mouth with an elegant floral finish. Hawkes Ridge Wine Estate Tempranillo 2009 is deep ruby red. Brighter on the nose and palate than a traditional Spanish version, it has flavors of black cherry and dark plums with healthy doses of spice and tomato leaf.

MISSION ESTATE

198 Church Road, Napier, Hawke's Bay,
+64 6 845 9350,
www.missionestate.co.nz

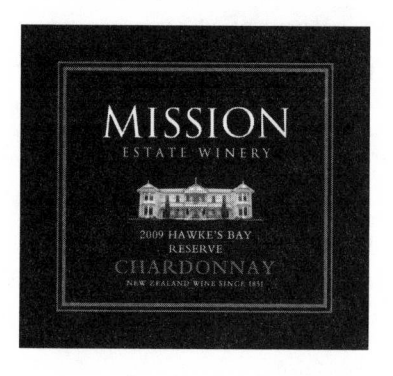

French Catholic missionaries from the Marist order arrived in Hawke's Bay in 1838 and planted their first vineyards in 1851— to make both sacramental and table wine.

Today, Mission Estate is New Zealand's oldest winery, steeped in tradition but with an eye to the future. Winemaker Paul Mooney has been here for more than 30 years; his original training was under the Marist winemaking priests. In the driveway of the imposing Grande Maison, you will spot one surviving row of Muscat that was grafted from original French rootstock in 1838. The tasting room and restaurant are housed in the seminary building, which itself dates back to 1930; the nearby winery underwent a major expansion and renovation in 2007. Viticulturist Caine Thompson manages the 323 hectares (798 acres) of estate vineyards. A broad variety of wines are produced under the Mission Estate, Vineyard Selection, Reserve, and Jewelstone labels. Mission Estate Reserve Chardonnay 2009 has flavors of white peach and apricot, with notes of toasted almond and buttered toast. It has full mouthfeel and a lingering finish. Mission Estate Jewelstone Syrah 2008 is dark red violet with a nose and palate of black cherry, raspberry, five-spice powder, and Sichuan pepper. Well-structured tannins and a touch of acidity play across the tongue for a balanced finish.

SACRED HILL

1033 Dartmoor Road, Napier, Hawke's Bay,
+64 6 844 0138,
www.sacredhill.com

David Mason and his brother Mark grew up in a family of Hawke's Bay grape farmers. In 1986 they decided to complete the process and open their own winery. In the 25 years since, the operation has grown considerably, and their wines have received accolades in the New Zealand and international wine press; but Sacred Hill remains a family affair. Four brands are produced under the Sacred Hill label: Special Selection, Wine Thief Series, HALO, and Reserve. These wines are made from estate vineyards in both Hawke's Bay and Marlborough, with Pinot Noir sourced from growers in Central Otago. With more than 175 hectares (432 acres) in Hawke's Bay—including some precious Gimblett Gravels land—and 60 hectares (148 acres) in Marlborough, there is a lot of fruit passing through the door of Sacred Hill's modern winery, built in 1995, to keep winemaker Tony Bish busy. Sacred Hill Halo Hawke's Bay Merlot-Cabernet Sauvignon-Cabernet Franc is inky violet red, with a strong nose of black cherry, cassis, chocolate-covered espresso bean, and toasted almond. In the mouth it showcases all these and more, with an elegant balance of bright fruit and spice notes washing over the entire palate before winding down to a long, silky finish. Sacred Hill Reserve Hawke's Bay Chardonnay 2010 exhibits scents of nectarine and marzipan, joined in the mouth by pink grapefruit and crème brulée, all wrapped in a luscious mouthfeel.

SILENI ESTATES

2016 Maraekakaho Road, Hastings, Hawke's Bay,
+64 6 879 8768,
www.sileni.co.nz

Named after the followers of Dionysus, the Greek god of wine, Sileni has a state-of-the-art winery that combines the old and the new, from open-top fermenters and naturally cooled barrel cellars to temperature-controlled cooling tanks and airbag presses. Its 106 hectares (262 acres) are managed by a trio of viticulturists who bring out the best in estate-grown Sauvignon Blanc, Sémillon, Chardonnay, Pinot Gris, Riesling, Syrah, Merlot, Cabernet

Franc, and Malbec. These are vinified by chief winemaker Grant Edwards and his team. Four ranges are produced at a variety of price points: Cellar Selection, Satyr Selection, Estate Selection, and Exceptional Vintage—the latter, only produced in the best years. Sileni Cellar Selection Sauvignon Blanc 2010 is a refreshing burst of tropical fruit with a dash of chopped green herbs and refreshing acidity. It is perfect on its own or alongside selections from the raw bar. Sileni Estate Selection The Triangle Merlot 2008 has intense flavors of blackberry, blueberry, licorice, and cocoa, with soft tannins and a smooth finish.

STONECROFT

121 Mere Road, Hastings, Hawke's Bay,
+64 6 879 9610,
www.stonecroft.co.nz

Stonecroft's vineyards were some of the first in Gimblett Gravels. They were planted in 1982 by Dr. Alan Limmer, who has remained as a consultant since selling the winery and vineyards to Dermot McCollum and Andria Monin in 2010. McCollum studied winemaking and viticulture at Tairawhiti Polytechnic in Gisborne, and Monin is an attorney by trade, but they have both received training through the WSET in London. The estate's almost 7 hectares (16 acres) of vineyards are divided among two plots, one on Mere Road and the other at the foot of Roy's Hill. McCollum is a "minimal interventionist" winemaker who uses traditional techniques to vinify the estate-grown Syrah, Cabernet Sauvignon, Gewürztraminer, Merlot, Chardonnay, and Zinfandel. Stonecroft Old Vine Gewürztraminer 2009 gives a full sense of umami in the mouth, alongside flavors of peach, rose petal, and clove. The small amount of botrytized grapes in the mix adds to the sweetness of this off-dry wine, but balanced acidity keeps it in check. Stonecroft Reserve Syrah 2009 is a mouth-pleaser in every way, combining voluptuous flavors of blueberry, cassis, toffee, honeysuckle, and anisette in a series of bursts and volleys that keep on keeping on.

TE MATA ESTATE

349 Te Mata Road, Havelock North, Hawke's Bay,
+64 6 877 4399,
www.temata.co.nz

Named for a giant whose fallen body is said to form nearby Te Mata Peak, Te Mata Estate has roots that reach back to 1854, when John Chambers started farming this land. It was his son, Bernard, who first planted grapevines and built a winery, which was purchased by the Buck and Morris families in 1978. The original winery building has been restored and is joined by a modern winemaking complex and the

Buck family home; what remains of Bernard Chambers's 1,960 hectares (4,843 acres) are 240 hectares (593 acres) of land spread over three sites, half of which are planted to vines. Winemaker Phil Brodie and viticulturist Larry Morgan coax the best qualities out of estate-grown fruit to produce six wines: Coleraine, Awatea, Bullnose Syrah, Cape Crest Sauvignon Blanc, Elston Chardonnay, and Zara Viognier. Over two-thirds of the production is devoted to Syrah, Cabernet/Merlot blends, and Chardonnay. Te Mata Estate Coleraine 2009, the estate's flagship wine, blends 52 percent Cabernet Sauvignon, 43 percent Merlot, and 5 percent Cabernet Franc into an exceptional wine with aromas of cassis, clove, and Turkish delight. In the mouth berries explode and then quietly recede, to be replaced by heady spice and an impressive finish. Te Mata Estate Woodthorpe Syrah 2010 is deep red with a bright rim, bearing scents of cherries, pepper, and honeysuckle, the last of which is probably due to the use of 4 percent Viognier. In the mouth black cherry and blackberry are aided by notes of clove, black pepper, and rose petal; its soft tannins dissolve into a delicate finish.

TRINITY HILL

2396 State Highway 50, RD 5, Hastings,
+64 6 879 7778,
www.trinityhill.com

Trinity Hill planted its first Cabernet Sauvignon, Merlot, Syrah, and Chardonnay vines in 1994 and produced its first wine, albeit offsite, in 1996. The following year heralded the completion of its winery—just in time for the 1997 harvest. A partnership between John Hancock, Trevor and Hanne Janes, and Robert and Robyn Wilson, Trinity Hill has helped set the international standard of Gimblett Gravels Hawke's Bay wines. It is a founding member of the Gimblett Gravels Winegrowers Association and, in 2007, created a joint venture with Pascal Jolivet of Sancerre, France. Its wines have won multiple awards, especially the Trinity Hill Homage Syrah line, named for Gerard Jaboulet, who gave John Hancock vine cuttings after he worked a Rhône Valley harvest in 1996. Trinity Hill Homage Syrah 2007 is inky purple and composed of 91 percent Syrah and 9 percent Viognier. It has aromas of black plums, black cherry, blackberry, and cassis. Big and fruity in the mouth

with a firm tannic structure, this delicious wine is one that will continue to get better over the next 10 years. Trinity Hill by John Hancock Gimblett Gravels Viognier 2008 is pale straw, with flavors of lemon, white nectarine, orange blossom, and jasmine. It is crisp and fresh and not overly perfumed. Trinity Hill Gimblett Gravels Tempranillo 2008 is garnet colored, with aromas of red and black raspberries, dark plums, and baking spices. Full-bodied in the mouth, it finishes with a light touch of vanilla and a lovely persistence.

UNISON

2163 Highway 50, Hastings, Hawke's Bay,
+64 6 879 7913,
www.unisonvineyard.co.nz

A small, family-owned estate in the midst of Gimblett Gravels, Unison Vineyard is run by husband and wife Philip and Terry Horn—with help from winemaker Jenny Dobson.

Since 1993 the heart of its production has been fine red wine, showcasing the best this gravel-strewn alluvial soil has to offer. Wine is hand-crafted in small batches using a hand-cranked wooden basket press; cases generally number in the hundreds rather than hundreds of thousands. Unison Classic Blend 2007 is a Merlot-Cabernet Sauvignon blend with a "splash" of Syrah. The nose is all fruit, with black cherry and cassis up front. These are joined by friendly pepper and mint notes on the palate. Unison Reserve Merlot 2008 could never be a spy; it gives up its flavors of red plum, gingerbread spice, and Mediterranean herbs with just one sniff. These continue on to a satin-rich, satisfying finish.

VIDAL WINES

913 St Aubyn Street East, Hastings, Hawke's Bay,
+64 6 872 7440,
www.vidal.co.nz

Spaniard Anthony Joseph Vidal purchased this former Hawke's Bay horse racing stable and transformed it into a winery and cellar in 1905. He planted vines and was one of New Zealand's pioneering winemakers. Today, Vidal Wine is owned by Sir George Fistonich of Villa Maria. It continues to make quality wine using grapes from various premium New Zealand regions. The head winemaker is Hugh Crichton,

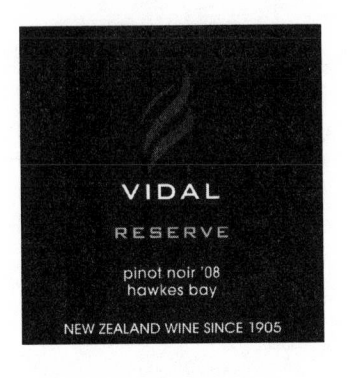

who started his career at Vidal in 2006. He has international experience, having worked harvests in France and Italy—both of which show in his finished products. Vidal's restaurant, opened in 1979, is adjacent to the winery, and has been the recipient of many accolades, most recently for its chef and maître d'. Vidal Reserve Chardonnay 2008 is straw colored, with both floral and citrus aromas. In the mouth there is a flinty characteristic along with fresh fruit notes. The finish has nice acidity with crisp minerality. Vidal Reserve Syrah 2005 is deep red garnet, with a nose of dark plums, purple flowers, and rose petals. In the mouth there are spicy notes—think freshly ground black pepper—and big fruit. It has a pleasant mouthfeel with a persistent finish. Vidal Reserve Hawke's Bay Pinot Noir 2008 is medium red, with aromas of black cherry and violets. In the mouth the flavors are elevated by fresh-picked red raspberry. It has a good length and pleasant post-palate sensation.

WILD ROCK

143 Mere Road, Hastings, Hawke's Bay,
+64 6 873 7126,
www.wildrockwine.co.nz

Owner TJ Peabody and viticulturist Steve Smith MW set out to craft distinctive, well-priced wines from a variety of prime New Zealand sites. Freed from the constraints of creating single-vineyard wines (at Craggy Range), here they produce Syrah, Merlot, and Malbec from Hawke's Bay, plus two Pinot Noirs (one from Martinborough and one from Central Otago), and Sauvignon Blanc from—you guessed it—Marlborough. Their irreverent yet still serious spirit is carried through by the winemaking team of Matt Stafford, Pieter Koopman, and Rod Easthope. Think "bad kids in the honor class" and you get the idea: showing up late without a pass, listening to their iPods during lectures, and still acing every exam. Wild Rock Gravel Pit Red Merlot Malbec Gimblett Gravels Vineyard Hawke's Bay 2009 is a blend of 73 percent Merlot, 23 percent Malbec, and 2 percent each Cabernet Sauvignon and Cabernet Franc. Deep ruby in color, it has a nose of blackberry and black currants with a whiff of violet. On the palate black fruits, violet, and a gravel-driven minerality make way for a tongue-coating dose of velvet. Wild Rock Angels Dust Reserve Syrah Gimblett Gravels Vineyard Hawke's Bay 2007 is an intense garnet with bright highlights. Fresh blueberry scents are accompanied by chocolate and portabello mushrooms—with the dirt still clinging to them. Rich blueberry and plum flavors merge with licorice and dried sage on the palate, leading to a long, plush finish.

WAIRARAPA

Wairarapa is in the southeast of the North Island. It includes the well-known Wellington and Martinborough, to the south, as well as Gladstone, which is in the center of the region, and Masterton, in the north. The nation's capital, Wellington, has been described as "The Coolest Little Capital in the World," a reference to its hip quotient, not its weather. The vineyards around Martinborough are some of the oldest in the area, having been planted in the 1970s, after soil testing determined that this was ideal *terroir* for Pinot Noir. Alluvial soils derived from the region's rivers, including the Ruamahanga, tend to be silt loam over limestone. Wairarapa's vineyards are low, ranging from sea level to 90 meters (295 feet). Average summer rainfall is 385 millimeters, or 15 inches, near Martinborough and 450 millimeters, or 18 inches, farther north toward Masterton. Although the total plantings in this region is small, with grapevines covering only 871 ectares (2,152 acres), it is known for exceptional quality wines. Vineyard area is expected to grow marginally; total plantings by 2012 are estimated at 885 hectares (2,187 acres).

Pinot Noir, well known here long before anyone had heard of Central Otago, is planted on 465 hectares (1,149 acres), or 54 percent of Wairarapa's vineyards. Sauvignon Blanc grows on 197 hectares (487 acres) as of 2010 and is predicted to increase to 217 hectares (536 acres) by 2012. Wairarapa is well known for its Chardonnay too; 70 hectares (173 acres) are planted in its sheltered valleys. Pinot Gris and Riesling have a strong presence, growing on 48 and 32 hectares (118 and 79 acres) respectively. Wairarapa is also noted for its Bordeaux varietals; Cabernet Sauvignon and Merlot are grown here in small but significant quantity—the former on 14 hectares (35 acres) and the latter on 12 hectares (30 acres). As might be expected, miniscule amounts of Cabernet Franc, Malbec, and Petit Verdot call Wairarapa home.

ALANA ESTATE

133 Puruatanga Road, Martinborough,
+64 6 306 9784,
www.alana.co.nz

Ian and Alana Smart say of their estate's wines: "Hands-on, hand-picked, hand-sorted, and handcrafted." The estate grows Pinot Noir, Chardonnay, Sauvignon Blanc, and Riesling on almost 17 hectares (42 acres) of terraced vineyards. Ian works alongside vineyard manager John Jones on every aspect from vine to bottle—Alana takes over from there. Alana Estate's gravity-flow winery is perfectly suited to small-batch wines that represent the terroir, climate, and art of the winemaker. Alana Sauvignon Blanc 2010 has a nose of lemon sorbet and toasted pineapple. In the mouth tropical fruits are entwined with flavors of peach, lemon zest, chopped parsley, and freesia—kept in balance by zippy acidity. Alana Rapture Pinot Noir 2010 exemplifies the varietal, with flavors of raspberry, black cherry, chocolate, and tangerine peel.

ATA RANGI

14 Puruatanga Road, Martinborough,
+64 6 306 9570,
www.atarangi.co.nz

Founded by Clive Paton in 1980, Ata Rangi translates as "new beginning" or "dawn sky." The business expanded in 1982, when Clive's sister Alison bought adjoining land, and then again in 1987, when Clive married Phyll Pattie. The family brought in winemaker Helen Masters, and together the team makes 15,000 cases of quality wine each year, from 35 estate-owned hectares (86 acres). Ata Rangi has thrice won the prestigious Bouchard Finlayson Trophy for Best Pinot Noir at the International Wine and Spirit Competition in London, as well as numerous gold medals, awards, and accolades. We visited Clive, Phyll, Alison, and Helen and enjoyed some delicious wine, tasty food, and lots of laughs. Ata Rangi Sauvignon Blanc 2010 is pale straw, with aromas of lemon rind, cut grass, tropical fruits, and pink grapefruit. In the mouth it is young, fresh, and vibrant, with flavors of honeysuckle and guava. It's crisp and persistent. Ata Rangi Craighall Chardonnay 2009 is straw yellow, with aromas of stone fruits, yellow peaches, apricot blossoms, and a touch of grapefruit rind. In the mouth it is velvety smooth yet refreshing at the same time. The persistence is fruity, long, and pleasant. This is a delicious Chardonnay. Ata Rangi Pinot Noir 2009 is medium cherry colored, with aromas of dark plums, raspberries, cherries, and a top note of sage. In the mouth it is smooth and voluptuous, with a surprising burst of fruit through the finish.

CAMBRIDGE ROAD VINEYARD

32 Cambridge Road, Martinborough,
+64 6 306 8959,
www.cambridgeroad.co.nz

When winemaker Lance Redgwell decided to set out on his own, he took a few words of advice from James Millton—the person widely acknowledged as the father of biodynamic winemaking in New Zealand. Redgwell studied the art and science of biodynamic viniculture and then set to work bringing out the best from just over 2 hectares (5 acres) on Cambridge Road. Planted in 1986 with Syrah and Pinot Noir, Cambridge Road is blessed with some of the oldest vines in the region. Quantities are tiny; only two barrels of the highly acclaimed and hard to get Noblestone Pinot Noir are made in a given year. Cambridge Road Martinborough Syrah 2008 has had its edges softened by the addition of 9 percent Pinot Noir. It is black cherry in the glass, with a nose and palate of vibrant cherry, raspberry, fennel seed, and a jubilant hint of jalapeño. In classic Rhône style it is lightly oaked with soft tannins and a satiny finish.

DRY RIVER

Puratuanga Road, Martinborough,
+64 6 306 3988,
www.dryriver.co.nz

The history of Dry River was immortalized by the name chosen by Neil and Dawn McCallum when they first planted vineyards here in 1979. It's named after a circa-1877 sheep farm—one of the first in Wairarapa. Over the years, the McCallum's acquired additional plots; three vineyards totaling just under 12 hectares (30 acres) are planted with Syrah, Pinot Noir, Gewürztraminer, Chardonnay, Sauvignon Blanc, Riesling, Pinot Gris, and Viognier. In 2002, Dry River was purchased by Julian Robertson and viticulturist Reg Oliver. Former hedge fund manager Robertson takes his New Zealand investments seriously; in addition to Dry River, he is also the owner of three of New Zealand's premier resorts: Kauri Cliffs Lodge, Matakauri Lodge, and The Farm at Cape Kidnappers. Neil McCallum stayed on for a while but has since retired; chief winemaker

is now Katy Hammond. Dry River remains a *terroir*-driven boutique winery, producing only 3,000 cases of wine per year. Dry River Pinot Noir 2009 is bright cherry red, and like many a fine New Zealand Pinot Noir, it tends toward the savory end of the spectrum, featuring both a nose and palate of black cherry, blackberry, black olive, and dried Mediterranean herbs, intertwined with floral notes, cooling spices, and a well-rounded finish. Dry River Lovat Gewürztraminer 2010 is a refreshing burst of ripe nectarine, Turkish delight, orange zest, and Chinese five-spice powder, with both good weight and lovely acidity.

ESCARPMENT

Te Muna Road, Corner New York Street and
Boundary Road, Martinborough,
+64 6 306 8305,
www.escarpment.co.nz

Larry McKenna and Robert Kirby were introduced to each other in 1999, and the friendship was fast and furious. Together with their partners, Sue and Mem, they established Escarpment Vineyard in the same year. They planted their favorite variety, Pinot Noir, which makes up 70 percent of their total vineyard. The remaining 30 percent is planted with Chardonnay, Pinot Gris, Riesling, and Pinot Blanc. Most of the grapes they use are estate grown, but they also have long-term grower contracts with Station Bush and Cleland Vineyard. The name "Escarpment"—a long ridge of land that was created by a fault— came to Robert's brother-in-law, David Glass, when he was out on a short "walk-about" in the neighboring foothills. Escarpment Martinborough Pinot Noir 2008 is bottled with a synthetic cork, rather than screwcap. It is a classic Pinot Noir, with colors of black cherry and medium garnet. It has aromas of dark red fruits and toffee, while on the palate flavors of tart cherry, raspberry, vanilla, anise, violet, and orange zest combine to produce a wonderful finish. Escarpment Chardonnay 2008 is straw colored, with aromas of flinty minerality and white stone fruits. In the mouth it is round and soft. Escarpment Pinot Gris 2008 is straw colored, with aromas of ripe pears and a touch of residual sugar in the mouth. It is creamy and full-bodied.

GLADSTONE VINEYARD

Gladstone Road, Carterton, Wairarapa,
+64 6 379 8563,
www.gladstonevineyard.co.nz

This was the first of a series of boutique wineries built along the Ruamahanga River in 1986. Gladstone was purchased by Christine and David Kerohan a decade later, with Christine learning winemaking under the tutelage of Jean Charles van Hove. Today, Christine retains her position as chief winemaker, in addition to her duties as managing director. David is the director of quality control, having continued teaching architecture at Wellington's Victoria University. In 2005, a new winery was built; the original building now houses a tasting room and café. With 12 hectares (30 acres) of estate-owned vineyards and 9 (22 acres) more under lease contracts, Gladstone works with Sauvignon Blanc, Pinot Gris, Riesling, Viognier, Pinot Noir, Merlot, Malbec, and Cabernet Franc. The 12,000 Mile range of wines reflects Christine's transition from her native Scotland—and you can count the number of female Scottish winemakers in the world on one hand—to New Zealand vigneron. Gladstone Vineyard Riesling 2010 is a citrus trifecta in the nose and mouth, with strong flavors of lemon, lime, and grapefruit. Nice minerality and soft floral notes balance the fruit toward the crisp finish. Gladstone Vineyard Pinot Noir 2009 is a finely tuned mix of sweet and tart black cherry, violet, dried sage, and licorice root. Its firm tannins underlie a beguiling complexity.

MARTINBOROUGH VINEYARD

Princess Street, Martinborough,
+64 6 306 9955,
www.martinborough-vineyard.co.nz

Inspired by a 1978 soil and climate study stating that Martinborough should be able to produce wines equal to those of Burgundy, Dr. Derek Milne—one of the report's co-authors—banded together with five other wine lovers and bought about 7 hectares (17 acres) of Martinborough land. Today, several of the original shareholders remain and are involved in varying aspects of viticulture and production. Founding pharmacist/winemaker Russell Schultz worked side by side with winemaker Larry Schultz until Schultz's departure in 2000, at which time Claire Mulholland took the helm as head winemaker. Mulholland and her team handcraft small amounts of Pinot Noir, Chardonnay, Pinot Gris, Sauvignon Blanc, and Riesling. In March 2011, at a blind tasting in California, a bottle of Martinborough Vineyard Pinot Noir from 1998 took the number one position among the "World's Twenty Best Pinot Noirs," beating—among others—Domaine de la

Romanée-Conti La Tâche 1990, a wine priced about 70 times above the price of a bottle of Martinborough. Martinborough Vineyard Te Tara Pinot Noir 2009 has a nose of cherry and raspberry with hints of spice. It is generous in the mouth, with strong berry flavors, a touch of coffee bean, and a splash of orange zest. Martinborough Vineyard Chardonnay 2008 exhibits flavors of peach and vanilla with a dusting of baking spices and dusky minerality. Full, creamy mouthfeel and a keen splash of acidity add up to a wine well worth holding on to for a few more years.

MURDOCH JAMES WINERY

284 Dry River Road, Martinborough,
+64 6 306 9165,
www.murdochjames.co.nz

More than 40 years ago, Roger Fraser worked as a vineyard hand during school holidays. He dreamed of one day owning a winery. Life took him in another direction, but in 1986 he and his wife, Jill, bought a plot of land in Martinborough and personally planted the first of their Pinot Noir and Syrah vines. Pinot Gris, Chardonnay, and Riesling were later added, and they now own and manage 20 hectares (49 acres) of vineyard. Roger and Jill still run the business. Son Carl is the winemaker, aided by Steve Plowman and Cliff de Jong. The estate's airy tasting room and restaurant are among the most visited in the region; its chef specializes in pairing locally sourced produce with the estate's wines. Murdoch James Fraser Pinot Noir 2008 tastes of black cherry, toasted almond, baking spices, and a touch of bell pepper, with good mouthfeel and soft tannins. Murdoch James Blue Rock Riesling 2010 has a nose of key lime pie and fresh chalk. It tastes of peaches, apricots, and lemongrass—with a combination of bold minerality and bracing acidity playing across the palate.

PALLISER ESTATE

State Highway 53, Kitchener Street,
Martinborough,
+64 6 306 9019,
www.palliser.co.nz

Named after the nearby Cape Palliser—which Captain James Cook named to honor his mentor, Rear Admiral Sir Hugh

Palliser—Palliser Estate is a "boutique vineyard with an international outlook." Palliser has won many gold medals and trophies including the Air New Zealand Wine Awards and Sydney International Wine Competition. The estate has 85 hectares (210 acres) of Pinot Noir, Sauvignon Blanc, Chardonnay, Pinot Gris, and Riesling. Its first harvest was in 1989. Palliser makes wines at two levels—Palliser Estate and Pencarrow—but we especially enjoyed the line of Pinot Noir wines named after the estate's dogs: The Great Marco, The Great Bear, The Great Harry, and The Great Walter. On our most recent visit to Palliser Estate, winemaker Allan Johnson, associate winemaker Pip Goodwin, and managing director Richard Riddiford greeted us warmly and then told us that the winery was in full swing harvest. If we planned on eating with them, we would have to work for our lunch. Mike got the dirty end of the stick and was put on manual punchdown duty, while Jeff got off slightly easier and operated the hydraulic press. After that, we were forced to measure the acidity and residual sugars of multiple barrel samples in the laboratory. Thankfully, we only had to observe the winemakers shoveling the fermented grapes out of the tanks. Lunch was well worth waiting for—Chef Jo Crabb fried up some Paua fritters and grilled some of the best lamb chops that we have ever eaten. Palliser Estate Martinborough Riesling 2010 is straw colored, with aromas of lime and lemon rinds and a touch of tangerine blossom and jasmine. It has lovely mouthfeel and flavors of citrus peel breaking through to a crisp, refreshing finish. Palliser's Pencarrow Martinborough Sauvignon Blanc 2010 is a lovely expression of the variety. It has notes of lemon peel, pea shoots, asparagus, and green herbs. It has a rich and luxurious weight on the palate and a long, clean finish. We hope that the 2011 Pinot Noir (which we punched down before lunch) is as good as the Palliser Estate Martinborough Pinot Noir 2008. It has aromas of fresh red fruit, especially raspberry and cherry. In the mouth the savory notes of sage, rosemary, Mediterranean herbs, and thyme are nicely framed in oak. The finish is long with round, sweet tannins.

SCHUBERT WINES

57 Cambridge Road, Martinborough,
+64 6 306 8505,
www.schubert.co.nz

Kai Schubert and Marion Deimling both studied viticulture and enology in Germany before setting out to find a vineyard of their own. They wanted to work with Pinot Noir and other varieties, and "searched the world" before choosing Wairarapa in 1998. They started with a small plot of 1.4 hectares (3.5 acres) that had already been planted; this Martinborough vineyard is home to Pinot Noir, Syrah, Merlot, Chardonnay, and Müller-Thurgau vines. In 1999 and 2000 they planted a further 40 hectares (99 acres) of vineyard, mostly with red grapes, including eight clones of Pinot Noir plus Syrah, Cabernet Sauvignon, Merlot, Pinot Gris, Chardonnay, and Sauvignon Blanc. In short order they've since collected a showcase of awards and medals. Schubert Sauvignon Blanc 2010 has a nose of straight-up citrus, but in the mouth there are distinct flavors of grapefruit, lime, and orange blossom; in short, it is a zesty palate pleaser! Schubert Marion's Vineyard Pinot Noir 2009 is complex on the nose—where it gives off aromas of blackberry, cherry preserves, lemon zest, and violet—and also in the mouth where you will taste concentrated black cherry, clove, and truffle. Just before the Pinot Noir gets too heavy, firm tannins are held in check by a spray of acidity.

TE KAIRANGA

Martins Road, Martinborough,
+64 3 306 9122,
www.tkwine.co.nz

The name Te Kairanga is Maori for "where the soil is rich and the food is plentiful." Te Kairanga has many vineyards spread across Wairarapa's soil—a combination of small blocks and two larger vineyards, one of 32 hectares (79 acres) and one of 46 (114). Viticulturist Gary Wood and chief winemaker Wendy Potts work mostly with Pinot Noir and Chardonnay, though some Bordeaux varieties and aromatic whites are also in the mix. Te Kairanga has some of the oldest vineyards in the region; its John Martin Reserve Pinot Noir is named after the founder of Martinborough and its "old vines" Draper Vineyard is named after Te Kairanga's founder, Tom Draper. Te Kairanga Martinborough Chardonnay 2009 has a nose and palate of ripe summer stone fruits and a palate showcasing Christmas spices and a creamy mouthfeel. Te Kairanga Estate Pinot Noir 2009 is deep cherry in the glass, with a nose of wild cherry, cassis, and cigar box. In the mouth cherry and stewed black fruits give way to soft waves of clove, anise, and vanilla bean.

SOUTH ISLAND

NELSON

Nelson is the northernmost wine region on the South Island. It sits at southern latitude 41.17—the same as Wellington in Wairarapa (the southernmost region on the North Island). Divided from Marlborough by the Richmond Mountains, Nelson is bordered by mountains to the west and the sea to the east. Its main regions are the Waimea Plains, closest to the city of Nelson, and Upper Moutere, a series of hills stretching toward Golden Bay. Some vineyards are now planted in the immediate vicinity of Golden Bay as well. Upper Moutere features alluvial clay and gravel soils, while Waimea, which means "river garden" in Maori, are silt and gravel loam over clay. Average summer rainfall at the entrance to the plains (closest to the airport) is about 550 millimeters, or 22 inches, while at the far end of Moutere, near the mouth of the Mateuka River, it can be as high as 700 millimeters, or 28 inches. Nelson was once known more for apples and tobacco, but viticulture is now on the rise: there were 25 wineries here in 2000 but by 2010 that number had grown to 36. On top of that, 62 grape growers farm the rolling green hills here.

In 2010 there were 842 hectares (2,081 acres) of grapevines in Nelson, an increase of 60 percent over 2003. More is to come: by 2012,

880 hectares (2,175 acres) should be under vine. Sauvignon Blanc is the leading variety of the region, blanketing 323 hectares (798 acres); it is estimated that an additional 10 hectares (25 acres) of this French native will be under cultivation by 2012. The second most cultivated grape here is Pinot Noir with 183 hectares (452 acres). The majority of Nelson Pinot Noir is made into still wine; less than 3 percent is transformed into sparkling wine. Total Pinot Noir plantings are predicted to increase to 220 hectares (544 acres) by 2012. Chardonnay comes in at number three, with 121 hectares (299 acres) under cultivation. A trio of aromatics round out the bulk of Nelson's vineyards: Pinot Gris grows on 70 hectares (173 acres), Riesling on 56 hectares (138 acres), and Gewürztraminer on 28 hectares (69 acres). Of the three, Pinot Gris is supposed to achieve significant gains and will grow on 85 hectares (210 acres) by 2012. This is no surprise, considering Nelson is building a reputation for its aromatic varietals, and in 2010 an industry-wide Aromatics Symposium was held here.

NEUDORF

138 Neudorf Road, Upper Moutere, Nelson,
+64 3 543 2643,
www.neudorf.co.nz

Animal behaviorist cum agricultural scientist Tim Finn and his wife, former journalist Judy Finn, first planted grape vines here in 1979. Today they have 33 hectares (82 acres) of vines split between the Moutere Hills and the Waimea Plains. Tim especially likes the latter for his Sauvignon Blanc because "about fifty percent of our grapes come from the Brightwater Township at the bottom of the Waimea plains where the soils are light, young, and stony. They are very similar to Marlborough—it's where we like to grow our Sauvignon Blanc." A boutique winery with cult wine status, Neudorf has its eye on quality and consistency. In 2010, its total production was a mere 165,000 bottles. We enjoyed dinner, great conversation, and fantastic wines with Tim and Judy at their home/winery in Nelson. Neudorf Moutere Riesling 2010 is pale straw, with aromas of lemon, lime, and jasmine. It would be hard for most wine lovers to tell this Kiwi wine from an Austrian Spätlese. With 55 grams of residual sugar per liter, this wine is slightly sweet on the palate, yet it has balanced acidity to prevent it from being cloying. This young, pretty wine would pair well with hot, spicy, Pan-Asian cuisine or be perfect on its own as an aperitif. Neudorf Sauvignon Blanc 2010 is a brilliant straw color, with musky, tropical fruit notes and the smell of freshly mowed grass in the bouquet. It is rich in the mouth with voluptuous heft. A beautiful, crisp finish with balanced acidity rewards the most sophisticated palate—this is not your typical New Zealand Sauvignon Blanc. Neudorf Moutere Chardonnay 2009 is elegant and restrained. It has aromas of toasted and buttered brioche, stone fruits, and white peaches. It has a sultry feel in the mouth, with flavors of caramelized pineapple, slate, flint, and a finish of clarified white peach essence. It is a wonderful example of a fine Chardonnay from the northern part of New Zealand's South Island and is reminiscent of a Grand Cru style of Chablis. Neudorf Moutere Home Vineyard Pinot Noir is only made in exceptional years; only 1,200 bottles were made in 2009. It is garnet to ruby red in color, with aromas of confectioners' sugar, red cherry—both fresh and dried—rosemary and Mediterranean spices. It has a savory feel on the mid palate and balanced acidity. Velvety tannins are very pleasing—but watch out for that burst of bright fruit at the back of your throat. The finish is long, persistent, and elegant.

MARLBOROUGH

The Marlborough region celebrated the thirtieth anniversary of its first commercial Sauvignon Blanc vintage in 2009—which is a long time ago on the New Zealand wine time line and a very short time in most other wine regions in the world. In 2000, the gravel, sand, and loam soils of New Zealand's largest wine region supported a total of 62 wineries—and at last official count, in 2010, that figure had risen to 137 wineries. This region is also home to 568 grape growers, an increase of almost 100 percent since 2003. With 18,401 hectares (45,470 acres) of grapevines, Marlborough is responsible for 58 percent of all the viticulture vineyards in the nation. It is expected to retain its hold on production, with an anticipated increase to 19,570 hectares (48,359 acres) by 2012.

Marlborough is a low-lying green northern plain. Until the late nineteenth century it was a vast marsh, and it was only when the swamp was drained that the way was paved for habitation and agriculture. Scottish farmer David Herd planted the first vineyard here in 1873, but sheep farms and fruit orchards were the main industry until Frank Yukich, of Montana Wines, planted the first Sauvignon Blanc vines in 1973. Since then, Marlborough has become almost one contiguous wine farm. In addition to big players like Montana (now Brancott) and Corbans—both of which are owned by Pernod

Ricard—Marlborough is home to a variety of boutique, medium-sized, and industrial-scale vineyards and wineries making wine at all levels of quality and price point.

Marlborough is divided into two large sub-regions: the Wairau Valley, closest to Blenheim, and the Awatere Valley to the south, nearby to the town of Seddon. The Wairau River runs east to west, across the top of the Wairu Valley, marking its border with the Richmond Range. The Awatere River is on the north side of the valley of the same name and runs parallel to the Wither Hills, which divide the two valleys. While Awatere has its fair share of vineyards, the bulk of the wineries are in the Wairau Valley. Wairau features deep alluvial and granite soils, with more gravel in the north and higher concentrations of clay in the south. Awatere soils tend to be sedimentary mineral soils, layered with sandstone and volcanic debris. Average summer rainfall in Awatere is around 300 millimeters, or 12 inches, while over the hills in Wairau, 400 millimeters, or 16 inches, is expected each summer.

Of course, Sauvignon Blanc rules the roost in Marlborough: of 18,401 total planted hectares (45,470 acres), 13,943 (34,454 acres) are the "savage white" varietal. This means that 76 percent of all the grapes grown across the region are Sauvignon Blanc, and more than 90 percent of all the Sauvignon Blanc grown in the country is grown here. The second most widely planted Marlborough varietal, Pinot Noir, thrives on 2,000 hectares (4,942 acres), of which 8.4 percent will be made into sparkling wine. Chardonnay is planted on 1,085 hectares (2,681 acres), Pinot Gris on 546 hectares (1,349 acres), and Riesling on 446 (1,102 acres). Merlot is planted on 89 hectares (220 acres), Gewürztraminer on 84 hectares (208 acres), and Sémillon on 78 (193 acres). Cabernet Sauvignon, Viognier, Pinotage, Syrah, and Malbec are all planted here, but in numbers that might be significant in a smaller region but hardly make a dent in the workhorse that is Marlborough.

ALLAN SCOTT WINES

Jacksons Road, Blenheim, Marlborough,
+64 3 572 9054,
www.allanscott.com

A family affair in every sense of the word, Allan Scott Wines was established by Allan and Catherine Scott in 1990. They are joined in the business by their son Josh (winemaker) and daughters Sara (viticulturist) and Victoria (marketing manager). The family has vineyards here in Marlborough and farther south, in Central Otago. Wines are bottled under four ranges: Estates, Single Vineyard, Methode Traditionelle, and Scott Base. Several of the higher-end wines are available only at the

cellar door tasting room and associated Twelve Trees Restaurant. Allan Scott Les Joues Rosé Méthode Traditionelle NV, made from 100 percent Pinot Noir, exhibits aromas of just-baked strawberry pie. It is medium pink in the glass, with delicate *perlage* and elegant flavors of raspberry, strawberry, and brioche. From the Single Vineyard range, Allan Scott Millstone Marlborough Sauvignon Blanc 2009 has a bright nose of passion fruit, citrus, and honeydew. Clean fruits continue onto the palate aided by toasty notes, a taste of earth, and a dash of zippy acidity.

BLIND RIVER

1667 Redwood Pass, Blenheim, Marlborough,
+64 3 575 7704,
www.blindriver.co.nz

With a label featuring an eel in the curved Maori *koru* position—signifying creation, perpetual movement, and a return to the point of origin—it's easy to imagine that the people behind Blind River are first and foremost about the land and the grapes. Founders Barry and Dianne Feickert farm 11 hectares (27 acres) of Awatere Valley vineyards planted with just two varieties, Pinot Noir and Sauvignon Blanc. Daughter Wendy is Blind River's viticulturist, while her sisters, Debbie and Suzie, are the winemaker and business manager, respectively. Blind River Sauvignon Blanc 2010 gives off strong aromas of passionfruit and citrus. In the mouth rich flavors of grapefruit, pineapple, and guava are run through with a rich vein of minerality. Blind River Pinot Noir 2009 is cherry red in the glass. On the nose it is full of berries and spice; the tongue breaks it down into black cherry, cassis, licorice, and clove, with a full mouthfeel and velvety texture.

BRANCOTT ESTATE

State Highway 1, Riverlands,
Blenheim, Marlborough,
+64 9 336 8300,
www.brancottestate.com

Brancott Estate began life in 1934 as Montana Wines, founded by Croatian immigrant Ivan Yukich. It is New Zealand's largest winemaking company. Via a recent series of acquisitions, takeovers, and mergers, Brancott Estatae is now part of the multinational Pernod Ricard brand, which produces wine in New Zealand under the Brancott, Church Road, Deutz, and

Lindauer labels and owns and manages vineyards across the entire country. Although the general belief until the early 1970s was that grapes would never ripen on the South Island, Ivan's son Frank dismissed that bit of superstition when he planted his first Sauvignon Blanc vines here, claiming that someday, "Wines from here will become world famous." That prognostication was the beginning of the Marlborough Sauvignon Blanc era; Montana's first commercial vintage of M.S.B. was 1979.

Chief winemaker Patrick Materman began his career here with the 1990 harvest, and today he is in charge of an enormous team of winemakers and viticulturists. Although owners of smaller Marlborough estates still refer to the behemoth as "Mon-tah-nah" with a dismissive wave of the hand, it pays to remember that without its pioneering efforts in Marlborough, an entire category of wine might never have happened. Fruit from Marlborough is vinified here into two ranges, the entry-level Classic range of Sauvignon Blanc, Pinot Noir, and Pinot Gris and the higher-end Letters series, with the distinctive gold initial on the bottle. Brancott Estate Brancott "B" Sauvignon Blanc 2010 has a bouquet of citrus fruits mingling with fresh chopped herbes de Provence. In the mouth grapefruit and passionfruit are accompanied by jalapeño, fresh and dried herbs, and crystal-clear acidity. Brancott Estate Terraces

"T" Marlborough Pinot Noir 2009 is deep ruby in the glass, from which it releases aromas of black cherry, cinnamon toast, and flowers. In the mouth it opens to reveal flavors of height-of-summer cherry, raspberry, chocolate, and spiced truffles. Smooth tannins and balanced acidity taper off to a satisfying finish.

CLOS HENRI

693 State Highway 63, Blenheim, Marlborough,
+64 3 572 7923,
www.closhenri.com

After ten generations in France's Loire Valley—the other "home" of Sauvignon Blanc—Henri Bourgeois took his love of Sauvignon Blanc and Pinot Noir and his dislike for the rules that bind winemakers' hands in his home country and planted 109 hectares (269 acres) of these varieties in Marlborough. His goal was to combine a history of French winemaking with New Zealand varietal character, and by all accounts, he has succeeded. The focal point of Clos Henri is the St. Solange Chapel, a deconsecrated chapel relocated here from a nearby town, which functions as a tasting room and is named in memory of Henri's wife, Solange. Clos Henri Sauvignon Blanc 2009 is a wine with aromas of citrus fruit, lemon peel, and chopped green herbs, which continue onto the palate with strong minerality and nice mouthfeel. Clos Henri Bel Echo Pinot Noir 2009 exhibits aromas and flavors of slightly tart cherry, anise, and sage, with powerful viscosity and grippy tannins.

CLOUDY BAY

Jacksons Road, Blenheim, Marlborough,
+64 3 520 9197,
www.cloudybay.co.nz

Cloudy Bay was one of the first five wineries in Marlborough. It was started in 1985 as an offshoot of Australia's Cape Mentelle and is now part of the LVMH Group. Cloudy Bay makes delicious, excellent quality, and highly regarded wines. Visitors to the winery are welcomed with stunning views through soaring floor-to-ceiling windows across the Richmond Mountains as well as views over the working barrel room. There are many

interesting activities in which to participate; we especially like the "Forage Cloudy Bay," where guests are scattered in four directions, north, south, east, and west, to forage for artisanal produce to bring back to Cloudy Bay's chefs. The produce is then transformed into an amazing meal paired with Cloudy Bay wines, and all are invited to sit, eat, and drink. The winemaking team consists of Nick Blampied-Lane, Sarah Burton, Jim White, and Tim Heath. We sat down to dinner with Heath and his wines, and he told us about an experience that we can't miss next year: Pinot at Cloudy Bay. Nick picks 18 different Pinot Noirs from all around the world, and consumers and journalists alike are led through a thought-provoking blind tasting. Tim Heath told us that the lunch served after the tasting is worth flying back to New Zealand for. He also promised us a day of fly-fishing and mountain biking on our next visit—and we intend to hold him to that. He introduced us to his Cloudy Bay Pinot Noir 2009, which has aromas of freshly cut mushrooms, strawberries, and red fruits. In the mouth it is smooth and silky, almost creamy. It finishes with fine tannins. Cloudy Bay Sauvignon Blanc 2010 has aromas of grapefruit, tropical fruits, and lime zest. It has an herbal quality in the mouth with a refreshingly acidic finish. We also got to hear the legend of Te Koko-O-Kupe, where the great explorer rested in Cloudy Bay and used his scoop (or *Te Koko*) to gather oysters from the shallows of the sheltered bay. We enjoyed Te Koko Sauvignon Blanc 2007 paired with briny, fresh oysters. It has aromas of mandarin zest, white peach, lemon pith, and Mediterranean herbs. In the mouth it shows tropical flavors with a touch of ginger. It finishes with bracing minerality and refreshing acidity—it was just perfect with the oysters.

DOG POINT VINEYARD

Dog Point Road, Renwick, Marlborough,
+64 3 572 8294,
www.dogpoint.co.nz

A collaboration between two couples, Ivan and Margaret Sutherland and James and Wendy Healy, Dog Point's name goes back to the earliest settlers in Marlborough, when this was sheep country. With no fences in place, sheep dogs had the run of the land, and

several generations of sheep in the area were overrun by packs of wild dogs. Fruit is selected from Doug Point's late-1970s-era vineyards in the Wairau Valley; both couples are involved hands-on from vineyard to bottle. Dog Point Vineyard Sauvignon Blanc 2010 has the nose of a lemon tree blossoming in an herb garden. In the mouth it is rich, with flavors of citrus, pineapple, and tomato leaf and a suggestion of wet river rocks. Dog Point Vineyard Chardonnay 2009 exhibits a bouquet of lemon, lime, ripe pear, and toasted cashews. On the palate lemon marmalade is the main flavor, mingling with toast spread with nut butter. It is a beautifully textured wine.

DRYLANDS

237 Hammerichs Road, Blenheim, Marlborough,
+64 3 570 5252,
www.drylands.co.nz

With some of Marlborough's oldest established vines, Drylands Home Block vineyard was originally owned and planted by Ewan Robinson in 1980. Owned today by the Constellation NZ group, the current plantings include 43 hectares (106 acres) of Sauvignon Blanc, 1.5 hectares (4 acres) of Sémillon, and 1.5 hectares (4 acres) of Chardonnay. The on-premise Drylands Restaurant is under the command of Chef Liz Parkes, and winemaking is overseen by Master Winemaker Darryl Woolley. We had a chance to cook a meal with Darryl, chat about New Zealand, and taste his wines. Drylands Sauvignon Blanc 2010 is straw yellow with tints of green. It has aromas of guava, passionfruit, and a touch of citrus flowers. It is lively and bright on the palate, with a delicious expression of tropical fruit and lemon zest. Drylands Pinot Noir 2009 is garnet ruby red, with aromas of black raspberry, black cherries, and a touch of vanilla. In the mouth it shows some heft on the tongue and has a lovely, silky, tannic finish.

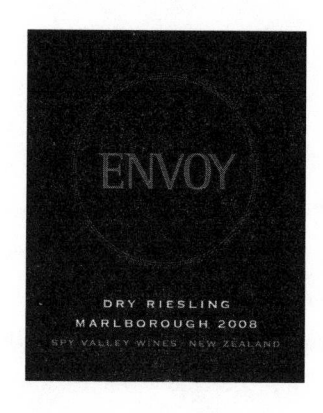

ENVOY BY SPY VALLEY

37 Lake Timara Road, Blenheim, Marlborough,
+64 3 572 9840,
www.spyvalleywine.co.nz

When you approach the main winery by car, it's easy to figure out why it's called Spy Valley. Named for its proximity to a satellite communications monitoring station, Spy Valley was originally called Johnson Estates when it was founded in 1993 by Bryan and Jan Johnson. Spy Valley Winery is a past winner of the New Zealand Institute of Architects Supreme Commercial Award for design, and its environmentally conscious landscaping has won the Marlborough Environmental Award. The team is extremely socially conscious and

"Believes that it is important to give back to the local community, almost as much as they believe in making award-winning wine." When visiting Spy Valley, be sure to stay at its Timara Lodge, a four-bedroom, private residence set among vines and beautifully manicured gardens—complete with an idyllic lake. Spy Valley's Envoy range of wines is made from specially selected single plots within the Johnson Estate vineyards. Envoy Pinot Noir 2009 is ruby red, with notes of red cherries, raspberries, dark spices, and cocoa powder. In the mouth there is nice sweetness with sweet round tannins and a mocha finish. Envoy Gewürztraminer 2009 is light straw colored, with aromas of white stone fruits, cloves, and wet earth. In the mouth it is fruit-forward and floral, with a crisp finish. Envoy Dry Riesling 2008 is light straw colored, with a nose of spice and citrus fruits. On the palate it is crisp with balanced acidity and a clean finish.

FORREST ESTATE

Blicks Road, Renwick, Marlborough,
+64 3 572 9084,
www.forrest.co.nz

Drs. John and Brigid Forrest both come from New Zealand farming families. Together they have combined their scientific backgrounds and knowledge of working the land to create one of New Zealand's finest family-owned estates. Between the seven vineyards they own and the two they manage, they have a total of 130 hectares (321 acres). John shares the winemaking duties with Dave Knappstein, and the vineyards—which stretch from Hawke's Bay to Central Otago, with the bulk here in Marlborough—are looked after by Tim Alexander. Forrest Estate's range consists of six different labels: Forrest, The Valleys, The Doctors (named for John and Brigid), John Forrest Collection, Tatty Bogler, and Newton Forrest, which is a Hawke's Bay collaboration with Australian viticulturist Bob Newton. The Hawke's Bay vineyard is home to Bordeaux varieties and Syrah, while closer to home they work with Sauvignon Blanc, Pinot Noir, and aromatic whites such as Riesling, Gewürztraminer, and Gruner Veltliner. John Forrest Collection Sauvignon Blanc 2009 showcases aromas of lemon, geranium leaf, and oregano. In the mouth lemon, lime, and chopped herbs share the spotlight, with

gorgeous mouthfeel and crisp acidity singing backup. The Doctors Riesling 2010 has a classic nose of green apple and lime and tastes of lemon-lime and star anise, with just a notion of florality yet balanced by dynamic acidity.

FROMM WINERY

Godfrey Road, Blenheim,
+64 3 572 9355,
www.frommwinery.co.nz

Owners Pol Lenzinger and George Walliser carry out founder Georg Fromm's philosophy of crafting single-vineyard wines in a European fashion. Winemaker Hatsch Kalberer prepared a wonderful tasting for us, while William Hoare guided us through the vineyards and took us to the highest point of the region to show us the lay of the land. Grapes are grown in the Fromm, Clayvin, William Thomas, and Quarters vineyards, all of which are now run using organic and biodynamic principles. Traditional practices are used at Fromm, and

Kalberer proudly defends his decision to use cork closures in his quality bottles of wine. Fromm Riesling Spätlese 2009 is pale straw, almost clear, with aromas of green apple and white flowers. In the mouth it has elegant fruit sweetness with bright acidity and flavors of ripe Granny Smith apples. Fromm Brancott Valley Chardonnay 2006 is pale straw, with notes of peach, apricots, and toasted brioche. On the palate you taste gentle white peach, green apple, and light flowers and sense a texture of buttered toast. Fromm Vineyard Syrah 2007 is ruby red with a violet rim. It has aromas of licorice and freshly ground black pepper backed by notes of cassis and candied cherries. There is more fruit in the mouth than on the nose, with flavors of slightly tart cherry, strawberry, raspberry, and suggestions of chocolate, coffee, and white pepper in the post palate.

GROVE MILL

13 Waihopai Valley Road, Renwick, Marlborough,
+64 3 572 8200,
www.grovemill.co.nz

In 2006, Grove Mill became the world's first "CarboNZero" wine producer, because of its ongoing actions to minimize and offset the winery's carbon footprint. Its actions also help counteract the negative impacts of climate change. The same year, it released the world's first "CarboNZero" certified wines. Head enologist Dave Pearce has been with Grove Mill since 1988 and is highly regarded as one of New Zealand's most innovative winemakers. The winery has 118 hectares (292 acres) of vines planted with Sauvignon Blanc, Riesling, Pinot Gris, Chardonnay, Gewürztraminer, and Pinot Noir. The winery is dedicated to protecting the Southern Bell Frog, who proudly adorns each label, by launching a long-term rehabilitation program for the estate's neighboring wetlands. Grove Mill Marlborough Sauvignon Blanc 2009 is pale straw, with notes of tropical fruits, citrus blossoms, freshly mowed grass, and mango. In the mouth it is full-bodied for the variety and finishes with herbaceous notes. Grove Mill also produces wines under the Black Birch label; its Black Birch Vineyard Marlborough Sauvignon Blanc 2010 is straw colored, with aromas of passionfruit, wheatgrass, and citrus rind. It is crisp, pleasant, and refreshing on the palate. Grove Mill Marlborough Riesling 2008 is a nice representation of what the variety can do in Marlborough *terroir*. It is pale gold in color, with notes of lemon, honeysuckle, honeycomb, and a touch of clove in the bouquet. In the mouth there is a hint of sweetness, but it is offset by balanced acidity. Very elegant, this is the type of wine that has you begging for another glass.

HERZOG ESTATE

81 Jeffries Road, Blenheim, Marlborough,
+64 3 572 8770,
www.herzog.co.nz

Hans Herzog's family has made wine near Zurich since 1630, but when he and his wife, Therese, investigated options for grape growing outside cold-weather Switzerland, they found their ideal spot in New Zealand. In the mid-1990s they planted 11 hectares (27 acres) of vineyards on the banks of the Wairau River, and in 2000 they closed their Michelin-starred restaurant, Taggenberg, and set up shop in Marlborough. Hans's domain is winemaking—he has degrees in both viticulture and enology,—but Therese rules the roost in the restaurant, which is simply named "Herzog." In addition to growing Sauvignon Blanc, Pinot Noir, and Chardonnay in his organically managed vineyards, Hans also utilizes traditional, hands-on methods with Arneis, Barbera, Tempranillo, and Zweigelt.

Meanwhile, Therese applies time-honored European technique to locally sourced meat, fish, and other produce. Hans Herzog Pinot Gris 2009 bears fragrances of green pear and rose petal. Fresh fruit, floral, and spice flavors linger in the mouth, where full body and vigorous acidity make for an engaging finish. Hans Herzog Pinot Noir 2008 has a full nose of red and black fruit, which is just a tease compared to the luscious black cherry and raspberry flavors that delight the taste buds—along with gentler notes of chocolate and forest mushrooms. Equal proportions of robust tannins and spry acidity create a memorable finish.

HUNTER'S WINES

603 Rapaura Road, Blenheim, Marlborough,
+64 3 572 8489,
www.hunters.co.nz

Irishman Ernie Hunter arrived in Blenheim in 1979, when the idea of Marlborough as wine country was barely a twinkle in anyone's eye. Still, he bought farmland and planted Riesling, Gewürztraminer, Cabernet Sauvignon, Chardonnay, Pinot Noir, and Sauvignon Blanc. His first vintage was 1982, and from it Ernie won six medals at the National Wine Show. He met and married Jane in 1984, who was at that time the national viticulturist for Montana Wines. Ernie was tragically killed in

HUNTER'S

Jane Hunter

Region : Marlborough Wairau Valley
Winemaker : Gary Duke
Brix at Harvest : 24.35
Harvest Date : 30 March - 15 April 2010

2010
PINOT GRIS
MARLBOROUGH

a 1987 accident, and Jane Hunter stepped in to keep the winery running. Today, Hunter's vineyards are more than double the size Ernie originally planted and have continued to produce award-winning wines season after season. Hunter's is still family owned; Jane leads a team alongside general manager Peter Macdonald, winemaker Gary Duke, and viticulturist Bryan Vickery. The café, set in a half hectare (two acres) of gardens landscaped with indigenous plants, is a lovely spot to enjoy a bite of food alongside a glass—or bottle—of Hunter's. Hunter's Marlborough Sauvignon Blanc 2010 has a fruit salad nose of Granny Smith apple, passionfruit, and grapefruit. On the palate citrus predominates, joined by notes of lavender, fennel seed, and chopped parsley. Hunter's Marlborough Pinot Gris 2010 showcases a Bartlett pear and jasmine bouquet. Pear perseveres in the mouth accompanied by ripe stone fruits and baking spices, with a gentle splash of acidity.

ISABEL ESTATE VINEYARDS

70-72 Hawkesbury Road, Renwick, Marlborough,
+64 3 572 8300,
www.isabelestate.com

Michael and Robin Tiller started out as contract grape growers in 1982 and 12 years later produced their first vintage under the Isabel Estates label. One of the largest family-owned vineyards in Marlborough, Isabel Estate grows Sauvignon Blanc, Chardonnay, Riesling, Pinot Noir, and Pinot Gris. Son Brad Tiller is the head viticulturist. Winemaker Patricia Miranda hails from Chile, but she has been here since 2004 and sees great potential in cool-climate varieties such as Riesling and Pinot Gris. Isabel Pinot Gris 2009 has a heady nose of nectarine and toffee; in the mouth fruit and vanilla meld with delicate spice and refreshing acidity. One whiff of Isabel Sauvignon Blanc 2010 will make you think that you're drinking lemonade while mowing the lawn. On the palate, up-front citrus and cut grass recede quickly and are replaced by flavors of mango, guava, jasmine, and French herbs, making for a delightful, mouth-filling glass of wine.

JACKSON ESTATE

Jackson Road, Renwick, Marlborough,
+64 3 579 5523,
www.jacksonestate.co.nz

The Jackson family arrived in New Zealand from England in 1842. Adam Jackson bought a large plot of land on what is now Jackson's Road in 1855. The ancient soaring gum tree that stands to this day behind the family homestead, Runnymede, is pictured on every bottle of Jackson Estate wine. In 1987, a fifth-generation descendant of Adam Jackson, John Stichbury, planted vines here, and in 1991 John and his wife, Jo, welcomed the first vintage of Jackson Estate. Together they oversee five vineyards in three different areas of Marlborough; the Grey Ghost, Stonewall, Blue Hills, Somerset, and Gum Emperor vineyards are planted with Sauvignon Blanc, Chardonnay, Riesling, and Pinot Noir. Viticulturist Geoff Woollcombe is responsible for what goes on in the fields, while the new state-of-the-art winery is the domain of wine-maker Mike Paterson. Jackson Estate Stich Sauvignon Blanc 2010 showcases aromas of citrus fruits and basil pesto. In the mouth flavors of passionfruit, nectarine, and lemon zest dominate, with equal proportions of natural fruit sweetness and zesty acidity. Jackson Estate Gum Emperor Pinot Noir 2008 is deep garnet in the glass, with a nose of perfumed black cherries. The rich palate opens to reveal ripe black and red fruit, lavender, and a touch of peat.

KIM CRAWFORD WINES

45 Station Road, Huapai, Auckland,
+64 9 412 6666,
www.kimcrawfordwines.co.nz

The virtual concept of Kim Crawford wines began in the 1990s, and in 2000, Crawford leased his first brick-and-mortar winery. His wines were well received nationally and internationally, and in 2005 *Wine Spectator* magazine named a Kim Crawford wine as one of the Top 100 Wines of the Year for the second time. The company is now owned and managed by Constellation NZ, while Crawford has become a self-declared "house husband." Anthony Walkenhorst is the chief winemaker, based at the company's Riverlands Winery in Blenheim. Kim Crawford Pinot Noir 2009 is medium ruby claret colored. It has aromas of black cherry and smoky bacon, and in the mouth flavors of sweet black cherry and vanilla come to life. Kim Crawford Marlborough Sauvignon Blanc 2010 is yellowish green in the glass, with aromas of tropical fruits and Mediterranean herbs. In the mouth it is crisp with a balanced acidity.

LAWSON'S DRY HILLS

Alabama Road, Blenheim,
+64 3 578 7674,
www.lawsonsdryhills.co.nz

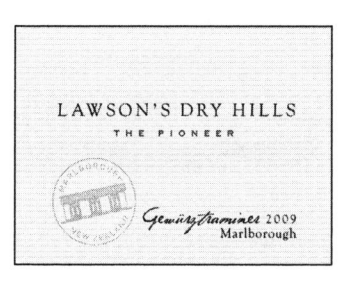

Owner Barbara Lawson started Lawson's Dry Hills in 1992 with her late husband, Ross Lawson, who is widely considered to be the major force in converting New Zealand winemakers from cork to screwcap. Barbara told us the story over a home-cooked lunch of green-lipped mussels and her delicious aromatic white wines. "Ross and I experienced a bad run of cork taint over two or three years, and in 2001 he was so fed up that he formed a committee, whose members included John Belsham, John Forrest, and John Stichbury. Together, they confronted the Portuguese cork growers and suggested that they were sending inferior corks to New Zealand. The guys weren't happy with the answers they received from the Portuguese so that year, Ross and I and a bunch of other winemakers switched to screwcap and have never looked back." Barbara's winemaker, Marcus Wright,

has been with Lawson's Dry Hills since 2001, and together they craft some of the best aromatic wines that we have ever tasted. Lawson's Dry Hills The Pioneer Gewürztraminer 2009 is named in honor of Ross Lawson. It is remarkably floral with notes of jasmine, honeysuckle, almond blossoms, gardenia, and citrus top notes, especially mandarin rind and Clementine pith. It's a complex bouquet! On the palate there is full mouth richness and an elegant balance of acidity. All we can say is, "Wow—pour me some more of that!" Lawson's Dry Hills The Pioneer Pinot Gris 2010 is a brilliant straw color with a green hue. The aromatics are generous and lovely, while the palate is extremely focused. This is a beautifully elegant wine. Lawson's Dry Hills White Label Pinot Noir 2010 is garnet to ruby colored, with aromas of bright cherry, dried black cherries, and raspberry. In the mouth it is fruity and lush and finishes with touches of coffee and vanilla bean. The tannins are soft, the acidity is balanced, and the finish is long.

MONKEY BAY

45 Station Road, Huapai, Kumeu, Auckland,
+64 9 412 6666,
www.monkeybay.co.nz

Monkey Bay gets its name from the legend that a pet monkey escaped from an early American whaling ship in these parts. Monkey Bay wines are made by the Nobilo Wine Group in Auckland. The Sauvignon Blanc grapes are sourced from the company's Marlborough Rarangi vineyards as well as other areas in Gisborne and Hawke's Bay. The company is especially proud of the quality of its wines given the affordable asking prices. Monkey Bay Sauvignon Blanc 2010 is pale yellow with touches of green. The nose offers tropical fruits and fresh cut grass, and the wine is fresh and lively on your palate. This is the perfect wine to be pulled from a tub of ice and served nice and cold at a backyard barbecue or pool party.

NAUTILUS

12 Rapaura Road, Renwick, Marlborough,
+64 3 572 6008,
www.nautilusestate.com

Winemaker Clive Jones—known to his friends as CJ—has been with Nautilus since 1998 and tells us, "Nautilus remains a work in progress; the winery was started in 1985, the dedicated Pinot Noir winery and cellar were built in 2000, and the new white winery was finished in 2006." To commemorate the completion, the owners, Australia's Hill Smith family, commissioned Wanganui artist Dale Hudson to create a giant Nautilus shell sculpture crafted from stainless steel and copper. CJ continues, "The company currently has no plans for expansion, except that we are continuously fine-tuning to make a quality product for our consumer. We're also seeing what we can do to create another layer of complexity to our wines." We enjoyed hanging out with CJ at the winery and again in New York City for lunch. Nautilus Sauvignon Blanc 2010 has aromas of sage, cut grass, and dried rosemary. It is seamless in the mouth with clean, bright acidity and a finish that invites you in for another glass. Opawa Pinot Noir 2009 (named after the Opawa—meaning "smoky" or "foggy"—River, which runs through this region) is light cherry red in color. It has aromas of red cherry and red raspberry, with nice equilibrium in the mouth and pleasant fruit flavors balanced by fresh acidity. Nautilus Pinot Noir 2009 is brilliant garnet in color, with aromas of spiced black cherry, clove, cinnamon, and spring floral notes. It has many layers of delicious flavor that continually surprise the palate. This is an elegant yet restrained example of a super Pinot Noir.

SAINT CLAIR ESTATE

13 Selmes Road, Rapaura, Blenheim,
+64 3 570 5280,
www.saintclair.co.nz

Neal and Judy Ibbotson started growing grapes in 1978 but it wasn't until 1994 that they decided to stop selling their prized fruit to other winemakers and began making their own wines. Their decision proved to be a smart one when their wine won gold medals the very first year. Today their children, Tony, Sarina, and Julie, are involved in the family business. The winemaking team includes chief winemaker Matt Thomson, who was present at the inception of Saint Clair in 1994, and senior winemaker Hamish Clark, who joined the team in 2001 (after a career as a forensic scientist and medical laboratory technician). Brie Hughes and Kyle Thompson round out the winemaking team for white wines and red wines, respectively. We had the opportunity to meet with Kyle Thompson and taste some of Saint Clair's excellent wines. Saint Clair Vicar's Choice Pinot Noir 2010 is garnet colored with an indigo rim. On the nose aromas of black cherry, dark fruit, and raspberry are present, while in the mouth there are flavors of strawberry and dark fruits. The mid palate is voluptuous with a fine-grained tannic finish. Saint Clair Pioneer Block 12 Lone Gum Gewürztraminer 2010 is pale

yellow-gold, with aromas of pink roses, rosewater, spice, and candied violets. It is textured on the mid palate, with a rounded feel on the back of the tongue. It has flavors of dark spice and flowers in the finish. Saint Clair Omaka Reserve Chardonnay 2010 is gold colored, with a nose of white peach and white flowers. In the mouth it is full-bodied with balanced acidity and a persistent finish.

SERESIN

85 Bedford Road, Renwick, Marlborough,
+64 3 572 9408,
www.seresin.co.nz

Michael Seresin, director of photography on films such as *Midnight Express* and more recently the Harry Potter series, uses the symbol of the human hand to mark his work on each bottle of wine his estate produces. The grapes are grown both organically and biodynamically, and the founder believes that the hand is "a symbol of the individual and of creative

endeavor; it represents our philosophy to work traditionally with natural elements." Seresin also makes quality olive oils, and its converted timber restaurant, Waterfall Bay, is worth a visit. Seresin Reserve Chardonnay 2008 has aromas of peach, flint, and grapefruit rind. In the mouth flavors of jasmine, white peach, and buttered toast come shining through. The finish is elegant and restrained. Seresin Rachel Pinot Noir 2008 is dark cherry colored, with notes of mushroom, cocoa, and dark red fruits in the bouquet. In the mouth the red fruits shine through and a touch of smoke is detected on the post palate. The tannins are big and smooth with a lingering finish.

TERRAVIN

367 Brookby Road, Blenheim, Marlborough,
+64 3 572 9890,
www.terravin.co.nz

Mike Eaton spent most of his life making wine for other people, but in 1998 he and his wife, Jo, bought a 12-hectare (30-acre) vineyard in the Omaka Valley and struck out on their own. Surrounded by a sea of Sauvignon Blanc, TerraVin quickly made its name with hand-crafted, unfiltered Pinot Noir. Mike handles the vines and the wines and also assists Jo with marketing. In 2007, they sold a portion of their vineyard, retaining 4 hectares (10 acres) of Pinot Noir, Pinot Gris, and Bordeaux varietals, which are used in their "J" blend; they also lease some vineyards but manage the vines themselves. Mike's training in France plus many years of experience in New Zealand shine through in each of the estate's limited edition bottlings. TerraVin Pinot Noir 2009, like many things with roots in France, is a living, breathing contradiction. It is at once delicate and powerful, walking the tightrope between fruit and spice, and its finish is a rich mélange of tannins and acidity.

VAVASOUR

26 Rapaura Road, Blenheim,
+64 3 575 7481,
www.vavasour.com

The Vavasour family arrived to New Zealand in 1890; family history shows that one of their ancestors was a "taster" for William the Conqueror. The wines are a joint effort of Stu Marfell, winemaker; Allan Croker,

VILLA MARIA ESTATE

Corner of Paynters Road and New Renwick Road,
Fairhall, Blenheim, Marlborough,
+64 3 520 8470,
www.villamaria.co.nz

viticulturist; and Mat Duncan, vineyard manager. Together these guys make delicious, high-quality wines from the estate's 85 hectares (210 acres) of vines. Vavasour Pinot Noir 2008 is red with a violet rim. Aromas of fruits of the woods, raspberries, and blackberries are present in the bouquet. In the mouth flavors of cherry, vanilla, and crème brûlée are noted, leading to a fruity yet elegant finish. Vavasour Awatere Valley Pinot Noir 2009 is medium to deep cherry in color. The nose shows spice, a hint of bitter almond oil, and red fruits. In the mouth there is a touch of spice, black cherry, blueberry, and toasted cashews. The mid palate is rounded with a touch of licorice root. The finish is nice and long.

Sir George Fistonich began his career in the wine world in 1961 with the start of his Auckland winery. In the mid-1990s he started building his Marlborough winery, which was completed just in time for the 1999 harvest. George Geris is the chief winemaker at Marlborough and has been with the company for 14 years. Before landing at Villa Maria, he was a flying winemaker who worked in Stellenbosch, Sicily, Puglia, and Tokaj. His goal in New Zealand is "to make wines that highlight the characteristics of the climate, varietal, and the region. I also believe that we have a special climate here, and that New Zealand is a very special place. Our maritime climate has high sunshine hours, a long growing season, and cool nights, which are especially important. It's like having a natural refrigerator, and because of this, we are able to get many layers of flavors and create wines that have a lot of elegance." Villa Maria Private Bin Sauvignon Blanc 2010 is pale straw in color, with aromas of freshly cut grass, vibrant herbs, fruit salad, mango, and guava. It is refreshing on the palate with a long crisp finish. Villa Maria Cellar Selection Riesling 2010 is fruit-forward with floral notes. In the mouth it is dry but has a touch of pleasant sweetness. It has lemon and lime flavors in the mouth, good acidity, and a pleasant finish. Villa Maria Reserve Pinot Noir 2008 is garnet colored, with full in-your-face classic Pinot Noir aromas of red cherry, red raspberry, and red plum. On the palate it is perfumed and elegant with silky tannins. Its fresh-fruit attack also fills your mouth with a touch of spice. This is a textbook, Old World–style Pinot Noir.

WITHER HILLS

211 New Renwick Road, Blenheim, Marlborough,
+64 3 578 4036,
www.witherhills.co.nz

Since 1994, Wither Hills has turned out a series of impressive vintages of Sauvignon Blanc, Chardonnay, Pinot Noir, and Pinot Gris. Its modern winery, tasting room, and restaurant are of more recent vintage, having been completed in 2005. Chief winemaker Ben Glover worked in California, Australia, France, and Italy before heading back to work alongside viticulturist and general manager Geoff Matthews and a stable of three other winemakers. Named for the dramatic hills that are a backdrop to this corner of the Wairau Valley, Wither Hills' four vineyards—Rarangi, Taylor River, Benmorven, and St. Leonard—are certified sustainable. In May 2011 they won a Habitat Enhancement Award for the restoration of native wetlands in the Rarangi Vineyard. Wither Hills Pinot Gris 2010 delivers aromas of juicy peach, jasmine, and red apples, with a hint of Asian spice. Fruit, spice, and flowers coalesce on the palate in a wine with generous mouthfeel and a long, invigorating finish. Wither Hills Pinot Noir 2008 is medium to dark garnet in color, with aromas of red cherry and raspberry in the bouquet. On the palate this is a fruit-forward wine with flavors of red cherry, raspberry, and a light vanilla finish. The tannins are smooth and silky.

CANTERBURY/WAIPARA

Almost midway along the east coast of the South Island, we come to the city of Christchurch, which suffered from a devastating series of earthquakes between September 2010 and February 2011. It is hard to believe when visiting the plains to the north and east of Christchurch, known as the "Gateway to the Antarctic," that such extensive damage took place anywhere near this bucolic rural setting. The Waimakariri River divides the large Canterbury Plains, which spread out to the northeast of the city; vineyards also run directly south, along the western hills of the Banks Peninsula. Waipara, a more confined vineyard area, near the Teviotdale Hills, is about 50 kilometers (31 miles) north of Christchurch, also along the coast. Stony alluvial soils cover most of the area; due to excellent drainage, irrigation is necessary. The soil of Waipara is mainly limestone-rich loam. In an average summer, 320 millimeters, or 13 inches, of rain falls.

One of New Zealand's fastest-growing areas, Canterbury/Waipara is home to 1,763 hectares (4,356 acres) of vines—an amount which has nearly tripled since 2003! As of 2010, there were 61 wineries in the region. Although Waipara covers a tighter area, it has more than four times the number of planted hectares of Canterbury; Waipara has 1,442 hectares (3,563 acres) and Canterbury 321 hectares (793 acres) of vines. Waipara's main varieties are Sauvignon Blanc, 656 hectares (1,621 acres), Pinot Noir, 311 hectares (768 acres), Riesling, 285 hectares (704 acres), Pinot Gris, 84 hectares (208 acres), and Chardonnay, 68 hectares (168 acres). Small

amounts of Merlot, Cabernet Sauvignon, Syrah, and Merlot are also planted in Waipara.

In the more southerly Canterbury, Pinot Noir is the most propagated variety, on 125 hectares (309 acres). The rest of the lineup is an all-star roster of whites, with Chardonnay planted on 57 hectares (141 acres), Riesling on 51 hectares (126 acres), Sauvignon Blanc on 36 hectares (89 acres), and Pinot Gris on 33 hectares (82 acres), trailed by much smaller plantings of Gewürztraminer, Müller-Thurgau (one of the first commercially planted grapes in New Zealand), and Pinot Blanc.

BELL HILL VINEYARD

State Highway 7, Waikari, North Canterbury,
+64 3 379 4374,
www.bellhill.co.nz

Husband-and-wife owners Marcel Giesen and Sherwyn Veldhuizen are both trained in viticulture and enology; they consider themselves wine growers rather than winemakers. Bell Hill's 2 hectares (5 acres) of vineyards are divided into seven individual blocks. Its vines are planted in the dense style of Burgundy, and grapes grown in the lime-rich soil are also vinified in a Burgundian fashion. Blocks are picked, fermented, and barrel-aged individually and then bottled separately or blended together. Most of the production is Pinot Noir, supplemented by small amounts of Chardonnay and Riesling. This last is a nod to Marcel's studies in Germany. Bell Hill Pinot Noir 2007 exhibits aromas of black cherry, plum, and clove. On the palate it is fruit-forward with elegantly textured flavors of wild cherry, lightly stewed plums, clove, and oregano. Grippy minerality and a strong tannic structure are clues to its aging potential.

MOUNTFORD ESTATE

434 Omihi Road, State Highway 1, Waipara,
Amberley, North Canterbury,
+64 3314 6199,
www.mountfordvineyard.co.nz

Winemaker C.P. Lin lost his sight at the age of two to retinal carcinoma. When he was 13, he and his family emigrated from Taiwan to New Zealand. He has a eidetic memory for taste and smell, which in conjunction with his love of wine, allows him to create masterpieces in the barrel and bottle. He is considered one of New Zealand's premier winemakers. Mountford Estate's vineyards were planted in 1991, mainly with Pinot Noir and Chardonnay. Owners Kathryn Ryan and Kees Zeestraten recently added more Pinot Noir, Chardonnay, and Riesling vines, bringing the total plantings here to 10 hectares (25 acres). Mountford Estate's premier Pinot Noir, The Gradient, is made in

very limited quantities and is crushed by both hand and foot using whole bunches of Pinot Noir grapes in French oak casks. Mountford Estate Hommage a' l'Alsace 2009 has aromas of roses, pear, and fragrant white flowers with bracing minerality. In the mouth it is crisp and refreshing with a touch of residual sweetness followed by a dry finish. Mountford Liaison Pinot Noir 2007 is garnet colored, with notes of smoked meats, black plum, intensely sweet black cherry, Mediterranean herbs, vanilla, and Japanese plums. In the mouth velvety tannins linger for a good, long time.

MUDDY WATER

42 Omihi Road, Waipara,
+64 3 314 6964,
www.muddywater.co.nz

Muddy Water takes its name from the Maori word *Waipara*, used to describe the region, *wai*—"water" and *para*—"mud." Fifteen hectares (37 acres) of organically grown Pinot Noir, Riesling, Chardonnay, and Pinotage are used to make Muddy Water wines. Originally owned by Michael and Jane East and recently purchased by neighboring Greystone Wines, the viticulturist is Miranda Brown and former French chef and sommelier Sylvain Taupenas is the assistant winemaker. Muddy Water Chardonnay 2009 is straw colored, with notes of white flowers, Bartlett pear, and citrus blossoms. In the mouth it is generous with flavors of citrus and buttered brioche. It has a pleasant finish too. Muddy Water James Hardwick Riesling 2008 is pale straw with a floral nose. Notes of slate and wet river rock are detected also. In the mouth it tastes of honeycomb, Granny Smith apples, and lemon peel. This Riesling invites you in for another sip.

PEGASUS BAY

Stockgrove Road, Waipara, North Canterbury,
+64 3 314 6869,
www.pegasusbay.com

The wonderful wines are enough to demand a visit, but if you need more incentive: Pegasus Bay's winery restaurant is one of only a few New Zealand restaurants to be awarded Cuisine NZ Winery Restaurant of the Year. They achieved this honor four years in a row: in 2008, 2009, 2010, and 2011. Pegasus Bay is truly a family affair; Ivan and Christine Donaldson started planting grapes in the 1970s, and now the entire family is involved. Ivan is also a consulting neurologist, associate professor, wine writer, and wine competition judge. Sons Matthew, Eduard, and Paul are all involved, as is Matthew's wife, Lynnette Hudson, who works as one of the winemakers. The family works 40 hectares (99 acres) of land, growing predominantly Riesling and Pinot Noir. Ivan and Lynnette agree that the goal of the company in the next 10 years is "not to get bigger, but to get better. We are happy with what we do, and we want to concentrate on the varieties that we are growing and the wines that we are currently making." Each year the estate produces 250,000 bottles of Pegasus Bay and 250,000 bottles of the "second" label, Main Divide. Pegasus Bay Sauvignon-Semillon 2009 has aromas of fresh cut grass, lemon blossoms, citrus fruit, and delightful green herbaceous notes. Full and round in the mouth, there is a nice level of complexity with a bit of fun on the palate. No malolactic fermentation gives this wine a crisp, clean, and refreshing finish. Lynnette says, "2009 was an absolute stellar vintage, with very cool nights, so we had great retention of acidity and fruit flavors." Pegasus Bay Waipara Valley Bel Canto Dry

Riesling 2009 is crisp, fruity, and floral, all at the same time. It is rich and viscous in style. Ivan says of this wine, "It is reminiscent of the Mosel style," and we couldn't agree more. Main Divide Tehau Reserve Pinot Noir 2008 is named after Ivan's family; he is part Maori on his father's side. The name Tehau means "the wind." We sat on the beautifully manicured outdoor terrace lawn with Ivan and Chris and enjoyed the gentle breeze while sipping this delicious wine. It had aromas of black cherry, red raspberry, red plum, and a touch of cocoa powder. In the mouth, it is a fruit bomb, with beautiful viscosity, a hint of dark chocolate, and a lingering, smooth tannic finish.

PYRAMID VALLEY

548 Pyramid Valley Road, Waikari,
North Canterbury,
+64 3 314 2060,
www.pyramidvalley.co.nz

Mike and Claudia Weersing came to New Zealand in 1996, when Mike began working at Neudorf Vineyards. He had previously studied in Burgundy and perfected his winemaking skills in France, Spain, Germany, and Australia. German-born Claudia, a fashion designer by trade, has embraced both the land and the principles of biodynamics. Together they farm four vineyards of Pinot Noir and Chardonnay and produce natural wines from their own vineyards and select growers. Each vineyard block is named for the most populous weed in its soil, which also gives name and sense of place to their Earth Smoke, Angel Flower, Lion's Tooth, and Field of Fire bottlings. Pyramid Valley Lion's Tooth Chardonnay 2008 has hues of bright straw and a nose of just-picked pear and honeysuckle. In the mouth flavors of green apple, brown pear, buttered toast, and almond paste pave the way for a satisfying finish. Pyramid Valley Angel Flower Pinot Noir 2009 is medium cherry in the glass. This cherry extends to both the nose and palate, where it mingles with cassis, baking spices, orange zest, and a hint of rose petal.

WAITAKI VALLEY

The newest of New Zealand's wine regions, Waitiki Valley is on the border of Northern Otago and Canterbury. Vineyards were first planted here in 2001, and the majority of them are about 65 kilometers (40 miles) from the Pacific Ocean, near the town of Kurow. A cool climate and limestone soils provide the ideal environment for about 100 hectares (247 acres) of mainly Pinot Noir, Pinot Gris, Riesling, and Gewürztraminer. There are a handful of family-owned wineries in this pioneering valley, mainly near the Waitaki River in the north.

OSTLER

45 Bledisloe Street, Kurow, Waitaki Valley,
+64 3 436 0545,
www.ostlerwine.co.nz

When physician Jim Jerram and his brother-in-law, sommelier and winemaker Jeff Sinnott, set out to find land suitable for a vineyard, they found exactly what they were looking for in Waitaki. In 1998, there were no commercial winemaking ventures here, which did not stop Jerram and Sinnott. In the pioneering spirit of Jim's great-grandfather, William Ostler, who had emigrated from Yorkshire, England, in 1852 and purchased Waitaki land, they forged ahead with their plan. By 2002 their first small vineyard was planted, with the first harvest two years later. Further vineyards were added, and today they have 8 hectares (20 acres) planted to Pinot Noir and Pinot Gris. An additional site was planted further inland in 2008, and in 2009 they opened Vintner's Drop, a regional tasting room featuring the wines of Waitaki. Along with Jim's wife, Anne—Jeff's sister—they employ traditional Burgundian and Alsatian techniques to handcraft high-quality wine from estate-grown fruit, plus some that is purchased from trusted growers. Ostler Blue House Vines Waitaki Riesling 2009 showcases fragrances of lime and geranium with what may be a whiff of seawater. Flavors of fresh lime, lemon zest, and

white flowers glide across the tongue; a touch of sweetness is kept from becoming overbearing by a final citrus splash. Ostler Caroline's Pinot Noir 2008 is "berry-licious," with beautiful fruit flavors of strawberry and raspberry mixing it up with clove and eucalyptus on the nose and in the mouth, where they are further joined by chopped Mediterranean herbs and silky tannins. It all draws to a lasting finish.

WAITAKI BRAIDS

Grants Road, Otiake, Waitaki Valley,
+64 2 173 8733,
www.waitakibraids.co.nz

A joint venture between investment banker Stephen Cozens, award-winning winemaker Michelle Richardson, New Zealand–born celebrity Chef Peter Gordon (of Providores in London and Dine by Peter Gordon in Auckland) and his partner Michael McGrath, Waitaki Braids is named for the distinctive braided rivers of the Waitaki Valley. Its 8 hectares (20 acres) of vineyards are home to Pinot Noir, Pinot Gris, Riesling, and Chardonnay. Because of limited quantities of these artisanal wines, they are available only via direct order or at a handful of fine dining restaurants around the world. The first vintage was 2004. Waitaki Braids Pinot Noir 2008 leads on the nose with blackberry, plum, and clove notes. On the palate these are enhanced by secondary characteristics of truffle and sage.

CENTRAL OTAGO

New Zealand is one of the most beautiful nations in the world, and Central Otago is its most beautiful wine-growing region. It is also both the highest altitude wine region in the country and the southernmost wine region in the world. As if that is not enough, the reputation of its Pinot Noir has it on par with Burgundy in the eyes of many wine lovers, especially those who are not bound to Old World tradition. Because of its extreme southern location and its proximity to the Southern Alps, whose peaks reach 3,000 meters (9,843 feet), Central Otago is a cold-weather region as well. Lower daytime temperatures combine with long hours of sunshine to provide ideal conditions for the ripening of its key varieties. In keeping with these conditions, there is a high risk of frost throughout the entire year. Thus, frost-fighting wind machines are a common sight in most vineyards. Central Otago is characterized by steep hillside vineyards and a crisscrossing network of rivers; its rugged allure can hardly be overstated. Summer rainfall can average between 200 millimeters, or 8 inches, and 350 millimeters, or 14 inches, depending on exact location. Glacial soils are rich with mica and schist. Central Otago is divided into four subregions: Alexandra, Cromwell Basin, Gibbston, and Wanaka.

If grapes were books, Pinot Noir would be a runaway bestseller: of 1,532 hectares (3,786 acres) of vineyards in Central Otago, 1,201 hectares (2,968 acres) are covered with Pinot Noir. Essentially all of this is made into table wine, with a small amount reserved for sparkling. The region also grows 143 hectares (353 acres) of Pinot Gris, 67 hectares (166 acres) of Chardonnay, 61 hectares (151 acres) of Riesling, 33 hectares (82 acres) of Sauvignon Blanc, 14 hectares (35 acres) of Gewürztraminer, and small amounts of Merlot and Syrah.

AMISFIELD WINE COMPANY

1113 Wanaka Cromwell Road, Cromwell,
+64 3 445 4901,
www.amisfield.co.nz

Established in 1999 and with 67 hectares (166 acres) of Pinot Noir, Pinot Gris, Sauvignon Blanc, and Riesling vines, Amisfield Wine Company wines have received high praise from *Wine Spectator*, New Zealand wine writer Michael Cooper, and US *Wine & Spirits* magazine. Stephanie Lambert is the head winemaker, and Andre Lategan is the vineyard manager. Together the team crafts sustainable wines at one of Central Otago's largest wineries. Be sure to visit the Amisfield Bistro to dine near the

vines and try the "Trust the Chef" menu; you won't be disappointed. Amisfield Pinot Noir 2008 is dark garnet in the glass with aromas of red raspberry, black raspberry, cassis, and a hint of cocoa. In the mouth the initial attack comes from dark cherries, and the finish has a touch of powdered sugar. Amisfield Pinot Gris 2009 is light straw colored, with notes of stone fruits, spice, and Anjou pear. This wine has wonderful texture. The mid palate brings out flavors of buttered toast.

BALD HILLS

46 Cornish Point Road, Cromwell, Central Otago,
+64 3 445 3161,
www.baldhills.co.nz

After a far-flung career that brought Blair Hunt and his wife, Estelle, to Australia, Fiji, and California, the couple returned to Estelle's home country, New Zealand, and founded Bald Hills. Their more than 7 hectares (17 acres) of

vineyards are planted mostly to Pinot Noir, with about 1 hectare (2.5 acres) each of Pinot Gris and Riesling. Highly lauded winemaker Grant Taylor, owner of nearby Valli Wines, lends his talents, but daily operations are managed by winemaker Christopher Keys and viticulturist Grant Rolston. Small batch wines are produced from grapes that are hand-picked and handsorted. The cozy tasting room is set among Estelle's rose gardens, and she and Blair are usually on hand to chat about the wines and the history of the winery. Bald Hills Pigeon Rocks Pinot Gris 2009 exhibits notes of ripe pear alongside Chinese five-spice powder and rose petal on both the nose and palate. This wine has mouth-filling texture, nurtured by crisp acidity. Bald Hills Single Vineyard Pinot Noir 2007 is red violet in the glass. Its delicate nose is slow to reveal its charms, but strong flavors of black cherry, plum, fennel seed, and violet mingle on the palate, drawing to a full-textured finish.

CARRICK WINES

247 Cairnmuir Road, Bannockburn, Central Otago,
+64 3 445 3480,
www.carrick.co.nz

Steve Green is a busy man! He is the self-described "owner, general manager, assistant winemaker, marketer, and overseas traveler" at the helm of Carrick Wines. With vineyards and a winery located on the Cairnmuir Terraces in Bannockburn, Steve has to rely on the home team while he's spreading the word about Carrick Pinot Noir around the world. The vineyards were planted in 1994 with Pinot Noir, Chardonnay, Riesling, and Pinot Gris vines— with additional plantings in 1998. Under the direction of winemaker Jane Docherty and viticulturist Blair Deaker, Carrick produces award-winning and highly praised wines from its own vineyards plus some outside fruit. The Carrick Restaurant has beautiful views of the Bannockburn Inlet, but more importantly turns out delicious seasonal, locally sourced cuisine prepared by Chef de Cuisine Janet Lyall. Carrick Chardonnay 2008 has a nose of just-picked peach and lovely flavors of peach and apricot buoyed by toasty vanilla and zippy acidity. Carrick Crown & Cross Pinot Noir 2008 is deep garnet in color, with a beautiful nose of black cherries and violet candy. Its silky tannins caress the mouth, unleashing flavors of cherry, blackberry, violet, and mocha.

FELTON ROAD

Bannockburn, Central Otago,
+64 3 445 0885,
www.feltonroad.co.nz

Owner Nigel Greening has assembled an amazing team of biodynamic experts to make his highly rated (and delicious) organic and biodynamic wines. We were lucky enough to stay with winemaker Blair Walter and his charming American wife, Erin, in their beautiful home just minutes from the vineyards. They invited the winery staff, including Todd Stevens, assistant winemaker, and Gareth King, head viticulturist, for an amazing dinner prepared by French chef Gilles Thebault. Gilles was unable to return to his regular job at a restaurant in Christchurch because the building was declared unsafe after the earthquake of 2011. (Thankfully, he has since returned to work.) We were the lucky ones that evening, because he prepared an amazing dinner using the winery's organically raised milk, eggs, goats, cows, and chickens. The meal was expertly paired with Felton Road's stunning wines. In our discussion over dinner, Blair explained the difference between biodynamic and organic to the table: "Organic wine-growing is all about what you are NOT allowed to do, while biodynamic says that organic is a given, but here are the things that you CAN do to grow better vines and make better wines." Felton Road has 32 hectares (79 acres) of vines. As Blair explains, "All of our grapes are estate grown, and we have a limited amount of land, but that's not a bad thing because we want to make quality wines while controlling all of the variables. We want to make consistently good wine for our consumers." Felton Road Cornish Point Pinot Noir 2009 is garnet to black cherry in color. It immediately wowed us with aromas of lovely rose and violet flowers, followed by black fruits with accentuated red jammy characteristics. It is creamy in the mouth with notes of vanilla bean and strawberries. The long, balanced finish is immensely rewarding with post-palate flavors of chocolate-covered cherries sprinkled with orange zest. Felton Road Bannockburn Pinot Noir Central Otago 2009 is garnet to black cherry colored, with aromas of black cherry, aromatic spices, sage, and thyme. It is rich in the mouth, with full fruit flavors and a long, balanced, tannic finish. Felton Road Bannockburn Pinot Noir Central Otago 2010 is garnet to black cherry red, with aromas of sage and thyme bramble. There are more notes of complex earth in the mouth, and it is less fruit-forward than the 2009, but this is certainly an Old World–style Pinot Noir, with a long, elegant, and balanced finish. There is a surprising burst of young red fruit in the posterior palate. Felton Road also makes fantastic Chardonnay and Riesling, and when you visit the winery, you can faintly hear the classical music, especially Beethoven and Mozart, which Blair plays to his wines aging in barrels.

GIBBSTON VALLEY WINES

1820 State Highway 6, Gibbston, Central Otago,
+64 3 442 6910,
www.gibbstonvalleynz.com

Alan Brady is widely credited as the first person to plant grapes in Gibbston in the early 1980s. He opened the first commercial winery in Central Otago shortly thereafter. He boasts New Zealand's "largest and most innovative wine cave"—blasted and carved out of the schist below the Central Otago Mountains. This cave, besides being the ideal temperature-controlled space in which to store his highly acclaimed wines, is hired out for weddings and special functions. Winemaking here is under the direction of Christopher Keys and Sascha Herbert. Gibbston Valley Le Maitre Pinot Noir 2009 is cherry red with aromas of fruits of the wood, raspberry, dark cherry, and a touch of spicy earthiness. In the mouth it is soft and supple with a pleasant finish. Gibbston Valley La Dulcinee Pinot Gris 2009 is straw colored, with notes of fresh white stone fruits and honeysuckle. It is creamy and elegant on the palate, with a refreshing finish.

MOUNT DIFFICULTY

Felton Road, Cromwell, Central Otago,
+64 3 445 3445,
www.mtdifficulty.co.nz

Founded in 1998, Mount Difficulty continues to make quality wines from its Pinot Noir, Chardonnay, Pinot Gris, Riesling, and Sauvignon Blanc vines planted on the Templars Hill, Pipeclay Terrace, Mansons Farm, Target Gulley, and Long Gully vineyards. Winemaking is under the direction of Matt Dicey, and the kitchen is headed by Chef Werner Hecht-Wendt. Visitors to the winery can enjoy leisurely lunches paired with Mount Difficulty wines seven days a week. Mount Difficulty Pinot Noir 2008 is dark garnet, with a nose of dried cherries, coffee,

cherry liqueur, and a touch of menthol. In the mouth it is full-bodied with a cooling finish. Mount Difficulty Roaring Meg Pinot Gris 2010 is perfumed with Anjou pears, honeydew melon, and a hint of guava. In the mouth it has complex fruit flavors and a rounded mouthfeel. The finish has a touch of pleasant sweetness.

MOUNT EDWARD

34 Coalpit Road, Gibbston, Central Otago,
+64 3 442 6113,
www.mountedward.co.nz

Alan Brady founded Mount Edward in 1997 with a commitment to making high-quality, small-batch Pinot Noir, Chardonnay, and Riesling from estate-owned vineyards and trusted contract growers. He continues to do just that, alongside winemaker Duncan Forsyth and viticulturist Tim Austin Moorhouse. Mount Edward has two vineyards in Cromwell and a third in Gibbston; all three are certified Bio-Gro organic. Mount Edward Morrison Vineyard Pinot Noir 2009 reveals scents of black cherry and violet. In the mouth ripe black cherry and a hint of zested orange play off against floral notes and spicy earth.

PEREGRINE WINES

Kawarau Gorge Road, RD 1 Gibbston, Queenstown,
+64 3 442 4038,
www.peregrinewines.co.nz

The soaring canopy of this stunning modern winery mimics the rise of the surrounding mountains, but also appears as if it's a bird taking flight. The native habitat of this winery's namesake bird, the peregrine falcon, is one of rugged mountains laced with rivers and streams emptying into crystalline lakes; in short, the landscape of Central Otago. As with every winery in the region, winemaker Peter Bartle's emphasis is on Pinot Noir harvested from a variety of local vineyards, with an ample amount of aromatic whites among the mix. Peregrine Pinot Gris 2010 is full-fruited with ripe flavors of green pear, nectarine, and grapefruit—and just the right dose of floral-dominated spice. At the high end of the price spectrum, house icon Peregrine The Pinnacle Pinot Noir 2007 is deep red in the glass, with a nose of black cherry and chocolate-covered espresso bean. On the palate fruit, chocolate, and coffee unfold to reveal layers of rich spice and a dash of dried herbs. This is a luxurious, mouth-filling wine.

QUARTZ REEF

8 Hughes Crescent, Cromwell, Central Otago,
+64 3 445 3084,
www.quartzreef.co.nz

Named for the large deposit of quartz crystals running beneath its vineyards, Quartz Reef is owned by Trevor Scott, John Perriam, and Austrian-born Rudi Bauer (who is also Quartz Reef's winemaker). Bauer has been named Winemaker of the Year in the New Zealand National Wine Awards more than once and was the recipient of the prestigious Der Feinschmecker Wine Award for International Winemaker of the Year. He has worked at wineries in Oregon, Burgundy, and Sonoma, and his wines have an international appeal. Bauer and Quartz Reef are committed to making delicious, high-quality wines in Central Otago. Quartz Reef Pinot Noir 2008 is medium cherry colored, with notes of dried cherry, red ripe cherry, raspberry, licorice, and a touch of cocoa. In the mouth the fruit flavors are accentuated by a pop of chocolate-covered cherry at the end. The finish is long, sophisticated, and fun. Quartz Reef Methode Traditionelle NV is made from 75 percent Pinot Noir and 25 percent Chardonnay and is straw colored with *petit perlage*. The nose reveals Granny Smith apples, floral touches, citrus peel, baking bread, and a hint of spice. It is elegant on the mid palate and refreshing in the post palate. The finish invites you in for another sip.

TWO PADDOCKS

315 Strode Road, Alexandra, Central Otago,
+64 3 449 2756,
www.twopaddocks.com

Well-known actor Sam Neill started Two Paddocks in 1993 with a grand ambition: to produce a Pinot Noir that would be enjoyed by his family and friends. Almost 20 years on, Neill must have a lot of friends; from 2 hectares (5 acres), Two Paddocks has grown to include three vineyards, including Redbank, a 53-hectare (130-acre) farm that is also home to fruit orchards and medicinal herbs. The focus is on Pinot Noir, Central Otago's calling card, but small amounts of Chardonnay, Riesling, and Sauvignon Blanc are bottled under the entry-level Picnic label. When Neill is off on location filming, the vineyards and winery remain in the capable hands of lead winemaker Dean Shaw and vineyard manager Mike Wing. The Redbank and Last Chance vineyards gained full organic status in 2008, and Two Paddocks has a firm commitment to producing wine using sustainable, ecologically sound methods. The jewel in the crown is the single-vineyard The Last Chance Pinot Noir, made only in top years. Two Paddocks Picnic Riesling 2009 has a nose of grapefruit and shale and flavors of lemon-lime sorbet with a dusting of spice. Off-dry in style, its mineral-rich acid finish keeps it from feeling too sweet. Two Paddocks Pinot Noir 2009 is deep red in the glass, with a nose of cherries and herbes de Provence. On the palate rich red and black fruit are complemented by smoked meat and herb flavors—all moving toward a rich, smooth finish.

VALLI

29 The Mall, Cromwell, Central Otago,
+64 3 442 6778,
www.valliwine.com

Grant Taylor, the great-great-grandson of Italian immigrant Giuseppe Valli, has racked up an enviable string of awards and accolades for his Pinot Noir. After 13 years in the Napa Valley and another 5 years at nearby Gibbston Valley, Taylor struck out on his own in 1998 with the establishment of Valli Wines. Mining the best of the region's terroir, Valli has two vineyards in the region: a Bannockburn Vineyard, planted in 1996, and a Gibbston Vineyard, planted in 2000. Valli also has a vineyard further north, in the up-and-coming Waitaki region. Taylor is assisted by vineyard manager and assistant winemaker Duncan Billing and also by his first cousin, Tim Valli. Valli Vineyards Old Vine Riesling 2010 has a luxurious nose of nectarine laced with jasmine and orange blossom. In the mouth balanced fruit, floral, and light spice notes play off one another until the last lick of a bright finish kicks in. Valli Bannockburn Vineyard Pinot Noir 2008 is full of ripe red fruits. Its perfumed nose blends cherry, herb, and spice notes, which then extend to the palate before drawing to a well-structured finish.

RECIPES

WAIPARA LAMB CHOPS

✳

*Recipe courtesy of Chef Oliver Jackson, Pegasus Bay Restaurant
at the Pegasus Bay Winery in Canterbury*

✳

SERVES 4

Pegasus Bay Restaurant has the distinct honor of being named "New Zealand Restaurant of the Year" by *Cuisine* magazine for three consecutive years: 2008, 2009 and 2010. Chef Jackson consistently turns out food that keeps people coming back for more. The dining room is under the watchful eye of Belinda Donaldson and winery owners Ivan and Christine Donaldson. Visitors can also dine outside on the meticulously kept lawn and garden with sweeping views to their duck-filled lake.

FOR THE LAMB

2 lamb racks, each rack
    cut in half
1 whole garlic bulb, cloves
    slightly crushed
Fresh oregano, chopped
5 tablespoons olive oil, divided
4 ounces balsamic vinegar
2 tablespoons butter
Salt to taste

FOR THE GARNISH

¼ pound pancetta or bacon,
    cut into small batons
1 (8-ounce) can cannellini beans,
    drained and rinsed
2 ounces fresh peas
10–12 mint leaves, washed and
    patted dry
¼ cup chicken stock
2 tablespoons butter
Salt and pepper, to taste
½ cup ricotta

MARINATE THE LAMB

Combine lamb, garlic cloves, and oregano in a large baking pan. Add 4 tablespoons olive oil and the balsamic vinegar, and toss to combine all ingredients. Marinate lamb for at least 1 hour and up to 24 hours. (If marinating the lamb for more than an hour, the mixture should be covered and refrigerated.)

COOK THE LAMB

Preheat oven to 400°F.

Heat a large heavy frying pan over moderately high heat until hot but not smoking, then add the remaining tablespoon of oil and 2 tablespoons butter. Remove the lamb from the marinade, and sprinkle with salt. Place racks fat side down in skillet to render some of the fat. Turn the racks onto their sides to brown slightly. Transfer lamb in skillet to oven, and roast lamb for 3 minutes. Turn lamb racks over with tongs, and return to oven for another 3 minutes. Remove the skillet from the oven and transfer the lamb to a cutting board. Cover with foil and let rest for 10 minutes.

MAKE THE GARNISH

Fry pancetta in frying pan over low heat to render fat. Add cannellini beans, peas, mint, stock, butter, salt, and pepper, and cook just until all ingredients are warmed through.

TO SERVE

Dollop ricotta around 4 serving plates, then place pea and bean mixture on plates. Cut lamb racks into chops and arrange on top of the vegetables. Pour pan juices over the lamb.

PAUA FRITTERS

✳

Recipe courtesy of Jo Crabb,
chef and cooking school instructor, Palliser Estate

✳

SERVES 4

According to Jo, *paua*, or "abalone," grow on the rocky coasts of New Zealand and especially around the Chatham Islands. They take between four to eight years to reach legal marketable size. Most New Zealander's gather their own *paua* because the cost can be over NZ$50 (US$42) per pound. It is common for families on vacation to collect *paua*, take it back to their seaside cottages, and prepare *paua* fritters. Jo invited us into her kitchen at Careme, Palliser Estate's cooking school, where she teaches. She graciously showed us the secrets of making delicious *paua* fritters—and she would be happy to show you too. We enjoyed them paired with a crisp, clean Palliser Estate Chardonnay 2008.

1 pound fresh abalone, stomach sack removed, frilly "skirt" trimmed

1 large onion, cut into large chunks

1 cup fresh bread crumbs

½ teaspoon salt

½ teaspoon fresh black pepper

½ cup plain flour

1 egg, lightly beaten

2 tablespoons cooking oil

Lemon wedges for serving

Using a grinder, coarsely mince the abalone twice; then put the onion through the mincer. (This helps get the last of the abalone through the grinder.)

Stir in the bread crumbs, salt, pepper, flour, and egg until combined.

Heat a heavy skillet or barbecue grill plate until hot but not smoking, add oil and cook a large tablespoon of the abalone mixture in the oil for about 2 minutes on each side until just cooked.

Form 16 to 20 small patties, about 1 tablespoon each and cook, as above, in small batches. (Don't overcook, or the fritters will be tough. The fritters should feel just a little soft when you push them.)

Serve hot with lemon wedges.

"HAWKE'S BAY" BASIL CRUSTED LAMB LOIN SERVED OVER EGGPLANT & FINE RATATOUILLE

✳

Recipe courtesy Chef Leyton Ashley,
Terroir Restaurant, Craggy Range Winery

✳

SERVES 4

We had a fantastic dinner with Craggy Range's director of wine and viticulture, Steve Smith MW, and his delightful wife, Laura. Chef Leyton Ashley had not yet included this recipe on the menu at Terroir, but he decided to try it out on us. Terroir restaurant was awarded "Winery Restaurant of the Year 2009" by *Cuisine* magazine. We enjoyed this delicious lamb dish with Craggy Range Bannockburn Sluicings Pinot Noir 2009 from Central Otago.

FOR THE LAMB LOIN

4 lamb loins, sirloin, boneless
Extra virgin olive oil

FOR THE BASIL CRUST

1 quart vegetable oil for frying
1 cup packed basil leaves
½ cup fine panko bread crumbs
1 small clove garlic
Salt and pepper to taste

FOR THE RATATOUILLE

Olive oil for cooking
1 yellow bell pepper, finely diced
1 red bell pepper, finely diced
1 zucchini, finely diced
1 large eggplant, finely diced
1 cup tomato sauce
Salt and pepper to taste

FOR THE EGGPLANT PUREE

1 large eggplant
Salt and pepper to taste
1 cup cream
1 teaspoon cumin, toasted
2 teaspoon tahini
Extra virgin olive oil

FOR THE AU JUS

1 cup lamb stock
1 sprig rosemary leaves

FOR THE FINAL STEPS

1 egg yolk
1 teaspoon Dijon mustard
Splash of water
About 1 cup plain flour
2 tablespoons vegetable oil for
    searing lamb
1 tablespoon butter

PREPARE AND SEAR THE LAMB LOINS

Prepare a water bath at 140°F. and prepare an ice bath in a large bowl or sink.

Remove any sinew from the lamb loins, then put 1 loin in a zippered plastic bag, add a splash of the extra virgin olive oil, and seal to remove air. Repeat for all remaining loins. Place bags in water bath for 12 minutes, then remove bags and place them directly into the iced water. Set aside to cool completely. (Alternatively, the loins can be seasoned with salt and pepper, seared in a hot pan, and then roasted in a moderate oven for 2 to 3 minutes until rare. Let cool.)

PREPARE THE BASIL CRUST

In a large heavy-bottomed saucepan or a deep fryer, heat about one quart of vegetable oil to 345°F. Using caution, fry the basil leaves in two batches until they are totally crispy, about 20 seconds. (Be very careful, as the leaves will explode as the water in them hits the oil.) Remove basil with a slotted spoon onto paper towels to drain. Let cool and dry. Put the basil, panko, and garlic in a food processor and process until fine and vibrant green. Season with a little salt and ground black pepper.

MAKE THE RATATOUILLE

Heat 4 saucepans with a little olive oil until they begin to smoke. Keeping vegetables separate, fry them quickly. Try to retain their color without overcooking. Set them aside to cool; then mix together with the tomato sauce. Season with salt and pepper.

MAKE THE EGGPLANT PUREE

Preheat the oven to 375°F.

(continued on the following page)

(continued from the previous page)

Pierce the eggplant skin, lightly salt, and roast the eggplant in the oven until it collapses. Meanwhile heat the cream and cumin in another saucepan and season with salt to taste. Remove eggplant from the oven, and while it is still warm, press it through a colander, discarding the skin. Place the eggplant flesh in a blender and blend, slowly adding the warm cumin cream from the feed tube while the blender is running. Season with tahini, the extra virgin olive oil, and salt and pepper to taste. Set aside.

MAKE THE AU JUS

Reduce a good-quality lamb stock with a little rosemary until about 20 percent of its original volume. The consistency should be somewhat sticky.

THE FINAL STEPS

Preheat the broiler.

In a small bowl, whisk together the egg yolk and Dijon mustard with a splash of water.

Place some plain flour on a plate.

Take the prepared lamb loins and—on the presentation side only—dust them in the plate of flour. Shake off excess flour. Brush the floured side of the lamb with the egg wash, and press the basil crust on top. Heat a heavy frying pan until hot but not smoking, add a little vegetable oil and a pat of butter, and gently sear the uncrumbed side of the lamb for about 30 seconds. Transfer the pan under the broiler for 1 to 2 minutes, until the lamb is warmed through. Let rest.

Reheat the eggplant puree and ratatouille. Add fresh chopped basil to the ratatouille once it is hot.

TO SERVE

Using a spatula, neatly spread the eggplant puree onto four serving plates. Spoon the ratatouille onto the plate. Place one lamb loin on top of the eggplant puree and ratatouille, and drizzle with the reduced jus to finish.

IN THEIR OWN WORDS

BOB CAMPBELL MW

Bob Campbell is one of New Zealand's premier wine writers. He is a Master of Wine, the author of the *New Zealand Wine Annual*, and a contributor to Jancis Robinson's *Oxford Companion of Wine*. He is an international wine judge and the founder of The Wine Gallery, a New Zealand wine school boasting more than 15,000 graduates.

How did you get involved in the world of wine?

I am an accountant by qualification and joined a winery (Montana, now Brancott Estate) as their financial accountant. All my friends thought that because I worked for a winery I must know about wine. I didn't. So I joined a tasting group, read every wine book I could lay my hands on, and tasted every wine I could afford (and some I couldn't afford). After a while I knew about wine.

What are some of the biggest changes you have seen in winemaking or wine styles since you began your career?

New Zealand wine was, by today's standards, mostly undrinkable when I joined the industry in 1973. We drank it anyway because we didn't know any better. On special occasions we drank imported wine. Now pretty well all New

Zealand wine is fault-free, and most of it is delicious. On special occasions we now drink top-flight New Zealand wine (as well as imports).

What are some of the exciting changes that you see happening in your country?

The rise in quality and quantity. It's been a hell of a ride. The year I joined the industry was the first year that grapes were planted in Marlborough. The quality potential had always been there—it simply took a brave soul to turn the key by planting the right sort of grape varieties there. Exciting pioneering stuff!

Pinot Noir didn't arrive until the early eighties, and now we make world-class wines from what I confess is my desert island grape variety. Sauvignon Blanc didn't appear until the early seventies. We've come a long way in a short time.

I find the experimental nature of the wine industry very stimulating. At first they planted every available grape variety in the first available and often highly unsuitable site. A few worked but many didn't. The experiments continue but are now based on good science. Unsurprisingly the failure rate has fallen considerably.

Have you ever worked as a winemaker—even for just a harvest? Where? How does that experience inform your writing?

I have never worked as a winemaker, but I have made wine at my home over many years. That has helped me understand the process as well as appreciate the difficulties involved in making a drinkable, let alone a good, wine. The best wine I made was a Zinfandel from Dusi Ranch in San Luis Obispo. I was living in Los Angeles at the time and made wine for the first time on a grand scale—half-a-ton of grapes all fermented in my garage. I still have a few bottles of this 1980 wine left, and it's still drinking well.

Do you think that the market should influence winemaking, or do you think that winemaking should influence the market?

I think that winemakers should lead the market, although that's probably truer at the top end rather than the more commercially driven bulk end of the market.

What is your opinion on screwcap versus cork closures?

When New Zealand winemakers started experimenting with screwcaps in 2001, I purchased 12 cases of 12 different wines from Sauvignon Blanc to Cabernet Sauvignon— 6 bottles of each under screwcap and 6 under cork. After three years I was convinced that there should be a law against bottling white wine under cork. I'm now 95 percent convinced that red wines perform better under screwcap but need a little more time before making the leap to 100 percent. Screwcaps were at first quite divisive in our industry, but winemakers now respect the rights of anyone to use any closure they like. Currently 99.5 percent of New Zealand wines are sealed with a screwcap.

If you could invite anyone from history, living or dead, to your home for dinner, who would it be? What food would you serve? What wine would you serve?

Auberon Waugh (deceased English wine writer who is the son of Evelyn Waugh), a man with a keen palate and good sense of humor. He once described a wine as "smelling of French railway station and ladies underwear"—brilliant. Waugh counseled wine writers to "camp it up a bit, and don't try to simply write sensible wine notes."

As for wine and food—I have a bottle of Japanese Merlot that would stimulate conversation. I'd probably also serve a bottle of Craggy Range 2009 Quarry blind alongside a masked bottle of 2009 Haut Brion. Waugh might prefer the Haut Brion (but then again he might not), but he would certainly admit that, at around one-twentieth of the price, Craggy Range punched well above its weight. I'd serve the wines with my famous (within my own family at least) seared lamb fillets on a white bean puree.

If you were to stay home tonight for a relaxing evening, drinking wine while watching a movie, which movie would you watch? Which wine would you drink? Explain.

I'd watch an old favorite—*The Blues Brothers*. It would be accompanied by a Syrah from the Gimblett Gravels district of Hawke's Bay—Trinity Hill 2008 "Homage" Syrah— *en magnum*.

Do you collect wine? If so, what is in your cellar?

I have around 1,500 bottles—many New Zealand but also a not inconsiderable collection of Mosel Rieslings, northern Rhône (particularly Côte Rôtie) and red Burgundy.

If you weren't involved in wine, what would you be doing?

I'd be a sad accountant who regretted never having made a career change.

TIM HEATH

Tim Heath has been a winemaker at Moët Hennessy's Cloudy Bay winery since 2005 and has worked in Australia's Clare Valley and Eden Valley as well as France's Rhône Valley. He loves the great outdoors, fly-fishing, his dog, Buster, and of course, his wife, Amy. We shared a delightful and delicious French meal together—perfectly paired with Tim's wines.

How did you get involved in the world of wine?

I started studying organic chemistry at university and quickly became a little disillusioned. . . . I didn't want to spend the rest of my life wearing a white lab coat and safety glasses. At the time I was working part time in a kitchen. I have always loved to cook even as a young kid. I fell in love with the fast-paced action and creativity of the environment, but the life of a chef is too hard for my liking. It's like doing harvest all year long with no break! It was about then that the wine industry caught my eye. It seemed to offer a great mix of variety and challenge and a chance to work in a sensory world full of aroma, flavors, and texture. It has proven to be a good choice.

What are some of the biggest changes you have seen in winemaking since you began your career?

A move away from heavily oaked, overripe styles of wine to more balanced, sensitively crafted wines that are more respectful to the fruit.

What are some of the exciting changes that you see happening specifically in your country?

The most exciting thing for New Zealand is the continued evolution and development in Pinot Noir that is occurring around the cooler regions of the country. There has been a huge amount of work done on clonal selection and site selection over the last 10 to 15 years, and we are really seeing the reward of that effort now that we are entering into a phase of more mature vine age. Also Kiwi Syrah from Hawke's Bay . . . some amazing wines come out of this region that have many similarities to northern Rhône Syrah.

Where else in the world have you studied, trained, or worked a harvest? How did that influence your winemaking?

Australia—Clare Valley and Barossa; France—northern Rhône, Champagne, Alsace; India—Nashik; Time spent in Spain—Penedes; Germany—Mosel.

Time in the Old World helped to broaden my winemaking horizons beyond that of a sometimes very clinical New World approach and really highlight the importance of a great site when trying to make great wine.

Which varietals are you working with? Are you experimenting with anything new?

Sauvignon Blanc, Chardonnay, and Pinot Noir for sparkling, and still wine, Pinot Gris, Riesling, Gewürztraminer. Experimenting with a little bit of Malbec . . . but it never sees the light of day . . . usually ends up in our own cellars!

Are there any new areas that you have identified for potential vineyard sites?

We have a vineyard called "Barracks" in the Southern Valleys region of the Wairau Valley in Marlborough for Pinot Noir. This was planted in 2004 and is showing some amazing potential.

What challenges have you faced as a winemaker or winery owner?

The biggest challenge would have to be having Mother Nature as your boss. At the end of the day she has the biggest influence on what ends up in the glass.

What is your winemaking philosophy?

Sensitive, respectful winemaking that allows the wine to show a true sense of place in the glass. An approach of less is more is often the best and allows the vineyard site to do the talking (minimal fining, natural yeast fermentation, careful use of new oak et cetera).

What would you hope people say about your wines?

That they show a true sense of place, are distinctive, and go beyond just simple fruit flavors. Most of all I hope that people say they are delicious.

Do you think that the market should influence winemaking, or do you think that winemaking should influence the market?

Winemaking should influence the market (answered like a true winemaker).

Besides your own wine, what are some of your favorite wines? What do you like about them?

German Rieslings (love the structural interplay between acidity and sweetness), northern Rhône Syrah (the amazing array of styles that come from this region—it's the "Burgundy of Syrah"), Champagne (it's delicious).

What is your opinion on screwcap versus cork closures?

Screwcap. There is no such thing as a perfect closure, but it's the closest we have got, particularly for aromatic white varieties and Pinot Noir.

If you could invite anyone from history, living or dead, to your home for dinner, who would it be? What food would you serve? What wine would you serve?

Grace Kelly, Leonardo da Vinci, Albert Einstein, Ricky Gervais, Johnny Cash, Sean Connery in character as James Bond, Brigitte Bardot, John Lennon, Queen Mary I of England, Nikola Tesla, Ernest Hemingway, Salvador Dali, Ayrton Senna, Winston Churchill, John Cleese, and Kermit the Frog.

Wine: It would be a BYO dinner party with the theme of "bring the best wine from your era." More interesting that way.

Food: A "no-holds-barred Medieval feast" cooked by Heston Blumenthal. But pigeon would have to be off the menu if Nikola Tesla ended up making it.

If you were to stay home tonight for a relaxing evening, drinking wine while watching a movie, which movie would you watch? Which wine would you drink? Explain.

Monty Python's *The Meaning of Life* and a bottle of red Burgundy. Serious wine for a not so serious film.

How do you like to spend your time away from the winery?

Fly-fishing, hunting, time in the outdoors in general, cooking and hanging out in my vegetable patch with my dog.

Do you collect wine? If so, what is in your cellar?

Yes, a variety of things from all over the place.

If you weren't involved in wine, what would you be doing?

Fly-fishing.

STEVE SMITH MW

In 1985, Steve was awarded the Winston Churchill Memorial Trust Scholarship to study grape vine disease in California. He is the only specialized viticulturist to have achieved the Master of Wine. In 1996, *Decanter* magazine named him "One of the Fifty Most Influential People in the World of Wine." He was also named one of the "Top 50" by *Wine & Spirits* magazine in 2005. He is the cofounder, part-owner, and director of wine and viticulture at the Craggy Range winery. We've had a lot of fun hanging out with Steve in New Zealand and the United States. He has been to a rum tasting/barbecue party in our New York City backyard, and we're still angry with him for showing up with a case of Craggy Range wine for our friends—nobody drank the 25 bottles of rum we had lined up for the tasting. We're still trying to figure out a way to send him the 25 half-empty bottles!

How did you get involved in the world of wine?
Entirely by chance. I wanted to be an architect and still have hidden ambitions here; however, straight out of high school I was offered a scholarship from the New Zealand Ministry of Agriculture as an agricultural researcher, and by chance the first project I was seconded to was set up to study the effects of grapevine phylloxera in the vineyards of New Zealand. From there I got a taste for it, firstly as an academic specializing in viticulture, then in commercial viticulture moving through wine to the business of wine, passing my Master of Wine, and now having the great privilege of being charged with establishing Craggy Range—the vineyards, the winery, the brand, and the business. It has been and still is a great ride.

What are some of the biggest changes you have seen in winemaking since you began your career?
In New Zealand it has been all change. From broad-acre viticulture with low-value Germanic wine styles to the New World's preeminent producer of fine, cool-climate white wine in less than 30 years, I have seen and been part of that happening. The realization in the New World that, for fine wine, site is everything, not the winemaker. A move back to natural farming and winemaking, but now with a great scientific base of knowledge about what natural actually means.

What are some of the exciting changes that you see happening specifically in your country?
In New Zealand it is the belief that we can make world-class, very fine red wines. Obviously Pinot Noir is the star here, and it has found a home in a number of locations that share the variety's natural requirement for cool, sunny, autumn conditions. However, it is not the only red wine story, in the gravelly soils of the Gimblett Gravels wine-growing district, the red wines from the Bordeaux red varieties show a distinctive stamp of ripeness and richness combined with a fragrance and lightness that is hard to find in many warmer locations.

Where else in the world have you studied, trained, or worked a harvest? How did that influence your winemaking?
I was lucky enough to have trained and studied under Dr. Richard Smart, so that's a global encyclopedia right there, and obviously the study for the Master of Wine took me around the world. I studied and trained more formally in California and worked a harvest at Louis Jadot in Burgundy. However I would have to say I've avoided doing harvests in wineries, mainly because I love the vineyards more. I believe you can honestly learn more visiting producers when they are not frantic and stressed out, walk the vineyards, taste their wines, listen, and question. Bordeaux had the greatest influence on me, the absolute perfection in the vineyards and cellars of the great producers, the glamour of the place, the incredible business of wine, and the most remarkable link between nature and technology. That had the greatest influence on me, to make wine naturally you need to be very smart, very perceptive, and very decisive when you need to—and surround yourself with great technology and the odd person who wears lab coats!

Which varieties are you working with? Are you experimenting with anything new?
Well we are in New Zealand so Sauvignon Blanc is a cornerstone, and we take it very seriously with a lot of craftsmanship and a distinctive house stamp of restraint and texture rather than the typical abundance of fruit. Pinot Noir occupies a lot of our red wine ambitions, and there is a lot going on in the vineyard with management and various selections of planting material to keep me intellectually occupied. Syrah has been our experiment, and it has become a rock star for the Craggy Range brand, so once again clonally and in the vineyard lots to learn. The whole Gimblett Gravels red wine story is pioneering and finding new red varieties that may suit this place. It will be interesting. New Zealand is the land of

the aromatic white wine, and there are people playing with all sorts of interesting varieties to keep the world interested way beyond just Sauvignon Blanc.

Are there any new areas that you have identified for potential vineyard sites?
I guess the Gimblett Gravels is new, as is the Te Muna Road area of Martinborough that was essentially unplanted when I purchased that land. For neither of these though could I claim "first there" rights, but I certainly believe we have had a significant influence on the reputation and discovery of these places by the wine people of the world.

What challenges have you faced as a winemaker or winery owner?
As a viticulturist and someone responsible for the wine that goes in the bottle, I would never claim I made it, because winemaking facilities and me are not good bedfellows— the greatest challenge we face is each season. They can be remarkably different and sometimes dramatically different at different times of the season, not just at harvest. The Crowded House (great New Zealand rock band, not Australian!) had a song called "Four Seasons in One Day," that's New Zealand weather. Farming your way through the season is the greatest challenge and the greatest pleasure. As a winery

owner, and I am sure Terry Peabody who is essentially the owner of Craggy Range (I have my little corner!), would agree in the 12 years since we started Craggy Range we have had everything thrown at us. One in a hundred year frosts in the spring, one in a hundred coldest Decembers on record, January another year and February another year. The global financial crisis, erratic exchange rates and in all of this managing what is a legacy investment to be profitable. The requirement to be multidisciplined does not even come close to summing it up.

What is your winemaking philosophy?
Natural where possible; create wines that capture the essence of where the grape is grown without being fruity or simple; wines with beauty in aroma, ripeness yet a sense of lightness, balance, and a lasting textural element that really does come from the soul of the vineyard.

What would you hope people say about your wine?
"Nice" would be the worst word. "Pleasure" would be the best, and realization once the glass or bottle was finished that "I really enjoyed that wine; I need to have a bottle close in times of need."

Do you think that the market should influence winemaking, or do you think that winemaking should influence the market?

You will only ever be able to sell wine that people want to drink, however you can lead people. Look at New Zealand Sauvignon Blanc, it came at a time where the new wine drinkers of the world were looking for freshness and flavor and purity and zing although that was never, ever said. New Zealand singlehandedly created the market boom for Sauvignon Blanc by creating a category of fresh, flavorsome, zingy white wines. I think the key is to understand what the macro trends are in the world with everything, particularly with lifestyle, health, and food and create something that fits into those, then you can lead the market but not rebel against a trend.

Besides your own wine, what are some of your favorite wines? What do you like about them?

Bordeaux and Barolo. I love the places, the people, and the top wines from these great producers.

What is your opinion on screwcap versus cork closures?

I am actually sick of the discussion, but briefly, white wines must be under screwcap for drinking and aging; lighter to medium-bodied red wines will likely give a better experience new and old under screwcap; the jury is out

on fuller bodied red wines particularly with bigger, savory tannins.

If you could invite anyone from history, living or dead, to your home for dinner, who would it be? What food would you serve? What wine would you serve?

Charles Darwin. The food would be a new species that he never found. Château Latour, the greatest living thing on earth.

If you were to stay home tonight for a relaxing evening, drinking wine while watching a movie, which movie would you watch? Which wine would you drink? Explain.

It all depends on who you are with. With my wife, probably *Ghost*, with some Taittinger Comte de Champagne 1995, the year we got married; she and the wine would have to console me. I'm tragic at that movie. By myself, probably *Midnight Express*, and I would probably need more than one bottle of a great traditional Napa Cabernet, Stags Leap Cellars from the '80s probably just to keep the heart pumping.

How do you like to spend your time away from the winery?

Two teenage daughters take care of that. We have a great beach house an hour from the winery that is a great refuge, and I am trying to find time to pick up a golf club a lot more . . .unsuccessfully at this point!

Do you collect wine? If so, what is in your cellar?

Bordeaux and Barolo.

If you weren't involved in wine, what would you be doing?

Good question, although architecture would definitely be there somewhere. It would need to be something on the land so it would be rural architecture, and there would be a lot of flowers and fruits around.

MICHAEL BRAJKOVICH MW

Michael Brajkovich was the first New Zealander to earn the coveted Master of Wine. He grew up making wine at the elbow of his father, Maté, and his mother, Melba. He received his bachelor's degree in enology and returned to the family vineyard—at Kumeu River Wines—to continue the Brajkovich winemaking legacy. We were invited to lunch at the Brajkovich family home. Melba presided over the table of her four adult children with a sense of pride, joy, and grace. We were honored to be guests at the table of this wonderful family.

How did you get involved in the world of wine?
I was born into it. My father started making wine here in Kumeu in 1944. He always hoped that maybe one of his children might come back into the business and carry it on. Now there are all four of us, plus Mum, back in the business and carrying on his vision.

What are some of the biggest changes you have seen in winemaking since you began your career?
The grapes. When I started in the 1980s the biggest variety was Müller-Thurgau; now it hardly figures in the national statistics. Vineyards have changed rapidly in terms of their varietal makeup, their trellising design, their management, and their location. A great deal of work has gone into the viticultural side of our business, because that is ultimately what determines the quality and the distinctiveness of our wines. We have better rootstocks now, better planting material in terms of clones, and a much better understanding of vineyard microclimate and how that can be improved through cultural techniques such as trellising, pruning, shoot positioning, and trimming. The use of bird netting to effectively exclude birds has been a major improvement in the last 20 years and has enabled a significant rise in maturity levels in grapes and much cleaner fruit too.

What are some of the exciting changes that you see happening specifically in your country?
Much better expression of varietal character and regional character in our wines as a result of better viticultural and enological practices. The move toward screwcap closures has also been significant in showing these characters in a much better light. There continues to

be discovered new viticultural regions with potential for producing wines of great character.

Where else in the world have you studied, trained, or worked a harvest? How did that influence your winemaking?

My tertiary level training was at Roseworthy College in South Australia, which is now part of the University of Adelaide. While there I worked a harvest in Coonawarra in the southeast of South Australia, then a few years later worked the harvest with Jean Pierre Moueix in Libourne.

My Australian training was crucial in ensuring that our wines are produced correctly and free of obvious fault. I still think that Australian winemakers are the most technically competent in the world. My French experience was even more important in exposing me to some of the greatest wine regions in the world and getting to understand the concept of terroir and tradition. With my technical background it opened up all sorts of possibilities to be tried out in our own conditions at Kumeu.

Later on I had the opportunity to learn even more about French wine, in particular through our English wine importers (Hugh Phillips and Kit Stevens) and from that experience went on to sit and pass the Master of Wine exam in London in 1989. I was the first New Zealand MW.

My own path into the MWs is a bit of a long story, I'm afraid.

I had first heard about the Masters of Wine from my father, then again when I was studying at Roseworthy College in the early '80s, and was always very much in awe of their ability to identify wines down to the particular terroir and vintage et cetera.

In 1983 I had a tremendous opportunity to work in Pomerol and St. Emilion with Christian Moueix and Jean-Claude Berrouet, where I learned a great deal about viticulture and winemaking in that part of France, and I also traveled through Burgundy and Alsace. This experience greatly influenced our winemaking at Kumeu River, in terms of technique, for many years to come.

I was always interested in wine styles and quality from around the world, as I am certain that such knowledge makes you a better winemaker. You cannot make good wine unless you know what good wine tastes like. And, similarly, a wide knowledge of the world of wines gives you a much greater appreciation of where your own wine fits in the greater scheme of things. However, this interest did not ever extend toward any aspiration to become a Master of Wine.

In 1987, I was judging at the Air New Zealand Wine Awards at the Château Tongariro and had the opportunity to judge with our overseas guest judge, Sarah Morphew MW. Sarah was the first woman MW, passing in 1971, I believe. She was also the current chair of the Institute of Masters of Wine, which was undergoing a few major changes at the time.

After the judging, Sarah commented to me that she thought I had the wine-tasting ability to be able to pass the MW exam, which took me aback a little. She then went on to ask, "Why not have a go?" My immediate reaction was that I could not justify spending that much time in the UK in order to qualify for the exams. In those days you had to have had five years' experience in the UK wine trade first. Sarah then told me that the institute was about to expand its frontiers and go international and part of that process was to allow candidates with five years' experience in the wine trade anywhere in the world the chance to sit. I still wasn't convinced, so that idea stayed in abeyance for a while.

Then in 1988 Michael Hill Smith became the first non-UK Master of Wine. Michael had been in London for a while working toward the exam, and then the rules had changed to allow internationals to sit as well. This was a fantastic and inspirational achievement and especially so as Michael took the examination tasting prize as well.

After Michael had passed, Sarah Morphew telephoned me and said why shouldn't I also have a go and pass too? It was a challenge, so I agreed to submit an entrance essay, which was accepted and away it all went.

At the same time, Bob Campbell was also interested in having a go at the exam, so we got together a (very) small tasting group to try out exam-style tasting conditions under the tutelage of Sam Weaver (now a winemaker with his own Churton label in Marlborough, but back then working for an Auckland wine merchant). Sam had passed the tasting section of the exam and so had an intimate knowledge of how the papers and questions were structured. He was immensely helpful in getting us used to the required examination technique. This exercise in itself was a wonderful learning experience, and working through the examination questions took me way outside my normal work and experience with wine. It was great discipline and very rewarding.

When it came time to plan for the May '89 exam in London, Bob felt he wasn't quite ready, so it was myself and Christchurch's Professor Ivan Donaldson who traveled from New Zealand for the exam. Ivan, of course, went on to create Pegasus Bay in Canterbury, a great success story. Expatriate New Zealander Margaret Harvey, who had been working in the trade in London for several years previously, was the other New Zealander sitting the exam that year.

In 1988 we had also started exporting wine, principally Chardonnay, to the UK for the first time. Our agent was and still is, Hugh Phillips of the Boxford wine company. We were introduced to Hugh by an old friend of his, Kit Stevens MW, who was at the time resident in Auckland. My brother and I traveled to the London Wine Fair in 1988 to show our wares. Paul had to return to New Zealand immediately afterward to sit university exams, but I stayed on in Europe to take an extraordinary tour of France for two weeks with Monsieur Stevens (Kit).

It was one of the most eye-opening experiences of my life, and I had the opportunity to taste a range of wines and meet a collection of people that I believe one could only dream about today. I thought I knew a thing or two about wine, but it was people like Kit Stevens and Hugh Phillips that extended my knowledge, particularly of French wine, way beyond what I could have learned back in New Zealand, or even Australia.

It was the broadening of my wine experience in this way that gave me the confidence to attempt the MW exam. Many people have asked why I sat the exam, and I have always answered, "Because it was there." At first it seemed unattainable, for one reason or another, then gradually the barriers disappeared, and Sarah Morphew's

prickly challenge pushed me into it.

I was out of wine college recently enough to be quite confident about the theory parts of the exam, all I had to do was improve the breadth and quality of my tasting, which I did through these incredible experiences, and to improve my essay writing.

To be honest, I did not expect to pass. I had seen previous exam papers, and they seemed very difficult and perhaps doable. I fully expected that this would be an interesting, if stressful, experience, but that afterward I would appreciate just how difficult the exam was and therefore have some idea if I was actually capable of pursuing it and eventually passing it. Because I fully expected to fail on this occasion, I had no fear of failure. I was a young(ish) winemaker trying to make an impression on the world of wine, but if I missed out, it was no big deal. As it happened, I passed on this first attempt and became New Zealand's first MW. The effect on my reputation and that of Kumeu River was immediate. Having been adventurous in winemaking with a few radical innovations such as wild yeast ferments, malolactic in Chardonnay, et cetera, the MW qualification saved me from being quirky and odd and instead gave everything a certain legitimacy.

Through membership of the institute I have met and associated with some very interesting people over the years, but the distance from London means there is limited scope for such interaction. I have attended some MW conferences and went on a tour to Tokaj, and just last year attended my first-ever General Meeting of the institute at Vintners Hall and that has all been very worthwhile. However, the most stimulating and rewarding experiences have been getting involved with the education side of the institute in New Zealand and Australia and in mentoring and teaching MW students. I regret that I do far too little of this sort of stuff and have resolved to contribute again to the MW education program soon.

Which varieties are you working with? Are you experimenting with anything new?
Chardonnay accounts for about 65 percent of our production and is clearly very important to us. Pinot Gris is 22 percent, Pinot Noir 8 percent, and Merlot 5 percent. We are experimenting with a very small area of Gewürztraminer.

Are there any new areas that you have identified for potential vineyard sites?
Not yet, but we are always interested in how we may progress into the future, and that certainly might include establishing vineyards in other regions.

What challenges have you faced as a winemaker or winery owner?
Back in the 1980s when interest rates went up to 19 percent and sales plummeted in the opposite direction, things got really tough in the wine business. Dad had to sell off some land to keep our business afloat, but at the same time we were making big strides in improving wine quality and concentrating on varieties that we can do well. This has placed us in very good stead to ride through the recent global financial crisis, and we continue to do what we do well, but it has still been very difficult in the trade over the last two years. We have avoided the temptation to grow too fast and instead have concentrated on our core values, which leads to the next question.

What is your winemaking philosophy?
We aim to produce grapes of the highest possible quality that reflect the nature and characteristics of our land, then sensitively transform that fruit into wine in such a way as to maximize the quality potential. Winemaking is a series of small steps, all of which are crucial to the quality of the finished wine. We are not prepared to compromise any of these steps, whether it be mechanical harvesting as opposed to our careful hand-picking, or using a crusher instead of slow, whole-bunch pressing in a pneumatic press, or relying on an

outdated technology such as cork stoppers, instead of the much more reliable and consistent screwcap.

What would you hope people say about your wine?

That our wine smells and tastes really good, that it enhances their enjoyment of the food they are eating, and that it reminds them of the countryside that produced it.

Do you think that the market should influence winemaking, or do you think that winemaking should influence the market?

In my experience, it has always been innovative, creative, and smart winemakers who have made the significant improvements in wine quality that have led consumers along in the same direction. This has always been true at the top end of any craft or art; it is the inspirational ones who take everyone else along with them, and the market follows. We try to produce wines that we think are excellent and represent the very best we can do. We then offer them for sale and hope that there are enough customers out there with similar (good) taste.

Besides your own wine, what are some of your favorite wines? What do you like about them?

At the winery we often taste wines from all around the world, but particularly from classic regions such as Burgundy, Bordeaux, Alsace, Mosel, Rheingau, Piedmont, and Tuscany. To me these great wines represent the epitome of wine style, honed over centuries of experience. They are a guide and inspiration to us and have led us to many of the ideas we have incorporated into our viticulture and winemaking over the years.

What is your opinion on screwcap versus cork closures?

No question, in my experience with our wines, the screwcap is a vastly superior closure to the cork stopper. It is much more consistent in its ability to seal the bottle and exclude the damaging effects of excessive oxygen, while at the same time allowing the gentle development of bottle bouquet in a very similar fashion to that seen with the very best of corks.

If you could invite anyone from history, living or dead, to your home for dinner, who would it be? What food would you serve? What wine would you serve?

I think Sir Winston Churchill would be a great deal of fun to have as a dinner guest. One could start with Champagne (Pol, I believe) and oysters, move on to Kumeu River Chardonnay with New Zealand lobster, and then magnificently rare beef with a local

Merlot that hopefully reminded him of his club's best old Claret. Finish off with a glass of very old vintage Port, a New Zealand sharp blue cheese, and a decent cigar. Sprinkled throughout the dinner would be numerous witty anecdotes from the man himself, to whom we all owe a greater debt of gratitude than we realize.

If you were to stay home tonight for a relaxing evening, drinking wine while watching a movie, which movie would you watch? Which wine would you drink? Explain.

Bertolucci's *1900*, which is one of the best films I've ever seen, but also one of the longest. Great story, great actors. We don't make a Riesling, but I would love to. I would watch the movie with a fine, fresh, and fruity bottle of Mosel, only about 8 or 9 percent alcohol so I wouldn't miss any of the movie by falling asleep.

How do you like to spend your time away from the winery?

Travel has always interested me, but it is usually associated with selling wine, or visiting wine areas. When my family and I travel we like to go to the beach, somewhere warm. Last year we enjoyed a fabulous holiday visiting relatives in our homeland of Croatia, soaking up the sun for several glorious weeks. On a more day-to-day level, Kate and I are involved in sports with the children, particular rugby and cricket for Markus and netball for Milla. It's great fun getting involved with the children's sporting pursuits.

Do you collect wine? If so, what is in your cellar?

Many examples of the kinds of wines described above, plus a few bottles of more simple styles of wine as well, often from Italy, Spain, and France, but also New Zealand and Australia, for everyday enjoyment. I don't often drink my own wine at home, I get to see them so often I would hate to develop a "cellar palate."

If you weren't involved in wine, what would you be doing?

Producing food of some description . . . cheese perhaps, or olive oil, or simply farming the best beef or lamb that I possibly could.

HELEN MASTERS

Helen Masters has been the winemaker at Ata Rangi for many more years than she's willing to admit. She first worked there in 1990, immediately following high school, and then set off to study at Massey University. After working harvests around the world, she returned to Ata Rangi in 2003 and has been making high-caliber wine ever since. We met Helen at a tasting in New York City and were intrigued by this fireball of a woman. We had the pleasure of visiting her during the harvest of 2011 and shared a few laughs and more than a few glasses of wine.

How did you get involved in the world of wine?

I was lucky enough to grow up in a family that was interested in wine, especially New Zealand wine. At the end of high school I researched the best wineries around—there was a much smaller number back then—and wrote letters asking for work experience. Ata Rangi took me on, and I worked there for a year before going off to study and explore the world. It was a formative part of my life, and here I am back at Ata Rangi 20 years later.

What are some of the biggest changes you have seen in winemaking since you began your career?

The growing interest and awareness of sustainable farming has been a major shift. This has moved through to the winery where we see a lot more wines made with less intervention.

What are some of the exciting changes that you see happening specifically in your country?

Greater understanding of how crucial vine age is to quality has led to more confidence—we see wine styles that have been evolving really being cemented as regional differences. There is a greater understanding of the best way to work with our piece of land. There is certainly a real sense of how New Zealand fits in the international picture.

Where else in the world have you studied, trained, or worked a harvest? How did that influence your winemaking?

I have worked a number of harvests in Oregon and California and different regions in New Zealand. These help you to understand the many shapes and forms a wine can take, especially with a variety such as Pinot Noir.

Which varieties are you working with? Are you experimenting with anything new?

I work mainly with Pinot Noir, Chardonnay, and Pinot Gris. I also enjoy working with Sauvignon Blanc, expressing the texture and structure to produce a style that works well with food and has longevity. On a small scale we play with blends of white varieties, Syrah, and red blends.

Are there any new areas that you have identified for potential vineyard sites?

Now that would be giving away secrets! There are pockets of land around the Wairarapa that could be interesting, especially in the long term when we understand how much climate change will impact on our present sites.

What challenges have you faced as a winemaker or winery owner?

We work hard to maintain a balanced ecosystem within the vineyard. One of the ways we do this is to try to incorporate as many plants native to New Zealand as possible within the surrounds of the vineyard.

What is your winemaking philosophy?

To get it right in the vineyard; in terms of yield, canopy, and health; to achieve this in the most natural and sustainable way. In the winery to do as little to change the inherent

character of the site and vintage while guiding the wine toward texture and length.

What would you hope people say about your wine?

It would be great if they said "it has texture, length, and elegance combined with an ethereal, almost indescribable character."

Do you think that the market should influence winemaking, or do you think that winemaking should influence the market?

We as wine growers must make wines that are authentic examples of the place they are grown. The consumer can then take from them what they will.

Besides your own wine, what are some of your favorite wines? What do you like about them?

In New Zealand there are a lot of exciting producers who are really thinking about the wines they make. I really enjoy Rieslings from Waipara, Gewürztraminer from some small boutique producers in Marlborough such as Te Ware Ra. Syrah from Hawke's Bay—a small producer Bilancia always excites. I am never disappointed with the Pinot Noir from Felton Road.

What is your opinion on screwcap versus cork closures?

I have bottled wines under screwcap for nine

years, both red and white. The same wine is bottled under cork each year, so we have a library from which we do blind comparisons. Screwcap is showing to be not just a good short-term closure but one that allows wine to age with integrity. Like any closure it has its weakness—it being that it is an external seal and requires care in handling to ensure that it is not damaged.

If you could invite anyone from history, living or dead, to your home for dinner, who would it be? What food would you serve? What wine would you serve?

Well one of them would have to be Malcolm Abel, who was responsible for the proliferation of the Abel clone—a Pinot Noir clone illegally imported into New Zealand in the '70s. Sadly Malcolm, who was the quarantine officer at the Auckland airport when this cutting was found on an intrepid kiwi, died not long after. With him we lost some of the details of what happened and who the character was. I would serve him Ata Rangi Pinot; our original plants plus a major portion of all our vineyards are planted with this clone; so he could see what his foresight has resulted in. I would do a classic Pinot matching: lamb stuffed with rosemary and anchovies with lentils and Jerusalem artichokes. We would also serve some older vintages of La Tache as this was reportedly where the cutting of the Abel clone was nabbed from.

If you were to stay home tonight for a relaxing evening, drinking wine while watching a movie, which movie would you watch? Which wine would you drink? Explain.

I would watch *Being John Malkovich*, a nicely twisted, dark comedy. I would start off with a good Oloroso Sherry and then move to something from the Piedmont region in Italy that could match the drama of the movie.

How do you like to spend your time away from the winery?

Catching up with friends and family. This involves a lot of eating and drinking so I try to temper this with as much outdoor activity as possible.

Do you collect wine? If so, what is in your cellar?

I collect as much wine as I can get away with—don't tell my husband; mostly Burgundies, with a splattering of Italian, German, and Alsatian wines, and a few good vintages of Bordeaux.

If you weren't involved in wine, what would you be doing?

I would be a furniture designer. I love the form, shape, and the feel of the materials.

SIR GEORGE FISTONICH

Sir George Fistonich founded Villa Maria Estate in Auckland in 1961 and thus began his lifelong commitment to produce exceptional New Zealand wines. In 1976, he purchased Vidal Winery, and in 1987, he acquired Esk Valley Estate, but he proudly states, "My greatest honor to date was being knighted in 2009." We had a leisurely lunch with Sir George and his enchanting wife, Lady Gail, on the outdoor terrace of their Auckland winery.

How did you get involved in the world of wine?
I grew up in a Croatian winemaking family that made wine on a small scale for friends, personal consumption, and neighbours. I also associated with many Croatian families who also made wine and become convinced that was my future dream and career—so I abandoned my building career and became a winemaker.

What are some of the biggest changes you have seen in winemaking since you began your career?
New Zealand moving away from being a fortified wine market and shifting from hybrid to *Vitis Vinifera* grape varieties. Having to almost create a new wine industry from no background.

What are some of the exciting changes that you see happening specifically in your country?
Consumers have become very knowledge-able about quality at all levels and the styles of wine produced by different grape varieties. The great interest in wine and food matching and the industry in general.

Where else in the world have you studied, trained, or worked a harvest? How did that influence your winemaking?
While I have not worked a harvest overseas, I have visited wineries in France, Italy, USA, Canada, and spent time with the winemakers and viticulturists. I have also kept a watching brief on what is happening in the wine industry and wines over the years, and have employed many talented winemakers who have brought their own level of experience and expertise to Villa Maria.

Which varieties are you working with? Are you experimenting with anything new?
Key varieties we work with are Chardonnay, Sauvignon Blanc, Riesling, Gewürztraminer,

Pinot Gris, Cabernet Sauvignon, Merlot, Pinot Noir, and Syrah. New varieties we are experimenting with in New Zealand include Verdelho, Arneis, and Grenache.

Are there any new areas that you have identified for potential vineyard sites?

At this stage Villa Maria has developed, over many years, a number of great vineyard sites, single-vineyards, and variety-specific in Marlborough, Hawke's Bay, Gisborne, Otago, and Ihumatao (Auckland), which currently meet our needs. However we are always keeping our eyes and ears open for new opportunities.

What challenges have you faced as a winemaker or winery owner?

Very volatile and competitive environment, very capital hungry, fluctuating exchange rates, and weather patterns.

What is your winemaking philosophy?

To make some of the world's greatest wines at all levels, that is everyday consumer and ultra-premium. Consistently high quality where quality of wines exceeds value and over-delivers to the consumer.

What would you hope people say about your wine?

"I drink your wines as they are consistently great wines." They always deliver or exceed expectation. We have been fortunate that many wine experts and writers have already acknowledged our status.

Do you think that the market should influence winemaking, or do you think that winemaking should influence the market?

As New Zealand is a relatively young wine industry, winemaking does influence the market as many New Zealand consumers are still learning about wine. However, we are rapidly becoming a knowledgeable wine country. Winemakers must be aware that consumers will dictate the styles and varieties of wine they prefer in the future. It would be dangerous to ignore that shift in consumer behavior.

Besides your own wine, what are some of your favorite wines? What do you like about them?

I enjoy great Burgundies for their structure, elegance, and subtle flavors, and classic Bordeaux reds for their complexity and longevity. Tawny Ports have a beautiful nutty character, and Sauternes exhibit wonderful layers of flavors of apricots, mandarin, and honey. I am also very partial to Italian reds.

What is your opinion on screwcap versus cork closures?

It has been proven that corks are unreliable

as a wine closure. Buying a cork-sealed wine is like playing Russian roulette, you never know if the wine will be OK until you open it. With a screwcap you know that the wine will not be negatively influenced by the cork. The wine will taste as the winemaker intended it to taste. Ninety percent of all New Zealand wines are now sealed with screwcaps. New Zealand is leading the way.

If you could invite anyone from history, living or dead, to your home for dinner, who would it be? What food would you serve? What wine would you serve?

Robert Mondavi, as he did so much to promote the enjoyment of wine with food. I would serve him great New Zealand lamb with a glass of our glorious Villa Maria Reserve Pinot Noir.

If you were to stay home tonight for a relaxing evening, drinking wine while watching a movie, which movie would you watch? Which wine would you drink? Explain.

I would watch the great New Zealand film *Whale Rider* while enjoying a glass of finely structured and complex Villa Maria Cellar Selection Syrah.

How do you like to spend your time away from the winery?

While I have a great staff, managing one of the world's top wine companies demands a lot of my time; however, I do like to get away to our holiday home in the north of the North Island and to Fiji in winter for a brief seaside holiday—it is a great place to unwind and rest. My occupation also allows me to travel to many countries of the world promoting Villa Maria, great New Zealand wine, and the tourist industry while also allowing my wife, Gail, and myself to take some extra time exploring and relaxing.

Do you collect wine? If so, what is in your cellar?

Yes I do. A large selection of old vintages from my own wines and a large selection from New Zealand's many outstanding producers. I have a temperature-controlled cellar of about 3,000 bottles. It also includes Bordeaux, Burgundies, and Champagnes, and some of Australia's top producers.

If you weren't involved in wine, what would you be doing?

Wine has always been my passion in life, and I would find it difficult to do anything else; wine covers many areas starting at grape growing through to fine dining and many other disciplines in between.

SOUTH AFRICA

"IT IS THE MOST BEAUTIFUL WINE REGION I have ever seen" is a common refrain among those who have visited South Africa's Cape Winelands. As wine regions in general tend to be beautiful, this is indeed a bold claim, but if you place yourself—as we have—on a stretch of windswept mountainside with row upon row of climbing green vines in the near and middle distance, with Cape Town itself and the iconic Table Mountain in the far distance, and the Cape of Good Hope and both the Atlantic and Indian Oceans just

beyond—well, you can't help but agree. Wine lovers have also been known to proclaim, "The best New World wines I have ever tasted are from South Africa," and it is here that we must disagree—not about the quality of the wine, but whether in fact South Africa falls into the category known as New World.

Winemaking in South Africa dates back to 1659, when Jan van Riebeeck, the founder and first commander of the Dutch settlement that is now Cape Town, made wine from vines that had been planted there four years earlier. The grape cuttings had been transported for cultivation by the Dutch East India Company, which had established Cape Town as a "refreshment station" with one goal: to provide fresh food to the company's merchant fleet on their voyages to India and the Far East. (It was mistakenly thought that drinking wine would prevent sailors from developing scurvy.) Unlike the elegant, highly quaffable wines that are crafted in South Africa today, the vintage of 1659 and those to follow were most likely barely palatable, having been made by people with no real knowledge of viticulture or winemaking.

It is said that the quality of wine improved somewhat 20 years later, when Simon van der Stel took over as commander of the Dutch colony at the Cape of Good Hope. Van der Stel, apparently, had some experience with vines and winemaking and soon produced drinkable wines on his estate in Constantia. In 1691, the Dutch East India Company, which still controlled the Cape, replaced the title of "Commander" with "Governor," and effectively granted van der Stel a promotion. The first governor of Cape Town is notable on two counts beyond improving the local wine: the town of Stellenbosch, which is the seat of South African wine production, is named for him, and, as the son of a Dutch man and an Indian woman, he was the first mixed-race

politician in the history of the nation of South Africa.

Its first governor notwithstanding, what really changed the history of winemaking at the southernmost point in Africa was the October 1685 issue of the Edict of Fontainebleau by French king Louis XIV. With one stroke of his royal pen, the "Sun King" undid the Edict of Nantes, which until that time had granted protection to Protestants living in Catholic France. Known as Huguenots, many of them fled to the Dutch colony in South Africa, where they were offered protection and farmland. Most settled in the area previously called Elephant's Corner, which is now named *Franschhoek*, the Afrikaans term for "French Corner." Bringing with them both their Old World love of wine and proficiency in the vineyard and winery, the seventeenth-century French settlers in South Africa improved upon the tradition started by van Riebeeck three decades before.

Most of the wine made in the region for the next hundred years went to domestic consumption or sailing ships; there was little in the way of an international market for South African wine. This changed in the beginning of the nineteenth century—at the same time that Dutch occupation of the Cape gave way to British. Britain and France were at war and, for its duration, there was no way anyone in England could buy French wine. This created a thriving export market for wine from South Africa. Fortunately, after van der Stel's abandoned 750-hectare (1,853-acre) Constantia estate was purchased and rehabilitated by Hendrik Cloete in 1778, the delicious nectar Vin de Constance gained a worldwide following and, over time, created a demand for all of the wines from this country at the bottom of the map. This is the same Vin de Constance memorialized by Charles Dickens and Jane Austen and requested by Napoleon on his deathbed. It is still made today by Klein Constantia.

As war between Britain and France raged on for almost 50 years, wine production blossomed on the Cape, growing exponentially. By 1865, when Britain and France finally came to terms, output had increased to 4.5 million liters per year. Gold and diamonds were discovered near the Orange River in 1867; the rush was on, and Cape Town became a magnet for men seeking their fortune from the ground. With a large population of miners on hand, plenty of sailors still passing through, and a constant military presence, a significant portion of wine went on to be distilled into brandy. As phylloxera made its way to South Africa and obliterated the vines there, the brandy distillers turned to the grain fields of Wellington, and the domestic whiskey industry took off.

Sadly, the wine industry did not fare as well—at least at that time. The export market dried up in 1865, when French wine was once again available in England, and by 1886, when phylloxera swept through the Cape decimating vines, many grape farmers turned their hand to raising ostriches and running fruit orchards. It took years to replant vineyards using imported rootstock, and it wasn't until January 1918 and the creation of KWV, or Koöperatieve Wijnbouwers Vereniging van Zuid-Afrika Bpkt (or more simply, the "Cooperative Winemakers' Society of South Africa"), that the wine business rebounded.

KWV was an organization set up to control and regulate the sale of its members' wine. It did much to stabilize the foundering industry. Although it is widely acknowledged as the body that saved the grape farmers and winemakers of South Africa from disaster, KWV, as with many large cooperatives, was concerned more with output and production than quality. (Fortunately, KWV evolved with the times and exists today as a private corporation whose wines are renowned for their high caliber.) Importantly, in 1918 the University of Stellenbosch was founded, and it today boasts one of the finest viticulture studies programs in the world.

For Europe and the United States, South Africa "fell off the map" as a wine-producing nation for almost the whole of the twentieth century, as a result of the combined effects of World War I, Prohibition, the Great Depression, and World War II. Apartheid, South Africa's system of racial segregation, came into effect in 1948 and did not end until 1993. These events and resultant trade sanctions (meant to force the government to abolish the shameful practice of apartheid) kept the wines of South Africa from reaching an international market, but winemakers and viticulturists continued to ply their trade and sell into the South African domestic market. In 1925, Stellenbosch University's first professor of viticulture, Abraham Izak Perold, crossed Pinot Noir and Cinsault, creating Pinotage, which is considered by many to be South Africa's "signature grape." In 1937, German immigrant Johann Graue bought the Nederburg Estate, where he was the first in South Africa to utilize the cold fermentation process. Stellenbosch Farmers' Winery, or SFW, was founded in 1935, and in 1945, Dr. Anton Rupert founded the Distillers Corporation. These two merged in 2000, forming the Distell Corporation, which is South Africa's leading producer of fine wine and spirits today.

Lieberstein, a semidry white wine produced by SFW, was first released in 1959. It is said to have revolutionized wine-drinking habits in South Africa, and in 1964, more than 41 million bottles of Lieberstein were consumed, making it the world's highest selling wine. In 1955, the Viticultural and Oenological Research Institute, now known as Nietvoorbij, was founded. The Stellenbosch Wine Route, the first in the country, had its start in 1971. Two years later, the country's "Wine of Origin" laws were instituted. The inaugural Nederburg Auction of Rare Cape Wines took place in 1975; this annual event now showcases the finest wines the nation has to offer and draws buyers and wine lovers from around the world. The Cape Wine Academy, or CWA, the nation's main educational body for the wine industry, started in 1979. The Cape Winemakers' Guild was established in 1983; it is an independent, invitation-only organization whose goal is to increase the overall quality of the region's wine. In 1990 Nelson Mandela was released from prison, laying the groundwork for a series of reforms that would restore South Africa's reputation in the global marketplace, allowing South African wine to be enjoyed by wine lovers the world over.

Ever since, change has occurred at a rapid pace in the vineyards and wineries of South Africa. KWV dropped its restrictive quota system in 1992—it had maintained a firm grip on grape growth, production, and sales—and became a private corporation in December 1997. In 2004 KWV entered into an historic agreement with the Phetogo Consortium, in which 25.1 percent of the company's assets were sold to a Black Economic Empowerment group. Various organizations promoting specific varieties have sprung up over the years, including the Pinotage Association in 1995, the Chenin Blanc Association in 2000, and the Shiraz Association in 2002. This is the same year that WIETA—Wine Industry Ethical Trade Association—got its start. This association is dedicated to improving the working conditions of all persons employed in the wine industry.

With the arrival of democracy in 1994, and Nelson Mandela's election to the presidency, the financial and intellectual assets of South Africa increased exponentially. Winemakers began traveling to other countries, in both the Northern and Southern Hemispheres, to gather knowledge from experts in the field. Under the old cooperative system, vineyards were only permitted in designated zones, which were not always the best for cultivation of grapes. Now, viticulturists could expand the boundaries of planted areas and search for the best possible combination of soil, exposure, and altitude—and focus on varieties best suited to the *terroir*.

Simultaneously, those in the business end of winemaking became educated in international markets and consumer demand. Hardly more than 20 years old, the modern South African wine industry has adapted well to its new role in the worldwide market. Between 2000 and 2010, the number of wine producers doubled to 600. From 1995 to 2007, exports grew by 335 percent. The harvest of 2011 created 969.1 million liters of wine, a 0.3 percent drop from the previous year, due to low rainfall and heat waves during the summer growing season and flooding in the Orange River region in December 2010, during the height of summer. South Africa ranks ninth in terms of overall wine production by country, accounting for 3 percent of total world yields.

The majority of South Africa's 102,000 hectares (252,047 acres) of grapevines are concentrated in the Cape Winelands. More than 275,000 people are employed directly or indirectly in the South African wine industry, including wine tourism. Of these, upward of 160,000 are from historically disadvantaged groups. There are multiple trusts and initiatives aimed at furthering their education, and several Cape wine farmers have set up joint ventures with their employees to increase their management and winemaking skills. Initiatives include daycare and schooling for vineyard and winery employees' children, scholarships, and money toward improved housing. Programs to allow groups of people living in winemaking regions to take over vineyard ownership are also underway. Wines of South Africa, in conjunction with the national wine industry, created a new premium wine brand, Fundi, in advance of the 2010 FIFA World Cup in South Africa. All the proceeds from this wine went toward training 2,000 wine stewards from the "colored" and indigenous African populations in preparation for the vast influx of tourism in the wake of the event.

The distinctness of South African *terroir* was fully recognized and given protected status in 1972, when the Wine of Origin Scheme came into effect. For the first time in the history of South African winemaking, claims made on labels had to be substantiated by fact; that is, grapes had to be raised where the maker stated they were grown, and they had to be vinified from the variety stated on the label. When the words "Wine of Origin" or the abbreviation "WO" appear on a label—along with the name of a production area, such as Durbanville or Walker Bay—it is confirmed that 100 percent of the grapes used to produce the wine are from the area stated. The Wine of Origin Scheme was modeled on European Union wine regulations, partly because so much wine from South Africa is exported there.

The broadest geographic term is "unit," of which there are four: Eastern Cape, KwaZulu-Natal, Northern Cape, and Western Cape—the last of which contains the majority of producing regions. The geographic term "region" refers to a large area within a unit, such as the Breede River Valley or Cape South Coast. Districts are more narrowly defined: they are smaller geographical areas contained within the larger regions. Stellenbosch, Paarl, and Franschhoek—some of the best-known districts in the country—are just three of the eight contained within the Coastal region. Wards are even smaller units inside districts. For example, Stellenbosch's borders contain seven wards, including Bottelary, Polkadraai Hills, and Simonsberg-Stellenbosch. Traditionally, estate wines could only be made from grapes grown on the producer's land. That status was updated in 2004, and now takes into account grapes grown on adjoining plots that are farmed together, regardless of ownership. However, to be labeled an "Estate Wine," every stage of winemaking, including bottling, must take place on the estate.

All of the varieties grown in South Africa belong to the *Vitis vinifera* species, first imported from Europe. Although approximately 75 varieties are recognized under the Wine of Origin Scheme, meaning they may be listed on a wine label, only about 25 are seen with any frequency. In addition to the international varieties grown within its borders, South Africa can claim two cross-bred cultivars as its own: the well-known Pinotage, a cross between Pinot Noir and Cinsault, and Nouvelle, an up-and-coming white grape that is a cross between

Cape Riesling and Ugni Blanc. In order to label a wine as a single varietal, at least 85 percent of the wine must be produced from that grape. (Prior to January 1, 2006, a minimum of 75 percent had to be used.) The vintage year on a wine produced prior to January 1, 2006, attests to the fact that at least 75 percent of that wine is made from grapes harvested in that year; since then, 85 percent of the wine must be from the indicated vintage.

South Africa's Wine and Spirit Board sets out labeling requirements for wine. If authorized by the Labeling Committee, a wine label will include the geographical area, such as estate, ward, region, or geographical unit. It will list the names of the grape varieties, the vintage year, and the term "Wine of Origin," in addition to stating the alcohol content.

Much of the increase in wine quality in South Africa is attributed to the Vine Improvement Program, or VIP. Begun in the closing years of the twentieth century, this program is directed in the areas of clonal research and the creation and cultivation of virus-resistant and yield-controlling rootstock. Other aims include coordinating grape varieties, clones, and rootstock with the most appropriate *terroir*. International consultants have brought their expertise to the country, including Michel Rolland at Remhoogte Estate, where he became a partner in 2001; Alberto Antonini

at Hartenberg Estate; and noted husband-and-wife team Phil Freese and Zelma Long, the viticulturist and winemaker who joined forces with Mike Ratcliffe to form Vilafonte.

South Africa is also an international leader in *terroir* research, and since the mid-1990s researchers at the University of Stellenbosch and the Nietvoorbij Institute of Viticulture and Oenology have worked to unlock the secrets of the land and the role it plays in grape quality and style. Besides its impact on the match between cultivars and location in customary wine-growing areas—and the establishment of new ones—it has had an effect on vineyard practices such as trellising and canopy management.

Wide differences in topography and geology account for the varied soils on the Cape. South Africa has one of the highest levels of biodiversity in the world; its fertile earth is home to a startling number of plant species.

Near the coast, we see sandstone mountains atop underlying granite, while at lower altitudes, shale predominates. Rich, brown soil with tints of red and yellow cover the granitic hills of the Bottelary, Maimesbury, and Darling, as well as the lower foothills of Table Mountain, Stellenbosch Mountain, and Simonsberg Mountain. At altitudes ranging between 150 and 400 meters (492 and 1,312 feet), these ancient soils are well drained but capable of holding the water necessary for healthy grape growing. The rolling hills between the mountains, at heights ranging from 20 to 150 meters (66 to 492 feet), contain brown-yellow gravel and clay. Shale-based soils tend to be rockier toward low-lying peaks, with an abundance of nutrients in soils farther down the slopes.

The influence of two oceans is felt across vineyards as prevailing winds shift throughout the day and the season. To the east, the Indian Ocean is warmed by the tropical Mozambique Current, while the Atlantic Ocean, on the west side of the Cape, is cooled by the icy Antarctic Benguela Current. The Mediterranean climate features hot, breezy summers and cool, wet winters. In addition to cultivation of grapes, the topography and climate foster the propagation of a distinct floral phenomenon, *fynbos* and *renosterveld*, known elsewhere as the Cape Floral Kingdom. Table Mountain alone supports 2,200 of this kingdom's 9,000 species. In 2004, the Biodiversity and Wine Initiative (BWI) was formed as a partnership between the wine industry and conservation sector. Wine producers are encouraged to utilize sustainable farming and winemaking practices, and also to protect the natural habitat. Out of respect for this varied assortment of endemic plants, in 2006 Wines of South Africa asked winemakers and producers to sign "The Wine Grower/ Producer's Commitment." This contract among members of the wine industry set out to protect the native *fynbos* within the framework of the landscape and environment as a whole, and to recognize the natural boundary between vineyards and undomesticated terrain. Many wine estates retain large swaths of land planted with wildflowers and native species rather than grapevines.

The Cape is crossed by five river systems; of these, the Breede River is the largest. The Western Cape is irrigated by the Oliphants River, while the same purpose is served to the east by the Baviaanskloof and Gamtoos Rivers. The Berg River runs from the Drakenstein Mountains, just below Franschhoek, to the Atlantic. The Gourits and Groot Rivers run through the Little Karoo basin before spilling their waters into the Indian Ocean.

MAJOR GRAPE VARIETIES

CABERNET FRANC

This parent of Cabernet Sauvignon is most at home in Bordeaux-style blends, where it is noted for its contribution of assertive peppery character. The strong smell of pepper is joined by flavors of cherry, cassis, and earth. The small, blue black, thick-skinned fruit thrives in sand- or granite-based soils. It is a component in several "Cape Blends," including Simonsig's Tiara, although it is also being used more frequently as a single varietal, as in Bruwer Raats's version at his family estate.

CABERNET SAUVIGNON

Cabernet Sauvignon covers more vineyard area than any other red grape in South Africa, accounting for 12 percent of total plantings. Cabernet sauvignon is a small grape with thick skin and a high seed-to-pulp ratio, which helps it impart a strong dose of tannin to a wine—leading to its ability to age gracefully for long periods of time. From its home in Bordeaux, Cabernet Sauvignon is the most widely traveled grape in all the world, laying down roots everywhere grapes are grown. A prime component of most "Cape Blends," which often include Pinotage, Cabernet Sauvignon lends flavors of black cherry, black currant, graphite, and cedar. It is the backbone of Kanonkop's Paul Sauer, the estate's iconic blend, and an excellent example of single-varietal Cabernet Sauvignon is found in Rustenberg's Peter Barlow. South African wine simply labeled "Cabernet" will be made from this grape, not Cabernet Franc. Cabernet Sauvignon is grown in every region, but it does particularly well in Durbanville, Lower Orange, Paarl, Philadelphia, Robertson, Stellenbosch, and Swartland.

CAPE RIESLING (CROUCHEN BLANC)

Misidentified for many years as Rhine Riesling, Crouchen Blanc—known here as Cape Riesling—is grown far more in South Africa than in its native France, where it is almost completely unknown today. (In Australia, it is called Clare Riesling.) Under perfect conditions, this green grape produces a highly aromatic wine with essences of green apple, citrus, and clover; despite its name, it has much more in common with Sauvignon Blanc than with (unrelated) Riesling. While the grape is often mixed with other white varieties, Nederburg's Foundation Cape Riesling is noted for its crisp palate of pineapple and citrus fruits.

CARIGNAN

A native of Spain that gained its fame as the most widely planted Rhône varietal, Carignan is a large, dark, round grape that grows in tight clusters. The wine made from it tends to have strong acidity and tannin and a deep red color. It is primarily used for blending, although the right combination of *terroir* and winemaking skill can make the best of its bright flavors of red cherry and mace. While Fairview's The Back Road is a prime example of Carignan at its finest, small amounts of the grape show up in bottles from several other top producers.

CHARDONNAY

One of the most widely planted cultivars in the world, Chardonnay, like the Huguenots, more than just survived its voyage from France to the Cape. It now makes up 8 percent of all grapes planted here. Its green apple and light citrus flavors can turn buttery-rich with the right amount of oak aging. The bulbous green grapes form conelike clusters on the vine, which thrive in limestone and chalk soil. Delicious on its own, South African Chardonnay is often blended with Sauvignon Blanc or Riesling. Lightly oaked DeMorgenzon DMZ Chardonnay highlights the variety's citrus and tropical fruit aromas, and Thelema Chardonnay's light notes of toast will mature to a distinct nuttiness if allowed to rest for a few years before drinking. Chardonnay is also used as the base for many *Cap Classique* sparkling wines. It is grown in Durbanville, Lower Orange, Stellenbosch, and Swartland.

CHENIN BLANC

The most widely planted grape in South Africa, blanketing 18 percent of the nation's vineyards, this transplant from France's Loire Valley is known locally as Steen. It is also one of the oldest cultivars in the country, having made its way here among original cuttings in the seventeenth century. The conical bunches of green grapes are among the last to be harvested each season. Its versatility provides a beautiful canvas for the effects of *terroir* and the artistry of the vintner; it is found in many different types of wine, from bone dry to sparkling to syrupy sweet. Its flavors of apple and underripe pear are complemented by high acidity and more than a suggestion of minerality. Bellingham's Bernard Series Old Vines Chenin Blanc is done in a rich, ripe style. Mulderbosch's Chenin Blanc, with a touch of late-harvest grapes added, is bright and racy. It grows most everywhere, but some of the finest examples come from Lower Orange, Paarl, Stellenbosch, Swartland, and Wellington.

CINSAULT

Once known as Hermitage in South Africa, this French blending variety provided one-half of the parentage for Pinotage. Bearing an aroma of strawberry with a light earthiness, it adds elegance and bouquet that its partners-in-wine, such as Carignan, often lack. Cinsault's large, cylinder-like clusters of grapes are relatively resistant to drought, so it does well during dry Cape summers. Elsewhere in the world, it is often found in the bottle alongside Cabernet Sauvignon. Boekenhoutskloof's The Wolftrap Rosé contains 20 percent Cinsault blended with a majority of Syrah and a smaller amount of Grenache. Howard Boysen bottles a highly regarded single varietal at his eponymous Stellenbosch winery.

GEWÜRZTRAMINER

Notable for its floral bouquet, particularly rose petal, this northern Italian native is abundantly raised in Germany and the Alsace region of France. Particularly difficult to grow, "Gewürz" (as it is more informally known) yields small bunches of pink grapes that are made into a strongly aromatic off-dry white wine. It brings rich fragrance to any wine it is blended with. Paul Cluver's single varietal from Elgin shows typicity with lychee and spice flavors. Robertson Special Late Harvest Gewürztraminer tastes of ripe peaches and honey. Because of their acidity and sweet, floral characters, South African Gewürztraminers are well suited to spicy Cape Malay cuisine, especially curries.

GRENACHE

Believed to be the most widely planted red grape on the planet, Grenache—called *Garnacha* in its home country of Spain—is happy to share the bill with other grapes or play a starring role on its own. It prospers in hot, dry climates; the medium purple, thin-skinned grapes are low in tannin, leading to smooth wines that can be easily drunk young. A common flavor profile of Grenache includes notes of red fruits, such as strawberry and raspberry, honeysuckle, and light spice. Ken Forrester's The Gypsy combines 60 percent Grenache with 40 percent Shiraz, and the hallmark flavors of raspberry, cherry, and baking spices shine through. Fairview Caldera is made with almost 50 percent Grenache, blended with Mourvèdre and Shiraz. It takes its name from the Catalan calderata, a nod to the grape's place of birth, but the winemaking style is clearly a nod to the Rhône Valley.

MALBEC

Blended in France and left to its own devices in Argentina, this spicy red seems comfortable pretty much however it is bottled in South Africa. Although total plantings are relatively small, a large percentage of "Cape Blends" list a small amount of Malbec on the back label. The deep, inky purple color of grapes on the vine carries over into the glass, where its strong tannic structure and flavors of black fruits, violets, and spice are highly regarded the world over. Annex Kloof Malbec from Malmesbury is full-bodied with ripe, red fruit flavors. A host of top South African wineries such as De Toren, Mulderbosch, and Mvemve Raats produce delicious blends buoyed by the addition of this versatile cultivar.

MERLOT

Seven percent of all the grapes planted in South Africa are Merlot, another transplant from Bordeaux that is doing well in the southern sun. With flavors of blueberry, sweet cherry, elderberries, and cooling herbs, Merlot has a deep, inky purple color on the vine and in the bottle. Merlot is less tannic than Cabernet Sauvignon and is thus a perfect blending partner for the softness it brings to wine, whether well-aged or drunk young. Indaba makes an affordable, approachable single-varietal Merlot that has all the classic fruit notes on the palate,

backed up by a suggestion of chocolate and spice. Grand Vin de Glenelly's bold Shiraz and Cabernet Sauvignon profile is tamed by the addition of 24 percent Merlot. This grape has done well for many years on the cool, higher-altitude vineyards of Paarl and Stellenbosch, and it also thrives in Durbanville, Klein Karoo, Lower Orange, Philadelphia, and Walker Bay.

MUSCAT

It is thought that most *Vitis vinifera* grapes are descended from Muscat. Four varieties are cultivated in South Africa: Muscat d'Alexandrie, (also called Hanepoot and Muscat of Alexandria), Muscat de Frontignan (a.k.a. Muscadel), Muscat de Hambourg (or Black Muscat), and Muscat Ottonel. Although Muscat of Alexandria is now grown around the world, it originated on the African continent, where it was used in winemaking by the ancient Egyptians. This variety of Muscat was also among the first plantings brought to South Africa by Jan van Riebeeck in the seventeenth century. Its local name, *Hanepoot*, is Afrikaans for "cockerel's foot," a reference to the shape of the leaves. While this grape is large, oval, and pale amber, Muscat de Hambourg's berries are the same shape but a much darker color, hence the descriptive Black Muscat. Muscat de Frontignan can run the full grape color spectrum, from pale whitish-green to dark purple; the South African version tends to run toward the darker end of the scale. In contrast, Muscat Ottonel is known to be the lightest in color of all the Muscats. Raised mostly in Constantia, Breede River Valley, Klein Karoo, and Lower Orange, Muscat is mainly made into sweet wines, although some dry versions can now be found as well. Without a doubt, the finest example of Muscat in South Africa is Klein Constantia's Vin de Constance, made from 100 percent Muscat de Frontignan. Muscat is known for its sweet floral aroma, and fortified or botrytized versions will have flavors of peach, apricot, and honey.

NOUVELLE

Developed by Stellenbosch University's Professor C.J. Orffer, Nouvelle is a cross between Cape Riesling and Ugni Blanc (Trebbiano). (Its parents were previously thought to be Sémillon and Ugni Blanc, which genetic testing in 2007 proved to be incorrect.) Total plantings are insignificant at this time, although it is gaining traction in Paarl. Most winemakers think it will work well as a blending grape, in particular with Sauvignon Blanc. Boland Cellar Nouvelle World First was made from 2005 through 2009.

PETIT VERDOT

This red grape is commonly used in small quantities in Bordeaux-style blends, although its use as a single varietal is on the rise in South Africa. It adds color, tannin, and a characteristic violet flavor to blends such as Rustenberg's John X Merriman and Mvemve Raats de Compostella.

PINOTAGE

South Africa's hometown favorite, Pinotage was created in 1925 by Professor Abraham Izak Perold, the first professor of viticulture at Stellenbosch University. A cross between Pinot Noir and Cinsault, the deep ruby red wine carries the flavors of blackberry and mulberry and can have notes of smoke and leather as well. Although early versions were criticized for their tendency toward paint and nail polish aromas, improved winemaking technique in recent years, such as cold fermentation, has helped to tame these unfavorable qualities. About 6 percent of all the grapes grown in South Africa are Pinotage, which is grown across all of the country's wine regions, most notably in Bot River, Lower Orange, Paarl, Stellenbosch, Swartland, and Walker Bay. Pinotage vines were first planted in 1941 at Kanonkop Estate, which is still known as one of the finest producers of the varietal. Beyerskloof is also noted for its fine Pinotage, especially the artisanally crafted Diesel Pinotage, named for the winemaker's dog, not the flavor profile. "Cape Blend" is an unofficial term for a wine made from Bordeaux varieties and Pinotage; at this time, there is no standard as to specific proportion of Pinotage or any of the blending components. (In fact, many wines labeled with this designation are Cabernet Sauvignon–dominant rather than Pinotage-dominant.) Prime examples of Cape Blend wines are Bellingham St. Georges and Warwick Estate Three Cape Ladies. A newer style of Pinotage is also noted for its distinct coffee-bean aroma and flavor—in addition to dark fruit and berry notes—such as the aptly named Barista Pinotage and Café Culture Pinotage.

PINOT NOIR

Far from its home in Burgundy, this grape—which grows in pinecone-shaped clusters—is commonly used in sparkling *Cap Classique* wines, but more and more vintners are bottling it in its more recognizable form. Although the berries are dark purple, the resultant wine is often more of a cherry to garnet red. Expect cherry on the nose and palate too, as well as blackberry, chocolate, coffee bean, and citrus zest. You can expect rich plum and violet flavors as well from Bouchard Finlayson Galpin Peak Pinot Noir, while Elgin Vintners' rendition will bear the classic cherry, chocolate, and orange flavor trifecta. Pinot Noir

is grown in small amounts throughout various areas, but the majority of it is found in Stellenbosch.

PORTUGUESE VARIETIES

Touriga Nacional, Tinta Barocca, Tinta Francisca, Tinta Rouriz, and Souzão—among others—are used to make fortified sweet wines with the addition of brandy. These can no longer be labeled "Port" in the international market, due to European Union regulations. Although fortified wines have long been the province of Paarl, Franschhoek, and Tulbagh, and may be labeled under the Boberg appellation, Calitzdorp in Klein Karoo is also known for its emphasis on this style. Look for bottlings from Axe Hill or Boplaas.

RIESLING

Vinified into dry, off-dry, and sweet wines, Riesling balances high acidity with strong fruit and floral flavors. It is also known in South Africa as Rhine Riesling and Weisser Riesling, both nods to its native Germany. Riesling seems to be decreasing in importance here as vineyards are replanted with more popular varieties. The bulbous yellow-green berries, often tinged with purple, grow best in cold-weather areas, such as Overberg's Elgin ward, where Paul Cluver's Close Encounter Riesling is made. A nice balance of natural fruit sweetness, mineral notes, and acidity is found in this classic version. Fairview Riesling combines lemon-lime and tropical fruit notes with floral aromas and a hint of spice.

ROUSSANNE

When Roussanne grapes are fully ripe they are a deep brown with an orange red–tinged color (*roux* in French), hence their name. Roussanne is a Rhône grape seen both as a single varietal or in white blends in South Africa. With notes of honeysuckle and pear and a floral aroma, it shows elegance and structure on the palate. Bellingham's The Bernard Series Whole Bunch Roussanne tastes of tropical fruit and jasmine with light spice notes, while Rustenberg's fruit notes are nicely combined with flavors of almond paste and baking spices.

SAUVIGNON BLANC

Sauvignon Blanc's name originates from the French words for "wild" (*sauvage*) and "white" (*blanc*). The round, green-skinned grape is thought to originate in France as well; it is the main white variety grown in Bordeaux, although it is now at home around the world. It accounts for 9 percent of wine grapes grown in South Africa and can be found on valley floors and hillsides alike in Bot River, Cape Agulhas, Cape Point, Constantia, Darling, Durbanville,

Olifants River, Overberg, Plettenberg Bay, Robertson, Swartland, and Walker Bay.

Classic South African Sauvignon Blanc will be crisp and clean with strong citrus and tropical fruit flavors. Notes of green bell pepper, fresh-cut grass, or asparagus are found as well and are possibly the reason for its *sauvage* reputation. Buitenverwachting Sauvignon Blanc, from Constantia, maintains a nice balance between lime, green fig, and freshly cut herbs. Sutherland's offering hails from cool-climate Elgin, and its pink grapefruit and lemon bouquet are supported on the palate by bracing minerality.

SÉMILLON

In a true-life "riches-to-rags" story, Sémillon once blanketed an astonishing 93 percent of planted vineyard areas in South Africa but now accounts for less than 1 percent of total plantings. Locally, it also goes by the name *Groendruif* (Afrikaans for "green grape"), and it was once so popular that it was simply called *Wijndruif*, or "wine grape." As in its native France, it is vinified into both dry and sweet wine. Sémillon is often blended with Sauvignon Blanc, in amounts too small to be noted on the label; it adds texture and weight to the finished wine. It is found in Constantia, Franschhoek, and Cape Agulhas. Boekenhoutskloof Sémillon is lemony crisp with just a touch of roasted vanilla bean.

SHIRAZ/SYRAH

Known almost everywhere else in the world—with the exception of Australia—as Syrah, dark purple clusters of Shiraz cover 10 percent of South Africa's vineyards. Shiraz's origins are shrouded in mystery: it may be named for a city in Persia, which may be where the grape originated, and it may have been called either Syrah or Shiraz first. At any rate, its current home base is France's northern Rhône, but it is another wonderful example of a "French" variety that is more than just thriving in the ancient soils of South Africa.

Shiraz is known as a big, round, jammy wine, with flavors of black cherry, plum, cassis, licorice, black pepper, smoke, and leather—in short, a powerful, masculine wine, perfect to go along with a *braai* covered with red meat. DeMorgenzon DMZ Shiraz starts off with the delicate fruit and floral notes of a Rhône-style version, but opens up to juicy berry flavors and touches of fresh ground pepper and gingerbread spice. Domain Org de Rac Shiraz, from Swartland, tastes of black plum and blackberry, backed by notes of truffle and smoked meat.

UGNI BLANC

Known in Italy as Trebbiano, Ugni Blanc is a medium-green grape that grows in long, cylindrical bunches. The most widely planted white wine grape in France, and the second most widely planted grape in the world, Ugni Blanc is grown in South Africa (as it is elsewhere) almost exclusively for brandy production. It is also one of the parents of Nouvelle.

VIOGNIER

With its highly aromatic, almost perfumed nose, flavors of white peach, apricot, honey, and soft spice, Viognier has branched out from its perceived home in the northern Rhône and is now a cult favorite among consumers and winemakers alike. The early-ripening, green-skinned grape forms cascading clusters on the vine. It is frequently blended with Shiraz, often without credit, in order to soften out the darker grape's rough edges with delicate floral notes. Elgin Vintners Viognier demonstrates height-of-season apricot and nectarine on the nose and palate, while the honeysuckle, orange zest, and lavender flavors of Fairview La Capra Viognier are capped by a rich, lightly oaked finish.

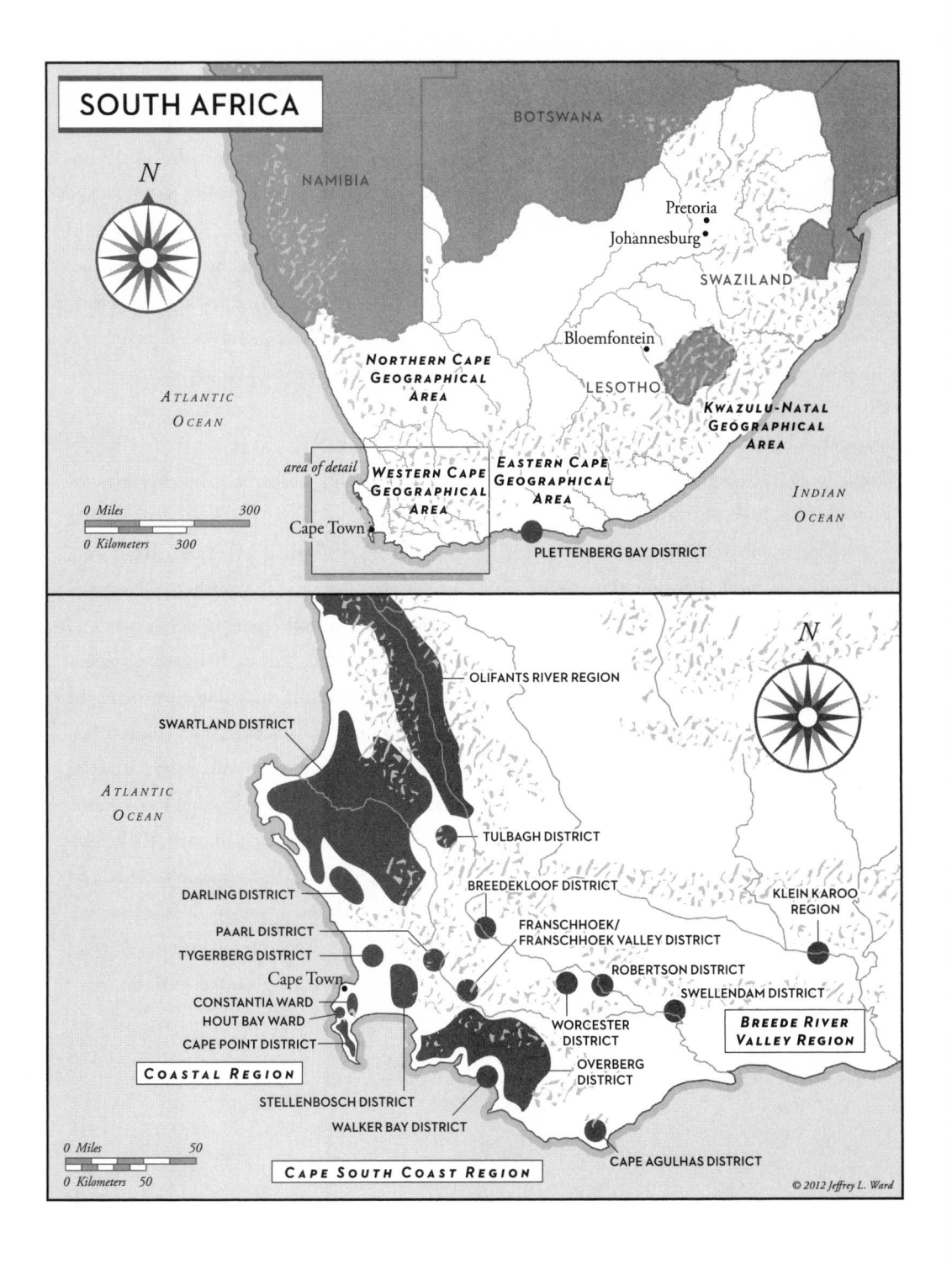

SOUTH AFRICA

N

BOTSWANA

NAMIBIA

Pretoria
Johannesburg

SWAZILAND

Bloemfontein

*ATLANTIC
OCEAN*

NORTHERN CAPE
GEOGRAPHICAL
AREA

LESOTHO

KWAZULU-NATAL
GEOGRAPHICAL
AREA

area of detail

WESTERN CAPE
GEOGRAPHICAL
AREA

EASTERN CAPE
GEOGRAPHICAL
AREA

*INDIAN
OCEAN*

0 Miles   300
0 Kilometers   300

Cape Town

PLETTENBERG BAY DISTRICT

N

OLIFANTS RIVER REGION

SWARTLAND DISTRICT

*ATLANTIC
OCEAN*

TULBAGH DISTRICT

DARLING DISTRICT

BREEDEKLOOF DISTRICT

KLEIN KAROO
REGION

PAARL DISTRICT

FRANSCHHOEK/
FRANSCHHOEK VALLEY DISTRICT

TYGERBERG DISTRICT

Cape Town

ROBERTSON DISTRICT

CONSTANTIA WARD

SWELLENDAM DISTRICT

HOUT BAY WARD

CAPE POINT DISTRICT

WORCESTER
DISTRICT

BREEDE RIVER
VALLEY REGION

COASTAL REGION

OVERBERG
DISTRICT

STELLENBOSCH DISTRICT

WALKER BAY DISTRICT

CAPE AGULHAS DISTRICT

0 Miles   50
0 Kilometers   50

CAPE SOUTH COAST REGION

© 2012 Jeffrey L. Ward

WINE AREAS, REGIONS, DISTRICTS, AND WARDS

COASTAL REGION

Spreading mainly north and east from Cape Town, the Coastal region incorporates the most well-known and most highly concentrated districts, such as Paarl, Stellenbosch, and Franschhoek, as well as the ward of Constantia. It also includes the districts of Cape Point, Darling, Swartland, Tulbagh, and Tygerberg, and the Hout Bay ward. It is dominated by a series of striking mountain ranges and green valleys.

CAPE POINT DISTRICT

Near the western edge of the Cape Peninsula, vineyards run to within a kilometer (just over half a mile) of the sea. Sauvignon Blanc and Sémillon are the standouts from this cool-climate district, although newly planted red varieties are also showing promise.

CAPE POINT VINEYARDS

1 Chapman's Peak Drive, Noordhoek,
+27 21 789 0900,
www.noordhoekvineyards.co.za

On a narrow peninsula between the cold Atlantic Ocean and the more temperate waters of False Bay, Cape Point Vineyards enjoys a maritime climate that surely contributes to the high quality of winemaker Duncan Savage's output. Grapes have been grown on this site since 1752; in 1996 owner Sybrand van der Spuy replanted the vines, which are on the world-renowned Chapman's Peak. A stroll through the vineyards reveals some of the most beautiful views available anywhere in the world, but the focus rightfully remains on what's in the bottle. The Cape Point Vineyards label remains the upper end of the winery's two labels, while a new addition to the family, Splattered Toad, draws attention to the plight of the western leopard toad, which is being driven toward extinction due to an influx of automobile traffic. Toad breeding sites have been set up on the property, and a portion of each bottle sold goes toward a sustainability fund. The general mix at the winery has been 75 percent whites and 25 percent reds, and the emphasis going forward will continue to be on white wine, in particular Sauvignon Blanc and Chardonnay. Cape Point Vineyards Sauvignon Blanc Reserve 2009 gains its creamy mouthfeel from partial barrel fermentation and 10 months ageing on lees; its notes of freshly chopped parsley and pea shoots are backed by zesty citrus flavors and invigorating acidity. Cape Point Vineyards Chardonnay 2009 balances rich flavors of apricot, white peach, and clover honey with a hint of buttered toast; the fruit wins out in the end, with a bright finish. Splattered Toad Sauvignon Blanc 2010 combines lime and pink grapefruit flavors with just-mowed grass; it is as wonderful an aperitif as it is an accompaniment to an icy platter of oysters and clams on the half shell.

CONSTANTIA WARD

The oldest ward in South Africa—and the site of Simon van der Stel's original wine farm—Constantia is home to a handful of high-quality producers. A short drive south of Cape Town, the cooling effect of the sea breeze from False Bay contributes to a long ripening season for Sauvignon Blanc and Muscat de Frontignan. Altitudes on the southern slopes of the Table Mountain Range run as high as 300 meters (984 feet) above sea level, and soils are mainly decomposed granite and clay. Constantia receives an average of 1,056 millimeters, or 42 inches, of rainfall per year; 335 millimeters, or 13 inches, of that falls during the summer.

BUITENVERWACHTING

Klein Constantia Road, Constantia, Cape Town,
+27 21 794 5190,
www.buitenverwachting.co.za

Part of the original estate founded by Simon van der Stel in 1685, Buitenverwachting is known for its elegant white wines. Although van der Stel's legacy changed hands and fell into disrepair, since its purchase in 1981 by the Mueller family and its transition to current managing partner, Lars Maack, Buitenverwachting lives up to its name, which is Dutch for "beyond expectation." Its privileged position on the east-facing slope of the dramatic Constantiaberg Mountain yields Sauvignon Blanc and Chardonnay of exceptional quality. Full-flavored Cabernet Sauvignon and Bordeaux blends are produced for the domestic and European markets. Vineyards here are irrigation-free; holistic farming practices are put to use; and a portion of the vineyards are undergoing organic certification. A temperature-controlled barrel cellar holding up to 3,000 barrels is one example of the state-of-the-art technology utilized by winemakers Hermann Kirschbaum and Brad Paton. The on-site restaurant is among South Africa's finest, combining local flavors and Continental cuisine. Buitenverwachting Chardonnay 2009 could potentially lead even the most sophisticated wine drinker to believe he had a fine Burgundy in the glass: enticing aromas of Bartlett pear, honeydew melon, and green fig mingle with scents of caramel-toasted almonds, creating a Chardonnay with timeless appeal. Buitenverwachting Sauvignon Blanc 2010 flashes its lime, fig, and green herb notes before revealing an elegant structure supported by chalky minerality. Sourced from a single parcel named after the American heiress who owned the estate in the early twentieth century, Buitenverwachting Husseys Vlei Sauvignon Blanc 2010 is even more elegant; complex layers of lime, green pepper, and yellow currant mingle on the tongue with bright spring ferns and notes of flint and shale that linger all the way to the next sip.

CONSTANTIA UITSIG

Constantia Uitsig Estate, Constantia,
+27 21 794 1800,
www.constantia-uitsig.com

Known as Constantia View until 1940, Constantia Uitsig was the home of the Lategan family for five generations. It was a portion of Simon van der Stel's original land grant of Groot Constantia, but it was purchased in 1988 by David and Marlene McCay, who renovated the farm and the estate buildings into a 16-room hotel, spa, three restaurants, and a private cricket oval. Restaurant La Colombe was rated number twelve in the San Pellegrino Fifty Best Restaurants of the World Awards in 2010. Constantia Uitsig Semillon 2009 is pale yellow with aromas of honeycomb, honeysuckle, lemon zest, and thyme. It is round and smooth in the mouth, with balanced acidity and a clean finish. Constantia Uitsig White 2009 is a blend of 70 percent Sémillon and 30 percent Sauvignon Blanc. It is straw colored, with aromas of asparagus, tropical fruits, pineapple, and passionfruit. It is smooth on the palate with a pleasant citrus finish.

GROOT CONSTANTIA

Groot Constantia Estate, Constantia,
+27 21 794 5128,
www.grootconstantia.co.za

On November 13, 1716, Swedish-born Oloff Bergh bought a portion of Simon van der Stel's original holdings, just four years after van der Stel's death. Oloff fell in love with Anna de Koningh, married, and together they had eleven children. The property was inherited and changed hands numerous times through the 1700s, 1800s, and 1900s. Today, it is owned by the Groot Constantia Trust, a government agency committed to maintaining this national historical monument. The estate encompasses Jonkershuis Restaurant, Simon's Restaurant, and the Izoko Museums of Cape Town. Groot Constantia Gouverneurs Reserve White 2009 is a blend of 85 percent Sémillon and 15 percent Sauvignon Blanc. It is straw yellow with a greenish hue and has notes of citrus blossoms and toasted hazelnuts in the bouquet. In the mouth refreshing flavors of jalapeño and white stone fruits shine through before a crisp finish. Groot Constantia Sauvignon Blanc 2010 has aromas of cut grass, passionfruit, and a touch of guava. In the mouth it is crisp with a decided minerality on the finish.

KLEIN CONSTANTIA

Klein Constantia Estate, Constantia,
+27 21 794 5188,
www.kleinconstantia.com

The words "Napoleon" and "baboons" don't usually belong in the same sentence, but when we visited Klein Constantia the first time with Adam Mason, the winemaker from 2004 until 2011, our tour was interrupted by the howling of baboons who had invaded the uppermost slopes of the historic vineyards. Apparently those baboons have very good taste: they were eating clusters of Muscat de Frontignan destined for Vin de Constance, beloved not only by Napoleon who requested it on his deathbed, but by Jane Austen, Charles Dickens, Baudelaire, and countless lovers of wine worldwide. Renovated and reinvigorated by the Jooste family, who purchased the estate in 1980, Klein Constantia stands on a portion of Simon van der Stel's seventeenth-century wine farm. In May 2011, Lowel Jooste entered into an agreement to sell the historic property to investment bankers Zdenek Bakala and Charles Harmen. In addition to Vin de Constance, a full range of varieties is grown and vinified here, including Chardonnay, Sauvignon Blanc, Riesling, Cabernet Sauvignon, and Shiraz. Outside Vin de Constance, the entire ward's reputation seems to be built on Sauvignon Blanc—although this did not stop Klein Constantia Cabernet Sauvignon 2008 from placing among the top contenders in the internationally judged "Top 100 South African Wines 2011" competition. Klein Constantia Vin de Constance

2005, comprised of 100 percent late-harvest Muscat de Frontignan allowed to shrivel on the vine (to concentrate its sugars) fills the mouth with intricate tiers of fresh and dried apricot, honey, orange zest, jasmine, and honeysuckle. Far from cloying, the sweetness is kept in check by vivid acidity. Klein Constantia Riesling 2009 is a fresh splash of lime, orange blossom, rose petal, and jasmine. Klein Constantia Sauvignon Blanc 2010 is a riot of tropical fruit and lemon blossom on the nose and continuing across the palate. Extended skin maceration and the addition of 3 percent Sémillon are at least partly responsible for the luscious texture.

STEENBERG

Steenberg Estate, Constantia,
+27 21 713 2222,
www.steenberghotel.com

Another parcel of the Cape's oldest farm, Steenberg was purchased in 1990 by a large mining consortium that reinvented the tatty buildings into a wine estate—complete with luxury accommodation, two restaurants, and a golf course. Catharina's Restaurant, run by Chef Garth Almazan, is decidedly the upscale venue, while Bistro Sixteen82 has simpler fare with lovely views over the gardens. TripAdvisor named Steenberg the Best Luxury Hotel in Africa in 2011. There are 60 hectares (148 acres) of vines planted, and guests can enjoy sampling Steenberg's wines at both the Wine Tasting Bar or the Tasting Lounge. Steenberg Sauvignon Blanc Reserve 2010 is pale straw, with notes of lime zest, wet river rocks, asparagus, and cut grass. In the mouth it is fruity but with a creamy texture and a long finish. Steenberg Merlot 2008 is indigo purple, with aromas of fennel seed, licorice, blueberry, and cocoa. On the palate flavors of raspberry and black cherry come to life. There is a touch of spice in the pleasant finish.

DARLING DISTRICT

Northeast of Cape Town, Darling sits close to the cold Atlantic Ocean, whose presence is felt in the Sauvignon Blanc that flourishes here, especially within the Groenekloof ward. A base of granite is overlaid with red and yellow brown soils, and annual rainfall averages 586 millimeters, or 23 inches. Summer rainfall is approximately a third of the annual total.

GROOTE POST

Darling Hills Road, Darling,
+27 22 492 2825,
www.grootepost.com

In 1972, Peter and Nick Pentz purchased and subsequently revived an historic eighteenth-century farm. The property includes a winery, tasting room, and Groote Post Restaurant, which can accommodate 120 of your closest friends. Winemaking is under the direction of Lukas Wentzel. Groote Post Unwooded Chardonnay 2010 is straw colored, with aromas of citrus blossoms, lime zest, and a touch of spice. On the palate it is full-bodied with a lasting finish. Groote Post Shiraz 2008 is indigo purple red with notes of black pepper and purple flowers in the bouquet. It has good heft on the tongue, with a hint of spice on the finish.

FRANSCHHOEK/ FRANSCHHOEK VALLEY DISTRICT

First settled by Huguenots, Franschhoek has retained its French charm and is known as the "gourmet capital" of the Cape. The Franschhoek Valley is surrounded on three sides by dramatic mountains: the Groot Drakenstein and Franschhoek Mountains, which join at the top of the valley, and further down, the Klein Drakenstein and Simonsberg Mountains. The Berg River, fed by melting snow from the looming peaks via a series of streams, snakes through the valley floor. Cool winds enter the valley from the south, and contribute to the sheltered microclimate that fosters the balance between sugar and acidity in ripening grapes. A multitude of white varieties are cultivated

here including Chardonnay, Chenin Blanc, Sauvignon Blanc, and Sémillon; reds such as Cabernet Sauvignon, Merlot, Pinot Noir, and Shiraz flourish here as well. Both Chardonnay and Pinot Noir are used in sparkling wines made via the *Méthode Cap Classique*.

BOEKENHOUTSKLOOF WINERY

Excelsior Road, Franschhoek,
+27 21 876 3320,
www.boekenhoutskloof.co.za

Established in 1776 by French Huguenots, Boekenhoutskloof translates as "beech tree ravine." The farm was purchased in 1993 by a group of businessmen committed to South African enterprise. Winemaking is under the direction of Marc Kent, who is sometimes referred to as "Maverick Marc" for his unconventional approach to his craft. Boekenhoutskloof Semillon 2008 is straw colored, with aromas of Anjou pear, lemon rind, and grapefruit peel.

It has medium body on the palate, and the finish is crisp and clean. There is a lingering sensation of wet river rocks in the post palate. Boekenhoutskloof Cabernet Sauvignon 2007 is dark garnet, with notes of blackberry, red plum, cigar box, and baking spice in the bouquet. It is generous in the mouth with smooth tannins and a firm, acidic finish.

fruits dance on your tongue before a crisp, pleasing finish. Boschendal Lanoy 2009 is a blend of 48 percent Cabernet Sauvignon, 41 percent Merlot, 6 percent Cabernet Franc, and 5 percent Malbec. It is garnet colored, with aromas of black plum, red raspberry, and cassis. There's a hint of peppermint on the palate before a long, smooth, tannic finish.

BOSCHENDAL WINES

Route 310, Franschhoek,
+27 21 876 3320,
www.boschendalwines.com

Boschendal comes from the Afrikaans word for "wood and dale." It is one of South Africa's oldest wine farms with a viticultural history dating back to 1685. The elegant manor house was built in 1812, and the estate boasts three restaurants. Boschendal is at the entrance to the beautiful Franschhoek Valley and is a must see for any visitor to South African wine country. JC Bekker is the cellar master, whom we have visited in Franschhoek and have had as a guest at our New York City dining table. We have tasted his wines many times and shared quite a few bottles together. The only problem is that we have too many favorites to mention. Boschendal Chenin Blanc 2010 is straw colored, with notes of tropical fruits, guava, and honeysuckle in the bouquet. In the mouth flavors of apple and white

GRAHAM BECK

Route 45, Franschhoek,
+27 21 874 1258,
www.grahambeckwines.co.za

Although Graham Beck passed away in July 2010, the family legacy that he began with the 1983 purchase of his first farm in Robertson certainly lives on. His second farm in Franschhoek is well appointed and is a lovely winery to visit. Graham was an avid horse racer and golfer, and his family is known for its stud farms. Graham Beck wines have achieved local and international acclaim and are especially well received in the British wine press. Graham Beck Viognier 2009 is straw colored with hints of green and aromas of Granny Smith apples and orange blossoms. It is broad on the palate with a balanced finish. Graham Beck Pinotage 2009 is ruby red, with notes of cherry, tropical fruit—especially guava—and a touch of spice. In the mouth it is balanced and has an elegant, persistent finish.

HAUTE CABRIÈRE.

Pass Road, Franschhoek,
+27 21 876 8500,
www.cabriere.co.za

Granted to Pierre Jourdan on December 22, 1694, Haute Cabrière is composed of two farms located at opposite ends of the Franschhoek Valley. Cellar master Achim von Arnim oversees winemaking of the house's two lines of wine, Haute Cabrière and Pierre Jourdan. The farm has a wonderful restaurant and is popular for wedding receptions, partly because the bride and/or groom can arrive in a helicopter and land on Haute Cabrière's heliport. Founder Pierre Jourdan was a lover of French Champagne, and the house makes many sparkling wines for weddings and other celebrations. One of our favorites however is Pierre Jourdan Tranquille, which is a similar blend of Pinot Noir and Chardonnay grapes, but doesn't have the bubbles associated with Champagne. It is blush pink in the glass, with notes of Granny Smith apple and a hint of fresh strawberry in the bouquet. It is round in the mouth with a pleasant finish that keeps inviting you back for another sip. Haute Cabrière Pinot Noir 2007 is medium red, with aromas of red cherries, dried black cherries, and a touch of black pepper. It is soft and fruity on the palate with a lingering cherry flavor.

LA MOTTE

R45 Main Road, Franschhoek,
+27 21 876 8000,
www.la-motte.com

The La Motte farm was purchased by Dr. Anton Rupert in 1970. Today his daughter Hanneli, the famous South African mezzo-soprano, runs the estate. She also owns the nearby Rupert and Rothschild estate with her brother Johann, the result of the Rupert family's partnership with the Rothschild family of France. Visitors to La Motte can enjoy monthly classical concerts, the family museum, and a wonderful restaurant. La Motte Chardonnay 2009 is straw yellow, with aromas of yellow peach and apricot in the bouquet. In the mouth, pineapple and tropical fruits come alive before the refreshing finish. La Motte Shiraz 2009 is dark reddish-purple with scents of clove and licorice over deeper black raspberry and black plum notes. On the palate black plum and black cherry flavors are present with chewy tannins.

SOLMS-DELTA

Delta Road, Groot Drakenstein,
+27 21 874 7811,
www.solms-delta.co.za

Professor Mark Solms returned home in 2002 to take custodianship of his ancestors' farm. He formed a partnership with British

in the mouth with a pleasant finish. Solms-Delta Hiervandaan 2006 is composed of Shiraz, Mourvèdre, Grenache, Carignan, and Viognier. It is dark red, with notes of blackberries, black plums, and crystallized orange peel. On the palate it displays nice weight, ripe tannins, and an elegant finish.

HOUT BAY WARD

An independent ward outside the confines of a district, Hout Bay is a short drive south of Cape Town. The ward itself is of recent vintage, and it is home to only a handful of wineries, mainly growing Chardonnay, Sauvignon Blanc, and the traditional Bordeaux varieties.

philanthropist Richard Astor and did something many South African landowners (or for that matter, landowners from anywhere) wouldn't dream of doing—he gave a one-third ownership of the estate's profits to the employees, many of whom were descendants of the estate's former slaves. The wine farm also houses the Museum van de Caab, dedicated to the history of this painful past. Mark opened Solms-Delta Fyndraai Restaurant and trained both men and women who had never eaten in a restaurant to become waiters and cooks. Mark Solms was also the first winery owner to hire a black woman as one of his winemakers. We had the distinct honor to sit, have lunch, and get to know this visionary man while enjoying his delicious, exquisitely crafted wines. Solms-Delta Amalie 2010 is a blend of Viognier and Grenache Blanc. It is straw yellow with golden reflections and has aromas of white fruits, white flowers, a touch of freesia, and a hint of vanilla. It is medium-bodied and round

HOUT BAY VINEYARDS

High Meadows Estate, Grotto Road, Hout Bay,
+27 21 790 2372,
www.houtbayvineyards.co.za

One day when Peter Roeloffze and Catherine Lacey were clearing the boulders around their home on Skoorsteenkop Mountain they imagined a homegrown project to make their own bubbly. This dream has become far bigger than either could ever have imagined. A series of setbacks—including accidentally spraying the vines with herbicide and destroying their vineyard—caused them to source grapes for their first several vintages, which gave them time to experiment and plot their course in the world of wine. They currently make two different *Méthode Cap Classique* sparkling wines with Chardonnay and Pinot Noir, and also produce single-varietal Sauvignon Blanc, Cabernet Sauvignon, and Merlot. Fortified Port-style wines and other dessert wines are in the works; the wines from their first 2011 harvest of Chardonnay, Pinot Noir, and Pinot Meunier are expected to be on the market by the time of publication. Hout Bay Vineyards Merlot 2008 packs a punch of blueberry and black cherry, softened by vanilla and light toast flavors.

PAARL DISTRICT

Named after one of three rounded granite domes (Paarl Rock, *paarl* is Afrikaans for "pearl") that dominate its landscape, Paarl is one of the most important wine-producing districts in South Africa with one of the highest concentrations of vineyards and wineries. Two relatively new wards, Simonsberg-Paarl, in the foothills of the Simonsberg Mountains, and Voor Paardeberg, show real promise. Although summers are generally warm, snow can cap the mountaintops throughout winter. Paarl receives 945 millimeters, or 37 inches, of rain annually, out of which 273 millimeters, or 11 inches, fall in summer. The Wellington ward, in the north of the district, is significantly drier, receiving only 279 millimeters, or 11 inches, over the whole year, with 104 millimeters, or 4 inches, during summer. Granite and shale underlie soils throughout the district, which tend to be red to yellow with good water retention in the southern portion and run more toward strongly structured, nutrient-rich brown soil in the north, nearer Wellington. There are more than thirty grapevine nurseries in Wellington, which provide the South African wine industry with 90 percent of its plant material. A series of microclimates, including alluvial terraces in the direction of Swartland and miniature valleys at the base of the Hawequa Mountains, provide a variety of conditions for the Chenin Blanc, Chardonnay, Cabernet Sauvignon, Shiraz, and Pinotage cultivated here. The Boberg designation may be used for fortified wines grown and produced here and in nearby Tulbagh.

DGB ESTATE

Lady Loch Road, Wellington,
+27 21 864 5300,
www.dgb.co.za

We visited JC Bekker (DGB Group winemaker) and Niel Groenewald (Bellingham chief winemaker) at the DGB winery in Wellington, at the foot of the beautiful Bainskloof Pass. DGB— named after Douglas Green, who pioneered the sales model for wholesale wine distribution in

1938 and is considered one of Paarl's first true *négociants*—was formally established in 1990, but its viticultural history goes back to 1693. Today it is one of South Africa's largest independent wine and spirit producers. Douglas Green Cabernet Sauvignon 2009 is ruby colored, with aromas of red and black fruits with a touch of bell pepper. In the mouth it is fruit-forward with a pleasant finish. Douglas Green Vineyard Creations Chardonnay 2009 is pale straw, with aromas of white stone fruits and citrus blossoms. In the mouth this is an easy-drinking Chardonnay, perfect for your next poolside party.

FAIRVIEW

Suid Agter Paarl Road, Suider-Paarl,
+27 21 863 2450,
www.fairview.co.za

Although archives show that wine was made on Fairview Farm in 1699, the modern-day story begins in 1937 with the farm's purchase by Lithuanian immigrant Charles Back. Today Charles Back II is in charge of the day-to-day operations of Fairview's attractions, including the Goatshed Restaurant and Vineyard Cheesery, as well as the picturesque herds of Jersey cows and Fairview goats. Fairview La Capra Chenin Blanc 2009 is pale straw colored, with aromas of honeydew melon and Anjou pear. In the mouth the flavors turn to tropical fruit salad, with a deliciously crisp finish. Fairview Weisser Riesling 2008 is light straw, with beautiful aromas of white flowers, wet river rocks, and honeycomb lifted over the fruit notes. In the mouth it has lovely roundness, with a slightly perfumed finish.

GLEN CARLOU

Simondium Road, Klapmuts,
+27 21 875 5528,
www.glencarlou.co.za

Glen Carlou was founded in 1985 and has been under the management of Hess Family Estates since 2003. The farm is also home to the Hess Collection Contemporary Art Museum, which features exhibitions from the Hess Art Collection. The restaurant features inspired preparations of duck and foie gras, but don't miss out on your opportunity to try a Kudo burger. Winemaker Arco Laarman's creations pair beautifully with the chef's cuisine. Glen Carlou Pinot Noir 2009 is ruby colored, with notes of raspberry and spice. On the palate flavors of black raspberry and cassis open up before a balanced, acidic finish. Glen Carlou Chardonnay 2009 is straw yellow with green tints and has aromas of citrus peel and Granny Smith apples. It is soft in the mouth, with vanilla undertones to the finish.

KWV

Kohler Street, Paarl,
+27 21 807 3007,
www.kwv.co.za

Now privately owned, KWV was originally a cooperative founded in January 1918. Its aim back then was to help stabilize the wine industry. Since becoming a private corporation in December 1997, the shift of focus from quantity to quality has been largely successful. KWV is one of the five largest wine and brandy producers in South Africa, turning out close to 20 million liters of wine each year, almost evenly divided between red and white. Labels include Laborie, Cathedral Cellars, Mentor Selection, KWV Reserve, KWV Lifestyle, Roodeberg, Bonne Esperance, Pearly Bay, Café Culture, and Golden Kaan. Each label is handled as its own separate winery, with on-site viticulture and winemaking teams. Visitors to the Paarl Emporium can expect a tour of what is billed as the largest cellar complex in the world. The high-end Laborie range's focus is on Rhône-style blends and *Cap Classique* sparkling wine, while the KWV Mentors' winemaker Richard Rowe is fixing his gaze on single-vineyard selections. The Cathedral Cellars brand, named for the recently renovated, circa 1930, barrel cellar featuring vaulted ceilings and stained glass windows, is good value. Café Culture is a new single-product label featuring funky graphics on the bottle; the 2009 turned out to be an easy-drinking Pinotage with dark berry flavors accented by notes of chocolate-covered espresso bean and hints of caramel. From the Lifestyle collection, KWV Shiraz 2008 is a classic rendition of the grape, with strong fruit flavors of black cherry and raspberry, spice, and pepper notes and tobacco on the finish. KWV Roodeberg White 2008 is a blend of 45 percent Chardonnay, 36 percent Chenin Blanc, 14 percent Sauvignon Blanc, and small amounts of Viognier, Sémillon, and Grenache Blanc. Refreshing notes of lime, passionfruit, green fig, and yellow currant mingle on the nose and palate. KWV Cathedral Cellar Cabernet Sauvignon 2006 tastes more expensive than it is: dark berries and a hint of eucalyptus mingle with baking spices, caramel, and candied violets, winding down to a long, smooth finish.

NEDERBURG

Sonstraal Road, Daljosafat, Paarl,
+27 21 862 3104,
www.nederburg.co.za

Nederburg was founded in 1791 by German immigrant Philippus Wolvaart, who planted 49 hectares (121 acres) of vines. Today the company is owned by Distell, and the cellar master is Romanian-born Razvan Macici. The white wines are made by Tariro Masayiti, and the red wines are made by Wilhelm Pienaar. Nederburg Lyric 2009 is a blend of 56 percent Sauvignon Blanc, 23 percent Chenin Blanc, and 21 percent Chardonnay. It is straw colored with green tints and has aromas of white stone fruit, cut grass, and tropical fruits. It is crisp in the mouth with balanced acidity. Nederburg Cabernet Sauvignon 2007 is dark ruby red, with notes of dark fruit, black plums, cassis, and cocoa. On the palate it has flavors of ripe dark fruits and a firm tannic finish.

VILAFONTÉ

Bosmans Crossing, Paarl Simonsberg,
+27 21 886 4083,
www.vilafonte.com

A joint venture between Californian Zelma Long (formerly of Mondavi, Simi, and LVMH), her husband, viticulturist Phil Freese, and Mike Ratcliffe of nearby Warwick Wine Estate, Vilafonté is named for the soil type found in the vineyards. The 12 hectares (30 acres) of vines here were planted in 1998 and 1999, and only two wines are made, both red—the Series M, which is Merlot-dominant, and Series C, which is Cabernet Sauvignon–dominant. Vilafonté also makes a cigar that is specifically designed to be enjoyed with fine red wines. We tasted these wines outdoors over dinner with Zelma, Phil, and Mike in South Africa on a perfect star-filled night. Vilafonté Series M 2007 is dark, dark red, with aromas of dark cherry, purple flowers, dried cherries, and powdered cocoa. It is generous in the mouth with lovely fruit and persistent tannins. Vilafonté Series C 2007 is ruby to garnet colored, with notes of anise, cassis, black cherry, saddle leather, and chocolate. On the palate the fruit jumps out and delights your entire mouth. This big wine can stand up to South African *braai*, and maybe even a cigar or two.

STELLENBOSCH DISTRICT

When it comes to winegrowing areas, Stellenbosch is truly blessed. With a variety of microclimates, rich red and yellow soil above well-draining shale and granite, more than adequate rainfall, and foothills and mountains giving shelter to a multitude of grape varieties, it is home to some of the finest vineyards and wineries the world over. Wine has been made here since the seventeenth century, and today historic estates sit cheek-to-jowl with modern wineries boasting the latest innovations in viniculture. It is subdivided into the Banghoek, Bottelary, Devon Valley, Jonkershoek Valley, Papegaaiberg, Polkadraai Hills, and Simonsberg-Stellenbosch wards, further testament to its diversity of terrain. Stellenbosch's annual rainfall totals 713 millimeters, or 28 inches, and the amount received in summer is 229 millimeters, or 9 inches. The southern end of the district, closer to False Bay, is a bit drier; summer brings 177 millimeters, or 7 inches, of rain, with a total of 542 millimeters, or 21 inches, falling over the course of the year.

The town of Stellenbosch is home to Stellenbosch University, the country's only university offering a degree in viticulture and enology. Both the Nietvoorbij Institute of Viticulture and Oenology and the Elsenberg Farm Cape Institute for Agricultural Training are located nearby. The former performs ongoing research into rootstock, clones, and new varieties. Stellenbosch University lists an impressive roster of celebrated winemakers among its graduates. Stellenbosch maintains some of the finest examples of original Cape Dutch architecture, and as home to many students, it boasts a lively café and nightlife culture.

BEYERSKLOOF

Route R-304 Koelenhof, Stellenbosch,
+27 21 865 2135,
www.beyerskloof.co.za

Beyerskloof's logo is a red Pinotage leaf, and for good reason: Beyers Truter is indisputably one of the finest Pinotage crafters in the country. From his early days at Kanonkop through the founding of Beyerskloof in 1988 to the current vintage, he has proven time and again that Pinotage—a homely offspring of mismatched parents—is capable of becoming a world-class wine. The estate's Nooitgedacht Farm had belonged to the Beyers family,

Truter's ancestors, until 1895, and with his purchase of the estate, he brought the land back under family control. His current business partner is Simon Halliday of Raisin Social, and winemaking duties are shared with Anri Truter and Travis Langley. Their Bottelary Road estate is 77 hectares (190 acres), with 50 hectares (124 acres) of those planted to vine: Pinotage covers 30 hectares (74 acres), a third of which are bush vines, 15 hectares (37 acres) are devoted to Cabernet Sauvignon, and Merlot and Cinsault are grown, respectively, on 10 hectares (25 acres) and 5 hectares (12 acres). After Pinotage, the winemaker's second love is Cabernet Sauvignon, which is fermented in traditional open tanks for the Beyerskloof blend. The on-site Red Leaf restaurant is a lovely spot to enjoy the signature Pinotage Burger. In the realm of social responsibility, the Beyers Truter Faith Fund is a nonprofit set up to prevent Fetal Alcohol Syndrome through outreach and education. The fund's namesake wine, Beyerskloof Faith 2007, is an inky black cherry colored blend of 30 percent Cabernet Sauvignon, 30 percent Merlot, 20 percent Pinotage, and 20 percent Shiraz. It is as bold in flavor as it is in color; intense berry with a burst of pepper and spice are in harmony with toasted vanilla bean and orange peel notes, leading to a long, sleek finish. Beyerskloof Diesel Pinotage 2008 is deep cherry red with a bright meniscus. Black cherry and raspberry share the stage with anise, fennel, oregano, and a whiff of violet. Careful vineyard selection and 19 months in new French oak have led to a wine of outstanding depth and complexity. Beyerskloof Chenin/Pinotage 2010, made from 75 percent Chenin Blanc and 25 percent Pinotage, is a white wine with the vaguest hue of pink. An aroma of apple and light floral notes is joined on the palate by flavors of Anjou pear, strawberries, and freesia; soft tannins are complemented by bright acidity.

BOTANICA

Devon Valley Road, Stellenbosch,
+27 21 865 2313,
www.botanicawines.com

Botanica is named for the beautiful botanical images and collages created by the artist Mary Delany in the late 1700s. The winemaking at Botanica is under the direction of Ginny Povall, and the grapes are grown at Protea Heights Farm, which was the first farm to grow and export protea flowers. There is a beautiful four-star guesthouse, Sugarbird Manor, on the property that is the perfect place to relax for a few days. Botanica Chenin Blanc 2009 is straw colored, with white stone fruit aromas with a touch of lifted apricot. It is generous in the mouth with a fair bit of minerality and balanced acidity.

DELAIRE GRAFF ESTATE

Helshoogte Pass, Stellenbosch,
+27 21 885 8160,
www.delaire.co.za

Poised on the slopes of historic Botmaskop Peak, on the pass linking Stellenbosch and Franschhoek, Delaire Graff Estate boasts a winery, hotel, and spa of unparalleled luxury. The former Avontuur farm was renamed Delaire, meaning "from the sky," by its previous owner, John Platter, the renowned South African wine writer. Its purchase in 2003 by Laurence Graff of Graff Diamonds International meant not just a major building effort, but a replanting program as well. A careful selection of varietal clones matched to vineyard sites provides winemaker Morne Vrey with the best fruit possible to be vinified in the state-of-the-art winery—said to be one of the most technologically advanced in the entire Southern Hemisphere. With beautifully landscaped gardens, a sensational art collection, the well-appointed Wine Lounge, two restaurants—Delaire Graff and Indochine— ten private lodges, and an opulent spa rated among the world's finest, this is one estate not to be missed on your trip to the Cape. Delaire Red 2006 combines 43 percent Cabernet Sauvignon, 32 percent Merlot, 11 percent Petit Verdot, 9 percent Shiraz, 4 percent Cabernet Franc, and 1 percent Malbec into a rich palate pleaser with striking flavors of black cherry and cassis, backed by anise, chocolate, and cinnamon. Delaire Shiraz 2009 is deep, red violet and tastes of fruits of the wood, white pepper, and herbes de Provence, with a lingering finish. Delaire Sauvignon Blanc 2010 has flavors of pineapple and papaya with freshly shelled pea and chopped herb notes.

DEMORGENZON

Stellenboschkloof Road, Stellenbosch,
+27 21 881 3030,
www.demorgenzon.co.za

Wendy and Hylton Appelbaum chose the name DeMorgenzon—meaning "morning sun"— because their Stellenboschkloof estate is the first in the area to catch the rays of the rising sun. After purchasing the land in 2003, they ripped out more than 50 hectares (124 acres) of grapevines, leaving only some Chenin Blanc bush vines intact, began replanting in earnest, and conducted serious site analysis in order to match varieties to *terroir*. DeMorgenzon now consists of 55 hectares (136 acres) of mountainside vineyard interspersed among 91 hectares (225 acres) of wildflowers and native flora. Hylton Appelbaum has a strong belief in the beneficial effects of music on plant growth. Baroque music plays throughout the vineyards and cellars 24 hours a day via a series of well-spaced speakers; they believe there is evidence to suggest that the music's effects lead to balance and complexity in the wines of DeMorgenzon. There is a newly built amphitheater on the premises as well, to showcase the best Baroque talent the Cape has to offer. The estate's most acclaimed bottling is the old vine Chenin Blanc, made by consulting winemaker and Chenin expert Teddy Hall. Winemaker Carl van der Merwe is a new addition to the DeMorgenzon team. The value range DMZ label uses a combination of estate-grown fruit and purchased grapes. DeMorgenzon Chenin Blanc 2009, made from select 38-year-old bush vines, opens with aromas of white peach, lemon, and toast, which extend on the palate to flavors of ripe nectarine, honeysuckle, and toffee. DMZ Chardonnay 2009 tastes of peach and passionfruit with touches of vanilla and toasted almond. DMZ Syrah 2009 reveals a rich, juicy burst of blackberry and plum instilled with pinches of vanilla, black pepper, and gingerbread spice.

DE TOREN

Polkadraai Road, Stellenbosch,
+27 21 881 3119,
www.de-toren.com

When Emil and Sonette den Dulk left the frenetic pace of life in Johannesburg behind in order to reconnect with nature in the Cape Winelands, they came across what they rightfully refer to as a "little piece of heaven" in the Polkadraai Hills. With the assistance of experts from the University of Stellenbosch, they accomplished their goal of creating what is hailed as South Africa's first five-varietal Bordeaux blend: the celebrated Fusion V. Twenty-two of the estate's 26 hectares (64 acres) are planted with Cabernet Sauvignon, Merlot, Cabernet Franc, Malbec, and Petit Verdot. De Toren Private Cellar's moniker is a nod to the tower for which it is named, an elevator shaft housing a 4,000-liter pressure tank used in gravity-flow winemaking.

Technology here ranges from high-tech to traditional: infrared aerial imaging monitors vineyard blocks to help pick the perfect time of ripeness, but harvesting is done by hand, and after being carried to the winery in small baskets, grapes are hand-sorted and basket-pressed. From the start the den Dulk's joined forces with winemaker Albie Koch, whose first vintage here, the 1999 Fusion V, was received with great reviews—and is quickly becoming the bottle of choice among South African wine collectors. De Toren Z, a Merlot-based Bordeaux blend, was created in 2004, and it's an able companion to the Cabernet Sauvignon–based blend. De Toren Fusion V 2008 is a near perfect amalgam of 56 percent Cabernet Sauvignon, 20 percent Cabernet Franc, 12 percent Malbec, 7 percent Merlot, and 5 percent Petit Verdot. Well-integrated flavors of cassis and black plum mix with licorice and Mediterranean herbs on the palate, winding down to an exquisite finish. De Toren Z 2008, a combination of 45 percent Merlot, 27 percent Cabernet Sauvignon, 15 percent Malbec, 7 percent Cabernet Franc, and 6 percent Petit Verdot, tastes of black cherry, blueberry, and black currant with notes of cigar box, cinnamon, and Turkish delight.

DE TRAFFORD WINES

Mont Fleur, Stellenbosch,
+27 21 880 1611,
www.detrafford.co.za

The Trafford family purchased land for grazing, but after finding that the land was suitable for growing grapes, they started planting vines in 1983. Architect-turned-winemaker David Trafford began making wines for family and friends and was eventually persuaded to share his quality wines with the wine-drinking consumer. De Trafford 2007 Blueprint Shiraz is vibrant red, with aromas of black raspberries, red raspberries, dark spices, and a touch of green juniper. It has sweet fruit on the palate, with a touch of spice before a fine tannic finish. De Trafford Cabernet Sauvignon 2009 is medium red, with notes of blueberry, red plums, and cigar box on the nose, with good heft and soft tannins on the palate.

ERNIE ELS WINES

Annandale Road, Stellenbosch,
+27 21 881 3588,
www.ernieelswines.com

The friendship between Ernie Els and Jean Engelbrecht of Rust en Vrede winery is responsible for the 1999 establishment of Ernie Els Wines. Ernie, a well-known professional golfer, has won more than sixty tournaments since

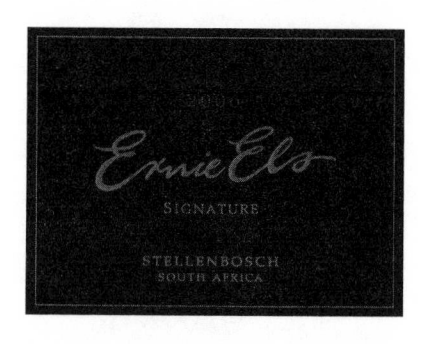

turning pro in 1989. Since teaming up with winemaker Louis Strydom, his wines have also achieved international acclaim. He has six wines in his portfolio, all at different price points, and Ernie remains active in the tasting and blending process. His flagship, Ernie Els Signature 2006 is dark ruby garnet, with aromas of blackberries, cassis, cinnamon, nutmeg, and a touch of cedar. It is big on the palate, with rich fruit flavors and a touch of menthol on the well-structured finish. Ernie Els Proprietor's Blend 2007 is ruby colored, with notes of red and black fruits and a hint of chocolate in the bouquet. In the mouth it is generous with fruit flavors before finishing with savory notes.

GLENELLY

Lelie Street, Idas Valley, Stellenbosch,
+27 21 809 6440,
www.glenellyestate.com

Located on the southern slopes of Simonsberg Mountain, Glenelly Estate was an established fruit farm for 138 years until May-Eliane de Lencquesaing—who was previously the owner of famed Bordeaux estate Château Pichon Longueville Comtesse de Lalande—bought it in 2003. Since then Mme. de Lencquesaing has had the 128-hectare (316-acre) property planted with 60 hectares (148 acres) of red grapes, including Cabernet Sauvignon, Shiraz, Merlot, Petit Verdot, and Cabernet Franc, and 6 hectares (15 acres) of Chardonnay. The parcel's east-facing slopes allow for cool daytime breezes, facilitating a longer ripening process than that of many neighboring vineyards. The year 2007 saw the successful harvest of the first estate-grown fruit, and in that same year winemaker Luke O'Cuinneagain came on board, after five years at nearby Rustenberg. In 2009, Glenelly's winery was completed; it combines technology with a respect for the environment and operates completely on gravity-flow. With the aim to combine French style with South African *terroir*, Glenelly produces a full range of distinctive wines—from the entry-level Glass Collection to the Grand Vin de Glenelly red blend to the crown jewel, the Bordeaux-style Lady May Cabernet Sauvignon. We were honored to sit with Lady May and have a civilized chat over a pot of tea. In her eighth decade, Lady May is a force of nature. Glenelly Glass Collection Chardonnay 2010 has clean flavors of pineapple, mango, and lemon peel. It is a perfect example of why Chardonnay does not need to be slathered in oak. Glenelly Grand Vin de Glenelly 2007, the winery's signature red blend, is made of 44 percent Shiraz, 31 percent Cabernet Sauvignon, 24 percent Merlot, and 1 percent Petit Verdot. Flavors of cherry, wild raspberry, and black currant mingle in the mouth with violet and spice notes. Glenelly Lady May 2008, a blend of 91 percent Cabernet Sauvignon and 9 percent Petit Verdot, displays all of the strength and elegance of a fine Bordeaux without the overpowering tannins one would expect from a Bordeaux of the same age. Complex flavors of blackberry, black cherry, and cassis are layered over clove, lavender, and thyme.

HARTENBERG

Koelenhof,
+27 21 865 2571,
www.hartenbergestate.com

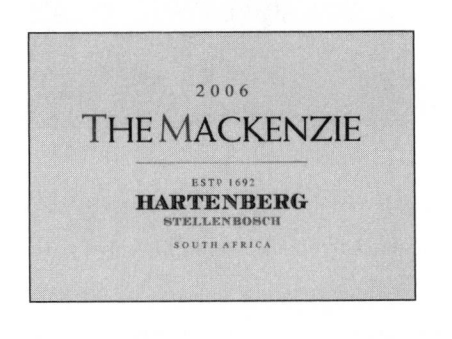

The earliest record of the Hartenberg estate goes back to 1692, and recent ownership has included Dr. Maurice Finlayson (1948), the Gilbey family (1985), and Ken Mackenzie, the owner since 1987. Along with winemaker Carl Schultz and consultant Alberto Antonini, the Mackenzie family makes wines of international appeal. Hartenberg Eleanor Chardonnay 2007, named for Eleanor Finlayson, is straw colored, with citrus blossom, hazelnut, and white flower aromas. It is creamy in the mouth, with a lemon curd, zesty finish. Hartenberg Mackenzie Cabernet Sauvignon Merlot 2006 is 85 percent Cabernet Sauvignon, 10 percent Malbec, and 5 percent Merlot. It is dark garnet, with aromas and flavors of red berries and black cherries in the mid palate, and hints of smoke, cocoa, and geranium leaf on the post palate. It is full-bodied with a smooth, tannic finish.

HOWARD BOOYSEN

Stellenbosch,
+27 72 414 5458,
www.howardbooysenwines.com

After graduating from Elsenburg Agricultural College, Howard Booysen was the recipient of the Protégé Award from the Cape Winemakers Guild. This distinction allowed him to hone his winemaking skills with various mentors at different wine estates. He is one of a handful of black winemakers in South Africa and currently moonlights as a sommelier at Restaurant Auslese. Booysen only makes one wine at this time, a delicious Riesling that has been highly scored by South African publications. It is our firm belief that this talented winemaker will be giving up his restaurant job soon to concentrate on making other quality wines. Howard Booysen Riesling 2010 is straw colored, with aromas of white stone fruits, nectarine, and a whiff of apricot. It has pleasant peach nectar flavors in the mouth with gentle sweet honeysuckle on the finish.

JARDIN / JORDAN

Stellenboschkloof Road,
+27 21 881 3441,
www.jordanwines.com

We visited Gary and Kathy Jordan at their beautiful estate and shared a delicious lunch made only more enjoyable by the stunning view over their Stellenbosch vineyards, Table Bay, and False Bay. They were wonderful hosts, and we learned that their winery restaurant has been rated one of South Africa's best, and that they are also the owners of one of our favorite restaurants in London: High Timber. In South Africa the estate's wines are available under the family name, Jordan, but in North America they are sold under the name Jardin. These are wines certainly worth seeking out. Jardin Chardonnay 2009 is medium straw colored, with aromas of white stone fruits, green apple, and buttered brioche toast. It is full-bodied in the mouth with a pleasant finish and a lingering nuance of toasted almonds and citrus zest. Jardin Cabernet Sauvignon 2008 is ruby red, with notes of black currants, black raspberry, and vanilla. It is generous in the mouth with a slight tannic grip. Perfectly enjoyable now, this wine will continue to improve with age.

KANONKOP

Route R44, Stellenbosch,
+27 21 884 4719,
www.kanonkop.co.za

Kanonkop's name is derived from a small hill, or *kopje*, on the property, from which a cannon was fired in the seventeenth century, announcing that trading ships from the Dutch East India Company had arrived at Table Bay. One hundred hectares (247 acres) of vineyards on the lower slopes of Stellenbosch's Simonsberg Mountain are planted with some of the oldest Pinotage vines in the region, with an average age of 50 years. The fourth-generation family farm has been owned by the Sauer-Krige family for 80 years; brothers Johann and Paul Krige are currently at the helm, with the assistance of winemaker Abrie Beeslaar, who has been here since 2003. With the introduction of its first estate-bottled wines in 1973, Kanonkop ushered in a new era of respect—or better yet reverence—for Pinotage. Both the single-varietal Pinotage and Cabernet Sauvignon–based Paul Sauer have garnered multiple accolades and awards over the years. Grapes are both picked and sorted by hand, and open-topped concrete fermentation tanks are punched down manually twelve times per day. We spent several nights at the small on-site cottage during harvest one season, and the winery buzzed all night with noise, activity, and light, in stark contrast to the nearly desolate road we pulled in from after a day visiting other wineries. One night when we just couldn't fall asleep, we helped the winemakers with the punchdowns. Kanonkop Pinotage 2009 comes across in waves of black cherry, cassis, and red plum with notes of banana and chocolate-covered espresso, culminating in a lightly grippy finish; this is truly a benchmark for the varietal. Kanonkop Paul Sauer 2007 is a luscious mélange of 68 percent Cabernet Sauvignon, 17 percent Cabernet Franc, and 15 percent Merlot. Expect flavors of cassis, blackberry, and star anise with touches of smoke and violet. The entry-level Kanonkop Kadette 2009 is a blend of 46 percent Pinotage, 30 percent Cabernet Sauvignon, 18 percent Merlot, and 6 percent Cabernet Franc. Blackberry, coffee, and plum mingle on the tongue with oregano and fennel. A great barbecue wine!

KANU

Polkadraai Road, Stellenbosch,
+27 21 865 2351,
www.kanu.co.za

The appearance of a *kanu*, a "mythical bird of promise," in the African sky is said to herald a bountiful harvest for all who fall under its passing shadow. Kanu wines celebrate the folkloric bird and its legend. Grown and produced on the Goedgeloof farm in the Polkadraai Hills, these vineyards once belonged to the Spier Wine Estate, established under the auspices of Governor Simon van der Stel in 1692. Purchased in 1997 by Hydro Holdings, the property underwent a total renovation. Chief winemaker Richard Kershaw arrived at Kanu in 2003, continuing the legacy begun by Teddy Hall, the noted Chenin Blanc authority. Chenin Blanc, the winery's flagship variety, is produced in three editions: a fresh, steel-fermented bottling under screwcap, a more complex barrel-fermented version, and the curiously named Kia-Ora, a sweet dessert wine. Kanu also bottles Sauvignon Blanc, Chardonnay, and Shiraz. Kanu Chenin Blanc 2009 goes down easy, with flavors of white peach, cantaloupe, and orange zest tinged with hints of white flowers and spice. It is comprised of 92 percent Chenin Blanc, 7 percent Viognier, and 1 percent Sauvignon Blanc. Richard Kershaw's winemaking experience in Hungary shines through in his Kanu Kia-Ora Noble Late Harvest 2005, a blend of botrytized 95 percent Chenin Blanc and 5 percent Sauvignon Blanc. Rich flavors of passionfruit, apricot marmalade, honey, and almond are lightly dusted with a trace of five-spice powder. Bright acidity keeps it from feeling tooth-achingly sweet.

KEN FORRESTER WINES

Corner Route R44 and Winery Road,
Stellenbosch,
+27 21 855 2374
www.kenforresterwines.com

Ken Forrester, a seasoned hospitality industry professional, and his wife, Teresa, purchased one of the oldest wine farms on the Cape, in 1993. Teresa set about restoring the 1694 Cape Dutch farmhouse that would become their home, while Ken and his winemaker friend, Martin Meinert, began replanting the vineyards, aiming to create the finest wine

minerality. Ken Forrester The Gypsy 2007, a blend of 60 percent Grenache and 40 percent Shiraz, exhibits luscious flavors of blackberry, cherry preserves, espresso bean, and clove. This Rhône blend from the Icon range is an exquisite combination of elegant and earthy qualities.

possible, with the spotlight on Chenin Blanc. To this day Ken Forrester is considered one of the pioneers of the South African Chenin Blanc transformation; FMC, or Forrester Meinert Chenin, produced from almost 40-year-old bush vines, is a shining example of prime old-vine Chenin Blanc. Their 50-hectare (124-acre) wine farm contains 34 hectares (84 acres) of grapevines; the estate vineyards are organically farmed, and a 2-hectare (5-acre) marshland on the property is set aside for preservation of local flora and fauna. There are three ranges of wine under the Ken Forrester label: the entry-label Petit series, the Ken Forrester brand, which is the flagship of the brand, and the high-end, low-volume Icon range. Ken Forrester Petit Pinotage 2009 is a sprightly red, whose cherry and black plum flavors are joined by characteristic tastes of smoked meat and nettles. Ken Forrester Chenin Blanc 2009 is a mouthpleasing synthesis of melon and passionfruit flavors with hints of honey and satisfying

KLEINE ZALZE

Strand Road, Stellenbosch,
+27 21 880 0717,
www.kleinezalze.co.za

We had a wonderful dinner at Kleine Zalze's Terroir Restaurant with wine pairings by Chef Michael Broughton. The cuisine, ambiance, company, wine, and weather could not have been more perfect. Kleine Zalze makes wines in five ranges from grapes grown on this family-owned estate. There are a luxurious lodge, condominiums for rent, and on-premise golf should you decide to take a day off from visiting the Stellenbosch Wine Routes. Kleine Zalze Family Reserve Sauvignon Blanc 2010 is straw yellow with green tinges and has aromas of pea shoots, freshly mowed grass, white flowers, and green figs. It is medium-bodied on the palate with a refreshing finish. Kleine Zalze Cellar Selection Gamay Noir is medium ruby red, with notes of wild strawberries, red cherries, and dried black cherries in the bouquet. It is light-bodied and fruity on the palate. It is a very refreshing wine served chilled on a warm South African day.

MEERLUST ESTATE

Meerlust Estate, Stellenbosch,
+27 21 843 3587,
www.meerlust.com

Johannes Albertus Myburgh bought his beloved Meerlust Estate in 1757. Eight generations later, his descendent, Hannes Myburgh, owns the farm and heads the winemaking team. Hannes's previous experience includes Château Lafite in France and von Oetinger in Germany. His wines have a decidedly European–South African taste profile and have won numerous international awards. Meerlust Rubicon 2006 is a blend of 74 percent Cabernet Sauvignon, 18 percent Cabernet Franc, and 8 percent Merlot. It is deep garnet with a violet rim and has aromas of black plums, cassis, crystallized violet, cigar box, and baking spices. In the mouth it is generous with persistent rounded tannins. Meerlust Chardonnay 2007 is pale straw colored, with notes of citrus blossom, Granny Smith apple, and freshly ground almond paste in the bouquet. It is creamy and full in the mouth with crisp minerality and balanced acidity.

MILES MOSSOP WINES

Stellenbosch,
+27 21 808 5900,
www.milesmossopwines.com

Miles Mossop is the winemaker at Tokara and makes excellent wines under the Tokara label, but true wine geeks should seek out his exceptional eponymous wines. We had the chance to hang out with him in Stellenbosch and catch up over a few glasses. Max, his red blend, is named for his son Maximilian, and Saskia is named after his daughter, Saskia-Jo. Miles Mossop Max 2006 is a combination of 54 percent Cabernet Sauvignon, 23 percent Merlot, and 23 percent Petit Verdot. It is dark garnet, with aromas of baking spices, black cherry, cassis, anise, and a top note of menthol in the complex bouquet. In the mouth the fruit flavors jump to life and tickle the post palate, and there is a touch of black licorice in the finish. Miles Mossop Saskia 2008 is a blend of 71 percent Chenin Blanc and 29 percent Viognier. It is straw colored, with notes of toasted hazelnut, white flowers, lime zest, and white stone fruits in the nose. In the mouth tropical flavors like pineapple and mango pop out before the crisp clean finish.

MORGENHOF

Klapmuts Road, Stellenbosch,
+27 21 889 5510,
www.morgenhof.com

Alain Huchon and Anne Cointreau Huchon purchased the historic 1692 Morgenhof Estate in 1993, and in 1998 achieved "estate status." Today all wines are made from grapes grown on premise, and the family takes great pride in this fact. The estate boasts both the Morgenhof restaurant and the Morgenhof Manor House (which sleeps ten people). This makes the estate a desirable wedding venue and popular tourist destination. Morgenhof Chardonnay 2009 is straw colored, with aromas of lime zest, lemon blossoms, and tropical fruit. It is creamy in the mouth with a long finish. Morgenhof Fantail Pinotage 2008 is dark cherry colored, with notes of wild strawberries and fruits of the wood in the bouquet. It is fruit-driven in the mouth with a soft tannic finish.

MULDERBOSCH

Polkadraai Road, Stellenbosch,
+27 21 881 3514,
www.mulderbosch.co.za

In 1989, medical doctor Larry Jacobs bought a run-down Stellenbosch fruit farm and enlisted rising-star winemaker Mike Dobrovic to assist him in building a winery and planting vineyards. Their first release of Sauvignon Blanc garnered a fair share of attention, and Mulderbosch has turned out excellent wines and earned accolades ever since. Of the farm's 46 hectares (114 acres), 26 hectares (64 acres) are covered with vines. The property was planted with awareness of the environment; 25 percent of the farm is set aside as a nature conservancy. When Mike Dobrovic moved on in 2009, his protégé Richard Kershaw was appointed head winemaker, and in late 2011,

Adam Mason, formerly of Klein Constantia, took the reins. A bottle of Mulderbosch is easy to spot in a wine shop; the unusual narrow paper label is modeled after a Cuban cigar band. Mulderbosch Chenin Blanc 2009 is a delicious union of tropical fruits, lime sorbet, and oak-derived spice. Mulderbosch Cabernet Sauvignon Rosé 2010 is an appealing bright pink in the glass, and on the tongue flavors of Turkish delight, raspberry, and strawberry marmalade are infused with touches of lavender, rosemary, and white pepper. Mulderbosch Faithful Hound 2007, a blend of 62 percent Cabernet Sauvignon, 10 percent Malbec, 10 percent Petit Verdot, 10 percent Merlot, and 8 percent Cabernet Franc, was named by winemaker Mike Dobrovic in homage to the loyal dog who kept watch over the farm for three years after his owner's death, waiting for him to return. Strong flavors of cassis, wild raspberry, espresso bean, star anise, and clove are joined in the mouth by touches of pencil lead and cedar.

MVEMVE RAATS

Vlaeberg Road, Polkadraai, Stellenbosch,
+27 21 881 3078,
www.raats.co.za

Mzokhona Mvemve and Bruwer Raats are one of the first black-and-white winemaking teams

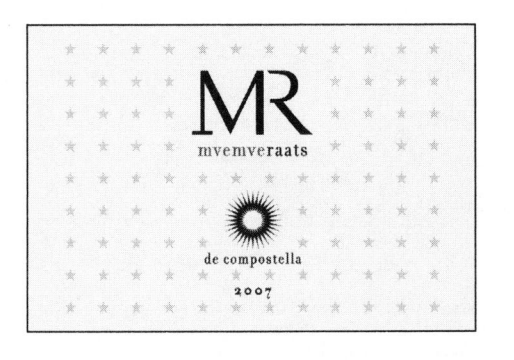

in South Africa. Started in 2004, Mvemve Raats makes wines that have garnered high points from international publications—its first three vintages of MR de Compostella (2004, 2005, and 2006) received 93 points from US *Wine Spectator* magazine. The pair met while working at Delaire winery and decided to make great wines without the constraints of tradition, style, or grape variety. Their philosophy seems to be working exceedingly well. Mvemve Raats MR de Compostella 2007 is a blend of 32 percent Cabernet Franc, 24 percent Cabernet Sauvignon, 20 percent Malbec, 16 percent Petit Verdot, and 8 percent Merlot. It is garnet colored, with notes of black cherry, black plum, cigar box, forest floor, and cocoa. It is big and bold in the mouth and certainly a wine to be reckoned with. It has balanced acidity and a lingering finish that keeps inviting you into the glass for more.

NEIL ELLIS

Helshoogte Road, Stellenbosch,
+27 21 887 0649,
www.neilellis.com

Neil Ellis began making wine utilizing a *négociant* model in 1986. After years of successful winemaking and international accolades, he joined forces with his landowner neighbor, Hans Peter Schroder, to create some amazing wines. Neil Ellis Zwalu 2009 is a blend of 35 percent Shiraz, 35 percent Cabernet Sauvignon, and 30 percent Cabernet Franc. It is medium red colored, with aromas of black raspberries, black plums, cassis, cigar box, purple flowers, and a touch of menthol. It is big across the tongue with a pleasing mouthfeel and persistent finish. Neil Ellis Sauvignon Blanc 2010 is medium straw colored, with notes of green apple and lemon zest in the nose and on the palate. It has balanced acidity and refreshing brightness.

POST HOUSE

Helderberg,
+27 21 842 2309,
www.posthousewines.co.za

In 1981 Hermann Gebers purchased the farm that would become Post House, and in 1996 Nick Gebers made his first wines from it. He decided to call them Post House Wines because the farm previously served as a postal station for the small missionary community of Raithby. Post House Missing Virgin 2008, named for a collectable postage stamp, is a combination of Pinotage and Petit Verdot that is dark, dark red (almost blue black) in color. It has aromas of blueberry, black currant, and Christmas baking spices. In the mouth it is an extremely fruity and generous wine with a lovely finish. Post House Penny Black 2008, named for the world's first printed stamp, is a blend of red varieties and has a nose of violet, freshly ground black pepper, and fruit cake. It is round in the mouth with a firm tannic finish.

RAATS FAMILY WINES

Vlaeberg Road, Polkadraai, Stellenbosch,
+27 21 881 3078,
www.raats.co.za

Bruwer Raats isn't afraid to put his money where his mouth is. We have been to dinner with him—informal testosterone-driven blind tastings, as they sometimes turn out to be—where he has compared his wines to those of fine French Bordeaux, and more often than not, his

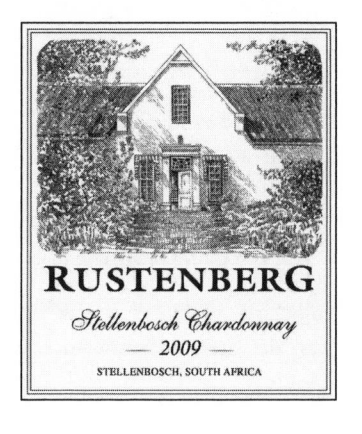

wine is the table's favorite. Bruwer is a great guy and a fantastic *braai* master who loves to create wines under his own label because, "You don't have to worry about shareholders or catering to a market or to keeping within a cellar's style. You can have freedom of expression in something that you believe in." His philosophy certainly comes through in the glass—we're big fans of Raats wines. Raats Original Chenin Blanc 2009 is straw colored, with aromas of honeycomb, tropical fruits, pineapple, and wet river rocks. It is bright and zesty in the mouth with a crisp finish. Raats Cabernet Franc 2008 is purplish-red, with notes of black raspberry, cassis, mocha, and tobacco leaf. It is silky on the palate, with a touch of smoke in its lingering finish.

RUSTENBERG WINES

Stellenbosch,
+27 21 809 1200,
www.rustenberg.co.za

One of South Africa's oldest wine farms, established in 1682, Rustenberg has achieved international acclaim in various forms of media. The Barlow family has owned the farm since 1941, and in 1987, Simon Barlow took over management. He is responsible for wide-scale replanting, winery renovations, and hiring the new winemaking team. Rustenberg is also committed to conservation and is a proud member of the Biodiversity and Wine Initiative. Rustenberg Chardonnay 2009 is straw colored, with notes of Macintosh apples, orange blossom, wet river rocks, and hazelnuts. It has a nice balance between minerality and acidity on the palate. Rustenberg John H Merriman 2007 is a Bordeaux-style blend with ruby garnet coloring. It has aromas of tobacco leaf, anise, and black plum and flavors of rich, dark fruits and spice. It has a persistent finish with smooth, tannic structure.

RUST EN VREDE

Annandale Road, Stellenbosch,
+27 21 881 3881,
www.rustenvrede.com

Chosen by President Nelson Mandela to be served at his 1993 Nobel Peace Prize dinner in Oslo, Rust en Vrede was part of Governor Willem van der Stel's original farm in 1694. Since 1977 the estate has been owned and managed by the Engelbrecht family, who are known worldwide for their quality wines. Rust en Vrede Merlot 2009 is dark garnet, with aromas of coffee, chocolate, black raspberry, and black plum. In the mouth it is generous with hints of vanilla and a smooth tannic finish. Rust en Vrede Syrah 2008 is deep purple colored, with notes of violet, black fruits, and coffee. On the palate it displays nice heft and has a smooth, tannic finish.

SIMONSIG

Kromme Rhee Road, Stellenbosch/Simonsig,
+27 21 888 4900,
www.simonsig.co.za

Owned and managed by the Malan family since 1688, Simonsig is run by three brothers who are all direct descendants of the founder Jacques Malan. The farm consists of 210 hectares (519 acres) and is known nationally and internationally for its quality wines. The Malan family is dedicated to social responsibility and sponsors a "Reach for Gold" program to assist farm workers with daycare and preschool for their children, as well as tuition assistance for continuing education. Simonsig Sunbird Sauvignon Blanc 2010 is pale straw, with aromas of tropical fruits, guava, mango, and passionfruit. In the mouth it is creamy with fruit overtones of mango and pineapple. It finishes with a pleasant floral touch. Simonsig Frans Malan Reserve 2007 is a Cape Blend of 64 percent Pinotage, 31 percent Cabernet Sauvignon, and 5 percent Merlot. It is garnet colored, with aromas of black raspberries, black plums, cedar shavings, and graphite. It is a big wine with generous mouthfeel and a smooth, tannic finish.

SPIER

Annandale Road, Stellenbosch,
+27 21 881 8400,
www.spier.co.za

Records show that grapes were first pressed at Spier in 1712, and the estate boasts one of the Cape's oldest wine cellars, dating back to 1767. Spier Estate is one of the most visited and most beautiful destinations on the Stellenbosch Wine Trail. With stunning views of the Helderberg Mountains, award-winning wines, a gourmet restaurant, luxury hotel, Cheetah Outreach Program, Eagle Encounter, horseback riding, and their Camelot Spa, guests might not want to ever leave the property. Spier Cabernet Sauvignon 2007 is garnet colored with a ruby violet rim. It has aromas of cassis, cigar box, and fresh black raspberries. It is smooth on the palate, with a lingering finish. Spier Sauvignon Blanc 2008 is straw colored with green tints and has notes of cut grass, mango, and pineapple in the bouquet. It has a crisp finish with a lingering sensation of fresh cut herbs.

Winemaking is under the direction of cellar master PG Slabbert and winemaker Juan Slabbert. Stellenbosch Hills Chenin Blanc 2010 is straw yellow, with aromas of tropical fruit, pineapple, and white stone fruits. It is crisp, clean, and refreshing, with balanced acidity and a lingering finish. Polkadraai Pinotage-Merlot 2009 is dark garnet, with enticing fruit aromas of blackberries, black plums, cassis, and a touch of new leather. In the mouth it offers big fruit flavors and a smooth, round, tannic finish.

STELLENBOSCH HILLS

Vlottenburg Road, Stellenbosch,
+27 21 881 3828,
www.stellenbosch-hills.co.za

Stellenbosch Hills evolved from the Vlottenburg Cooperative founded in 1945, but the name was changed in 2003 because *Vlottenburg* means "small parcel of land" and does not accurately represent the land holdings of the 16 growers currently involved.

THELEMA

Helshoogte Pass, Stellenbosch,
+27 21 885 1924,
www.thelema.co.za

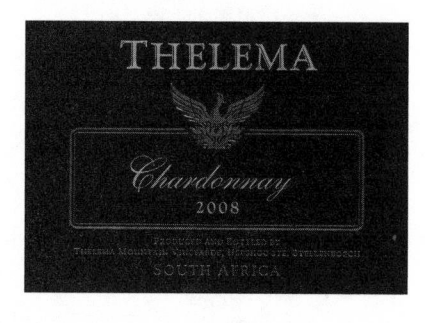

Gyles Webb and Barbara McLean Webb established Thelema Mountain Vineyards in 1983, after the McLean family purchased an old fruit farm at the top of the Helshoogte Pass outside of Stellenbosch. Their first order of business was to plant vines, and in 1988 they produced their first vintage. Gyles retains the position of cellar master, while winemaking is under the direction of Rudi Schultz. Thelema Chardonnay 2008 is medium straw colored, with aromas of Anjou pear, green fig, and citrus blossom. In the mouth the flavors of fruit come through with a vanilla toasted brioche finish. Thelema Merlot 2007 is garnet colored, with notes of raspberries, red plums, cassis, forest floor, and tobacco leaf. In the mouth it is smoky with firm tannins and calls out for barbecued meats.

THE WINERY OF GOOD HOPE

Main Road M9,
+27 21 855 5528,
www.wineryofgoodhope.com

The Winery of Good Hope produces wines under four labels: Land of Hope, Vinum Africa, Winery of Good Hope, and Radford Dale. Founded in 1998 by Australian Ben Radford and South African Alex Dale, the winery has an impressive team, including Rhône-expert Edouard Labeye and Australia's Robert Hill Smith. Radford Dale Shiraz 2008 is dark garnet, with aromas of black fruits, freshly ground black pepper, and a hint of violet. It is generous in the mouth with ripe

yet firm tannins and a pleasing finish. Radford Dale Pinot Noir 2008 is medium red, with lovely aromas of red cherry, dried cherry, and a touch of cherry vanilla ice cream. It is medium bodied on the palate, with a touch of spice in the persistent finish.

TOKARA

Helshoogte Road, Stellenbosch,
+27 21 885 2550,
www.tokara.co.za

We were amazed at the stunning view of Table Mountain and False Bay when we visited mountaintop Tokara Winery with our friends Sue and Cris. Winemaker Miles Mossop explained to us that he sources fruit from Tokara's Home vineyard, Highlands Vineyard, and Siberia Vineyard, then showed us around the beautiful property before guiding us through a tasting of Tokara's delicious wines. Tokara Collection Stellenbosch Chardonnay 2009 is straw colored, with aromas of tropical fruits, lemon zest, lime juice, toasted brioche, and roasted hazelnuts in the bouquet. It is medium-bodied on the palate, with a creamy texture and pleasant finish. Tokara Pinotage 2008 is deep garnet, with baking spice, anise, smoked meat, and black fruit notes on the nose. In the mouth it is generous with a persistent finish.

VERGELEGEN

Lourensford Road, Somerset West,
+27 21 847 1334,
www.vergelegen.co.za

From the Dutch word *vergelegen*—meaning "remotely situated"—Vergelegen Estate has been famous since the early days of its first owner, Governor Willem van der Stel and its subsequent owner, Lady Phillips. Since 1987 the estate has been managed by the Anglo American company and is known for its production of fine South African wines. Visitors to Vergelegen can visit the lovely gardens, have a delicious meal at one of its two restaurants, or relax under 300-year-old camphor trees with a glass of wine and a picnic. Vergelegen Merlot 2007 is dark garnet, with aromas of ripe black plums, black cherries, and cocoa powder. It is soft in the mouth with smooth tannins. Vergelegen Cabernet Sauvignon 2006 is deep ruby garnet, with a nose of cassis, dark spice, and black plum. It is generous in the mouth with a fine tannic finish.

WARWICK ESTATE

Route 44 between Stellenbosch and Klapmuts,
+27 21 884 4410,
www.warwickwine.com

Warwick Estate was named by Colonel William Alexander Gordon in 1902 and

purchased by Stan and Norma Ratcliffe in 1964. Norma was one of the first female winemakers in South Africa and is the chairperson of the Cape Independent Winemakers Guild. Today, her son, the affable and gregarious Mike Ratcliffe, who championed the concept of the "Cape Blend" in South Africa and continues to maintain a close involvement with black economic empowerment, runs Warwick Estate. When not tending to the vines or overseeing the winemakers, Mike can be found blogging, tweeting, or Facebooking something newsworthy; he is an avid social media promoter of South African wine. Mike has also landscaped the estate to include lovely areas for picnics and the estate's fun Big Five Wine Safari. We had dinner with Mike and his delightful wife, Pip, on the outdoor terrace of their home amidst the vines, and have since shared many bottles of wine on various continents. Warwick, The First Lady Cabernet Sauvignon 2009, named for Norma, is ruby garnet colored, with aromas of red fruits, black cherries, and a touch of vanilla toast. In the mouth it is big, but elegant, with smooth round tannins and a persistent finish. Warwick Chardonnay 2009 is straw colored with green hints and has notes of orange blossom, Granny Smith apple, and coconut. It is full-bodied with nice heft on the palate and a fresh finish.

SWARTLAND DISTRICT

Meaning "The Black Land," Swartland takes its name from the "rhino bush" or *renosterbos*, which covers the landscape in dark tones similar to the hide of a rhinoceros. This district has traditionally been recognized for its rich reds and sweet fortified wines, which have recently been joined by high-quality bottlings of Chardonnay, Chenin Blanc, and Sauvignon Blanc. Prior to Swartland's emergence as a winegrowing area, plantings of grain predominated, although now patches of green vineyard are seen climbing the foothills of the Perdeberg, Piketberg, Porterville, and Riebeek Mountains. Trellising has replaced bush vines as the vineyard management style of choice. On average, 523 millimeters, or 21 inches, of rain fall each year; 154 millimeters, or 6 inches, of these touch ground in summer. In addition to the aforementioned white varieties, the wards of Malmesbury and Riebeekberg are noted for Pinotage, Shiraz, and Cabernet Sauvignon.

A.A. BADENHORST FAMILY WINES

Siebritskloof Road, Paardeberg, Malmesbury,
+27 22 487 3351,
www.aabadenhorst.com

Cousins Hein and Adi Badenhorst restored a winery and a Swartland vineyard that had been neglected since the 1930s. Winemaking is obviously in their DNA, as their grandfather was the farm manager at Groot Constantia for 46 years. AA Badenhorst White Blend 2008 is composed of seven varieties, but mostly Chenin Blanc. It is straw colored, with aromas of citrus flowers, white peaches, apricots, and lifted floral notes in a complex bouquet. It is full textured in the mouth with a persistent finish. AA Badenhorst Red Blend 2007 is a combination of 80 percent Shiraz, 10 percent Mourvèdre, 7 percent Cinsault, and 3 percent Grenache. It is dark red, with aromas of anise, black pepper, black plums, and a hint of violet. It is big in the mouth with juicy fruit flavors and a long spicy finish.

ORG DE RAC

Piketberg, Swartland,
+27 22 913 2397,
www.orgderac.co.za

The team at Org de Rac is committed to organic and sustainable farming. It uses no chemical additives and only one-half the amount of sulfur

as conventional wines. Org de Rac wines just might prevent those horrible headaches some people get due to sulfur dioxide. The best part though is that they make delicious, quality wines. Org de Rac Cabernet Sauvignon 2009 is dark cherry red, with aromas of cassis and blackberries. It shows lots of fruit on the palate with ripe tannins. The finish is balanced and elegant. Org de Rac Merlot 2009 is deep garnet, with a nose of black raspberries, black currants, and a whiff of mint. It is soft and pleasant in the mouth with a lingering persistence.

SADIE FAMILY WINES

Aprilskloof Road, Paardeberg, Malmesbury,
+27 22 482 3138,
www.thesadiefamily.com

Eben Sadie began his commercial winemaking career when he was hired as the first winemaker at Charles Back's Spice Route winery in Malmesbury. He was the first South African

to earn a 95-point score from *Wine Spectator* in 2007. Part philosopher, part visionary, and a whole lot of winemaker make him a wine person to watch. Sadie Columella 2008 is medium garnet, with complex aromas of black plum, black currant, and wet river rocks. On the palate the dark fruit flavors elegantly dance on your tongue before a luxurious silky-smooth finish. Sadie Palladius 2009 is an intricate blend of white grape varieties with a predominance of Chenin Blanc. It is straw colored and presents with an enticing blend of both fruit and floral aromas, especially ripe stone fruits and white flowers. In the mouth it has good heft, Rubenesque curves, and fresh fruit flavors—before a refreshing finish keeps inviting you back for another sip.

TULBAGH DISTRICT

Ninety minutes north of Cape Town by car, Tulbagh's vineyards are surrounded by the Groot Winterhoek, Obiekwaberg, and Witsenberg Mountains and are interspersed with fruit orchards and wheat fields. Yellow, stony soils are layered over sandstone boulders and schist. Yearly rainfall is low with only 551 millimeters, or 22 inches, on average per year; summer's share is just 175 millimeters, or 7 inches. Modern viticultural techniques and advanced water management make the best use of available water resources. The horseshoe-shaped valley creates a "cold trap," in which cold nighttime air does not move out of the geographic basin during the day; rather, it is trapped under warmer daytime air, providing lower daily temperatures and therefore lengthening the ripening period of the grapes. Boasting just under twenty wineries, some of which are essentially brand new, Tulbagh's reigning pride is Shiraz and *Méthode Cap Classique*. The Boberg designation may be used for fortified wines grown and produced here and in neighboring Paarl.

SARONSBERG

Tulbagh,
+27 23 230 0707,
www.saronsberg.com

In 2002, Saronsberg rejoined two farms that had been split by brothers more than 50 years ago. The company planned to gradually replant the vineyards, but a wildfire that swept through the farm just two months after the acquisition forced immediate and total replanting. The saving grace of the replanting was that it allowed winemaker Dewaldt Heyns to reverse outdated viticultural traditions in one fell swoop. Saronsberg Shiraz 2008 is deep, dark purple in color, with aromas of dark plums, black raspberries, and candied violets. It has a balanced structure, firm tannins, and a long finish. Saronsberg Full Circle 2008, named for the earthquake epicenter of 1969, is dark reddish-purple, with notes of raspberry, cassis, and baking spices. It has a big mouthfeel with firm tannins.

TYGERBERG DISTRICT

The majority of grape growing occurs in the Durbanville and Philadelphia wards, the first of which borders Cape Town's northern suburbs. Durbanville's vineyards climb as high as 380 meters (1,247 feet) above sea level; many south-facing slopes have views of Table Mountain and both the Atlantic and Indian Oceans. Durbanville's yellow brown and red soils lie over shale. Average summer rainfall is just 121 millimeters, or 5 inches; but then the annual average is a miserly 353 millimeters, or 14 inches. Breezes from False Bay and Table Bay combine with afternoon mists to keep the grapes from burning under full sun. Main varieties here include Sauvignon Blanc, Chardonnay, Merlot, and Cabernet Sauvignon, while the focus in Philadelphia, just to the north, is on reds such as Cabernet Sauvignon and Merlot. With vineyards as high as 260 meters (853 feet), cool sea breezes, and a strong contrast between day and night temperatures, Philadelphia's climate facilitates the kind of slow ripening that leads to the best expression of these grapes.

CAPAIA

Botterberg Road, Philadelphia,
+27 21 972 1081,
www.capaia.eu

Established in 1997 by Baron Alexander and Baroness Ingrid von Essen, Capaia has been making quality estate-produced wines in Philadelphia since its first harvest in 2003. Tibor Gal designed the state-of-the-art winery, and consultants Stephan Graf Neipperg and Armin Tement manage the winemaking. Capaia Sauvignon Blanc 2010 is straw colored, with aromas of bell peppers, pea shoots, and white flowers. There is a nice minerality to the palate, balanced acidity, and a long, crisp finish. Capaia Blue Grove Hill Merlot Cabernet Sauvignon 2008 is garnet red, with a nose of red fruits and cocoa powder. In the mouth it is fruit-driven, with a touch of clove in the post palate.

D'ARIA

Racecourse Road, Durbanville,
+27 21 801 6772,
www.dariawinery.co.za

In 1999 the Barinor Holding Company bought two adjacent farms owned by a mother and daughter, both widows. Barinor board member Johan von Waltsleben is now the viticulturist, and his son Rudi is the winemaker. D'Aria has

lovely guest cottages for visitors, a restaurant named Poplars, and a summer concert series. D'Aria Soprano Shiraz 2008 is dark red, with aromas of raspberry, red plum, and freshly ground pepper. It has a bit of spice in the mid palate, with a dark chocolate flavored finish. Music by D'Aria Red 2009 is a blend of Shiraz, Cabernet Sauvignon, and Merlot. It has juicy fruit flavors of red berries in the mouth with a soft tannic finish.

DE GRENDEL

Plattekloof Road, Durbanville,
+27 21 558 6280,
www.degrendel.co.za

Loosely translated as "lock" or "latch," the winery name of De Grendel goes back to the original 1600s owner, who stabled Arabian horses on the property. The farm has been owned by the Graff family since the 1800s and is now under the management of Sir David Graff. Charles Hopkins is the cellar master, and Elzette du Preez is the winemaker; together they make De Grendel's award-winning wines. De Grendel Winifred 2009 is a white varietal blend, Sémillon-dominant, with aromas of citrus blossoms and tropical fruits. In the mouth flavors of pineapple and lemon zest dance on your palate before a firm, yet balanced acidic finish. De Grendel Shiraz 2007 is purple colored, with a nose of black fruits, purple flowers, and black pepper. It is fruity in the mouth with a balanced, tannic finish.

DURBANVILLE HILLS

Route M13, Durbanville,
+27 21 558 1300,
www.durbanvillehills.co.za

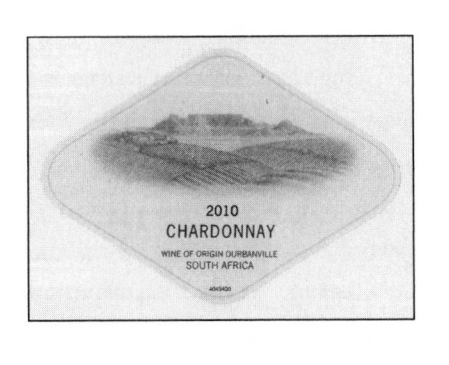

DIEMERSDAL

Adderley Road, Durbanville,
+27 21 976 3361,
www.diemersdal.co.za

The Louw family has been making wine at Diemersdal for six generations—since 1885. The farm has 180 hectares (445 acres) under vine, and Tienie Louw, Thys Louw, and Mari van der Merwe artistically perform the winemaking. Diemersdal Eight Rows Sauvignon Blanc 2010 is straw colored, with aromas of tropical fruits, wet river stones, and just a hint of juniper. It is crisp and clean on the palate with a refreshing finish. Diemersdal Merlot 2010 is garnet, with notes of red plums, ripe raspberries, cigar box, dark spice, and menthol. The fruit comes alive on the palate, with a touch of mint at the finish.

The Durbanville Hills winery has amazing views; it has both Table Mountain and Table Bay in its crosshairs. This winery is a collaboration between nine individual vineyard owners and the Distell Corporation. Under the capable direction of gregarious winemaker Martin Moore, it only uses fruit from shareholder growers within the ward of Durbanville. This fruit is then vinified into the Hills range, Rhinofields Reserve range, and Single Vineyard range of wines. While bottlings within the Hills range may include grapes from any of the growers, only fruit from two or three selected vineyards will find its way into the Rhinofields wines; the variation in *terroir* provides a fuller expression of flavors due to different ripening conditions. The Single Vineyard label is the winery's premier expression of the winemaker's craft. In addition to employing sustainable vineyard practices, Durbanville Hills also administers several social initiatives for employees and their families, including a daycare center for young children and a scholarship program for workers and their children. From the Single Vineyard range, Durbanville Hills Pinotage 2009 arouses the sense of smell with strawberry and lychee notes, followed by flavors of black cherry, red raspberry, and a touch of jalapeño pepper in the mouth. Durbanville Hills Rhinofields Shiraz 2008 has a nose of raspberries and black plums with hints of baking spice, all of which carry over onto the palate, culminating in a silky finish with a touch of oak. Durbanville Hills Chardonnay 2010 is an easy-quaffing mouthful of white peach, lemon, and butterscotch, with a bright, refreshing finish. These and many more of the wines are available at the on-site Hills Restaurant.

CAPE SOUTH COAST REGION

Running southeast from Cape Town and bordering the ocean, the Cape South Coast region consists of the cool-weather districts of Cape Agulhas, Overberg, Plettenberg Bay, and Walker Bay.

CAPE AGULHAS DISTRICT

Summer in Cape Agulhas brings strong, cooling winds to Africa's southernmost point. Most vineyards in this area surround the village of Elim, a Moravian mission village dating back to 1824, which is a recognized ward of the district, as well as a national monument. The cool maritime climate produces excellent Sauvignon Blanc and is expected to do the same for newer plantings of Sémillon and Shiraz.

OVERBERG DISTRICT

Southeast of Stellenbosch, and partially bordering Walker Bay, Overberg contains the Threewater, Greyton, Klein River, and Elgin wards. The best known is Elgin, whose high-lying vineyards grow on the slopes of the Hottentots Holland Mountains. Pinot Noir, Riesling, Sauvignon Blanc, and Shiraz have replaced apple orchards across the district. The Klein River ward is just starting to achieve notice for its viticultural output.

ELGIN VINTNERS

Beaulieu Farm, Viljoenshoop Road, Elgin,
+27 83 225 1884,
www.elginvintners.co.za

Six dedicated grape growers choose the best varieties from their holdings to craft their quality wines under the Elgin Vintners label.

garnet red, with aromas of dark plums, black raspberries, baking spices, and with hints of tobacco leaf and cedar. It has nice heft on the palate with ripe tannins.

CATHERINE MARSHALL WINES

41 Viljoenshoop Road, Elgin,
+27 21 788 5427,
www.cmwines.co.za

The combined vineyards of the growers total 101 hectares (250 acres), and the group uses a variety of winemakers based on that winemaker's style, affinity, and flair with a particular varietal. Elgin Vintners Viognier 2009 is pale straw in color, with the nose and the flavor running more fruit than floral. Aromas of custard apple, quince paste, Anjou pear, lime sorbet, and baked apple are present in the bouquet. It has a creamy mouthfeel, with flavors of baked apple, Turkish delight, and sparkling apple cider on the palate leading up to a refreshing finish. Elgin Vintners Pinot Noir 2008 is medium red, with a nose of red raspberry, red cherry, and a hint of caramelized orange. It has balanced tannic structure and a persistent finish. Elgin Vintners Agama 2007 is a blend of 70 percent Cabernet Sauvignon and 30 percent Merlot and is named for the agama lizard that lives in the brush near the Merlot vineyards. It is ruby

Catherine Marshall started Barefoot Wine Company in 1996 and is the first woman in South Africa to market wine using her own name on the label. In 1997 Catherine Marshall Wines started producing one wine, a Pinot Noir, at a time when there were very few South African producers of the variety. She graduated from school in Stellenbosch and worked harvests in France, California, and Australia, and her wines have a decidedly international taste profile. Her Catherine Marshall Eleven Barrels Reserve Pinot Noir 2009 is medium red, with aromas of black cherry, black plum, fruits of the wood, and a touch of graphite. The palate is supported by a nice backbone of minerality and smooth tannins.

IONA

Route 44, Elgin,
+27 28 284 9678,
www.iona.co.za

Named after the small Scottish island visited by Nordic Vikings in 900 AD, Iona Winery was a run-down apple farm until 1997, when the Gunn family lovingly rescued it. The winemaking team consists of winemaker Werner Muller and assistant winemaker Thapelo Hlasa. Iona Sauvignon Blanc 2010 is straw colored, with aromas of lemon blossom, grapefruit rind, white flowers, and honeycomb. It has medium body with nice minerality and a balanced acidic finish. Iona Chardonnay 2009 is medium straw, with notes of lemon blossoms, white stone fruits, lightly buttered brioche, and toasted hazelnuts. It is creamy in the mouth, with English lemon curd flavors and a balanced finish characterized by a crisp minerality.

PAUL CLUVER
ESTATE WINES

De Rust Estate, N2, Grabouw,
+27 21 844 0605,
www.cluver.com

Currently run by four of the five Cluver siblings, Paul Cluver Estate Wines has been making wine since 1896. Paul Cluver IV is the managing director, while his sisters Liesl, Inge, and Karin handle administrative roles. The winemaker is Andries Burger (who is married to Inge), and he's assisted by Nina Sweigelaar and viticulturist Craig Harris. The estate has a lovely amphitheater and sponsors a musical concert series each year. Paul Cluver Riesling 2009 is medium straw colored with a greenish tint. Aromas of tropical fruits, pineapple, lychee, and mango are present in the bouquet. In the mouth flavors of grapefruit, guava, rose petal, and a light sprinkling of Chinese five-spice powder are evident. The finish is crisp and lightly floral. Paul Cluver Gewürztraminer 2010 is straw colored, with a nose of citrus blossom, rose petal, and lime marmalade. It is dry on the palate with a persistent, perfumed finish.

SHANNON

Dunmanway Farm, Elgin,
+27 21 859 2491,
www.shannonwines.com

Named for the Shannon family's ancestors from County Cork, Ireland, the Downes brothers Stuart and James established their winery within the Kogelberg Biosphere. Kogelberg is the first UNESCO-designated biosphere in Africa, and the brothers take their environmental responsibility seriously. Winemaking is carried out at their college water polo teammate's Newton Johnson winery. Shannon Mount Bullet Merlot 2008 is garnet colored, with aromas of cassis, black raspberry, Mission fig, saddle leather, and cigar box. On the palate it displays voluptuous presence, fresh fruit flavors, and a smooth tannic finish. Shannon Sauvignon Blanc 2010 is medium straw, with a nose of asparagus, pea shoots, freshly cut straw, and tropical fruit underpinnings. It is refreshing in the mouth, with vibrant acidity and a persistent finish.

PLETTENBERG BAY DISTRICT

Plettenberg Bay is both the newest and easternmost district on the coast, with vines dating back to just 2000. With its mountainous terrain, untarnished Indian Ocean beaches, and cool, coastal climate, it might seem more suitable for adventure tourism than grape growing, but its carbon-based soils provide Sauvignon Blanc vines a place to put down roots and flourish.

WALKER BAY DISTRICT

The district surrounds the seaside town of Hermanus. Pinot Noir and Chardonnay have long been the varieties of note from the wards of Hemel-en-Aarde ("Heaven in Earth") Ridge, Hemel-en-Aarde Valley, Upper Hemel-en-Aarde Valley, and Sunday's Glen. The weathered shale soil and maritime breezes provide an ideal climate for the superior Pinotage, Sauvignon Blanc, Merlot, and Shiraz now also coming from these wards. The district's Bot River ward runs from the Bot River Lagoon to the foothills of the Groenlandberg and Babylonstoren Mountains. Its soils consist of shale and Table Mountain sandstone, and it too is noted for its cool, maritime microclimate. Noted varietals from this ward include Chenin Blanc, Pinotage, Sauvignon Blanc, Shiraz, and other Rhône varietals.

BOUCHARD FINLAYSON

Valley Road, Hermanus,
+27 28 312 3515,
www.bouchardfinlayson.co.za

Bouchard Finlayson, a boutique winery in the seaside town of Hermanus, is a joint

project begun by Paul Bouchard, formerly of Burgundy, France's Bouchard Ainé and Fils, and South African wine legend Peter Finlayson. Since 1989 the estate has been dedicated to the production of cool-climate varieties such as Pinot Noir, Chardonnay, and Sauvignon Blanc. Head winemaker Peter Finlayson is assisted by winemaker Chris Albrecht and farm manager Mortimer Lee. Bouchard Finlayson Galpin Peak Pinot Noir 2009 is medium cherry to garnet in color, with aromas of black raspberry, black currants, and black plums. In the mouth the fruit flavors come forward before refreshing mineral characteristics. It finishes with good persistence and a touch of black pepper. Bouchard Finlayson Kaaimansgat Chardonnay 2010 is straw colored, with aromas of white stone fruits, Anjou pears, and citrus zest. It is crisp and flavorsome with a refreshing finish.

GABRIELSKLOOF

Swart River Road, N2, Bot River,
+27 28 284 9865,
www.gabrielskloof.co.za

Gabrielskloof planted its vines in 2002 and today the company is run by Barry Anderson, Bernhard Heynes, and winemaker Kobie Viljoen. Gabrielskloof also produces its own olive oil and lavender soaps from estate-grown produce. The restaurant serves inspired cuisine prepared from seasonal and locally sourced products. Gabrielskloof Five Arches 2008 is a blend of 29 percent Cabernet Franc, 24 percent Cabernet Sauvignon, 24 percent Malbec, 18 percent Petit Verdot, and 5 percent Merlot. It is dark purple garnet in the glass, with aromas of cocoa powder, black fruits, tobacco leaf, and baking spices. Big in the mouth, it has firm tannins and a long finish.

HAMILTON RUSSELL VINEYARDS

Hermanus,
+27 28 312 3595,
www.hamiltonrussellvineyards.com

Tim Hamilton Russell purchased the land that was to become Hamilton Russell Vineyards in 1975 and sold it to his son Anthony in 1994, who made the commitment to produce only estate grown, vinified, and bottled wines.

Hamilton Russell Chardonnay 2010 is straw colored, with aromas of white stone fruits, Bosc pear, toasted brioche, and roasted hazelnut. In the mouth it is fruity and crisp with rounded edges and a delicious finish. Hamilton Russell Pinot Noir 2009 is medium red, with enticing notes of fruits of the wood, red cherry, and vanilla. It is generous with a touch of minerality in the mid palate and a pleasant finish.

HERMANUSPIETERSFONTEIN

Hemel-en-Aarde Village, Hermanus,
+27 28 316 1875,
www.hpf1855.co.za

Winemaker Bartho Eksteen was the proud recipient of the Diners Club Winemaker of the Year Award in 2010, and together with viticulturist Ernst Bruwer they believe that "Good earth makes better wines." In 2007 the winery became a member of the Biodiversity and Wine Institute and is dedicated to limiting the loss of jeopardized natural habitat for a variety of animals and species. Hermanuspietersfontein Sauvignon Blanc 2010 is straw colored with greenish tints and has aromas of citrus blossoms, dried stone fruits, and toasted coconut. It is full-bodied and rich, with a balanced acid finish.

BREEDE RIVER VALLEY REGION

Named after the river that cut through rock, leaving alluvial soils on the fertile valley floor, the Breede River Valley borders the northern portion of the Coastal region to the west, and sits atop the Cape South Coast region as it stretches east toward the Indian Ocean.

BREEDEKLOOF DISTRICT

An hour from Cape Town, this broad river valley features vineyards with alluvial soils over river stones. Home to 27 wineries—and leopards roaming the hills—the district's Goudini and Slanghoek wards expect to receive 641 millimeters, or 25 inches, of rainfall per annum; of that, 196 millimeters, or 8 inches, arrive during the summer season. Traditionally the home of Muscat, a wide range of red and white grapes now flourish among diverse species of *fynbos*.

ROBERTSON DISTRICT

Fertile alluvial soils layered over shale in the "The Valley of Vines and Roses" make a suitable home for both grapes and racehorses, as evidenced by the number of both being raised here. Total rainfall averages 280 millimeters, or 11 inches, per annum; 116 millimeters, or 5 inches, of that can be expected in the summer. The Breede River provides much-needed water throughout the valley. Hot summers are tempered by cool winds that also bear otherwise-deficient moisture. Once known only for fortified dessert wines and whites such as Chardonnay and Sauvignon Blanc, Robertson has diversified into reds as well, now producing fine examples of Shiraz and Cabernet Sauvignon. Its many wards include Agterkliphoogte, Bonnievale, Boesmansrivier, Eilandia, Hoopsrivier, Klaasvoogds, Le Chasseur, McGregor, and Vinkrivier.

DUVON

Goree Valley, Robertson,
+27 82 341 1059,
www.duvon.co.za

Armand Hercolaas du Toit and his uncle Alex Karl von Klopmann combined the "du" and "von" of their names to come up with DuVon Wines. They maintain two guesthouses available for hire with views of their Little Italy farm and vineyards. DuVon Cabernet Sauvignon

2008 is garnet colored, with aromas of raspberries, black plums, and a touch of green pepper. It is generous on the palate, with a firm tannic backbone. DuVon Shiraz 2008 is dark reddish-purple, with aromas of black pepper, black raspberry, and dark chocolate. In the mouth there are dark fruit flavors with a smooth, tannic finish.

EXCELSIOR ESTATE

Route R317, Ashton,
+27 23 615 1980,
www.excelsior.co.za

The de Wet family first bought a large expanse of land alongside the Breede River in 1859; shortly thereafter, they planted the region's first vineyards. In 1870 the tract was divided among the founder's three sons; the portion named "Excelsior" is now owned by Freddie and Peter de Wet, the fourth and fifth generation of the family to farm this estate. Excelsior Estate encompasses 200 hectares (494 acres) of grape vines, predominantly Cabernet Sauvignon, Chardonnay, and Shiraz. The de Wets believe that great wine begins in the vineyard; it was with this in mind that they installed what is claimed to be the first vineyard drip irrigation system in South Africa. Winemaker Johan Stemmet has been at the helm since 2003, producing wines that are repeatedly lauded for their excellent value-to-price ratio. In an area renowned for its stud farms, the de Wets have recently turned to breeding championship racehorses, a theme echoed on Excelsior's distinctive packaging. Excelsior Chardonnay 2010 delivers flavors of Granny Smith apple, pineapple, and lemon zest, with a soft, buttered toast finish. Excelsior Shiraz 2009 gets a floral lift from the addition of 11 percent Petit Verdot. A jammy concoction tasting of blackberry, cherry, licorice, and chocolate, this one over-delivers for the price. Excelsior Cabernet Sauvignon 2009 blends 85.5 percent Cabernet Sauvignon with 4 percent Petit Verdot, 7.5 percent Merlot, and 3 percent Shiraz and has flavors of black cherry, cassis, black pepper, clove, and chocolate.

SWELLENDAM DISTRICT

About a three-hour drive due west of Cape Town, Swellendam's long summer days, mild winters, and general Mediterranean-like climate provide good conditions for Cabernet Sauvignon, Chardonnay, Sauvignon Blanc, and Shiraz. There are three main wards within its boundaries: Stormsvlei, Malgas, and Buffeljags.

WORCESTER DISTRICT

In combination with the Breedekloof district, this is the largest winegrowing area in the nation in terms of plantings and total volume. Its 19,000-plus hectares (46,950-plus acres) of vineyards account for 20 percent of all the grapevines in the country, and its wineries turn out more than 25 percent of the country's wine and spirits. It is the most important brandy-producing area in all of South Africa. The wards Aan-de-Doorns, Hex River Valley, Nuy, and Scherpenheuvel sit inside its borders.

KLEIN KAROO REGION

This is the easternmost wine-producing region in South Africa, and also the driest; due to lower levels of rain, many vineyards are managed organically. A wide strip of territory bordered by striking mountains, Klein Karoo features vines grown in the alluvial soils of ancient riverbeds. Traditionally the home of Muscat-based dessert wines, Port-style wine from the Portuguese varieties, and pot-distilled brandy, Klein Karoo is just realizing its potential for crisp whites and well-balanced reds, most of which are centered in the cooler areas bordering the Swartberg,

Langeberg-Garcia, and Outeniqua Mountains. Running from De Rust and Oudtshoorn in the east, through Calitzdorp and Ladismith, and then on to Barrydale and Montagu in the west, the region is divided into three main wine-growing areas. The highest concentration of vineyards and wineries is near Calitzdorp, long known for its fortified "sweeties" made from Touriga Nacional and Tinta Barocca. Recently, there has been a trend toward dry wines from these and similar varieties. Besides the afore-mentioned areas, Klein Karoo also takes in the freestanding wards of the Tradouw Highlands, Upper Langkloof, and Bamboes Bay.

OLIFANTS RIVER REGION

Consisting of the Citrusdal Mountain, Citrusdal Valley, and Lutzville Valley districts and the Bamboes Bay ward, the Olifants River Valley is home to citrus trees and grape vines. Its proximity to the Atlantic Ocean accounts for summers that are warm to cool (compared with other areas), and rainfall is on the low side. Misty mornings provide moisture and a cool-ing effect on the grapes, while judicious canopy management ensures the sun's harmful effects are minimized. The Lutzville Valley district, in the northwest of the region, takes in the wards of Koekenaap, Spruitdrift, and Vredendal.

The Citrusdal Valley and Citrusdal Mountain districts, to the south of the region, benefit from sandy alluvial soils. The Piekenierskloof ward is noted for its superlative Grenache. The area closest to the Atlantic Coast is becom-ing known for impressive Sauvignon Blanc. Cabernet Sauvignon, Chenin Blanc, Merlot, Pinotage, and Shiraz also thrive throughout this long, narrow river valley.

NORTHERN CAPE GEOGRAPHICAL AREA

The Northern Cape Geographical Area encom-passes the Douglas and Sutherland-Karoo districts and the Hartswater, Rietrivier, Central Orange River, and Lower Orange wards. Lower Orange, with its vineyards running along the Orange River, is South Africa's northernmost wine-growing area and is also the nation's fourth largest, with more than 17,000 hect-ares (42,008 acres) of planted vines. Grapes are grown on islands bounded by the river and its tributaries; each presents its own particu-lar microclimate. Varied trellising systems are employed as well, such as T-trellises, gable, and hut, which shelter the grapes from the effects of the hot sun. Varieties cultivated here include Chenin Blanc, Chardonnay, Pinotage, Shiraz, Cabernet Sauvignon, Merlot, Petit Verdot, Muscadel, and Muscat of Alexandria.

WESTERN CAPE GEOGRAPHICAL AREA

The Western Cape is a broad geographical area encompassing the Breede River Valley region, Coastal region, Klein Karoo region, Olifants River region, and Overberg district. It also includes the freestanding wards of Cederberg, Ceres, Lambert's Bay, Prince Albert Valley, and Swartberg, none of which technically falls into a recognized region or district. Cederburg is just outside the Olifants River region, to the west of Citrusdal, while Ceres, named for the Roman goddess of grain, is to the north of the Breede River Valley region and east of the Tulbagh district. Lamberts Bay sits on the Atlantic Coast, west of Olifants River. Prince Albert Valley is slightly north of the uppermost border of the Klein Karoo region, due north of Oudtshoorn. Swartberg is southwest of Prince Albert, again north of all of Klein Karoo and the city of Calitzdorp.

CEDERBERG

Dwarsriver, Cederberg,
+27 27 482 2827,
www.cederbergwine.com

When visiting wineries in South Africa, it is not common to leave the paved highway and drive 46 kilometers (29 miles) on a gravel and dirt road—but the visit to Cederberg is worth the effort. Located in the Cederberg Wilderness Area in the Cape Floral Kingdom, Cederberg makes some wonderful wines that we like very much. They have also been highly rated in *Wine Spectator* and *Decanter* magazines. Winemaker David Nieuwoudt and his family grow grapes in Dwarsriver (named for the Dwars River,) which is a town populated by 29 families. The local primary school, the Dwarsriver Primer Skool, has only 18 students as of this writing. When visiting David, be sure to enquire about staying at the family's Sanddrif Holiday Resort or camping nearby on the banks of the river. Cederberg Shiraz 2008 is inky purple red, with aromas of black plums, cassis, espresso, and dark chocolate. It is well structured in the mouth with a smooth tannic finish. Cederberg Chenin Blanc 2010 is pale straw with silver highlights. Aromas of lime zest, lemon juice, white peach, fresh rosemary, and chopped parsley are present in the bouquet. In the mouth it has crisp, clean astringency, with flavors of lemon, lime, pineapple, and lemongrass.

EASTERN CAPE GEOGRAPHICAL AREA

There is but one wine-producing locale in the Eastern Cape, the stand-alone ward of St. Francis Bay, which is in an area best known for hiking, boating, and waterfront vacation homes. With unpredictable rainfall and land highly prized by residential developers, it may be too soon to predict how this area will fare in the realm of grape-growing and wine production.

KWAZULU-NATAL GEOGRAPHICAL AREA

Although it is in fact a very large geographical area, covering the province of the same name, KwaZulu-Natal has a miniscule number of vines under cultivation. Grapes were first planted here in the early 1990s, with the first estate vineyard planted in 2000. Sauvignon Blanc is said to be doing well here, and Chardonnay, Pinot Noir, and Pinotage have taken root as well.

ABINGDON

Hilton, KwaZulu-Natal,
+27 33 234 4335,
www.abingdonestate.co.za

We first met Ian and Jane Smorthwaite while we were visiting our friend, winemaker Adam

Mason, when he was still making wine at Klein Constantia. They had come down for a look-around and a chat with Adam, and invited us to taste their wines. They regaled us with stories of the challenges of being one of the few wineries with estate-grown grapes in KwaZulu-Natal. We especially got a kick out of their first-year Chardonnay story—it seems that local wildlife love the sweet taste of Chardonnay grapes, and before Jane and Ian could do anything about it, a troop of wild monkeys had picked their vines clean. The next year they invested in monkey-proof netting, and the problem was solved. For this reason we didn't get to taste Abingdon's white wines, but we enjoyed the Abingdon Estate Cabernet Sauvignon 2008. It is ruby red in the glass with aromas of dark berries, cassis, and a pleasant vegetal note. In the mouth it is well structured, with balanced tannins and a lingering finish.

RECIPES

12-HOUR BRAISED SHORT RIBS
AND PAN-SEARED RIB EYE

Served with Porcini Mushrooms and Cauliflower Puree

✳

*Recipe courtesy of Louise le Riche, owner of Leriche-Jardine Restaurant,
and Gary and Kathy Jordan, owners of Jordan Winery in Stellenbosch*

✳

SERVES 6

We had a perfect lunch on a gorgeous, sunny day perched high above the vines of Stellenbosch. The cuisine, setting, wine, and company were perfectly delightful. This is one winery and one winery restaurant that you should not miss if you're visiting Stellenbosch. We can't wait until we return! Gary and Kathy's wines are sold under the Jardin label in the United States, and we think that Jardin Cabernet Sauvignon 2007 is the ideal match for this hearty dish.

FOR THE SHORT RIBS

6 Angus beef short ribs, bone in
Flour, seasoned with salt
    and pepper to taste
Cooking oil
Butter
1 cup carrot, diced
1 cup onion, diced
1 cup celery, diced
1 cup leek, sliced
1 cup mushroom, sliced
1 bottle good-quality South
    African red wine
1 quart good quality beef
    or veal stock
2 sprigs thyme
1 bulb of garlic, crushed
6 white peppercorns
2 star anise

FOR THE CAULIFLOWER PUREE

1 head cauliflower, cut
    into florets
2 potatoes
1½ cups milk
2 tablespoons butter
3 tablespoons grated parmesan

FOR THE ANGUS RIB EYE
AND PORCINI MUSHROOMS

6 porcini mushrooms, sliced
2 pounds Angus rib-eye fillets
Coarse sea salt
Pepper
Cooking oil
Butter

PREPARE THE SHORT RIBS

Preheat the oven to 250°F. Lightly dust the short ribs in seasoned flour, dusting off any excess.

Heat a large heavy-bottomed pan until hot but not smoking, then add a little cooking oil and butter. Once the butter has stopped foaming, add the short ribs and brown evenly all over. Transfer to a platter. Add the vegetables to the pan and cook, stirring, until caramelised. Deglaze the pan with the red wine, adding a little at a time, until two-thirds of the bottle has evaporated. Transfer the short ribs back to the pan. Add the stock and the remaining ingredients, cover, and braise in the oven for 12 hours, until the ribs are falling off the bone. Remove the ribs carefully from the pan and cool. Retain the braising juice for cooking the mushrooms, below.

PREPARE THE CAULIFLOWER PUREE

Thinly slice the cauliflower and potatoes, and boil in milk until soft. Remove from milk, and place in a blender or food processer. Process until smooth. Add butter and parmesan, and stir to combine,

PREPARE THE ANGUS RIB EYE AND PORCINI MUSHROOMS

Heat the reserved braising juices from the short ribs in a small pan, add the sliced porcini mushrooms, and cook until tender.

Meanwhile, season the rib-eye fillets with coarse sea salt and pepper. Heat a large heavy-bottomed frying pan until hot but not smoking, then add a little oil and butter. Once the butter has stopped foaming, add the fillets, sear on both sides, and cook to desired temperature. Transfer to a cutting board and let rest.

TO SERVE

Reheat the short ribs and transfer to a large platter. Slice the rib-eye steak and arrange on platter with the ribs. Pour braising juice with porcini mushrooms on top of the meat. Meanwhile, warm the cauliflower puree separately and transfer to a serving bowl.

BELLINGHAM *BRAAI* PIE

*

Recipe courtesy of Niel Groenewald, winemaker, Bellingham Wines

*

SERVES 8

While Mike and our friends, Sue, Cris, J.C. Bekker, and the team of Bellingham winemakers, were enjoying a crisp glass of Chenin Blanc on the Bellingham Manor House lawn, Jeff was in the kitchen with Niel learning how to construct Niel's now-famous (at least, in our New York foodie circle of friends) *Braai* Pie. *Braai* is the Afrikaans word for "barbecue," and this delicious pastry delight is a meat and cheese pie that is cooked outside on the barbecue. We have since made it for Sue, Cris, and other friends in our New York City backyard, and it comes out perfectly every time. Niel recommends serving it with one of his Bernard Series Old Vine Chenin Blancs. Whether you drink the current year or a past vintage, it makes a fantastic combination with this dish.

2 (1-pound) packages ready-to-bake puff pastry

1 onion, chopped

8 ounces bacon, diced

1 yellow pepper, sliced

10 sweet Peppadew peppers, sliced

Olive oil

Salt and pepper to taste

1 bunch of spinach, cleaned and coarsely chopped

3 smoked (or grilled) chicken breasts, sliced

8 ounces white mushrooms, sliced

½ cup crumbled feta cheese

½ cup grated Cheddar cheese

1 cup grated mozzarella cheese

Prepare a barbecue grill for grilling over hot coals.

Roll out the dough into two equal pieces.

Fry the onion, bacon, and peppers in olive oil. Season as desired.

Layer the ingredients in the following order on one sheet of dough: half of the spinach; smoked chicken; onion, bacon, and peppers; mushrooms; all three of the cheeses; remaining spinach.

Using your fingertips, wet the edges of the bottom sheet of dough, and cover with the second sheet of dough. Fold over the edges, and crimp down using the tines of a fork (or use your fingers for a more rustic look). Brush both sides with generous amounts of olive oil, and place the pie into a folding grill cage.

Cook over barbecue coals for approximately 15 minutes, turning regularly until golden brown. Be careful to not burn the *Braai* Pie. Let it rest for 10 minutes. Slice and serve.

GRILLED YELLOWTAIL
OR BRANZINO

✳

Recipe courtesy of Durbanville Hills Eatery,
Durbanville Hills Winery

✳

SERVES 4

On the south side of the Tygerberg Mountains, Durbanville Hills Eatery has some of the most stunning views of Table Mountain, Table Bay, and Robben Island that we have seen. The bistro-style restaurant has soaring glass walls that run from floor to ceiling, so it's the perfect place to enjoy a lazy lunch while touring wine country. The emphasis is on fresh and local produce sourced from quality providers. We enjoyed this fish with winemaker Martin Moore and tried more than one of his wines, forcing us to have our own lazy lunch. Martin suggests pairing it with Durbanville Hills Rhinofields Sauvignon Blanc 2010.

Olive oil

Lemon juice

1 garlic clove, crushed

Salt and pepper to taste

Chili flakes (optional)

About 2½ pounds whole
   Yellowtail or Branzino,
   or any fresh white fish,
   cleaned and scales removed,
   or 2½ pounds fish fillets

4 lemon slices (optional)

4 tomato slices (optional)

Chopped fresh herbs (mint,
   chervil, basil, chives or
   a combination of these)

Turn the oven onto broil or heat two ridged grill pans.

Whisk together equal quantities of olive oil and lemon juice, and add garlic, salt, and pepper (and chili flakes, if you are using) to taste.

If you are using a whole fish, clean it, pat it dry, and leave the head intact. Score two slices on either side of the fish. Pour the oil and lemon juice mixture into the cuts and lightly dribble the liquid over the rest of the fish. (If using fish fillets, lightly cover the pieces in the liquid.) Place a slice of lemon and a slice of tomato into the cuts in the whole fish or place on top of each fish fillet.

Grill for 8 to 12 minutes until done, sprinkle with fresh herbs and serve with baby potatoes and a green salad.

IN THEIR OWN WORDS

BEYERS TRUTER

Beyers Truter is indisputably one of South Africa's foremost masters of Pinotage—a grape that invokes much controversy among wine lovers. Although Pinotage was dismissed early on as a variety that would never be tamed into drinkable wine, Beyers Truter has proved that assumption wrong at two prestigious wine competitions, and in every bottle he has ever produced, first at Kanonkop, and, since 1988, at his eponymous Beyerskloof winery. His first major accolade was winning the Diners Club Winemaker of the Year award in 1987. In 1991, Beyers scored a major coup for both himself and his grape of choice when he was named International Winemaker of the Year at the International Wine and Spirits Competition.

How did you get involved in the world of wine?
I started collecting wine—red wine—when I was still at school, so you could say my hobby became my job.

What are some of the biggest changes you have seen in winemaking since you began your career?
Machinery is more sophisticated, although I still believe in making our reds in open fermenters—cement *lagares*—and punching the cap every two hours. Winemakers are much more knowledgeable than years ago, and it should be like that, because it is important for

a winemaker to understand the chemistry of the wine, rather than trying to be an artist.

What are some of the exciting changes that you see happening specifically in your country?
Winemakers are much more in sync with their *terroir*, and also vineyard practices have improved tremendously. The old saying that wine is made in the vineyard is true.

Where else in the world have you studied, trained, or worked a harvest? How did that influence your winemaking?
I am a firm believer of first doing your basic

studies and also gaining experience in your own country before touring the world, because in the end you have to make wine in your own country under your own conditions.

Which varieties are you working with? Are you experimenting with anything new?

Mainly Pinotage, but also Cabernet Sauvignon and Merlot. I have planted Pinot Noir Clone 777 and 115. Clone 115 is known as Pinot Fin. We also have a small vineyard of very old bush vine Cinsault. So I am experimenting with a blend of Pinotage, Pinot Fin, and Cinsault. Because of the long walk with Pinotage, I will call this wine "Trail Dust," after Louis L'Amour's saying, "Trail dust is thicker than blood."

Are there any new areas that you have identified for potential vineyard sites?

In South Africa, there are a lot of new and exciting areas. I have stuck to one of the oldest and well-known regions in South Africa, namely Stellenbosch. Our farm of 133 hectares [329 acres] is 70 percent planted with Pinotage, and the climate and gravel soils of the Bottelary area are great for this home-grown variety.

What challenges have you faced as a winemaker or winery owner?

To make wine is one of the most rewarding and enjoyable jobs on earth. Challenges—no, never! Only opportunities.

What is your winemaking philosophy?

First of all, the God-given factors play the biggest role in winemaking. If you accept that, you have learned a lot about your own philosophy, and you can take the crown off your head and start working. Value for money at all price levels. I still like hard work—punching the cap every two hours and ageing the wine in French oak barrels for 18 months, without a lot of interference.

What would you hope people say about your wine?

That they enjoy it and will come back to buy more.

Do you think that the market should influence winemaking, or do you think that winemaking should influence the market?

I believe, especially at the higher price levels, that winemaking will influence the market. At lower price levels it is vice-versa.

Besides your own wine, what are some of your favorite wines? What do you like about them?

I am a red wine lover—I even drink young Pinotage with ice after I have practiced. Bordeaux and Burgundies. Wines like Kanonkop

Paul Sauer, Vriesenhof Pinot Noir, Ettiene Le Riche Cabernet, and Kaapzicht Pinotage and Vision. They are all well made, with complexity and classic balance.

What is your opinion on screwcap versus cork closures?

They are both only stoppers. I believe if you are in a hurry, without anything to open a bottle, and in need of a glass of wine, a screwcapped wine could save your life. But I am a traditionalist, in the sense that I prefer and love cork.

If you could invite anyone from history, living or dead, to your home for dinner, who would it be? What food would you serve? What wine would you serve?

I would like to invite two people. The first would be Paul, from the Bible, for his passion for Christ. The second would be Professor Abraham Izak Perold, the maker of Pinotage, to ask him about the future of the wine industry, because he was one of the best agriculturalists that walked the planet. With Paul, we would have Karoo rack of lamb and the 1968 Lanzerac Pinotage, and with Professor Perold, it would be a medium-rare rump steak and a bottle of Simonsig 1972 Pinotage.

If you were to stay home tonight for a relaxing evening, drinking wine while watching a movie, which movie would you watch? Which wine would you drink?

Any army, cowboy, or comedy—it does not really matter. I also love Will Smith and Jackie Chan movies. In South Africa, a relaxing evening is a *braai* with a good bottle of Pinotage, watching our home team, the Stormers, playing rugby.

How do you like to spend your time away from the winery?

I like diving—snorkeling for giant periwinkle and crayfish. An hour or two under water clears all the cobwebs. I also enjoying playing golf, and I like fishing from the rocks.

Do you collect wine? If so, what is in your cellar?

Yes, it is one of my hobbies. At this point I am into South African Pinot Noir from Hamilton Russell Vineyards, Vriesenhof, Bouchard-Finlayson, Newton Johnson, and Paul Cluver.

If you weren't involved in wine, what would you be doing?

Without a doubt, a doctor of medicine.

ADAM MASON

Adam Mason was the winemaker at Klein Constantia from 2004 until 2011. In late 2011 he took over the reins at Mulderbosch. We have visited Adam in South Africa and have had the pleasure of cooking for him as a guest at our dining table.

How did you get involved in the world of wine?

I have always had a love for plants. To me, winemaking seemed the logical conclusion of gardening and growing things. There's that, and the alchemist within. I still find the process absolutely magical.

What are some of the biggest changes you have seen in winemaking since you began your career?

Knowledge of the process has improved in giant leaps compared to even 10 years ago, with specific regard as to how microorganisms (both beneficial and not) play their role in the process both in the vineyard and the cellar. I would say that global quality of wine has improved as a result. Hats off to the wine researchers!

What are some of the exciting changes that you see happening specifically in your country?

The current generation of winemakers has been exposed to international markets, their wines, as well as viticultural and winemaking practices through travel and cultural exchange programs that the preceding generation missed. This has had an enormous influence on the quality of South African wines since 1994. I get pretty excited thinking of where we'll be in 10 years from now.

Where else in the world have you studied, trained, or worked a harvest?

I worked vintages in France after finishing my studies and, since working at Klein Constantia, have been fortunate enough to travel to some of the greatest vineyards in the world. Each visit forces me to re-evaluate my winemaking practices. It's important to question oneself. Mostly though it makes me realize how ancient our relationship with wine is, and in order to continue enjoying it, we must remain open to new wine experiences. Visiting places like Tokaj and Jerez, where winemaking has continued unabated for over three hundred years, really puts one's own position in the grand scheme of things into perspective.

Which varieties are you working with?

At Klein Constantia I worked mostly with Sauvignon Blanc and Muscat de Frontignan, but like all good South Africans we always had about a dozen varieties growing. At Mulderbosch we are working with quite a few varieties as well. The Muscat de Frontignan raisins that I used to produce Vin de Constance are quite possibly the most forgiving of any grape I have ever worked with. That opened up a world of possible fermentation options with fairly high success rates. Every winemaker's dream, right?

What challenges have you faced as a winemaker or winery owner?

The most difficult is balancing commitment to work with a healthy family life. In a way I dread harvest as it becomes a bit like living with strangers for a few months each year. Not so *lekker*—or "cool"—as we say here in South Africa.

What is your winemaking philosophy?

I would say I have a mantra more than a philosophy: "Don't F*ck It Up."

What would you hope people say about your wine?

Let's drink another bottle.

Do you think that the market should influence winemaking, or do you think that winemaking should influence the market?

That is a brilliant question. Both are true to a certain extent, but I think certainly at the upper level the top wines are seen to be defining the market, while at the lower end a wine's very survival depends on conforming to the market's wishes (i.e., the least offensive to the most number of people and offering the biggest discount!).

Besides your own wine, what are some of your favorite wines? What do you like about them?

It does not matter which wines they have been, but my most memorable wines have been the ones least expected to provide something special. Be it a 1970s Cabernet Sauvignon from South Africa or a fresh Muscat from Piedmont, they have been wines that have stopped me in my tracks and forced me to savor each little moment together.

What is your opinion on screwcap versus cork closures?

Put a cork in it.

How do you like to spend your time away from the winery?

Cape Town offers amazing walks on Table Mountain and the peninsula's beaches so we generally load up the car with children and dogs and take off for a few hours. Family holidays are mostly spent close to the ocean.

Do you collect wine? If so, what is in your cellar?

Not yet. But if money were no object I would collect exceptionally old and rare wines and make it a house rule not to drink anything younger than me.

If you weren't involved in wine, what would you be doing?

Landscape architect for sure. With a small coffee shop and bistro on the side selling organic veggies, free-range, acorn-fed, 18-month air-dried hams and home-distilled grappa. There is still time!

NORMA RATCLIFFE

One of South Africa's first female winemakers, Norma Ratcliffe escaped the cold winters of Edmonton, Canada, moved to the Cape Winelands, planted Cabernet Sauvignon vines in the late 1960s, and has never looked back. She was one of the original founders of the Cape Independent Winemakers Guild, their first female member, and an avid supporter of empowerment initiatives for black winemakers. She is the owner and one of the winemakers at Warwick Wine Estate.

How did you get involved in the world of wine?
By default and through passion. I came to South Africa, married a South African yachtsman and farmer who had bought the current piece of land in 1964, started to plant Cabernet Sauvignon vineyards (then almost unheard of in South Africa, where they were planting more obscure varieties) but grew fruit and vegetables to make some cash. What was originally a pumpkin (*pampoen* in Afrikaans) patch is now our top Cabernet Sauvignon vineyard and is still referred to as "*Pampoen* land." Where we once had a peach orchard (Professor Black was the name of the peach variety), we now have our top Sauvignon Blanc vineyard, now named after that "Professor Black" peach variety. I started experimenting with winemaking in 1974. First Cabernet Sauvignon, as it was all we had. It was stomped by the feet of great friends, swilling wine glasses and having fun in half barrels. Slowly we added more

vineyards, introducing international varietals that were rare in South Africa at the time. I studied wine and winemaking and took short, informal courses and then went to work at a château in Bordeaux. That year, at the château, the winemaker broke her leg, and I was left holding the baby. So with my baptism by fire, I returned to Warwick where we made our first commercial (read: *legal*) Cabernet Sauvignon in 1984 and went from strength to strength (the first official vintage was 1985 as we forgot the minor detail of getting a wine licence in 1984!).

What are some of the biggest changes you have seen in winemaking since you began your career?
The introduction of new small French oak barrels (*barriques*) in the '70s was a leap forward for new tannin profiles in the wine. Controlling vineyards to maintain natural

acid in grapes so as not to need acid additions. Riper fruit but an increase in alcohol. Temperature control at all stages of the winemaking process so that wine is not exposed to spikes. The biggest steps forward have been in viticulture. The gradual elimination of leaf roll virus in our main red varieties means fruit ripens easily and evenly.

What are some of the exciting changes that you see happening specifically in your country?
Experimentation with new varieties and blends. Opening up of new wine areas that hadn't even been considered before and are producing new flavor profiles and area-specific wines, particularly in cool regions. The planting of vineyards with the *terroir* in mind and not just the commercial value. The bombardment of the South African winemaking scene by extremely highly educated and talented female winemakers. We broke the ground, they are setting the pace. I was inducted into the all-male group of the Cape Winemakers Guild in 1989 and became chairman in 1993. I guess that I am the only lady to ever chair that group. The opportunities that have been taken by black women (and men) to enter the winemaking world are transforming the industry. The development of our own variety, Pinotage, as a world-class wine. I was a leader in developing a Cape Blend with Pinotage as

a component when I made Warwick Three Cape Ladies in 1997.

Where else in the world have you studied, trained, or worked a harvest? How did that influence your winemaking?
I did a bachelor of science at university in Canada in the frozen north. Basically untrained in a formal wine school. Did courses, devoured books, and did short courses available to me here. Lots of mentorship from male winemakers in the area who wanted me to be successful to give the area the great name that it has now. Worked a harvest in the southern Medoc when even the men in South Africa were not doing their time overseas because of our political views in this country and the apartheid regime. We learn as we go and are always learning. I still travel plenty to wine areas to keep abreast of what is happening. I did a stint in Bulgaria last summer to see what was going on and saw exciting things and varieties.

Which varieties are you working with? Are you experimenting with anything new?
Cabernet Sauvignon, Merlot, Cabernet Franc, Pinotage, Shiraz, Chardonnay, Sauvignon Blanc. We are mostly tweaking new blends. We have tried lots of other varieties but over 45 years have planted and replanted the things that work best for us. It doesn't mean we won't

change. We have developed a real name for Cabernet Franc as a single variety, and it forms a large component of our Trilogy blend. Cabernet Sauvignon will always be king!

Are there any new areas that you have identified for potential vineyard sites?

There are lots of new sites with potential, but we still have undeveloped land at Warwick that we can work with. Should we explore new areas, we would probably buy in the fruit from that area first and experiment with it, before investing in the land itself. We have slowly been planting Sauvignon Blanc higher and higher up the mountain to take advantage of the cooler elevations. We are mad about the fruit quality that we get in the Stellenbosch-Simonsberg region and don't plan to stray far off the mark.

What challenges have you faced as a winemaker or winery owner?

I suppose the main challenge is to produce an even greater wine every year. I was self-taught so my winemaking career as a whole was a learning curve. I often say that "if I had had the modern winemaking equipment of today I may have produced greater wines!" Not true, it just would have made it easier. We really didn't have access to export markets until President Mandela was released in 1990. We

had to start from scratch to build an overseas brand. My son Michael has been the person who has done that and built on what I started.

What is your winemaking philosophy?

I believe in keeping the whole process simple but to use modern technology in its most useful way. Quality without compromise. Don't kill an elegant wine with too much wood.

What would you hope people say about your wine?

Let's order another bottle.

Do you think that the market should influence winemaking, or do you think that winemaking should influence the market?

The clear answer is that *terroir* solidly influences wine style as does vintage. Discerning consumers recognize this and love the personalities of different areas and years. Commercial wines are all pretty uniform even at the top end. At a price, consumers look for this. France has been hugely influenced by the market . . . less wood, more ripe fruit, and rising alcohols. They have to compete with other areas and stay in business.

Besides your own wine, what are some of your favorite wines? What do you like about them?

In South Africa, I love the Sauvignon/Sémil-

lon blends from Constantia and Cape Point
and Cape Agulhas. I like them for their
tightness and natural acidity, as well as their
minerality. Great wines for warm climate.
Love the German Rieslings with food choices.
Love the aromatics, and I am addicted to that
"diesel-y" nose. Top-class chenins from South
Africa are exciting. Dusty and fruity. Love
the Pinot Noirs from New Zealand. Rich and
seamless. These all would be chosen for my
mood and menu. Cabernet Sauvignon in the
Simonsberg appellation of Stellenbosch rules
the roost though.

What is your opinion on screwcap versus cork closures?

The debate goes on. I love the screwcap. What
great convenience for a lovely wine that is to
be drunk young. My age group is particularly
keen on them. However, you will not wean me
off the old wines in my cellar with big long
corks that give me such pleasure when I pull
them. A cork has a presence. I have drunk
fine wines from Australia with a screwcap that
were 15 years old and perfect. The problem
may be solved for most of us eventually as the
supply of really fine quality cork is diminish-
ing and probably not sustainable. We do not
ever want to have Warwick defined by its
bottle closure.

If you could invite anyone from history, living or dead, to your home for dinner, who would it be? What food would you serve? What wine would you serve?

I would have had Maggie Thatcher when
she was prime minister. She was a great role
model for our era. Serve good South African
leg of lamb done on the *braai*. Sauce Nivernais
[hollandaise with mint], fresh garden vegs,
fabulous local South African cheeses, and my
mother's famous Panna Cotta. Cannot get
away from Cabernet Franc, but would serve
my own Warwick Cabernet Franc.

If you were to stay home tonight for a relaxing evening, drinking wine while watching a movie, which movie would you watch? Which wine would you drink? Explain.

Braveheart for the umpteenth time, with a bottle of South African Cabernet. Gutsy movie,
gutsy wine. Love old movies like *Brideshead
Revisited*, with an elegant Sauvignon/Sémillon
from South Africa or Château Canon.

How do you like to spend your time away from the winery?

I am an avid hiker with Table Mountain and
the Simonsberg Mountain on my doorstep,
and I do play golf. I collect antique silver wine
funnels so I follow the auctions. Love spending time with my children and grandchildren.

Do you collect wine? If so, what is in your cellar?

Enough wine to keep my family drinking for 50 years. My late husband and I had different tastes in wine. We collected wine and had two separate cellars so there is a diverse collection. Interesting to see what the mature wines are like now. I lean heavily on old Bordeaux from the northern Medoc. St. Julien being one of my favorite areas. Château Ducru-Beaucaillou. Yum, yum. I am passionate about Cabernet Franc and collect every bottle that I can lay my hands on no matter where I might be. I have a 1995 Château Ausone lurking around. I should get started on the 1948 Vieux Château Certan that I was saving for my sixtieth birthday and forgot to drink. The 1982 Cheval Blanc should be perfect. Oops, I have drifted to the right bank. Hope my children don't read this, or they will want me to start pulling corks immediately.

If you weren't involved in wine, what would you be doing?

My whole life is wine related. One doesn't have to do an either/or scenario. I would like to be more involved in the arts again. I did serious porcelain ceramics in the '70s and then got too busy. I would head that way again or maybe pick up a paintbrush. I am busy with mentorship programs for women (and men) in the wine industry from previously disadvantaged South African backgrounds. There is lots of work to be done there.

PHILIP VAN ZYL

Platter's South African Wine Guide, conceived by John and Erica Platter in 1978, is considered to be the first and best-selling annual wine guide in South Africa. The first printing was in 1980, and three decades later the guide has sold more than 1.4 million copies to wine lovers around the world. Philip is the editor of the *Platter's Guide*. He has been with Platter's since 1998 and, with his team, received the 2007 Champagne Louis Roederer International Wine Writer's Domaines Ott Award for Best Annual Wine Guide.

How did you get involved in the world of wine?
My dad, being from the Western Cape, enjoyed the occasional glass of wine and his favorite was a semisweet white, Tasheimer Goldtröpfchen. I suspect Dad was as tickled by the name, which translates as "droplets of gold," as the flavor. Occasionally he'd let me taste. Having imbibed something as magical as "droplets of gold" as a youth, maybe it was inevitable that I'd end up in wine.

What are some of the biggest changes you have seen in winemaking or wine styles since you began your career?
I became involved with *Platter's Guide* mid-1998, four years after the first democratic elections and South Africa's re-admission to the community of nations. The wine industry has since changed out of all recognition. For starters it's twice the size, in terms of the number of brands. It's more focused, more scientific, more competitive, more environmentally aware. It's also more interesting, with a diversity of styles, grape varieties, and regions having come into play. For me one of the most significant and encouraging trends is the respect for old vines, as seen in Eben Sadie's landmark Ouwingerdreeks ("Old Vine" series), Johann Rupert's Cape of Good Hope bottlings, and others.

What are some of the exciting changes that you see happening in your country?
South Africa's wines are improving by the vintage and gaining more recognition internationally, which is tremendously exciting. There is a perception in some quarters, though, that the wines pre the '90s are somehow inferior. That's simply not true. There are some world-class reds from the '50s, '60s, and '70s, and I'd urge anyone who gets the opportunity to open a bottle. Unfortunately they're becoming rare, but so worth seeking out.

Have you ever worked as a winemaker even for just a harvest? Where? How does that experience inform your writing?

Living and working in the Cape Winelands, there's no way one could resist making wine. This past vintage my wife, Cathy, and I made a Syrah with friends at Joostenberg Wine Estate. Our "finest" achievement, though, would be the Cinsault we made some years ago from a 23-year-old vineyard, since uprooted, on nearby Somerbosch Farm. We called the wine Screaming Eaglet, an allusion—sad to say—to the loudness of the new American oak rather than the quality. Making wine myself made me aware of the myriad factors impacting quality, and hence much less inclined to criticize others' wines harshly.

If you could invite anyone from history, living or dead, to your home for dinner, who would it be? What food would you serve? What wine would you serve?

It would have to be former president Nelson Mandela. I'd do exactly as his caregivers say, bearing in mind he's 92 years of age, but if the opportunity arose I'd offer him a glass of Klein Constantia Vin de Constance. This is a brilliant re-creation of the world-renowned Constantia sweet wines of the eighteenth and nineteenth centuries, and a wine befitting South Africa's global icon.

If you were to stay home tonight for a relaxing evening, drinking wine while watching a movie, which movie would you watch? Which wine would you drink? Explain.

Left to my own devices I'd watch a Fellini movie and drink one of the small but growing number of locally vinified Italian varieties, like Steenberg Vineyards' Nebbiolo or Altydgedacht Estate's Barbera. But with a young fan of South Africa's "prank king," Leon Schuster, in the household, it's more likely to be a rerun of *You Must Be Joking!* or *Mr. Bones*, which probably calls for a glass of Pinotage.

Do you collect wine? If so, what is in your cellar?

"Collect" isn't the word. More like "agglomerate." It's a chaotic process, so everything in the cellar ends up being a surprise. As of recently, however, at least it's an air-conditioned surprise.

If you weren't involved in wine, what would you be doing?

Wishing I were involved in wine.

MAY DE LENCQUESAING

May de Lencquesaing is the owner of Glenelly Estate. She is a member of one of Bordeaux's oldest wine families. She is known worldwide for the wines of Château Pichon Longueville Comtesse De Lalande. *Decanter* magazine named her "Woman of the Year" in 1994, and she maintains the vice presidency for the International Wine and Spirits Competition and the presidency of the Medoc Legion of Honor. Lady May is a force of nature; we had the extreme honor and privilege to sit, chat, and share a pot of tea with this amazing octogenarian.

How did you get involved in the world of wine?
I was born into the world of wine. It really wasn't a choice, but I am happy about it. My family is one of the oldest *négociant* families in Bordeaux.

What are some of the biggest changes you have seen in winemaking since you began your career?
The fact that we are able to get consistent quality year after year is one of the biggest changes I have seen in the industry. When I was very young, you would have good years and bad years, because we didn't have the technology to correct faults in the wine. I remember that from 1928 until 1945, nobody was making good wine. We had many problems with the economic recession of the time.

Where have you studied, trained, or worked a harvest? How did that influence your wine-making?

I grew up in the world of wine. All of the discussion at the dinner table was about the vines, the grapes, the weather—you could say that was my early training as a winemaker. I have since been formally trained—I always want to make sure that I know a little bit more than I need to know, when I am talking to winemakers.

Which varieties are you working with? Are you experimenting with anything new?
We are working with Bordeaux varieties in the South African *terroir*. The Glenelly Lady May 2008 is 91 percent Cabernet Sauvignon and 9 percent Petit Verdot.

Besides your own wine, what are some of your favorite wines? What do you like about them?
Well, I do love so many of our wines from France and from South Africa, but I also love wines from Burgundy too.

What is your opinion on screwcap versus cork closures?

Cork is a natural product that comes from trees, as does the wood to make barrels. I feel that it is a natural choice to use cork when you are making wines that will be aged for a long time. I am also very respectful of nature and our environment, so I do not think that we should waste this wonderful natural resource on a wine that will be opened and drunk within two years. I wrote a book many years ago entitled *The Magic of Wine*, where I tell a story of how when the wine is in the barrel, it is like a young child. He can breathe and interact with all of his friends in the other barrels. At this point, he has not learned to become formal and keep to himself—like a child learns when he begins to enter adulthood. Once we put the wine into a bottle, it is separated from all of the other wine, it is alone, setting out in the world on its own and destined to be shipped to other countries. This is like adult children when they set out on their own to go to college, or enter the work environment. I feel that the little bit of cork in the bottle allows the child in the bottle to interact with the environment. I also love the moment when a cork is pulled, the table is set with silver and candles, and the wine is poured from a lowly glass bottle into a beautiful crystal decanter.

It is in this moment that the wine can express itself, to be who he really wants to be. In this moment, the wine is the center of attention—the star.

If you could invite anyone from history, living or dead, to your home for dinner, who would it be? What food would you serve? What wine would you serve?

I would invite Thomas Jefferson. I have great respect for him and his wine knowledge. You know, of course, that he was a great admirer of Château Haut Brion, one of our friends in Bordeaux. I think that I would serve him my 1982 Château Pichon Longueville Comtesse de Lalande. He would like that, I think. I would also love to have Napoleon at the same table. Everybody knows that he loved Klein Constantia Vin de Constance, and that he was a lover of this South African wine, but this is a white wine, so I would like him to try a red wine from South Africa. So I think that I would serve him my Grand Vin De Glenelly. I think that he would enjoy our red wines.

How do you like to spend your time away from the winery?

I love to travel. I really enjoy visiting Paris and New York. I have so many friends in those cities, I feel like I am at home.

Do you collect wine? If so, what is in your cellar?

Yes, I have wines from my friends and neighbors in South Africa and France.

If you weren't involved in wine, what would you be doing?

As I said earlier, I was born into the world of wine. I couldn't imagine doing anything else.

URUGUAY

KNOWN MORE FOR THE COSMOPOLITAN vibe of its capital, Montevideo, and the swank beaches and resorts of Punta del Este, the small country of Uruguay is often overlooked when New World wines are being discussed. However, it is the fourth most important wine-producing country in South America—after Chile, Argentina, and Brazil. Uruguay is situated between the 30th and 35th parallels of latitude in the Southern Hemisphere, much like the vineyards of its neighbors, Argentina and Chile, as well as grape-growing areas of South Africa and Australia.

Wine production arrived in Uruguay in much the same way as the rest of the continent. It is widely agreed that the Spanish conquistadors Francisco Cervantes and Hernando de Montenegro brought vines from the Canary Islands to Cuzco and Lima. This is documented by the Peruvian poet Garcilaso de la Vega, a.k.a. "El Inca," in his *Comentarios Reales* of 1606, which is considered one of the best books on the history of the New World. After

Peru, from vines first grown in Cuzco, the practice of planting vines took hold in Chile and Buenos Aires. It is thought that the first vines in Uruguay came from Buenos Aires along with the movement of the Spanish colonists.

The end of the nineteenth century brought with it a wave of immigrants from Spain, especially from the Basque region in the north. They carried over vines and rootstock from their home country and began making wine in the New World. In addition to familiar varieties they also brought Tannat, a grape variety from Madiran in southwestern France. It was originally known as Harriague, honoring the French Basque settler who introduced the varietal to the region.

Like many of its neighbors, including Argentina, Brazil, and Chile, Uruguay had a first wave of European immigrants that were Spanish, followed by Italian immigrants in the late nineteenth century. Beginning in approximately 1870 and well into the early twentieth century, Italians from the length of their home country made their way to this small South American nation. Today, 40 percent of the population of Uruguay claims Italian descent, and the ancestors of nearly two-thirds of the residents of Montevideo hailed from Italy.

Many of the early Italian settlers worked in construction and farming, and their influence is felt in many areas of Uruguayan culture. Pasta runs neck and neck with grilled beef as the national dish, and wine is enjoyed alongside most meals. While one would expect a preponderance of Italian varieties such as Sangiovese or Trebbiano to be grown here, the Italian families who own wineries have allowed both the climate and *terroir* to speak when choosing which grapes to grow.

Uruguay is bordered to the north by Brazil; to the west by the Uruguay River and the country of Argentina; to the southwest by the Rio de la Plata; and to the southeast by the Atlantic Ocean. There are about 3.5 million people living in Uruguay; 88 percent are of European descent. Uruguayans drink an average of 35 liters of wine per year, which is almost four times the average US consumption. Most of the top wine-consuming countries in the world are in Europe, but Argentina and Uruguay hold their own in South America.

In the past 20 years, many Uruguayan vineyards have been replanted with new rootstock. More and more wineries now grow Cabernet Sauvignon, Merlot, Cabernet Franc, Syrah, Pinot Noir, Chardonnay, Sauvignon Blanc, and Sauvignon Gris alongside their hundred-year-old Tannat vines. The newer vines are just beginning to hit their stride, which makes it an exciting time to explore the wines of Uruguay. The past 20 years have also brought modern winemaking techniques. Agronomists now limit the number of grape bunches on each vine, manage water needs, and prune more drastically. This is all in the spirit of cutting back grape yields and increasing quality. Winemakers use more modern techniques such as temperature-controlled stainless-steel tanks for fermentation and air-conditioned storage facilities. Many have been educated in other countries and have worked harvests in the United States, Europe, Chile, Argentina, South Africa, and Australia and have returned to Uruguay with new ideas and techniques.

Uruguay's climate is temperate and receives maritime influences from the Atlantic Ocean. There are four well-defined seasons, with hot, sunny, summers and cool, wet winters. Most vineyards are planted at a hundred or so meters (a few hundred feet) above sea level, contrasted with neighboring countries Chile and Argentina, where vines are planted at substantial elevation in the foothills of the Andes Mountains. This gives Uruguay a broad diversity of microclimates in which to grow grapes. There are vines planted in sixteen of nineteen *departamentos* (departments) in the country, but the most important are in Colonia, Montevideo, Maldonado, and Canelones in the south, where approximately 90 percent of the country's vineyards are located. Although

the terms are not exactly the same, departamento, or "department," is analogous to "province" or "state." There are 9,000 hectares (22,239 acres) of vines in this relatively flat country and many people have compared the Mar de la Plata region to Bordeaux. There are a few differences, of course. The soil in Bordeaux tends to be more gravel, thus giving better drainage, while the departments of San José and Canelones have soil comprised of mostly clay. With annual rainfalls of 1,600 millimeters, or 63 inches, the Uruguayan winemakers had to find a sturdy grape, which is why the thick-skinned Tannat variety has been so popular.

Tannat is notorious for being a tough grape variety to tame; this is especially due to the variety's thick skin and subsequent abundant tannins. Many winemakers have overcome this challenge by proper vineyard management, modern cellar techniques, and even more modern techniques such as microoxygenation. Blending Tannat with other varieties, most commonly Merlot and Pinor Noir, is often used as a way to soften Tannat's strong tannins.

Many winemakers are making quite good, representative Tannat either as a single varietal or blended with other grapes to make interesting blends. The Tannat variety is generally characterized by its dark red, bluish, almost black color, often with violet reflections, and aromas of mature, ripe dark fruits, tobacco, and saddle leather. In most of the best varietal representations, the tannins are strong but supple.

Many wines from Uruguay—including those made from Tannat, Tannat blends, and other international varietals—have won medals at prestigious international wine competitions including Challenge du Vin, Bacchus, Chardonnay du Monde, Ljubljana, Mondial de Bruxelles, and Vinitaly. Unfortunately, many of these award-winning wines are not exported to the US or UK markets. Many are made for domestic consumption as well as export to other South American countries, Canada, Mexico, and Poland.

MAJOR GRAPE VARIETIES

CABERNET FRANC

A native of France, this red grape tastes of cherry, currants, violet, and pepper. Often found blended with Tannat, Cabernet Sauvignon, or Merlot, it is also vinified individually into red and rosé wines.

CABERNET SAUVIGNON

Rich tannins and flavors of black cherry, cassis, violet, baking spices, and pencil lead lend themselves to single varietal or blended bottlings of this French grape.

CHARDONNAY

Flavors of tropical fruit and green apples abound in one of Uruguay's most popular white varieties, which is made in a light fruity style in stainless steel or a heavier oaked style with barrel-enhanced aromas of caramel, butter, and toasted bread.

MERLOT

The small almost-black grape takes its name from the French word for blackbird, *merle*. Soft tannins and flavors of cherry, dark berries, and mint are found whether made as a single varietal or blended with Tannat and Cabernet Sauvignon.

PINOT NOIR

This French native, mainly used here for blending in order to soften the harsher edges of Tannat, is increasingly being seen bottled on its own. Pinot Noir's black clusters of grapes yield a red wine noted for its flavors of cherry and chocolate with a splash of refreshing acidity. It is also vinified singly or blended with Chardonnay to make sparkling wine.

SAUVIGNON BLANC

Bright notes of tropical fruit and fresh-cut herbs are this French native's characteristic traits. Bottled either singly or blended with other whites, it is found in moderate amounts throughout many Uruguayan vineyards.

SHIRAZ/SYRAH

Bottlings that use the former synonym for this deeply colored grape lean toward the big, bold New World style, while those that use the latter name, Syrah, are usually made in a more elegant French fashion. Either way, look for flavors of blackberry, spice, and ground pepper, bottled varietally or mixed with Tannat, Cabernet Sauvignon, and Merlot.

TANNAT

Uruguay's signature red grape hails from southwest France and was introduced here by nineteenth-century Basque settlers. The dark purple berries are characterized by strong, supple tannins and aromas of dark fruits, tobacco, and saddle leather. Old-vines Tannat may come from plantings that are more than one hundred years old, and newer clones are often blended with Bordeaux varieties or Pinot Noir.

URUGUAY

BRAZIL

N

Uruguay River

Rio Negro

COLONIA

CANELONES

Rio de la Plata

Montevideo

MONTEVIDEO

MALDONADO

ATLANTIC OCEAN

ARGENTINA

0 Miles 100
0 Kilometers 200

© 2012 Jeffrey L. Ward

WINE REGIONS

CANELONES

Of the four major Uruguayan wine regions, Canelones produces the most wine—approximately 60 percent of the country's wines are produced in this department alone. Canelones is located in the southern part of the country and is 15 miles north of the capital city, Montevideo.

ANTIQUA BODEGA STAGNARI

Ruta 5, Kilometer 20, La Paz, Canelones,
+598 2 362 2137,
www.antiguabodegastagnari.com.uy

Pablo Stagnari Casall left the port of Genoa, Italy, in 1898, to start a new life in Uruguay. A few years later, he purchased 3 hectares (7 acres) of land in Santos Lugares and planted vines. The current bodega remains in Santos Lugares, but the family now has 30 hectares (74 acres) in both Santos Lugares, where they grow Sangiovese (imported from Italy) and Merlot, and in Melilla, where they grow Chardonnay, Sauvignon Blanc, Tannat, Cabernet Sauvignon, Cabernet Franc, Merlot, and Syrah. Agronomist

Carlo Meneguzzi Stagnari limits his vineyard planting to 4,000 vines per hectare (2.5 acres) and oversees every aspect of tending the vines. Winemaker Mariana Meneguzzi Stagnari has worked harvests in Australia and California and crafts quality wines with co-winemaker Laura Casella. Del Pedregal Estival 2009 is 80 percent Sangiovese and 20 percent Cabernet Franc and is rich garnet colored, with fresh red fruit and blueberries on the nose. The body is medium density with smooth tannins. Antiqua Bodega Stagnari Osiris Reserva Tannat 2005 is ruby red with fruits of the wood and blueberry in the bouquet. There are persistent yet smooth tannins on the finish.

ARIANO HERMANOS

Ruta 48, Kilometer 15, El Colorado, Canelones,
+598 2 364 5290,
www.arianohermanos.com

In 1927, Adelio and Amlicar Ariano, two brothers from Italy, purchased 8 hectares (20 acres) of land in La Colorado, Canelones. Today the family manages well over 100 hectares (247 acres) of vines in Paysandu and Canelones

WINES OF THE SOUTHERN HEMISPHERE

and produces more than 1.5 million liters of wine. Various Ariano family members make up the Bodega's team of winemakers, agronomists, vineyard workers, export department, and management. Varieties include Cabernet Sauvignon, Cabernet Franc, Merlot, Syrah, Chardonnay, Muscat Ottonel, Sémillon, and Sauvignon Blanc. The harvest in Paysandu occurs in February, while in Canelones the harvest is later, usually in March. Irrigation is generally not required, as average rainfall is adequate; however Ariano does have the ability to irrigate one of its 15–hectare (37-acre) plots, which historically receives the lowest rainfall. Ariano Hermanos Tacuabé Semi Reserva Tannat-Cabernet Sauvignon 2005 is dark cherry in color, with red fruits and toasted wood notes in the bouquet. On the palate it is smooth and supple. Ariano Hermanos Don Nelson Special Reserve Tannat 2006 is dark ruby in the glass with a spicy yet floral nose. It is full-bodied and well-rounded in the mouth.

CASTILLO VIEJO

Ruta 68, Kilometer 24, Canelón Chico,
Las Piedras, Canelones,
+598 2 368 9606,
www.castilloviejo.com

One of the larger estates in Uruguay, with more than 130 hectares (321 acres), Castillo

Viejo owners Ana, Edgardo, and Alejandro Etcheverry oversee production of more than 1.5 million liters of wine per year. Their grandfather, Don Santos Etcheverry, emigrated to Uruguay from the French Basque town of Hasparren and started the company in 1927. The family has three categories of wine: Catamayor, Reserva, and Reserva de la Familia. It has been making French varietal wines since the mid-1980s. Castillo Viejo Catamayor Cabernet Franc 2005 is red cherry in color with a bouquet of ripe red fruits. In the mouth it has a soft tannic finish. Castillo Viejo Reserva Tannat Cabernet Franc Blend 2005 is deep purple in the glass. The nose has notes of soft vanilla and hazelnut with ripe tannins prevalent on the palate. Castillo Viejo Reserva de la Familia Tannat Vieja Parcela 2004 is deep purple, with a bouquet of cherry preserves and dried figs. The finish presents a firm tannic structure.

CÉSAR PISANO E HIJOS

Ruta 68, Kilometer 29, Progresso, Canelones,
+598 2 368 9077,
www.pisanowines.com

A leisurely drive from Montevideo along Route 5 brings you to the coastal region of Progreso; both the Pisano and Arretxea families arrived here from Europe in the second half of the nineteenth century. With the marriage

of Italian César Pisano to Basque Doña María Elsa Arretxea and the subsequent birth of their sons, Daniel, Eduardo, and Gustavo, the modern company of César Pisano e Hijos was born. The grapes for their iconic wine, Pisano-Arretxea Gran Reserve 2001, are sourced from vines that were planted by César Pisano's father, Don Cesare Pietro Pisano, in 1942. Made from Cabernet Sauvignon, Merlot, and Tannat from their Viña Barrancal Estate, the color is inky purple, with coffee and baking spices on the nose. In the mouth it has powerful tannins with lingering fruit flavors of blackberry and cherry. The family's Exte Oneko Tannat 2004 is a fortified, sweet red wine made from Tannat grapes that are allowed to shrivel on the vines. The resulting wine is intensely purple, with a bouquet of raspberries, white pepper, black plum, and cocoa. It is dense in the mouth, with the flavor of mixed black and red berry jam.

ESTABLECIMIENTO JUANICÓ

Ruta 5, Kilometer 37,500, Juanicó, Canelones, +598 4 335 9735, www.juanico.com.uy

One of the largest wineries in Uruguay, with more than 250 hectares (618 acres) of vineyards and a production capacity of over 4 million liters, Establecimiento Juanicó continues to make distinctive wines. Run by the Deicas family, in 1996 it was the first winery in Uruguay to produce a late-harvest wine utilizing Botrytis. It was also the first Uruguayan bodega to create a joint venture with a French winery; Gran Casa Magrez was produced by Establecimiento Juanicó and Château Pape Clément for the French market in 1999. The bodega introduced Cuvée Castelar, its first *Méthode Champenoise* product, in 2001 and soon won international medals for this delicious sparkling wine. Don Pascual Sauvignon Gris 2008 is dark yellow to gold, with tropical fruits on the bouquet. On the palate guava and mango explode in your mouth before a pleasant, lingering finish. Bodegones del Sur Shiraz Tannat Reserve 2004 is Shiraz prominent and deep ruby in color. Light floral top notes over aromas of ripe red fruits are noted in the bouquet. Strong tannins are present in the finish. Deicas Family Botrytis Noble is deep gold in color and is made from Sauvignon

Blanc, Sauvignon Gris, Gros Manseng, Gewürztraminer, and Petit Grain varieties. The bouquet reveals dried fruit, honey, and rose aromas, while on the palate the natural acidity complements the sweetness and prevents it from being cloying.

FILGUEIRA

Ruta 81, Kilometer 6,500, Cuchilla Verde, Canelones,
+ 598 2 336 6868,
www.bodegafilgueira.com

A native of Galicia, Spain, Don Manuel Filgueira sailed to Uruguay at the beginning of the twentieth century and began planting vines and making his wines. In 1992 he handed over management of the company to his son's wife, Dr. Martha Chiossi Filgueira, who replanted the original vineyards with French varieties. All of the grapes for the family's wines are estate grown. Tannat, Cabernet Sauvignon, Merlot, Cabernet Franc, Pinot Noir, Syrah, Chardonnay, Sauvignon Gris, and Sauvignon Blanc are the current varieties used in the production of Filgueira's fine wines. The family also had the foresight to hire the French consultant Pascal Marty, who implemented many modern techniques used in the winery today. Filgueira Family Reserve Chardonnay 2007 is aged for eight months in French oak

and is medium yellow in color. Notes of vanilla, toasted brioche, and pears are evident on the bouquet, and on the palate this wine is very well balanced. The Filgueira Fuga Cabernet Sauvignon 2009 is aged for six months in oak and has a red cherry color, with notes of white pepper and red plums. The finish lingers elegantly on the palate. Filgueira Tannat 2009 is ruby colored, with aromas of black plums and blackberries and has well-rounded tannins in the mouth.

GIMENEZ MENDEZ

Batlle y Ordoñez 165, Canelones,
+598 4 332 0307,
www.gimenezmendez.com

The Gimenez Mendez family owns four vineyards near Uruguay's Rio de la Plata, where the daily temperature can fluctuate between 32 degrees Celsius (90 degrees Fahrenheit) during the day to a mere 10 degrees Celsius (50 degrees Fahrenheit) at night. This large temperature spread allows the sun to concentrate the grapes' sugars and tannins, while allowing the berry ample time at night to cool down. Winemakers Luis Gimenez Mendez, Mauro Gimenez Mendez, and Gaston Vitale craft superior wines from the estate's vines of Sauvignon Blanc, Chardonnay, Viognier, Torrontés, Tannat, Merlot, Cabernet Sauvignon, Cabernet Franc,

Shiraz, Marcelan, Petit Verdot, and Arinarnoa (the latter is a grape variety developed in 1956 by crossing Merlot with Petit Verdot). More than a few of Gimenez Mendez's wines have earned gold medals at international competitions. Gimenez Mendez Tannat Alta Reserva 2008 is ruby red in color, with aromas of black raspberry and dark plums. It is full-bodied, with persistent tannins on the palate. Gimenez Mendez Alta Reserva Arinarnoa 2007 is inky purple in color, with cooling notes of menthol and eucalyptus. In the mouth black raspberry and blueberry flavors lead to a lasting finish. Las Brujas Sauvignon Blanc 2008 is named for the Las Brujas ("The Witches") region and is pale straw, almost clear in color. Tropical fruits and citrus aromas give way to a crisp refreshing wine on the palate.

MARICHAL VINOS FINOS

Ruta 64, Kilometer 48,500, Canelones,
+598 4 332 1949,
www.marichalwines.com

University-educated winemakers and agronomists Juan Andrés Marichal and Alejandro Marichal run the family business under the watchful eye of their parents. Founded by Isabelino Marichal in 1938, the family maintains traditional winemaking techniques but also utilizes modern technology. Located in rolling hillsides 29 kilometers (18 miles) from the ocean, this small winery picks most of its grapes by hand. Two lines of wine are made at Marichal Vinos Finos: a Premium Varietal line and a Reserve Collection. Marichal Cabernet Franc Rosé 2009 is a beautiful light pink color and is refreshing on the palate. It is an ideal wine to sip while sunning on the beach, whereas the Marichal Reserve Pinot-Chardonnay 2008 stands up to delicate sauces and is more of a food wine. Other well-made wines include Marichal Chardonnay, Marichal Sauvignon Blanc, Marichal Merlot, Marichal Tannat, Marichal Reserve Pinot Noir Tannat Blend, Marichal Reserve Pinot Noir, and Marichal Reserve Tannat. Juan Andrés Marichal recommended that we try his chef Luis Zunino's *Cazuela de Cordero* with Marichal Reserve Tannat 2009. It was a perfect pairing, and we can't wait until we visit all of our friends in Uruguay to eat this delicious lamb dish again.

PIZZORNO FAMILY ESTATES

Ruta 32, Kilometer 23, Canelón Chico, Canelones,
+598 2 368 9601,
www.pizzornowines.com

Only 20 kilometers (12 miles) south of Montevideo, the Pizzorno family combines estate-grown grapes, modern technology, and artisanal style to its handcrafted wines. Founded by Don Próspero José Pizzorno, whose family emigrated from Italy, the estate has 20 hectares (49 acres) of Tannat, Cabernet Sauvignon, Petit Verdot, Cabernet Franc, Sauvignon Blanc, Chardonnay, Pinot Noir, Ugni Blanc, and Moscatel de Hamburgo. A boutique winery in every sense of the word, no fertilizers nor irrigation are used; grapes are manually harvested; and corks and labels are placed by hand. Don Prospero Sauvignon Blanc 2009 is straw colored and has a floral and tropical fruit bouquet. It is light and fresh in the mouth with a light citrus finish. Pizzorno Espumoso Natural Reserva is pale straw with fine persistent bubbles. On the nose citrus blossom and yeast aromas are evident, with a balanced acidity in the mouth. Pizzorno Tannat 2008 is dark garnet with a violet rim. Red cherry and black raspberry explode in the mouth, with a balanced tannic finish. The Pizzorno family also makes a line of Alphabet Wines which are imported into the US market. Its C Tannat-Malbec 2009 is 50 percent of each and is ruby red colored. Aromas of spice, cassis, and cocoa are present on the bouquet. It is medium- to full-bodied with a long, elegant finish. Don't forget to bring this wine the next time your brother-in-law is grilling some prime steaks on the barbecue.

REINALDO DE LUCCA

Ruta 48, Kilometer 13,100, El Colorado,
+598 2 367 8076,
www.deluccawines.com

Reinaldo De Lucca has an extremely hands-on approach to making wine at Bodegas De Lucca. He wears three hats and serves as vineyard worker, business director, and winemaker. His 50 hectares (123 acres) of vertically trellised vineyards in Rincón del Colorado, El Colorado Chico, Progreso, and El Colorado grow predominantly Cabernet Sauvignon, Tannat, and Merlot grapes. De Lucca Rio Colorado Reserva 2006 is a blend of Cabernet Sauvignon, Tannat, and Merlot and has an intense ruby color. On the nose, red fruit and aromatic herbs are evident. In the mouth it is rich and supple. De Lucca Tannat-Merlot Reserva 2007 has a bouquet that includes notes of raspberry and red fruit and a rich, rounded mouthfeel.

TOSCANINI E HIJOS

Ruta 69, Kilometer 30, Canelón Chico, Canelones,
+598 2 368 9697,
www.toscaniniwines.com

Don Juan Toscanini and his wife, Doña Maria Bianchi, left Geneva in 1894, and settled in Canelón Chico, just 30 kilometers (19 miles) north of the port of Montevideo. They rented

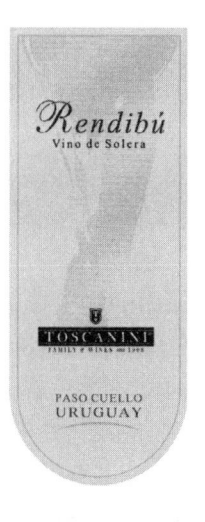

tannins. Toscanini Reservado Supremo Tannat Cabernet Franc 2006 is deep red, with spice and ripe, red fruit on the bouquet. The soft tannins and full-bodied nature of this wine are found on the palate. Rendibú Dessert Wine NV is a blend of Chardonnay and Sauvignon Blanc grapes that have been allowed to dry on the vines. Only four bunches of grapes are allowed per vine, so there is intense concentration of white stone fruits and honey flavors in this gold-hued wine. On the palate there is restrained sweetness, balanced by good acidity.

a plot of land to grow grapes and eventually saved enough money to buy it in 1908. Their family now owns 80 hectares (198 acres) in Paso Cuello and Canelón Chico and grows grapes in soil that is clay and calcareous. They make their wines using many varietals including Gewürztraminer, Chardonnay, Sauvignon Blanc, Trebbiano, Sémillon, Cabernet Franc, Tannat, Merlot, Cabernet Sauvignon, and Pinot Noir. The family's wines have won international awards. It has recently collaborated with the Massenez family from France, known for its *Eaux-de-vie* production in Alsace. Toscanini's French winemaker Stephane Geneste is especially proud of the Casa Vialona Private Reserve Tannat 2002, which is aged for 12 months in oak. It is ruby red in color, with aromas of mature red and black fruits. Oak aging is noticeable on the palate with balanced

VINOS FINOS H. STAGNARI

Ruta 5, Kilometer 20, La Puebla, La Paz,
Canelones,
+598 2 362 2940,
www.stagnari.com

Located on the banks of the Uruguay River, near Salto Grande—which is a large lake—Vinos Finos H. Stagnari benefits from the wide daily temperature variations of this prime location. The soils are sandy clay on the surface, with abundant pebbles for drainage 1 meter (3 feet) down. Winemaker and owner Hectar Stagnari graduated from winemaking school in 1978, worked at châteaux in both Bordeaux and Châteauneuf du Pape, and developed his international winemaking style. He grows Cabernet Sauvignon, Syrah, Merlot,

Gewürztraminer, Viognier, and Chardonnay, and all of his wines are made from grapes grown on his own land. He is very proud that one of his wines claimed the title "Best Red Wine in the World" at an international competition in Ljubljana, Slovenia. Stagnari Dayman Castel La Puebla Tannat 2003 is oak-aged for 12 months in the caves of the La Puebla Castle. It is made only in exceptional years. It is rich garnet in color, with mature fruit aromas on the bouquet. In the mouth it is robust yet elegant with well-structured tannins. Vinos Finos H. Stagnari Selección La Puebla Syrah 2009 is not aged in oak and is a rich, purple garnet color, with young fresh fruits on the nose. It has a supple mouthfeel with balanced tannins.

VIÑA VARELA ZARRANZ

Ruta 74, Kilometer 29, Joaquin Suárez,
Canelones,
+598 2 364 4587,
www.varelazarranz.com

Brothers Don Ramón and Don Antonio Varela emigrated from Spain in 1933 and established the family wine business. It was the third generation that modernized the winery in 1986. The family now owns 110 hectares (272 acres) of vineyards in the towns of Joaquín Suárez and Cuatro Piedras in Canelones. Agronomist Ricardo Varela oversees Chardonnay, Sauvignon Blanc, Merlot, Cabernet Franc, Cabernet Sauvignon, Tannat, Muscat de Frontignan, Muscat de Ottonel, and Viognier vines, while winemaker Enrique Varela supervises the winery. Viña Varela Zarranz has won numerous gold and silver medals in international competitions. Its barrel-aged Tannat Crianza 2004 is a worldwide favorite, with deep ruby color and notes of ripe red fruits and vanilla on the bouquet. On the palate it is balanced with a persistent tannic finish. Viña Varela Zarranz Cabernet Sauvignon 2009 only sees one month of oak aging and presents notes of raspberry and red cherry. In the mouth cocoa and smooth tannins are evident. Fusion Roble 2009 is oak-aged for 10 months and is a blend of 50 percent Cabernet Sauvignon, 30 percent Tannat, and 20 percent Merlot. It is intensely red, with aromas of eucalyptus, mint, and caramelized sugar. It has a pleasant mouthfeel and a balanced tannic structure.

COLONIA

Colonia is located west of Montevideo in the southwest corner of the country. It is bordered on the south by the Rio de la Plata and is directly across the river from Argentina and the city of Buenos Aires.

DANTE IRURTIA

Ramal Ruta 97, Kilometer 2300, Carmelo,
Colonia,
+598 4 542 2323,
www.irurtia.com.uy

Located 250 kilometers (155 miles) west of the capital, Montevideo, the town of Carmelo has the good fortune to be the crossing point of the Parana River and the Uruguay River. Together they form the De La Plata River, making this an ideal area for grape growing and wine production—due to the dark sandy soils rich in phosphorus, potassium, and calcium. Don Lorenzo Irurtia emigrated to Uruguay in the early twentieth century and had his first successful harvest in 1913. Today, the winery manages 360 hectares (890 acres) and produces 4,450,000 liters of wine from Pinot Blanc, Sauvignon Blanc, Chardonnay, Riesling, Gewürztraminer, Viognier, Sémillon, Cabernet Sauvignon, Cabernet Franc, Tannat, Merlot, Malbec, Pinot Noir, Nebbiolo, and Syrah vines. Average vine age on the estate is an impressive 22 years. Dante Irurtia received three gold medals in 2009 in Ljubljana, Slovenia, for its Cosecha Particular Cabernet Sauvignon 2005, Reserva del Virrey Tannat 2004, and Botrytis Excellence 2002. Cosecha Particular Cabernet Sauvignon 2005 has a deep red color and spicy aromas. It has round, pleasant tannins on the finish. Reserva del Virrey Tannat 2004 is deep violet red, with aromas of dried fruit and cocoa. It has soft, supple tannins on the palate. Botrytis Excellence 2002, made from vine-dried Gewürztraminer, is gold toned with notes of peach and apricot. On the palate there is a complex balance between sugar and acid.

MALDONADO

Maldonado is located east of Montevideo and is bordered on the southwest by the Rio de la Plata and the southeast by the Atlantic Ocean. The beautiful seaside resort town of Punta del Este is located in this department.

ALTO DE LA BALLENA

Ruta 12, Kilometer 16,400, Sierra de la Ballena,
Maldonado,
+598 9 441 0328,
www.altodelaballena.com

Alvaro Lorenzo and Paula Pivel planted their first vines in 2001 on land that they had purchased one year earlier. Their vineyards and winery are only 12 kilometers (7 miles) from the ocean and a short distance from Punta del Este, the largest seaside resort in all of South America. They have planted 8 hectares (20 acres) with Merlot, Tannat, Cabernet Franc, Syrah, and Viognier. Their first harvest was in 2005, and the wines were brought to market

BODEGA BOUZA

Cno. de la Redención 7658, Montevideo,
+598 2 323 7491,
www.bodegabouza.com

in 2007. Alto de la Ballena Reserva Cabernet Franc Varietal 2007 is deep garnet, with red fruit, eucalyptus, and vanilla on the nose. A soft tannic structure is evident in the mouth with a final note of dark chocolate. Alto de la Ballena Tannat, Merlot, Cabernet Franc Blend 2008 is cherry red, with red fruits of the wood on the nose. It is round and smooth in the mouth. Alto de la Ballena Syrah 2008 is deep red with a violet rim and has notes of dark fruits and spice on the nose. In the mouth the complex tannic structure is evident with a long finish.

MONTEVIDEO

The department of Montevideo, in the south central area of Uruguay, sits like a jewel on the Rio de la Plata. It is one of the smallest departments in total area but has the highest number of inhabitants due to its namesake capital city. It is also home to the country's chief maritime port.

The Bouza family grows grapes in its Melilla and Las Violetas vineyards, both located in the Montevideo region of Uruguay. The winery produces 90,000 bottles per year from Albariño, Chardonnay, Merlot, Tempranillo, and Tannat vines. Bouza Albariño 2010 is crisp, clean, and refreshing, while the Bouzo Tannat A6 Parcela Unica 2008 is ruby red, with a bouquet of red and black plums. Round in the mouth, it has a soft tannic finish. Bouza wines are paired with Uruguayan specialties, such as Patagonian blackfish (*Merluza Negra*), in the family's on-premise restaurant. After a dessert of Crème Caramel with Dulce de Leche, take a stroll through the winery's Automobile Museum, which has more than thirty classic cars on display.

GRUPO TRAVERSA

Avenida Pedro de Mendoza, Montevideo,
+598 2 222 0035,
www.grupotraversa.com.uy

The origins of the Traversa family in Uruguay begin with the emigration of Carlos Domingo Traversa from Asolo, Italy, in the Veneto, 50 kilometers (31 miles) north of Venice. Grupo Traversa now owns one of the largest wineries (if not *the* largest) in Uruguay. It is responsible for approximately 14 percent of the country's grape production; it both grows its own grapes and buys grapes from growers. Grupo Traversa produces about 10.5 million liters of wine per year, much of which is sold within the Uruguayan market. Its domestic portfolio includes the Faisan line, which comes in the Tetrabrick, or 3-liter jug, format. Viña Salort Chardonnay Roble 2010 is aged for four months in new French barrels and has a straw yellow color. Aromas of tropical fruits, including pineapple and guava, are present with a crisp, clean finish. Traversa Tannat Merlot Blend 2007 has 80 percent Tannat and 20 percent Merlot, is purple red in color and has notes of red fruits and spicy black pepper. It is powerful and fresh on the palate.

URUKA VINOS FINOS

Avenida José Belloni, 9031, Montevideo,
+598 2 222 0065,
www.urukawines.com

The love affair began when South African winemaker Riaan van der Spuy met Uruguayan chemist Claudia Lugano during the 2000 harvest in California. Riaan began working for the Lugano family winery, founded in 1920, and incorporated the innovative ideas he'd learned in faraway lands. The name "Uruka" comes from the fusion of the first three letters of "Uruguay" and the last two letters of "Suid Afrika." The couple was married in 2003 and have given birth to the future generation of winemakers, Lucia and Felipe. The couple grows Tannat, Cabernet Sauvignon, Cabernet Franc, Merlot, and Malbec on 35 hectares (86 acres) in the Montevideo region. Uruka Tannat Roble Ecologico 2009 is purple red in appearance, with aromas of tobacco and stewed red fruits. In the mouth mature tannins are present. Uruka Tannat Merlot 2008 is comprised of 70 percent Tannat and 30 percent Merlot and is ruby red in color. Raspberry and red cherry notes are present in the bouquet, with soft round tannins in the mouth. Uruka Syrah Malbec Blend 2007 contains 50 percent of each and is a deep red color. Ripe red fruits with a touch of smokiness are noted on the nose. On the palate soft tannins pleasantly fill your mouth.

VINOS FINOS J. CARRAU

César Mayo Gutiérrez 2556, Montevideo,
+598 2 320 0238,
www.bodegascarrau.com

Ten generations of winemaking—and counting—the Carrau family began growing grapes and making wine in a small village north of Barcelona, Spain, in 1752. The family emigrated to Uruguay in 1929 and planted vines in Las Violetas in the Canelones region. Their wines are well received the world over. In 1997, the family bought a parcel of land in the Cerro Chapes region and built a modern winery that was considered to be a major innovation in Uruguay at the time. It was designed with the environment in mind, to blend into the local hillsides, while using minimal energy expenditure to produce wine. Bodegas Carrau Amat 2004, named for Don Francisco Carrau Amat, an ancestor from Catalunya, is a wine not to miss. Made from 100 percent Tannat, the color is deep purple, with rich aromas of anise and black plums.

Tobacco and caramel notes are also found on the bouquet. Chewy tannins and a luxurious mouthfeel lead the way to a persistent finish. Bodegas Carrau Vilasar 1999 is made from Nebbiolo and Marzemino grapes. It has a ruby red color and notes of strawberries and blackberries on the nose. Firm tannins with ripe red fruit explode in the mouth. Bodegas Carrau Vivent Licor de Tannat 2006 is the family's fortified wine. It is intense purple in the glass, with a bouquet of dark chocolate and tobacco. Eighty grams of residual sugar per liter make this a pleasant sweet wine. It's a perfect way to end a lovely dinner.

VIÑEDOS Y BODEGA SANTA ROSA

César Mayo Gutiérrez 2211, Montevideo,
+598 2 320 9921,
www.bodegasantarosa.com

Founded in 1898, Viñedos y Bodega Santa Rosa has been winning international medals for a long time. In 1910 it received a gold medal in Buenos Aires and 1993 brought a silver medal at the prestigious Vinexpo in Bordeaux. It currently has 280 hectares (692 acres) of planted vines in Las Violetas, in Juanicó, north of Montevideo. Santa Rosa Tannat del Museo Reserva 2005 is bright ruby red, with aromas of raspberries and red plums and balanced tannins on the finish. Santa Rosa Juan Bautista Passadore 2006 is a blend of Tannat, Merlot, Cabernet Franc, Cabernet Sauvignon, and Malbec. It spends 24 months in French and American oak barrels and is deep purple. Notes of black truffles, mint, and caramelized sugar are present on the bouquet. It is full-bodied with well-structured tannins. Santa Rosa Chardonnay 2009 is yellow gold in color, with aromas of white flowers, ripe pears, and melon. It is refreshing and crisp on the palate.

RECIPE

CREOLE LAMB CASSEROLE

✳

Recipe courtesy of Chef Luis Zunino of Bodegas Marichal

✳

SERVES 6

Chef Luis Zunino supplied us with this delicious Creole Lamb Casserole (*Cazuela Criolla de Cordero*) recipe. Juan Andrés Marichal paired it perfectly with his Marichal Tannat Reserve 2009. This dish is ideal for those autumn nights when there's a chill in the air and winter is waiting right around the corner.

Olive oil

2 pounds leg of lamb, cut into chunks

Salt

Pepper

4 ounces smoked bacon

2 bay leaves

1 sprig fresh rosemary

2 celery stalks, sliced

5 scallions

3 garlic cloves

2 large Spanish onions, diced

1 red pepper, sliced

1 green pepper, sliced

2 large tomatoes, quartered

4 carrots, sliced

4 potatoes, cubed

2 cups cooked chickpeas

1/2 cup frozen green peas

1 cup Marichal Tannat wine

1 loaf focaccia

Heat a cast iron pot and add olive oil. Add the cubed lamb and season with salt and pepper. When brown, remove and set aside.

Add more olive oil if necessary, then add bacon, bay leaves, rosemary sprig, celery, scallions, garlic, and onion and sauté for 5 minutes.

Add the bell peppers and tomatoes and cook for approximately 10 minutes.

Add the carrots, lamb cubes, and potatoes and cook for 10 to 20 minutes.

Add the chickpeas and green peas and cook until heated through. Season with salt and pepper.

Add 1 cup red wine and continue cooking for 10 minutes.

Remove from heat, and let rest 15 minutes.

Serve in small bowls with sliced focaccia.

IN THEIR OWN WORDS

CARLOS PIZZORNO

Carlos Pizzorno is a third-generation winemaker of his family winery. The Pizzornos have been making quality wines since 1910; Carlos's grandfather was one of the pioneers of the winemaking industry in Uruguay.

How did you get involved in the world of wine?
I come from a traditional viticulture family in Uruguay, located in the Canelón Chico region close to the River Plata. I am the third generation of the family here. The winery was founded in 1910 by Don Próspero José Pizzorno, an Italian visionary and enterprising immigrant. He was the inspiration of a century-long family tradition. I grew up in Canelón Chico; my house was at the estate, so every morning I could see the vineyard. I can remember riding my bicycle around the vineyard—it was fun. In 1978 I had completed my enology degree, and in 1983, I took the management of the company.

What are some of the biggest changes you have seen in winemaking since you began your career?
The first and biggest change I could see was preparing the vineyard to produce fine wine—selecting the soil to plant different varieties of French rootstock. We strongly believe that the quality of our wines begins in the vineyard. This is why we only make wine from grapes produced on our own plantation, and that the results obtained in the vineyards fully meet our expectations of high standards and exclusive character of the wines we produce.

We also renovated our winery. We acquired modern technology so that we can ensure perfect control of the winemaking process, while also maintaining hygienic conditions. We began selling our wines in the international market in 1999, so we now attend wine shows, fairs, visit our customers, and continuously promote Uruguay and Uruguayan wine.

What are some of the exciting changes that you see happening specifically in your country?

Firstly, many winemakers are replanting their vineyards and making fine wines. We are happy to show our country's viticulture tradition. Also, many people are now growing Tannat, the signature grape variety of our country. People are beginning to appreciate how special it is due to its great body, tannic structure, intense color, and aromatics.

Where else in the world have you studied, trained, or worked a harvest? How did that influence your winemaking?

I visited Europe in 1987. In France, I studied the behaviors of different varieties before deciding which rootstocks to plant in Uruguay. I also met Professor Alan Carboneau at INRA in Bordeaux. He was a major influence and helped us select which rootstock would work the best. After that I visited Champagne to learn about the traditional Champenoise method. This was very important to me because now I have the experience to produce sparkling wine at our winery. We also have Duncan Killiner working with us as a consultant since 2003. It is a large investment for our boutique winery, but our goal is to create quality wines.

Which varieties are you working with? Are you experimenting with anything new?

Tannat has its origins in Madiran, southwest France, but it has proven to be ideally suited to the local *terroir*. Considerable care is taken to source premium Tannat grapes at optimum states of maturity, and to highlight the variety's complex fruit. The grape is also well suited to blends, particularly with classic grape varieties such as Cabernet and Merlot. It is a strong wine with a great personality and ideal with barbecued red meats.

Sauvignon Blanc is another special variety at our vineyard, and we are sure that the influence of our Kiwi winemaker makes the difference in our Don Próspero Sauvignon Blanc. Pinot Noir has been our latest experiment, and we seem to be having successful results with American consumers.

What challenges have you faced as a winemaker or winery owner?

Finding the niche market to sell our wine. Pizzorno is a boutique winery, and our goal is to reach the consumer who is interested in purchasing handcrafted Uruguayan wines. We also strive each year to improve our quality and stay up to date. The support of our consultant, Duncan, helps us achieve that goal.

What is your winemaking philosophy?

Our wines are the result of a distinctive winemaking style based on the combination of artisanal handwork and technology. It is also important for us to produce limited production wines that have a good balance between fruit and oak.

What would you hope people say about your wine?

We hope that they would know and respect our brand because of our commitment to quality. We also would like people to think that our quality-to-price ratio makes our wines good value.

Do you think that the market should influence winemaking, or do you think that winemaking should influence the market?

We have our style of winemaking. Our aim is to produce quality handcrafted wines from grapes grown on our own estate. We use low production vines and gentle, careful winemaking techniques. We feel that this best represents the spirit and character of our *terroir* and the essence of our Uruguayan wine country.

Besides your own wine, what are some of your favorite wines? What do you like about them?

At this moment I have in mind two wines, for a red wine, I had the chance to taste Château Pierrail 2004 Grand Vin de Bordeaux, and it was really amazing. For a white wine, I like St Hallett Poacher's Blend 2005 Semillon-Sauvignon Blanc from Australia.

What is your opinion on screwcap versus cork closures?

We use screwcap for young white wine and rosé. The English were the first to ask for it, and now we're using it in all of our markets. It is safer than cork, and wines do not lose their vibrancy. We understand that all consumers are not yet open to using screwcaps, because the perception is that they are used for cheaper wines. For our reserve wines, we always use natural cork.

If you could invite anyone from history, living or dead, to your home for dinner, who would it be? What food would you serve? What wine would you serve?

I would invite Jancis Robinson—that would be an unforgettable experience. I would serve her Uruguayan barbecued lamb and the wine would be Pizzorno Primo 2004, it was an excellent vintage for us. We launched this wine in 2010 at our 100-year anniversary. The blend was Tannat, Cabernet Sauvignon, Merlot, and Petit Verdot, all from our best plots. They were vinified separately, aged separately in French oak, and then blended. I feel that this wine reflects both the passion and commitment of the Pizzorno family.

If you were to stay home tonight for a relaxing evening, drinking wine while watching a movie, which movie would you watch? Which wine would you drink? Explain.

The Concert is the latest movie I watched. It had great music that matched perfectly to our Pizzorno Tinto Reserve. It is my favorite wine, a blend of Tannat, Cabernet Sauvignon, and Merlot, and aged for 12 months in French oak. It is a complex wine, with a long finish.

How do you like to spend your time away from the winery?

Traveling, and getting to know new countries, and of course tasting new and exotic wines!

If you weren't involved in wine, what would you be doing?

Winemaking is an art and a style of life. It is a project that my whole family is involved in, and it is a great experience for us to work together. Also, my son, Francisco, is 17 years old and is studying to become an agronomic engineer. I couldn't imagine working far from nature, and I couldn't imagine working in an office all day. I love my work.

ACKNOWLEDGMENTS

We love having friends who live and work in the Southern Hemisphere, and love them even more when we are able to visit during the Northern Hemisphere's dark winter months. This book was made possible thanks to those who opened their cellars, kitchens, and hearts to us.

We would like to thank the wonderful team at Sterling Epicure, especially our editor Carlo DeVito. His support, guidance, and friendship are gratefully appreciated. We also want to thank his lovely wife Dominique and their two sons, Dylan and Dawson, for their indulgence when we interrupted their weekend family time. Diane Abrams deserves our heartfelt thanks for building this book from a pile of paper, and keeping us organized in her gentle, calm, and efficient manner. We're thankful to Brita Vallens for keeping the tornado of artwork in one place, Scott Amerman for his sharp eyes, and Campbell Mattinson for his gracious assistance. We would like to thank the sales and marketing teams at Sterling for their vision in getting this book out to the world.

No expression of gratitude would be complete without thanking our manager and friend, Peter Miller, the "Literary Lion," who after all these years, we just call "Lion." We are equally grateful to our friend, Michel Rolland, the world-renowned wine consultant, for positively changing the face of Southern Hemisphere wine forever.

Thanks so much to Lori Tieszen and Jake Pippin of Wines of Chile; Nora Favelukes from Wines of Argentina; James Gosper, Antonia Muir, and Angela Slade from Wine Australia; Su Birch and Rory Callahan from Wines of South Africa; Clive Weston and Narida Hooper from New Zealand Family of Twelve; Ranit Librach from New Zealand Winegrowers; Andreia Gentilini Milan, Barbara Ruppel, Ana Paula Kleinowski, and Edgar Sinigaglia from Wines of Brazil; and the Winemakers of Uruguay.

We would also like to thank Mauricio Banchieri, Alfredo Bartholomaus, Marybeth Bentwood, Alba Botha, Linda Bragaw, Claudia Centola, Molly Choi, Oz Clarke, Cris Crisp, Helen Gregory, Joe Janish, Susan Kostrzewa, John Larchet, Robin Kelley O'Connor, Don Opici, TJ Peabody, Rebekah Polster, Rebecca Rader, Anne Riives, Ivan Ruiz, Bethany Burke Scherline, Steve Smith, Mary Anne Sullivan,

Sam Timberg, Marcy Walsh, Donna White, and Kevin Zraly.

Heartfelt thanks to all of our friends and colleagues in the world of wine. Without your knowledge, support, and hand-holding skills, this book would not have been possible.

Thank You, Gracias, Merci, Baie Dankie, Kia Ora, Obrigado, Ta, Murromboo, Grazie, Cheers, Sulpayki, Arohanui, Chaltu Mai.

CREDITS

All interior photos by Mike DeSimone and Jeff Jenssen

Jacket photo by Geoffrey Michaels

Label images featured in the book were generously provided by the following:

ARGENTINA: 14: Colomé/The Hess Collection; 18: Bodegas San Huberto; 21: Callia/Palm Bay International, Graffigna/Pernod Ricard Argentina; 25: Bodega Los Toneles; 26: Bodegas Santa Ana; 28: Achaval Ferrer; 29: Alta Vista/Lutecia, Altos Las Hormigas; 30: Andeluna Cellars; 31: Bodega Benegas; 32: Bodega Catena Zapata/Winebow; 33: Cheval Des Andes/Gregory White PR; 34: Dominio del Plata, Doña Paula; 36: Kaiken, Viña Las Perdices; 37: La Rural/Rutini Wines; 38: Bodega Luigi Bosca; 39: Mendel Wines, Bodega Navarro Correas/DIAGEO Wines; 40: Bodega Norton; 41: Pascual Toso; 42: Pulenta Estate, Bodega Renacer; 44: Bodega Ruca Malen/Opici Wines; 46: Terrazas de los Andes/ Gregory White PR; 47: Trapiche, Trivento/Banfi; 48: Viña Alicia; 50: Familia Zuccardi; 51: Almanegra/ Winebow, Close de los Siete/Nike Communications; 53: Bodega Diamandes, Finca Sophenia; 54: Flechas de los Andes S.A., François Lurton; 57: Bodegas Salentein; 63: Bodega Chacra/Kobrand Wine and Spirits

AUSTRALIA: 98: Ferngrove; 99: Frankland Estate; 100: Plantagenet Wines; 102: Cape Mentelle; 103: Cullen Wines; 104: Howard Park Wines, Leeuwin Estate; 105: Moss Wood Wines; 107: Peel Estate Wines; 108: Picardy Winery; 110: Sandalford; 112: Petaluma Wines; 113: Shaw + Smith Wines; 115: Château Tanunda/Banfi; 117: Glaetzer Wines; 121: Penfolds Wines/Treasury Wine Estates; 122: Peter Lehmann, Schild Estate Wines; 124: St. Hallett, Standish Wine Company; 126: Yalumba; 128: Jim Barry Wines; 129: Kilikanoon, Mount Horrocks Wines; 131: Balnaves of Coonawarra; 132: Bowen Estate Wines; 134: Henschke Wines; 135: Pewsey Vale/Negociants USA; 138: Chapel Hill; 139: d'Arenberg, Hardys/Accolade Wines; 140: Kangarilla Road; 142: Mollydooker Wines; 143: Spring Seed Wine Company; 144: Wirra Wirra; 146: Tapanappa Wines; 155: Greenstone Vineyard; 156: Shadowfax/ Minc Communications; 157: Brown Brothers; 163: Dalwhinnie Wines; 166: Coldstream Hills Winery/ Treasury Wine Estates; 168: Five Oaks Wines; 169: Giant Steps/Innocent Bystander; 172: Yering Station/ Rathbone Wine Group; 178: Brokenwood Wines; 179: Hope Estate; 181: Tempus Two/Australian Vintage; 183: Tyrrell's Wines

BRAZIL: 216: Santo Emilio Vinícola; 217: Boscato Vinhos; 218: Vinícola Perini/Comunicative; 220: Vinícola Aurora; 221: Basso Vinhos e Espumantes Ltda.; 223: Casa Valduga; 225: Miolo Wine Group; 226: Don Laurindo; 227: Don Giovanni Vinhos Vinhedos Pousada; 228: Vinícola Geisse

CHILE: 248: Viña Falernia; 250: Maycas del Limari/ Banfi, Viña Tabali; 253: Arboleda/Wines of Chile USA; 254: Errazuriz/Wines of Chile USA, Viña San Esteban; 255: Seña/Wines of Chile USA; 258: Viña Casablanca/Carolina Wine Brands, Casas del Bosque;

259: Kingston Family Vineyards; 260: Loma Larga/ Mas Diseno; 262: Veramonte/Huneeus Vintners; 265: Leyda/Winebow; 267: Matetic/Quintessential Wines; 269: Antiyal; 270: Carmen/Trinchero Family Estates; 272: Cousino Macul/Winebow; 273: Concha y Toro /Wines of Chile USA; 274: De Martino/Opici Wines, Domus Aurea/Wines of Chile USA; 275: El Principal; 276: Haras de Pirque/Ste. Michelle Wine Estates, Intriga/MontGras Properties; 278: Portal del Alto; 279: Santa Carolina; 280: Santa Ema/TGIC Importers; 281: Santa Rita/Palm Bay International, Tarapaca/Wines of Chile USA; 283: Tres Palacios/ Michael Skurnik Wines, Undurraga/Vision Wine & Spirits; 284: Viñedo Chadwick/Wines of Chile USA; 285: Ventisquero, William Fevre/Sommelier Imports; 289: La Rosa, Morande; 292: Caliterra/ Wines of Chile USA; 293: Casa Lapostolle/Wines of Chile USA; 295: Cono Sur/Vineyard Brands, Estampa; 296: Hacienda Araucano/Winesellers, Ltd.; 297: Koyle/Quintessential Wines, La Playa/Wines of Chile USA; 298: Los Vascos/Pasternak Wine Imports, Montes; 299: Viña MontGras/Palm Bay International; 301: Viñedos Emiliana/Wines of Chile USA; 303: Miguel Torres; 304: Viña Valdivieso; 306: La Reserva de Caliboro/Palm Bay International, Bodega y Viñedos O. Fournier; 307: Terranoble/Winebow; 308: Via Wine Group

NEW ZEALAND: 350: Babich Wines; 353: Mudbrick Vineyard; 354: Nobilo/Constellation NZ; 356: Villa Maria Estate; 357: Mills Reef; 359: The Millton Vineyard; 360: Vinoptima; 363: CJ Pask Winery, Craggy Range; 365: Mission Estate Winery; 366: Sacred Hill Winery; 368: Te Mata Estate; 369: Trinity Hill; 370: Vidal Wines; 372: Ata Rangi; 374: Dry River, Escarpment Vineyard; 376: Martinborough Vineyard; 377: Palliser Estate; 380: Neudorf Vineyards; 383: Allan Scott Family Winemakers; 384: Clos Henri; 385: Cloudy Bay/

Palliser Estate Wines; 387: Spy Valley Wines; 388: Fromm Winery; 389: Grove Mill Wine Company, Ltd./The New Zealand Wine Company, Ltd.; 391: Hunter's Wines; 393: Lawson's Dry Hills; 394: Nautilus Estate; 395: Saint Clair Estate; 396: Seresin; 397: Vavasour/Foley Family Wines, Villa Maria; 401: Pegasus Bay; 405: Amisfield; 406: Felton Road Wines, Ltd.; 408: Mount Difficulty; 409: Quartz Reef

SOUTH AFRICA: 462: Buitenverwachting/Cape Classics; 464: Klein Constantia/Cape Classics; 466: Boekenhoutskloof Winery; 469: Solms-Delta, 472: KWV/Opici Wines; 473: Nederburg/Distell; 474: Beyerskloof/Cape Wine Match; 476: DeMorgenzon/ Cape Classics; 477: De Toren/Cape Classics; 479: Ernie Els Wines/Terlato Wines International, Glenelly/Cape Classics; 480: Hartenberg Estate; 481: Jordan Wines; 482: Kanonkop/Cape Classics; 483: Kanu/Cape Classics; 484: Ken Forrester Wines/ Cape Classics; 485: Miles Mossop Wines; 486: Mulderbosch/Cape Classics; 487: Mvemve Raats/ Cape Classics; 488: Post House Wines; 489: Raats Family Wines/Cape Classics, Rustenberg/Cape Classics; 491: Stellenbosch Hills/Cape Wine Match, Thelema/Cape Classics; 493: Warwick Estate; 495: Org de Rac/Cape Wine Match; 497: D'Aria/Cape Wine Match; 498: Durbanville Hills/Distell; 500: Elgin Vintners/Cape Wine Match; 501: Iona/Terry Seitz Inc.; 503: Bouchard Finlayson; 505: DuVon/ Cape Wine Match, Excelsior Estate; 508: Cederberg Estate; 509: Abingdon Estate

URUGUAY: 543: Pisano Wines; 547: Toscanini Wines; 550: Alto de la Ballena, Bodega Bouza; 552: Bodegas Carrau

INDEX

Note: Page ranges in parentheses indicate non-contiguous/intermittent references. Page numbers in **bold** indicate main discussions of grape varieties.

(Continued on next page)

(Continued on next page)

(Continued on next page)